THE CAMBRIDGE HISTORY OF

COMMUNI᷍᷍

CW00815814

The third volume of *The Cambridge H*
the period from the 1960s to the pres
two decades of the global Cold War
socialism. An international team of sc
China as a global power continuing to proclaim its Maoist
allegiance, and the transformation of the geopolitics and
political economy of Cold War conflict in an era of increasing
economic interpenetration. Beneath the surface, profound
political, social, economic and cultural changes were occurring
in the socialist and former socialist countries, resulting in the
collapse and transformations of the existing socialist order and
the changing parameters of world Marxism. This volume draws
on innovative research to bring together history from above and
below, including social, cultural, gender and transnational history
to transcend the old separation between communist studies and
the broader field of contemporary history.

JULIANE FÜRST is Reader in Modern European History at the
University of Bristol. She is the author of *Stalin's Last Generation:
Soviet Post-War Youth and the Emergence of Mature Socialism* (2010) and
the editor of *Late Stalinist Russia: Society Between Reconstruction and
Reinvention* (2006).

SILVIO PONS is Professor of Contemporary History at the University
of Rome "Tor Vergata." He is the president of the Gramsci
Foundation in Rome and a member of the Editorial Board of the
Journal of Cold War Studies. His main publications include *Stalin and
the Inevitable War* (2002), *Reinterpreting the End of the Cold War* (2005), *A
Dictionary of Twentieth-Century Communism* (2010) and *The Global
Revolution: A History of International Communism* (2014).

MARK SELDEN is a Senior Research Associate in the East Asia
Program at Cornell University, and Editor of *The Asia-Pacific Journal:
Japan Focus*. His research on modern and contemporary geopolitics,
political economy and history of China, Japan and the Asia-Pacific
ranges broadly across themes of war and revolution, inequality,
development, regional and world social change, and historical
memory. Books include *China in Revolution: The Yenan Way Revisited*
(1995), *Chinese Society: Change, Conflict and Resistance* (2010), *The
Resurgence of East Asia: 500, 150 and 50 Year Perspectives* (2003) and
Chinese Village, Socialist State (1993).

THE CAMBRIDGE HISTORY OF
COMMUNISM

GENERAL EDITOR

SILVIO PONS, *Università degli Studi di Roma "Tor Vergata"*

The Cambridge History of Communism is an unprecedented global history of communism across the twentieth century. With contributions from a team of leading historians, economists, political scientists and sociologists, the three volumes examine communism in the context of wider political, social, cultural and economic processes, while at the same time revealing how it contributed to shaping them. Volume I deals with the roots, impact and development of communism, analyzing the tumultuous events from the Russian Revolution of 1917 to World War II, and historical personalities such as Lenin, Stalin and Trotsky. Volumes II and III then review the global impact of communism, focusing on the Cold War, the Chinese Revolution, the Vietnam War and the eventual collapse of the Soviet Union. Together the volumes explain why a movement that sought to bring revolution on a world scale, overthrowing capitalism and parliamentary democracy, acquired such force and influence globally.

VOLUME I

World Revolution and Socialism in One Country 1917–1941

EDITED BY SILVIO PONS AND STEPHEN A. SMITH

VOLUME II

The Socialist Camp and World Power 1941–1960s

EDITED BY NORMAN NAIMARK, SILVIO PONS AND SOPHIE QUINN-JUDGE

VOLUME III

Endgames? Late Communism in Global Perspective, 1968 to the Present

EDITED BY JULIANE FÜRST, SILVIO PONS AND MARK SELDEN

THE CAMBRIDGE
HISTORY OF
COMMUNISM

*

VOLUME III
Endgames? Late Communism in
Global Perspective, 1968 to the Present

*

Edited by

JULIANE FÜRST
University of Bristol

SILVIO PONS
Università degli Studi di Roma "Tor Vergata"

MARK SELDEN
Cornell University

CAMBRIDGE
UNIVERSITY PRESS

CAMBRIDGE
UNIVERSITY PRESS

University Printing House, Cambridge CB2 8BS, United Kingdom

One Liberty Plaza, 20th Floor, New York, NY 10006, USA

477 Williamstown Road, Port Melbourne, VIC 3207, Australia

4843/24, 2nd Floor, Ansari Road, Daryaganj, Delhi – 110002, India

79 Anson Road, #06–04/06, Singapore 079906

Cambridge University Press is part of the University of Cambridge.

It furthers the University's mission by disseminating knowledge in the pursuit of education, learning, and research at the highest international levels of excellence.

www.cambridge.org
Information on this title: www.cambridge.org/9781107135642
DOI: 10.1017/9781316471821

© Juliane Fürst, Silvio Pons and Mark Selden 2017

First published 2017
Paperback edition first published 2020

Printed in the United Kingdom by TJ International Ltd. Padstow Cornwall

A catalogue record for this publication is available from the British Library.

Three Volume Set ISBN 978-1-316-63458-5 Hardback

Volume I ISBN 978-1-107-09284-6 Hardback
Volume II ISBN 978-1-107-13354-9 Hardback
Volume III ISBN 978-1-107-13564-2 Hardback

Three Volume Set ISBN 978-1-316-63457-8 Paperback

Volume I ISBN 978-1-107-46736-1 Paperback
Volume II ISBN 978-1-107-59001-4 Paperback
Volume III ISBN 978-1-316-50159-7 Paperback

Contents

v

Contents

Contents

Plates are to be found between pp. 336 and 337

Plates

1. Demonstrations and student revolt in Berlin. Young protesters carry flags and a poster of Ho Chi Minh, February 1968. Wolfgang Kunz / ullstein bild via Getty Images.
2. Students demonstrating in Prague, 1968. Imagno / Getty Images.
3. Members of the Xiangyang commune in Jiangsu province take part in the campaign to "Criticize Lin Biao and Confucius." Early 1970s. Bettmann / Contributor / Getty Images.
4. Josip Broz Tito, Prime Minister Indira Gandhi of India and Tanzanian president Julius Nyerere talk while they attend the third conference of the Non-Aligned Movement, Lusaka, Zambia, September 1970. John Reader / The LIFE Images Collection / Getty Images.
5. Veteran US militant Angela Davis is welcomed upon her arrival in Moscow, 29 August 1972, by Valentina V. Nikolseva-Tereshkova, president of the Soviet Women's Committee, and members of the Central Committee of the Communist Party of the Soviet Union. AFP / Getty Images.
6. Mao Zedong and Richard Nixon with Zhou Enlai and Henry Kissinger in Beijing, 21 February 1972. Bettmann / Contributor / Getty Images.
7. Russian writer and Nobel Prize winner Aleksandr Solzhenitsyn is mobbed by journalists on his arrival in Zurich after being deprived of his Soviet citizenship following the publication of *The Gulag Archipelago*, 1974. Keystone / Staff / Getty Images.
8. Liberation of Saigon (now Ho Chi Minh City), May 1975. Jean-Claude LABBE / Gamma-Rapho via Getty Images.
9. Mao Zedong with Khmer Rouge leaders Pol Pot and Ieng Sary in Beijing, June 1975. API / Gamma-Rapho via Getty Images.
10. At the Montreal Olympic Games, Romanian Olympic gymnastics champion Nadia Comaneci celebrates as the scoreboard shows the perfect score of 10 after her acrobatic compulsory on the uneven bars. AFP PHOTO.
11. Tashkent 1978. Private collection. Photo by Igor Palmin.
12. Beriozka store in Moscow, 1970s. Private collection. Photo by Fine Art Images / Heritage Images / Getty Images.
13. Raul Castro, Fidel Castro and Haile Mengistu of Ethiopia in Havana, 1 May 1978. Francois LOCHON / Gamma-Rapho via Getty Images.

14. Popular meeting in the Nicaraguan capital of Managua after the Sandinista victory, 1979. Tony Comiti / Sygma via Getty Images.
15. Mass grave of victims of the Pol Pot regime near the hills of the former Cambodian capital of Oudong, 40 km north of Phnom Penh. Roland Neveu / LightRocket via Getty Images.
16. A Solidarity rally during Pope John Paul II's visit to Kraków, Poland, June 1979. Bettmann / Contributor / Getty Images.
17. Deng Xiaoping and Hu Yaobang, Beijing, September 1981. Stringer / Getty Images.
18. Funeral of Enrico Berlinguer, 13 June 1984. Mondadori Portfolio via Getty Images.
19. Leaders of the Warsaw Pact at a meeting of the Political Consultative Committee in Prague, 1983. ITAR-TASS / Vladimir Musaelyan; Eduard Pesov. Photo by TASS via Getty Images.
20. East German television filming the celebration ceremony of the fortieth anniversary of the capitulation of Nazi Germany to the Soviet Union in World War II, 8 May 1985. Mehner / ullstein bild via Getty Images.
21. Chernobyl Nuclear Reactor No. 4, which exploded on 26 April 1986. Oktay Ortakcioglu / Getty Images.
22. Secondhand market at the Skala-Expo fairground in Budapest, 1982. Keystone Pictures USA / Alamy Stock Photo.
23. A new shipment of shoes immediately attracts a line of people in Moscow, 1980s. Bettmann / Contributor / Getty Images.
24. Residents chatting at modern concrete housing project in a southwestern suburb of Prague, 1980s. Chris Niedenthal / The LIFE Images Collection / Getty Images.
25. Mikhail Gorbachev and Ronald Reagan in Red Square, Moscow, May 1988. TASS via Getty Images.
26. Soviet withdrawal from Afghanistan: The last battalion crosses the Soviet–Afghan border along the bridge over the Amu-Dar'ia River near the town of Termez, Uzbekistan, 15 February 1989. Sovfoto / UIG via Getty Images.
27. Mikhail Gorbachev on an official visit in Beijing meeting with Deng Xiaoping, May 1989. Jacques Langevin / Sygma / Sygma via Getty Images.
28. Students protesting in Tiananmen Square in Beijing, May 1989. dpa picture alliance / Alamy Stock Photo.
29. Arrest warrant on China's state television for Chinese scientist and dissident Fang Lizhi, a key figure in the pro-democracy movement that inspired the Tiananmen Square protests in 1989, and his wife Li Shuxian. AFP / Stringer / Getty Images.
30. Academician Andrei Sakharov addressing the final session of the First Congress of USSR People's Deputies, June 1989. ITAR-TASS Photo Agency / Alamy Stock Photo.
31. Women veterans in the cathedral area of the Kremlin, Moscow, 9 May 1989. Vladimir Bogdanov / FotoSoyuz / Getty Images.
32. The Berlin Wall, November 1989. Pool BOUVET / MERILLON / GammaRapho via Getty Images.

33. Václav Havel waves to people crowding Wenceslas Square in Prague on Human Rights Day, 10 December 1989. Sovfoto / Contributor / Getty Images.
34. Nelson Mandela at the airport to greet Alfred Nzo, the secretary general of the African National Congress, and Joe Slovo, the secretary general of the South African Communist Party back from exile, Cape Town, 1990. Lily FRANEY / Gamma-Rapho via Getty Images.
35. Abandoned Soviet statues in Moscow, late 1991. Arnold H. Drapkin / The LIFE Images Collection / Getty Images.
36. Che Guevara mural in the center of Sumbe, Kwanza Sul province, Angola. Zute Lightfoot / Alamy Stock Photo.
37. A worker inspects motherboards on a factory line at the Foxconn plant in Shenzen. VOISHMEL / AFP / Getty Images.
38. A peddler sells potatoes in Beijing. LIU JIN / AFP / Getty Images.
39. Boats on the dried-out Aral Sea (formerly the world's fourth-biggest lake), Muynak, Uzbekistan. Daniel Kreher / Getty Images.
40. The Great Hall of the People as Chinese president Xi Jinping gives a speech marking the 150th anniversary of the birth of Sun Yat-sen on 11 November 2016 in Beijing. Etienne Oliveau / Getty Images.
41. József Somogyi, *Smelter (Martinász)*, 1953. Postcard, 1963.
42. István Tar, *Welder*, 1950. Source: *Új Magyar képzőművészet* (Budapest, 1950), n.p.
43. Sándor Mikus, *Male Choir*, 1961. Source: Rezső Szij, *Mikus Sándor* (Budapest, 1977), p. 36. Photographer: Balla Demeter.
44. Sándor Mikus, *Stalin Statue*, 1951. www.fortepan.hu / FOTO:FORTEPAN / Gyula Nagy.
45. István Kiss, *Republic of Councils Memorial*, 1969. De Agostini / Santini / D'Alessio / Getty Images.
46. István Kiss, *Workers*, 1982. FOTO:Fortepan — ID 26629; Adományozó / Donor : Angyalföldi Helytörténeti Gyűjtemény.
47. Dušan Otašević, *Towards Communism on Lenin's Course*, 1967. Copyright held by the Museum of Contemporary Art, Belgrade.
48. Milan Knížák, *A Walk Around the New World – A Demonstration for All the Senses*, 1964. Reproduction courtesy of Olomouc Museum of Art.
49. Map of socialist countries in the world in the 1980s.

Every effort has been made to contact the relevant copyright-holders for the images reproduced in this book. In the event of any error, the publisher will be pleased to make corrections in any reprints or future editions.

Figures

Contributors to Volume III

JAN C. BEHRENDS is a senior research fellow at Potsdam's Centre for Contemporary History (ZZF) and lecturer in East European history at Humboldt Universität zu Berlin. His publications include *Die erfundene Freundschaft. Propaganda für die Sowjetunion in Polen und in der DDR* (2005) and *Underground Publishing and the Public Sphere: Transnational Perspectives* (2015, with Thomas Lindenberger).

STEPHEN V. BITTNER is Professor of History at Sonoma State University in California. He is the author of *The Many Lives of Khrushchev's Thaw: Experience and Memory in Moscow's Arbat* (2008), and the editor of Dmitrii Shepilov's *The Kremlin's Scholar: A Memoir of Soviet Politics Under Stalin and Khrushchev* (2007).

MARK PHILIP BRADLEY is the Bernadotte E. Schmidt Professor of History at the University of Chicago, where he also serves as the faculty director of the Pozen Family Center for Human Rights and chair of the Committee on International Relations. He is the author of *The World Reimagined: Americans and Human Rights in the Twentieth Century* (2016) and *Vietnam at War* (2009), and the coeditor of *Familiar Made Strange: American Icons and Artifacts After the Transnational Turn* (2015).

MICHELE DI DONATO is Marie Skłodowska-Curie Fellow at the Centre d'Histoire of Sciences Po, Paris. Among his publications are *The Cold War and Socialist Identity: The Socialist International and the Italian "Communist Question" in the 1970s* (2015) and *I comunisti italiani e la sinistra europea. Il PCI e i rapporti con le socialdemocrazie, 1964–1984* (2016).

CELIA DONERT is Senior Lecturer in Twentieth-Century History at the University of Liverpool. She is the author of *The Rights of the Roma: State Socialism and the "Gypsy Question"* (2017) and articles in *Past & Present, Contemporary European History* and *Vingtième Siècle*.

MARKO DUMANČIĆ is Assistant Professor at Western Kentucky University. His work has appeared in the *Journal of Cold War Studies, Cold War History* and *Studies in Russian and Soviet Cinema*. He also wrote the introduction to the edited volume *Gender, Sexuality, and the Cold War: A Global Perspective* (2017).

REUBEN FOWKES is Curator and Co-Director of the Translocal Institute for Contemporary Art in Budapest. His publications include two special issues of *Third Text*, journal articles and book chapters.

JULIANE FÜRST is Reader in Modern European History at the University of Bristol. She is the author of *Stalin's Last Generation: Soviet Post-War Youth and the Emergence of Mature Socialism* (2010) and the editor of *Late Stalinist Russia: Society Between Reconstruction and Reinvention* (2006).

KARL GERTH is Professor of History and Hwei-chih and Julia Hsiu Endowed Chair in Chinese Studies at the University of California San Diego. He is also the author of *As China Goes, So Goes the World: How Chinese Consumers Are Transforming Everything* (2010) and *China Made: Consumer Culture and the Creation of the Nation* (2003).

ROBERT GILDEA is Professor of Modern History at the University of Oxford. His publications include *Europe's 1968: Voices of Revolt* (2013, edited with James Mark and Anette Warring), *Marianne in Chains: In Search of the German Occupation, 1940–1945* (2002) and *Fighters in the Shadows: A New History of the French Resistance* (2015).

PIERO GLEIJESES is Professor of US Foreign Policy at Johns Hopkins University (School of Advanced International Studies). His most recent book is *Visions of Freedom: Havana, Washington, Pretoria and the Struggle for Southern Africa, 1976–1991* (2013).

HO-FUNG HUNG is the Henry M. and Elizabeth P. Wiesenfeld Associate Professor in Political Economy at Johns Hopkins University. He is the author of *The China Boom: Why China Will Not Rule the World* (2015) and *Protest with Chinese Characteristics: Demonstrations, Riots, and Petitions in the Mid-Qing Dynasty* (2011).

POLLY JONES is Associate Professor of Russian and Schrecker-Barbour Fellow at University College, University of Oxford. Her publications include *Myth, Memory, Trauma: Rethinking the Stalinist Past in the Soviet Union, 1953–1970* (2013) and *The Dilemmas of De-Stalinization* (2005).

ARTEMY M. KALINOVSKY is Assistant Professor of East European Studies at the University of Amsterdam. He is the author of *A Long Goodbye: The Soviet Withdrawal from Afghanistan* (2011) and coeditor, with Sergey Radchenko, of *The End of the Cold War and the Third World* (2011), the *Routledge Handbook of the Cold War* (2014, with Craig Daigle) and *Reassessing Orientalism: Interlocking Orientologies in the Cold War Era* (2015, with Michael Kemper).

BEN KIERNAN is the A. Whitney Griswold Professor of History and Professor of International and Area Studies at Yale University. His books include *How Pol Pot Came to Power* (1985), *The Pol Pot Regime* (1996), *Genocide and Resistance in Southeast Asia* (2008), *Blood and Soil: A World History of Genocide and Extermination from Sparta to Darfur* (2007) and *Việt Nam: A History from Earliest Times to the Present* (2017).

STEPHEN LOVELL is Professor of Modern History at King's College London. His books include *Summerfolk: A History of the Dacha, 1710–2000* (2003), *The Shadow of War: Russia and the Soviet Union, 1941 to the Present* (2010) and *Russia in the Microphone Age: A History of Soviet Radio, 1919–1970* (2015).

CHARLES S. MAIER is Leverett Saltonstall Professor of History at Harvard University. His main publications are *Recasting Bourgeois Europe* (1975), *Dissolution: The Crisis of Communism and the End of East Germany* (1997), *Leviathan 2.0: The Making of Modern Statehood* (2014) and *Once Within Borders: Territories of Power, Wealth, and Belonging Since 1500* (2016).

JAMES MARK is Professor of History at the University of Exeter, UK. He is the author of *The Unfinished Revolution: Making Sense of the Communist Past in Central-Eastern Europe* (2011) and coauthor of *Europe's 1968: Voices of Revolt* (2013, with Robert Gildea and Anette Warring).

JAN PLAMPER is Professor of History at Goldsmiths, University of London. His major publications include *The Stalin Cult: A Study in the Alchemy of Power* (2012) and *The History of Emotions: An Introduction* (2015).

SILVIO PONS is Professor of Contemporary History at the University of Rome "Tor Vergata." He is the president of the Gramsci Foundation in Rome and a member of the Editorial Board of the *Journal of Cold War Studies*. His main publications include *Stalin and the Inevitable War* (2002), *Reinterpreting the End of the Cold War* (2005), *A Dictionary of Twentieth-Century Communism* (2010) and *The Global Revolution: A History of International Communism* (2014).

SOPHIE QUINN-JUDGE is the author of *Ho Chi Minh: The Missing Years* (2003) and *The Third Force in Vietnam: The Elusive Search for Peace* (2017). She was Associate Professor of History and Associate Director of the Center for Vietnamese Philosophy, Culture and Society at Temple University before retiring in 2015.

CARL RISKIN is Distinguished Professor of Economics at Queens College, City University of New York, and Senior Research Scholar at the Weatherhead East Asian Institute, Columbia University. He is the author of *China's Political Economy: The Quest for Development Since 1949* (1987) and *Inequality and Poverty in China in the Age of Globalization* (1987, with A. R. Khan) as well as editor of *China's Retreat from Equality*.

TOBIAS RUPPRECHT is Lecturer in Latin American and Caribbean History at the University of Exeter, UK. He is the author of *Soviet Internationalism After Stalin: Interaction and Exchange Between the Soviet Union and Latin America During the Cold War* (2012).

MARK SELDEN is a Senior Research Associate in the East Asia Program at Cornell University, and Editor of *The Asia-Pacific Journal: Japan Focus*. His research on modern and contemporary geopolitics, political economy and history of China, Japan and the Asia-Pacific ranges broadly across themes of war and revolution, inequality, development, regional and world social change, and historical memory. Books include *China in*

Revolution: The Yenan Way Revisited (1995), *Chinese Society: Change, Conflict and Resistance* (2010), *The Resurgence of East Asia: 500, 150 and 50 Year Perspectives* (2003) and *Chinese Village, Socialist State* (1993).

STEPHEN A. SMITH is a historian of modern Russia and China. He is a Senior Research Fellow of All Souls College, Oxford and a Professor of History at Oxford University. His most recent book is *Russia in Revolution: An Empire in Crisis, 1890–1928* (2017). He is currently working on a book on "supernatural politics" that compares the ways in which peasants in Soviet Russia (1917–41) and in China (1949–76) used the resources of popular religion and magic to make sense of the turbulent changes that overwhelmed their lives in the course of the communist revolutions.

ANDRÉ STEINER is Senior Research Fellow at the Center for Contemporary History, Potsdam, and Professor for Economic and Social History at the University of Potsdam. He is the author of *Die DDR-Wirtschaftsreform der sechziger Jahre* (1999) and *The Plans That Failed: An Economic History of the GDR* (2013), and the editor of *Der Mythos von der postindustriellen Welt* (2016, with Werner Plumpe).

DOUGLAS R. WEINER is Professor in the Department of History at the University of Arizona. He is the author of *Models of Nature: Ecology, Conservation and Cultural Revolution in Soviet Russia* (2000) and *A Little Corner of Freedom: Russian Nature Protection from Stalin to Gorbachev* (2002), and editor of *Shades of Green: Environmental Activism Around the Globe* (2006, with Christof Mauch and Nathan Stoltzfus).

MARILYN B. YOUNG is Professor of History at New York University. She is the author of *The Vietnam Wars, 1945–1990* (1991), and editor of *The New American Empire: A 21st Century Teach-in on US Foreign Policy* (2005), *Iraq and the Lessons of Vietnam* (2008) (both with Lloyd C. Gardner) and *Bombing Civilians: A Twentieth-Century History* (2010, with Toshiyuki Tanaka).

VLADISLAV M. ZUBOK is Professor of International History at the London School of Economics and Political Science. His books include *A Failed Empire: The Soviet Union in the Cold War from Stalin to Gorbachev* (2009), *Zhivago's Children: The Last Russian Intelligentsia* (2009) and *The Idea of Russia: The Life and Work of Dmitry Likhachev* (2017).

Introduction to Volume III

JULIANE FÜRST, SILVIO PONS AND MARK SELDEN

This third and final volume of *The Cambridge History of Communism* spans the period from the 1960s to the present. It is a period dominated by the collapse of socialism in Eastern Europe and beyond, the demise of the Soviet Union and the resurgence of China as a global power, and the emergence of a new post-Cold War era of global interdependence, competition and conflict. It also displays, however, certain surprising continuities with the past. Communism, declared dead twenty-five years ago, has left many legacies in the geopolitical, political, social and cultural spheres, which still inform both individual and collective identities all over the world and continue to shape the faultlines in an ever more integrated world. And yet, compared to the 1960s – when communist parties held power in half of Eurasia, communists were important players in Africa and Latin America, and communism was a feared spectre in the Western world – one hundred years after the Russian Revolution, communism is represented on the political stage only by the state capitalism of a nominally communist China, Vietnam, Laos and Cuba, an isolated authoritarian regime in North Korea, a number of backward-looking former ruling parties in Eastern Europe and Russia, and fragmented relics of communist parties elsewhere. In the new millennium, the communist project seems a thing of the past, while its old adversary, nationalism, is thriving under conditions of uncertainty and dissatisfaction with capitalism.

Francis Fukuyama famously proclaimed the demise of communism in the late 1980s and early 1990s as "the end of history." While history clearly has marched ahead steadily ever since, there is no doubt that an epoch did come to an end. Indeed, there is abundant evidence that things were "ending" long before the eventful years of the late 1980s, even predating the timeframe of our volume. And while few predicted the spectacularly swift demise of communist reality that took place within only a few years, many, including some communist officials and intellectuals, had long recognized the enormous challenges faced by communism and its multiple failings in all sectors of life throughout the postwar period.

The decades under investigation here also examine the multiple strategies advanced by communist rulers, economists, ideologues, intellectuals and activists to transform and reform communism. These attempts stretch from the largely unsuccessful Kosygin reforms in the Soviet Union in 1965 to the more successful market transformation of the Deng Xiaoping era in China in the 1980s and beyond, and from East European attempts to create "socialism with a human face" in the 1960s to the attempts by New Left forces worldwide in 1968 and its aftermath to rescue the lost radicalism of Marxist ideas, to the emergence of the Eurocommunist project from the mid 1970s. It includes the efforts of socialist elites to face up to their history as well as the deliberate obscuring of this history. It is visible in the many structures built since the 1960s which were meant to embody communist principles in everyday life as well as in many cultural policies appealing not only to those living within the communist sphere but also to a global audience. The failure of Mikhail Gorbachev's reforms marked the end of these diverse attempts in European and Soviet communism, while the "Chinese way" (including variants such as those in Vietnam, North Korea and perhaps Cuba) remained to suggest that communist regimes could survive and advance only by adapting to world capitalism – its historical antagonist. In certain ways the search for new applications of socialist ideas may still be ongoing, but nowadays these are rarely couched in communist terms.

It is communism's late twentieth-century and, for China and Vietnam, even early 21st-century struggle to redefine itself in order to remain relevant – East and West, geopolitically as well as culturally, economically and ideologically, in the eyes of the world and in the hearts and minds of its subjects and its proponents – that provides the main narrative of this volume and the multiple perspectives of its contributions. All of these topics have been the subjects of innovative research in recent years. We draw on rapidly evolving historiographical and methodological approaches – notably in social, cultural, gender and transnational history – to transcend the old separation between communist studies and the broader field of contemporary history, particularly global history.

Hindsight is a dangerous historical tool, but it is also one that cannot be ignored. We have titled our volume *Endgames? Late Communism in Global Perspective, 1968 to the Present*. We posit that we cannot overlook the fact that communism ended in Europe and the Soviet Union (and, de facto, economically and socially even in Asia), but we wish to avoid a definitive judgement, which in our opinion is still premature. Rather than labeling our volume "the end" we deliberately place the emphasis on "games." The period 1960 to the present, rather than being exclusively one of decline or collapse, is multivalent. First of all, not only for those who lived under communism, but also for many avid Western observers and political actors, Alexei Yurchak's title for his study of late Soviet society astutely captures the fact that "Everything was forever, until it was no more."[1] Communism's end as a political force in Europe paradoxically arrived both as a surprise and as a long-predicted event. Communist shortcomings were a favorite topic not only of the Western press, but also around East European and Soviet kitchen tables and among the intelligentsia – and not least in the ranks of the Chinese political elite during and after the Cultural Revolution. And yet, the effort to survive both within and with communism continued to the very end and, for some, beyond.

Second – and this was another reason why we felt the term "endgames" captured the spirit of the times well – the games could be seen as "endgames" with two possible outcomes. On the one hand, we now see that communism played its final games on numerous battlefields – not only in Eastern Europe and the Soviet Union but also among Western sympathizers and Latin American and African revolutionaries and on several Asian fronts. In the 1960s and 1970s communism was fighting on more international fronts than ever before. It reached into the newly decolonized world in Africa and Asia, it attracted many Latin American rebels leading to revolutions in Cuba, Nicaragua, El Salvador and elsewhere, and it found new credibility, though only in its Maoist or Castroist incarnations, among the young global counterculture and New Left protest movement in Europe, North America and beyond. On the other hand, for a while, especially in the late 1960s and early 1970s when the West was battling with political upheaval and economic crisis, it appeared that the "endgames" could have resulted in very different outcomes – ones that left capitalism, not communism, in tatters.

1 Alexei Yurchak, *Everything Was Forever, Until It Was No More: The Last Soviet Generation* (Princeton: Princeton University Press, 2006).

Finally, our narrative stresses the international and global aspects of the era. Not only the vision and ideology of communism but also the reality of diverse state socialisms were international phenomena that fueled transnational connections. As the contributions to this volume make clear, there were multiple ways in which people understood communism, what they hoped for, how they assessed their experiences and what they feared. This was true not only of those living under communist rule but also of people throughout the world.

This period also contains a narrative of divergence, not least symbolized by the different fates of the two main players in the communist "endgames" as they were earlier: The Soviet Union and China in the 1950s boasted of "the greatest friendship" and a productive alliance and aid relationship. Within a decade this turned into bitter rivalry fought out within the communist sphere and beyond. And yet this was also an age of solidarity and mutual support among people and causes that could loosely be defined as being on "the left." The Soviet Union had long proclaimed decolonization, social rights and labor movements worldwide as communist causes, albeit not always priority issues. China too promoted Maoism across the globe at times, not merely competing with Western capitalism and imperialism, but from the 1960s above all challenging its one-time ally, the Soviet Union. In both East and West many people rallied in solidarity with the Vietnam revolutionaries and supported anti-colonial liberation movements throughout Africa, Asia and Latin America. They aligned with popular movements, striking workers and peasants everywhere, and some hailed China's Red Guards (however hazy their idea about realities on the ground). At the same time, a predatory capitalist West was a constant presence in the mind of communist leaders and many communist subjects. "Those in authority taking the capitalist road" served as whipping boys in the Chinese Cultural Revolution, while the challenge of a vibrant but exploitative capitalism provided a constant catalyst for competition for communist rulers. Yet the powerful attractions of Western civilization throughout remained a benchmark for dreams and aspirations for many people in communist countries. In this global age, communism was an ideological and systemic challenge, one that was supported or rejected by diverse global players.

In short, for many reasons we decided to put a question mark after "Endgames." This is not only because the world's most populous country, and one of its most dynamic, is still nominally communist. It is also because much of what defined the period under discussion has left deep traces, despite the demise of the communist superstructure that once seemed so formidable. Not only are continuities of regimes in China, Vietnam, North Korea and Cuba noticeable, but it is important to recognize more subtle legacies in terms of social practices and habits, ways of thinking, power networks and institutional forms that have affected the evolution of postcommunist Russia and Eurasia.[2] Russia and the West, and China and the West, remain locked in power struggles that rest not only on political interests but also on deep mutual misunderstandings and different concepts of the relationship between democracy and sovereignty, the nature of power politics and interdependence, multipolarity and the international community. Many formerly communist countries are now pursuing neo-authoritarian politics under the mantle of nationalism and "managed" democracy, while many rights associated with civil society are sharply restricted. And the question that confronted communism (and indeed capitalism) in the later half of the twentieth century – how to keep ideas of social justice relevant while achieving economic success – remains unresolved.

It quickly became apparent that in the period covered by this study – possibly even more than at any other time – there was not one but multiple histories of communism. The very notion of communism never ceased presenting ambivalent and multifaceted meanings. What was communism? From the standpoint of Marxist utopian visions, communism never existed, never could exist, as a political and economic entity, but only as an ideology proclaiming a future prosperity for all and the end of class differentiation. While the Soviet Union declared on several occasions that socialism had been achieved and China claimed to be on the eve of communism during the Great Leap Forward, no communist leader dared to declare a society communist, which in Marxist-Leninist eschatology represented the end of struggle and the perfection of a classless society in an age of abundance for all. Yet, while this distinction was still used by Soviet leaders Nikita Khrushchev and Leonid Brezhnev, when promising communism "in our lifetime" or extolling the necessity of "developed socialism," de facto in popular parlance in East and West "communism" and "socialism" were freely interchangeable and used for both ideological ascriptions as well as descriptions of social, economic and cultural policies and practices. The polarization of the Cold War did little to clarify the

---

2 Mark R. Beissinger and Stephen Kotkin (eds.), *Historical Legacies of Communism in Russia and Eastern Europe* (New York: Cambridge University Press, 2014).

terms and much to blur the boundaries between aspiration and reality and endow the term "communism," depending on the standpoint of the speaker, with a whole host of negative or positive associations. We have sought to illuminate the concepts of socialism and communism and commissioned work that ranges from the exploration of late twentieth-century communist political and socioeconomic praxis to essays on the lived reality of socialism, from communism as expressed not only verbally but also visually, to the transmuted and manipulated forms that existed over the past half-century.

Our awareness that the history of communism has to be told in multiple different yet interlinked registers, has led us to group the chapters into three parts, each of which conveys an important, yet not exclusive story. Following on from the second volume, which charts communism's rise across the globe, we begin with a part on the new global role of communism in what, as is now apparent, was the heyday of its international reach. Communism shaped Cold War geopolitics, a significant part of the world economy and even a substantial part of global youth culture. The Soviet Union had apparently stabilized its East European sphere of influence after the repression of the Prague Spring in 1968, and competed with the West and China in the global South. Communist-inspired movements struggled and in some cases came to power in Asia, Africa and Latin America, while the West faced turmoil and predicament throughout the 1970s. Yet communism also confronted fractures and predicaments. Mao continued following the independent path he had taken from Moscow already in the 1950s, culminating in the Cultural Revolution, and then in the 1970s rapprochement with the United States. The Sino-Soviet conflict erupted everywhere, destroying the former unity of international communism. Western communist parties struggled for identity and legitimacy in this field of contention, distancing themselves from the Soviet Union after the crushing of the Prague Spring. The New Left and other left-leaning protest movements adopted elements of communist thought, but they also declared many of its state proponents (particularly the Soviet Union), and even communist parties, morally and politically bankrupt. Global presence entailed a global price in funds, arms and political capital. The Cold War created deep strains for the Soviet Union, particularly the war in Afghanistan and social turmoil in Poland. Western-led global economic expansion exacted a toll on stagnant Soviet-type economies as Eastern Europe became dependent on Western capital. In Europe, early attempts to construct new forms of legitimacy were confined to West European communism, and emerged in Moscow belatedly only under Gorbachev. Europe's 1989 was a global event in itself, leading shortly to the collapse of Soviet communism and amplifying its consequences.

At the same time, communism in its historical heartland was beset by other problems, which were consequences of the fact that communism existed not merely as an ideology and player on the global stage, but as a lived reality – what Rudolf Bahro has termed "actually existing socialism."[3] In 1917 communism had established itself as the creed of the most revolutionary and radical party – the Bolsheviks, victors in the Russian Revolution. Half a century later, communist parties had seized power in countries ranging across Eastern Europe, Asia, Africa and Latin America, with robust communist parties vying for power in many other countries. Seventy years later, the labels of revolutionary and radical were in tatters as Soviet and East European realities suggested an aging bureaucracy fighting not only severe economic problems but also, most importantly, a general sense of ennui among communist subjects with the very ideology and praxis that were supposed to generate enthusiastic participation. Yet here too it would be wrong to assume a unidirectional trajectory. As our essays on the lived experience of communism demonstrate, late socialist life was not devoid of its own dynamics and movements, some of which were initiated by ruling communist parties, and some of which were the result of variations, subversion and autonomous action by various actors who would not be bound by Soviet orthodoxy and who sensed the weakening of Soviet power. Yet all of these aspects made up the world of late communism as played out on the ground, and it is at times hard to draw the line between its history and the history of the countries in which socialism provided not only the state system but the social, cultural and economic framework. In particular, Soviet and East European historiography has posed critical questions of the lived communist experience.

The diverging fates of Soviet and Chinese communism are at the center of our third part. Despite many similarities, communist policy as well as communist experience in China were always distinct from those of the Soviet Union or Eastern Europe. China's revolution emerged from protracted guerrilla warfare centered in revolutionary base areas and, with the subsequent Great Leap Forward and Cultural Revolution, it embarked on its own distinctive path long before the final decades of communism in Europe. But at no time were differences more profound than in the late 1980s when

---

3 Rudolf Bahro, *The Alternative in Eastern Europe* (London: New Left Books, 1978).

China's regime crushed student protests in Tiananmen Square and throughout the nation, while Gorbachev sought to reform the Soviet system with *glasnost'* and *perestroika*. The results, however, were counterintuitive. As Gorbachev appeared to unintentionally instigate political collapse in the Soviet Union and the Soviet economy went into free fall, China's communist leaders engineered a top-down as well as market-driven transition in a postsocialist economy and society, which is best understood as state capitalism with Chinese characteristics. Continued communist party rule and maintenance of the Chinese empire, together with that country's dynamic economic, financial and geopolitical resurgence, contrast sharply with the experience of the Soviet Union and Eastern Europe. But it would also be premature to dismiss the significance of communist legacies in Europe or predict the "endgame" for either China or Russia.

Contents

The first part of the volume deals with the impact of transnational events and processes from the 1960s onward, the gradual transformation of the Cold War order and major geopolitical factors resulting in the crisis and eventual demise of Soviet socialism and the collapse of the Soviet empire. The elements of strength and the expansive thrust of communism as they were long perceived by many contemporaries concealed profound contradictions and flaws culminating in the fissiparous events of 1989–91 in Europe and the Soviet Union. Severe international political and economic challenges had combined and surfaced by the early 1980s. The chapters in this part reveal multiple intertwined developments. Together they show how the "endgames" of communist history may be understood in a global context in which communist forces were less and less capable of decisively shaping outcomes.

The multiple ambivalent meanings of 1968 in communist history provide ample material for reflection and periodization. As Robert Gildea argues in "The Global 1968 and International Communism," by the end of the 1960s dominant cultural and political landscapes of the postwar era were profoundly changing. In particular, a new generation of young revolutionaries shared languages of anti-imperialism and Third Worldism with the communists, but identified most communist establishments in the Soviet Union, Eastern Europe and beyond with Stalinism and rejected their bureaucratic, dictatorial or imperialist evolution. Consequently, they created diverse revolutionary trajectories and political spaces, which diverged from dominant traditions – though some were inspired by new icons such as Mao, Che Guevara and Ho Chi Minh. The impact of 1968 was multidimensional and its meanings differed from the perspectives of the First, Second and Third Worlds. Disaffection created by the repression of the Prague Spring, penetration of countercultures beyond the Iron Curtain, China's tumultuous Cultural Revolution and the development of new languages forged by social movements in capitalist countries in both core and periphery converged to displace orthodox communist beliefs and self-confidence.

Even the pivotal international event of the 1970s, the Vietnam War – which catalyzed the hopes and projects of global revolt – may be said to have left a contradictory legacy. Marilyn Young and Sophie Quinn-Judge show the far-reaching implications of Vietnam, beyond the war itself, both at the level of governments and people – as it was connected for many to "a shared sense of liberation from repressive social conventions." The transnational antiwar movement had a worldwide impact and particularly stimulated anti-imperialist feelings throughout the Third World. Activists and militants saw the war as a prelude to revolutionary engagements from the Middle East to Latin America. However, the capacity of communists and revolutionaries to build on the symbolic effect of Vietnam was limited both because the Cambodian Revolution showed a very different face of communism and because a new intra-communist conflict arose in Indochina in the immediate aftermath of the Vietnamese victory. As Ben Kiernan puts it, "The Cambodia–Vietnam conflict that began in 1977–78 signaled a final collapse of the global communist vision," a reference both to the massacres conducted by Cambodian forces led by Pol Pot and to the Cambodia-Vietnam-China wars that were among its legacies. The long-term legacy of the Vietnam War for international civil society was to underline the illegitimacy of violent interventions by the great powers to shape societies and polities in their own image, lessons that would reverberate into the new millennium.

Artemy Kalinovsky reflects on how Moscow's policies shifted from strategies of modernization in the Third World – which pivoted on the attractiveness of the Soviet model – to military interventions in postcolonial conflicts. For a decade or more after Stalin's death, the Soviets prioritized support for state-led development and state-socialist ideology in the decolonizing world. Military aid was a component of this strategy, but it increasingly became the focus of bipolar global confrontation in the era of détente with the West. A new wave of revolutionary movements in Africa after the fall of the Portuguese empire in 1974 was the turning point. Paradoxically, the peak of Soviet influence in the Third World coincided with the decline of its appeal as an economic and ideological model. Direct intervention in Ethiopia and Afghanistan had a ruinous effect, undermining the credibility of the Soviet Union as an anti-imperialist power. Contrary to conventional wisdom, the Afghan War did not significantly weaken Moscow in economic terms, but it did lead to ideological retreat from the Third World, a course which Gorbachev completed. Piero Gleijeses integrates this picture by providing a perspective on the Cold War in Latin America and Africa. By the end of the 1960s, the ability of Cuba to mobilize revolutionary forces in Latin America and Africa had declined. However, by the mid 1970s new revolutionary upsurges were underway in Africa and then in Latin America. The Cuban internationalist initiative was crucial in Angola both to force Moscow's hand and to defeat South African subimperialism. Then Cuba and the Soviet Union coordinated their action in Ethiopia. A few months later, the Sandinista revolution in Nicaragua secured Cuban help. In other words, Cuba played a role in promoting revolutionary actions that influenced and changed Cold War frameworks, particularly in Africa and Latin America – though only after earlier dreams of revolutionary independence and internationalism had been shattered.

At the same time, communist internationalism was unable to maintain its previous place in diverse global discourses. Mark Bradley shows that socialist advocacy for collective economic and social rights and the backing of postcolonial self-determination persisted in the 1970s, but the most radical change came with the development of human rights discourse, which challenged state-based politics and ideologies. In socialist societies, human rights as a moral language had an impact both through the official discourse on détente and the Helsinki agreements, and because dissidents had already forged a "repertoire of thought and action" which sought to deepen post-Stalin concerns with humanistic socialism. As Bradley remarks, the new human rights discourse established by dissidents such as Aleksandr Solzhenitsyn, Andrei Sakharov and Václav Havel transcended the boundaries of the Cold War to assume transnational significance for intellectuals and shape public opinion. They contributed to delegitimizing communism while ensuring the longlasting and universal influence of human rights perspectives even beyond the end of the Cold War. In the communist world, attempts were made to carry out reforms and redefine the terms of human rights. Michele Di Donato and Silvio Pons maintain that "reform communism" was a reactive component of communist political culture whose legacy crucially influenced Gorbachev's *perestroika*.

In the aftermath of de-Stalinization, reform attempts were confined to the sphere of economics. However, the implications of change emerged fully in the Prague Spring's call for "humanistic socialism." After its repression, transnational ideas of reform were inherited by Eurocommunism, and the quest to renovate communist legitimacy inspired Gorbachev – though in contradictory ways that ended by calling into question communist identity as such. In short, reform-inspired communist culture proved central to the fading away of Marxist revolutionary traditions in Europe and Russia.

We see communism's problems of legitimacy in the wider context of changes taking place in global capitalism, transnational connections, the digital revolution and postindustrial transformations East and West, which have shaped the world since the last quarter of the twentieth century. This was the context that brought to a head the combination of ideological decline and economic predicament of Soviet socialism. Charles Maier points retrospectively to the shocking effects of the transformations of global political economy on state socialism and its claims of industrial modernity and legitimacy, as "[a]ll the premises that earlier had helped make Marxian economics plausible were changing from the mid 1960s through the 1980s." André Steiner analyzes the problems that made Soviet-type economies uncompetitive in the realm of global transformations. The attempts to reconcile planning with the market by means of economic reforms came to an end in 1968. The gap in technology, productivity and consumer goods with the West increased. East European countries turned to an import-led strategy of growth, which increased debt with Western countries. The 1973 oil shock had mixed consequences, as the Soviet Union benefited from rising prices in the world market, but its satellites faced rising prices even within the framework of Comecon. In the wake of the second oil shock of 1979, Eastern Europe faced a debt crisis and Poland came close to bankruptcy. Economic performance worsened in the region, and the Eastern bloc countries "lived beyond their means for many years." However, Steiner concludes that the basic limits to economic change lay in the political sphere, as party officials, planning authorities and bureaucratic interests opposed any reform that could jeopardize their power. Gorbachev dismantled planning structures without establishing a new system to allocate resources, which led to disruptive economic crisis.

Still, the peaceful demise of communist regimes throughout Eastern Europe and the Soviet Union should not be seen as inevitable. It involved complex interactions between long-term processes and contingency, resulting in a decline in legitimacy and self-confidence. James Mark and Tobias Rupprecht show the fateful convergence between the political, economic and imperial predicaments of Soviet communism in 1989 by offering a global perspective. The neoliberal consensus that emerged in the West and extended to Latin America and elsewhere strongly influenced the economic reforms in Eastern Europe. The thrust toward peaceful democratization which was powerfully initiated with Poland's Solidarność reflected wider change that had taken place in Southern Europe in the 1970s and implied a new inclusive role for the European Community.

The retreat of the Soviet Union from its sphere of influence in Eastern Europe, too, echoed ideas of East–West interdependence that formed the core of Gorbachev's "new thinking" and discredited the old-fashioned link between communist internationalism and authoritarianism, while encouraging national self-determination. The transformations of Europe's 1989 fueled an expansion of all these processes and influenced other regions, resulting in new geopolitical formations and democratization struggles and, notably in China, accelerated market transition combined with authoritarian rule. Vladislav Zubok's chapter provides insights on the correlation between the fall of communist regimes in Eastern Europe and the dissolution of the Soviet Union. Zubok demonstrates how international political and economic pressures limited the choices of the Soviet leadership as "the Cold War ended not on Gorbachev's terms, but on the terms of the West." The attempt to integrate the Soviet Union into the international system and world economy gave rise to reforms that in fact accelerated Soviet disintegration by dismantling communist institutions.

Yet communism did not merely fight a battle for superiority and survival in the world arena. Most urgently it also fought to remain credible among hundreds of millions of people who were its subjects around the globe. As the preceding volume has shown, this took many different forms including cultural revolution that kept the young engaged, political reform to heal the wounds of Stalinism, and a zigzag pattern from liberalization and conservative entrenchment to stem the tide of demands from left and right. Most significantly, however, the internal travails of communism were among the great domestic and international events, responses to myriad quotidian problems and challenges – many of which it had created and set itself. Throughout the postwar years, communism was a global force in motion that shaped people's lives, spaces and landscapes, artifacts, everyday objects and social relations.

The Soviet Union, as the oldest "actually existing" socialist society, provided the blueprint for much of post-1945 Eastern Europe in establishing a world that was communist not only in outlook but also in deed and appearance. The specificities of everyday "socialism" (with which, as noted, "communism" was at times used interchangeably, especially outside the Soviet Union) have been most attentively researched even as socialist societies emerged across East Asia and beyond. Analysis of the Soviet bloc nations in the 1950s through the 1980s ironically seems to suggest a decline of communism as an ideology, just as more people were living in communist-inspired societies than ever before. It seems that communism as a lived experience did not necessarily further communism as an ideological force, but rather caused its subversion, manipulation and adaptation. The second part hence opens with a chapter by Juliane Fürst and Stephen Bittner, which emphasizes that the Soviet Union was by no means doomed in the 1970s – indeed it had found an uneasy equilibrium between a modicum of material comforts and tacit acceptance – but that the lack of belief in a communist eschatology meant that what shaped late socialism was not communism but practices of accommodation. One of the peculiarities of late socialism was that it existed as a physical, visual and social reality but was propped up mainly by the *performance* of ideology rather than its content. This fact forces us to rethink what communism actually meant in the last few decades of the twentieth century, since clearly Marxist, Leninist or Maoist thought no longer determined it in its entirety. The following chapter, by Stephen Smith, looks at another longstanding battle of communism, that with its greatest ideological foe: religion. Smith too argues that there is no easy linear history of communism's relationship with religion and that practices could differ widely from ideologically pure interpretations of Marxist doctrine, depending on the expediencies of time. Ultimately, there was no clear winner or loser in the contest for people's faith. From the Soviet Union to China, communism left societies secularized yet not devoid of religious beliefs. Communist rationale found itself in the end as embattled as religious devotion, while neither was ever completely eradicated.

Various chapters in this part take up the issue of communism as a force that created a lived reality, which reflected ideological premises but existed regardless of belief. Reuben Fowkes looks at one of the most obvious visual interventions of communism into the European landscape: the construction of iconic buildings and monuments all across Eastern Europe. While designed to express and further communist ideology, they also have a life as physical objects that shape and change spaces and landscapes. They can be read in a multitude of ways and change meaning according to circumstance, creating a dynamic that owes its existence, but not necessarily its content, to communist state projects. They are also potent reminders that the collapse of communism in Europe in 1989–91 did not mean the end of many communist realities, underlining the point that the lived experience of communism developed an existence that was not inextricably linked to the ideology that once inspired it. Similarly, the history of communist propaganda in all its new media presence, as discussed by Stephen Lovell in his chapter on Cold War media in the Soviet Union and Eastern Europe, demonstrates that late or developed socialism was shaped less by fervent ideological belief than by creating a set of familiar tropes that might fail in their initial aim of inciting ideological conviction yet, with hindsight, left an enduring legacy of a shared communist past. Film, newspapers, radio, television and even literature all showcased the limitations of the heavily regulated communist propaganda machine, especially when compared to its slick Western counterparts in Hollywood and New York, but it created a dense net of images, impressions and associations that in total made up a strong framework of experience. In short, the output of late socialist media and propaganda, as described by Lovell, failed on many fronts, including its primary one of effectiveness, but nevertheless was an important constituent of the experience of living under communism.

Polly Jones in exploring the "zones of late socialist literature" dispels the notion that late socialism – as the lived communist experience is mainly referred to by scholars – can be neatly divided between those "for" and "against" the regimes and their ideology or even into "official" and "unofficial." Nominally there were three zones operating in literature – state publishing, self-publishing, which became known by its Russian term "samizdat," and publishing abroad, also called "tamizdat." Yet, a closer look at literary production demonstrates that many actors worked in several spheres, often under different names, and that there was not much homogeneity within these spheres. Rather than clinging to Cold War dichotomies of communist and anti-communist or even East and West, a more differentiated view is needed to come to terms with what communist reality meant. This is also apparent in Celia Donert's discussion of feminism, globalism and communism. Feminism was one of the forces that emerged from the global 1960s counterculture; it swept through the West in the 1970s, changing both legislation and minds (to what extent, of course, is still hotly debated). Meanwhile in Eastern Europe and the Soviet Union the women's question had been raised much earlier and had achieved much in terms both of legislation and of changing minds and praxis. Women who lived under communism in the Soviet Union and Eastern Europe but also in China and Vietnam felt entitled to a working life to an extent that has still not been achieved in the West. By contrast, Western feminism decided to make the personal political, demanding a type of equality that was not even debated in communist societies and was considered unnecessary in communist doctrine. Donert looks at how these two worlds nonetheless became entangled in each other, but concludes that ultimately they remained separate entities, each in its own way incomplete. Marko Dumančić picks up this theme in his discussion of gender identities in the Soviet Union and China, in both their socialist and postsocialist incarnations. He emphasizes how profoundly communist policies affected both genders, creating not only a specifically socialist female experience, but also a certain type of masculinity that still reverberates in Russia and China today. He neatly anticipates in his conclusions the issues raised by Jan Behrends and Jan Plamper, both of whom point to a number of continuities from the socialist to the postsocialist world, thus justifying the question mark in our title. Seventy-plus years of lived communism altered not only the world but also communism itself. Where communism ended and other ideologies, identities and ideas picked up is difficult to tell – not only in the case of the Soviet Union and Eastern Europe but possibly even more so in China.

The simultaneous collapse of communism across the countries of Eastern Europe and the dismantling of the Soviet Union led many to conclude that the death knell of communism as a world phenomenon was at hand."'A spectre is haunting Europe . . . ' The most famous phrase to emerge from the revolutions of 1848 has come true in a totally unintended way: 170 years later, communism in Europe is just a spectre, a ghostly memory," Charles Maier concludes. Looking beyond the collapse of ruling communist parties to "the more general loss of collectivist vision East and West," he finds that this was part of a major systemic transition in the global political economy that has played out in different ways across the world. On the eve of the 100th anniversary of the Bolshevik Revolution, Jan Plamper finds that the very recollection of communism in Russia seems to be disappearing from popular memory as 1917 yields to commemoration of 4 November 1612 (the liberation of Moscow from Polish rule) and especially 9 May 1945. This date – the Soviet victory in World War II – has become the archetypal national holiday and celebration of the strong Soviet state, while the embrace of the Russian Orthodox Church rather than the revolutionary promise of the Bolsheviks is celebrated by the contemporary Soviet state in official and popular memory.

What of those regions, primarily in Asia, where communist parties not only continue to dominate the political realm but also have exhibited extraordinary economic dynamism? Ho-fung Hung and Mark Selden observe that it was precisely in the final decades of the twentieth century that China drew attention, as a result of three decades of the world's most dynamic economic growth in a nation that proclaimed its own distinctive socialist – but in fact postsocialist – path, even as it redefined its relationship with the United States and the world economy. Within decades China's economic resurgence forced a rethinking of two propositions: that communism could not compete economically with capitalism and that the Chinese Communist Party (CCP) could not sustain power in a market-driven economy like those that emerged in China and Vietnam. Along with Maier, they find that economic transformation was possible precisely by jettisoning the core elements of state socialism for a market-driven state capitalism without abandoning the one-party communist state. The large economic gains and the consolidation of China as a major power went hand in hand with the continued repressive apparatus dominated by the CCP.

What explains China's economic resurgence and relative political stability? Mao's successor Deng Xiaoping is frequently credited with China's great postsocialist transformation, but Karl Gerth insists that the most powerful impetus toward a market economy and freedom of movement came from below, from farmers and petty entrepreneurs who fueled the drive that enabled China to emerge as the world's second-largest economy and the workshop of the world. Assessing China's transformation from a human relations perspective, Carl Riskin documents contradictory elements: "[T]he great majority of the population experienced a huge improvement in living standards, along with advances in longevity and nutrition, and greatly expanded personal freedom – all principal components of 'human development.'" At the same time, inequality has increased, worker security has evaporated, the natural environment has deteriorated, and an oppressive reproductive policy led to serious demographic imbalances, "all impediments to human development." Many of these phenomena could be found not only in China but also in the former socialist states and in capitalist countries in the global phenomenon of neoliberalism that has reshaped economies everywhere since the 1980s along lines of rampant inequality and precarity.

All of these authors raise important questions about what remained of the socialist promise and the hopes for development, not least by drawing attention to the threat posed by environmental crises that have accompanied China's and other countries' race to industrialization and urbanization. Douglas Weiner points out that "because communist societies' [developmental] goals have been largely borrowed from those of the capitalist world, they share many of the same features of resource management, beginning with a reliance on fossil fuels and nuclear energy," leading to the climate crisis that currently confronts humanity, with neither market nor regulatory state-driven policies thus far demonstrating the capability of resolving the fossil fuel crisis. He concludes that in both market and communist regimes, concerns "about human health, habitat preservation, species extinction and planetary environmental systems all took a back seat to shorter-term development goals." The question remains whether postcommunism or capitalism can effectively confront the environmental crisis borne of shared development priorities that transcend the statist and market-driven paradigms.

What, then, will be the lasting legacy of communist experience? Jan Behrends notes that, a century after the October Revolution, the legacies of the communist movement and communist power vary, but "the most lasting legacy of communist rule is the Leninist party-state," one that takes different forms in the former Soviet Union, Eastern Europe and beyond, depending crucially on the destruction or continued rule of the party, but also on the subsequent experience of war and militarized violence, as in the Soviet invasion of Afghanistan and the war in Chechnya. While sprouts of democracy emerged in the Balkan states in the wake of the collapse of communism in Eastern Europe, nearly everywhere democracy was soon discredited and, as in the states that comprised the former Soviet Union, oligarchs linked to the army prevailed. In Russia, moreover, Behrends finds, Putin initiated a re-Sovietization of political culture including political repression, the cult of the leader and strategic use of mass organizations.

Evaluating Late Communism

Why did the communist global project fail, notably with the demise of communism in Eastern Europe and the Soviet Union, but also, from another perspective, in China where the CCP is firmly entrenched and presides over a dynamic development agenda even as it leads the nation toward a distinctive form of state capitalism? How can we locate the collapse of the Soviet Union and its empire not only as a landmark event in the history of communism but also as a world-historical event? What were the consequences of this event, which for so long looked suspiciously like a seamless transition to democratic forms of government? How are we to assess the transformation and resurgence of China with respect to continuity and rupture as new social and economic forms emerge even if the CCP retains its monopoly on power? Such questions will continue to fuel debates not only among historians of communism but also among students of global social and political change, as they are crucial for assessing the great transformations of the long twentieth century with critical implications for our times and the future.

In particular, we would underline two key implications. First, there was a significant shift in how people viewed communism from the late 1960s onward in both East and West as well as in North and South. The fact that communism already had a lived history of fifty years, a record in the international arena and tangible policy results significantly shaped its perception. Most notably, communism fragmented in the minds of people – indeed long before its fragmentation on the global stage. In the West, communism was reimagined in terms of variants associated with national traditions, or in various New Left variations, while in the East it became a way of life that was only tenuously anchored in ideology. Svetlana Boym has identified this shift in sentiment in the Soviet Union as one from ideology to nostalgia. Communism lived there as a memory of a more youthful, radical past that was desirable, but of a different era.[4] Everyday communism, however, was bound up with the grind of daily life. In the West, Soviet communism's loss of faith in itself did not go unnoticed. Hardly anyone referred to Soviet reality as a guiding light, as many had in the 1930s. Yet this did not mean that none of the tenets of communism was appealing, albeit they were repackaged to the point of nonrecognizability. It would be foolish not to acknowledge the impact of Marxist ideas on Western societies to this very day, especially since its old adversary, capitalism, still reigns supreme, yet deeply troubled.

Second, the different paths of communism's downfall and multiple transformations are inextricably part of the remaking of the contemporary world.

4 Svetlana Boym, *Another Freedom: The Alternative History of an Idea* (Chicago: University of Chicago Press, 2010).

Communist experiences were not simply the outcome of globalization; they also sprang from domestic dynamics, forces both from above and below, external and internal to national communisms. This should lead us to perceive contemporary global processes as more multifaceted than triumphal public discourses in the West have often assumed. Narratives that exclusively focus on US-led Western nations as the driving force of global change, and deterministic assumptions about the inevitable breakdown of the communist "anomaly," fail to capture the varied outcomes described here. This volume seeks to provide perspective on the multiple and open-ended trajectories of communism as well as on its crises, failures and changes through lenses of world interdependencies, state resilience and global capitalism that continue to shape our present and future.

PART I

*

GLOBALISM AND CRISIS

The Global 1968 and International Communism

ROBERT GILDEA

In June 1962 a meeting of Students for a Democratic Society (SDS) at Port Huron, Michigan, of whom Tom Hayden was the leading light, published a statement expressing anxiety about the current situation in the United States. While they had been raised on the American dream of "freedom and equality for each individual, government of, by, and for the people," they were now confronted by what they called "the Southern struggle against racial bigotry" and "the Cold War, symbolized by the presence of the Bomb," the "military-industrial complex" and the "Warfare State." The current political system, they held, was "an organized political stalemate" based on the "paranoia" of anti-communism, which shut down social and political criticism, even in the universities. Their demands for a "participatory democracy" that involved ordinary citizens in decision-making at the grassroots became the founding manifesto of the New Left.[1]

Two years later, in November 1964, two Polish students, Karol Modzelewski and Jacek Kuroń, drafted an open letter to the Polish Workers' Party, the ruling party of communist Poland. The letter accused their communist rulers of having forgotten their anti-fascist and Marxist ideals and of erecting a "central political bureaucracy" that regarded youth, the working class and peasants as their enemy. They called for freedom of speech, meeting, research and artistic creation, a plurality of political parties, trade unions that were independent of the state and had the right to strike, and workers' councils to be set up in factories. Modzelewski and Kuroń were arrested, put on trial in July 1965 and sentenced to three years in prison.[2]

---

1 Richard Flacks and Nelson Lichtenstein, *The Port Huron Statement: Sources and Legacies of the New Left's Founding Manifesto* (Philadelphia: University of Pennsylvania Press, 2015), 239–43, 249–59.
2 Jacek Kuroń and Karol Modzelewski, *An Open Letter to the Party Written in a Polish Prison* (London: Socialist Review, 1969), 8, 51–63.

The original draft was confiscated but a redraft was circulated in secret from hand to hand and internationally.

Political Revolt

Although written more than 4,000 miles apart, these texts came out of a certain global context. World War II had been over for twenty years, but there was a feeling among many young people that many of the legacies of Nazism and fascism were still present. On either side of the Cold War divide, liberal democracies or people's democracies flourished, but both the American and Soviet regimes might be criticized as military-industrial-security regimes geared to developing nuclear weapons, motivated by anti-communist or communist ideologies and setting firm limits on individual freedom. Opposition to this stalemate came less from political radicals in Europe than from the American South where the civil rights movement took off, and from the Third World of underdeveloped Latin America, Africa and Asia where peasant and urban revolutions against corrupt local regimes supported by American imperialism spread like wildfire in the 1960s. Opposition also came from global cultural movements of young people challenging their parents' generation and the postwar world in general and providing a broad context of discontent and creativity in which more political avant-garde protest could flourish.

These texts also reflected other protest movements in the 1960s in that they occupied a broad and diverse political field between anti-Stalinism on the one hand and anti-imperialism, anti-capitalism and anti-racism on the other. Stalinism, seen to be embodied by official communist parties, stood for militarism and bureaucracy, purges and the Gulag system. Protest was revolutionary, and revolutionary often meant Marxist, but Stalinism was deemed the opposite of revolution. A Marxist revolutionary might be a Trotskyist, inspired by the Bolshevik avant-garde of 1917, a Maoist, inspired by the Long March and the Chinese Cultural Revolution, or a Castroist or Guevarist, inspired by the leaders of Third World revolutions against American imperialism. Not all revolutionaries, however, were Marxists. They might be anarchists, hating the dictatorship of the proletariat and loving the councils movement that swept across Europe from Kronstadt to Spain at the end of World War I. They might be architects of the New Left, which broke with communism after the 1956 Soviet invasion of Hungary and developed libertarian Marxist ideas. They might be militants of the civil rights movement in the United States, which in turn inspired many protest movements in Europe. Or they might belong to much wider cultural rebellions and countercultural revolts that swept up young people in the long 1960s.

Protest movements emerged in a similar global context, but they were inflected according to local political circumstances. The so-called free world headed by the United States and including Japan was fiercely anti-communist, communist parties being banned in South Africa in 1950, the United States in 1954 and West Germany in 1956. In the Eastern bloc of Europe, communist regimes banned all other political parties and clamped down on all noncommunist views. Northern Europe was run by democratic regimes while Mediterranean countries – such as Spain under Francisco Franco and Greece, where the communist party was banned in 1947 and the colonels seized power in 1967 – were dictatorships supported by the USA as bastions against communism. In the global South, meanwhile, from the American South to Africa and Asia, a fightback was taking place in the 1960s against racial segregation, the oppression of the European colonial powers and American imperialism, which in turn had a huge impact on protest movements in Europe and North America.

There were significant encounters, connections and transfers between these protest movements, at the level of individuals, organizations and images. For example, the Students for a Democratic Society in the United States was the twin of a movement of the same name in West Germany, which in 1965 was shaken up by the arrival of Dieter Kunzelmann. Contacts between these movements, however, also threw up misunderstandings and conflicts. When Rudi Dutschke traveled to Leningrad in 1965 to meet Komsomol activists, he was horrified to discover how far they followed the communist party line and took the side of Lenin, who had crushed the Kronstadt sailors' revolt of 1921, which Dutschke admired.[3] By contrast, when he visited Prague during the Prague Spring of 1968, Dutschke was frustrated by the fact that the Czechoslovak students were only too keen to abandon Marxist socialism, which they experienced as Stalinist, for democracy and free speech.[4] Likewise, Seweryn Blumsztaijn, an activist in Poland's 1968, was bemused by Western radicals' commitment

3 Rudi Dutschke, *Jeder hat sein Leben ganz zu leben. Die Tagebücher, 1963–1979* (Cologne: Kiepenheuer & Witsch, 2003), 31–32.
4 James Mark and Anna von der Goltz, "Encounters," in Robert Gildea, James Mark and Anette Warring (eds.), *Europe's 1968: Voices of Revolt* (Oxford: Oxford University Press, 2013), 150–51.

to Marxism: "[W]e were fighting for what they were rejecting," he later said; "For us democracy was a dream – but for them it was a prison."[5]

Protesters had a wide variety of means of protest at their disposal, and often divided between those who favored only nonviolent protest and those who were prepared to resort to violence. In societies that were basically democratic, protest tended to be peaceful, symbolic, even subversive, unless and until it came up against state violence. In other societies, marked by the legacies of fascist and Nazi Europe, imperial and colonial power, and white supremacism, violent action was much more likely to be an option. Disagreement on this question broke out between protesters in the same country and between those in or from different countries. Greek students who fled the brutal colonels' regime to study in France, for example, commented that the May events were little more than a fiesta.[6]

The term "1968" is a shorthand for a range of political activities that took the world by storm from the early 1960s to the early 1970s. They began with the peace movement against the Bomb and the civil rights movement against segregation in the United States and other powers in which white domination was entrenched, such as South Africa. By the mid 1960s they were shaped by the repercussions of Third World revolutions against European colonialism and American imperialism, culminating in agitation over the Vietnam War. After the crushing of the events of 1968, some protesters went down the route of violence, inspired by the Palestinian uprising, while others turned away from violence and engaged in more cultural forms of protest.

The peace movement generally applied peaceful methods, but there were differences between Western Europe and Japan. In Britain, the Committee for National Disarmament (CND) organized marches from London to the nuclear weapons research establishment at Aldermaston from 1958, reaching peak numbers in 1962. In West Germany, where the United States had a powerful military presence, and where Hiroshima was compared to Auschwitz, the *Kampf dem Atomtod* organized Easter Marches from 1960, mobilizing 100,000 people in 1964.[7] Under the umbrella of labor and

5 Ibid., 144.
6 Kostis Kornetis, *Children of the Dictatorship: Student Resistance, Cultural Politics and the "Long 1960s" in Greece* (New York and Oxford: Berghahn Books, 2013), 62.
7 Holger Nehring, "Searching for Security: The British and West German Protests Against Nuclear Weapons and 'Respectability,' 1958–1963," in Benjamin Ziemann (ed.), *Peace Movements in Western Europe, Japan and the USA During the Cold War* (Essen: Klartext, 2001), 167–87.

Christian organizations, they were decidedly nonviolent. More independent and more confrontational, however, was Zengakuren, the National Federation of Student Self-Government Associations, which had grown up under the auspices of the Japanese Communist Party (JCP). In June 1960 the Japanese government set out to extend the 1951 Treaty of Mutual Cooperation and Security, which gave the USA the right to keep military bases in Japan. When 15,000 people protested outside the Japanese parliament and were driven back by police with truncheons and tear gas, one student died and hundreds of others were injured. Subsequently, the federation broke up, with revolutionary Marxist groups breaking away from the JCP and taking up helmets and staves for street fighting.[8]

The civil rights movement in the United States began as entirely peaceful. Dr. Martin Luther King, Jr., who emerged as its leader, had read Marx but could not abide what he saw as communist rejection of religion and individual freedom. Instead he was inspired by the nonviolent *satyagraha* or truth-force tactics of Gandhi, and visited India in 1959 in order to find out about them at first hand.[9] Peaceful activism was taken up by white and black young people who founded the Student Non-Violent Coordinating Committee (SNCC), which in 1961 organized Freedom Rides to test the official desegregation of interstate buses in the South. However, entrenched social and racial inequalities in the USA were dramatized by riots in the black ghettoes of northern cities during three hot summers of 1965–67. The SNCC became divided between activists who opposed violence and those who were prepared to embrace it, and on 17 June 1966 Stokely Carmichael announced, "We want black power!"[10] Later that year the Black Panthers were organized to provide self-defense against racist violence. Carmichael linked the riots in what he called the "internal colonies" of the black American to Third World struggles against imperialism. This he owed to the discovery of Frantz Fanon, the doctor and writer of French Caribbean origin who was bloodied by the Algerian War and whose 1961 *Wretched of the Earth* argued that the violence of the colonialists had to be confronted by violence of the colonized, which

---

8 Lawrence S. Wittner, *The Struggle Against the Bomb*, vol. II, *Resisting the Bomb: A History of the World Nuclear Disarmament Movement, 1954–1970* (Stanford: Stanford University Press, 1997), 42, 91, 244; Volker Fuhrt, "Peace Movements as Emancipator Experience: Anpo tôsô and Beheiren," in Ziemann (ed.), *Peace Movements*, 79–80.
9 Martin Luther King, Jr., *Stride Toward Freedom: The Montgomery Story* (London: Souvenir Press, 2011 [1958]), 71–85.
10 Simon Hall, *Peace and Freedom: The Civil Rights and Antiwar Movements in the 1960s* (Philadelphia: University of Pennsylvania Press, 2005), 56.

would cleanse them of their sense of powerlessness and bind them in their struggle for liberation.[11]

There was a direct link between the civil rights and the student movement. On campus, students were increasing in number and in politicization, but were frustrated by narrow academic subjects, hierarchical university structures and generalized bans on political activism. In the autumn of 1964, students who had taken part in the Freedom Rides returned to their home universities. At Berkeley they set up tables on Telegraph Avenue to publicize SNCC's work and collect donations. When this was banned by the university authorities, the administrative building was occupied on 2 December 1964, triggering a strike by 10,000 students. The university was forced to concede the principle of free speech, and a model was provided for other campus struggles both in the United States and elsewhere.[12] At its Frankfurt Congress in September 1967, the West German SDS declared its solidarity with Black Power, hoping to see American imperialism dismantled from within.[13]

In communist bloc countries, the grip of Stalinism had been undermined by Nikita Khrushchev's 1956 Secret Speech, but the limits on reform were dramatized by the Soviet suppression of the Hungarian uprising of that same year. Restrictions on free speech in the universities were demonstrated in Poland by the arrest and trial in July 1965 of Modzelewski and Kuroń. Leadership passed to a younger generation of students around Adam Michnik, who set up a group called the Commandos. Their aim was to infiltrate or disrupt meetings of the official Communist Youth organizations and turn them toward sharper criticism of the regime. In Czechoslovakia, the communist party was much bigger than in Hungary and Poland, its 1.5 million accounting for 10–12 percent of the population, and its Stalinist control was rigid after having seized power in 1948. Nevertheless, the system was increasingly questioned by economists such as Ota Šik, who argued the benefit of market forces against five-year plans, jurists such as Zdeněk Mlynář who promoted the rights of civil society against the party-state, and

11 Stokely Carmichael, speech to congress of Dialectics of Liberation, 18 Jul. 1967, in *Stokely Speaks: From Black Power to Pan-Africanism* (Chicago: Chicago Review Press, 2007), 86–94.
12 Gerd-Rainer Horn, *The Spirit of '68: Rebellion in Western Europe and North America, 1956–1976* (Oxford: Oxford University Press, 2007), 60–65.
13 Martin Klimke, *The Other Alliance: Student Protest in West Germany and the United States in the Global Sixties* (Princeton: Princeton University Press, 2010), 112.

a cultural renaissance of writers, artists and New Wave filmmakers.[14] All this had an influence on students who chafed against party domination of the Czechoslovak Youth Union. On 31 October 1967 they processed from their dim dormitory blocks to Prague Castle carrying candles, playing musical instruments and chanting "We want light!," only to be attacked and beaten by police.[15]

In Italy, the student movement drew on a long tradition of factory occupations going back to the *biennio rosso* of 1919–20, when metalworkers occupied car factories in Milan and Turin and set up factory councils, modeled on Russian soviets, and to an anti-fascist tradition that had climaxed in the wartime partisan movement. In fact, student occupations began at the new University of Trento, on the Austrian border, in January and October–November 1966. Students produced a "manifesto for a Negative University," embodying ideas of participatory democracy.[16] The occupation movement spread to the larger universities in Italy – Turin, Genoa, Milan, Pisa and Venice – in November 1967, and into the high schools during the winter.[17] The movement spread to France too, beginning at the University of Nanterre. Students led by anarchist Jean-Pierre Duteuil and Daniel Cohn-Bendit occupied the segregated women's dormitories in March 1967, organized a strike in November 1967 and occupied the university's administrative block on 22 March 1968, an event that is generally seen as the beginning of France's 1968.[18]

The events of 1968, in France or anywhere else, cannot be understood outside the context of the Third World revolutions, aimed at Western imperialist and colonial powers, that rocked the globe in the 1960s. The Soviet Union exploited the opportunity of offering support to these movements – even if they were not communist but rather "national-democratic"– to win Cold War advantage. Young activists across the world drew inspiration from the Third World in their protests, and in the Eastern

14 Vladimir V. Kusin, *The Intellectual Origins of the Prague Spring* (Cambridge: Cambridge University Press, 1971), 35, 59–88, 106–16; Jan Pauer, "Czechoslovakia," in Martin Klimke and Joachim Scharloth (eds.), *1968 in Europe: A History of Protest and Activism, 1956–1977* (Basingstoke: Palgrave Macmillan, 2008), 165–66.
15 Z. A. B. Zeman, *Prague Spring: A Report on Czechoslovakia 1968* (London: Penguin, 1969), 80–82.
16 Horn, *The Spirit of '68*, 75–80.
17 Sidney G. Tarrow, *Democracy and Disorder: Protest and Politics in Italy, 1965–1975* (Oxford: Clarendon Press, 1989), 151–52; Robert Lumley, *States of Emergency: Cultures of Revolt in Italy from 1968 to 1978* (London and New York: Verso, 1990), 79–96.
18 Jean-Pierre Duteuil, *Mai 68. Un mouvement politique* (La Bussière: Acratie, 2008), 93–102, 203–05.

bloc found room to criticize the USSR for not going far enough in its support. The powerful slogan was that young activists should bring the revolution back home to Europe and the United States. The question was: Would that revolution be real or symbolic?

The first breakthrough was the Cuban Revolution against the American-backed regime of Fulgencio Batista in 1959. Its leader, Fidel Castro, immediately became a figure on the world stage, as did his young comrade-in-arms, the Argentinean Ernesto "Che" Guevara. "The liberation of Cuba, in this moment of revolutionary thought, is found in the hands of the people," reported Jean-Paul Sartre, who visited Cuba in 1960. The war was "a people's war, a guerrilla war," emancipating a "semi-colony."[19] Régis Debray, a brilliant student of the École normale supérieure in Paris and member of the Union of Communist Students (Union des étudiants communistes, UEC), who had written an article on the Cuban Revolution for Sartre's Les Temps modernes, was invited by Castro to attend the Conference of the Organization of Solidarity with the People of Asia, Africa and Latin America, known as the Tricontinental, in January 1966. He took the opportunity to write a study of guerrilla warfare, and his best-selling 1967 book Revolution in the Revolution? highlighted the tactic of foquismo, actions by a vanguard (foco) of revolutionaries who could provide impetus for wider peasant uprisings.[20] But revolution was not child's play, That year, following Che on his campaign against the Bolivian government, Debray was captured, tried and sentenced to thirty years in prison, although he was released after four years following a worldwide campaign led by Sartre.[21]

If Latin America provided romance, Africa proved tragedy. The "winds of change" that swept the continent in 1960 brought independence to many countries, but also the fightback of neocolonial forces. The Sharpeville massacre of black demonstrators protesting against the pass laws in South Africa on 21 March 1960 brought into being a worldwide anti-apartheid movement.[22] Patrice Lumumba came to power in the Congo when the Belgians suddenly granted independence; he was welcomed as a "black Robespierre" by Sartre.[23] When he was overthrown and murdered

---

19 Jean-Paul Sartre, Sartre on Cuba (New York: Ballantine Books, 1961), 111, 157.
20 Régis Debray, Révolution dans la Révolution? Lutte armée et lutte politique en Amérique Latine (Paris: Maspero, 1967).
21 Le Procès Régis Debray (Paris: Maspero, 1968).
22 Hakan Thorn, Anti-Apartheid and the Emergence of a Global Civil Society (Basingstoke: Palgrave Macmillan, 2006).
23 Jean-Paul Sartre, "Préface," in Jean Van Lierde (ed.), La pensée politique de Patrice Lumumba (Paris: Présence africaine, 1963), xx.

in January 1961 by African rivals supported by a coalition of Belgian forces, other Western governments and the CIA, demonstrations broke out in cities from Montreal to Lahore. On 8 December 1964, the new Congolese premier, Moise Tshombe, who had helped to eliminate Lumumba with Western assistance, came to West Berlin in search of further support. He was met at the city hall by a powerful demonstration organized by SDS and African students. "Our friends from the Third World jumped immediately into the breach" in the police lines, remembered Dutschke; "it was up to the Germans to follow."[24] Three days later, Che Guevara addressed the UN and berated it for betraying Lumumba. "The free men of the world must be prepared to avenge the crime committed in the Congo," he declared, and in 1965 he formed a band of freedom-fighters in the Congo.[25]

In 1962, Algeria finally gained its independence from France after an eight-year war. This initially owed little to the French Communist Party which in 1956 had voted the government full powers to crush the rebellion. But after 1960 the communist party was involved in a campaign to end the war against the right-wing extremists of the Organisation armée secrète (OAS), which tried to hold on to French Algeria by terror attacks both in Algeria and in metropolitan France. After its liberation, Algeria became a center of transnational revolution. Che Guevara visited Algiers in July 1963 and was interviewed by Frantz Fanon's widow, Josie.[26] As the European settler *pieds noirs* fled to France, Tiennot Grumbach, a French law student, went as a so-called *pied rouge* with medical supplies to liberated Algeria and organized an international youth camp at Sidi Ferruch. This was a sort of North African '68 *avant la lettre*, and Grumbach later recalled that "all the young people who made 'May '68' passed through there – Italians you will find in Lotta Continua, together with German students."[27]

China became a focus of attention in 1960, when it broke diplomatically with its former mentor, the Soviet Union, and in 1966, when Mao launched the Cultural Revolution. It offered a Maoist alternative of revolution

---

24 Quinn Slobodian, *Foreign Front: Third World Politics in Sixties West Germany* (Durham, NC: Duke University Press, 2012), 73.
25 John Gerassi (ed.), *Venceremos! The Speeches and Writings of Ernesto Che Guevara* (London: Weidenfeld & Nicolson, 1968), 368.
26 Robert Young, *Postcolonialism: An Historical Introduction* (Oxford: Blackwell, 2001), 125.
27 James Mark, Nigel Townson and Polymeris, "Inspirations," in Gildea, Mark and Warring (eds.), *Europe's 1968*, 97.

based on commune organization that challenged Soviet bureaucracy and détente with the USA, scorning the "paper tiger" of Western imperialism. The mobilization of young people in the Red Guards as the vanguard of the revolution against the party bureaucracy in 1966–69 may be seen as a Chinese 1968, and it certainly had a galvanizing effect on young activists in Europe. In West Germany, Kunzelmann and his comrades set up Kommune I that month to promote free love and political education, calling themselves Red Guards.[28] In France, enthusiasm for the Cultural Revolution provoked a breakaway in December 1966 from the Union of Communist Students by a Maoist group that called itself the Union of Communist Youth (Marxist-Leninist) or UJC(ml).[29] In July 1967 their leaders went on a pilgrimage to China. One of them, Jean-Pierre Le Dantec, recalled that, "We got an anti-Soviet and anti-Stalinist version of the story of the conquest of power in China ... there was a spiritual time bomb in Mao Zedong's saying that 'a revolution is not a dinner party' ... we liked Mao's idea that there had to be trouble."[30] In the Eastern bloc there was also enthusiasm for Maoism among young people who wanted a stick with which to beat the stultifying communist system. György Pór, a member of the Communist Youth (Magyar Kommunista Ifjúsági Szövetség, KISZ), formed a small Hungarian Revolutionary Marxist-Leninist Party, for which he was expelled from Budapest University in 1966, put on trial and convicted for "Maoist anti-state conspiracy" in June 1968.[31]

It was, however, the Vietnam War and massive American bombing raids on the north after February 1965 that catalyzed and universalized the student and youth movements. Vietnam was seen as the battlefield on which the struggle between imperialism and anti-imperialism would be decided. Street demonstrations became bigger and sometimes violent. Surviving ties between young people and communist organizations were ruptured, even in Eastern Europe, where the regimes were nominally on the side of North Vietnam, but were felt not to be fully committed to the people's struggle.

---

28 Slobodian, Foreign Front, 175–77.
29 Christophe Bourseiller, Les maoistes (Paris: Plon, 2007), 110–14; Richard Wolin, The Wind from the East: French Intellectuals, the Cultural Revolution and the Legacy of the 1960s (Princeton: Princeton University Press, 2010), 109–41.
30 Interview with Jean-Pierre Le Dantec, recorded by Robert Gildea, Paris, 24 Apr. 2007.
31 Robert Gildea, James Mark and Niek Pas, "European Radicals and the 'Third World': Imagined Solidarities and Radical Networks, 1958–1973," Cultural and Social History 8, 4 (Dec. 2011), 452–53; Rebecca Clifford, Robert Gildea and James Mark, "Awakenings," in Gildea, Mark and Warring (eds.), Europe's 1968, 25–27.

The first global anti-war demonstration took place on 24 April 1965 in Tokyo, where Zengakuren descended on the US embassy. "As part of Asia to which Vietnam belongs," they declared, "we will march." At Berkeley, California, a Vietnam Day Committee formed around Jerry Rubin and organized a "twenty-four-hour carnival of anti-war protest" on Vietnam Day, 21 May 1965, which mobilized a crowd of 10,000 people.[32] The anti-war movement soon spread to Europe. In France, it was promoted and exploited by the Trotskyists around Alain Krivine, who broke with the Union of Communist Students in April 1966 and founded the Revolutionary Communist Youth (Jeunesse communiste révolutionnaire, JCR). They organized a "Six Hours of the World" event in Paris on 28 November 1966, attended by 5,000 people, in order to spread National Revolution Committees throughout universities and high schools.[33] In Britain, a Vietnam Solidarity Committee was set up in 1966 by the Trotskyist International Group, later the International Marxist Group (IMG), notably by Tariq Ali, whose family had fled military dictatorship in Pakistan, and it organized demonstrations against the US embassy in Grosvenor Square in October 1967 and March 1968. West German students organized anti-Vietnam demonstrations on 2 June and 21 October 1967. Rudi Dutschke announced that, "A victory of the Vietnamese revolution would be the green light to social revolution movements across the whole world," toppling "international counterrevolution personified by the American elite."[34]

Agitation came to a climax after Che Guevara's letter to the Tricontinental Conference, read out on 16 April 1967. He urged creating "a Second or Third Vietnam, or the Second and Third Vietnam of the world!," which became the slogan of all young revolutionaries.[35] Che himself then went off to fight in Bolivia, where he was killed on 9 October 1967, a death which dramatized the global revolution even more than his life had done. The International Berlin Vietnam Congress, held in Berlin on 17–18 February 1968, was also inspired by the Vietnamese Tet Offensive of 29 January 1968. Marchers brandished banners of Ho Chi Minh and Che Guevara alongside those of German revolutionary Rosa Luxemburg.

---

32 Gerard J. DeGroot, "Left, Left, Left: The Vietnam Day Committee," in Gerard J. DeGroot (ed.), *Student Protest: The Sixties and After* (London: Longman, 1998), 85.
33 Niek Pas, "'Six heures pour le Vietnam.' Histoire des Comités Vietnam français, 1965–1968," *Revue historique* 302 (2000), 157–85.
34 Rudi Dutschke, *Écrits politiques, 1967–1968* (Paris: Christian Bourgois, 1968), 77.
35 Gerassi, *Venceremos!*, 420–22.

Cultural Revolt

Political activism in the leadup to 1968 took place within a much wider framework of the social and cultural changes of the 1960s. These provided a broader youth constituency into which this activism could tap but which might also offer a challenge to movements – not least communism – that were seen to be too narrowly political and not in step with social and cultural movements.[36]

These movements practiced a lifestyle revolt or cultural rebellion that may be seen as forming three concentric if overlapping circles. The first and widest circle was the emergence of a youth culture that was situated between mass culture and counterculture, and largely defined by enthusiasm for rock music, jeans and mini-skirts, and later the hippie long skirt and long hair. This in itself was a rebellion against conventional family values and social respectability. Youth enthusiasm was kindled by the arrival of the Beatles at the Star Club in Hamburg in 1963 and in the United States in February 1964. In Mexico, Spanish-language cover versions of Elvis gave way in late 1964 to bands like Los Dug Dugs, doing English-language cover versions of the Beatles, and with this came a fashion for long hair and mini-skirts known as *La Onda*, the wave.[37] Political conflict was often not far away. The Rolling Stones concert at Berlin's Waldbühne in September 1965 led to clashes with police, while attempts by the East German authorities to suppress performances they thought ferried American cultural imperialism in October 1965 triggered youth riots in Leipzig.[38]

The second circle was the world of hippies and dropouts. The hippie subculture, which began on the west coast of the United States, aimed to build an alternative society in which war, violence, racism and poverty were replaced by peace and love. It reached a high point with the Summer of Love 1967 in the Haight-Ashbury district of San Francisco, with free music, art, medical care and transport offered by the Diggers, and with the Monterey Pop Festival in California in June 1967, which featured Jimi Hendrix,

---

36 Arthur Marwick, *The Sixties: Cultural Revolution in Britain, France, Italy and the United States, c. 1958–c. 1974* (Oxford: Oxford University Press, 1998).

37 Eric Zolov, *Refried Elvis: The Rise of Mexican Counterculture* (Berkeley: University of California Press, 1999), 64–65, 93–114.

38 Timothy Scott Brown, *West Germany and the Global Sixties: The Antiauthoritarian Revolt, 1962–1978* (Cambridge: Cambridge University Press, 2013), 158–60; Mark Fenemore, *Sex, Thugs and Rock 'n' Roll: Teenage Rebels in Cold-War East Germany* (Oxford and New York: Oxford University Press, 2007), 177.

The Who, Janis Joplin and Jefferson Airplane.[39] This counterculture was political in that it battled with police over illegal drugs and resisted the draft for the Vietnam War, but also created separate spaces away from possible repression.[40] Hippies followed the hippie trail to Mexico, Morocco, Afghanistan, Kathmandu in Nepal and ultimately Goa in India, for midnight bathing and more on its Anjuna beach.[41]

The third and most intense circle was linked to the anarchist or libertarian Marxist critiques of advanced industrial society and linked cultural and political analysis. It drew on analyses of advanced industrial society by the likes of Herbert Marcuse, the German-American thinker whose *One-Dimensional Man* was published in 1964. Marcuse argued that advanced industrial society was highly productive and increased affluence but at the same time was scientifically and bureaucratically managed, promoted commodity fetishism and commodified culture through the mass media. Ordinary people were pacified, persuaded to conform and rendered insensitive to exploitation and mass slaughter. Individuality, creativity and critical thought were stifled. In opposition to this state of affairs, he argued, free play should be given to the imagination to bring about social transformation.[42]

In the mid 1960s a number of groups emerged to challenge the existing order by provocation through art, spectacle or "happening." The idea was to shock society through theatrical, symbolic gestures that were transgressive, collective and short-lived. In Amsterdam, the so-called Provos made their mark on 10 March 1966 when they threw stink bombs to disrupt the wedding of Princess Beatrix to a German diplomat who had fought in the Wehrmacht.[43] In West Germany the Subversive Aktion group, founded by Kunzelmann, planned to throw puddings at US vice-president Hubert

---

39 Detlef Siegfried, "Music and Protest in 1960s Europe," in Klimke and Scharloth (eds.), *1968 in Europe*, 57–70.
40 Joseph H. Berke, "The Creation of an Alternative Society," in Joseph H. Berke, *Counterculture* (London: Owen, 1969), 16, 40; Godfrey Hodgson, *America in Our Time: From World War II to Nixon. What Happened and Why* (Garden City, NY: Doubleday, 1976), 319–29.
41 Luther Elliott, "Goa Is a State of Mind: On the Ephemerality of Psychedelic Social Emplacements," in Graham St. John (ed.), *The Local Scenes and Global Culture of Psytrance* (New York and Abingdon: Routledge, 2010), 26.
42 Herbert Marcuse, *One-Dimensional Man* (London and New York: Routledge, 1991 [1964]).
43 Niek Pas, "Mediatization of the Provos: From Local Movement to a European Phenomenon," in Martin Klimke, Jacco Pekelder and Joachim Scharloth (eds.), *Between Prague Spring and French May: Opposition and Revolt in Europe, 1960–1980* (New York and Oxford: Berghahn Books, 2011), 157–76.

Humphrey when he visited in April 1967. Happenings also occurred on the other side of the Iron Curtain, where because of censorship political opposition often took artistic form. Vera Jirousová, who graduated from Prague's Philosophy Faculty, belonged to the Holy Cross School of Pure Humour Without Wit. "We did things in a spontaneous, creative manner," she recalled, "immediately, not to order: 'Walk down the street and crow.' 'Take off your jacket and throw it off the Charles Bridge.' 'I don't need to free myself because I am free.' That was the difference."[44] In the United States, former Marcuse pupil, civil rights activist and Digger Abbie Hoffman and anti-war activist Jerry Rubin founded the Youth International Party or Yippies on 31 December 1967. "The hippies see us as politicos and the politicos see us as hippies," complained Rubin.[45] Perhaps their most famous subversive stunt was to run a pig called Pigasus for the Democratic Party presidential nomination in 1968.

The Revolts of 1968

In these political and cultural contexts, the revolts of 1968 triggered each other in what David Caute called "a chain of insurrections" across the globe.[46] From San Francisco and Mexico City to Paris, Berlin, Cape Town and Tokyo, students occupied campuses and young people took to the streets. Communist parties and communist-dominated trade unions were wrongfooted by these events. They denounced them as student adventurism and either failed to gain purchase on them or applauded their defeat. In the long run, however, communist parties both in the Soviet bloc and beyond were among the great losers from 1968.

Although the high point of 1968 is often seen to be France's "May'68," the story might better begin in January 1968 in Prague, where Alexander Dubček took over as First Secretary of the Communist Party after a revolt in the Central Committee against the Stalinist Antonín Novotný. Jurist Zdeněk Mlynář was appointed to the Central Committee and was behind the party's Action Program of April 1968. Censorship was abolished, and people – disillusioned with the fact that Marxism-Leninism had promised so much but

---

44 Maria Černá, Joan Davis, Robert Gildea and Piotr Osęka, "Revolutions," in Gildea, Mark and Warring (eds.), *Europe's 1968*, 116.

45 Jerry Rubin, *Do It! Scenarios of the Revolution* (New York: Simon & Schuster, 1970), 85; Jonah Raskin, *For the Hell of It: The Life and Times of Abbie Hoffman* (Berkeley: University of California Press, 1998).

46 David Caute, *Sixty-Eight: The Year of the Barricades* (London: Hamish Hamilton, 1988), vii.

delivered so little – debated intensely how far communism could be reconciled with market forces, autonomous trade unions and associations, religious freedoms and the rights of national minorities.

This relaxation of the Stalinist system found echoes across the communist bloc in Central and Eastern Europe, although not always with the same room for maneuver. Student protest in Poland was triggered by the government's banning on 30 January of the play, *Forefather's Eve*, by Polish nationalist poet Adam Mickiewicz, on the grounds that it was anti-Russian. This provoked marches to the Mickiewicz monument in defense of free speech. When student leaders from the Commando movement, including Adam Michnik, were arrested, a strike movement spread across the universities in March 1968. There was, however, no response from the workers. Since many of the student leaders were of Jewish origin, the government of Władysław Gomułka took the opportunity not only to crush the strike but also to purge Jews from prominent positions in the communist movement.[47]

In Yugoslavia, which had broken with Stalinism in 1948, students in Belgrade trying to get to a concert clashed with police during the night of 2–3 June 1968. Together with their teachers, they occupied the university, which they renamed the Red University of Karl Marx, and went on strike, demanding free press and right of assembly. Communist leader Josip Broz Tito argued that the workers' self-management supposed to exist in Yugoslavia already gave them what they wanted and asked students and teachers to return to work.[48]

In Italy, where the student occupation movement was already well underway, the defining moment of 1968 was the Battle of Valle Giulia in Rome on 1 March 1968, between students, defying a ban on demonstrations, and the police. The Italian Communist Party was entirely unsympathetic: Communist filmmaker Pier Paolo Pasolini criticized what he called upperclass students and praised baton-wielding police who were recruited from the poverty-stricken south.[49] Students' relations with workers were nevertheless good, and workers came out on strike at the Pirelli works in Milan, Fiat in Turin and the Porto Marghera oil refinery outside Venice.[50]

---

47 Jerzy Eisler, "March 1968 in Poland," in Carol Fink, Philipp Gassert and Detlef Junker (eds.), *1968: The World Transformed* (Cambridge: Cambridge University Press, 1998), 244–50; Černá et al., "Revolutions," 109, 113–14.
48 Boris Kanzleiter, "1968 in Yugoslavia: Student Revolt Between East and West," in Klimke, Pekelder and Scharloth (eds.), *Between Prague Spring and French May*, 84–92.
49 Horn, *The Spirit of '68*, 142.
50 Lumley, *States of Emergency*, 181–213; Tarrow, *Democracy and Disorder*, 168.

In France, the events in Paris from 3 May 1968 were triggered by the disciplining of student leaders including Daniel Cohn-Bendit and Jean-Pierre Duteuil, who had occupied the administrative building of the University of Nanterre on 22 March 1968. The Sorbonne was occupied by police, and students mobilized to liberate it. Television images of the brutalization of students by police brought youths and workers onto the streets in support. At first, communist leaders were hostile, with Georges Marchais calling Cohn-Bendit a "German anarchist," but, when the workers began to mobilize, the communist-dominated CGT (Confédération Générale du Travail) union joined the call for a general strike on 13 May.[51] Factory occupations began on 14 May, and after the government reopened the Sorbonne it became the epicenter of a countercultural revolution, as well as a platform for Trotskyist and Maoist groups. Having briefly lost authority, Charles de Gaulle's government reached a deal with the trade unions to end the strike movement, banned the Trotskyist and Maoist groups and called elections, which were won by the Gaullist party's landslide on 23 and 30 June 1968.

In Central and Eastern Europe, the end came much more brutally, with the Soviet invasion of Czechoslovakia on 12 August 1968. Four other countries of the Warsaw Pact – East Germany, Poland, Hungary and Bulgaria – supported the invasion. Dubček and the reformist leadership were whisked away to Moscow, signed "confessions" and were sent home to dismantle their reforms. There was considerable resistance to the Soviet invasion in Czechoslovakia. Petr Uhl and his comrades set up a Revolutionary Youth Movement, which organized a university strike in November 1968. For this he was arrested, tried and sentenced to four years in prison.[52] In March 1969 the Czechoslovaks beat the Soviets in an ice hockey tournament, provoking demonstrations by half a million people. This led to the final dismissal of Dubček as First Secretary, the expulsion of half a million party members and indubitable proof that in the Soviet bloc communism and reform were incompatible.

The reverberations of 1968 were felt far outside Europe. At the University of Cape Town, 300 students of the National Union of South African Students (NUSAS) occupied the administrative building on 14 August 1968, after the university withdrew a job offer to

---

51 Maud Ann Bracke, "The Parti communiste français in May 1968: The Impossible Revolution?," in Klimke, Pekelder and Scharloth (eds.), *Between Prague Spring and French May*, 64–83.

52 Černá et al., "Revolutions," 121–22.

a Cambridge-educated black South African anthropologist. A sit-in lasted ten days, with seminars led by philosophy lecturer Rick Turner, who had written a thesis on Sartre at the Sorbonne.[53] But NUSAS represented white, mostly English-speaking students, so black students – confined under the apartheid regime to so-called tribal or bush universities such as Fort Hare and Turfloop – set up a South African Students' Organisation (SASO), led by medical student Steve Biko.[54]

In Chicago, the SDS, the Yippies and the SNCC spearheaded a challenge to the Democratic Party Convention, which was set to nominate Hubert Humphrey as its candidate for the presidential election. Abbie Hoffman borrowed the French slogan from May '68, "Be realistic. Demand the impossible."[55] A crowd of 10,000 young people gathered in Grant Park on 28 August, but when the US flag was lowered by the students, the police charged and used tear gas. The leaders, including Abbie Hoffman, Jerry Rubin, Tom Hayden of SDS and Bobby Seale of the Black Panthers, were arrested and – dubbed the Chicago eight – put on trial for "conspiracy" in 1969. The November 1968 presidential elections were won by the Republican candidate, Richard Nixon, who became the mouthpiece of the "silent majority" opposed to 1968 and all it stood for.

Nearly 2,000 miles south, in Mexico, the situation became much more serious. After the *granaderos* or riot police attacked a student demonstration on 23 July commemorating the beginning of the Cuban Revolution in 1953, strikes and occupations spread through the universities and high schools, mobilizing 250,000 students. The Zócalo (main square) in Mexico City, used for military parades, was taken over as a festive meeting place.[56] A strike committee tried to negotiate with the government and organized a silent procession on 13 September 1968. The aim, read one student flyer, was "to transform society . . . in this task we are not alone. For the first time youth around the world are identifying with each other in this common task."[57] An appeal was sent to the people of the United States "because Americans can speak their mind." They received a reply from black SNCC leader James Forman saying that all student movements were

53 John Daniel and Peter Vale, "South Africa: Where Were We Looking in 1968?," in Philipp Gassert and Martin Klimke (eds.), *1968: Memories and Legacies of Global Revolt* (Washington, DC: German Historical Institute, 2009), 142.
54 Saul Dubow, *Apartheid, 1948–1994* (Oxford: Oxford University Press, 2014), 129, 160–70.
55 Raskin, *For the Hell of It*, 155.   56 Zolov, *Refried Elvis*, 127.
57 Eric Zolov, "Protest and Counter-Culture in the 1968 Student Movement in Mexico," in DeGroot (ed.), *Student Protest*, 80.

confronted by capitalism, colonialism and racism and offering solidarity.[58] The government was keen to restore order before the opening of the Mexico Olympics, and on 2 October 1968 the police and army were sent to break up a demonstration in Tlatelolco Square, the square of the Three Cultures, killing more than 200 students.[59] The repercussions were legion. On 16 October two black American athletes, who had won gold and bronze in the Olympic men's 200 meters, raised black-gloved fists on the podium, while on 5 November a student-led meeting in Paris declared, "Paris–Mexico, same fight."[60]

After 1968: The Question of Revolution

The defeat of the movements of 1968 either at the ballot box or by force was not the end of the story. A Trotskyist book published in France in September 1968 entitled *May 68: A Dress Rehearsal*, had a picture of helmeted Japanese Zengakuren in battle.[61] Revolutionary networks were formed, from the Trotskyist International Socialists in Britain and the Weathermen in the United States, to Lotta Continua in Italy and the Gauche prolétarienne (GP) in France, which seriously debated a move to violent action. In areas where there had been considerable industrial strike activity in 1968, such as Italy and France, these activists tried to remobilize workers for the fight. Lotta Continua used the spectre of Third World revolution to intimidate the bosses: "Agnelli, Indochina is in your factory."[62] Elsewhere, links between students and workers failed to materialize. In Poland, the workers had not backed the students in 1968, and in December 1970, when the port workers of Gdańsk, Gdynia and Szczecin went on strike, the students were nowhere to be seen, and the state opened fire on the workers.[63]

The Vietnam War was still a model for American radicals, although the issue now was not only to stop American bombing but also to support the Vietnamese. At a mass rally of 500,000 people on Washington's Mall

---

58 Sarah Stokes, "Paris and Mexico City: 1968 Student Activism," D.Phil. thesis (Oxford University, 2012), 291.
59 Annick Lempérière, "Le 'mouvement estudiantin' à Mexico (26 juillet–2 octobre 1968)," in Philippe Artières and Michelle Zancarini-Fournel (eds.), *68. Une histoire collective (1962–1981)* (Paris: La Découverte, 2008), 291–98.
60 Stokes, "Paris and Mexico City," 321.
61 Daniel Bensaïd and Henry Weber, *Mai 68: une répétition générale* (Paris: Maspero, 1968); Alain Brossat, "La Zenkakuren japonaise: modèle pour les étudiants occidentaux?," in Artières and Zancarini-Fournel (eds.), *68. Une histoire collective*, 68, 102.
62 *Tout! Ce que nous voulons: Tout!* 1 (23 Sep. 1970).   63 Černá et al., "Revolutions," 128.

in November 1969, helmeted protesters stormed the Justice Department, clashed with police and hoisted the Vietcong flag in place of the Stars and Stripes. After the demonstration, the Weathermen declared, "It's not so much that we're against the war, we're for the Vietnamese and their victory."[64]

Western revolutionaries, however, were now inspired by a new wave of revolutions in the Third World. After the defeat of Gamal Abdel Nasser in the Six-Day War in 1967, leadership of the Arab struggle passed to the Palestinians. Stokely Carmichael told a meeting of Arab students in Chicago in August 1968 that "we feel very close to the commandos in Palestine ... We will help the struggle of the Arabs in any way we can."[65] Alain Geismar of the Gauche prolétarienne went to meet the Palestine Liberation Organization (PLO) in Jordanian refugee camps in the summer of 1969.[66] When the Jordanian army attacked those PLO camps in September 1970, Palestine Revolution Support Committees were formed in France. These acted as bridges between the GP and Arab students and workers from Algeria, Tunisia and Morocco.

Inspired by working with the PLO, a small minority of revolutionaries continued down the road of what they called revolutionary anti-imperialism by armed struggle or urban guerrilla tactics, which included bombings, kidnappings and ultimately killings. Among them were the Red Brigades in Italy, the Red Army Faction in West Germany, the American Weathermen and the Japanese Red Army, Nihon Sekigun, which perpetrated the Lod Airport massacre near Tel Aviv on 30 May 1972.[67] They also included the New Popular Resistance in France, the armed wing of the GP, the Iberian Liberation Movement, one of whose members, Salvador Puig Antich, was garrotted in March 1974, and the People's Revolutionary Resistance directed against the Greek colonels.[68] Whereas for most 1968ers, slogans such as "bring the war

---

64 Jeremy Varon, "Crazy for the Red, White, Blue and Yellow: The Use of the NLF Flag in the American Movement Against the Vietnam War," in Ziemann (ed.), *Peace Movements*, 235–36.

65 *Stokely Speaks*, 139–40. 66 Bourseiller, *Les maoistes*, 163.

67 Jeremy P. Varon, *Bringing the War Home: The Weather Underground, the Red Army Faction and Revolutionary Violence in the Sixties and Seventies* (Berkeley: University of California Press, 2004); Donatella della Porta, *Social Movements, Political Violence, and the State: A Comparative Analysis of Italy and Germany* (Cambridge: Cambridge University Press, 1995); William R. Farrell, *Blood and Rage: The Story of the Japanese Red Army* (Lexington, MA: Lexington Books, 1990).

68 Robert Gildea, Gudni Jóhannesson, Chris Reynolds and Polymeris Voglis, "Violence," in Gildea, Mark and Warring (eds.), *Europe's 1968*, 274–76.

home," "two, three, many Vietnams" and "revolution within the revolution" were understood symbolically and rhetorically, these violent groups took them literally. They saw themselves fighting the Vietnam War and Palestinian struggle on European and American soil, and also refighting the battles of anti-Nazi and anti-fascist resistance against regimes they saw as only nominally democratic and still run by politicians, soldiers and corporate bosses marked by that era. Although they prided themselves on acting for "the people," in the Third World as much as in Europe, they enjoyed very little popular support and were treated by the media simply as "terrorists."

The descent into terrorism not only alienated the wider public from those who were sometimes call "the monstrous children of 1968," but also divided the revolutionary movements themselves. When the PLO took Israeli athletes hostage at the Munich Olympics in September 1972 and eleven of them died in the ensuing battle, the GP, whose leadership was predominantly Jewish, denounced the attacks and increasingly distanced itself from violence. It became inspired by strike action that revived among skilled workers faced by layoffs as economic recession bit. The most famous was the Lip watch-making factory strike of 1973 in Besançon, when the workers took over the factory in an early version of *autogestion*. In conversation with Jean-Paul Sartre, the GP leaders concluded that the way forward was "a partial, local and in part symbolic taking of power" and subsequently dissolved themselves.[69] In Poland, shipyard workers went on strike at Radom in 1976 but this time, unlike in 1970, had the support of intellectuals such as Modzelewski, Kuroń and Michnik, who formed the Workers' Defense Committee (Komitet Obrony Robotników, KOR), which was a forerunner of Solidarity. In Greece, students occupied the Athens Polytechnic in November 1973, with the support of workers, and though the uprising was brutally repressed by the colonels' tanks, the regime did not have much longer to last.[70] In South Africa, black students organized by Steve Biko's SASO formed a Black People's Convention to undertake youth and community work in black communities. This led the way to strikes by 100,000 South African workers in 1973, to the trial of nine SASO activists in 1975–76 under the Terrorism Act and ultimately to the Soweto uprising of June 1976.[71]

69 Philippe Gavi, Jean-Paul Sartre and Pierre Victor, *On a raison de se révolter* (Paris: Gallimard, 1974), 254–55.
70 Kornetis, *Children of the Dictatorship*, 256–92.   71 Dubow, *Apartheid*, 166–89.

After 1968: Lifestyle Activism

This reaction against the ideology of revolution was part of a much wider movement that retreated from confrontation and violence and explored changing the world through lifestyle activism or cultural subversion that emerged from the deeper cultural and social movements of the 1960s and 1970s. This was symbolized by the Woodstock Festival of 15–18 August 1969, which gathered an audience of nearly half a million hippies and other fans. In Mexico, as if to forget the massacre of 2 October 1968, *La Onda* gained new momentum. Rock music proper arrived inside the Olympic stadium with the Byrds performing in March 1969. The hippie movement also took off, this time by Mexican *jipis* themselves, who turned the Zona Rosa of Mexico City into a countercultural center and went off to discover the Mexican countryside.[72] In Czechoslovakia, while Uhl indulged in revolutionary posturing, four teenagers from Prague formed an underground rock band called the Plastic People of the Universe. It triumphed at the Third Czech Music Festival, held in a half-frozen marshy meadow in February 1975, until the authorities clamped down on them and put the band on trial in 1976.[73]

Many former activists left street battles to experiment with communal living, either in squats in the city or in the countryside. Rather than confront the state and capitalism, they skirted round them, taking part in a sort of inner immigration to find free spaces in which they could build communities of equals pooling resources without authority, private property or nuclear families. In France, it was estimated that in the summer of 1972 there were between 300 and 500 communes in the Pyrenees, Cévennes and the Alps with about 30,000–40,000 communards.[74] In Denmark, the number of communes multiplied from 10 in 1968 to 700 in 1971 and 15,000 in 1974, with 100,000 inhabitants.[75] Communal experiments spread as far as Leningrad, where the Yellow Submarine commune was founded in 1977 by a group of young people hostile to the rigidities of the Soviet system.[76] In time, however, most of the communes either fell foul of the authorities, or broke up over

---

72 Zolov, *Refried Elvis*, 133–56.
73 Jonathan Bolton, *Worlds of Dissent: Charter 77, the Plastic People of the Universe, and Czech Culture Under Communism* (Cambridge, MA: Harvard University Press, 2012), 99–122.
74 Bernard Lacroix, *L'utopie communautaire* (Paris: PUF, 1981), 8.
75 John Davis and Anette Warring, "Living Utopia: Commune Living in Denmark and Britain," *Cultural and Social History* 8, 4 (2011), 515.
76 John Davis and Juliane Fürst, "Drop-outs," in Gildea, Mark and Warring (eds.), *Europe's 1968*, 193–210.

issues of authority, gender hierarchies, sharing resources or the raising of children.

One of the main legacies of 1968 was the feminist movement. Women were heavily involved in the movements that made 1968, but often came to realize that these were very male-dominated. Aggressive, theoretical debates left women voiceless, military-style tactics alienated them and the sexual exploitation of women by male leaders was standard. In 1964 two activists in the SNCC, Casey Hayden – the partner of Tom Hayden – and Mary King wrote a position paper arguing that "assumptions of male superiority are as widespread and deep-rooted and every much as crippling to the women as the assumptions of white superiority are to the Negro." The emergence of an autonomous black power movement was a powerful influence on feminism, but also a provocation, since Stokely Carmichael had quipped that "the only position for women in the SNCC is prone."[77] American women were ahead of the game, although many had been influenced by Simone de Beauvoir's *Second Sex*. When feminist organizations multiplied after 1968, there was a global dimension that was strongest across the Atlantic. The Redstockings, set up in 1969 to challenge American laws against abortion, was copied by a Danish group of the same name in 1970. Their campaign to change abortion laws was taken up in France, where 343 women in the public eye signed a manifesto in 1973, putting on record that they had had illegal abortions. These transnational encounters did not always result in a common view. When French feminist Annette Lévy-Willard went to meet American feminists in 1971, she said that there was "a real cultural gap" between them. "We were extremely chic, made up, hair done, while the American girls were wearing any old shirt, enormous glasses, had frizzy hair and didn't shave under their arms. They seemed rather lesbian to us, while we were very heterosexual."[78]

Afterlives of 1968 and International Communism

The Soviet invasion of Czechoslovakia in 1968 had a fatal effect, in the long run, on the communist movement. In the first place, it drove a wedge between communists in the Warsaw Pact who backed the Soviet Union's action and those, mainly in the West, who condemned it. In the mid 1970s they devised the option of Eurocommunism, which distanced itself from

---

77 Sara Evans, *Personal Politics: The Roots of Women's Liberation in the Civil Rights Movement and the New Left* (New York: Vintage Books, 1980), 84–87, 233–34.
78 Interview with Annette Lévy-Willard, conducted by Robert Gildea, Paris, 6 Jun. 2007.

Moscow by accepting NATO and the plurality of political parties. The Italian Communist Party (Partito Comunista Italiano, PCI) negotiated an "historic compromise" with the Christian Democratic Party and gave parliamentary support to its government. In the hope of one day being offered ministries it took a hard line against the Red Brigades. This was not to last. The Red Brigades' terrorist campaign climaxed with the kidnapping and murder of Christian Democratic president and former prime minister Aldo Moro in April–May 1978, which weakened the PCI and destroyed its chance of entering government.[79]

In 1975, in its eagerness to defend its borders through détente, the USSR signed the Helsinki Accords on Security and Cooperation, and committed itself to upholding human rights. This offered an opportunity to former '68ers to use this as a stick with which to beat the Soviet Union. Reinvented as "dissidents," they tried again to introduce democracy into the communist bloc. Former revolutionary Petr Uhl, jurist Zdeněk Mlynář and playwright Václav Havel were among the signatories in January 1977 of Charter 77 which asserted the right of "all the citizens of Czechoslovakia to work and live as free human beings." This included "the freedom to play rock music" denied to the Plastic People of the Universe.[80] The regime was not ready to give ground, and in October 1977 Uhl and Havel were sent to trial, while Mlynář fled to Vienna. However, the fuse of the human rights bomb had been lit. Mikhail Gorbachev had studied law with Mlynář in Moscow in the 1950s and talked with him about the possibility of reforms in Czechoslovakia in 1967. In 1987, as he pushed through *glasnost'* and *perestroika*, he was interviewed by Mlynář, who said, "In the Soviet Union they are doing what we did in Prague in the spring of 1968, perhaps acting more radically. But Gorbachev is General Secretary and I am still in exile."[81]

Change finally came to Eastern Europe with the Velvet Revolutions of 1989. The new leaders of postcommunist countries in Central and Eastern Europe often traced a link back to 1968. Václav Havel, of course, became the first president of postcommunist Czechoslovakia, then of the Czech Republic. Karol Modzelewski and Jacek Kuroń were leaders of the

79 Donald Sassoon, *The Strategy of the Italian Communist Party from the Resistance to the Historic Compromise* (London, Francis Pinter, 1981), 223–30.
80 Václav Havel, *The Power of the Powerless: Citizens Against the State in Central-Eastern Europe* (London: Hutchinson, 1985), 46–47, 221.
81 Mikhail Gorbachev, *Memoirs* (London: Bantam Books, 1997), 623; Mikhail Gorbachev and Zdeněk Mlynář, *Conversations with Gorbachev on Perestroika, the Prague Spring and the Crossroads of Socialism* (New York: Columbia University Press, 2002), 44–46, 65.

Solidarity movement that came to power in Poland. Gábor Demszky, who became liberal mayor of Budapest after 1990, argued that "'68 brought a real change, after that the world turned to a more cultured and fortunately more westernized direction, and it was already neither necessary nor possible to live or think in these older ways, it was the end of the eastern Soviet system . . . Our young heroes of '68 were Daniel Cohn-Bendit in Paris, Rudi Dutschke in Berlin, Tom Hayden and Abbie Hoffmann in the US."[82]

The year 1989 might have been the apotheosis of all 1968 activists, but it was not so simple. Many found themselves discredited by their association with communism, even if their brand had always been an anti-Stalinist Marxism. Attacks were mounted on 1968ers from France and Denmark to Poland, Hungary and the Czech Republic as apologists for communist dictatorship and violence from whom repentance was now due.[83] Meanwhile, many of the 1968ers who had formerly embraced the promise of Third World revolution saw their dreams turn into nightmares when the entry of the Vietcong into Saigon in 1975 drove out the Vietnamese boat people. Former Young Communist Bernard Kouchner, one of the founders of Médecins sans frontières, chartered the *Île de lumière* to rescue them in the China Sea.[84] The triumph of Pol Pot's Khmer Rouge in Cambodia and Mengistu Haile Mariam's Marxist regime in Ethiopia suggested that wars of liberation could lead to dictatorships more cruel than the democracies against which they were fighting. In 1978 former Maoist Jean-Pierre Le Dantec published an attack on Third Worldism in *Le Nouvel Observateur*: "We invented the Third World" as a myth to help change the world, he confessed, but now realized that "one barbarism can hide another."[85]

Many former 1968 activists nevertheless kept the faith and reinvented their protests in different ways that were not tainted by communism. Some joined the struggle against global capitalism that took off after the end of the Cold War. Tom Hayden, for example, spoke at the Seattle anti-World Trade Organization protest in 1999 and urged support for Barack Obama as

82 Kristin Ross, *May 1968 and Its Afterlives* (Chicago: University of Chicago Press, 2002); James Mark, Anna von der Goltz and Anette Warring, "Reflections," in Gildea, Mark and Warring (eds.), *Europe's 1968*, 287, 336.
83 Mark, von der Goltz and Warring, "Reflections," 315–31.
84 Eleanor Davey, *Idealism Beyond Borders: The French Revolutionary Left and the Rise of Humanitarianism, 1954–1988* (Cambridge: Cambridge University Press, 2015), 193–200.
85 Jean-Pierre Le Dantec, "Une barbarie peut en cacher une autre," *Le Nouvel Observateur* 717 (22 Jul. 1978); Ross, *May 68 and Its Afterlives*, 158–69.

US president in 2008 because the former continued the tradition of opposition to what he called "grave threats to our democracy when shaped only by the narrow interests of private corporations in an unregulated global market-place. We should instead be globalizing the values of equality, a living wage and environmental sustainability." The wheel had come full circle. "What he needs, and what we need," concluded Hayden, forty-six years on from the Port Huron statement, "is a New Left."[86]

Bibliographical Essay

A good overview of the subject is David Caute, *Sixty-Eight: The Year of the Barricades* (London: Hamish Hamilton, 1988). Overviews which have a transnational but not necessarily global perspective include Ingrid Gilcher-Holtey, *Die 68er Bewegung. Deutschland, Westeuropa USA* (Munich: Beck, 2001), Gerd-Rainer Horn, *The Spirit of '68: Rebellion in Western Europe and North America, 1956–1976* (Oxford: Oxford University Press, 2007), and Paul Berman, *A Tale of Two Utopias: The Political Journey of the Generation of 1968* (New York and London: Norton, 1996).

There are some very useful edited collections on this subject. The ones with the most global reach are Carol Fink, Philipp Gassert and Detlef Junker (eds.), *1968: The World Transformed* (Cambridge: Cambridge University Press, 1998), and Philipp Gassert and Martin Klimke (eds.), *1968: Memories and Legacies of Global Revolt* (Washington, DC: German Historical Institute, 2009). Klimke has coedited two other important collections with a European focus: Martin Klimke and Joachim Scharloth (eds.), *1968 in Europe: A History of Protest and Activism, 1956–1977* (Basingstoke: Palgrave Macmillan, 2008), and Martin Klimke, Jacco Pekelder and Joachim Scharloth (eds.), *Between Prague Spring and French May: Opposition and Revolt in Europe, 1960–1980* (New York and Oxford: Berghahn Books, 2011). Philippe Artières and Michelle Zancarini-Fournel (eds.), *68. Une histoire collective (1962–1981)* (Paris: La Découverte, 2008), focuses on France but links into wider themes.

Studies using the oral history of 1968 activists began with Ronald Fraser et al., *1968: A Student Generation in Revolt* (London: Chatto & Windus, 1988). A new generation of research, with a mainly European focus, although taking in global influences, is highlighted by Anna von der

86 Tom Hayden, *The Long Sixties: From 1960 to Barack Obama* (Boulder and London: Paradigm Publishers, 2009), 171, 185.

Goltz (ed.), "*Talkin' 'Bout My Generation*": *Conflicts of Generation Building and Europe's "1968"* (Göttingen: Wallstein Verlag, 2011), and Robert Gildea, James Mark and Anette Warring (eds.), *Europe's 1968: Voices of Revolt* (Oxford: Oxford University Press, 2013). A related series of articles, "Voices of Europe's 1968," was published in a special issue of *Cultural and Social History* 8, 4 (Dec. 2011).

Global connections operating at a national or local level have been explored by Martin Klimke, *The Other Alliance: Student Protest in West Germany and the United States in the Global Sixties* (Princeton: Princeton University Press, 2010), Quinn Slobodian, *Foreign Front: Third World Politics in Sixties West Germany* (Durham, NC: Duke University Press, 2012), and Richard Wolin, *The Wind from the East: French Intellectuals, the Cultural Revolution and the Legacy of the 1960s* (Princeton: Princeton University Press, 2010). An interesting comparative study is Sarah Stokes, "Paris and Mexico City: 1968 Student Activism," D.Phil. thesis (Oxford University, 2012).

Studies that prioritize transnational cultural and countercultural movements include Arthur Marwick, *The Sixties: Cultural Revolution in Britain, France, Italy and the United States, c. 1958–c. 1974* (Oxford: Oxford University Press, 1998), Axel Schildt and Detlef Siegfried (eds.), *Between Marx and Coca-Cola: Youth Cultures in Changing European Societies, 1960–1980* (New York and Oxford: Berghahn, 2006), and Eric Zolov, *Refried Elvis: The Rise of Mexican Counterculture* (Berkeley: University of California Press, 1999).

Among works that deal with questions of violent and peaceful protest are Donatella della Porta, *Social Movements, Political Violence, and the State: A Comparative Analysis of Italy and Germany* (Cambridge: Cambridge University Press, 1995), Jeremy Varon, *Bringing the War Home: The Weather Underground, the Red Army Faction and Revolutionary Violence in the Sixties and Seventies* (Berkeley: University of California Press, 2004), Benjamin Ziemann (ed.), *Peace Movements in Western Europe, Japan and the USA During the Cold War* (Essen: Klartext, 2001), Håkan Thörn, *Anti-Apartheid and the Emergence of a Global Civil Society* (Basingstoke: Palgrave Macmillan, 2006), and Eleanor Davey, *Idealism Beyond Borders: The French Revolutionary Left and the Rise of Humanitarianism, 1954–1988* (Cambridge: Cambridge University Press, 2015).

Specialized studies on particular areas with a wide resonance include Jonathan Bolton, *Worlds of Dissent: Charter 77, the Plastic People of the Universe, and Czech Culture Under Communism* (Cambridge, MA: Harvard

University Press, 2012), and Kornetis Kostis, *Children of the Dictatorship: Student Resistance, Cultural Politics and the "Long 1960s" in Greece* (New York and Oxford: Berghahn Books, 2013).

Speeches, letters and memoirs by activists themselves may be used to trace global connections. Among these may be highlighted John Gerassi (ed.), *Venceremos! The Speeches and Writings of Ernesto Che Guevara* (London: Weidenfeld & Nicolson, 1968), Dany [Daniel] Cohn-Bendit, *Nous l'avons tant aimée, la révolution* (Paris: Barrault, 1986), Rudi Dutschke, *Écrits politiques, 1967–1968* (Paris: Christian Bourgeois, 1968), Rudi Dutschke, *Jeder hat sein Leben ganz zu leben. Die Tagebücher, 1963–1979* (Cologne: Kiepenheuer & Witsch, 2003), Luisa Passerini, *Autobiography of a Generation: Italy 1968* (Hannover and London: Weslyan University Press, 1996), Tariq Ali, *Street-Fighting Years: An Autobiography of the Sixties* (London: Collins, 1987), Petr Uhl, *Le socialisme emprisonné* (Paris: Stock, 1980), Adam Michnik, *Letters from Prison and Other Essays* (Berkeley: University of California Press, 1985), and Mikhail Gorbachev and Zdeněk Mlynář, *Conversations with Gorbachev on Perestroika, the Prague Spring, and the Crossroads of Socialism* (New York: Columbia University Press, 2002).

2

The Vietnam War as a World Event

MARILYN B. YOUNG AND SOPHIE QUINN-JUDGE

At its center, the Vietnam War involved three countries outside Vietnam itself: China, the Soviet Union and the United States. If one widens the lens there were many more: the Indochinese neighbors who were drawn into the fray, Cambodia and Laos; the allies who sent ground troops (in varying numbers) – South Korea, the Philippines, Australia, New Zealand, Britain, Thailand and Taiwan on the US side; some Soviet and many more Chinese anti-aircraft troops – around 320,000 in all – supporting Hanoi. Pull back still more and one can include the countries from whose US bases the military flew its hundreds of thousands of bombing missions, or refueled its aircraft carriers, or offered weary troops "rest and recreation": above all Thailand, but also the Philippines, Japan (in particular, Okinawa) and South Korea. Add to these countries such as Canada, which were important suppliers of war material, and the war widens further. Europe, and indeed the world economy, also experienced a variety of political and economic tremors from the war, especially in 1971 when Richard Nixon took the United States off the gold standard, terminating the Bretton Woods financial system. But perhaps the most notable way in which the Vietnam War was a world event was in terms of an ever-widening gyre of protest, beginning of course in the USA but spreading literally worldwide, gathering as it went issues well beyond the war itself.

The Vietnam War and the Communist World

The Vietnam War affected political thinking worldwide, both at the governmental and the popular level; it concluded with a victory (an immensely costly one in terms of lives and destruction) for Vietnamese forces and a defeat for the United States and its allies. But the war also played a pivotal role in intensifying Soviet–Chinese conflict as a result of the solidification of a US–China economic and strategic partnership that became clear in the years 1970–72. The Vietnam War for independence from France had been internationalized into an anti-communist crusade in 1950, when the United States began to shoulder the cost of the French war effort. By the time the United States was sending its own forces to advise and build up the southern Vietnamese state created in 1954–55, the Republic of Vietnam, the conflict was on its way to becoming a long-term feature of the Cold War, part of the US offensive predicated on the "domino theory," the purported threat of expanding communist influence throughout Southeast Asia. US fears of Soviet and Chinese subversion blinded the administrations of Dwight Eisenhower and John F. Kennedy to the roots of the war in the Vietnamese struggle for independence; US actions to a large extent brought about the Chinese and Soviet involvement that they had ostensibly worked to prevent.

Both the Soviet Union and China had been happy to promote the Geneva Agreements to end the French–Viet Minh War in 1954. But after the United States made clear its intent to support an anti-communist southern government in breach of the international promise made at Geneva to hold national elections in 1956, the Chinese began to adjust their thinking. By late 1962, while the Soviet Union began to focus on promoting détente with the USA, the Chinese had come to consider the US involvement in southern Vietnam as a threat to their security. By 1963 they were expanding their supply of military equipment and discussing their response to possible US aggression against North Vietnam. In June 1964, Mao Zedong told Van Tien Dung, the visiting Chief of Staff of the Democratic Republic of Vietnam (DRV), that "if the United States risks taking the war to North Vietnam, Chinese troops should cross the border." And, "The more you fear the Americans, the more they will bully you . . . You should not fear, you should fight."[1]

Following the overthrow of Nikita Khrushchev in 1964, Soviet leaders continued to view the Vietnam War as an obstacle to détente, even as they promised military aid to the DRV when the US troop buildup began in 1965. For the Chinese, however, it presented opportunities. The war for them became a "litmus test for 'true communism,'" a way to prove "that the center of the world revolution had moved from Moscow to Beijing."[2] At the same time, Mao could use the escalation of the war to promote his domestic revolution and mass mobilization: The "Resist America and Assist Vietnam Movement" that began in August 1964 "would penetrate into every part of

---

1 Chen Jian, *Mao's China and the Cold War* (Chapel Hill: University of North Carolina Press, 2001), 208–09.
2 Ibid., 212.

Chinese society," making it a "dominant national theme" as the Cultural Revolution got off the ground.[3]

Gradually the Soviets came to replace the Chinese as the main suppliers of military aid to the DRV. And, as the Sino-Soviet rift deepened in 1968, the Chinese became less focused on Vietnam and more concerned about the threat from their erstwhile Big Brother. At the same time, the instability and political overspill from the Cultural Revolution and mounting Sino-Soviet tensions caused the Vietnamese to become wary of China's intentions – the earlier closeness between the neighbors devolved into a relationship of mutual suspicion. The People's Republic of China (PRC) was less than enthused to see Vietnam unified so quickly in 1975–76 with the departure of US forces and with the aid of surface-to-air missiles and other Soviet weapons.

The United States shared Chinese apprehension of what it now viewed as a Soviet client state in the heart of Southeast Asia. Thus, by the end of the Vietnam War the old fears of falling dominoes had been replaced by a more concrete menace in the minds of US strategists: Now it was the possibility of Soviet bases in Vietnam, especially Soviet use of the US-built facilities at Cam Ranh Bay, that concerned the analysts.

On the other hand, the Soviet Politburo gained new confidence in Third World revolutions from the outcome of the Vietnam War. As Ilya Gaiduk explains, "Instead of seeing the US defeat in Indochina as a warning against similar adventures of their own, Soviet leaders, blinded by Marxist-Leninist philosophy and the conviction that the revolutionary trend of history was on their side, believed that where imperialism had failed they would certainly succeed."[4] Under the leadership of the aging Leonid Brezhnev, the Soviet Union began to take a more active role in support of communist-led African liberation movements, while the Chinese chose to support groups unfriendly to Moscow. The 1979 Soviet occupation of Afghanistan followed.

The ultimate lesson of the Vietnam War for Moscow, however, would be quite different. By the late 1980s the Soviets had discovered that a foreign army, however mighty, cannot impose its system on a client state, especially when that client regime has only a thin layer of support within its own society. The military planners in Washington and Moscow tried for a decade to impose their wills on Vietnam and Afghanistan, but the veterans who fought in these countries understood the vanity of these campaigns much sooner.

3 Ibid., 214.
4 Ilya V. Gaiduk, *The Soviet Union and the Vietnam War* (Chicago: Ivan R. Dee, 1996), 250.

Economic Impact of the Vietnam War

From the economic angle, the Vietnam War could be said to have lifted many boats, while devastating the mainly rural economies of the Indochinese countries. It was a bonanza for the economies of East Asia, namely Japan, Singapore, South Korea and Thailand. Singapore, an island entrepot, shipped bargeloads of air conditioners to Saigon, along with other items vital to the survival of US troops in the tropics; the shipyard at Sembawang repaired US naval ships, even as Singapore claimed to be nonaligned. The US airbases in Thailand supported whole communities in the country's impoverished northeast, while the "rest and recreation (R and R)" industry for US GIs that flourished in Bangkok and Pattaya created the sex tourism industry. The base cities of Olongapo and Angeles in the Philippines, and the Okinawan bases and others in Japan, all experienced the same mix of economic boom and cultural degradation. (South Vietnam lived through a similar transformation, but paid the added price of destruction of the countryside and the death and dislocation of its population.)

The Republic of Korea (ROK) sent more troops than any other ally to support the South Vietnamese army, the ARVN (Army of the Republic of Vietnam), driving a hard bargain for this aid. From 1964 until 1973, around 300,000 ROK citizens served in Vietnam, in the parts of central Vietnam where the National Liberation Front (NLF) resistance was especially fierce. In exchange the US government agreed to maintain the US Military Assistance program to the ROK at the 1965 level and to use "offshore procurement from Korea" for items such as petroleum, oil, lubricants and construction materials.[5] The ROK contingent cost the United States approximately US$ 2 million annually, after a much larger payout of around US$ 43 million in the first year of their deployment.

The short- and long-term effects of the decade of war mobilization on the US economy will continue to be debated. But there is consensus that the flow of dollars overseas to pay for the war was a primary cause of the inflation that became a hallmark of the 1970s. Nixon's 1971 decision to end the gold standard helped to ease pressure on the dollar, but interest rates remained high. The OPEC oil price shock in the last years of the war added to pressure on the military budget. The inflation and deficits caused by the war exacerbated the domestic loss of confidence in the US government, which exploded during and after the Watergate hearings and President Nixon's resignation.

---

5 US Army Center of Military History, ch. 6, "The Republic of Korea," www.history.army .mil/books/vietnam/allied/ch06.htm, 126.

In July 1975 a Lou Harris poll reported that confidence in the military had dropped from 62 percent to 29 percent during the period from 1966 to 1975; over the same time span, confidence in business plummeted from 55 percent to 18 percent and that in both the president and Congress fell from 42 percent to 13 percent.[6]

Vietnam and Worldwide Resistance

The protest movement that grew out of the Vietnam War was marked by extreme disillusionment with governments, but for many it also gave rise to a shared sense of liberation from repressive social conventions. The US demonstrations attracted more than 100,000 people by the fall of 1967 and the March on the Pentagon. And they would continue to grow. An international gathering in 1968 attracted some 10,000 delegates from France, Germany, Italy, Greece, Norway, Denmark, Austria, Canada, the UK and the USA. This was the International Congress on Vietnam at the Free University in what was then West Berlin. They cheered speeches by Tariq Ali, Robin Blackburn, Rudi Dutschke, the poet Erich Fried, Bahman Nirumand, an Iranian revolutionary, and a nephew of Salvatore Allende among many others; the next day some 20,000 people marched to the Berlin Opera House chanting revolutionary slogans and carrying placards with portraits of Lenin, Rosa Luxemburg, Karl Liebknecht, Che Guevara and of course Ho Chi Minh. Protests against the war spanned the globe, from London and Lisbon to Tokyo, from Mexico to Chile. Che Guevara called for "two, three, many Vietnams." In the event there was only one; nevertheless, the world – or much of it – was present in Vietnam and Vietnam in the world.

Let us focus on Vietnam War protest in the United States first. Mass protest against the war was not immediate but rather grew with the intensity of the US military effort in Vietnam and its patent failure to produce proclaimed results. Nor did it occur outside the larger context of American political and social movements. The Sixties – to use the general noun currently in use – were centrally about the recognition, on the part of an ever-growing number of Americans, that the country in which they thought they lived – peaceful, generous, honorable, just – did not exist and perhaps never had. The emergence of a more nuanced history of the United States, as opposed to the patriotic metanarrative taught in US schools, began not with

6 Cited in Howard Zinn, *A People's History of the United States* (New York: Harper Perennial, 2003), 557.

the war but with the civil rights movement. Criticism of US policy was couched initially in the familiar rhetoric of the Cold War, but it quickly developed in new directions. The new directions in which the civil rights movement took the country began with a set of tactics, the images that went with them and a new set of questions: What was the nature of the federal government's commitment to universal suffrage? Would it use federal troops to enforce equal rights for all its citizens? Questions about contemporary racial arrangements led inevitably to historical ones and an uneasy recognition of the contradictory nature of the entire national narrative, from Founding Fathers to contemporary racism to nation-building in Vietnam.

While the press and pundits debated what was to be done in Vietnam, those Americans who were politically active by and large focused on civil rights and nuclear disarmament. The 1963 March on Washington for Jobs and Freedom drew 250,000 people to Washington, and no one talked about Vietnam. But the organizers of rallies for peace and nuclear disarmament found that the issue of Vietnam increasingly intruded. For one thing, the tactics the United States was using had begun to receive critical attention. On 23 March 1963, the *New Republic* denounced the use of defoliants in an editorial that began: "The silent war in South Viet-Nam (or should one say *silenced?*) has entered a new phase in the wake of Communist charges that the United States has used 'poison gas.'" The Pentagon argued that technically the Geneva Convention on the use of such weapons did not apply, but the editors dismissed this and instead described, in some detail, the nature of the chemicals used and the peasants they harmed. "All such considerations may be just so many sentimentalities to the hard, young *realpolitiker* and perhaps they are right that the chemicals being sprayed were not really banned by the Geneva Convention of 1925." But the editors doubted that the "dubious military effectiveness" of the weapon was worth the adverse political reaction.[7] According to David Zierler's study of scientists' opposition to the use of Agent Orange, the editorial "reverberated through the scientific community," although it was not until October 1964 that the issue was raised by the board of the Federation of American Scientists.[8] And it would not be until 1971, after 1.8 million hectares of Vietnamese jungle and farmland had been poisoned by the dioxin in Agent Orange that the spraying would end.

7 "One Man's Meat," *New Republic* (23 Mar. 1963), 5–6.
8 David Zierler, *The Invention of Ecocide: Agent Orange, Vietnam, and the Scientists Who Changed the Way We Think About the Environment* (Athens: University of Georgia Press, 2011), 96.

The genetic damage caused by exposure to Agent Orange is still coming to light in a second generation of victims.

Bertrand Russell's denunciation of American tactics, published as a letter to the editor of the *New York Times* on 8 April 1963, had a different tone. It began: "The United States Government is conducting a war of annihilation in Vietnam," and went on to describe the war as one whose sole purpose was "the protection of economic interests and the prevention of far-reaching social reforms in that part of the world." Moreover, the *way* the war was being conducted itself was an "atrocity": napalm "used against whole villages, without warning" and chemical warfare "for the purpose of destroying crops and livestock and to starve the population." After comparing US tactics to those of the Germans in Eastern Europe and the Japanese in Southeast Asia during World War II, Russell concluded: "How long will Americans lend themselves to this sort of barbarism?" To this, the editors of the newspaper responded that, despite his eminence as a philosopher, Russell's letter represented "something far beyond reasoned criticism. It represents distortions or half-truths from the first to the last sentences." The editors did not defend the government's ongoing support for the Diem dictatorship or US military tactics; against Russell's ethical critique, the *New York Times*'s editors offered *Realpolitik*. Having long urged the implementation of social and economic reforms as the way to turn the tide, they now warned against "the increasing military commitment in South Vietnam." Clearly, the editors did not share Washington's excessive optimism about American successes.

Still, the *New York Times* insisted, American advisors and trainers *had* done "a great deal of good." As for Russell's specific charges: Napalm, a thickened oil incendiary agent, may have killed innocents "as other weapons have done in all wars," and US advisors opposed its use except against "clearly identified military targets." Defoliants ("common weed killers," as the *New York Times* described Agent Orange) were used with limited success to clear the jungle around enemy base areas. Russell's failure to acknowledge the "Communist push for domination against the will of the inhabitants of Vietnam" made a "mockery of history," the newspaper declared.[9]

Russell was present at the first public demonstration against the war in the form of buttons worn by large numbers of people that read: "I like Bertrand Russell." The occasion was the 1963 Easter Peace Walk organized by SANE

9 The full exchange can be read online at *War Crimes in Vietnam*, part 1, "The Press and Vietnam: The New York Times, March–July 1963," www.big-lies.org/vietnam-war-crimes/russell-67-war-crimes-vietnam-1.html, including the letter the *New York Times* published, without Russell's permission, in a radically edited form.

(Committee for a Sane Nuclear Policy) to coincide with the Aldermaston march in Britain. Between 5,000 and 7,000 people (the lower figure was reported by the *New York Times*, the higher by the organizers; Aldermaston, it should be noted, drew 70,000 marchers) gathered at UN Plaza in New York to call for the ratification of a test ban treaty and an end to the arms race. On the fringe of the crowd several people carried signs calling for a total US withdrawal from Southeast Asia. Angered at this "confusion" of issues, SANE officials asked the speakers, Bayard Rustin and Dave Dellinger, to get rid of them; Rustin tried, but Dellinger refused and at the close of his prepared speech called on the assembled crowd to "organize against the threat of US intervention in Vietnam."[10]

When the *New York Times* reported on the event the next day, there was no mention of the signs. Indeed, there was not much about the rally itself. On page 63 of the paper, Murray Illson reported that 5,000 pickets, from church, labor and community groups, had called for a nuclear test ban and full disarmament. Illson also noted the presence, five blocks away, of twenty-five members of the US Nationalist Party whose signs read "Bomb the Ban" and "Ban the Reds, Not Our Bomb." At about the same distance, eight high school students carried placards that were somewhat more prolix: "Commies, Nazis, Black Muslims and Fascists Are One and the Same – They Must All Go" and "100 Megatons Makes a Hell of a Hole, but Is Life Under Communism Better?" Toward the end of the story, the reporter returned to UN Plaza where, he noted, most of the participants in the rally seemed to be women and children.

But it was the Diem regime's suppression of Buddhists and, in particular, the 11 June 1963 self-immolation of Thich Quang Duc that seems to have focused the attention of activist groups on Vietnam. On 27 June, the *New York Times* ran a full-page ad featuring a photograph (on page 21) of the burning monk and under it, in large black capital letters:

WE, TOO, PROTEST. We, American clergymen of various faiths also protest. We protest: 1. Our country's military aid to those who denied him religious freedom. 2. The immoral spraying of parts of South Vietnam with crop-destroying chemicals and the herding of many of its people into concentration camps called "strategic hamlets." 3. The loss of American lives and billions of dollars to bolster a regime universally regarded as unjust, undemocratic, and unstable. 4. The fiction that this is "fighting for freedom."

---

10 Andrew Hunt, *David Dellinger: Life and Times of a Nonviolent Revolutionary* (New York: New York University Press, 2006), 124.

The ad was signed by Harry Emerson Fosdick, James Pike and Reinhold Niebuhr, among other religious leaders. In smaller print, the ad quoted from Senator Mike Mansfield's pessimistic February 1963 report on the prospects for victory in Vietnam; below that was a quotation from a *New York Times* editorial, warning Diem that he could not "discriminate against the majority of the people of South Vietnam and win his war against the Communists." The campaign had been organized by the Rev. Donald Harrington, founder of the Ministers' Committee on Vietnam. It included an appeal for funds, and on 15 September the ad ran again, this time on page 9 with the added words: "17,358 American clergymen of all faiths have joined this protest. Will you?"[11]

From this point on, the traditional pacifist groups – the War Resisters League (WRL), the Women's International League for Peace and Freedom (WILPF), the Fellowship of Reconciliation (FOR) and the Committee for Non-Violent Action (CNVA) – all began to organize around the issue of Vietnam, though, as Tom Cornell pointed out years later, "we never had a demonstration of more than 250 people until the war got going."[12] WRL formed special action committees whose task it was to respond to an immediate crisis with instantaneous pamphlets and demonstrations. It was not always easy. Women Strike for Peace (WSP), organized in 1961, for example, struggled with whether to include Vietnam in their protest agenda. "A standing joke in Washington headquarters," WSP's historian recalled, "was 'a not-so-funny thing happened to us on the way to disarmament – the Vietnam war.'"[13] At the second national conference in 1963, a motion from the floor to condemn US intervention led to a lengthy debate that ended finally in a decision to pay attention to Vietnam in the coming year and "alert the public to the dangers and horrors of the war in Vietnam and to the specific ways in which human morality is being violated by the US attack on . . . women and children."[14]

The US visit of Madame Nhu, the de facto first lady as sister-in-law of South Vietnamese president Ngo Dinh Diem, inspired demonstrations by peace groups on and off campuses (300 people at Columbia University, for

11 *New York Times* (27 Jun. 1963), 21. A two-paragraph story about the ad appeared on p. 8 of that day's paper. On 15 August 1963, p. 3, the newspaper carried a brief story with the headline "US Clergymen Score US Aid to Diem." Again, there was no byline, and the story simply stated that Harrington, as head of the Ministers' Committee on Vietnam, had sent a letter to Kennedy protesting ongoing support for Diem.
12 Hunt, *Dellinger*, 134.
13 Amy Swerdlow, *Women Strike for Peace: Traditional Motherhood and Radical Politics in the 1960s* (Chicago: University of Chicago Press, 1993), 129.
14 Ibid.

example), and the hotels where she stayed were noisily picketed: "No Nhus Is Good Nhus." It should be noted that *LIFE* magazine easily rivaled the pickets in the misogynistic relish with which they reported the tour. The same issue carried the cover story, "Mac Finds Out What's Gone Wrong," referring to the latest troubleshooting mission by Defense Secretary Robert McNamara. Inside, huge black letters announced: "Now We Talk Tough: Shape Up or We'll Cut Our Aid." Nevertheless, *LIFE* remained committed to the general enterprise. In the words of its Southeast Asia correspondent: "Vietnam must be held – a primitive, complex mixture of East and West and a bastion against the Chinese from the north."[15] At this point, in spite of the severe political crisis in Saigon, no major media outlet would depart from its overall support of US goals in Vietnam.

At the same time, a call for a new kind of radical politics, more a mood than a movement, had begun to coalesce into the New Left, and there were nascent protests against the draft. In retrospect, 1963 was the antechamber to the anti-war movement. Some of the divisions that would mark its progress were already visible, such as the reluctance of groups that had focused on broader issues of peace and disarmament or civil rights to shift gears to full-time anti-war work. The repertoire of protest actions developed in the civil rights movement, from sit-ins to educational projects (Freedom Schools/teach-ins) did not appear all at once but rather expanded in pace with the war itself. The first teach-in against the war was organized at the University of Michigan in 1965, to be followed by countless others around the country. By then it was abundantly clear that the sullen acceptance with which the Korean War had been tolerated would not prevail this time.

On a note both lighter and darker, Russell Baker summarized the state of the union on Christmas Day, 1963. His column that day reviewed American policy in general and Vietnam policy in particular. It concluded: "[N]obody in authority considers [Vietnam] a war, and your Government urges you not to think of it as a war. In fact, your Government urges you not to think of it at all."[16] By 1965 it was impossible for anyone *not* to think about Vietnam.[17]

Early on in the war, some leaders of the civil rights movement began to connect racial justice at home and the war abroad. Malcolm X, for example, denounced the war in December 1964 and, before the year was out, he was

15 *LIFE* (11 Oct. 1963), 25. 16 Russell Baker, "Observer," *New York Times* (25 Dec. 1963), 36.
17 See Douglas Robinson, "Policy in Vietnam Scored in Rallies Throughout the US," *New York Times* (16 Oct. 1965). Some 10,000 marchers tried to reach the Oakland army base but were blocked by 300 Oakland policemen.

joined by James Forman, executive secretary of the Student Non-Violent Coordinating Committee (SNCC). In 1965, the McComb, Mississippi, branch of the Freedom Democratic Party explicitly called for draft resistance: "No one has a right to ask us to risk our lives and kill other Colored People in . . . Vietnam so that the White American can get richer. We will be looked upon as traitors to the Colored People of the world if Negro people continue to fight and die without a cause . . . . We can write our sons and ask if they know what they are fighting for. If he answers Freedom, tell him that's what we are fighting for here in Mississippi. And if he says Democracy tell him the truth – we don't know anything about Communism, socialism, and all that, but we do know that Negroes have caught hell under this American democracy."[18] World heavyweight boxing champion Muhammad Ali brought the issue of black resistance to the war to a far larger audience, when he refused to be drafted in 1967, saying "I ain't got no quarrel with those Vietcong." For this, Ali was stripped of his title, sentenced to jail (the Supreme Court eventually threw the conviction out) and barred from the ring for three years.

By 1967 Martin Luther King, Jr., had not only endorsed draft resistance, but had also expressed unexpected empathy for the "desperate, rejected and angry young men" who had set ghettoes from Watts to Washington, DC, on fire: "As I have walked among [them] I have told them that Molotov cocktails and rifles would not solve their problems . . . But they asked – and rightly so – what about Vietnam? . . . Their questions hit home, and I knew that I could never again raise my voice against the violence of the oppressed in the ghettos without having first spoken clearly to the greatest purveyor of violence in the world today – my own government."[19] A May 1967 FBI report on the potential for racial violence in the summer of that year noted the link between the civil rights movement and anti-Vietnam War movement with considerable alarm: "King has now joined [Stokely] Carmichael [of the SNCC], [Floyd] McKissick [of the Congress of Racial Equality], and other civil rights extremists in embracing the communist tactic of linking the civil rights movement with the anti-Vietnam-war protest movement . . . King's exhortation to boycott the draft and refuse to fight could lead eventually to dangerous displays of civil disobedience and near-seditious activities by Negroes and whites alike."[20]

---

18 Quoted in Marilyn B. Young, *The Vietnam Wars, 1945–1990* (New York: HarperCollins, 1991), 198.
19 Martin Luther King, Jr., *I Have a Dream: Writings and Speeches That Changed the World*, ed. James Melvin (New York: HarperCollins, 1992), 135–52.
20 Federal Bureau of Investigation, "Racial Violence Potential in the US This Summer," 23 May 1967, www.ddrs.psmedia.com.

The assassinations of King and Malcolm X short-circuited what might have been a powerful, united movement against the war and for fundamental social justice. In the event the mainstream of the anti-war movement narrowed its focus to a single goal: to end the war in Vietnam.[21] This focus was adopted by a wide range of groups, from Students for a Democratic Society to traditional peace churches and more mainstream denominations, represented by the National Council of Churches, and GI anti-war groups such as Veterans for Peace. The destruction of a small Southeast Asian country by the most powerful military machine in the world, which unfolded daily in the press and on TV screens, never felt ordinary. Rather, for many Americans, it assumed nightmare proportions, requiring an ever-greater need to protest and somehow bring it to an end.

Richard Nixon, like Lyndon Johnson before him, was extremely sensitive to the anti-war movement and monitored it closely. "Realizes," his aide Bob Haldeman noted in his diary for 29 September 1969, referring to the president, that "war support is more tenuous every day and knows we have to maintain it somehow." Fearful of the coming October moratorium, Nixon considered scheduling a press conference that would "preempt coverage of the day's activities." The point, Haldeman told his diary, was to "try to make the innocents see they are being used . . . Hard to do much because momentum is tremendous and broad based." The November moratorium – a nationwide call to suspend "business as usual" in order to protest the war – disturbed Nixon even more. He thought hard about it and had "helpful ideas like using helicopters to blow their candles out." Much in the style of his superior's later observation of the Great Wall of China, that it was a great wall, Haldeman noted that "the big march turned out to be huge." Even, "really huge."[22] In fact, as many as 500,000 people turned out for the demonstration in November, making it the largest of the war.

At the same time, many Americans were as upset by the demonstrators as by the war. Indeed, their opposition to Washington's war frequently took the form of urging that the government go "in" or get "out" – where going in meant unleashing the yet more total destruction of Vietnam as a means of getting out victorious. As George Packer described it, the Sixties, "which

21 Factions of Students for a Democratic Society and the Weather Underground embraced a more militant agenda, convinced that an armed uprising in the United States was not only necessary but possible. For them, the war in Vietnam was no more than another instance of American imperialism which would end only when capitalism itself was overthrown.

22 H. R. Haldeman, *The Haldeman Diaries: Inside the Nixon White House* (New York: Berkley, 1995), 110, 129.

began in liberal consensus over the Cold War and civil rights, became a struggle between two apocalyptic politics that each saw the other as hell-bent on the country's annihilation. The result was violence like nothing the country had seen since the civil war."[23] Republican politicians skillfully manipulated these enmities (and still do).

Finally, Ho Chi Minh *did* win. His colleagues and heirs had defeated the world's preeminent military power. And the anti-war movement had succeeded as well, if not in ending the war then at least in contributing to its end. It took more than a decade to achieve this, but the legacies of the anti-war movement, like the legacies of the war itself, lingered and for a time seemed to have an effect, albeit limited. The resistance to the war within the military was the exception – this was a phenomenon that changed American war-making over the long term. The GI anti-war movement brought about the end of the draft and the switch to an all-volunteer military force. Not just the future senator and secretary of state John Kerry, but eventually 25 percent of enlisted men engaged in some form of anti-war action. David Cortright writes that, "In virtually every corner of the military, the burden of fighting an unpopular and unwinnable war caused social disruption and institutional decay. It is probably safe to say that no institution in American society suffered more from the Vietnam War than the military itself. This was due not only to the horrific human cost of the war – more than 59,000 fatalities and hundreds of thousands of severe injuries – but also its profound social and political impact in generating widespread internal opposition and disaffection."[24]

International opposition to the crusade in Vietnam began even before the United States officially committed its troops to the battle in 1965. And President Johnson met a cool response when he tried to persuade European leaders to contribute troops, as the British, Belgians, French and Dutch had done under UN auspices for the Korean War.

Bertrand Russell wrote his letter of denunciation to the *New York Times* in 1963, and in 1966 he founded the International War Crimes Tribunal in which representatives of some eighteen countries participated in hearings on the war held in Sweden and Denmark. They concluded, unanimously, that the United States had been guilty of committing war crimes in Vietnam.

---

23 George Packer, "The Fall of Conservatism," *New Yorker* (26 May 2008).
24 David Cortright, "Resistance in the Military: How Dissent and Defiance in the Ranks Helped to End the Vietnam War," paper delivered at conference "The Vietnam War, Then and Now: Assessing the Critical Lessons" (Washington, DC, 29–30 Apr. 2015), 3.

The force of the international movement around Vietnam was only in part about Vietnamese victimization. Rather it took its force and substance from the multiple connections made by anti-war activists across all borders – including those of North Vietnam and the NLF. And, as in the United States, the power of the movement was linked to domestic issues in each country so that, by 1968, while Vietnam was never absent it had also, to some degree, become connected, in each country, to a wider set of issues. The movement against the war in Vietnam was, at the same time, a movement for fundamental change of the society itself. In the United States, the anti-war movement led to a new consciousness and the rewriting of national history, with a broader focus on women, Native Americans, slavery and social movements. It pried open the selection of political candidates, giving a larger voice to ordinary citizens in the primary process. It is possible the iconic events in France in May 1968 would have taken place anyway – but the mobilization against the war made it easier, even more likely. This was the start of a challenge to the right of patriarchs to control world affairs, which continues today.

In varying degree, anti-war activists across the globe embraced Vietnam as a revolutionary exemplar, as the embodiment of all Third World hopes, as contributing to the end of imperialism everywhere. The International Congress on Vietnam held at the Free University in West Berlin is a case in point. The flag of the National Liberation Front was raised alongside a banner quoting Che: "The duty of a revolutionary is to make a revolution." There were speakers from West Germany, Chile, France, the UK, the USA, Iran and Italy. Rudi Dutschke, mixing Maoist metaphors with New Left rhetoric, called for a "long march through institutions," the building of counterinstitutions and, in defiance of the vast historical difference between China in the 1930s and Europe in the 1960s, the construction of liberated zones. The West German government had originally banned a public demonstration but the injunction was overturned in court, and a crowd of some 20,000 marched along Kurfürstendamm. There was a sense, one observer said, of "breaking the ice that has frozen over Europe's history."[25]

In Japan, in that same winter of discontent, demonstrators gathered to protest the docking of the aircraft carrier USS *Enterprise* – which was on its way to Vietnam – at the Sasebo naval base. Some 47,000 protesters gathered at the harbor to protest while small boats carrying demonstrators who

25 Tariq Ali and Susan Watkins, *1968: Marching in the Streets* (London: Bloomsbury/ New York: Free Press, 1998), 48.

appealed to the crew to desert circled the ship. Direct challenges to the ability of the United States to fight the war characterized the peace movement in Japan, from welcoming and aiding soldiers and sailors who opposed the war and deserted, to efforts to block the transport of arms and ammunition.

With the 1968 Tet or New Year's Offensive, the international expressions of solidarity became even more fervent. The offensive, which had been organized too fast for the southerners to prepare adequately, did not succeed in triggering a mass uprising in South Vietnam, as Lien-hang Nguyen has pointed out, but it did serve "as a catalyst in other social protest movements in Europe, Asia and Latin America."[26] And, she might have added, Africa. "We stand with them," Frelimo (Frente de Libertação de Moçambique, Mozambican Liberation Front) guerrillas fighting against the Portuguese were said to have cheered as they listened to an account of Tet over the radio. The Pakistani poet Habib Jalib openly warned the government: "The cloud of dynamite that covers Vietnam is moving your way."[27] In El Salvador the growing guerrilla movement saw armed struggle as the only way forward, and Cuba and Vietnam their models.

In Paris a section of the Left Bank was renamed "The Heroic Vietnam Quarter," and the NLF flag flew over the Sorbonne. Meanwhile in London, the numbers of demonstrators grew from 25,000 people who gathered in Trafalgar Square in March to the 100,000 who came out to protest in October 1968. It would perhaps be easier to name the countries in which demonstrations did not take place, thanks to authoritarian right-wing governments (Argentina, Greece), than those in which they did.

Among the most significant ways in which Vietnam was in the world and the world in Vietnam was its assiduous pursuit of what its chronicler Robert Brigham has called "people's diplomacy." The support of communist governments – even when they were most at odds, as was the case with China and the Soviet Union in this period – was assured. But both Hanoi and the NLF sought the support of peace groups everywhere and, for obvious reasons, most particularly in the United States. The more pressure that could be brought on the US government to negotiate on acceptable terms, the closer Vietnam could come to an end to the killing. As Lien-hang Nguyen puts it, the Vietnamese "utilized . . . transnational revolutionary circuits in the 1960s

26 Lien-hang Nguyen, "Revolutionary Circuits: Toward Internationalizing America in the World," *Diplomatic History* 39, 3 (2015), 413.
27 Ali and Watkins, *1968*, 36.

and 1970s."[28] These circuits included distinctly nonrevolutionary individuals – pacifists and a variety of political activists from the novelist Grace Paley to the historian Staughton Lynd. In many ways the most fruitful connections came through the efforts of Vietnamese women organized in the north as the Vietnam Women's Union and in the south as the Women's Union of Liberation.

The notion of a global sisterhood, attractive to newly energized feminist groups in the United States, was put to good use by the Vietnamese in numerous international meetings, including one held in Paris in 1968, shortly before the inauguration of formal peace talks. The Conference of Concerned Women to End the War included representatives from Japan, the UK, Australia, New Zealand, West Germany, Canada and the United States. The impact on the Americans who attended was particularly strong.

At the same time, veterans and young volunteers from the International Voluntary Service, American Friends Service Committee and other peace churches returned home from serving in South Vietnam and brought back tales of the senseless violence being perpetrated by the United States. From the Indochina Mobile Education Project to the Winter Soldier hearings in 1971, the American people were receiving first-hand reports of the war that were far more troubling than the scenes on their brief evening newscasts. These projects brought the voices of the Vietnamese people, unfiltered by politics, directly into American communities. The US press, as well, increasingly played this role.

Vietnamese efforts were not limited to Europe or North America but were also directed toward Third World struggles elsewhere. Vietnamese met with and apparently inspired members of the Popular Front for the Liberation of Palestine, Vietnamese texts were translated and circulated to activists throughout the Middle East, Asia, Africa and Latin America. Particularly effective were the travels of Madame Nguyen Thi Binh, a member of the Paris peace delegation, who "toured the world in 1970, meeting with antiwar activists, heads of state, and revolutionary leaders." With the aid of not one but two African heads of state (Julius Nyerere and Milton Obote), Binh arrived in Lusaka to participate in the Non-Aligned Conference despite the fact that Zambia did not recognize the NLF's Provisional Revolutionary Government (PRG). When some delegates protested that the NLF was hardly nonaligned, a representative from Algeria questioned the nonalignment credentials of those in attendance whose countries served as bases for

---

28 Nguyen, "Revolutionary Circuits," 412.

the US war against Vietnam; Fidel Castro himself insisted that Vietnam "was the most excellent example of the soul and spirit of the non-alignment movement," and Binh's subsequent speech was held up by the African press as "the rallying cry of the entire summit."[29]

It was the combination of the war as a revolution to be admired or even emulated and the war as an example of the victimization of a Third World country by the most powerful military in the world that made the movement against the war so nearly universal. The Vietnamese struggle was seen as a struggle to defend "all of humanity."[30]

Not until February 2003 would the world again witness such widespread protest against the war-making of a major power. But US war-making in the twenty-first century, with a volunteer army, is different from war-making in the twentieth, and Iraq was not, after all, Vietnam. The end of conscription in the United States, a direct result of Vietnam anti-war activism, meant that most American men of college age were not touched by the war. The US armed forces had learned other lessons from their failure in Vietnam: Journalists were no longer so free to helicopter in and out of battle zones, but mostly covered the war as "embedded" correspondents with US units. TV coverage of the coffins of dead soldiers arriving on US soil was also placed off-limits. If Vietnam became a television war, the war in Iraq was almost invisible to the general public, a war spun and managed by press spokespeople.

Conclusion

The Vietnam War's impact on the United States and the world would be hard to overestimate. The United States, the major military, economic and technological power of the post-World War II era, was defeated by a poor, underdeveloped country. The country went through a tremendous loss of faith in war-making as a viable solution to imagined or real threats – this self-doubt and disillusionment are still referred to as "the Vietnam syndrome." But the new Socialist Republic of Vietnam, formally unified in 1976, did not win much more than national glory. The geopolitical advantage that Vietnam, along with their Soviet patrons, expected to gain quickly dissolved, as a new conflict, this time with the Khmer Rouge regime in Cambodia, came

29 Nguyen, "Revolutionary Circuits," 421.
30 Marc Lazar, "Le Parti Communiste Français et l'action de solidarité avec le Vietnam," in Christopher Goscha and Maurice Vaisse (eds.), *La Guerre du Vietnam et l'Europe (1963–1973)* (Brussels and Paris: Bruylant/LGDJ, 2003), 250.

to absorb Vietnam's resources. As Vietnam was drawn into a decade-long occupation of Cambodia and economic stagnation, their new rivals to the north, the Chinese, embraced economic reform and stoked a border confrontation with Vietnam that lasted until 1990. This shift from a monolithic communist bloc in Asia to a fragmented state of hostility was one of the outcomes of the Vietnam War, for China's ties with the United States came about as a result of the diplomacy to end the war.

The war was a major turning point in the Cold War, coming to life at a moment when there was a strong impetus for détente in the world, at the end of the Korean War and the first Indochina War. The US decision not to implement the peace process delineated at Geneva in 1954 kept the Cold War alive and led gradually to the transformation of a colonial war for independence into a vastly destructive proxy war among the superpowers.

For the communist world, the Vietnam War became a test of alliances and long-term ideological goals. In the end, the war both changed and was changed by these alliances. The People's Republic of China at first viewed the war as a means of mobilizing its population and keeping the US military tied down in Southeast Asia. Chinese military and material aid to Vietnam also helped Mao Zedong to increase his prestige in the Third World as a true supporter of world revolution, at the expense of the USSR. But as the Sino-Soviet split grew more bitter in the mid 1960s and, after ideological debate gave way to warfare on their northern border in 1969, the Chinese leadership became more concerned with the threat to their nation from the Soviet Union. With the United States admitting after 1968 that the war was a stalemate, the Chinese found themselves being courted by the Nixon administration. Henry Kissinger, the key architect of US foreign policy under Nixon, saw that the best escape from the Vietnam quagmire would be to normalize relations with China, thus ending the threat of monolithic communism in Asia and depriving Vietnam of its once-trusted ally. Nixon's visit to China in the spring of 1972 was the start of an economic relationship that has grown today into perhaps the most influential factor in the health of the world economy. The strategic partnership to counter Soviet hegemony that began in that year has, on the other hand, lost its force with the end of the Soviet Union.

The international impact of the Vietnam War at the popular level has been longlasting. The power of leftist theory regarding economic justice may have ebbed with the death of European communism in 1989–91. But the passions stirred by the war in the 1960s and 1970s have not disappeared, and in fact international civil society seems better prepared than ever to track the true facts on the ground when war breaks out. The Iraq War was remarkable for the attention paid to civilian casualties and international efforts to record these deaths by groups such as Iraq Body Count. We retain the revulsion against the high-tech cruelty of modern warfare, especially indiscriminate bombing, that we once felt at the sight of children flaming with napalm, running down a country road. The fact that the US administration is reluctant to hold a congressional vote to sanction the continuing wars in the Middle East, in the face of popular opposition to the ongoing "war against terror," says much about popular feelings about war.

Bibliographical Essay

New political histories of the Vietnam War now appear with regularity, as scholars gain access to more archives of the US State Department, some from the Pentagon and written by official Armed Forces historians, as well as collections of presidential papers and tapes in the libraries of Presidents Truman, Eisenhower, Kennedy, Johnson and Nixon. A few examples: books by Fredrik Logevall, *The Embers of War: The Fall of an Empire and the Making of America's Vietnam* (New York: Random House, 2012), and *Choosing War: The Lost Chance for Peace and the Escalation of War in Vietnam* (Berkeley: University of California Press, 2001), Mark A. Lawrence, *Assuming the Burden: Europe and the American Commitment to the War in Vietnam* (Berkeley: University of California Press, 2005), Mark Philip Bradley, *Imagining Vietnam and America: The Making of Postcolonial Vietnam, 1919–1950* (Chapel Hill: University of North Carolina Press, 2000), and William J. Rust, *Eisenhower and Cambodia: Diplomacy, Covert Action, and the Origins of the Second Indochina War* (Lexington: University Press of Kentucky, 2016), all provide valuable context and multiarchival scholarship on the origins of the US war. David Halberstam's *The Best and the Brightest* (New York: Random House, 1972) is one of several excellent books by journalists about the failures of US policymaking for Vietnam. Several scholars have utilized Nixon's White House papers and tapes to write on the final years of the war, including Jeffrey Kimball in *Nixon's Vietnam War* (Lawrence: University Press of Kansas, 1998).

For general US histories of the war, from its origins up to 1975 and beyond, one can single out George Herring's *America's Longest War: The United States and Vietnam, 1950–1975* (New York: John Wiley and Sons, 1979) as a concise and objective study; Marilyn B. Young's *The Vietnam Wars: 1945–1990* (New York: HarperCollins, 1991) covers all three Indochina Wars with great thoroughness and a strong critique of US policy. Essential eyewitness accounts of the way the war was fought include the two books by Jonathan Schell, *The Village of Ben Suc* and *The Military Half*, now combined in one paperback volume entitled *The Real War: The Classic Reporting on the Vietnam War* (New York: Pantheon Books, 1988). For in-depth scholarly research, David Elliott provides a two-volume work on the communists (known as the Viet Cong by the US military) in the Mekong delta: *The Vietnamese War: Revolution and Social Change in the Mekong Delta, 1930–1975* (Armonk, NY: M. E. Sharpe, 2003). Mai Elliott, who worked with David for the Rand Corporation, has contributed a study of *Rand in Southeast Asia: A History of Vietnam War Era* (Santa Monica, CA: Rand, 2010). Rand, a contractor to the US military, was responsible for much of US government analysis, and as Mai Elliott shows, in the early days it was strongly influenced by one analyst who saw the bombing of the DRV as the key to winning the war. His ideas later lost favor.

"International history" of the Vietnam War, covering all the state actors with a major influence on the war, is a genre pioneered by British scholar Ralph B. Smith. His three-volume *An International History of the Vietnam War* (London: Palgrave Macmillan, 1984, 1986, 1991) is still the most in-depth work of this type, using the BBC Monitoring service and the CIA's Foreign Broadcast Information Service as basic sources for the communist bloc. His inclusion of economic analysis keeps his study relevant, even though he wrote without the archival information on Soviet and Chinese policies that would become available in the 1990s. His successors include Singaporean scholar Ang Cheng Guan, who completed the Smith opus with a final volume entitled *International History of the Vietnam War: The Denouement, 1967–1975* (London: Routledge, 2011).

More recent international histories using Hanoi archives by Pierre Asselin, *Hanoi's Road to the Vietnam War, 1954–1965* (Berkeley: University of California Press, 2013), and Lien-Hang T. Nguyen, *Hanoi's War: An International History of the War for Peace in Vietnam* (Chapel Hill: University of North Carolina Press, 2012), purport to be the final word on Hanoi's role and thinking regarding the war. However, both authors take a revisionist view that puts strong emphasis on Hanoi's actions without providing a balanced view of US war planning. The old issue of whether the Vietnamese had the right to fight to unify their country after the failure of the Geneva Agreements goes unaddressed.

Studies based on communist archives: The partial opening of archives in China, Eastern Europe and Russia during the 1990s has provided a deeper understanding of attitudes within the socialist bloc to the Vietnam War. For China, Chen Jian, *Mao's China and the Cold War* (Chapel Hill: University of North Carolina Press, 2001), and Qiang Zhai, *China and the Vietnam Wars, 1950–1975* (Chapel Hill: University of North Carolina Press, 2000), have set the pace with their overviews. Ilya Gaiduk, a Russian historian, has written two books using the Soviet archives: *The Soviet Union and the Vietnam War* (Chicago: Ivan R. Dee, 1996) and *Confronting Vietnam: Soviet Policy Toward the Indochina Conflict, 1954–1963* (Washington, DC, and Stanford: Woodrow Wilson Center Press and Stanford University Press, 2003). Norwegian scholar Mari Olsen has also contributed a study based on the Soviet Foreign Ministry archive: *Soviet–Vietnam Relations and the Role of China, 1949–1964: Changing Alliances* (London: Routledge, 2006). All of these studies confirm the reluctance of the USSR to become involved in the second Vietnam War, until 1965.

The anti-war movement, in the United States and worldwide: We recommend the exhaustive bibliography established by Ed Moise on this topic (edmoise.sites.clemson.edu/antiwar.html), but will select a few examples, specifically on the world movement: Tariq Ali and Susan Watkins, *1968: Marching in the Streets* (London: Bloomsbury/New York: Free Press, 1998), is heavily illustrated and covers protest demonstrations in many countries. Christoper Goscha and Maurice Vaïsse (eds.), *La guerre du Vietnam et l'Europe (1963–1973)* (Brussels and Paris: Bruylant/LGDJ, 2003), is a collection of papers, some in French and some in English. Among the ones dealing with the anti-war movement are: Jost Dülffer, "The Anti-Vietnam War Movement in West Germany," 287–305; Nadine Lubelski-Bernard, "L'opposition à la guerre du Vietnam en Belgique (1963–1973)," 307–26; and Kim Saloman, "The Anti-Vietnam War Movement in Sweden," 327–37.

Reports from the sessions of the International War Crimes Tribunal (founded by Bertrand Russell) are online at raetowest.org/Vietnam-war-crimes/russell-vietnam-war-crimes-tribunal-1967.html. The complete transcripts of the Winter Soldier Investigation are available at www.wintersoldier.com/index.php?topic=CompletWSI. This includes the introduction by Senator Mark Hatfield, when he presented the testimonies to the Senate on 5 April 1971. The three-day event was organized by Vietnam Veterans Against the War, on 31 January, 1 February and 2 February 1971.

Two other sources on US war crimes are books by German writer Bernd Greiner, *War Without Fronts: The USA in Vietnam* (New Haven: Yale University Press, 2009 [2007]); and Nick Turse, *Kill Anything that Moves: The Real American War in Vietnam* (New York: Metropolitan Books, 2013).

Both use the Pentagon's own investigations into reported war crimes, after the My Lai massacre came to light.

On the anti-war movement within the US armed forces, David Cortright's *Soldiers in Revolt, 1975* (Chicago: Haymarket, 2005) is an excellent source by a participant-observer.

3

The Soviet Union and the Global Cold War

ARTEMY M. KALINOVSKY

The Soviet Union always claimed to be an anti-imperialist power. What this meant in practice differed throughout the USSR's seventy-year history, but between the 1950s and mid 1980 the decolonization of European empires and the Cold War confrontation with the United States (as well as the Sino-Soviet split) drew Moscow into ideological, economic and military competition for the so-called Third World. At the same time, engaging with the Third World meant confronting internal contradictions (such as the fact that the USSR was itself an empire) as well as the limits of the USSR's model and its might.

This chapter will attempt a history of that engagement. Although it will not offer a comprehensive overview of Soviet foreign relations in the period, it will examine the changing role of Soviet power along several lines. This chapter will examine, first, the attractiveness of the Soviet model of development to countries in the Third World; second, the Soviet Union's role in the militarization of postcolonial regimes and interventions in postcolonial conflicts; third, tensions between pursuing détente and the Soviet interest in the Third World throughout the 1970s; and, finally, the Soviet intervention in Afghanistan and its significance for Soviet relations with the Third World in the 1980s and the end of the Cold War.

Reengaging the World: Decolonization and the Cold War

The early Cold War confrontation did not immediately awaken Moscow's interest in the colonial world, despite the clear pressures for independence growing throughout the European empires. Skeptical of the prospects for revolution in India and Pakistan, Stalin limited engagement with these new states. The experience with Israel and Iran seemed to deepen his suspicions.

Stalin had been among the first to recognize Israel in 1948, hoping that the new country's strong communist and socialist parties would give the Soviet Union a bridgehead in the British-dominated Middle East. By the end of the year, however, he was convinced that pro-American feeling in the young state was too strong; his paranoia about the loyalty of Soviet Jews, many of whom had been inspired by the creation of the Jewish state, led to a domestic crackdown known as the "anti-cosmopolitan campaign."

After World War II, Stalin tried to stimulate a separatist movement in Iranian Azerbaijan through the Azerbaijani Soviet Socialist Republic. The attempt not only failed, but it also discredited the Iranian communists who had supported it. A disappointed Stalin wrote to Ja'afar Pishevari, the leader of the separatist Azerbaijan People's Government in Iran, that there was no hope for a revolution in Iran, because, "There are few workers in Iran and they are poorly organized. The Iranian peasantry still does not show any serious activism."[1] Later, when a genuinely anti-imperialist (though not communist) movement took root under Mohammed Mossadeq, Stalin was indifferent. Moscow followed the situation in Iran closely but refused to help Mossadeq. From Stalin's point of view, Mossadeq was too weak to carry out a genuine revolution of national liberation, and Britain's loss would just end up being the United States's gain.

It would take Nikita Khrushchev, who gradually consolidated power after Stalin's death, to make the Soviet Union a truly global player. Khrushchev and the other Soviet leaders who succeeded Stalin shared a general belief in the need to lessen tensions with the United States and West European powers, but they also needed to demonstrate their continued commitment to revolution. They were thus more open to working with the colonial and postcolonial world than Stalin had been. In 1955, Khrushchev and fellow Presidium member Nikolai Bulganin undertook a whirlwind tour of South Asia that included stops in India, Burma and Afghanistan. Recognizing that there was an interest in Soviet technology and military support, Bulganin prevailed on colleagues who thought Khrushchev's commitments to these emerging countries were too expensive. What motivated Khrushchev and the colleagues who supported him? Was it a desire to find alternatives for trade, to expand the USSR's horizons of partners for exchange? Was it the wave of decolonization acting like a caffeine kick to Soviet anti-imperialist ideology, reawakening it from a long slumber? Was it a desire to rejuvenate the revolutionary project at home, by reclaiming the Soviet Union's position

---

1 Joseph Stalin to Ja'afar Pishevari, 8 May 1946, translated by Vladislav Zubok, in Natalia I. Yegorova, *The "Iran Crisis" of 1945–1946: A View from the Russian Archives*, Working Paper no. 15 (Washington, DC: Cold War International History Project, 1996), 23–24.

in the leadership of all oppressed peoples? Or perhaps it was the personal feelings of men like Khrushchev, who saw in the wave of revolutionary leaders younger versions of themselves?

The answer, most likely, is all of the above. The Soviet Union did need to expand its trade horizons if it was going to successfully raise standards of living at home. It also needed to secure allies, since the United States and United Kingdom were preparing to engage in long-term security relationships with countries in the Middle East and South Asia, through alliances such as the Baghdad Pact and the South East Asian Treaty Organization (SEATO). The ideological fervor that decolonization inspired cannot be overlooked, however. Neither Khrushchev nor any other Soviet leader could claim to be returning the country to Leninist principles while ignoring the anti-imperialist movements and new postcolonial states looking for models and support. Leaders may have used ideology to mobilize and discipline populations during the Cold War, but ideology also disciplined leaders themselves.

This ideology could be flexible, however. The Soviet Union would support "big umbrella" anti-imperialism, meaning in practice that almost all postcolonial states and anti-colonial movements could find a way to establish good relations with the Soviet Union if they chose to do so. Antagonism with the United States or European countries was not even a prerequisite. Thus, Soviet technical and military aid began to flow to Afghanistan and India in the 1950s, even as both countries sought the same from Washington. Khrushchev's call for peaceful coexistence meant that one could pursue the battle for the Third World even *within* postcolonial states, working alongside capitalists while proving the USSR's superiority. Nothing illustrated the change better than the reassessment of Mossadeq's tenure. When Viacheslav Molotov joined the anti-Khrushchev conspiracy in 1957 and was subsequently ousted, his earlier "misreading" of the situation in Iran was used against him. Molotov had mistakenly seen "the conflict surrounding the Anglo-Iranian Oil Company not as a conflict between Iran and the colonizers of the West," but as an intra-imperialist squabble, thus missing the fact that Iran was in the midst of a "revolution of national liberation."[2]

Engagement with the wider world required the creation of new institutions at home that would provide expertise and facilitate relations

---

2 Artemy M. Kalinovsky, "The Soviet Union and Mossadeq: A Research Note," *Iranian Studies* 47, 3 (2014), 401–18.

between Moscow and its new friends. These institutions, and the people who staffed them, would become interpreters of the world for Soviet decision-makers and even drivers of foreign policy. Institutes of Africa and Latin America were set up for the first time, under the Academy of Sciences. The Institute of Oriental Studies in Moscow got a new director, the Tajik party leader Bobojon Ghafurov, to oversee its engagement with contemporary issues and use scholarship as a way of demonstrating Soviet commitment to the "East." Organizations such as the Society for Solidarity with the Countries of Asia and Africa (Sovetskii komitet solidarnosti stran Azii i Afriki, SKSSAA) built upon earlier institutions like the All-Union Society for Cultural Ties (Vsesoiuznoe obshchestvo kul'turnoi sviazi s zagranitsei, VOKS) but, with a much larger budget and staff, came to play a key role in domestic mobilization, cultural exchange and expertise. SKSSAA's board included the Tajik poet Mirzo Turson-zade, Foreign Minister Andrei Gromyko and a number of specialists and party advisors. In the decades that followed, a person might train at the Institute of Oriental Studies, working with the SKSSAA, and eventually move on to the foreign ministry or KGB. These individuals became a pressure group of sorts within Soviet foreign-policy circles, not just interpreting the Third World for Soviet officials but often lobbying for engagement.

Nonalignment and the Sino-Soviet Split

The Soviet engagement with the postcolonial world faced two significant external challenges that affected Moscow's policy throughout the Cold War. The first, nonalignment, challenged the bloc-making of Cold War adversaries as yet another attempt by "Europeans" to divide the world between them. The internal contradictions of the movement ultimately limited its impact on the Cold War confrontation. The second was the growing confrontation with communist China, which posed a more formidable challenge to the Soviet position in the Third World and transformed Moscow's thinking and approach.

Nonalignment emerged out of a desire by Josef Broz Tito's Yugoslavia, which had broken with Moscow in 1948, and postcolonial elites to avoid getting pulled into the US–Soviet confrontation. Together they hoped to maintain agency in the face of universalizing projects and to achieve, through solidarity in numbers, the parity with great powers that was elusive to each of these states individually. The Korean War, the struggle in Vietnam and the French tenacity in North Africa all demonstrated the distance still to cover to get rid of European colonialism, and the dangers of the Cold War created new excuses for intervention and domination. Delegates from across Asia and Africa gathered in Bandung in 1955; there they criticized the Soviet domination of Eastern Europe and Central Asia. The American author Richard Wright felt that "Russia had no defenders at Bandung."[3] This was not quite accurate, but the conference did threaten to undermine the Soviet Union's bid for leadership. Even more troubling was the 1961 Conference of Heads of State of Non-Aligned Governments, hosted by Tito in Belgrade in 1961. Many of the protagonists from the Bandung meeting, including Jawaharlal Nehru, Kwame Nkrumah, Sukarno and Gamal Abdel Nasser, took part.

The Non-Aligned Movement, as it became known, struggled to maintain coherence throughout the Cold War period, and as a result it never proved much of a threat to either Washington or Moscow. Some countries, such as Cuba, were outright Soviet allies. Indonesia remained a key member even after Sukarno seized power in a military coup and took the country closer to the United States. India and China, two of the leading nations at Bandung, went to war in 1962. Indeed, India was the great prize for both Washington and Moscow: It was important strategically (due to its location, territory and population), and it had the potential to demonstrate the success of each side's respective development policies. Yet while India remained formally neutral, it often sided with Moscow at crucial moments, at least tacitly. Moscow rewarded New Delhi with generous economic and especially military aid.

China posed a bigger problem. Historians have offered different takes on the causes of the Sino-Soviet split, some emphasizing domestic power struggles, others ideology. Most recently, Austin Jersild has drawn our attention to the role of everyday interactions between Soviet advisors and their Chinese partners in pushing the two countries apart – the Soviets were too similar to the Europeans who had lorded it over the Chinese during the era of "concessions."[4] Whatever the causes of the split, by the early 1960s Beijing and Moscow were on their way to becoming competitors for the Third World. Wright had already noticed at Bandung that Chinese

---

3 Richard Wright, *The Colour Curtain: A Report on the Bandung Conference* (London: Dennis Dobson, 1955), 134.
4 Austin Jersild, *The Sino-Soviet Alliance: An International History* (Chapel Hill: University of North Carolina Press, 2014).

prime minister Zhou Enlai had ably won over the delegates, avoiding any discussion of the Soviet Union, instead focusing on a common history of oppression and the willingness to resist it. China, Wright felt, "could walk as a fellow guest into an anti-Western house built by a reaction to colonialism and racialism."[5] In 1955 Moscow and Beijing were still allies, and the performance was coordinated.[6] As Khrushchev sought better relations with the West, Beijing warned that Moscow was giving up on world revolution and anti-imperialism. Increasingly, China would indeed use the advantage identified by Wright against its former ally.

The Soviet Union, Jeremy Friedman has convincingly argued, was trying to pursue two contradictory policies, and China reveled in exposing the contradiction.[7] Moscow wanted to pursue "peaceful coexistence" with the United States, in part to help its own standing with the European working class. But Moscow also wanted to support national liberation movements. China could, and did, point out that the two were not easily reconcilable. While the Soviets held out on recognizing the Provisional Government in Algeria for fear of alienating the French, Beijing provided aid and weapons. The Soviet Union could respond by attacking "excessive nationalism" – pointing out that the kind of nationalist regimes Beijing was willing to support were just handmaidens of colonial powers – and by becoming more generous with economic and military aid. The latter, Friedman suggests, also pulled China into a competition it could not yet sustain, giving the Soviets some breathing room.

For some postcolonial states, the split was a boon – they had two and sometimes three "superpowers" to play off against each other. The North Vietnamese communists spent the first half of the 1960s trying to stay neutral and maintain friendly relations with both Beijing and Moscow. Eventually, they learned to attract increasing aid from both with minimal interference in how they pursued the war for South Vietnam. Sometimes Soviet equipment piled up in ports collecting rust; the abundance of Soviet materiel served as a potent reminder to Beijing that Hanoi was not dependent on Chinese patronage.

---

5 Wright, *The Colour Curtain*, 140.
6 See Shu Guang Zhang, "Constructing 'Peaceful Coexistence': China's Diplomacy Toward the Geneva and Bandung Conferences, 1954–1955," *Cold War History* 7, 4 (Oct. 2007), 509–28.
7 Jeremy Friedman, *Shadow Cold War: The Sino-Soviet Competition for the Third World* (Chapel Hill: University of North Carolina Press, 2015).

Trade and Development

Starting with Khrushchev's 1955 tour of South Asia, the Soviet Union began fighting the Cold War using trade and aid. Some historians have recently argued that Soviet leaders were simply searching for new trade outlets; moreover, the leaders believed that the Soviet Union's economy was tiny compared to that of the United States, and thus never had much to offer. Yet this misses the complex mix of motivations that drove Soviet leaders to offer aid and seek out trade relationships. It also ignores the very real ways in which Soviet economic achievements appealed to postcolonial states. Few of them were interested in importing the Soviet model as such. But many believed that the USSR's crash transformation from an agricultural country to one that could take on and defeat Nazi Germany, build nuclear weapons and send rockets and humans into space meant that there was much the USSR could teach them. The Soviet Union was riding a wave of economic growth as the postwar recovery finally took off; palpable achievements in industry and science added to a sense of optimism in Soviet officials, which in turn encouraged them to offer Soviet aid abroad.

Afghanistan, Egypt and India were among the first to attract significant Soviet aid and projects. In all three cases, the USSR was not interested in wholesale economic transformation, nor was it trying to transform the political system. The Soviets were not the only players in any of these countries, but just one of the "donors" building roads, dams and factories. Moscow's engineers, professors and economic advisors sometimes even worked alongside counterparts from the United States and Europe. In Egypt, Nasser's ambitions for postcolonial development made him look to the United States for help in building the Aswan Dam; when the USA pulled funding, he decided to nationalize the Suez Canal, prompting an Anglo-French-Israeli attack. In the end the Soviet Union stepped in to build the dam and also began an extensive security relationship that lasted throughout the 1960s. But, as it would do elsewhere, Moscow tolerated Nasser's ongoing relationship with the West, as well as his persecution of domestic communists.

Just as Moscow was not interested in a wholesale export of the Soviet system, the "recipient" countries were similarly intent on attracting maximum advice while preserving maximum autonomy. Countries such as India and Afghanistan that experimented with "five-year plans" were not interested in a Soviet-style planned economy, but rather in ways to bring knowledge into their countries and target plans accordingly. As David Engerman has argued, the "net effect of all the foreign advice" solicited by India was close to zero.[8] Indian leaders were interested in the specific techniques economists from around the world offered, and they (selectively) used the opinions of foreign experts to justify their own economic policies. Beyond that, they were determined to forge their own path.

India not only provided the biggest platform for competing Cold War development and modernization schemes, it also gave Soviet economists food for thought. The interaction between Soviet and Indian economists in the late 1950s pushed the former to develop the idea of a "noncapitalist path" to development. They observed the diverse approaches of Indian leaders to their country's problems, the concurrent growth of the state sector and the vibrant private sector alongside it. These observations, in turn, fed into the formulation used by Khrushchev in 1956 in speaking of "noncapitalist paths" to development. Khrushchev's formulation harked back to Lenin's observation in 1920 that backward nations might not have to go through the capitalist stage of development. Yet Khrushchev was also drawing on what Soviet economists were writing about India, articulating a flexible approach that allowed the Soviet Union to engage the United States in a competition for the Third World that played out through economic aid.[9]

As Guy Laron and others have argued, the Cold War in the Third World was not a zero-sum game.[10] Indeed, in a number of cases the Soviet Union and the United States were effectively working side by side even as they were competing for influence. Nowhere was this more true than in the case of Afghanistan, where the monarchy and, after it was overthrown, the republic under Mohammed Daoud tried to pursue state-building and modernization programs with aid from the United States and the Soviet Union, as well as a group of other states and private foundations. The Soviets and Americans built parallel projects – dams, roads and schools – but they also interacted with each other and occasionally tried to coordinate their efforts. Both Soviet and American advisors later spoke warmly about the relationships they had developed with their counterparts.

8 David Engerman "Learning from the East: Soviet Experts and India in the Era of Competitive Coexistence," *Comparative Studies in South Asia, Africa, and the Middle East* 33, 2 (2013), 230.
9 Ibid.
10 Guy Laron, *Origins of the Suez Crisis: Postwar Development Diplomacy and the Struggle over Third World Industrialization, 1945–1956* (Washington, DC: Woodrow Wilson Center Press, 2013).

Soviet aid was ideologically flexible, but this did not mean that Soviets provided aid free of ideology. At the most fundamental level, the very idea of development was ideological. Of course, Soviet engineers, teachers and economists were supposed to demonstrate the superiority of their system. Moreover, they were supposed to play an active role in shaping "modern" subjects. By working on Soviet-led construction projects or studying in Soviet technical schools, young men (and, in fewer cases, women) oriented toward their family, village and tradition were supposed to reorient themselves toward their profession, their nation-state and the future. Teachers and trainers working in Afghanistan wrote home about the relative successes and obstacles in creating such new men and women. In this sense, the Soviet approach mirrored that of Western development specialists, who were similarly convinced of the need to create a new middle class for "modernization" to properly take hold.[11]

If Soviet aid in India was a "drop in the bucket," considering India's overall size and the enthusiasm of various donors, in some of the postcolonial states of sub-Saharan Africa the Soviet Union had the opportunity to make a much larger economic and political impact. In the case of Ghana, however, despite leader Kwame Nkrumah's interest in socialism, they found that Anglo-American influence was far too strong. Soviet offers of aid were met with polite resistance. In Guinea, which faced a more severe economic rupture after independence from France (the country voted against remaining in the French community in a referendum, prompting an economic blockade by Paris), there was much greater interest in Soviet involvement. Yet by 1961 Soviet officials were increasingly disappointed with what they saw as Guinean mismanagement of the economy and an emphasis on "prestige" projects such as a stadium and a presidential palace. In December 1961 the Soviet ambassador was expelled from the country, accused of being involved in a plot against the Guinean leader Sékou Touré.[12]

The relationship with west Africa showed the limits of Soviet economic development assistance. Countries such as Ghana were clearly integrated into the capitalist world (most of Ghana's main export crop, cocoa, was still marketed through a British company), and Moscow could not replace these trading partners completely. Moscow was willing to barter finished

11 Antonio Giustozzi and Artemy M. Kalinovsky et al., *Missionaries of Modernity: Advisory Missions and the Struggle for Hegemony in Afghanistan and Beyond* (London: Hurst, 2016).
12 Alessandro Iandolo, "The Rise and Fall of the 'Soviet Model of Development' in West Africa, 1957–1964," *Cold War History* 12, 4 (Nov. 2012), 683–704.

goods for primary export products, but these countries preferred hard currency. Second, Moscow's resources were limited. By the early 1960s the economic growth of the 1950s was reaching its limits. Harvests in the Virgin Lands, which Moscow had shown off to visitors from postcolonial states as an example of how to achieve agricultural independence, were declining. In 1963 the Soviet Union was forced to import grain. Khrushchev's opponents were increasingly critical of "wasteful" foreign engagements that used precious Soviet resources without creating stable allies or markedly advancing the cause of revolution. From the early 1960s, in fact, Moscow would try to establish more economically advantageous forms of trade. If Soviet economists had championed economic self-sufficiency in the 1950s (with the implication that the USSR could help postcolonial countries achieve that status through aid), by the 1960s they were increasingly tolerant of primary commodity exports, provided those exports went to socialist countries. The USSR's own needs and economic weakness limited its effectiveness as a "donor country."

This did not mean that the period of Soviet aid was finished. One of the longlasting legacies of the 1950s was the assortment of agencies and committees charged with studying, articulating and implementing policies for the Third World. The State Committee for Economic Cooperation (Gosudarstvennyi komitet po vneshnim ekonimicheskim sviaziam, GKES) continued to build roads, power plants and factories in India, Afghanistan and other countries. Even as official discourse proclaimed the end of economically senseless aid, Moscow continued to make commitments to its allies. Afghanistan would be one of the largest recipients of Soviet aid, but in the 1970s newly decolonizing or revolutionary states such as Ethiopia also managed to get major Soviet investments.

The "ideological" factor in Soviet aid and trade never disappeared. Even as some Soviet institutions, such as the Ministry of Trade, tried to get trading relationships on a more "rational" footing by insisting on balanced trade and the fulfillment of loan obligations, other, more ideologically oriented ones such as the SKSSAA or even the International Department of the Communist Party of the Soviet Union (CPSU) often overrode such concerns. Moscow's friends grew practiced in the art of appealing to anti-imperial solidarity. Afghanistan once again provides an interesting example. Soviet officials hoped that Afghan exports of gas and other products would pay for Soviet goods and economic aid; in reality they never even came close. Moreover, Afghan officials from the early 1960s also appealed to Moscow for help in repaying loans to the United States. Trade officials tried many times over the following decades to put pressure on their Afghan counterparts, but there was little the Afghans could really offer. Dried fruits and carpets, two of Afghanistan's main exports, were produced in Soviet Central Asia. At one point Afghan trade representatives wanted to export opium, but Soviet officials explained that it was a controlled substance and in any case the USSR had all the opium it needed. Yet time after time party officials stepped in to defray loans and approve new shipments of goods or new projects to be implemented by the USSR.

Overall, however, interest in Soviet technology declined in the 1960s and 1970s. Increasingly, even countries following the "noncapitalist path of development" were turning to the capitalist West for technology and economic assistance. The countries that continued to rely primarily on Soviet aid and development in the 1970s were either newer revolutionary regimes, such as the military committee (Derg) that took power in Ethiopia in 1973, or semi-isolated socialist states such as Cuba. This did not mean that the global Cold War was over for the Soviet Union – on the contrary, it was entering a new dimension, where Soviet involvement would primarily be military.

Military Aid, Intervention and the Rise and Fall of Détente

If Soviet economic and development aid was one way to solve the paradox of peaceful coexistence (normalizing relations with the imperialist powers while helping postcolonial states achieve full independence), then Soviet military aid was the continuation of the same in the era of détente. The ever-growing military-industrial complex was the only sector of the Soviet economy that could comfortably offer significant proportions of its output to foreign clients. And the Soviet Union had plenty of infrastructure in terms of bases, military academies and training grounds to easily take in thousands of aspiring officers from around the world and turn them into competent commanders. Yet what began as military aid (training, equipment, advising) led in more than one case, through chains of commitment, to direct involvement, and in the ultimate and tragic case of Afghanistan, intervention.

Cuba was among the most important early Soviet military commitments. Moscow had done nothing to support Fidel Castro's partisans, but it embraced him after he took power. John F. Kennedy's disastrous attempt to overthrow Castro in the Bay of Pigs invasion, while unsuccessful, nevertheless presented Khrushchev with a quandary. Could the Soviet Union help fledgling revolutions abroad? Or were they doomed to be choked by imperialist hands? The dilemma was accentuated by Khrushchev's domestic battles to shrink the size of the armed forces and the evolving Sino-Soviet split. If Moscow failed to protect Cuba, it would prove the Chinese claim that Khrushchev was ready to sell out revolutions in favor of friendship with the capitalist world. Placing nuclear missiles on Cuba was a way to prove the Chinese wrong and show domestic opponents that Soviet missile technology made power projection possible even with reduced military manpower. The resulting crisis needs no repeating here.[13]

Perhaps the most sustained Soviet involvement was in the Middle East, and particularly with Egypt and Syria. Egypt turned to the socialist bloc for military aid in 1955. As in 1948, when Moscow encouraged Czechoslovakia to sell arms to Israel, it now asked Prague to supply Gamal Abdel Nasser rather than supporting him directly. After the Suez crisis, Soviet aid gradually increased. Nasser became one of the Soviet Union's postcolonial celebrities, paraded around the country on his state visits, his image frequently appearing in papers across the USSR.

Just as economic aid allowed postcolonial regimes to pursue develop-ment and state-building schemes far more ambitious then those foreign advisors recommended, military aid allowed them to expand their own regional ambitions. This was arguably the case for aspiring regional powers such as Egypt (in the 1960s), Iraq (in the late 1970s) and India (throughout the Cold War). Military aid inevitably entangled Moscow in regional Cold Wars. In 1958 Nasser successfully forged a union with Syria, creating the United Arab Republic. Yet he was arrayed against a conser-vative monarchist coalition, including Saudi Arabia and Jordan, that drew support from the United States. The confrontation came to a head over Yemen, where a group of army officers ousted the country's leader, precipitating a civil war. With Soviet aid, Egypt was able to intervene on behalf of the new regime.

The high point of the Soviet relationship with Egypt was the Six-Day War and its aftermath. A (false) report from Soviet intelligence that Israel was planning a strike, passed on with the hope of drawing Arab leaders closer to Moscow, instead prompted Nasser to begin preparations for war. Both Moscow and Washington tried to defuse tensions, but eventually Israel

---

13 The literature is vast, but see Aleksandr Fursenko and Timothy Naftali, *One Hell of a Gamble: Khrushchev, Castro, and Kennedy, 1958–1964* (New York: W. W. Norton and Company, 1997).

decided to act on its own, wiping out the Egyptian air force and doubling its territory over the course of six days at the expense of Syria and Jordan, which had joined the fight. It was not lost on anyone that Moscow's military allies, equipped and trained by the Soviet Union, had been easily defeated. Desperate to prove its commitment to Egypt and Syria, Moscow (again) cut off relations with Israel. The Soviet friendship with Arabs and indignation at Israel were performed in demonstrations and party meetings across the country. The net effect, however, was to further erode any Soviet leverage with its allies. At the same time, Moscow needed to reclaim its credibility and showered Nasser with additional aid and advisors. Indeed, after Nasser began his "war of attrition" in the Sinai in 1969, the Soviets were drawn into the fighting, manning anti-aircraft batteries and fighter planes bearing Egyptian markings. In the long term, however, Moscow could not save its relationship. After Nasser died of a heart attack, his successor, Anwar Sadat, ejected Soviet advisors and turned to the United States. The loss of a country in which the Soviet Union had invested so much proved traumatic for Soviet leaders – for the rest of the Cold War they would fear that one of their allies would "pull a Sadat."

The confrontations in the Middle East also threatened to undermine the US–Soviet détente, which was reaching its zenith by 1973. Moscow and Washington had attempted to collaborate on a peace deal between Egypt and Israel in 1969, but when conflict broke out they retreated to familiar Cold War posturing. The Soviets had little leverage and had to prove their commitment and credibility; the United States distrusted Soviet intentions, and both sides initiated massive airlifts during the 1973 war. This would not be the only area where the US–Soviet détente found its limits. The Soviet conception of détente focused first and foremost on normalization in Europe and a recognition of postwar borders. It did not mean the abandonment of world revolution.

Odd Arne Westad has argued that, in effect, the Soviet Union was pursuing two foreign policies in the 1970s.[14] While the Foreign Ministry focused on US–Soviet détente, the International Department of the CPSU Central Committee was actively pushing for engagement with the Third World. Indeed, the Soviet Union had several powerful foreign-policy lobbies by this point, each pursuing a somewhat different agenda. There were external lobbies as well. Just as Soviet organizations such as SKSSAA helped Soviet

14 Odd Arne Westad, *Global Cold War: Third World Interventions and the Making of Our Times* (Cambridge: Cambridge University Press, 2005).

officials interpret the Third World, sometimes giving a different interpretation of developments than the Foreign Ministry did, foreign partners also offered a different perspective and often advocated a more activist approach than the ones the Soviets were (initially) prepared to follow. Piero Gleijeses, for example, has argued that Cuba was crucial for driving Soviet military engagement in southern Africa.[15] Natalia Telepneva has recently shown how the Soviet Union's "partners" in the socialist block, such as Czechoslovakia and East Germany, also helped to drive Soviet engagement.[16]

Indeed, the end of the Portuguese empire in 1975 launched a new wave of enthusiasm for socialist revolution on the African continent for the first time since the early 1960s. At the same time, the struggle that broke out for Angola demonstrated the implications of the global Cold War in the era of Sino-Soviet enmity. While Moscow and Cuba supported the Popular Movement for the Liberation of Angola (Movimento Popular de Libertação de Angola, MPLA), the United States threw its support behind the National Union for the Total Liberation of Angola and the National Front for the Liberation of Angola (Frente Nacional de Libertação de Angola, FNLA). The Chinese were also supporting the FNLA, meaning that along with the apartheid regime in South Africa they were fighting a postcolonial state. The Soviet Union was able to regain some of the ground lost to China in the 1960s by pointing out that Beijing was siding with racists, but the involvement of three superpowers (as well as Cuba and South Africa) meant that Angola would face a twenty-year civil war.

The 1970s were the peak of Moscow's Third World influence, but the weaknesses in the USSR's relationships and the limits of Soviet socialism's appeal were increasingly clear. Fewer and fewer postcolonial countries seemed interested in Soviet technology or economic planning. Moreover, fewer countries and movements were looking to the Soviet Union for ideological inspiration. Cuba remained a model for aspiring Latin American revolutionaries, and the Vietnamese victory against the United States inspired others. (That victory may also have made Soviet leaders more open to supporting other revolutionary movements.) Most importantly, perhaps, the dream of socialist revolution espoused by the USSR no longer inflamed passion the way it had in earlier decades. The kind of nationalism

15 Piero Gleijeses, "Moscow's Proxy? Cuba and Africa 1975–1988," *Journal of Cold War Studies* 8, 4 (Fall 2006), 3–51.
16 Natalia Telepneva, "Our Sacred Duty: The Soviet Union, the Liberation Movements in the Portuguese Colonies, and the Cold War, 1961–1975," Ph.D. thesis (London School of Economics, 2014).

the Soviet Union had supported since the 1950s had also begun to lose its luster. Contrary to the predictions of Soviet ideologists (and Western modernization theorists), religion and "tradition" were not fading away in the Third World, but often seemed to be making a comeback and playing an increasing role in political life. By the late 1970s, Soviet theorists had begun to acknowledge, openly, that in certain societies religion might serve as an important tool of anti-imperialist mobilization. It was a way of understanding developments in places such as Egypt, where Sadat had courted the previously outlawed Muslim Brotherhood, but this insight would also help the Soviet Union interpret the Iranian Revolution. According to one Soviet diplomat, the idea took hold that "fundamentalism could be seen as one detachment of the national-liberation movement."[17]

That ideological shift helps explain the perhaps surprising reaction of Soviet leaders to the revolution in Iran and the war with Iraq that followed. The Soviet Union had been involved in Iraq since 1958, and after 1972 Iraq became one of Moscow's main allies in the region. As in Syria, the Soviet Union found it could work with the Ba'th party and its particular version of socialism, even if this meant looking the other way while Saddam Hussein's regime slaughtered members of the country's communist party. The Soviet Union had also maintained a relatively good relationship with Iran since the shah's visit in 1956. Yet when the shah's regime fell in 1979, at least some Soviet analysts and officials saw in the anti-Americanism of Ayatollah Ruhollah Khomeini's followers something they could use to their advantage. When Hussein launched his attack on Iran in 1980, Soviet officials seem to have seriously considered supporting Iran. Hussein's treatment of communists, his increasingly close relationship with the United States and the fact that he lied to Moscow and promised not to go to war with his neighbor pushed Soviet officials to offer support to Iran. Not much came of this, however – as one KGB agent put it, "'death to the Soviet Union' could be heard as often as 'death to Israel' or 'death to America.'"[18] Moreover, the longstanding Soviet military relationship with Iraq meant that a loss by Iraq's army would undermine the USSR's prestige – just like Egypt and Syria's loss in 1967 had done.

Indeed, the Soviets' avowed friends were often more dangerous than their enemies. Nowhere was this more true than in the Horn of Africa. In Somalia, Mohammed Siad Barre, a military leader, had taken power in 1969 and

17 Oleg Grinevsky, *Tainy sovetskoi diplomatii* (Moscow: Vagrius, 2000), 209.
18 Vladimir Kuzichkin, *Inside the KGB: My Life in Soviet Espionage* (New York: Pantheon Books, 1991), 350–52.

embarked on a cautious state-building and modernization project. Although he could speak the language of Marxism-Leninism, Barre relied on the USSR primarily for military aid, allowing the Soviets to maintain a naval base at Berbera. In Ethiopia, a military coup had ousted the emperor, Haile Selassie, and moved steadily to the left. By 1975 its social programs were prompting rebellions throughout the country. Taking advantage of upheaval caused by the revolution, Barre began supporting an ethnic Somali insurgency in the Ogaden desert.

The Soviets were at an impasse – they had nothing to gain from the two countries going to war, and could not easily decide whom to support. Until 1977, it was the Ethiopian regime, now under the officer Haile Mariam Mengistu, that seemed the more erratic, and despite continuous requests for help Moscow had made only a limited commitment to the regime. Increasingly positive reports from the Soviet embassy in Addis Ababa, as well as a positive assessment from Fidel Castro (who found Mengistu a "serious" intellectual intent on fundamental social reforms, and Barre a "chauvinist"), finally swung the Politburo behind Ethiopia. Predictably, Barre kicked out Soviet military personnel and installations, hoping for aid from the United States. Over the next eight months, the Soviets sent more than US$1 billion worth of military equipment to Ethiopia, while Cuba sent thousands of soldiers and advisors.

The Soviet decision to back Ethiopia cost the Soviets their position in the Horn and aggravated relations with the United States. It also bound Moscow to protecting an increasingly erratic and isolated regime. The war against Somalia would be finished quite quickly, but Mengistu's fight against separatists and other opposition groups would consume his regime and, increasingly, Soviet attention as well. The Soviets found that their political and even economic advice went largely unheeded, as Mengistu continued to purge rivals and eventually led his country into a disastrous famine.

The Soviet involvement in Ethiopia's civil wars might have been considered the most tragic of Moscow's commitments abroad were it not for the parallel (and in many ways similar) but much deeper involvement in Afghanistan. Moscow had started providing arms to Afghanistan and training its officers in the 1950s, after the United States had turned down a request from Kabul for fear of alienating Pakistan. By the mid 1970s, there was a substantial pro-Soviet and communist-leaning body of officers that supported one of the two wings of the country's small communist party – Khalq and Parcham of the People's Democratic

Party of Afghanistan. In April 1979, these officers helped the party come to power, but the prevalence of Khalq supporters among them helped that wing consolidate control. Rather than following Soviet advice and building a broad coalition to pursue gradual reforms, the party's leaders proclaimed radical land and social reforms and fought with each other. Soon they were facing uprisings throughout the country and calling on the USSR for help. Soviet leaders refused until they felt that without a Soviet intervention the country would collapse into chaos and, ultimately, become vulnerable to US influence.

The intervention in 1979 dragged Soviet forces into a ten-year counterinsurgency and further undermined its longstanding claim to being an anti-imperialist power. European and Third World leftists criticized the Soviet Union. The United States, which had faced charges of imperialism for its war in Vietnam, and China, whose anti-imperial credentials were tarnished by its de facto support of apartheid South Africa, both supported the resistance against the Soviet Union and the communist regime's army.

One country that refrained from criticizing the Soviet Union was India. The intervention came at an awkward time in South Asia's own "internal" Cold War. Six years after the humiliation of Pakistan in the 1971 war, that country's left-leaning leader, Zulfikhar Ali Bhutto, was ousted by Zia ul-Haq, an army general with sympathy for Islamist movements. Under Zia ul-Haq, Pakistan would offer refuge, training and weapons to the *mujahedeen*, developing the idea of using Afghanistan for "strategic depth" against India – influence in Afghanistan would help it in any future confrontation against India. From New Delhi's point of view, a Soviet-supported communist regime in Kabul was preferable to most other options.

Beyond a mutual fear of Pakistan, however, there seemed to be less and less that India and the USSR could offer each other. As Sergey Radchenko has shown, by the 1980s Moscow was desperate to keep India on board, but found it had little to offer except for military technology and oil. An Indian official noted in 1985 that New Delhi "got practically everything from the USSR it asked for" but clearly this was not enough, as throughout the 1980s Indian leaders continued to make overtures to the United States. New Delhi wanted Washington to stop providing military support to Pakistan, but it also wanted US technology. Moscow could not compete. As Politburo member Lev Zaikov pointed out in 1986, "We give them outdated technology, and it compromises itself there, and [compromises] us as well."[19]

Limits of the Soviet Union's Global Cold War

There were substantial limits to the Soviet engagement with the Third World. Some, as we saw earlier, were related to Soviet economic capacity or the attractiveness of its technology. Other limits were set by Soviet priorities vis-à-vis Europe and the United States. There were still other limits that were defined primarily by how the Soviet Union thought about political actors in the world and where, geographically, it might be effective.

One such limit was in relations with nonstate actors. The Soviet Union was a fairly conventional power in that, its domination of Eastern Europe not-withstanding, it operated its foreign policy primarily through the nation-state system. Moscow maintained ties with communist parties in nonsocialist states through the International Department of the CPSU and the KGB, but it discouraged these parties from attempting violent revolution and generally pushed them to work with other "progressive forces" in their countries. Communist parties were expendable if Soviet relations with a given country were on the line, as we saw in the case of Iraq. As for stateless groups, such as the Kurds or the Palestinians, the Soviets were prepared to provide some support, particularly in propaganda, but largely refrained from direct involvement. Organizations such as the SKSSAA or the Committee for Solidarity with Chilean Democrats, which functioned after Augusto Pinochet's coup in Chile, sometimes allowed the Soviet Union to position itself as the champion of such groups without committing extensive resources or upsetting its relations with other states.

Geographically, Latin America is probably the area where Soviet involve-ment was most limited. The Cuban–Soviet relationship would endure throughout the Cold War, despite various ups and downs, but Moscow generally preferred to restrain rather than encourage Cuban ambitions to spread the revolution on the continent.[20] Still, in the 1950s and 1960s in particular the Soviet Union appeared to many Latin American leaders and

19 Sergey Radchenko, *Unwanted Visionaries: The Soviet Failure in Asia at the End of the Cold War* (Oxford: Oxford University Press, 2014), 95.

20 See Piero Gleijeses, "The Cuban Revolution: The First Decade," in Norman Naimark, Silvio Pons and Sophie Quinn-Judge (eds.), *The Cambridge History of Communism*, 3 vols. (Cambridge: Cambridge University Press, 2017), vol. II, ch. 15.

intellectuals to offer a model for their own developmental goals, especially those concerning industrialization, education and public health. Janio Quadros, a progressive (but not communist) president of Brazil, noted soon after taking office in 1961 that, "The scientific and technical knowledge of the Soviet Union can, in this phase of enormous movement of progress, contribute to the development of my country, in a time when Brazil has decided to burst its chains of poverty, disease and ignorance."[21] Where possible it tried to provide economic aid to progressive governments, but generally found that it could not compete in an area where American capitalism was so dominant.

Such links generally survived the leftist governments under which they were established; modernizing rightist regimes often found it expedient to maintain links with the Soviet Union, either to bolster their own regional ambitions or to secure an added source of technology and trade to support their domestic schemes. In the early 1980s, the Soviet Union bought grain from Argentina, sold arms to the anti-communist regime in Peru and discussed building a nuclear reactor for Brazil, then still under the rule of a right-wing military government. Most importantly, as Duccio Basosi has noted, the Soviet Union had nothing to offer in response to the debt crisis of the 1980s, when Latin American countries that had borrowed extensively from the United States in the previous decades found themselves facing rising interest rates and economic turmoil. If there was ever a moment for the Soviet Union to prove that it could offer an alternative to the predatory capitalism of the United States, this was it. Yet whether due to lack of resources (the collapse of oil prices in the early 1980s made it difficult for the USSR to earn dollars, limiting its ability to help countries indebted to the United States) or a lack of political will, Moscow did very little.[22]

Even before the debacles in Afghanistan and Ethiopia, many Soviet experts had begun to doubt the value of Soviet commitments abroad – for the revolution or for the USSR's interests. The war in Afghanistan may not have been a "bleeding wound" in the sense that it did not weaken the Soviet Union economically or militarily, but it upset the entire Soviet foreign-policy establishment. Liberal-minded advisors coalescing around

21 Tobias Rupprecht, "Socialist High Modernity and Global Stagnation: A Shared History of Brazil and the Soviet Union During the Cold War," *Journal of Global History* 6, 3 (Nov. 2011), 511–12.
22 Duccio Basosi, "The Missing Cold War," in Artemy M. Kalinovsky and Sergey Radchenko (eds.), *The End of the Cold War and the Third World: New Perspectives on Regional Conflict* (London: Routledge, 2011), 208–28.

Yurii Andropov and Mikhail Gorbachev, senior officials in the intelligence services and even the military leadership all agreed, although for different reasons, that Soviet involvement had gone too far.

Yet retrenchment proved even harder. One of Gorbachev's first priorities upon becoming general secretary in 1985 was getting the Soviet Union out of Afghanistan. The goal had never been the complete defeat of the insurgency, but rather to leave the regime able to stand on its own, with continued Soviet military aid. Eventually, Gorbachev's predecessors had hoped, the United States would understand that the regime was not going anywhere and stop supplying the resistance. By 1987, however, Gorbachev had become convinced that there was nothing that could be done in the country and placed his bets increasingly on the emerging relationship with Ronald Reagan. The next year, still short of an agreement with Washington, he announced a unilateral withdrawal. An eventual accord between Pakistan and Afghanistan, with the United States and Soviet Union acting as guarantors, provided for future noninterference, but also left the USA free to continue supplying the opposition as long as the USSR gave arms to its client in Kabul. The regime held out – barely – collapsing four months *after* the Soviet Union did, in 1992.

Gorbachev's hope, it seemed, was that he could leverage his new relationship with the United States to resolve some of the thorniest problems of the Cold War era – not just Afghanistan, but also the ongoing civil war in Angola, the conflict in Southeast Asia, the Arab–Israeli conflict and the continuing civil war in Nicaragua. The impact of Gorbachev's diplomacy is ambiguous. It became clear by 1989 that Soviet influence in the Third World was declining rapidly. Gorbachev increasingly saw not just Afghanistan, but also the Soviet Union's other commitments abroad as an albatross that complicated his relationship with Europe and the United States and distracted from domestic reform. Moscow was still willing to sell arms for hard currency, but it was no longer willing to spend its own resources to keep allied regimes on life support. Ideologically, the Soviet Union was moving away from its earlier key tenets, and it seemed to be set for a period of military retrenchment.

Even as Gorbachev was scaling down Soviet involvement in the Third World, Soviet anti-imperialism began to be brought home in unexpected ways. Some Central Asian intellectuals, for example, now began to turn anti-imperialist arguments against Moscow. This was particularly notable among precisely those individuals who had gone abroad as avatars of Soviet anti-colonialism to South Asia and the Middle East, including Afghanistan. The skepticism about foreign aid and involvement that had become more present in government and academic circles in the late 1970s and early 1980s now became politicized in the era of *glasnost'* (openness). As the USSR's own economic problems multiplied, entrepreneurial politicians and commentators asked why the country's resources were being sent abroad. The same arguments were increasingly being deployed among nationalist politicians in Russia and the Baltic states about subsidies for the USSR's "south." In both cases, Soviet investment and aid had been based on universalist ideas of social and economic development. Academic arguments from the late 1970s about the validity of these universalist ideas now resurfaced in often-nasty political debate: Why should the Soviet Union support the Third World? And, for that matter, why should the wealthier republics of the union support the poorer ones? The ties that bound the republics to each other, and the union to its Third World allies, were coming apart in tandem.

Bibliographical Essay

For a deeper understanding of the Soviet Union's role in the global Cold War, it is worth going back to Vladimir Lenin's *Imperialism: The Highest Stage of Capitalism* (1917), which laid out the Bolsheviks' approach to the colonial question. During the Cold War the question of the Soviet Union's role in the "Third World" was a topic frequently broached by European and American scholars. Among the most notable analysts were Alvin Z. Rubinstein, whose books include *Red Star on the Nile: The Soviet–Egyptian Influence Relationship Since the June War* (Princeton: Princeton University Press, 1977) and *Moscow's Third World Strategy* (Princeton: Princeton University Press, 1990); Mark N. Katz, *The Third World in Soviet Military Thought* (Baltimore: Johns Hopkins University Press, 1982); Fred Halliday, *Cold War, Third World: An Essay on Soviet–US Relations* (London: Hutchinson Radius, 1989); and Galia Golan, *The Soviet Union and National Liberation Movements in the Third World* (Boston and London: Unwin Hyman, 1988). A number of scholars have also explored the connection between the Soviet "south" and its policies abroad; notable works include Charles K. Wilber, *The Soviet Model and Underdeveloped Countries* (Durham, NC: Duke University Press, 1969), and Alec Nove and J. A. Newth, *The Soviet Middle East: A Communist Model for Development* (New York: Frederick A. Praeger, 1966). Still others focused on how the Soviet Union tried to use the heritage of its Muslim population in reaching out to countries in the Middle East and South Asia; these include Karen Dawisha and Hélène Carrere d'Encausse, "Islam in the Foreign Policy of the Soviet Union: A Double-Edged Sword?," in Adeeb I. Dawisha (ed.), *Islam in Foreign*

Policy (Cambridge: Cambridge University Press, 1985), 160–77, and Yaacov Ro'i, "The Role of Islam and Soviet Muslims in Soviet Arab Policy," *Asian and African Studies* 10, 2 (1974), 157–81, and 10, 3 (1975), 259–80. Although these works have been superseded in many cases, they are nevertheless valuable and insightful for scholars starting their research on these topics. The above list is representative rather than exhaustive.

Soviet writing on the Third World should also be of interest to scholars interested in these questions, for what they reveal about changing notions regarding development, revolution and Moscow's foreign-policy priorities. Most of this literature remains available only in Russian, but see for example Nodari Simonia, *Synthesis of Traditional and Modern in the Evolution of Third World Societies* (Westport, CT: Greenwood Press, 1992).

The end of the Cold War and the past fifteen years in particular have seen a proliferation of new studies on the Soviet Union and the global Cold War, taking advantage of archival resources in the former USSR and beyond. Many of the works of the 1990s included an explicitly Moscow-centric view, but shone new light on key episodes and problems in the history of Soviet foreign policy. These include Aleksandr Fursenko and Timothy Naftali, *One Hell of a Gamble: Khrushchev, Castro, and Kennedy, 1958–1964* (New York: W. W. Norton and Company, 1997), as well as Ilya V. Gaiduk, *The Soviet Union and the Vietnam War* (Chicago: Ivan R. Dee, 1996), and *Confronting Vietnam: Soviet Policy Toward the Indochina Conflict 1954–1963* (Washington, DC: Woodrow Wilson Center Press, 2003). At the same time, works taking a more international and even transnational approach began to appear, often engaging with a broader debate about the history of decolonization, postcolonialism and development in the twentieth century. An early example is Elizabeth Bishop's Ph.D. thesis, "Talking Shop: Egyptian Engineers and Soviet Specialists at the Aswan High Dam" (University of Chicago, 1997). Odd Arne Westad's *The Global Cold War: Third World Interventions and the Making of Our Times* (Cambridge: Cambridge University Press, 2005) helped catalyze the field and remains a crucial reference point.

Since then, the field has continued to expand. David Engerman's "The Second World's Third World," *Kritika: Explorations in Russian and Eurasian History* 12, 1 (Winter 2011), 183–211, remains a very useful guide to the literature, although many new works have appeared since the article came out. Important works on the Soviet Union and China include Lorenz Luthi, *The Sino-Soviet Split: Cold War in the Communist World* (Princeton: Princeton University Press, 2008); Sergey Radchenko, *Two Suns in the*

Heavens: The Sino-Soviet Struggle for Supremacy, 1962–1967 (Stanford: Stanford University Press, 2009); Austin Jersild, *The Sino-Soviet Alliance: An International History* (Chapel Hill: University of North Carolina Press, 2014); and Jeremy Friedman, *Shadow Cold War: The Sino-Soviet Competition for the Third World* (Chapel Hill: University of North Carolina Press, 2015). On the Soviet Union and the Middle East, see in particular Guy Laron's *Origins of the Suez Crisis: Postwar Development Diplomacy and the Struggle over Third World Industrialization, 1945–1956* (Washington, DC: Woodrow Wilson Center Press, 2013); and Jesse Ferris, *Nasser's Gamble: How Intervention in Yemen Caused the Six-Day War and the Decline of Egyptian Power* (Princeton: Princeton University Press, 2012). Craig Daigle's *The Limits of Détente: The United States, the Soviet Union, and the Arab–Israeli Conflict, 1969–1973* (New Haven: Yale University Press, 2012) is more focused on the US perspective but has valuable insights on Moscow's point of view, based on Soviet sources. On the USSR and Africa, see Sergey Mazov, *A Distant Front in the Cold War: The USSR in West Africa and the Congo, 1956–1964* (Stanford: Stanford University Press, 2010), as well as Alessandro Iandolo, "The Rise and Fall of the 'Soviet Model of Development' in West Africa, 1957–1964," *Cold War History* 12, 4 (Nov. 2012), 683–704, and Natalia Telepneva, "Our Sacred Duty: The Soviet Union, the Liberation Movements in the Portuguese Colonies, and the Cold War, 1961–1975," Ph.D. thesis (London School of Economics, 2014). On Latin America, see Tobias Rupprecht, *Soviet Internationalism After Stalin: Interaction and Exchange Between the USSR and Latin America During the Cold War* (Cambridge: Cambridge University Press, 2015); Michelle Denise Getchell, "Revisiting the 1954 Coup in Guatemala: The Soviet Union, the United Nations, and 'Hemispheric Solidarity,'" *Journal of Cold War Studies* 17, 2 (Spring 2015), 73–102; and Vanni Pettina, "Mexican–Soviet Relations, 1958–1964: The Limits of Engagement," Cold War International History Project e-dossier, www.wilsoncenter.org/publication/mexican-soviet-rela tions-1958–1964-the-limits-engagement

4

Marxist Revolutions and Regimes in Latin America and Africa in the 1970s

PIERO GLEIJESES

In January 1971 the CIA reported that the Tupamaros, the guerrilla movement in Uruguay, were "the most active and successful guerrilla group in South America."[1] This assessment was correct, given that elsewhere on the continent the situation of the guerrillas was desolate. The hope spawned by Fidel Castro's triumph over Fulgencio Batista had withered away. The victorious Cubans had believed that Latin America was "a tinder box to which one merely had to apply a spark . . . to set off the revolutionary explosion."[2] This spark would be created by what they called the *foco*, the small guerrilla vanguard that would launch armed struggle in the countryside. "We have demonstrated," Che Guevara wrote in 1959, "that a small group of men who are determined, supported by the people, and not afraid of death . . . can overcome a regular army." This was, he believed, the lesson of the Cuban Revolution.[3]

The Cubans urged the people of Latin America to follow their example. Guerrilla insurgencies erupted throughout the continent, only to be crushed, one after the other. After years of defeats, in 1966–67 Cuba made its strongest attempt to promote armed struggle in the hemisphere. It concentrated on four countries: Venezuela, Guatemala, Colombia and Bolivia.

It was a tragic failure. The guerrillas were crushed in Bolivia in October 1967, were virtually wiped out in Guatemala by 1968 and suffered cruel setbacks in Venezuela and Colombia. These defeats and, above all,

1 CIA, Directorate of Intelligence, "The Latin American Guerrilla Today," 22 Jan. 1971, CIA Records Search Tool (CREST), National Archives, College Park, MD (hereafter NA).
2 Hughes to Secretary of State, "Cuba in 1964," 17 Apr. 1964, Freedom of Information Act (FOIA), 1996/668.
3 Ernesto "Che" Guevara, "Proyecciones sociales del Ejército Rebelde," 27 Jan. 1959, in Juan José Soto Valdespino (ed.), *Ernesto Che Guevara. Escritos y discursos* (Havana: Editorial de Ciencias Sociales, 1977), vol. IV, 20.

Che's death in Bolivia, forced Castro to reevaluate the *foco* theory. He finally accepted that a handful of brave men was insufficient to ignite armed struggle in Latin America. "By 1970 Cuban assistance to guerrilla groups and other efforts to export revolution had been cut back to very low levels," US officials remarked.[4]

The ordeal of Francisco Caamaño, the military leader of a revolt in the Dominican Republic in 1965, illustrates the Cubans' hard-won maturity. Cuba's General Directorate of Intelligence (Dirección General de Inteligencia, DGI) had worked hard to persuade Caamaño to come to Cuba to prepare for armed struggle in his country.[5] He had arrived in Havana in November 1967, one month after Che's death, he stayed for five years, and he never lost confidence in the *foco* theory. The Cubans, however, had. They urged Caamaño to wait. "He kept insisting that he wanted to go," a knowledgeable journalist has written, "and the Cubans kept trying to convince him that it was not possible," that conditions in the Dominican Republic were not yet ripe. However, "Caamaño was not willing to stay in Cuba any longer," a member of his group explained, and the Cubans relented. With arms and money provided by the DGI and a yacht bought in Antigua, Caamaño and eight followers landed in the Dominican Republic in early February 1973. Within two weeks the Dominican armed forces had murdered him and wiped out his little band.[6] The Cuban press, which had vehemently supported the guerrillas in the 1960s, refrained from comment. When Castro evoked Caamaño's memory later that year, he referred to him only as the leader of the 1965 Dominican revolt.[7]

The point is not that Castro no longer supported armed struggle in Latin America. In those same years he helped the Tupamaros with military training, weapons and money.[8] This support, however, was far more discriminating and discreet than it had been in the 1960s. Castro no longer launched fiery appeals for revolution throughout Latin America. Instead, he began to build

4 US Department of State (DOS), "Cuban Presence in Africa," 28 Dec. 1977, FOIA, 1997/ 1334.
5 Hamlet Hermann, *Caamaño en Europa (1966 y 1967)* (Santo Domingo: Búho, 2011).
6 Alejandro Ovalles, *Caamaño, el gobierno y las guerrillas* (Santo Domingo: Taller de Impresiones, 1973), 13; and Hamlet Hermann, *Francisco Caamaño* (Santo Domingo: Alfa y Omega, 1983), 426. Hermann was one of the two survivors of Caamaño's guerrilla group.
7 Castro, 26 Jul. 1973 speech, *Granma* (28 Jul. 1973), 4.
8 Interview with Ulises Estrada, a senior Cuban intelligence officer, Havana, 25 Jun. 1997 (all interviews cited in this chapter are by the author); Pablo Brum, *The Robin Hood Guerrillas: The Epic Journey of Uruguay's Tupamaros* (Middletown, DE: Createspace Independent Pub., 2016), 133, 223; Sergio D'Oliveira, *El Uruguay y los Tupamaros* (Montevideo: Centro Militar, República Oriental del Uruguay, 1996), 31.

bridges. Since late 1964 Cuba had had diplomatic or economic relations with only one Latin American country, Mexico. But in February 1970 Havana signed a trade agreement with the Christian Democratic government of Chile, and the following August, one month before the Chilean presidential elections, Castro announced, "It is possible to arrive at Socialism through the polls."[9]

The Chilean election was won by Salvador Allende. Allende was a sincere democrat, but he was also a socialist who headed a coalition that included the communist party, and he was a friend of Fidel Castro. In Washington, President Richard Nixon and National Security Advisor Henry Kissinger considered Allende's victory at the polls a slap in the face for the United States and a dangerous example for Latin America.

The attempts of Nixon and Kissinger to prevent Allende from assuming the presidency in 1970 have been well documented.[10] Less is known, however, about the US role in the overthrow of Allende on 11 September 1973. US complicity was indirect, but important. Technically, the Chilean military acted on its own when it ousted Allende, but the CIA had engaged in a destabilization campaign and had aided groups that were fostering a coup. In the words of a leading expert, "By the most narrow definition of 'direct role' – providing planning, equipment, strategic support, and guarantees – the CIA does not appear to have been involved in the violent actions of the Chilean military on September 11, 1973."[11] What the CIA did is best summed up by Henry Kissinger: It "created the conditions as great as possible [for a coup]."[12]

The previous year the CIA had written, "By coming to power through legitimate electoral means, the Allende government has demonstrated the unsoundness of Castro's theory that armed struggle is the only path to power for a true 'revolutionary' government."[13] By helping overthrow Allende, however, Nixon and Kissinger suggested that Castro had been right.

9 Havana radio, 4 Aug. 1970, quoted by Edward Gonzalez, *Cuba Under Castro: The Limits of Charisma* (Boston: Houghton Mifflin, 1974), 142, n. 59. For the 20 Feb. 1970 trade agreement with Chile, see *El Mercurio* (Santiago) (20 Feb. 1970), 3 (editorial); (21 Feb. 1970), 1; (22 Feb. 1970), 25.
10 US Senate, Select Committee, *Alleged Assassination Plots Involving Foreign Leaders* (Washington, DC: US Government Printing Office, 1975), 225–54.
11 Peter Kornbluh, *The Pinochet File: A Declassified Dossier on Atrocity and Accountability*, rev. edn. (New York: New Press, 2013), 114.
12 Memo Telcon, Nixon and Kissinger, 16 Sep. 1973, Declassified Record, National Security Archive, Washington, DC (hereafter NSA).
13 CIA, Directorate of Intelligence, "Cuba's Changing Relations with Latin America," 28 Jan. 1972, CREST, NA.

Castro had understood from the very first moment that "the United States would do everything possible to bring down Allende," and that the Chilean upper class and a large sector of the military would collude with Washington.[14] This was also the view of the Movimiento de la Izquierda Revolucionaria (MIR), Chile's Castroite group, which was not part of Allende's Unidad Popular, the government's coalition. Miguel Henríquez, the leader of the MIR and a man for whom Castro had great respect, asked the Cubans time and again for arms to defend the government from the growing threat of a military coup, but Castro refused: He would not arm the MIR without Allende's permission.[15] He urged Allende to allow Cuba to arm the government parties. "We kept insisting that the situation required it and that Unidad Popular had to be ready," he told Erich Honecker, the leader of the German Democratic Republic. Finally, a few months before the September 1973 coup, Allende gave Castro the green light: "First he gave us permission to give weapons to the communist party [which was part of Unidad Popular]," Castro explained. "He had great confidence in the communist party . . . Ultimately he gave us permission to arm the socialists and the other parties of Unidad Popular . . . However . . . they were not ready. They took a few weapons, but far fewer than we wanted to give them . . . When the coup took place, there were enough weapons for a battalion in our embassy . . . Most were for the communist party. We had asked them to come and take them a few weeks before the coup, but they never did."[16]

Africa

In the mid 1960s many – in Havana, Moscow and Beijing – had believed revolution was imminent in Africa. Guerrillas were fighting the Portuguese in Angola, Guinea-Bissau and Mozambique. In Congo Brazzaville, a new government had proclaimed its Marxist-Leninist sympathies. Above all, there was the former Belgian Congo, then called Congo Leopoldville, where armed revolt threatened the corrupt pro-American regime that Presidents Dwight D. Eisenhower and John F. Kennedy had laboriously put in place.

14 Interview with Fidel Castro, Havana, 30 Jun. 2015.
15 Interviews with Estrada, Havana, 21 Jul. 1995; and Jorge Risquet, a close aide of Fidel Castro, Havana, 26 Jun, 2015.
16 Memcon (Castro, Honecker), 21 Feb. 1974, DY30, JIV 2/201/1157, Stiftung Archiv der Parteien und Massenorganisationen der DDR im Bundesarchiv, Berlin (hereafter SAPMO).

To save the Leopoldville government, in the summer of 1964 the adminis-tration of Lyndon B. Johnson raised an army of 1,000 white mercenaries in a major covert operation that provoked a wave of revulsion even among African leaders friendly to the United States. Both the Soviet Union and China responded by sending weapons to the rebels but, because the erstwhile harmony between the two communist giants had evaporated, they acted independently of each other. In Havana, Fidel Castro took a bold decision: Without informing Moscow or Beijing, he sent 120 Cubans, led by Che Guevara, to Congo Leopoldville to help the rebels. In August 1965, 250 more Cubans, under Jorge Risquet, a close aide of Castro, arrived in neigh-boring Congo Brazzaville at the request of that country's government, which feared an attack by the CIA's mercenaries.[17]

Central Africa, however, was not ready for revolution. By the time the Cubans arrived in Congo Leopoldville, Lyndon Johnson's mercenaries had broken the resolve of the rebels, leaving Che no choice in November 1965 but to withdraw. In Congo Brazzaville, Risquet's column saved the host govern-ment from a military coup and trained the rebels of Agostinho Neto's Popular Movement for the Liberation of Angola (Movimento Popular de Libertação de Angola, MPLA) before withdrawing in July 1967.

The guerrillas' defeat in Congo Leopoldville was followed by the over-throw of the two radical presidents of sub-Saharan Africa, Kwame Nkrumah in Ghana in 1966 (with CIA help) and Modibo Keita in Mali in 1968. Furthermore, as relations between the Soviet Union and China collapsed in bitter and even violent disputes, China's foremost goal in Africa was no longer to spark revolution, but to counter the Soviet Union. US officials celebrated: The communist threat to the continent had been defanged. They overlooked, however, the only communist country that had sent men to fight in Africa – Castro's Cuba – even though there were still Cubans in Guinea-Bissau, helping that country's guerrilla movement, the PAIGC (Partido Africano da Independência da Guiné e Cabo Verde) in its war against Portuguese colonial rule.

By the late 1960s Guinea-Bissau was one of the few colonies left in Africa. A decade earlier, France and Britain, the continent's major colonial powers, had concluded that trying to delay the inevitable would risk turning the local elites into enemies, whereas promptly granting independence would allow the metropoles to retain economic and political influence in their former

---

17 This paragraph and the next are based on Piero Gleijeses, *Conflicting Missions: Havana, Washington, and Africa, 1959–1976* (Chapel Hill: University of North Carolina Press, 2002), 77–184.

colonies. Belgium had followed suit. But Portugal had bucked the tide, as had South Africa, which ruled its neighbor, Namibia. In Rhodesia, the white minority proclaimed a Unilateral Declaration of Independence in 1965, derailing British plans to grant independence with majority rule, that is, with a black government. Thus southern Africa became the "White Redoubt" and remained a backwater of the Cold War. The Soviet Union, China and Yugoslavia gave some weapons and military training to the national liberation movements of southern Africa, but the impact was slight. The guerrillas who challenged Portuguese rule in Angola and Mozambique, white rule in Rhodesia and Namibia, and apartheid in South Africa seemed impotent. The stage was dominated by Washington's friends – apartheid South Africa and authoritarian Portugal.

The strongest of the guerrilla movements fighting colonial rule in Africa in the early 1970s was not in southern Africa, but in tiny Guinea-Bissau. Even unsympathetic US officials acknowledged that the PAIGC was "Africa's most successful liberation movement."[18] The war's foremost scholar, Patrick Chabal, concludes that its leaders were outstanding, above all Amílcar Cabral, the secretary general. While Cabral was influenced by Marxism, he was not a Marxist. "He came to view Marxism as a method rather than an ideology," Chabal remarks. "When useful in analyzing Guinean society it was relied upon. When it was no longer relevant, it was amended or even abandoned."[19] Cabral "was no communist," a Cuban intelligence officer who knew him well agreed; "He was a progressive leader with piercing insight into Africa's problems." He was also, as Chabal writes, "the undisputed commander and tactician of the war."[20] Cuban military instructors operated the increasingly sophisticated weapons sent to the PAIGC by the Soviet Union, and throughout the war most of the doctors in the liberated zones of the country were Cubans. In mid 1973 the rebels, who controlled two-thirds of the country and half the population, were decisively strengthened by the Soviets' delivery of surface-to-air missiles. A Portuguese officer who served in Guinea-Bissau noted, "Our unchallenged air superiority, which had been our trump card and the basis of our entire military policy . . . had suddenly evaporated."

18 DOS, Bureau of Intelligence and Research, "Africa: Prospects for Liberation from White Minority Regimes," 22 Sep. 1971, Pol 13 Afr, Subject – Numerical Files: 1963–73, Record Group 59, NA.
19 Patrick Chabal, *Amílcar Cabral: Revolutionary Leadership and People's War* (Cambridge: Cambridge University Press, 1983), 169.
20 Interview with Ulises Estrada, Havana, 16 Mar. 1994; Chabal, *Amílcar Cabral*, 98.

General António Spínola, one of Lisbon's top generals, recalled, "The situation deteriorated dramatically."[21]

The West and the Liberation Struggle

The United States was sympathetic, in principle, to the gradual progression of colonized people toward independence, but American empathy for the colonized faced two constraints: The metropoles were US allies in the struggle against the Soviet Union; and Washington insisted that the independence movements be free of the communist virus. Therefore, US policy toward decolonization often clashed with its rhetoric. The United States supported France's colonial war in Indochina because it believed, incorrectly, that the Viet Minh was a Soviet proxy. And it provided weapons to the French for their war in Algeria because France was a valuable NATO ally.[22]

Portugal, too, was a useful ally because the US Air Force maintained important military facilities at the Lajes air base in the Azores. This deepened the gap between Washington's rhetoric and its actions. From the Kennedy through the Nixon administrations, US officials asserted that the United States sold weapons to Portugal only on condition that they not be used in Africa. But the Portuguese diverted the weapons to their African wars anyway. "We would have been fools not to have done so," a Portuguese general remarked. "Now and then the Americans would grumble. It was all for show."[23] Washington's key European allies required no such figleaf: Britain, France and West Germany sold Portugal arms, no strings attached.

The honor of the West was upheld by Sweden and the other Nordic countries. On 9 December 1968, the Swedish foreign minister made what was, by Western standards, an extraordinary statement: "We are in touch with a number of leaders of the African liberation movements. We are prepared to help ... It is humanitarian aid that is in question. Aid that puts the members of those movements in a better position to continue their struggle for the liberation of their people."[24] Less than a year later, on

21 Carlos Fabião, "A descolonização na Guiné-Bissau," in Associação 25 de abril (ed.), *Seminário 25 de abril: 10 anos depois* (Lisbon: Fundação Calouste Gulbenkian, 1984), 310; António Spínola, *País sem rumo. Contributo para a História de uma Revolução* (Lisbon: Editorial SCIRE, 1978), 53–54. See also Gleijeses, *Conflicting Missions*, 185–213.
22 See Piero Gleijeses, "Decolonization During the Cold War," in Martin Thomas and Andrew Thompson (eds.), *The Oxford Handbook of the Ends of Empire* (forthcoming).
23 General Francisco da Costa Gomes, quoted in José Freire Antunes, *Nixon e Caetano. Promessas e abandono* (Lisbon: Difusão Cultural, 1992), 110.
24 Quoted in Tor Sellström, *Sweden and National Liberation in Southern Africa*, vol. II (Uppsala: Nordiska Afrikainstitutet, 2002), 52.

29 September 1969, the first shipment of a comprehensive Swedish support program to African liberation movements left Rotterdam. It was addressed to the PAIGC. With the hearty approval of the Swedish parliament, Stockholm became the first Western capital to extend direct humanitarian assistance to an African liberation movement. The competence and integrity of the PAIGC leaders deeply impressed the Swedes; the PAIGC was an "ideal organization for us," a Swedish aid official recalled.[25] The leader of the PAIGC, Amílcar Cabral, told East German officials in 1972, "Sweden ... is giving us more than a number of socialist countries put together."[26] Thus began a journey that saw Sweden provide assistance to liberation movements from Guinea-Bissau, Angola, Mozambique, Rhodesia, Namibia and South Africa – even though these movements got their arms from the Soviet Union (and, to a lesser extent, China). The Swedes accepted the right of those who were fighting for their freedom to receive aid from anyone willing to give it. They also believed that extending aid was the most effective way to counter communist influence. Norway, Denmark, Finland and the Netherlands followed in Sweden's footsteps.

Angola

In April 1974 Portuguese military officers overthrew their country's dictatorship. They moved quickly toward decolonization: Guinea-Bissau became independent in September 1974 and Mozambique the following June. In both countries there had been only one guerrilla movement, which inherited power in a smooth transition.

In Angola, however, there were three guerrilla movements, and they had fought each other as bitterly as they had the Portuguese. The leaders of the MPLA espoused an eclectic interpretation of Marxism-Leninism that was, Yugoslav officials noted, "adapted to the specific conditions and needs of Angola."[27] Even US officials who were alarmed by the MPLA's communist proclivities noted that it "stood head and shoulders above the other two

---

25 Quoted ibid., 56.
26 "Antwort des Generalsekretärs der PAIGC, Amilcar Cabral, auf die Ausführungen des Gen. Gerhard Grüneberg, Mitglied des Politbüros und Sekretär des ZK der SED, im der 2. Beratung zwischen den Delegationen der SED und der PAIGC am 27.10.1972 im Hause des ZK," 30 Oct. 1972, DY30 IVB 2/2.023/87, SAPMO.
27 Commission for International Cooperation and Relations of the League of Communists of the Socialist Federative Popular Republic of Yugoslavia, "Angola i Narodni Pokret za Oslobodjenje Angole /MPLA/," Feb. 1971, Arhiv Jugoslavije, Arhiv Josipa Broza Tito, Belgrade.

groups" (the FNLA and UNITA [União Nacional para a Independência Total de Angola, National Union for the Total Independence of Angola]) which were led by corrupt, unprincipled – but anti-communist – men.[28]

The new Portuguese government and the three Angolan movements agreed that a transitional government would rule Angola until independence on 11 November 1975. Civil war erupted, however, in the spring of 1975. Several months later, both South Africa and the United States began providing the FNLA and UNITA with weapons and military instructors to crush the MPLA. Pretoria's motivation was to shore up apartheid at home and eliminate any threat to its illegal rule over Namibia. South African officials feared the MPLA's implacable hostility to apartheid and its promise to assist the liberation movements of southern Africa. (UNITA and FNLA offered Pretoria their friendship.) Although US officials knew that an MPLA victory would not threaten American strategic or economic interests, Secretary of State Kissinger believed that success in Angola – the installation of a client regime – would provide a cheap boost to US prestige and to his own reputation, which had been pummeled by the fall of South Vietnam in April 1975. He cast the struggle in stark Cold War terms: The freedom-loving FNLA and UNITA would defeat the Soviet-backed MPLA.[29]

The war, however, did not progress as Kissinger expected. By September, it was evident that the MPLA – facing the FNLA and UNITA which were bolstered by arms and instructors supplied by Washington and Pretoria – was winning. It was winning because, as the CIA station chief in Luanda noted, it was "more effective, better educated, better trained, and better motivated" than its two rivals.[30]

To save the situation, Washington encouraged Pretoria to send troops. On 14 October, a South African armored column invaded Angola. As the column raced toward Luanda, MPLA resistance crumbled; the South Africans would have seized the capital had not Fidel Castro decided on 4 November to respond favorably to the MPLA's appeals for troops. The intervention "was a unilateral Cuban operation designed in great haste," the CIA noted.[31] Castro did not consult or even inform the Soviet

28 Tel. interview with US consul-general in Luanda, Tom Killoran (1974–75), 10 Apr. 1998 (quotation); interview with Robert Hultslander, CIA station chief in Luanda (1975), www.gwu.edu/~nsarchiv/NSAEBB/NSAEBB67/transcript.html.
29 This paragraph and the next three are based on Gleijeses, *Conflicting Missions*, 230–396.
30 Interview with Hultslander, www.gwu.edu/~nsarchiv/NSAEBB/NSAEBB67/tran script.html).
31 CIA, "Cuban Foreign Policy and Activities Abroad," 5 Feb. 1981, Executive Secretariat, Meeting Files, box 1, Ronald Reagan Library, Simi Valley, CA.

Union because he knew that the Kremlin would oppose his decision: Moscow distrusted the MPLA leaders and did not want to jeopardize the SALT II arms control negotiations with the United States. Castro defied the Soviet Union because of his commitment to what he has called "the most beautiful cause," the struggle against apartheid.[32] He understood that the victory of the Pretoria–Washington axis would have tightened the grip of white domination over the people of southern Africa. Even Kissinger acknowledged that Castro "was probably the most genuine revolutionary leader then in power."[33]

For two months the Cuban troops arrived in Angola aboard Cuban planes and ships, without any logistical assistance from the Kremlin, which was unhappy with Castro's decision. Despite their marked inferiority in numbers and heavy weapons, they halted the South African advance toward Luanda. Their numbers grew slowly until, by late December, they achieved rough numerical parity with the South Africans in Angola – approximately 3,500 soldiers each. In January 1976, the Soviets finally relented; their planes began transporting the Cuban troops to Angola, and the trickle became a flood; by April, when the operation ended, there were 36,000 Cuban soldiers in Angola. "Fidel thought, 'If we have to fight a decisive battle [against the South Africans] we have to be strong,'" a senior aide explained. "Furthermore, we thought that the South Africans might give up if they saw us coming with a massive force."[34] The South Africans retreated. By late March 1976 the Cubans had pushed them out of Angola.

The Cuban troops included white, mulatto and black soldiers. But for many the presence of black and mulatto soldiers meant that this was a nonwhite army. This had a particularly strong impact in South Africa and Namibia. The tidal wave unleashed by the Cuban victory washed over southern Africa. Its psychological impact and the hope it aroused are illustrated by two statements from across the political divide in apartheid South Africa. In February 1976, as Cuban troops were forcing Pretoria's army to retreat, a South African military analyst wrote: "In Angola, Black troops – Cubans and Angolans – have defeated White troops in military exchanges . . . and that psychological edge, that advantage the White man has enjoyed and

32 "Indicaciones concretas del Comandante en Jefe que guiarán la actuación de la delegación cubana a las conversaciones en Luanda y las negociaciones en Londres (23–4–88)," Centro de Información de las Fuerzas Armadas Revolucionarias, Havana (hereafter CF).
33 Henry Kissinger, *Years of Renewal* (New York: Touchstone, 1999), 785.
34 Interview with Jorge Risquet, Havana, 28 Feb. 1996.

exploited over 300 years of colonialism and empire, is slipping away. White elitism has suffered an irreversible blow in Angola, and Whites who have been there know it."[35] The "White Giants" had retreated and black Africans celebrated. "Black Africa is riding the crest of a wave generated by the Cuban success in Angola," noted the *World*, South Africa's major black newspaper. "Black Africa is tasting the heady wine of the possibility of realizing the dream of total liberation."[36]

The impact was more than psychological. As Pretoria had feared, the MPLA government welcomed guerrillas from South Africa, Namibia and Rhodesia. It became a tripartite effort: The Cubans provided most of the instructors, the Soviets the weapons and the Angolans the land.[37]

Angola's independence was particularly important for the South West Africa People's Organization (SWAPO), Namibia's guerrilla movement. SWAPO had begun fighting in 1966 but it had been hamstrung by geography. Only Zambia offered it safe haven, which meant that its fighters had to traverse either southeastern Angola or Namibia's Caprivi strip, a 250-mile panhandle squeezed between Angola, Zambia and Botswana that was dotted with South African military bases.

The MPLA victory changed this. "Our geographic isolation was over," SWAPO's president Sam Nujoma wrote. "It was as if a locked door had suddenly swung open . . . For us . . . [it] meant that . . . we could at last make direct attacks across our northern frontier and send in our forces and weapons on a large scale." The South African military commander in Namibia agreed: "For the first time they [SWAPO] obtained what is virtually a prerequisite for a successful insurgent campaign, namely a border that provided safe refuge."[38]

For the South Africans, the MPLA was a cancer that had to be eradicated. Pretoria was determined to bring to power in Angola Jonas Savimbi, the guerrilla chieftain who had been fighting the MPLA since the early 1970s. Thousands of Cuban soldiers remained in Angola to protect it from South African aggression. Even the CIA conceded that they were "necessary to preserve Angolan independence."[39]

35 Roger Sargent, *Rand Daily Mail* (13 Feb. 1976), 13.   36 *World* (24 Feb. 1976), 4 (editorial).
37 Piero Gleijeses, *Visions of Freedom: Havana, Washington, Pretoria and the Struggle for Southern Africa, 1976–1991* (Chapel Hill: University of North Carolina Press, 2013), 86–97.
38 Sam Nujoma, *Where Others Wavered: The Autobiography of Sam Nujoma* (London: Panaf Books, 2001), 228–29; Jannie Geldenhuys, *Dié Wat Gewen Het: Feite en fabels van die bosoorlog* (Pretoria: Litera Publikasies, 2007), 45.
39 CIA, "Angola Cuba: Some Strains But No New Developments," 9 Apr. 1979, CREST, NA.

Angola widened Castro's horizons. In March 1976, a prominent American journalist wrote, "Vistas that might seem dazzling to Fidel Castro's eye will open up with the victory in Angola ... For Fidel Castro there is no 'darkest Africa.' It is all ablaze with lights – the campfires of fellow revolutionaries ... So long as Castroite Cuba exists there will be armed Cubans in Africa, and they will be much more than shock troops for the Russians. Fidel Castro sees them as standard-bearers for the nonaligned countries of the third world."[40] One year later Castro told East German leader Honecker, "In Africa ... we can inflict a heavy defeat to the entire policy of the imperialists."[41] He was thinking of the final assault against the White Redoubt: Namibia, Rhodesia and South Africa itself, the bastion of apartheid. He told me, "I was also thinking of Ethiopia."[42]

The Horn of Africa

In Ethiopia, less than two weeks after President Jimmy Carter's inauguration, the military junta that had overthrown Emperor Haile Selassie in 1974 turned further to the left, quashing any lingering US hope of retaining influence there. In July 1977, the junta was rocked by Somalia's invasion of the Ogaden, a region in eastern Ethiopia inhabited by ethnic Somalis. The attack had been encouraged by ambivalent signals from Washington. The Somalis made swift progress, and by late August 1977 Secretary of State Cyrus Vance told the Chinese foreign minister, "I think they [the Somalis] will succeed ... They ... will be in control of the Ogaden."[43] Ethiopia's leader, Mengistu Haile Mariam, a self-proclaimed Marxist-Leninist, turned to Cuba, which had begun sending military instructors and doctors to Addis Ababa the previous April. He asked for troops.

Castro's reply was negative. A secret Cuban military history notes, "It did not seem possible that a small country like Cuba could maintain two important military missions in Africa."[44]

---

40 Herbert Matthews, "Forward with Fidel Castro, Anywhere," *New York Times* (4 Mar. 1976), 31.

41 Memcon (Castro, Honecker), 3 Apr. 1977, JIV 2/201/1292, SAPMO.

42 Interview with Fidel Castro, Havana, 30 Jun. 2015.

43 Memcon (Vance, Huang Hua), 23 Aug. 1977, 14, Declassified Documents Reference System (DDRS). The best source on US policy in the Horn is Nancy Mitchell's *Jimmy Carter in Africa: Race and the Cold War* (Washington, DC, and Stanford: Woodrow Wilson Center Press and Stanford University Press, 2016).

44 Ministerio de las Fuerzas Armadas Revolucionarias (Cuba), "Las misiones internacionalistas desarrolladas por las FAR en defensa de la independencia y la soberanía de los pueblos," n.d., CF.

However, as the Ethiopians' military situation deteriorated, the Cubans reconsidered. On 25 November 1977, Castro decided to send troops to Ethiopia to help repel the Somali attackers. Two days later, General Secretary Leonid Brezhnev of the USSR wrote Castro a warm message expressing "our complete agreement with your policy. We are pleased that our assessment of events in Ethiopia coincides with yours, and we sincerely thank you for your timely decision to extend internationalist assistance to socialist Ethiopia."[45] Over the next three months, 12,000 Cuban soldiers arrived in Ethiopia. As a 2000 study of the Russian Ministry of Defense said, the troops "were notable for their high degree of discipline and organization."[46] By March 1978, the Cubans and the Ethiopians had repulsed the Somalis.[47]

The contrast between the Soviet reaction to the dispatch of Cuban troops to Angola in November 1975 and to Ethiopia in November 1977 is stark: In Angola, Cuba acted without even informing the Soviet Union, whereas in Ethiopia there was close consultation; in Angola, for two harrowing months the Cubans operated without any logistical support from the Soviet Union, whereas in Ethiopia Moscow supported the airlift of Cuban troops from day one; in Angola, the Cubans planned military operations without any Soviet input, whereas in Ethiopia Soviets and Cubans worked together to help the Ethiopians plan military operations. As Castro told Angola's President Agostinho Neto, "In Angola we took the initiative, we acted on our own . . . It was a decision full of risks. In Ethiopia, our actions were coordinated from the very beginning with the Soviets."[48]

That Havana and Moscow agreed about the policy to pursue in Ethiopia does not mean that the Cubans were subservient to the Soviets. The key to explaining Cuban motivations may have been provided by National Security Advisor Zbigniew Brzezinski, who told Vice-President Walter Mondale, "Castro ended up more favorably impressed by the Ethiopians. He found the Somalis, who pressed their longstanding territorial demands on Ethiopia, more irredentist than socialist." Castro had been very impressed by the Ethiopian Revolution, and by Mengistu, whom he had met in March 1977. He told Honecker, "a real revolution is taking place in Ethiopia. In this

45 Brezhnev to Castro, 27 Nov. 1977, CF.
46 Republic of Russia, Ministry of Defense, *Rossiia (SSSR) v lokal'nykh voinakh i voennykh konfliktakh vtoroi poloviny XX veka* (Moscow, 2000), 111.
47 The best study of the war is Gebru Tareke, *The Ethiopian Revolution: War in the Horn of Africa* (New Haven: Yale University Press, 2009).
48 Memcon (Castro, Neto), 24 Jan. 1979, Consejo de Estado, Havana.

former feudal empire the land has been given to the peasants ... Mengistu strikes me as a quiet, honest and convinced revolutionary leader."[49] Hundreds of Cuban documents covering the critical period from late 1976 through the spring of 1978 make clear that Castro's feelings were shared by the three top Cuban officials in Addis Ababa: the ambassador, the head of the military mission and the head of intelligence.[50] Though the process was undeniably bloody, the Ethiopian junta had decreed a radical agrarian reform and taken unprecedented steps to foster the cultural rights of the non-Amhara population. Even the US government was impressed. The CIA noted "the new rulers' efforts to improve the lot of the disadvantaged," and the State Department reported that the government was focusing on "improving living standards for all" and that "much has been accomplished."[51] But soon the promises of the Ethiopian Revolution turned to mayhem: Mengistu launched a policy of land collectivization that ran roughshod over the will of the rural population; he adopted a series of measures that proved disastrous for the country's economy; he unleashed a brutal war against the Eritrean independence movement; and he was implacably repressive. The Cubans had defended Ethiopia from the Somali invasion that sought to dismember it; but they had helped sustain what became one of Africa's most oppressive and inept regimes.

Central America Explodes

In the early and mid 1970s Latin American revolutionary movements had been dealt a litany of defeats. The Tupamaros had been crushed by 1972; the following year Caamaño's guerrilla group had been annihilated and Allende overthrown. In Argentina the military inflicted devastating blows on the country's two guerrilla movements. By the time Carter ascended the presidency in Washington in January 1977 all that was left in South America – beside a doomed insurgency in Argentina – was Colombia's guerrilla movement, which struggled to survive without any hope of taking power.

And, in Central America, there was Nicaragua's Sandinista National Liberation Front (Frente Sandinista de Liberación Nacional, FSLN), founded

---

49 Brzezinski to Carter [late Mar. 1977], DDRS – Somalia; Memcon (Honecker, Castro), 3 Apr. 1977, DY30 JIV 2/201/1292, SAPMO.
50 These documents are located in the Centro de Información de las Fuerzas Armadas Revolucionarias in Havana. I have copies of all of them.
51 CIA, Weekly Summary, 28 May 1976, CREST, NA; DOS, "Current Foreign Assistance" and "The Case for Continued Assistance," enclosed in Tarnoff to Brzezinski [May 1978], Warren Christopher Papers, box 16, NA.

in the early 1960s by youths inspired by the Cuban Revolution. Despite their bravery and fortitude, the Sandinistas had not been able to forge a strong guerrilla movement. By 1975, writes the foremost historian of the FSLN, there were only a few dozen Sandinista guerrillas in the mountains of northern Nicaragua, "increasingly isolated from both their urban support networks and their peasant collaborators."[52]

Three years later Nicaragua exploded. In January 1978, following the assassination of the only charismatic leader of the moderate opposition, massive demonstrations erupted. They were followed by a popular uprising in the town of Masaya, twenty miles from Managua. These spontaneous outbursts took everyone, including the Sandinistas, by surprise. Then, in August 1978, a daring Sandinista feat – the occupation of the National Congress in Managua – sparked a revolt in the town of Matagalpa. The agony of the Somoza dictatorship had begun. Hundreds of thousands of Nicaraguans shed their fear and were ready to fight. They needed leaders. The Sandinistas had one great asset: They had fought the Somoza dictatorship for nearly twenty years. They alone had legitimacy, and they alone had trained combatants who could lead the struggle. The population responded, swelling the Sandinistas' ranks.[53]

The Sandinistas garnered growing support in Latin America. Venezuela and Panama sent weapons, and Costa Rica became the Sandinistas' rear base. Cuba also sent weapons – it had been the Sandinistas' lone and loyal supporter for almost twenty years – but the CIA did not immediately realize the extent of Havana's help. However, a few weeks after the fall of Somoza it reported that during the final two months of the revolt "some 36 support flights – primarily by Panamanian and Costa Rican aircraft – carried arms, ammunition, and other supplies from Cuba to the Sandinista forces."[54]

The men who had founded the FSLN in the early 1960s were Marxist-Leninists. But by the time Somoza fell there were not many communists among the Sandinista leaders. Furthermore, the two most powerful

52 Matilde Zimmermann, *Sandinista: Carlos Fonseca and the Nicaraguan Revolution* (Durham, NC: Duke University Press, 2000), 185.
53 The best accounts of the fighting against Somoza in Nicaragua in 1978–79 are Alan Riding's daily coverage in the *New York Times* and René de la Pedraja, *Wars of Latin America, 1948–1982: The Rise of the Guerrillas* (Jefferson, NC: McFarland & Co., 2013), 248–70.
54 National Intelligence Officer for USSR–EE to Director Central Intelligence, "Brzezinski Request for Communist Intervention Comparison," 13 Aug. 1979, enclosed in Turner to Brzezinski, 15 Aug. 1979, CREST, NA.

Sandinistas – Nicaragua's future president Daniel Ortega and his brother Humberto, the future defense minister – were not Marxist-Leninists.[55]

There are striking similarities between Eisenhower's handling of Cuba in 1958, when the prospect of Castro's victory over Batista became real, and Carter's handling of Nicaragua as the revolt against Somoza grew. Just as Eisenhower had deemed Castro an unsavory, dangerous figure, but not a communist (this would have justified extreme measures to prevent his victory), so, too, did Carter assess the Sandinistas. And just as Eisenhower had tried to push out Batista and replace him with a less odious figure who would defuse the crisis, so, too, did Carter try to nudge Somoza aside. But Batista and Somoza were clients, not proxies, and they held onto power as long as they could. When they finally fled, it was too late for Washington to forge an acceptable alternative.

The End of the Decade

On 19 July 1979, the Sandinista leaders entered Managua in triumph. Six weeks later, on 3 September, the Summit of the Non-Aligned Movement (NAM) met in Havana. Fidel Castro would preside, and he would chair the NAM for the next three years. His prestige in the Third World was at its peak – he had defeated apartheid South Africa and saved Angola.

It would be, many expected, a stormy summit. Castro had been insisting that there was a "natural alliance" between the Soviet bloc and the nonaligned world, and he wanted the NAM to recognize this. Those members of the NAM who opposed the idea – as well as the Carter administration – looked to Josip Broz Tito, the president of Yugoslavia and only surviving founding member of the NAM, to lead the battle against the Cubans. The clash had been simmering for more than a year, and the Cubans seemed prepared for a fight. "We are not afraid of confrontation," Cuba's vice-president told top Yugoslav officials, "no matter who is against us."[56]

---

55 This assessment of the Sandinistas is based on my own research. See Piero Gleijeses, "Nicaragua: Resist Romanticism," *Foreign Policy* 54 (Spring 1984), 122–38, and Gleijeses, "The Reagan Doctrine and Central America," *Current History* 85, 515 (Dec. 1986), 401–04, 435–37.

56 Carlos Rafael Rodríguez, quoted in Tvrtko Jakovina, *Treća strana hladnog rata* (Zagreb: Fraktura, 2011), 101. Jakovina provides an excellent account of the confrontation between Havana and Belgrade, based on Yugoslav documents (ibid., 101–23). The best book on the NAM is Jürgen Dinkel, *Die Bewegung Bündnisfreier Staaten* (Oldenbourg: De Gruyter, 2015).

Castro, however, knew when to retreat. Realizing the depth of opposition to his tilt of the NAM to Moscow, he did not force the issue at the summit. Many observers believed that it was only *partie remise* and that the battle would soon be resumed. They were wrong. Castro's campaign on behalf of the "natural alliance" had crested.

In late December 1979, the Soviet Union invaded Afghanistan, a non-aligned country. The invasion placed Cuba, the Kremlin's champion in the NAM, in a difficult position. "Afghanistan is an active member of the Non-Aligned Movement . . . and Cuba is now the president of the movement," Castro told the Soviet ambassador, Vitalii Vorotnikov.[57] To condemn Moscow openly, however, would align Cuba with the United States against the Soviet Union. When, on 14 January 1980, the General Assembly of the United Nations debated a resolution condemning the invasion, Cuba was one of 18 countries that opposed the resolution, while 104 voted in favor and 30 abstained. The vote damaged Cuba's international prestige and derailed its chance to win the UN Security Council seat reserved for Latin American countries. A few months later, Castro told Honecker, "The situation in Afghanistan has hurt us greatly, especially in the Third World. We were placed in an absolute minority . . . At the time we were fighting for a seat in the Security Council, and we had received approximately 90 votes . . . because of the events in Afghanistan we had . . . to abandon our quest. It would have been absurd [to have continued], we had lost many votes, and this has hurt the Non-Aligned Movement greatly."[58]

The 1970s ended with one important victory of the revolutionary movement: the surrender of the white minority regime in Rhodesia, defeated by the growing onslaught of the guerrillas armed by the Soviet Union and China, and by the implacable determination of the Carter administration to bring peace to the land. Washington insisted that no solution was possible unless the guerrillas were allowed to participate in free, internationally supervised elections. As Nancy Mitchell demonstrates, Carter was motivated by human rights considerations and by *Realpolitik*: He believed that the white regime was doomed and the longer the war continued the greater would be the opportunity for Moscow to extend its influence.[59] Finally, in April 1980, the elections were held, and Rhodesia became the independent country of

57 Vitalii Vorotnikov, *Gavana–Moskva: pamiatnye gody* (Moscow: Fond imeni I. D. Sytina, 2001), 108.
58 Memcon (Castro, Honecker), 28 May 1980, DY30 JIV 2/201/1365, SAPMO.
59 Mitchell, *Jimmy Carter in Africa*.

Zimbabwe. It would be, for a decade, the last victory of the revolutionary movement in Africa and Latin America.

One country paid a terrible price for the liberation of Rhodesia: Mozambique. Frelimo, the guerrilla movement that had led the struggle against the Portuguese and became the government of independent Mozambique in 1975, generously allowed the Rhodesian insurgents to use the country as a rearguard base. In response, the Rhodesian armed forces launched devastating crossborder raids into Mozambique, and the Rhodesian government helped create RENAMO (Resistência Nacional Moçambicana, Mozambican National Resistance), an anti-Frelimo guerrilla movement that wreaked havoc in Mozambique. When Rhodesia became Zimbabwe in 1980, there was no respite for Mozambique: Pretoria became RENAMO's patron because the Frelimo government was helping the rebels of the African National Congress of South Africa. Frelimo's errors helped RENAMO gather strength. Frelimo sought to transform the socioeconomic structure of Mozambique – its plans were well meant, but its policies and their implementation were often ill thought out and heavy-handed.[60]

Looking Back

In the early 1970s, the revolutionary movement was at a low ebb in both Africa and Latin America. The collapse of the Portuguese dictatorship in 1974 opened the door for dramatic change in Africa, and five years later the revolt of the people of Nicaragua, led by the Sandinistas, brought about the first victory of a guerrilla movement in Latin America since the triumph of the Cuban Revolution twenty years earlier.

The keynote of the revolutionary struggle of the 1970s in both Africa and Latin America is the heroism of the guerrillas. But heroism is not enough. Every guerrilla movement needs – desperately – weapons. Even the Sandinistas, despite massive popular support, could not have won without arms. What is special in the case of Nicaragua, however, is that the weapons did not come, mainly, from communist countries. Cuba's help to the Sandinistas in 1978–79, as a source of training, advice and weapons, was critical, but the role of noncommunist Latin American countries – Venezuela, Costa Rica and Panama – was as important. As for the Soviet

---

60 Allen Isaacman and Barbara Isaacman, *Mozambique: From Colonialism to Revolution, 1900–1982* (Boulder: Westview Press, 1983); Stephen Emerson, *The Battle for Mozambique: The Frelimo–Renamo Struggle, 1977–1992* (Solihull: Helion & Company, 2014).

Union, its involvement with Latin American guerrillas in the 1970s was minimal, and it played no role in the Sandinista victory over Somoza.

Africa was different. Guerrilla movements were more active there in the 1970s than in Latin America. Whereas the Latin American guerrillas were openly Marxist-Leninist (the Sandinistas were the exception) and this isolated them from large sectors of society, in Africa the guerrillas were members of national liberation movements fighting against a colonial power. Furthermore, the US presence in Africa was less oppressive than in Latin America, and the assistance of the communist countries was decisive in the victories of the African liberation movements. The Swedes, and the other Scandinavians, proffered precious economic aid to the African liberation movements (but none to the Latin American guerrillas). They refused, however, to provide weapons, even though they deemed the guerrillas' cause to be just. At times, Stockholm endorsed armed struggle with extraordinary lucidity, as when the Swedish representative at the United Nations said, "We recognize that the Namibian people have seen no other way out than to resort to armed struggle to free itself from foreign occupation. We know that this struggle is pursued with the goal [of creating] an independent and united Namibia. [It] has the full support of the Swedish government."[61] Nevertheless, Stockholm refused to supply the guerrillas with the aid most essential to their cause – arms. Many Swedes criticized this restriction, as did some leaders of the liberation movements, but in practical terms it was moot because others – the communist countries – provided the weapons.

One country did even more: Castro's Cuba. The Cubans' role was unique. Take, for example, the war of independence in Guinea-Bissau. Sweden and to a lesser degree Norway provided the bulk of the humanitarian assistance. The Soviet Union supplied virtually all the weapons. Cuba – and Cuba alone – sent military instructors who fought alongside the PAIGC and operated the sophisticated Soviet weapons. In the words of Guinea-Bissau's first president, "We were able to fight and triumph because other countries and people helped us . . . with weapons, medicine and supplies . . . but there is one nation that, in addition to material, political and diplomatic support, even sent its children to fight by our side, to shed their blood in our land . . . this great people, this heroic people, we all know that it is the heroic people of Cuba."[62]

---

61 Quoted in Sellström, *Sweden and National Liberation*, vol. II, 248.
62 President Luís Cabral, *Nõ Pintcha* (22 Jan. 1977), 4–6.

The guerrillas in Latin America and Africa were motivated by indigenous factors, but their insurgencies occurred within the larger context of the clash between two superpowers. The "hot" Cold War, in which blood was shed, was fought almost exclusively in the periphery, in the Third World. As Nancy Mitchell writes, "The Cold War was a contest that consisted of shadow-boxing in areas of marginal significance because real war in places that really counted – Berlin, Washington, and Moscow – was unwinnable."[63] It is impossible, however, to draw simple conclusions about the impact of the Cold War on the insurgencies of the 1970s.[64]

Look, for example, at southern Africa. It is likely that the United States would have been less dependent on the Azores air base without the Cold War. But what would the impact of a US refusal to supply weapons have been on the Portuguese war effort when France, Britain and West Germany were willing to sell Lisbon arms with no strings attached? Would these countries have acted differently without the Cold War? Furthermore, would Moscow have supplied weapons to the guerrillas had it not been locked in a confrontation with the United States? There are no clear answers.

South Africa invaded Angola in 1975 to defend apartheid. The Gerald Ford administration, on the other hand, was motivated by multiple factors that ranged from Kissinger's ego to the Cold War. For the subsequent fifteen years Pretoria's policy in the region continued to be driven by the defense of apartheid, and Washington's by the Cold War. It is likely that without the Cold War President Carter would have established diplomatic relations with Angola and exerted real pressure on South Africa to allow free elections in Namibia, while the Reagan administration would not have comforted the South Africans in their war of aggression against Angola and in their refusal to allow free elections in Namibia.

Turn the focus to Havana. Between 1975 and 1988, Castro helped change the course of history in southern Africa. Castro was motivated above all by his hatred of apartheid and his deeply held belief that it was Cuba's duty to help the people of the Third World achieve their liberation – these reasons transcended the Cold War. But Cuba could not have maintained its army in Angola without the massive economic and military aid it received from the Soviet Union. There may have been an element of idealism in the Kremlin's policy in southern Africa, a sense of internationalist duty that harkened to the

63 Nancy Mitchell, "The Cold War and Jimmy Carter," in Melvyn Leffler and Odd Arne Westad (eds.), *The Cambridge History of the Cold War* (Cambridge: Cambridge University Press, 2010), vol. III, 67.
64 See Gleijeses, "Decolonization During the Cold War."

origins of the Soviet Union. But Cold War considerations – the confrontation with the United States – were decisive. Without the Cold War the Soviet Union would not have underwritten the Cuban presence in Africa, and there would have been no Cuban troops to confront the South Africans – neither in 1975 nor in the years that followed. What then? Would US pressure have sufficed to restrain Pretoria? Or should we conclude that in southern Africa the Cold War had a beneficial impact because it made it possible for the Cuban troops to stop the South Africans?

The bipolarity of the Cold War – the capitalist West against the communist bloc – was disrupted by the eruption of the Sino-Soviet conflict in the 1960s. This conflict, however, did not significantly affect the liberation struggle in the 1970s. In Latin America, the Soviet Union played only a small role and China was irrelevant. Even in Africa, where both countries were active, their rivalry had little impact. In Guinea-Bissau, Namibia and Mozambique, where there was only one guerrilla movement, they did not vie for influence: The Soviets supported the PAIGC and SWAPO, whereas the Chinese supported Frelimo. In Rhodesia, where there were two guerrilla movements, one received aid from Moscow and the other from Beijing. Relations between the two Rhodesian movements were strained, but this was due to personal, military and ethnic rivalries, not to the Sino-Soviet rift. The only African country where the Sino-Soviet conflict mattered was Angola. Throughout the 1960s the MPLA received its weapons from the Soviet Union. But an ephemeral thaw in the MPLA's tense relations with Beijing in 1972–73 fanned Soviet suspicions that the movement was pro-Chinese. This was one reason – but not the only reason – that Soviet aid to the MPLA "virtually ceased" in 1973, as a KGB officer wrote.[65] China, however, which still considered the MPLA pro-Soviet, did not fill the gap. It was Yugoslavia that stepped in. When the civil war broke out in Angola in early 1975, the first important military aid to the MPLA came from Yugoslavia, in April.[66] Soviet weapons began arriving only in late August. As for the Chinese, in 1975 they helped the anti-communist and deeply corrupt FNLA, siding with South Africa and the United States. Then, in the late 1970s, they sent weapons to the guerrilla leader Jonas Savimbi, who continued his fight against the MPLA government with Pretoria's support. As the Zambian

---

65 Oleg Negin (pseudonym of Oleg Nazhestkin), "V ognennom kolze blokadi," in V. Karpov (ed.), *Vneshiaia Razvedka* (Moscow: XXI Veksoglasie, 2000), 240.
66 See Jovan Čavošky, "'Yugoslavia's Help Was Extraordinary': Yugoslavia's Political and Material Assistance and the MPLA's Rise to Power, 1961–1975," *Journal of Cold War Studies* (forthcoming). See also Gleijeses, *Conflicting Missions*, 243, 347–49.

chargé in Beijing reported, "China in its global policy, wherever Russia and Cuba appear, they will do the opposite."[67] But Chinese aid to UNITA did not affect the course of the civil war in 1975, or the situation in Angola in the late 1970s. It did, however, damage Beijing's prestige in the Third World.

The Cuban troops (and thousands of aid workers) remained in Angola through the 1980s, protecting it from South Africa and helping Namibia's SWAPO and Nelson Mandela's African National Congress. In 1988 the Cubans gained the upper hand over the South Africans in Angola, and Pretoria capitulated, ending its aid to Savimbi and agreeing to the independence of Namibia.[68]

The United States and South Africa led the struggle against the revolutionary forces. Having failed to prevent the "communist" victories in the 1970s they tried, in the decade that followed, to reverse the course of history.

The Reagan administration focused on Nicaragua, where the Sandinistas proved inept in handling the country's economy; they were arrogant, ignorant and repressive. But, as even a fierce critic noted, they also instituted important social reforms "targeted at improving the living standards of the Nicaraguan people," and they showed "real concern for the destitute."[69] This was an unprecedented departure for Nicaraguan rulers.

Had the Sandinistas been merely corrupt, impervious to social reform and repressive, they could have lived in harmony with the United States, as did, for example, the rulers of Mexico. Were Nicaragua in Africa, the Reagan administration would have been far less alarmed. But Ronald Reagan believed that the Sandinistas – in America's backyard! – were Marxist-Leninists. Therefore, he unleashed relentless economic warfare on the country and nurtured the anti-Sandinista army – the Contras. Nicaragua's *Via Crucis* had begun.

Like the Sandinistas in Nicaragua, the MPLA government in Angola faced an implacable enemy bent on its destruction: apartheid South Africa. The South Africans helped Savimbi with weapons, money, military advisors and even troops; they also launched bruising raids into southern Angola. However, they stopped short of attacking the Cuban troops who barred their access to the Angolan heartland. The Reagan administration helped Pretoria

---

67 S. A. Maonde, Zambian chargé in Beijing, to Zambian foreign minister Mwala [Aug. 1978], 151 UNIP 7/23/65, United National Independence Party archive, Lusaka.
68 Gleijeses, *Visions of Freedom*, 393–526.
69 Arturo J. Cruz, "Nicaragua's Imperiled Revolution," *Foreign Affairs* 61, 5 (Summer 1983), 1032. When he wrote this article Cruz had already joined the anti-Sandinista insurgency led by Eden Pastora (interview with Cruz, Washington, DC, 18 Mar. 1982).

by vetoing all UN Security Council resolutions that would have imposed sanctions on South Africa for its attacks on Angola. In 1986, it joined Pretoria in providing military assistance to Savimbi.[70]

The MPLA government had initially implemented policies that raised Angola's health and education levels, and improved the living conditions of the rural population. But as the country's security and economy deteriorated under the blows of Savimbi and his patrons, the MPLA leaders became increasingly corrupt, indifferent to the needs of the population and repressive. Even so, they were far better than the alternative, Savimbi. Unlike Savimbi, the MPLA did not burn its opponents at the stake, much less their wives and children. It repressed dissent but not as cruelly and absolutely as Savimbi, who imposed a "culture of zero tolerance of dissent and a personality cult that had parallels with those of Mao Tse-Tung and Kim Il-Sung."[71] Marrack Goulding, the British ambassador to Angola in 1983–85, branded Savimbi "a monster whose lust for power had brought appalling misery to his people."[72]

Looking back at the revolutionary movements of the 1970s there are a few obvious conclusions. Without the aid of the communist countries, it would have been far more difficult for the independence movements of Portuguese Africa to defeat Lisbon. Without Cuba's intervention in 1975, South Africa would have overrun Angola and installed its clients in Luanda. Beyond the undeniable benefits of independence, however, the dreams of the revolutionaries remain unfulfilled. It is likely that the MPLA government in Angola, Frelimo in Mozambique and above all the Sandinistas in Nicaragua would have improved the lot of their citizens had they not faced the determined aggression of the United States and South Africa. The responsibility for the plight of the people of Zimbabwe, Guinea-Bissau and Ethiopia, on the other hand, belongs to the governments in Harare, Bissau and Addis Ababa.

There is one very significant result of the revolutionary fervor of the 1970s. It was in that decade that the White Redoubt in southern Africa was shattered and apartheid South Africa suffered its first major defeat – at the hands of the Cubans in Angola. More than a decade later, in 1988, the Cubans again humiliated the South African army and forced Pretoria to accept the

---

70 An intriguing question about the Angolan operation is when it started. Until October 1985, covert operations in Angola were prohibited by the US Congress, but two US documents as well as South African sources suggest that, despite the strictures of Congress, aid to Savimbi began under Carter (Gleijeses, *Visions of Freedom*, 51–53).

71 Tony Hodges, *Angola: Anatomy of an Oil State* (Bloomington: Indiana University Press, 2004), 19. See also Gleijeses, *Visions of Freedom*, 298–304.

72 Marrack Goulding, *Peacemonger* (Baltimore: Johns Hopkins University Press, 2002), 193.

independence of Namibia. This hastened the demise of apartheid. In the words of Nelson Mandela, the Cuban victory "destroyed the myth of the invincibility of the white oppressor . . . [and] inspired the fighting masses of South Africa . . . [It] was the turning point for the liberation of our country – and of my people – from the scourge of apartheid."[73] Cuba helped change the course of history in southern Africa despite Washington's efforts to prevent it.

Bibliographical Essay

There is no counterpart for the 1970s of Richard Gott's classic survey of guerrilla movements in the 1960s, *Guerrilla Movements in Latin America* (London: Seagull Books, 2008). However, Timothy Wickham-Crowley, *Guerrillas and Revolution in Latin America: A Comparative Study of Insurgents and Regimes Since 1956* (Princeton: Princeton University Press, 1992), and René de la Pedraja, *Wars of Latin America, 1948–1982* (Jefferson, NC: McFarland & Co., 2013), are useful.

The most important accounts of Francisco Caamaño's guerrilla attempt in the Dominican Republic are two books by Hamlet Hermann: *El Fiero. Eberto Lalane José* (Santo Domingo: Búho, 2009) and *Caamaño, Biografía de una época* (Santo Domingo: Búho, 2013). (Hermann was one of the two survivors of Caamaño's guerrilla group and a gifted historian.) See also Brian Bosch, *Balaguer and the Dominican Military: Presidential Control of the Factional Officer Corps in the 1960s and 1970s* (Jefferson, NC: McFarland & Co., 2007); Manuel Matos Moquete, *Caamaño, la última esperanza armada* (Santo Domingo: Videocine Palau, 1999).

The two best books on the Tupamaros in Uruguay are Pablo Brum, *The Robin Hood Guerrillas: The Epic Journey of Uruguay's Tupamaros*, 2nd edn. (Middletown, DE: Createspace Independent Pub., 2016), and *Sendic* (Montevideo: Ediciones Trilce, 2000), by former Tupamaro Samuel Blixen. Régis Debray, *Les épreuves du feu* (Paris: Éditions du Seuil, 1974), vol. II, 125–278, is worth reading, although biased.

On the Sandinistas, see Matilde Zimmermann, *Sandinista: Carlos Fonseca and the Nicaraguan Revolution* (Durham, NC: Duke University Press, 2000); David Nolan, *The Ideology of the Sandinistas and the Nicaraguan Revolution* (Coral Gables, FL: Institute of Inter-American Studies, 1984); Dennis Gilbert, *Sandinistas: The Party and the Revolution* (New York: Blackwell, 1988);

73 Nelson Mandela, 26 Jul. 1991 speech, *Granma* (27 Jul. 1991), 3.

Shirley Christian, *Nicaragua: Revolution in the Family* (New York: Vintage Books, 1985); Nikolai Platoshkin, *Sandinistskaia revolutsiia v Nikaragua* [The Sandinista Revolution in Nicaragua] (Moscow: Russkiii fond sodeiist-viia obrazovaniiu i nauke, 2015). The authoritative account of the Reagan administration and Nicaragua is William Leogrande, *Our Own Backyard: The United States in Central America, 1977–1992* (Chapel Hill: University of North Carolina Press, 1998).

On the United States and the Allende government, see Peter Kornbluh, *The Pinochet File: A Declassified Dossier on Atrocity and Accountability*, rev. edn. (New York: New Press, 2013); Lubna Qureshi, *Nixon, Kissinger and Allende: US Involvement in the 1973 Coup in Chile* (Lanham, MD: Lexington Books, 2009); Jonathan Haslam, *The Nixon Administration and the Death of Allende's Chile: A Case of Assisted Suicide* (London: Verso, 2005).

Turning to Africa, on the war in the Portuguese colonies, see Patrick Chabal, *Amilcar Cabral: Revolutionary Leadership and People's War* (Cambridge: Cambridge University Press, 1983); John Marcum, *The Angolan Revolution*, 2 vols. (Cambridge, MA: MIT Press, 1969–78); Jean-Michel Mabeko Tali, *Dissidências e Poder de Estado: o MPLA perante si própio (1962–1977)*, 2 vols. (Luanda: Editorial Nzila, 2001); Allen Isaacman and Barbara Isaacman, *Mozambique: From Colonialism to Revolution, 1900–1982* (Boulder: Westview Press, 1983); Piero Gleijeses, *Conflicting Missions: Havana, Washington, and Africa, 1959–1976* (Chapel Hill: University of North Carolina Press, 2002).

On the Ethiopian revolution, see Marina Ottaway and David Ottaway, *Ethiopia: Empire in Revolution* (New York: Africana Publishing Co., 1978); René Lefort, *Éthiopie. La révolution hérétique* (Paris: Maspéro, 1981); Joseph Tubiana (ed.), *La révolution éthiopienne comme phénomène de société: témoignages et documents* (Paris: Éditions L'Harmattan, 1990); Andargachew Tiruneh, *The Ethiopian Revolution 1974–1987: A Transformation from an Aristocratic to a Totalitarian Autocracy* (Cambridge: Cambridge University Press, 1993); Gebru Tareke, *The Ethiopian Revolution: War in the Horn of Africa* (New Haven: Yale University Press, 2009). By far the best source on US policy in the Horn is Nancy Mitchell's *Jimmy Carter in Africa: Race and the Cold War* (Washington, DC, and Stanford: Woodrow Wilson Center Press and Stanford University Press, 2016). On Soviet policy in the Horn, see Odd Arne Westad, *The Global Cold War: Third World Interventions and the Making of Our Times* (Cambridge: Cambridge University Press, 2005), 250–87.

On the role of the two superpowers, Cuba and South Africa in southern Africa, see Mitchell's masterful *Jimmy Carter in Africa*; Gleijeses, *Conflicting*

Missions and *Visions of Freedom: Havana, Washington, Pretoria and the Struggle for Southern Africa, 1976–1991* (Chapel Hill: University of North Carolina Press, 2013); Vladimir Shubin, *The Hot "Cold War": The USSR in Southern Africa* (London: Pluto Press, 2008); Francois Jacobus du Toit Spies, *Operasie Savannah. Angola 1975–1976* (Pretoria: S. A. Weermag, 1989); Westad, *Global Cold War*, 207–49.

On Scandinavian assistance to African liberation movements, see Tor Sellström, *Sweden and National Liberation in Southern Africa*, 2 vols. (Uppsala, Sweden: Nordiska Afrikainstitutet, 1999–2002), and Piero Gleijeses, "Scandinavia and the Liberation of Southern Africa," *International History Review* 27, 2 (June 2005), 324–31.

5

Cambodia: Detonator of Communism's Implosion

BEN KIERNAN

The Cambodia–Vietnam conflict that began in 1977–78 signaled a final collapse of the global communist vision. "Indochine: guerre des socialismes, mort des peuples," proclaimed the cover of the January 1980 special issue of Jean-Paul Sartre's *Les Temps Modernes*. The Southeast Asia historian Benedict Anderson considered the open warfare between Cambodia, Vietnam and China in 1978–79 a "fundamental transformation in the history of Marxism and Marxist movements" with "the prospect of further full-scale wars between the socialist states."[1] In his 1983 book *Imagined Communities*, Anderson explained the Cambodia–Vietnam conflict as a function of nationalism, a contest between essentially similar dueling national visions shaped in part by the specific divide-and-rule territorial policies of French Indochina.[2]

But two historians of Indochina, Georges Boudarel and Daniel Hémery, took a different view. In a 1979 issue of *Problèmes Politiques et Sociaux* devoted to the theme "Indochina: The First War Between Communist States," they described Cambodia as the "detonator of the crisis."[3] In their view Cambodia's role was the key: Both its domestic regime and its foreign policy were explosive. Indeed, Cambodia had started the war with bloody cross-border attacks into Vietnamese territory in 1977 – even as it also attacked its other neighbors, Thailand and Laos.[4]

Anderson's view implied a continuity in Cambodian nationalist communism inherited from the anti-colonial struggle and still influential into the Pol

---

1 *Les Temps Modernes* 402 (Jan. 1980); *Nation* (6 Jun. 2016), 43.
2 Benedict Anderson, *Imagined Communities: Reflections on the Origin and Spread of Nationalism* (London: Verso, 1983), 11, 110–20.
3 Georges Boudarel and Daniel Hémery (eds.), "Indochine: première guerre entre états communistes," *Problèmes Politiques et Sociaux* 373 (12 Oct. 1979); Georges Boudarel and Daniel Hémery, "Le Cambodge, détonateur de la crise," ibid., 5–12.
4 Ben Kiernan, "New Light on the Origins of the Vietnam–Kampuchea Conflict," *Bulletin of Concerned Asian Scholars* 12, 4 (1980), 61–65.

Pot period.[5] By contrast, Boudarel and Hémery's analysis suggested that Cambodia's "detonator" role sprang not from historical structures of a colonially shaped nationalism but from specific choices made by the Pol Pot regime. Human agency, indeed, overrode colonial structures in Cambodian communist history. The first generation of Cambodian communists had ignored French territorial divisions and worked closely with Vietnamese communists. The discontinuity is clear once Pol Pot's group of foreign-educated Cambodians took over the party leadership in 1962. Their choice to take it in an anti-Vietnamese direction led to a genocide that is currently being judged by the UN-sponsored tribunal in Phnom Penh.

Anderson was right on a key issue: the importance of "print-capitalism" in the making of Cambodian nationalism. In a colonial peasant society, the late arrival of the first Khmer-language newspaper and novel (in 1936 and 1938, respectively) delayed the rise of a grassroots vernacular nationalism in Cambodia, and made its tender shoots vulnerable to uprooting by a postwar royalist dictatorship and to competition from an equally youthful communism, which eventually triumphed over both. The crux of the matter, then, is the nature of the communist regime that Pol Pot led, and how it came to power in Cambodia in 1975.

The "unexpected victory"[6] of Pol Pot's Khmer Rouge had required the emergence first of a nationalist movement and a colonial war within which a communist party could thrive, then of external backing for an extremist communist faction amid the internal suppression of more moderate and reformist groups, then the rise of a postindependence communist insurgency and, finally, an escalated, massively destabilizing war. If the Pol Pot regime, with its Chinese backing, was the detonator of communism's implosion, a series of wars imposed on Cambodia by other great powers – Japan, France and the United States – laid a long fuse that led to the Cambodian genocide.

Origins of Khmer Communism

Communism first appeared in the French Protectorate of Cambodia in the late 1920s, after a decade of agricultural expansion, including the establishment of

5 The continuity argument also appears in more recent work of Anderson's former student and later US intelligence officer, Steve Heder, *Cambodian Communism and the Vietnamese Model* (Bangkok: White Lotus, 2004). See Ben Kiernan, "Documentation Delayed, Justice Denied: The Historiography of the Cambodian Genocide," in Dan Stone (ed.), *The Historiography of Genocide* (London: Palgrave Macmillan, 2008), 472, 484.
6 Timothy Carney, "Cambodia: The Unexpected Victory," in Karl Jackson (ed.), *Cambodia 1975–1978: Rendezvous with Death* (Princeton: Princeton University Press, 1989), 13–35.

French-owned rubber plantations in the country's east. But Cambodians were unlikely communist recruits. The plantation workforce largely comprised press-ganged northern Vietnamese. Most of Cambodia's rural areas were the home of ethnic Khmer (Cambodian) rice-growing peasant farmers, 80 percent of whom in 1930 owned less than 5 hectares, totaling 44 percent of the cultivated land. Fewer than 4 percent were landless or tenant farmers.[7] The soil was poor, but fish and fruit were plentiful. Cambodia was underpopulated, and most peasants possessed the 2–3 hectares of rice land or half-hectare of riverbank land needed to support the average family of three to five people. The country's urban population comprised mostly ethnic Chinese and Vietnamese shopkeepers, laborers and clerks. Cambodia possessed almost no industrial sector. Its population was 80 percent rural, 80 percent ethnic Khmer and 80 percent Theravada Buddhist. The French Sûreté (security service) reported in 1929 that Cambodians "have not yet learnt how to organize meetings to hatch conspiracies. They know how to gather together only on pagoda feast-days and for funeral ceremonies."[8]

Vietnamese and Chinese underground communist and nationalist organizations spread into Cambodia in the late 1920s.[9] In October 1929 the Sûreté arrested Vietnamese activists in Phnom Penh and several Cambodian provincial capitals, including members of Ho Chi Minh's Revolutionary Youth League. In February 1930, Ho amalgamated the League with two other parties, forming the Vietnamese Communist Party (VCP), which soon proliferated throughout Vietnam and set up a cell in a Cambodian rubber plantation. The Chinese Communist Party (CCP) set up cells in Kompong Cham and Kratie provinces which survived the French repression of 1930–31. But the CCP failed to spread in Cambodia. After October 1930, when at the direction of the Communist International the VCP changed its name to the Indochina Communist Party (ICP), communist activity in Cambodia remained almost entirely confined to ethnic Vietnamese. In the prewar era the only ethnic Cambodian to join the ICP was Thach Choeun, a Khmer Krom, a member of the large Khmer minority in Vietnam's Mekong delta. Choeun was recruited at age twenty-eight while working as a fisherman on Cambodia's Tonle Sap Lake in 1932.

---

7 Ben Kiernan, "Introduction," in Ben Kiernan and Chanthou Boua (eds.), *Peasants and Politics in Kampuchea 1942–1981* (London: Zed, 1982), 4; Ben Kiernan, *How Pol Pot Came to Power: Colonialism, Nationalism and Communism in Cambodia, 1930–1975* (New Haven: Yale University Press, 2004), li.
8 *Le Khmer* (3 Aug. 1936); Kiernan, *How Pol Pot*, 13.
9 Geoffrey C. Gunn, "Reinterpreting Cambodian History: New Light on the Origins of Communism in Southern Indochina (1927–1939)," *Kabar Seberang* 16 (1985), 24–64.

The ICP program included the defeat of French colonialism and overthrow of Cambodia's monarchy, "with all the mandarins and notables." It envisaged a "fraternal alliance of all the peoples of Indochina," who would have the right "freely to manage their own affairs." The ICP tightened its control in 1934, specifying: "There is no question of a separate Cambodian revolution. There is only a single Indochinese revolution ... Cambodia does not have the right to a separate Cambodian communist party [which] would be to fall into the trap of racial division, set by imperialism." Then in 1935, the party restated: "After the eviction of the French imperialists," Cambodians "will have the right to manage their own affairs up to and including the right to secede and form an independent state."[10] This program attracted no Cambodian recruits.

Neither had the high taxes levied by the French nor the Great Depression made communism attractive to Cambodians.[11] In 1934 the Sûreté reported not "a single case of contamination of Cambodians." The next year the French arrested the three leading communists in Cambodia. Thach Choeun fled back to the delta. In 1937 he quietly returned to Cambodia and became a Buddhist monk in Takeo province, then left the *wat* in 1939 to take up the post of chief of the ICP for Svay Rieng province, near the Vietnamese border. But the ICP itself described its activities in Cambodia as "very weak ." The same was true of Cambodian nationalism, limited to a small circle in a country where only 60,000 Khmer pupils attended primary schools, the sole high school opened in 1935, and the first Khmer-language newspaper, *Nagaravatta*, was launched in 1936.

World War II and Colonial Warfare

Neither colonial domination nor socioeconomic conditions in Cambodia proved fertile ground for communism or nationalism. War would foster them: first, the Japanese occupation of Cambodia during World War II, and then a sustained French attempt to *re*conquer the country in 1945–54. These conflicts not only provoked Cambodian national sentiment, but in the absence of a strong nationalist movement they also enabled an initially small group of Khmer communists to compete for its leadership. By the time of the French defeat at the hands of Vietnam's communist movement, a significant Cambodian communist movement had emerged alongside it.

10 Kiernan, *How Pol Pot*, 12, 16, 17. Unless otherwise noted, this chapter draws on that work.
11 David P. Chandler, "The Assassination of Resident Bardez (1925): A Premonition of Revolt in Colonial Cambodia," *Journal of the Siam Society* 70, 1–2 (1982), 40–41, 47.

After the 1940 Nazi invasion of France, two Japanese divisions arrived in Cambodia in May 1941. Tokyo signed a treaty with the Vichy French representatives in Indochina, leaving them and Cambodia's young king Norodom Sihanouk in place. The colonial condominium encouraged the small group of middle-class Khmer nationalists to hope for Japanese support to oust the French. But the Japanese not only stood by while the French suppressed Cambodian nationalism; Tokyo also allowed its wartime ally Bangkok to seize Cambodia's northwest provinces, annexing them to Thailand until 1946. Youthful Cambodian noncommunist nationalism was crushed between French, Japanese and Thai colonialisms.

In resolutions passed in 1939 and 1941, the ICP determined to oppose both the French and the Japanese, and to help set up a "League for the Independence of Cambodia." But it acknowledged that there was "still no trace" of the ICP in Cambodia.[12] Thach Choeun had disappeared, but the next Cambodians to join the ICP were, like him, former Buddhist monks.

On 20 July 1942, the nationalists Son Ngoc Thanh and Pach Chhoeun, founders of *Nagaravatta*, organized a demonstration in Phnom Penh to protest the French arrest of two monks for preaching anti-French sermons: 700 Khmer monks and 2,000 lay supporters marched to the office of the French Resident Superior.[13] The hoped-for Japanese intervention never came. The French arrested Chhoeun with several others, and they spent the war in a colonial prison. Thanh escaped to Bangkok and then Tokyo, where he was hidden for three years. The French rounded up 200 other nationalists, crippling the movement. A few escaped to the countryside; some, including several former monks, joined the ICP.[14]

One of these ex-monks was a Khmer Krom named Achar Mean (an *achar* is a learned pagoda layman), a Pali-language teacher at the prestigious Wat Unnalom in the capital. He escaped to a *wat* in Kompong Chhnang and made contact with the ICP branch in Thailand. He became the first Khmer to join the ICP after the war, using the name Son Ngoc Minh. Another Pali teacher, a former monk from Kompong Speu named Achar Sok, was still at Wat Unnalom in February 1945 when US B-29s bombed Japanese-occupied Phnom Penh. Bombs fell near the *wat*, killing twenty monks. Sok made his

12 Kiernan, *How Pol Pot*, 42.
13 Author's interview with Venerable Chhun Chem, age 86, Wat Svay Att, Prey Veng, 17 Jan. 1986. Chem studied at the Higher Pali School in Wat Unnalom in 1939–44 and was present at the July 1942 demonstration.
14 Ben Kiernan, *The Pol Pot Regime: Race, Power, and Genocide in Cambodia Under the Khmer Rouge, 1975–1979* (New Haven: Yale University Press, 2008, 3rd edn.), 12; Kiernan, *How Pol Pot*, 43–45.

way to Vietnam, where under the name Tou Samouth he too worked with the ICP. These two Buddhist laymen became the founders of Khmer communism.

If not for the war, they might have taken another path. Samouth had begun his clerical career at Phnom Penh's Buddhist Institute, of which the nationalist leader Son Ngoc Thanh was deputy director in the late 1930s. But Thanh's unique mistake was to strongly support the Japanese in World War II. They kept him in Tokyo from 1942 until 30 May 1945, and in mid October the returning French arrested Thanh, dispatching him to six years' detention in France as a collaborator. Thus the founder of Cambodian nationalism spent only four months in the country during the decade 1942–51, the movement's formative years. Others, such as Tou Samouth and Son Ngoc Minh, took up the independence cause, forging what alliances they could against both French and Thai colonialisms. Both joined the ICP in the last quarter of 1946.

The French return in force to Phnom Penh in late 1945 again dispersed Cambodian anti-colonialists to the Thai and Vietnamese borders. This time they set up resistance bases there. Most of them now used the name Khmer Issarak, or "Independent Cambodians." On the Vietnamese border, working within the ICP alongside Ho Chi Minh's Viet Minh League, Son Ngoc Minh and Tou Samouth, briefly joined by Pach Chhoeun and other nationalist refugees from the French, built up a peasant guerrilla force. This Issarak branch, under communist leadership, slowly grew in numbers and effectiveness. By late 1948 it fielded forces alongside the Viet Minh in Cambodia's northeast, southeast and southwest. In mid 1949 the French reported Son Ngoc Minh, based in Kampot, leading "a well-armed band of about three hundred, including women ... equipped with a hospital where all the wounded of other rebel bands are cared for."[15]

A succession of Khmer Issarak committees on the Thai border ran into difficulties with domineering Thai government officials and increasingly turned to the Viet Minh for aid. The first committee, comprising twelve members in late 1945, included only one with communist links. A second was formed in Bangkok in early 1946; Thai officials ran its three subcommittees. In 1947 Thai officers had two of the fourteen Khmer committee members shot for insubordination. Massive defections followed, including some to the ICP. A new committee formed and, by 1949, the leading Issarak committee of seven included three close allies of the Viet Minh. In February 1950, it sent

---

15 Kiernan, *How Pol Pot*, 66.

a delegation to southern Vietnam, according to French intelligence, "to study the formation of a pro-Viet Minh Cambodian government."[16] On 17 April, some 200 delegates, including 105 monks, assembled in southwest Cambodia to form a national Khmer Issarak association (usually known as the Unified Issarak Front, or UIF), and a People's Liberation Central Committee headed by Son Ngoc Minh, with Tou Samouth and two other Khmer ICP members, Chan Samay (a Khmer Krom) and Sieu Heng, as vice-presidents.

For the next four years, the French pursuit of their reconquest of Indochina further radicalized the Cambodian nationalist resistance. The Khmer communists ran intensive political training programs for hundreds of rural recruits. In February 1951 the ICP resolved to form separate parties for the three countries of Indochina. In September the leading Khmer ICP members Son Ngoc Minh, Tou Samouth, Sieu Heng and Chan Samay became the founders of the Khmer People's Revolutionary Party (KPRP). Eastern Zone UIF leader Keo Moni and others joined them to form a KPRP provisional Central Committee. From a base of 40 Khmer ICP members in 1950, and 300 in early 1951, at year's end the KPRP claimed 1,000 Khmer members operating in 60 cells. French sources estimated only 150 members in 1952, but by July 1954 their estimate had risen to 400, while according to Vietnamese sources the KPRP then had 1,862 Khmer members operating in 136 cells. The difference may be explained in part by hundreds of probationary KPRP members, particularly in the armed forces, rising to full membership in the party ranks. By 1954 about 5,000 Khmers were enlisted in UIF and Viet Minh military units in Cambodia, excluding village militia. An effective UIF unit was led by So Phim, who had joined the ICP in 1950, headed Svay Rieng province and by 1954 had succeeded Keo Moni as chief of the KPRP's Eastern Zone branch. Former ICP members also led the party's Southwest, Northwest and Northeast Zones.

During the sustained anti-colonial conflict, a Cambodian communist movement sank roots in significant rural areas of the country. The KPRP's statutes stressed the struggle for independence, making no mention of Marxism-Leninism nor any revolutionary anti-feudal or land-reform program. Its underground party leadership in 1954 remained largely rural, Buddhist-educated, moderate and pro-Vietnamese. It was still a far cry from the group of urban origin, foreign education, extremist views and anti-Vietnamese inclinations who in 1975 would head the victorious Communist Party of Kampuchea.

16 Ibid., 78–79.

Meanwhile the French Communist Party (Parti communiste français, PCF) had recruited a younger generation of Khmer radicals, postwar students in France. About ten joined the PCF from 1950 on. Most were either of urban or middle-class origin like Khieu Samphan, the son of a judge, or were upwardly mobile Khmer Krom, such as Ieng Sary and Son Sen, who had moved to Phnom Penh from the Mekong delta. Unlike most KPRP members, they had little contact with rural Cambodia or its vernacular Buddhist culture. The oldest of this group was Saloth Sar, the future Pol Pot, who had grown up in Phnom Penh's royal palace, attended an elite Catholic school and received a scholarship to study in Paris at age twenty-four. En route there via Saigon in 1949, Sar and a fellow student visited the bustling ethnic Chinese market town of Cholon and came away feeling, one later recalled, "like dark monkeys from the mountains." In Paris in 1952 Sar signed his article "Monarchy or Democracy" with the pseudonym "Khmaer Daeum" (Original Khmer) that again suggested racial sensitivity and contrasted with the modernist pen-names chosen by other students, "Free Khmer" and "Khmer Worker." Sar lost his scholarship after failing his radio electricity course two years in a row. One of the first Khmer PCF members to return home, in August 1953 Sar joined the communist forces in eastern Cambodia and spent the last year of the war there, later complaining he was "kept in the background."[17] Son Sen and Ieng Sary came back from France in 1956–57, Khieu Samphan in 1959.

Meanwhile, in the wider Cambodian legal political arena, other forces had arisen to challenge French colonialism. The Democratic Party, founded in March 1946 by Prince Yuthevong on his return from France where he had joined the Socialist Party, easily won the French-sponsored national elections held in 1946 and 1947. But Yuthevong's death and the 1950 assassination of his successor by a conservative opponent, following Sihanouk's dissolution of the National Assembly in 1949, debilitated the Democrats. They won a reduced majority in the 1951 elections. Son Ngoc Thanh then returned from exile to a popular welcome, but in the face of royal and French opposition he made another disastrous decision: He took to the jungle and attempted to win leadership of the Issarak armed resistance. He failed, becoming a marginal figure with a small guerrilla force on the Thai border. In January 1953, Sihanouk again dissolved the National Assembly, declared martial law and jailed Democratic parliamentarians. Sihanouk began

---

17 Toni Stadler, personal communication (quoting Pol Pot's traveling companion Mey Mann), cited in Kiernan, *Pol Pot Regime*, "Introduction"; Kiernan, *How Pol Pot*, 123.

a "Royal Crusade for Independence" to pressure France to hand over power to him. In an example of what Anderson called "official nationalism,"[18] the previously compliant colonial monarch had jumped on the nationalist bandwagon, seized the reins and offloaded the youthful grassroots independence forces who had successfully set it on course.[19]

Independence

The French delivered most governmental (but not military) powers to Sihanouk in November 1953, and in July 1954 they agreed to withdraw from Cambodia, Vietnam and Laos. Over the next sixteen years, Sihanouk's independent regime oversaw the destruction of most of Cambodia's domestic opposition movements. He would be overthrown in 1970 only from within his royal government, which broke apart under the impact of the escalating war in neighboring Vietnam.

Sihanouk dealt a blow to his anti-colonial rivals in the 1955 elections stipulated by the Geneva agreement to end the Indochina War. In contrast to Ngo Dinh Diem of South Vietnam, Sihanouk agreed to hold internationally supervised elections in Cambodia. But the agreement had assigned the UIF no regroupment zone in Cambodia, unlike the communists in Vietnam and Laos. The UIF and KPRP had to put down their arms and contest the elections or, if they feared Sihanouk's repression, depart the country altogether. A thousand Khmer Issaraks left Cambodia for North Vietnam, including Son Ngoc Minh, Chan Samay, Sieu Heng, Keo Moni, So Phim, more than 500 other KPRP members, about 330 UIF fighters, a dozen women, 8 ethnic Thais, an ethnic Cham leader and 4 of the Paris-trained former PCF members.[20] After several months, Sieu Heng and So Phim returned to Cambodia on foot to join Tou Samouth in a KPRP "temporary" Central Committee. Phim was instrumental in disarming the Issarak forces in his Eastern Zone: A militia member recalled that Phim "collected all the guns we had and put them away."[21]

---

18 Anderson, *Imagined Communities*, 127, 104.
19 Ben Kiernan, "Myth, Nationalism, and Genocide," *Journal of Genocide Research* 3, 2 (2001), 197–201.
20 Kiernan, *How Pol Pot*, 154–55; Kiernan, *Pol Pot Regime*, 69; Thomas Engelbert and Christopher E. Goscha, *Falling out of Touch: A Study on Vietnamese Communist Policy Towards an Emerging Cambodian Communist Movement, 1930–1975* (Clayton: Centre of Southeast Asian Studies, Monash Asia Institute, Monash University, 1995), 46–47.
21 Kiernan, *How Pol Pot*, 154–55, 152.

Perhaps 200 others – led by 2 onetime ICP members, the UIF's former Southwest Zone chief Non Suon and the head of the KPRP's Phnom Penh branch Keo Meas – formed a legal party, the Krom Pracheachon (Citizens Group) to contest the elections, alongside the Democrats and a few Thanhists. But during the campaign Sihanouk's Sangkum Party mobilized state power, closing down opposition newspapers, firing upon and jailing opposition candidates and killing six Pracheachon workers. In the election there were significant allegations of vote-rigging, and the Sangkum took all ninety-one seats in the National Assembly, although on the basis of the voting Sihanouk later described as "red" or "pink" thirty-nine of the country's hundred or so districts. The last Thanhists retreated to the forest, and the Democratic Party dissolved itself in 1957 after its leaders were beaten up near a military barracks.

Only the leftist Pracheachon remained active above ground. But its members' identities were now known to the authorities, and they were subject to arrest and even assassination, as in the case of Nop Bophann, editor of the newspaper *Pracheachon*, shot dead in a Phnom Penh street in 1959. Meanwhile Tou Samouth, So Phim and Sieu Heng, former head of the UIF in the Northwest Zone, led the underground KPRP members remaining in Cambodia. The KPRP had divided into three groups that for reasons of distance or security had difficulty communicating. With hundreds in exile in North Vietnam, and hundreds of others publicly active, the cadre of KPRP officers able to hold secret party leadership posts in Cambodia was severely reduced.

Worse, in 1955 Sieu Heng, who headed the KPRP's rural committee, made secret contact with Sihanouk's Defense Minister Lon Nol, and began informing on his comrades. Many other KPRP members considered that with the French departure the cause of independence had been won, especially after Cambodia rejected US military bases and, in January 1957, officially adopted a foreign policy of neutrality. Significantly for the peasantry, too, the burdensome colonial taxation had ended; independent Cambodia imposed no income or head tax and now raised revenue from foreign aid and taxing rice exports. Hundreds of KPRP members, including So Phim, went back to their villages and attempted to settle down. In some cases this was not easy, perhaps because of Sieu Heng's betrayal. So Phim and his wife were twice tracked by the authorities and had to move fast to avoid capture before they could finally go home to Prey Veng. In Kompong Thom a young Issarak named Ke Vin (later known as Ke Pauk) was home just a few months before being arrested and jailed for three years. KPRP rural activism almost ceased.

Party membership fell to only 850 in 1957, and as few as 250 active members in 1960.[22] In the 1958 National Assembly elections, four Pracheachon candidates attempted to run for rural seats but government repression blocked them. Keo Meas, who managed to stand in Phnom Penh, was the last non-Sangkum candidate to contest any assembly seat until the Sihanouk regime fell in 1970.

The worst-affected KPRP zone was the Southwest, Son Ngoc Minh's base and site of his headquarters. His 1954 departure for Hanoi with his deputy Chan Samay and other members of the UIF Zone Committee, as well that of leading local military commander Nhem Sun, combined with former Southwest Zone UIF chief Non Suon's move into public life as a Pracheachon leader, meant that the local underground KPRP was deprived of senior leaders to run the zone. This depletion of the Southwest Zone leadership differed from the situation in the Northwest, whose military commander, former ICP member Muol Sambath, remained in place, and in the Eastern Zone, whose leader Keo Moni had regrouped to Hanoi, but his deputy Ney Sarann (alias Achar Sieng, who had joined the ICP in 1950) had returned to Cambodia with So Phim.

With Sieu Heng's defection, the KPRP's urban committee led by Tou Samouth became the de facto body running the underground party throughout the country. But as an urban committee it too was weakened. Samouth spent much time traveling in the countryside and conducting training in base areas, especially along the Vietnamese border. Keo Meas, former head of the KPRP's Phnom Penh branch, was now a public figure. He was not only too exposed to help run an underground party; he was also vulnerable to suggestions that he could not be trusted with secret information in case he were to be arrested.

The KPRP, a party of predominantly rural origin, was now susceptible to a takeover by a relatively small new group that was both more at home in the unfamiliar urban conditions and capable of gaining the encouragement of a large external communist power.

After his ten-month spell in the UIF zone in 1953–54, Saloth Sar worked with the Democratic Party's election campaign and also helped establish the Pracheachon Group. Twenty years later, awaiting execution in a Pol Pot prison, former UIF and Pracheachon leader Non Suon wrote in his "confession" that at that time he had often seen Saloth Sar "at Keo Meas's place." Sar "wore a white short-sleeved shirt, and drove a black Citroen 15, but I did not know his name then and did not ask Keo Meas."[23]

22 Engelbert and Goscha, *Falling*, 56.   23 Kiernan, *How Pol Pot*, 157.

Meas's role as secretary of the KPRP's Phnom Penh branch was now filled by Long Rith (later known as Nuon Chea, Pol Pot's number two). Born in Battambang, Rith had studied law at Thammasat University in Bangkok in the 1940s and worked as a clerk at Thailand's Foreign Ministry, secretly joining the Communist Party of Thailand. He returned to Cambodia's north-west around 1948 and transferred his membership to the ICP, and then in 1951 to the KPRP. He became a member of the UIF's Northwest Zone Committee under Sieu Heng and Muol Sambath, responsible for economics. But Long Rith's foreign education and urban experience also resembled those of Pol Pot and the other Paris-educated Khmer members of the PCF more than the Buddhist education and rural experience of the vast majority of KPRP members. Rith now moved to Phnom Penh and took over the capital's KPRP branch. "In order to deceive the enemy," Non Suon wrote in his "confession" about Long Rith in the late 1950s, "he worked in business." Around 1958, Rith passed the job of secretary of the Phnom Penh Party branch on to Saloth Sar, who later stated that this also put him "in charge of liaison with the countryside." In 1954 Sar had brought former Battambang student Ping Thuok (later known as Vorn Vet) into the KPRP, and he now appointed him to the Phnom Penh party committee, with responsibility for "workers and the city population." Long Rith/Nuon Chea and Saloth Sar/ Pol Pot were delegating party authority as each in turn moved up the KPRP ladder.[24]

Ieng Sary and Son Sen joined them in Phnom Penh in 1956–57 when they returned from Paris. Like Saloth Sar, they took up government-paid teaching posts, as did other French-educated radicals. The Sihanouk regime not only valued their academic credentials but hoped to buy them off with well-paid positions and opportunities for corruption in government service. In many cases (though not all), this succeeded. But, by contrast, no such offers were made to the grassroots rural leftists who had fought for Cambodia's inde-pendence. They faced continuing repression under Sihanouk's regime, while ironically it was these same veteran communists who most valued his foreign policy of independence and neutrality, which the younger generation tended to dismiss, seeing Sihanouk's regime as corrupt and feudal. They were ready to start their own revolution. That required a revolutionary party, foreign backing and a new insurgency.

After the open defection of Sieu Heng in 1959, the KPRP secretly convened for its Second Congress in a back room at Phnom Penh's railway station

---

24 Ibid., 157, 181.

in September 1960. The meeting changed the party's name to Workers' Party of Kampuchea (WPK), following the example of the Vietnam Workers' Party and claiming equal status. It also produced a new party Central Committee. Tou Samouth became secretary-general, but Nuon Chea gained promotion to deputy secretary-general, and Saloth Sar became number three in the party hierarchy and a member of the small Standing Committee. The rest of the WPK Central Committee included Mar Mang, Ieng Sary, Keo Meas, Son Ngoc Minh (absent in Hanoi) and So Phim.

Four observations may be made about this new Central Committee ranking. First is the sudden rise of two French-educated former PCF members, Saloth Sar and Ieng Sary, who now occupied positions three and five in the party hierarchy. Second, they had achieved this rise through the Phnom Penh KPRP branch, run first by Nuon Chea, educated in Bangkok and a former Communist Party of Thailand and ICP member, and then by Saloth Sar himself. Third, apart from Tou Samouth, the three other former ICP and founding KPRP members, Keo Meas, Son Ngoc Minh and So Phim, were all ranked at the bottom of the list of the eight members of the new Central Committee. As Keo Meas and Son Ngoc Minh were now unable to play much of a role in the party's secret deliberations, this left only So Phim, ranked number four in the 1954 Central Committee yet now demoted to number eight, three ranks behind Ieng Sary, who had been in Paris from 1950 until 1957. This might seem astonishing but for the close links forged in Paris between Ieng Sary, Saloth Sar and their future wives. Sar had married Khieu Ponnary, a sister of Sary's wife Khieu Thirith, in Phnom Penh on Bastille Day 1956. Finally, suddenly appearing in the number four position in the party hierarchy was Mar Mang, a cadre from the Southwest Zone whose name and aliases (Pang and Nhim) are not evident in records of the pre-1954 independence struggle.[25] The post-1954 depletion of the top KPRP leadership of the Southwest Zone enabled a new central leadership to dig deep there, select a new regional leader and promote him in the national hierarchy. By contrast,

---

25 I first mentioned Mang in this role as "Moong," citing a Vietnamese source (B. Kiernan, "Origins of Khmer Communism," *Southeast Asian Affairs* [1981], 177). My source had described him as a French-educated teacher. In 2004 Steve Heder, citing a 2001 interview with Mang's son Sou Met, former air force commander in the Pol Pot regime, asserted that Mang had been an "ex-ICP cadre" (Heder, *Cambodian Communism*, 84). Sou Met died in 2013 while under investigation for crimes against humanity by the UN-supported Extraordinary Chambers in the Courts of Cambodia. For more on Mar Mang, see "Planning the Past: The Forced Confessions of Hu Nim," in David P. Chandler, Ben Kiernan and Chanthou Boua (eds.), *Pol Pot Plans the Future: Confidential Leadership Documents from Democratic Kampuchea, 1976–1977* (New Haven: Yale Southeast Asia Studies, 1988), Document VIII, 248–49.

two senior cadres from the Southwest, Prasith, an ethnic Thai ICP and KPRP veteran, and Non Suon, gained only alternate or probationary membership of the Central Committee (ranks numbers 9 and ten), a demotion for both.

Few of the veteran, rural, ex-Buddhist KPRP leaders remained at the WPK helm. Tou Samouth now headed a Standing Committee that was largely a product of its relatively new, foreign tertiary-educated Phnom Penh branch. Yet the bulk of party members in the rural areas were veterans of a national independence struggle that had emerged from a Buddhist education and wartime destabilization of their village environment.

Of course we are talking here only about the party in Cambodia itself. By 1960 the Khmer Issaraks residing in North Vietnam had completed courses in Vietnamese and were playing roles in the Vietnamese and Asian communist worlds similar to those played by European communists in the early USSR. Son Ngoc Minh and Chan Samay, both Khmer Krom and therefore Vietnamese citizens, gained positions in the Vietnamese government. Others worked with the Lao and Thai communists. More than 100 Khmers graduated as military officers and became instructors in the Vietnam People's Army. About fifty completed several years' study in China; one worked at Beijing Radio's foreign broadcast service. By 1970, some 822 of these 1,000 Khmers gained admission to the party.

However, that party was changing fast. Sihanouk's favoritism for French-educated intellectuals had enabled them, including Saloth Sar's Phnom Penh group, to move freely about Cambodia and extend their influence, while government repression of the grassroots KPRP veterans allowed Sar's group to strengthen its grip on the underground party. In 1958 Sihanouk sponsored one of the most promising French-educated Ph.D. graduates, the Marxist agrarian economist Hou Yuon, as a Sangkum candidate for a seat in the National Assembly in his home province of Kompong Cham. Hou Yuon accepted the safe seat and became minister of commerce and industry after the election. Another Marxist, Hu Nim, also gained a seat in Kompong Cham and became an undersecretary of state. In the June 1962 elections, both men stood again with Sihanouk's backing, as did Khieu Samphan, a Marxist economist who had returned from Paris in 1959 and was now offered a seat in Kandal province. All three gained cabinet posts.

The KPRP faced yet more repression. In late 1961, with Tou Samouth's backing, the Pracheachon Group had begun preparations to run election candidates as in 1958. Sihanouk would not allow it. In January 1962, police arrested Non Suon and fourteen other Pracheachon members, sentencing them to death, later commuted to life imprisonment. The editor of

Pracheachon newspaper, Chou Chet, was also arrested, with a colleague. Each received a year in jail, and their paper was closed down. Tou Samouth rolled with the punches. His instructions to party members after a secret visit to Vietnam revealed the value that both Hanoi and the KPRP placed on Sihanouk's neutrality, despite his sporadic domestic repression: "In the upcoming elections there is no need for us to present candidates, since the results of these elections are known in advance." Moreover, "the solid implantation of Sihanouk's party on Cambodian soil" had to be recognized. However, Samouth went on, eventual communist victories in Vietnam and Laos would lead "immediately" to victory in Cambodia. "Our cadres and people should thus arm themselves with a little patience. For the moment they should remain relatively discreet . . . Our interest, therefore, is to make the confidence of the young intellectuals who sympathize with our move-ment, who have been successful in introducing themselves into the Sangkum." Samouth held to the policy of a united front with Sihanouk's regime.[26]

Then, in July 1962, Lon Nol's police arrested Tou Samouth near his safe house in Phnom Penh, dragged him off and assassinated him. The possibil-ities include a police swoop based on ex-party informant Sieu Heng's provision of 1950s information on Samouth's likely whereabouts (which probably happened, but may not have led the police to him); or an internal party source such as Saloth Sar, Ieng Sary or Nuon Chea allowing police to obtain the current information. Circumstantial evidence suggests the latter.[27]

Saloth Sar now became acting secretary-general of the party. Nuon Chea remained deputy secretary-general. They called a two-day Third Party Congress in February 1963 to confirm their positions, appoint a new Central Committee and take the party in a new direction. This produced a five-person Standing Committee: Saloth Sar, Nuon Chea, Ieng Sary, So Phim and Vorn Vet. With Keo Meas dropped from the Central

26 Kiernan, *How Pol Pot*, 196.
27 Ieng Sary revealed his hostility to Tou Samouth in 1974 when he distributed a new, edited version of the party history, based on a 1973 text published by So Phim's Eastern Zone. All six favorable references to Tou Samouth from the 1973 text were deleted in Ieng Sary's 1974 edited version. (See the relevant parts of the two texts side by side in Kiernan, *How Pol Pot*, 364–67.) In 1978 the Pol Pot regime went further and published hostile statements about Tou Samouth in the first edition of its *Black Book*, but then, perhaps realizing these implied its involvement in his 1962 murder, quickly deleted them in the more widely distributed second edition. That coverup itself was revealing enough. For more details suggesting CPK involvement in the murder, see ibid., 241, n. 135. As yet unexplained, too, is Lon Nol's 1969 statement that Tou Samouth remained "President of the clandestine Khmer Communist Party" (*Le Sangkum* [Nov. 1969]).

Committee and Son Ngoc Minh demoted, So Phim was now the only grass-roots rural KPRP leader in the top five. According to one participant, Phim stood against Sar for the party leadership and was defeated "not by a vote but by opinion." He regained his number four party ranking but was isolated on the new expanded Standing Committee. Phim was its sole member without experience in the Phnom Penh party committee. He was also the only one of the five holding a specific geographic responsibility, as party secretary of the Eastern Zone, his rural base where he would continue to spend most of his time. The other four members, the urban party leadership henceforth known as the party "Center" (*mocchim*), were now in control of the Standing Committee of a rural party.[28]

The other members of the Central Committee, in ranking order, were now Mang, Prasith (both from the Southwest Zone), Muol Sambath (Northwest), Mok (Southwest), Phuong (East), Son Sen (Phnom Penh) and Son Ngoc Minh (still in Hanoi). Pracheachon leaders Keo Meas and Non Suon were dropped altogether, while former students now occupied positions 1, 2, 3, 5 and 11. After the Phnom Penh Party branch, the Southwest Zone was most favored, holding positions 6, 7 and 9, in contrast to the Northwest (8) and East (4, 10). The new addition from the Southwest, Chhit Chhoeun alias Mok, had come to the notice of the French in 1949 as a tax-levying Issarak district commander in Takeo province, and was recalled locally as someone who "would kill ordinary people." The Center was now digging deeper for protégés in the Southwest, which in the years to come would become "the zone of 'Pol Pot-ism' *par excellence*."[29]

The party's new direction became clear within months. In May 1963, Saloth Sar and Ieng Sary disappeared from their teaching posts in Phnom Penh and moved to the border area of Kompong Cham province. Son Sen went underground in the capital, following them a year later, as did Nuon Chea. Khieu Ponnary, Khieu Thirith and Son Sen's wife Yun Yat joined their husbands in the forest in September 1965. This new foreign-educated leadership now had their revolutionary party, and they were preparing to launch an armed insurgency. In early 1965, the Third Plenum of the CPK Standing Committee passed a resolution stating: "To struggle against imperialism it is absolutely necessary to use revolutionary violence; that is one must use armed forces to win victory."[30] But the CPK Center also sought an external sponsor.

28 David P. Chandler, *Brother Number One: A Political Biography of Pol Pot* (Boulder: Westview, 1992), 80.
29 Michael Vickery, *Cambodia 1975–1982* (Boston: South End, 1984), 86.
30 Engelbert and Goscha, *Falling*, 64–66.

Chinese Backing

Saloth Sar set out on the journey up the Ho Chi Minh Trail to Hanoi, where he spent nine months, and then went on to Beijing for four months.[31] In Hanoi Sar had extensive meetings with Vietnam Workers' Party (VWP) leaders, and in June 1965 he shared with them "The Kampuchean Party Platform." This document asserted that "The Kampuchean revolution must have two forms of struggle," peaceful and "nonpeaceful," and it outlined Sar's view that Cambodia's class struggle pitted the rural areas against the cities, prefiguring the anti-urban policy to be pursued in 1975: "85% of the population lives in the countryside. There are sharp contradictions between the peasants on the one hand and landlords and feudalists on the other. Whenever there is a struggle for land reform, then, at that time, the massive force of the countryside becomes the great force of a revolution. The countryside plays an important role militarily . . . the national revolution is a revolution of the peasants." On the other hand, "The cities are the concentrated areas, the nerve-centre of the ruling class and the imperialists. Thus, the cities are the places where the revolutionary enemies can concentrate great power to suppress the revolution." VWP secretary Le Duan urged Sar not to provoke Sihanouk by armed rebellion, which might cause the Cambodian ruler to abandon his neutral foreign policy. Duan told Sar that, under Sihanouk, "Kampuchea is at the frontline in opposing American imperialism . . . In Kampuchea, we will go with Sihanouk."[32]

Sar's visit to China proved a turning point. There are several reasons why Beijing might have extended Sar the ideological backing he sought. The CCP's well-known distinction between "state-to-state" and "party-to-party" relations would have allowed it to justify fostering close relations with Sihanouk's communist opponents even while the Beijing government strongly supported Sihanouk's government. Second, in the 1950s Beijing had published its expansive territorial claims over the South China Sea, clearly impacting Vietnam, and China also encouraged Cambodia to dispute Vietnamese offshore territory: In 1960 Zhou Enlai had suggested to Sihanouk that Cambodia claim the undisputed Vietnamese island of Phu Quoc.[33] Finally, in this period Beijing was fostering the rise of breakaway anti-Soviet, pro-China communist parties around the globe, especially in

---

31 Chandler, *Brother Number One*, 73–78; cf. Kiernan, *How Pol Pot*, 219–24.
32 Engelbert and Goscha, *Falling*, 137, 146, 150–51.
33 See "A Map of China Published in 1954" (in Chinese), in *Kampuchea Dossier II* (Hanoi: Vietnam Courier, 1978), plate section; Norodom Sihanouk, *Souvenirs doux et amers* (Paris: Hachette, 1981), 311.

Southeast Asia where only the Vietnamese and Lao communist parties proved resistant. In 1965–66 it is highly likely that Beijing would have offered ideological backing to a visiting new Cambodian communist leader and encouraged him to distance his party from that of the Vietnamese.[34]

We may never know what happened during Saloth Sar's visit to China, partly because he never publicly admitted it occurred.[35] The party's later assertion in a "Lesson on the History of the Kampuchean Revolutionary Movement" that it took "secrecy as the basis" of its revolution seems to confirm that the visit was very important.[36] Reflecting on this period in 1978, the Pol Pot regime asserted: "In 1966, the Communist Party of Kampuchea ... clearly discerned the true nature of the Vietnamese." Moreover, "as early as 1966," the party *judged* that it could have only state-to-state and other public relations with Vietnam, for there was a fundamental contradiction between the Kampuchean revolution and the Vietnamese revolution."[37] The wording suggests that this judgement was unconveyed to the Vietnamese party.

Insurgency

In Cambodia in early 1966, the underground WPK adopted a new aggressive propaganda line against Sihanouk's regime, attacking him as "a secret agent of the United States." That September, Sar and the other WPK leaders again changed the party's name to the Communist Party of Kampuchea (CPK). This moved the Cambodians above the ideological level of the Vietnamese, on a par with the Chinese party. In another indication of the 1966 turning point, CPK Politburo member Vorn Vet looked back on this era in his 1978 "confession" in the last days of the Pol Pot regime. In early 1966, he wrote, "the Party raised the line of struggling for strength in the towns, and *preparing for armed struggle in the countryside.*" But there was disagreement within the party, at least from the senior surviving KPRP veteran. Vet continued: "In mid-1966 So Phim came from the base [and] raised with me the question

---

34 Kiernan, *How Pol Pot*, 220–23; see also Chandler, *Brother Number One*, 75–77, and Heder, *Cambodian Communism*, 92–100.

35 Sar's visit to China is excised from both *Livre Noir: faits et preuves des actes d'agression et d'annexion du Vietnam contre le Kampuchea* (Phnom Penh: Département de la presse et de l'information du Ministère des affaires étrangères du Kampuchea Démocratique, 1978), 38–39, and *Black Paper: Facts and Evidences of the Acts of Aggression and Annexation of Vietnam Against Kampuchea* (Phnom Penh: Department of Press and Information of the Ministry of Foreign Affairs of Democratic Kampuchea, 1978), 26.

36 Kiernan and Boua, *Pol Pot Plans the Future*, Document VII, 220.

37 *Livre Noir*, 33, 42 (emphasis added).

of the armed struggle – it had to be resisted [he said], the people did not want to spill blood."[38]

With population growth, rural debt and concentration of land ownership, Cambodia's agrarian problems were rising, but the vast majority of its rural population remained landowning peasants (unlike in neighboring South Vietnam or Thailand). From 1962, when 6 percent of farming families were landless tenants or sharecroppers, the figure would reach 20 percent by 1970.[39] But outside this growing poor peasant class, most Cambodian peasants were far from destitute or ready to rebel. Saloth Sar's vision of raging class conflict between peasants and landlords was a fantasy. In November 1964 Hou Yuon, the independent Marxist economist in the National Assembly who had served in the cabinet, published a book urging an alliance between socialists and the Sihanouk regime. He wrote that Sihanouk's 1963–64 economic reforms "have given a new lease of life for national capitalism to progress cleanly in the interests of the nation and the people," while bringing "bright new changes for the farmers and the workers."[40] The Cambodian economy was indeed improving.[41]

But in 1965 the economy suffered a major blow when US escalation of the war in Vietnam led to major rice shortages there and to massive smuggling of Cambodian rice across the border, depriving Sihanouk's government of two-thirds of its annual revenue in 1966.[42] At the same time the government responded to the CPK underground's new aggressive propaganda by increasing its repression of dissent in the rural areas in mid 1966, just as the CPK was preparing to launch its insurgency. The assembly elections of September 1966 brought General Lon Nol into government as prime minister, although Hou Yuon, now opposed by Sihanouk and shunned by the CPK underground, was reelected with 78 percent of the vote in his rural constituency. (Hu Nim and Khieu Samphan, secretly supported by the CPK, won smaller majorities.) Lon Nol's new government quickly set about rounding up the rice harvest and purchasing it from peasants at fixed low prices, which raised rural resentment.

The CPK-instigated insurgency against the Sihanouk regime, provoked in part by the Lon Nol government, began in early 1967. It continued in fits and

---

38 Vorn Vet's confession, S-21 prison, Dec. 1978, 54-page typescript, at p. 20 (emphasis added), Tuol Sleng Museum of Genocide, Phnom Penh (copy in author's possession).
39 Kiernan, "Introduction," in Kiernan and Boua (eds.), *Peasants and Politics in Kampuchea*, 4.
40 Hou Yuon, *Pahnyaha Sahakor* [The Cooperative Question] (Phnom Penh, 1964), 2, 3.
41 Kiernan, *How Pol Pot*, 208.
42 Rémy Prud'homme, *L'économie du Cambodge* (Paris: PUF, 1969), 255, Table 12, note a.

starts for the next three years. The 1967 revolt was most successful in the Northwest, North and Eastern Zones, but met defeat in the second half of the year and failed to get off the ground in the CPK Center strongholds of the Southwest and Northeast Zones. The Center relaunched the insurgency in January 1968, but this time So Phim's Eastern Zone proved recalcitrant, joining in as late as August and mounting only a limited military campaign. By 1969–70, the Center's strategy for a nationwide "people's war" had stalled, while the insurgency in the East had proven the most effective branch of the party organization due to its political entrenchment in that zone, military restraint and support from the Vietnamese communists.

In July 1969 the Center decided that they needed to win Sihanouk over, after all. But now at least they had not only acquired control of the top levels of the party and won foreign backing for their struggle, but they also had their own small insurgent force, by 1970 perhaps 3,000–5,000 guerrillas nationwide. And, for reasons unrelated to the CPK insurgency, the Sihanouk regime was about to fall, creating the chaos that offered the CPK its path to power.

The Impact on Cambodia of the US Escalation in Vietnam

Vietnamese communists increasingly resorted to Cambodian territory for sanctuary from American attack. At the end of 1965, US intelligence reported that they had established "probably temporary" bases there, sometimes clashing with Cambodian border forces. US fighter planes pursued them, shelling and strafing inside Cambodia, conducting 2,565 sorties and firing 214 tons of ordnance across the border from 1965 to 1968.[43] In 1966 Cambodia's Prince Norindeth protested this US bombardment of Cambodia, claiming that "hundreds of our people have already died in these attacks."[44]

Finally, in the year commencing 18 March 1969, the US Air Force flew more than 3,600 secret B-52 raids over Cambodian territory.[45] They dropped about 100,000 tons of bombs; the civilian toll is unknown. The goal was to destroy the Vietnamese communist forces in Cambodia or drive them back into Vietnam. But in September 1969, Lon Nol reported an *increase* in communist troops in the sanctuaries, which he said was partly "motivated by the cleaning-up operation" of the US–Saigon forces. He added that

43 Taylor Owen and Ben Kiernan, "Bombs over Cambodia," *Walrus* (Oct. 2006), 67.
44 *Australian* (15 Jan. 1966).
45 William Shawcross, *Sideshow: Kissinger, Nixon and the Destruction of Cambodia* (New York: Simon & Schuster, 1979), 27.

"nothing suggests that these foreign units will soon leave our territory."[46] Like the bankrupt budget resulting from the smuggling of Cambodian rice into South Vietnam, this proved the second major issue in Sihanouk's overthrow at Lon Nol's hands on 18 March 1970, precisely a year after the B-52 campaign began. Both factors were exacerbated by the US escalation of the Vietnam War.

The Second Indochina War

Lon Nol's coup, conducted in Sihanouk's absence on 18 March 1970, ended Cambodia's neutrality. It precipitated near-simultaneous March–April invasions by both Vietnamese armies in the civil war. President Richard Nixon's May–June ground invasion of Cambodia then created 130,000 Khmer refugees.[47] US aerial bombardments escalated. US intelligence discovered that many "training camps" on which Lon Nol's forces had requested air strikes "were in fact merely political indoctrination sessions held in village halls and pagodas." Lon Nol intelligence itself noted that "aerial bombardments against the villagers have caused civilian loss on a large scale," and that the peasant survivors of the US bombing were turning to the CPK for support.[48] But on 9 December 1970, after a conversation with Nixon, Henry Kissinger called General Alexander Haig to relay his new orders. "He [Nixon] wants a massive bombing campaign in Cambodia ... Anything that flies on anything that moves."[49] By 1971, 60 percent of refugees surveyed in Cambodia's towns gave US bombing as the main cause of their displacement.[50] The bombardment of the countryside continued until August 1973, when Congress imposed a halt. Nearly half of the 540,000 tons of US bombs dropped on Cambodia fell in six months from February to August 1973.[51]

From March 1970 the CPK insurgents (known as "Khmer Rouge") profited greatly from Sihanouk's newfound political support, mainly in radio broadcasts into Cambodia from his Beijing exile; from an influx into their

---

46 Kiernan, *How Pol Pot*, 286.
47 Seymour M. Hersh, *The Price of Power: Henry Kissinger in the Nixon White House* (New York: Summit Books, 1983), 202.
48 "Cambodia: Can the Vietnamese Communists Export Insurgency?," Research Study, Bureau of Intelligence and Research, US Department of State (25 Sep. 1970), 4, 6.
49 Owen and Kiernan, "Bombs over Cambodia," 66.
50 George C. Hildebrand and Gareth Porter, *Cambodia: Starvation and Revolution* (New York: Monthly Review Press, 1976), 109, n. 83.
51 Ben Kiernan, "The American Bombardment of Kampuchea, 1969–1973," *Vietnam Generation* 1, 1 (1989), 4–41.

insurgency of his loyalists in Cambodia; and from new military aid and training support from the Vietnamese communist forces; but also from the Cambodian popular reaction to the escalated US (and South Vietnamese) bombings. The CPK used the bombardments' devastation and massacre of rural civilians as recruitment propaganda, and as an excuse for their own brutal, radical policies and cover for their purges of more moderate communists and their marginalization of newly recruited Sihanoukists.

In the early years of the war, Sihanoukists, moderates and pro-Vietnamese communists still predominated in a regionalized even if not factionalized insurgency. The CPK Center ruled at the national level but admitted it still needed to "get a tight grasp, filter into every corner."[52] Before defeating Lon Nol's Khmer Republic (1970–75), it needed to eclipse its revolutionary rivals and allies. The war's destruction of much of Cambodian rural life helped. For instance, it provided cover for the systematic murders of nearly a thousand Khmer communists, half the party's membership, who had returned from North Vietnam in 1970–71 to join the struggle in Cambodia. One by one, CPK security squads called them to "meetings" and quietly killed them in the forest. Only a few dozen remained in North Vietnam or managed to defect to the Lon Nol regime or escape into South Vietnamese territory.[53]

The CPK was able to find new recruits. In 1970 a combined US aerial and tank attack in Kompong Cham province took the lives of 200 people. When another raid killed seven people nearby, a local peasant recalled, "some people ran away . . . others joined the revolution." One young Khmer joined the communists a few days after an aerial attack took the lives of fifty people in his village. After Chalong village lost more than twenty dead, an inhabitant said: "Many monasteries were destroyed by bombs. People in our village were furious with the Americans; they did not know why the Americans had bombed them. Seventy people from Chalong joined the fight against Lon Nol after the bombing." Anlong Trea was napalmed and bombed, killing three people. Sixty villagers joined the Khmer Communists "out of anger at the bombing," locals recalled.[54]

In 1973 the United States withdrew from Vietnam, but switched its air arm to Cambodia. The Secretary of the air force later said that Nixon "wanted to send a hundred more B-52's. This was appalling. You couldn't even figure out

52 Kiernan, *How Pol Pot*, 323.
53 See e.g., Georges Boudarel, "La Terreur au Cambodge: la liquidation des communistes cambodgiens formés au Vietnam (*Tap ket*)," in Boudarel and Hémery (eds.), "Indochine: première guerre entre états communistes," 5–7.
54 Kiernan, *How Pol Pot*, 350, 353.

where you were going to put them all."[55] In March 1973, the bombardment spread west across the country. Around Phnom Penh, 3,000 civilians were killed in three weeks, with "dozens of villages . . . destroyed and as much as half their population killed or maimed." As the bombardment intensified, it reached 3,600 tons per day.[56]

The CPK's recruitment highlighted the destruction. The CIA's Directorate of Operations, after investigations in the Southwest, reported on 2 May 1973: *"They are using damage caused by B-52 strikes as the main theme of their propaganda.* The cadre tell the people that the Government of Lon Nol has requested the airstrikes and is responsible for the damage and the 'suffering of innocent villagers' . . . The only way to stop 'the massive destruction of the country' is to . . . defeat Lon Nol and stop the bombing. This approach has resulted in the successful recruitment of a number of young men . . . Residents . . . say that *the propaganda campaign has been effective* with refugees and in areas . . . which have been subject to B-52 strikes."[57] A report for the US Army in July 1973 stated that "the civilian population fears US air attacks far more than they do Communist rocket attacks or scorched-earth tactics."[58]

In July and August 1973 the Southwest Zone was carpet-bombed in the most intensive B-52 campaign yet. Its political impact was to tip the uneasy CPK factional balance in the Southwest in favor of Pol Pot's Center. After Mang, Southwest Zone CPK secretary, died in 1968, Mok had succeeded him even though his deputy Prasith outranked Mok on the Central Committee. In 1973–74, with the Center's assistance, Mok purged four of the other five members of the Southwest Zone Committee. The Center summoned Prasith to a meeting in January 1974; its forces ambushed and murdered him. Mok's son-in-law became chief of a new Southwest Zone Brigade, and Mok's relatives filled many other zone positions.[59]

The divisions within the CPK soon became known. In a 1974 cable, Henry Kissinger pointed out that, in areas such as southwest Cambodia, the Khmer communists "not only had little training abroad but probably resent and compete with the better-trained men from North Vietnam." "The Khmer communists, such as Saloth Sar," Kissinger said, "are probably

---

55 Shawcross, *Sideshow*, 218–19.
56 *Boston Globe* (1 Apr. 1973); *Christian Science Monitor* (5 Apr. 1973).
57 "Efforts of Khmer Insurgents to Exploit for Propaganda Purposes Damage Done by Airstrikes in Kandal Province," CIA Intelligence Information Cable, 2 May 1973 (emphasis added).
58 "Effectiveness of US Bombing in Cambodia," US Army document, 21 Aug. 1973, 2.
59 Kiernan, *Pol Pot Regime*, 68, 87–88, 104–05; unless otherwise noted, sources for the remainder of this chapter may be found in that work.

xenophobic ... when it comes to Vietnamese." Yet Kissinger was unsure if the Cambodian insurgency was "regional" and "factionalized" with only "a veneer of central control," or whether "the real power" lay with Sar's central presidium.[60] If the former had still been true in 1972, the latter was largely the case by 1974.

US bombing killed 100,000–150,000 Cambodian civilians from 1969 to 1973. In that period, CPK forces grew from about 5,000 to more than 200,000 troops and militia. CPK cadres told peasant victims of the bombing that "the killing birds" had come "from Phnom Penh" and that Phnom Penh must pay for its assault on rural Cambodia. This echoed Saloth Sar's 1965 denunciation of Cambodia's cities. The day the bombing ended, CPK propaganda leaflets found in bomb craters attacked the "Phnom Penh warriors" who were, they vowed, soon to be defeated.[61] Cambodian popular outrage at the US bombing, manipulated by the CPK, proved fatal both for moderate Khmer communists and for Lon Nol's doomed regime, but even more for the 2 million inhabitants of Phnom Penh.

Democratic Kampuchea

After its armies marched into the capital on 17 April 1975, the victorious CPK regime labeled the conquered city dwellers "new people" (*neak thmei*). Driven from the capital in all directions, they were forcibly settled among the rural "base people" (*neak moultanh*) who had lived in the countryside under Khmer Rouge control during the 1970–75 war. They were put to work in agricultural labor camps without wages, rights or leisure time. Before the rice harvest in late 1975, the CPK again rounded up 800,000 of the urban deportees in various regions and dispatched them to the Northwest Zone, doubling its population. Tens of thousands died of starvation during 1976, while the new regime, which adopted the name Democratic Kampuchea (DK), began exporting rice. Meanwhile, it hunted down, rounded up and killed thousands of defeated Khmer Republic officials, army officers and, increasingly, soldiers, schoolteachers and alleged "pacification agents" (*santec sampoan*) who in most cases had merely protested the repression or just the rigorous living conditions imposed on them. In 1976–77, the CPK Center and its security apparatus, the Santebal, also conducted massive purges of the

---

60 "Emergence of Khmer Insurgent Leader Khieu Samphan on the International Scene," cable from Secretary of State to US Embassy, Phnom Penh, Apr. 1974.
61 US Army, Intelligence Information Report, "Bomb Damage Assessment, Cambodia," No. 2 725 1716 73, 22 Aug, 1973, 2.

Northern and Northwest Zone CPK administrations, arresting and killing large numbers of peasant "base people" related to the purged local officials. Starvation and repression escalated in 1977 and especially in 1978. By 1979, approximately 650,000 or one-quarter of the Khmer new people, and 675,000 Khmer base people (15 percent), had perished from execution, starvation, overwork, disease and denial of medical care.

The CPK began its rule with about 14,000 party members in 1975. The party Standing Committee still comprised Saloth Sar, Nuon Chea, Ieng Sary, So Phim and Vorn Vet. But according to two reports in 1975–76, Son Sen had been promoted to number 4, above Phim, reinforcing the dominance of the Paris-trained group. At any rate, from September 1975 to May 1976, So Phim attended none of the fourteen Standing Committee meetings for which records are extant, and then he was absent receiving medical care in China from May to August 1976. In March 1976 the government of Democratic Kampuchea announced its first cabinet. Pol Pot, using that name for the first time and concealing his real identity, became DK's prime minister, with three deputy prime ministers: Ieng Sary (foreign affairs), Vorn Vet (economy) and Son Sen (defense). When Pol Pot briefly stepped down as prime minister later in the year, Nuon Chea took his place. The power of the CPK Center was clear. Pol Pot's brief return to the shadows in 1976 signaled major secret purges of party veterans, who were now arrested, tortured and killed: Keo Meas, Non Suon, Ney Sarann, Keo Moni, Hou Yuon, Hu Nim and hundreds of others. Most were sent to the Santebal's secret "S-21" prison and forced to "confess" to having been lifelong agents of the CIA, the KGB, the Vietnamese communists or all three. Eventually Mok's Southwest Zone troops and Ke Pauk's northern troops spread out across the country and purged Muol Sambath's Northwest Zone CPK branch, Chou Chet's Western Zone and So Phim's Eastern Zone. Chet himself was arrested in March 1978, followed by Sambath in June.

The severe repression of the majority Khmer rural population and purges of the CPK and its regional administrations paralleled escalating waves of intense violence against Cambodia's ethnic minorities, even among the base people. Over half of the ethnic Chinese, a quarter of a million people, perished in the countryside in 1975–79, the worst disaster to befall the ethnic Chinese community of Southeast Asia. In 1975 the CPK expelled more than 100,000 Vietnamese residents from Cambodia and ferociously repressed a Cham Muslim rebellion on the Mekong River. Pol Pot then ordered the deportation of 150,000 Chams living on the east bank of the Mekong and their forced dispersal throughout the Northern and Northwest Zones.

In November 1975, a CPK official in the Eastern Zone complained to Pol Pot of his inability to implement "the dispersal strategy according to the decision that you, Brother, had discussed with us." Officials in the Northern Zone, he complained, "absolutely refused to accept Islamic people," preferring "only pure Khmer people."[62] In a message to Pol Pot two months later, Northern Zone leader Ke Pauk listed "enemies" such as "Islamic people."[63] Deportations of Chams began again in 1976, and by early 1979 approximately 100,000 of the country's Cham population of 250,000 in 1975 had been killed or worked to death. The 10,000 or more Vietnamese residents remaining in the country were all hunted down and murdered in 1977 and 1978. Other ethnic minorities, including the Khmer Krom, Thai and Lao, were also subjected to genocidal persecution. In all, about 1.7 million Cambodians died during the DK period from April 1975 to January 1979.

The 1975 Cham revolt, and an uprising in the Northern Zone in 1977, were followed in 1978 by a more serious rebellion in the Eastern Zone. From late 1976, the DK regime accelerated its violent internal purges of the Cambodian regional administrations. Between them, the Santebal, Mok's and Pauk's troops, and the CPK Center's armed forces subjected all five regions of the Eastern Zone to concerted large-scale arrests and massacres of local CPK officials and soldiers. So Phim's loyal ranks were purged from under him; he was unable to resist, and in May 1978 he was ambushed and committed suicide. The crescendo of repression provoked a mutiny by units of his remaining Eastern Zone armed forces. The rebels, led by Heng Samrin and Chea Sim, fought back against the Center, Southwest and Northern Zone troops.[64] They held out for several months before retreating across the Vietnamese border with thousands of civilians and requesting aid. Since early 1977, Phnom Penh had mounted many crossborder attacks on Vietnam, and Hanoi was ready to intervene. On 25 December 1978, 150,000 Vietnamese troops launched a multipronged assault. Phnom Penh fell on 7 January 1979. The Khmer Rouge fled to the Thai border, where they received assistance from Thailand, China and the United States. Most Cambodians welcomed the end of the genocide. The People's Republic of Kampuchea was established, led by Heng Samrin, Chea Sim and Hun Sen,

62 "To Comrade Brother Pol with Respect," signed Chhon, 30 Nov. 1975, Documentation Center of Cambodia, Phnom Penh, No001045 (01 bbk).
63 "To Brother Pol with Respect," signed "Comrade Pauk," 4 Feb. 1976, Documentation Center of Cambodia, Doc. No. No001187 (02 bbk).
64 On this Eastern Zone rebellion, see Ben Kiernan, *Genocide and Resistance in Southeast Asia* (New Brunswick, NJ: Transaction, 2008), chs. 1–2.

who became prime minister in 1985 and remained in power in 2017. Vietnamese troops withdrew in 1989.

Ideology

What drove the genocide? The phenomenon is notable for its explosive combination of totalitarian political ambition and a racialist project of ethnic purification.[65] Despite important Stalinist and Maoist influences, Democratic Kampuchea, unlike the communist regimes of the USSR, China and Vietnam, never established "autonomous zones" for its national minorities. After September 1975, DK even refused public recognition of Cambodia's specific minorities and asserted that they totaled a nominal 1 percent of the population rather than their actual 15–20 percent.[66] DK was the only communist regime systematically to disperse its minorities by force and to make punishable by death the use of minority and foreign languages. DK distinguished itself even from its Stalinist predecessors, Mao's China and Enver Hoxha's Albania. Those states also repressed religion and subjugated minority cultures. But China, which supplied DK with the military equipment that enabled the genocide, at least formally established its own minority "autonomous zones." Albania, home to 60,000 Greeks in what was otherwise "one of the most ethnically homogeneous populations in the world," enforced atheism, purged Christian names and removed crosses from graves, but formally recognized its Greek minority's existence and published a tightly controlled Greek-language periodical.[67] Only North Korea pursued no minority policy but, unlike other communist states, it had (apart from a small Chinese community) almost no ethnic minorities.[68] A close ally of DK, North Korea may have provided Pol Pot a model of ethnic as well as ideological purity, a view that disregarded Korea's distinct ethnic near-homogeneity. Yet even North Korea never attacked all its neighbors in a single year, as DK did in 1977, and Pyongyang has shown little interest in irredentism over the Korean-speaking border region in China, in contrast to the way DK allied with China to strengthen its hand in attacking Vietnam to "reconquer" the

---

65 See e.g. Ben Kiernan, "Le communisme racial des Khmers rouges. Un génocide et son négationnisme: le cas du Cambodge," *Esprit* 252 (May 1999), 93–127.

66 *Democratic Kampuchea Is Moving Forward* (Phnom Penh, Aug. 1977), 6.

67 Elez Biberaj, *Albania: A Socialist Maverick* (Boulder: Westview Press, 1990), 5, 89, 98–99, 95–96; R. Zickel et al., *Albania* (Washington, DC: Federal Research Division, 1994), 68–69.

68 Frederica M. Bunge (ed.), *North Korea: A Country Study* (Washington, DC: US Government Printing Office, 1981), 56.

long-lost Mekong delta, "Kampuchea Krom."[69] If the CPK attempted to reverse two centuries of territorial history, it also dismissed material facts in its economic program, setting production targets, for instance, without data on existing productivity.[70]

Racialist, territorial and ideological strands all intertwined in a tapestry of tragedy. On the one hand, the CPK labeled all Muslim Chams, though from a variety of social classes, as petit-bourgeois "whose lives are not so difficult." It considered Chams the only nationality with no "laborer" class. This clear-cut racial stereotype disguised as class discrimination served a policy of targeted ethnic repression. Conversely, the CPK often justified the liquidation of majority-Khmer political opponents or potential dissidents by a slogan with strong racialist overtones, in the name of wiping out those with "Khmer bodies and Vietnamese minds." The tragedy was twofold. In absolute numbers, most of DK's victims were from the Khmer majority, but the ethnic minorities suffered in severe disproportion. Political repression and genocide reinforced one another to exact a unique toll in the history of communist regimes: More than a fifth of a nation's population perished in less than four years.

Such a domestic catastrophe could have had only severe foreign-policy implications: in this case, the "detonation" of a massive explosion that dynamited Cambodia's relations with neighboring Vietnam and shattered any hope in a communist future.

Bibliographical Essay

The accessible primary sources for the history of the Communist Party of Kampuchea and the Democratic Kampuchea regime are probably richer than the sources for most other communist parties and regimes, given that the CPK not only was overthrown within four years of coming to power but also became the subject of a United Nations-backed criminal tribunal. Many of its records were preserved by the successor regime or have since come to light.

Other confidential CPK documents came into the hands of its opponents before its 1975 victory. Timothy Carney, a US State Department official in

---

69 Ben Kiernan, *Blood and Soil: A World History of Genocide and Extermination from Sparta to Darfur* (New Haven: Yale University Press, 2007), 552–54.
70 See Document II and "Introduction," in Kiernan and Boua (eds.), *Pol Pot Plans the Future*, 12. On Khmer Rouge anti-materialist ideology, see Ben Kiernan, "Kampuchea and Stalinism," in Colin Mackerras and Nick Knight (eds.), *Marxism in Asia* (London: Croom Helm, 1985), 232–49; and Kiernan, *Blood and Soil*, ch. 15, esp. 550–51.

Cambodia during Lon Nol's Khmer Republic, published the CPK's "Short Guide for Application of Party Statutes," along with 1972–73 eyewitness accounts written by a well-informed defector from the CPK zones, in his collection *Communist Party Power in Kampuchea (Cambodia): Documents and Discussion* (Ithaca: Cornell Southeast Asia Program, 1977). Carney also published the 1973 "Summary of Annotated Party History," by the Eastern Zone CPK branch, along with three post-1975 DK documents, in *Cambodia 1975–1978: Rendezvous with Death*, edited by Karl D. Jackson (Princeton: Princeton University Press, 1989). I juxtaposed the 1973 text with Ieng Sary's truncated 1974 version in my *How Pol Pot Came to Power: Colonialism, Nationalism and Communism in Cambodia, 1930–1975* (London: Verso, 1985; New Haven: Yale University Press, 2004), 364–67.

The 1965 exchange of documents in Hanoi between the Vietnamese and Cambodian communists appears in three appendices of Thomas Engelbert and Christopher E. Goscha, *Falling out of Touch: A Study on Vietnamese Communist Policy Towards an Emerging Cambodian Communist Movement, 1930–1975* (Clayton, Australia: Centre of Southeast Asian Studies, Monash Asia Institute, Monash University, 1995). These discussions are also mentioned in the 1978 DK publications, *Livre Noir. Faits et preuves des actes d'agression et d'annexion du Vietnam contre le Kampuchea* (Phnom Penh: Département de la presse et de l'information du Ministère des affaires étrangères du Kampuchea Démocratique, 1978), and the slightly different *Black Paper: Facts and Evidences of the Acts of Aggression and Annexation of Vietnam Against Kampuchea* (Phnom Penh: Department of Press and Information of the Ministry of Foreign Affairs of Democratic Kampuchea, 1978).

The Cambodian Genocide Program at Yale University published a series of online English translations of DK documents, including "The Khmer Rouge National Army Order of Battle: January 1976" (gsp.yale.edu/khmer-rouge-national-army-order-battle-january-1976); "The Pol Pot Files, 1975–1977" (gsp.yale.edu/pol-pot-files-1975–1977); "The Son Sen Files, 1976–1977" (gsp.yale.edu/son-sen-files-1976–1977); and "Ieng Sary's Regime: A Diary of the Khmer Rouge Foreign Ministry, 1976–79" (gsp.yale.edu/ieng-sarys-regime-diary-khmer-rouge-foreign-ministry-1976–79). Eight more DK texts in translation may be found in David P. Chandler, Ben Kiernan and Chanthou Boua (eds.), *Pol Pot Plans the Future: Confidential Leadership Documents from Democratic Kampuchea, 1976–1977* (New Haven: Yale Southeast Asia Studies, 1988). Tables outlining the CPK's political and military chain of command can be found in Ben Kiernan (ed.), *Genocide and Democracy in Cambodia* (New Haven: Yale Southeast Asia Studies, 1993), 14–15.

The August 1979 Phnom Penh trial in absentia of Pol Pot and Ieng Sary, while legally invalid, provided much valuable documentary and testimonial information. The documentation, including CPK meeting minutes and victim statements, is collected in *Genocide in Cambodia: Documents from the Trial of Pol Pot and Ieng Sary*, edited by Howard J. De Nike, John Quigley and Kenneth J. Robinson, with the assistance of Helen Jarvis and Nereida Cross (Philadelphia: University of Pennsylvania Press, 2000). Since 2006, the Extraordinary Chambers in the Courts of Cambodia have tried a number of cases of crimes against humanity and genocide. The ECCC website is a rich source of legal and historical information on the DK era: www.eccc.gov.kh.

6

Human Rights and Communism

MARK PHILIP BRADLEY

The relationship between human rights and communism in both theory and practice has often been in tension. In the ideational realm, Karl Marx famously dismissed the rights of man as a bourgeois fantasy that masked the systemic inequality of the capitalist system. "None of the supposed rights of man," Marx wrote, "go beyond the egoistic man, man as he is, as a member of civil society ... withdrawn into himself, wholly preoccupied with his private interest and acting in accordance with his private caprice."[1] Rights and liberties in bourgeois society, he argued, provided only an illusory unity behind which social conflict and inequalities deepened. Rhetorically, the Soviet Union, the People's Republic of China and most of the rest of the communist world followed Marx's lead. As the Chinese argued in 1961, "the 'human rights' referred to by bourgeois international law and the 'human rights' it intends to protect are the rights of the bourgeoisie to enslave and to oppress the labouring people ... [and] provide pretexts for imperialist opposition to socialist and nationalist countries. They are reactionary from head to toe."[2] Rejecting Enlightenment-era inalienable individual political and civil rights, communist states instead championed collective economic and social rights. The Soviets grew fond of annually celebrating International Human Rights Day, to mark the anniversary of the 1948 adoption of the UN Universal Declaration of Human Rights, by offering lectures to its citizens that contrasted the promotion of socialist rights in the Soviet Union with their violations in the capitalist world.

And yet state-orchestrated mass killings and what have come to be called gross violations of human rights were at times almost commonplace in

---

1 Karl Marx, "On the Jewish Question" (1843), in *The Marx and Engels Reader*, ed. Robert C. Tucker (New York: Norton & Co., 1979), 43.
2 Marina Svensson, *Debating Human Rights in China: A Conceptual and Political History* (Lanham, MD: Rowman and Littlefield, 2002), 233.

communist-led states. Between 1933 and 1945, more than a million people died in the Soviet Gulag system and likely at least 6 million more in politically induced Soviet famines, Stalin's mass executions in the great terror and in what Timothy Snyder has termed the "bloodlands" of Poland, the Baltic states, Ukraine, Belarus and the western edges of Russia. In Mao's China, as many as 45 million Chinese died of famine during the Great Leap Forward, while some 2.5 million were killed or tortured to death. During the Cultural Revolution, between 750,000 and 1.5 million were killed. In Pol Pot's Cambodia, 200,000 were executed and between 1.4 million and 2.2 million of the country's 7 million people died of disease and starvation. If the precise numbers have always been, and continue to be, in dispute, their order of magnitude is not.[3]

In fact the entanglements between human rights and communism in the twentieth century were more ambiguous than the chasm between ideology and these staggering numbers would suggest. The meanings of human rights themselves remained unstable over much of the second half of the century, as did the actors in the communist world who engaged with them. What promises of global human rights like those contained in the Universal Declaration might portend and the very claims about what constituted human rights were not fixed. Nor was the significance of human rights for the making of international politics or local lives as they were lived on the ground at all clear. The relationship between human rights and international communism after 1945 remained fluid. In the immediate postwar period, the Soviet Union played an active role in the creation of a global human rights order through the drafting of the Universal Declaration and the Genocide Convention and participating in the Nuremberg Trials. With the coming of decolonization, the Soviets and the Chinese would also help to open out the meanings of international human rights toward the rights to postcolonial self-determination and development. But human rights in the communist world largely became a polemical state posture within the broader Cold War ideological struggle. Indeed, the international project of human rights itself became a muted practice by the 1950s.

3 On these numbers, see Timothy Snyder, *Bloodlands: Europe Between Hitler and Stalin* (New York: Basic Books, 2010); Frank Dikotter, *Mao's Great Famine: The History of China's Most Devastating Catastrophe, 1958–1962* (New York: Walker Books, 2010); Roderick MacFarquhar and Michael Schoenhals, *Mao's Last Revolution* (Cambridge, MA: Harvard University Press, 2006), 262; and Cambodia Genocide Program, Yale University, www.yale.edu/cgp/.

The presence of human rights in global politics shifted dramatically beginning in the 1970s. It was not so much states, communist or otherwise, that contributed to this transnational explosion of human rights but nonstate actors, among them dissidents in the Soviet Union and Eastern Europe. Importantly, their engagement with human rights operated at multiple levels. At home the growing deployment of human rights sometimes bore considerable traces of a socialist past, suggesting that the turn to a global language of human rights in the 1970s remained enmeshed in other political and moral vocabularies. For their part, Eurocommunists created new contradictions within the communist world over the decade by using the language of human rights in their pleas to Moscow for freedom of expression for dissidents. On the global stage, the writings of Soviet and East European dissidents were appropriated and often reshaped in Western Europe, the United States and the global South, becoming a critical vehicle for articulating new understandings of what the protection of human rights could mean. This global florescence of human rights talk was not so much a Cold War project nor, as some scholars have argued, did human rights in the form of the 1975 Helsinki Accords bring an end to the Cold War. But the transnational circulations of socialist rights talk and local appropriations of it ultimately shaped the form and content of human rights as it became the dominant moral language of the late twentieth century.

The immediate post-World War II moment of the mid to late 1940s brought an unprecedented international effort to articulate transnational human rights norms. The Universal Declaration of Human Rights was the most dramatic instantiation of these new human rights concerns. The thirty articles making up the declaration were hammered out over a period of two years. The final document sought to protect not only individual civil and political rights, but economic and social rights as well. The rights to life, liberty and freedom of expression and religion along with freedom of movement and freedom from slavery and torture were articulated as international rather than solely national guarantees. The declaration's enumeration of economic and social rights was especially striking as it linked postwar global security with individual rights to an adequate standard of living, to work and equal pay, to education and to cultural wellbeing. Its sweeping guarantees of their protections were as expansive as its catalog of rights. "Everyone is entitled to all the rights and freedoms set forth in the Declaration," the authors promised, "without distinction of any kind."[4] Along with the Universal Declaration, 1940s human rights norm-making at the United Nations centered on a convention to outlaw genocide, a global freedom of information covenant, protective rights of asylum for refugees and the stateless and the drafting of legally binding guarantees of the political, economic and social rights enshrined in the declaration. Meanwhile, the International Military Tribunal (IMT) at Nuremberg, established to try alleged Nazi war criminals, began to develop new conceptions of universal justice.

Almost every member state of the United Nations voted in favor of adoption of the Universal Declaration of Human Rights when it came before the General Assembly on 10 December 1948. Only a handful abstained. The Soviet Union was one of them. The Soviets had been deeply engaged throughout the drafting of the declaration, sometimes shaping key provisions. The Soviet delegation, for instance, pushed strongly for inclusive and protective language regarding women's rights. The original preamble to the declaration referenced only men, prompting vocal objections from Hansa Mehta of the Indian delegation. Eleanor Roosevelt, who chaired the drafting committee, thought the issue was of no consequence. Intervening in this debate between the only two women members of the drafting committee, the Soviet delegation strongly supported the gender-neutral language "[a]ll human beings are born free and equal in dignity and rights" that became article 1 of the Declaration. The Soviet position on women reflected its own constitutional protections for the equality of men and women. As early as 1919, Lenin contrasted the idea of liberty in "the capitalist bourgeois republics" with what he termed "the disgustingly filthy coarse laws in which woman is treated as an inferior being," drawing particular attention to "laws dealing with marriage rights and divorce."[5] The Soviet Family Law Code accorded gender equality to divorce and strengthened child-support systems. In the drafting of the Universal Declaration, the Soviets successfully pushed against British and American objections to the right to equal pay for equal work (article 25) and to French and Saudi objections to the equal rights of men and women in marriage (article 16.1). The delegation was similarly vocal in drafting language to prohibit racial discrimination and to promote national self-determination. But they also fought against other provisions of the declaration, including articles guaranteeing freedom of expression and

4 Article 2, United Nations Universal Declaration of Human Rights, 10 Dec. 1948, www.un.org/en/documents/udhr/.
5 V. I. Lenin, "Soviet Power and the Status of Women," in *Collected Works*, vol. XXX (4th English edn., Moscow: Progress Publishers, 1965), 120–23.

the right to asylum. At the root of its broader unease with the declaration was Soviet insistence that states were the ultimate guarantors of individual and collective rights, an argument that shaped its public rationale to abstain in the final voting on adoption.

Abstention, however, was not straight-out opposition and reflected a broader Soviet concern with the promotion of international human rights as a form of public diplomacy. The Soviets played a more significant role at the Nuremberg trials than historians have sometimes acknowledged. As Francine Hirsch has recently argued, "the Soviet Union made significant contributions to the legal framework of the IMT and also to a new postwar vision of international law" by offering entirely novel theories about aggressive war, criminal responsibility, complicity and collective guilt. It was Soviet legal experts, for instance, who first invented the new international legal norm "crimes against the peace," which became central to the Nuremberg prosecutions. Ironically, Soviet eagerness to take the Nazis to trial, not initially shared by the Americans or the British, rested on their belief in the efficacy of political show trials. Indeed, Stalin appointed Andrei Vyshinskii, who had led the Soviet show trials of the late 1930s, to oversee planning for the IMT. Soviet prosecutors at Nuremberg were drawn from Vyshinskii's domestic team. The Soviet Union hoped to use the trials to craft a narrative of German fascist war guilt and to make a case for postwar reparations. But unlike the show trials at home, the Soviets could not control the testimony given at Nuremberg. Forced to deal with German evidence of Nazi–Soviet complicity in the early years of the war and of Soviet culpability in the Katyn forest massacres, in which more than 4,000 Polish military officers were killed in mass executions, the trials became an embarrassment for the Soviets.[6]

If the Soviet Union did not always do human rights diplomacy well, its anti-fascist sensibilities at Nuremberg carried over into its support and ratification of the Genocide Convention in 1948. Predictably perhaps, given the Stalinist state's own culpability in millions dying of political purges, the Soviets objected to including political groups in the convention and insisted that only proof of eliminationist intent could trigger its provisions. But on these issues the Soviets were not so different substantively in their positions than other big and small state powers at the UN. Similarly, Soviet opposition to provisions for an international court to make determinations of genocide

---

6 Francine Hirsch, "The Soviets at Nuremberg: International Law, Propaganda, and the Making of the Postwar Order," *American Historical Review* 113, 3 (Jun. 2008), 703.

was shared by other major powers. At the same time the Soviets did advocate more progressive positions on what constituted genocide than other powers. Despite its own very substantial record of ethnic cleansing, the Soviet Union insisted, for instance, that cultural genocide be a part of the convention's prohibitions. With the Genocide Convention in place in 1948, the Soviets also began to take an active role in UN negotiations to turn the Universal Declaration into a binding international covenant, playing an instrumental part in drafting and promoting what became provisions guaranteeing the right to work that would anchor the International Covenant on Economic and Social Rights.

Negotiations over the covenant would prove to be the last gasp of 1940s-era human rights norm-making. Human rights as they were championed in the immediate postwar period largely became a sideshow for international relations in the 1950s and 1960s. Escalating Cold War tensions between the Soviets and the Americans partly explain the decline, but so too does the global rupture of decolonization. The West European powers in particular, largely with the support of the United States, were keen to establish a firewall between colonialism and human rights, and ever vigilant to ensure that collective national self-determination did not become a part of the global human rights instruments of the 1940s. In the decolonizing global South, however, an alternative human rights discourse was beginning to take shape that would come to its fullest power in the UN General Assembly with the passage of the Declaration on the Granting of Independence to Colonial Countries and Peoples (1960) and the Declaration and Convention on the Elimination of All Forms of Racial Discrimination (1963, 1965), and in a growing transnational movement to oppose apartheid in South Africa. The Soviet Union lent its active support to these initiatives inside and outside the United Nations.

It did so increasingly in competition with the People's Republic of China (PRC). The PRC actively courted the support of newly postcolonial states, most notably at the Bandung conference of 1955, and later of the Non-Aligned Movement around questions of political and economic self-determination. The PRC attacked apartheid in South Africa as early as the 1950s and offered solidarity to the African-American struggle for civil and political rights. The competition between the Chinese and the Soviets over rights questions in the postcolonial world contributed to the increasingly public Sino-Soviet split that would divide the communist world after 1960. As the Sino-Soviet dispute deepened, China was also critical of Soviet oppression toward minorities, women and dissidents. Just as they were in the Soviet Union and for Marx, the PRC officially viewed human rights in their Enlightenment incarnation as without relevance to Chinese socialist society. A brief exception was the Hundred Flowers movement launched in 1956, through which Mao encouraged intellectuals – party members and nonparty people alike – to voice their concerns about the leadership and policies of the communist party. Some intellectuals, along with workers and minorities, spoke out in speeches, wall posters and essays that at times employed the language of human rights or *renquan*, one first popularized in China during the May Fourth era. A few went so far as to call for a bill of human rights to protect people's rights around political and civil rights. The Hundred Flowers movement was extremely short-lived. An anti-rightist campaign launched in the summer of 1957 rounded up more than half a million critics of the regime. Only in the late 1970s would the vocabulary of human rights begin to return to Chinese domestic politics.

Socialist advocacy for collective economic and social rights and the championing of postcolonial revolution and self-determination persisted in the international sphere in the 1970s. The Soviet Union and its East European allies ratified the Covenants on Civil and Political Rights and on Economic and Social Rights (1966) years before many of the Western powers did so (Bulgaria 1970; Yugoslavia 1971; Soviet Union, East Germany, Belarus and Ukraine 1973; Hungary and Romania 1974; Czechoslovakia 1975 – and by contrast UK 1976; Italy 1978; France 1980; Greece 1997; and the United States 1992, but only the Covenant on Civil and Political Rights). But the more dramatic and transformative human rights developments of the 1970s came at the nonstate rather than state level. Simply put, the decade of the 1970s brought an explosion of global nonstate human rights advocacy. Hundreds of local groups around the globe took up the banner of human rights, increasingly enmeshed in transnational networks of advocacy and information politics. The growth of Amnesty International is illustrative. It reported only 32,000 members worldwide in 1973. By 1980, the organization counted hundreds of thousands of members in 134 countries, including the Soviet Union, and a Nobel Peace Prize among its accomplishments.

The novel presence of transnational human rights politics and other forms of global social mobilizations in the 1970s simultaneously reflected and contributed to what was a profound shift in world order. On one level, the state-based political and economic structures that had formed the post-World War II international order began to come undone. While Soviet–American

Cold War tensions endured in the 1970s, notably in Indochina, but also helping to launch a new round of deadly proxy wars in such places as Angola, Afghanistan and Nicaragua, the forces of neoliberal globalization began to transform the contours and dynamics of world politics. An intensification of global capitalism, new patterns of international migration, the end of empire and the transnational diffusion of new technology and media all pushed against the nation-state-based international order that structured the high Cold War era. But, just as importantly, the rise of new affective bonds between the individual, the state and the world community, ones fashioned by the growing authority of moral witness in framing conceptions of suffering and injustice, started to reshape the kinds of political claims made in the international sphere. These transformations in world structure and affect deeply shaped transnational human rights politics in the 1970s and beyond.

In this, elements of civil society within the Soviet Union and Eastern Europe were central to almost entirely reshaping dominant understandings of human rights thought and practice on a world scale. The relationship between Soviet and East European dissidents and human rights has frequently been misunderstood. Too often the dissident embrace of global human rights talk is rendered as a transformative break in their own domestic oppositional practices or a simple causative force bringing about an end to the Cold War. In fact the political and moral lines that entangled dissent and rights were more complex. At the same time, a host of human rights actors in the West and some in the global South appropriated the languages of Soviet and East European dissidents for their own purposes to ultimately refashion human rights as the dominant moral language of the late twentieth century.

In what is sometimes termed the first nonstate human rights action in the Soviet Union, a crowd gathered on the evening of 6 December 1965 in Moscow's Pushkin Square, just a mile from the Kremlin, to protest the recent arrest of the writers Andrei Siniavskii and Yulii Daniel for the spread of anti-Soviet propaganda. Siniavskii, a prominent member of the Union of Soviet Writers, began to write novellas depicting a menacing and surreal Stalinist state during the cultural Thaw under Nikita Khrushchev. Although Daniel had a more muted public reputation before his arrest, he had also published several satirical novels about contemporary Soviet society. The mathematician and nonconformist poet Aleksandr Volpin, twice confined to psychiatric hospitals for writing "anti-Soviet poems" in the Stalinist era, organized the protest. He did so very deliberately on Soviet

Constitution Day, the state holiday honoring what was known as the Stalin Constitution of 1936, arguing that obedience to "Soviet legality" legitimated the protest and required a public trial to claim the civil liberties of Soviet citizens had been violated by the state. The crowd of 250 protestors and approving bystanders carried banners that read "We Demand an Open Trial for Siniavskii and Daniel" and "Respect the Soviet Constitution." The KGB quickly dispersed the protesters, confiscated the placards and detained some of the participants, including Volpin, for questioning. The harsh sentences ultimately imposed on the two writers at their trials sparked further protests, which continued over the next three years in what became a cycle of new arrests of dissidents, trials and renewed protest by dissident rights defenders.[7]

The failure of the Soviet state to respond to the strategy of socialist legality, according to what has been the dominant narrative of the emergence of a human rights movement in the Soviet Union, pushed activists toward the global language of human rights and the potential leverage of world opinion to make their case. In the late 1960s a group of activists founded the Initiative Group for the Defense of Human Rights, which sent letters to the United Nation Commission on Human Rights about rights violations in the Soviet Union. Another group began to publish the samizdat periodical *Chronicle of Current Events*, which quoted on each of its cover pages article 19 of the Universal Declaration promising that "Everyone has the right to freedom of opinion; this right includes freedom of opinion without interference and to seek, receive and impart information and ideas through any media and regardless of frontiers." In November 1970, a group of scientists formed the Committee on Human Rights, which encouraged what would become hundreds of letters and petitions from individuals to Soviet authorities about human rights violations. A Moscow section of Amnesty International was formed in 1973, linking Soviet activists to more transnational networks of human rights advocacy.

Most dramatically in this narrative of the transformational deployment of human rights by dissidents in the Soviet Union is the landmark Helsinki Final Agreement of 1975. Signed by the Soviet Union, the

7 Benjamin Nathans, "The Dictatorship of Reason: Aleksandr Vol'pin and the Idea of Rights Under 'Developed Socialism,'" *Slavic Review* 66, 4 (Winter 2007), 653–58; Joshua Rubenstein, *Soviet Dissidents: Their Struggle for Human Rights* (Boston: Beacon Press, 1985), 30–42; Ludmilla Alexeyeva, *Soviet Dissent: Contemporary Movements for National, Religious, and Human Rights* (Middletown, CT: Wesleyan University Press, 1985), 274–77 (quotes 275, 276).

United States, Canada and states in Western and Eastern Europe, the agreement in the moment was best known for its normalization of post-World War II borders in Europe, essentially legitimating Soviet control of Eastern Europe, to the delight of Soviet leader Leonid Brezhnev. But Helsinki also promised "respect for human rights and fundamental freedoms" within those borders, and included promises for cooperation of humanitarian contacts and the free flow of information. The human rights dimensions of the agreement largely rested on pressures from West European states. Neither the Soviets nor the Americans anticipated their subsequent force and power but acquiesced to them out of a broader desire to promote détente. Soviet dissidents seized on Helsinki, becoming a part of what became a global nonstate network of Helsinki Watch groups that put pressure on the Soviets and Soviet-bloc governments in Eastern Europe for human rights violations. The physicist Andrei Sakharov, a founding member of Moscow Helsinki Watch along with the earlier Committee on Human Rights, who would win the Nobel Peace Prize in 1975 as a spokesperson for what the Nobel committee termed the "conscience of mankind," quickly became the public face of the new human rights advocacy in the Soviet Union.

This new concern for human rights or the "Helsinki effect," some scholars have argued, ultimately undermined one-party communist rule and played a role in the collapse of communism in Eastern Europe in 1989 and the dissolution of the Soviet Union. In the view of its strongest proponents, Helsinki and human rights brought an end to the Cold War. They did not, nor is a Cold War framework essential for understanding what human rights were doing in the liminal moment of the 1970s. The apparent shift from a local vernacular of socialist civil rights law to the new language of global human rights by Soviet activists was not so much a rupture as an extension of an already existing dissident repertoire of thought and action. The term "human rights" was often used interchangeably with "civil rights" by leaders of the new Soviet human rights groups in the 1970s. The influential *Chronicle of Current Events*, for instance, was concerned with both socialist legality and the language of international human rights covenants and conventions. As the Soviet historian Ben Nathans writes, "the local and global dimensions of human rights activism were mutually constitutive." At no point in the Soviet Union, he argues, was "there a repudiation of, or a break with, civil rights or citizen-based strategies . . . to contain the power of the state." International "human rights became an additional method for achieving the same purpose – from outside as well as below."[8]

Indeed, socialist vernaculars mediated how global human rights talk was appropriated and transformed in the Soviet Union. Nathans suggests that the disenchantment of dissidents with the Soviet state, one that began during the period of de-Stalinization in the 1950s, was never accompanied by a full rejection of socialism as a "system of coordinated, equalitarian public welfare." Socialism as an ideology continued to inform the thought and practice of Soviet dissident human rights activists, and the emphasis on transnational solidarities in Soviet official thought may have shaped the initial inclination of dissidents to embrace a global language of human rights. For example, in setting up the Moscow section of Amnesty International in 1973, its local organizers sent the following message to Amnesty representatives in London:

> Since childhood we have been accustomed to hearing such phrases as "political action of the masses," "the active foreign policy of the government and party," the "struggle for social rights and the social reconstruction of society," "the scientific and technical revolution" – and these are the things we imagined the world was preoccupied with. As for words like "conscience," "dignity," "conviction" – we are accustomed to apply them exclusively to the exertions and strivings of individual human beings. For who can help one to value such words, and to preserve their value, other than oneself and those to whom one is closest? At first were we astonished, and could not grasp, that in fact total strangers can help people who live in the most distant countries in conditions utterly different from one's own, in other cultures. It is this above all that we value in your example and your activity.[9]

The global language of human rights that activists ascribed to Amnesty, Nathans argues, "represented not so much a new morality as a new way of deploying familiar, in fact intimately familiar moral ideas." Human rights did not so much displace socialism for dissident rights advocates in the Soviet Union as become entangled with it.[10]

---

8 Benjamin Nathans, "The Disenchantment of Socialism: Soviet Dissidents, Human Rights and the New Global Morality," in Jan Eckel and Samuel Moyn (eds.), *The Breakthrough: Human Rights in the 1970s* (Philadelphia: University of Pennsylvania Press, 2013), 42, 43.
9 Groupa-73, Moscow, to Amnesty International 6th International Council, Vienna, 15 Sep. 1973, cited and translated in Nathans, "Soviet Dissidents," 41.
10 Ibid., 41–42.

The rise of "Eurocommunism" among some European communists in the second half of the 1970s offered another reformulation of socialist thought that put pressure on the Soviet Union's attitude toward dissent and its position in the communist world. Led by the Italian Communist Party, Eurocommunists proposed a "third way" between social democracy and Soviet socialism and embraced the idea of a Western socialism based on pluralistic democratic principles. For the Soviets, this centrifugal movement was anathema. Tensions within the communist world rose further when at a June 1976 conference of European communist parties in Berlin, Eurocommunists referenced the human rights provisions of the Helsinki agreements to criticize Moscow's record on human rights. Increasingly loud criticism by the Italian Communist Party followed on the repression of dissidents in the Soviet Union and Eastern Europe, critiques just as loudly rejected by the Soviets. At a meeting in Moscow in October 1978, the Italian Communist Party's leader Enrico Berlinguer told the Soviets that "limitations on freedom of expression and opinion cause grave damage not to adversaries but to Communists and friends of the Soviet Union . . . You say there are few dissidents . . . and it is for this very reason that they should be allowed to display their opinions openly." To this a visibly agitated Mikhail Suslov, the Communist Party of the Soviet Union's chief ideologue, replied, "What you maintain is incomprehensible . . . we will not allow this – ever." One of Suslov's colleagues added, reinforcing the human rights dynamics of the Sino-Soviet split, "no one says anything about what's going on in China, with its concentration camps and where atrocious crimes have been committed." Later, when Italian Eurocommunists publicly criticized the use of force in Poland in 1981 to put down the Solidarity movement, *Pravda* denounced them as intent on rejecting "the Marxist-Leninist revolutionary platform."[11]

In Western Europe and the United States, the human rights dimensions of dissent came to powerfully shape new conceptions of what human rights were understood to be. Dissidents began to assume an unprecedented prominence on the world stage in the 1970s and became readily identifiable figures to a variety of global publics. The nonconforming dissident was

11 "Meeting Between Delegations of the Communist Parties of Italy and the Soviet Union, Moscow, 7 October 1978," and *Pravda* editorial, 24 Jan. 1982, in Silvio Pons, "Documents: Meetings Between the Italian Communist Party and the Communist Party of the Soviet Union, Moscow and Rome, 1978–1980," *Cold War History* 3, 1 (Oct. 2002), 159, 160, 166.

lionized, and those lifted up in the West tended to be males of "titanic stature," "courage" and "moral grandeur." In a typical representation of the era, an observer wrote in 1973 that "one has an initial duty as a human being to salute them; to salute them for existing, and, by doing that alone, making our world a better and more honourable place."[12] Increasingly seen as courageous defenders of universal moral truths, dissidents became instrumental in the making of a popular Western human rights consciousness in the 1970s. The local meanings of their work and politics became decoupled as their ideas moved across borders. As one scholar has remarked, "the West often thought it was listening in to a conversation that in fact it had staged by choosing and translating the thinkers ... that spoke most closely to its concerns."[13] In these exchanges, a particular view of dissidents began to anchor new ideas about human rights thought and practice outside the Soviet East.

Aleksandr Solzhenitsyn was without question the best-known of the era's dissidents and, as an emblem of the new global concern with human rights, the most controversial. He first became widely known inside and outside the Soviet Union for his novella *One Day in the Life of Ivan Denisovich*, published in the Soviet Union and the West in the early 1960s. The first major imaginative work to critically address the harrowing experiences of imprisonment in the vast network of Stalinist labor camps and prisons that Solzhenitsyn knew intimately from his eight-year sentence served in one of them, it was published with Soviet leader Nikita Khrushchev's permission in the cultural Thaw that was part of his larger de-Stalinization campaign. *Day in the Life* immediately became a world-wide literary sensation, recognized by critics as a "flawless classic" akin to Dostoevsky's *House of the Dead* and "one of the most important [books] that has come out of Russia in many years."[14]

With Khrushchev's fall from power, the Soviet state began to look on Solzhenitsyn with disfavor and launched a campaign of escalating repression against him and other dissidents. The manuscripts for his next two books, *First Circle* and *Cancer Ward*, were smuggled to the West and published in the

---

12 Bernard Levin, "We Must Not Leave It to That Nice Mr. Brezhnev," *Times* (London) (2 Oct. 1973), 16, cited in Robert Horvath, "'The Solzhenitsyn Effect': East European Dissidents and the Demise of Revolutionary Privilege," *Human Rights Quarterly* 29, 4 (Nov. 2007), 880.
13 Jonathan Bolton, *Worlds of Dissent: Charter 77, the Plastic People of the Universe, and Czech Culture Under Communism* (Cambridge, MA: Harvard University Press, 2012), 3.
14 Philip Rahv, "House of the Dead," *New York Review of Books* (1 Feb. 1963).

late 1960s. They also focused on the Soviet prison system Solzhenitsyn knew first-hand to, as one contemporary critic wrote, "compel the human imagination to participate in the agony and murder of millions that have been the distinguishing feature of our age."[15] Together *First Circle* and *Cancer Ward* solidified Solzhenitsyn's reputation as "the greatest living Russian writer," and he was awarded the Nobel Prize for Literature in 1970. In his acceptance speech, which he did not deliver in person, fearing the Soviet authorities would prevent him from returning home, Solzhenitsyn did not shy away from a vigorous critique of the Soviet system. He also drew explicit attention to human rights as a parable for understanding the devastating impact of the Soviet system on its individual victims. Lauding the Universal Declaration of Human Rights as the "best document of the last twenty-five years," he proceeded to chastise the United Nations human rights machinery for ignoring the plight of Soviet citizens, what he termed "the groans, screams and beseechings of humble individual PLAIN PEOPLE," and betraying "those humble people into the will of the governments which they had not chosen."[16]

At home Solzhenitsyn was also increasingly outspoken about the ills of the Soviet regime to the displeasure of the Brezhnev Politburo which banned his writings, had him barred from the Union of Soviet Writers and ordered the KGB to disrupt his work and family life.[17] Less than two months after the publication of Solzhenitsyn's magnum opus, *The Gulag Archipelago*, in Paris and New York in December 1973, based on microfilm of the manuscript smuggled out of the country by an international network of his supporters, Leonid Brezhnev had him arrested and expelled from the Soviet Union in February 1974. The world press breathlessly covered Solzhenitsyn's dramatic arrest and deportation, and after he and his family settled in a small Vermont town in the United States Solzhenitsyn quickly became a significant figure in American domestic Cold War politics. When President Gerald Ford declined to meet Solzhenitsyn at the White House, his challenger in the 1976 contest for the Republican presidential nomination, Ronald Reagan, told reporters Solzhenitsyn "would be welcome to eat dinner anytime at the Reagan White House." Ford and Reagan forces sparred over a "Solzhenitsyn

15 Patricia Blake, "A Diseased Body Politic," *New York Times* (27 Oct. 1978), BR2.
16 Nobel Lecture, www.nobelprize.org/nobel_prizes/literature/laureates/1970/solzhenitsyn-lecture.html.
17 This and the following two paragraphs draw upon Mark Philip Bradley, "American Vernaculars: The United States and the Global Human Rights Imagination," *Diplomatic History* 38, 1 (Jan. 2014), 17–19.

plank" at the Republican convention that turned him into a proxy for the internecine feuds within the Republican Party over the efficacy of détente. Conservative senator Jesse Helms sought to confer honorary citizenship on Solzhenitsyn. Solzhenitsyn's own public speeches in the United States in which he vehemently denounced what he saw as the tragically wrongheaded policies of détente and encouraged the United States to "intervene" in Soviet domestic affairs played into a hawkish Cold War reading of his views. Some American liberals took an increasingly skeptical attitude toward Solzhenitsyn's politics, alienated by his "far-fetched" Slavophile nationalism, put off by his "scorn for democracy" and distrustful of "the willful Russian autocrat in him."[18]

But Solzhenitsyn's great imaginative power, even his harshest critics acknowledged, did considerably more than rehash Cold War polemics. In *Gulag Archipelago*, Solzhenitsyn offered an entirely original lens through which to apprehend violations of individual human rights at a moment when the contours of a new global human rights politics were just coming into view. In part, the content and reception of *Gulag* are essential to understanding Solzhenitsyn's transformative impact on his readers. Over the course of three volumes, he traced the history of the imprisonment, brutalization and murder of tens of millions of Soviet citizens by their own government between 1929 and 1953 in "that amazing country of *Gulag* which, though scattered in an Archipelago geographically was, in the psychological sense, fused into a continent – an almost invisible, almost imperceptible, country." The book relied on eyewitness testimony related to him by more than 200 prisoners, interspersed with his own experiences in the camps and a sweeping account of how he believed Soviet political culture had brought about the destruction of millions of innocent lives.[19] The reception of *The Gulag Archipelago*, which appeared to rapturous reviews, was extraordinary. As one critic claimed, "it is clear that no writer in the world today has been able to explore the compelling experiences of his people as Solzhenitsyn has done or received such an enthusiastic audience."[20]

18 *New York Post*, 12 Apr. 1976; Jesse Helms, "Honorary Citizenship for Solzhenitsyn," *East Europe* 23 (Jul. 1974), 5; "Reagan's Plank Criticizes Ford–Kissinger Policies," *New York Times* (17 Aug. 1976), 1, 48; Arthur Schlesinger, Jr., "The Solzhenitsyn We Refuse to See," *Washington Post* (25 Jun. 1978), D1.
19 Aleksandr I. Solzhenitsyn, *The Gulag Archipelago: An Experiment in Literary Investigation* (New York: Harper & Row, 1973), x, 4–5, 587.
20 Joshua Rubenstein, "The Gulag Archipelago 1918–1956," *New Republic* (22 Jun. 1974), 22.

Even more important than *Gulag*'s subject and vast circulation for an emergent global human rights consciousness in the 1970s was the impact of its form. Holocaust memory hovered over its reception. As one reviewer argued, *Gulag* was an account of "the other great Holocaust of our century." Solzhenitsyn, many critics noted, was "a survivor himself" who sought to "sear" the experience of the Soviet Gulag "into the collective consciousness" by chronicling its "full horror."[21] *Gulag* made the imprisonment, brutalization and murder of Soviet citizens visible in the increasingly familiar testimonial mode of Holocaust survivors. Solzhenitsyn's own subtitle for the project was "An Experiment in Literary Investigation," and his method consciously relied on confronting readers with first-person testimony. He was intent upon viscerally pulling his readers into the narrative, insisting on their engagement with the clear purpose of altering how they saw and felt about an unfamiliar world. *Gulag* opens in this way:

> Down the long crooked path of our lives we happily rushed or unhappily wandered past a variety of walls and fences – rotten wooden palings, clay embankments, brick and concrete walls, iron railings. It never occurred to us to ask what was behind them, or to look or even think about it. But that was where gulag country began, two yards away ... All those gates were prepared for us, every last one! And then a fatal door opened and four white hands, unused to work but tenacious, grabbed us by the leg, arm, collar, cap, ear and dragged us like a sack, and slammed the door to our past life shut forever more. "You're under arrest!" And all you can manage to bleat out is, "M-me? What for?"

Readers might have easily pictured the white hands grabbing them as well. Solzhenitsyn uses this direct approach throughout *Gulag*, asking readers to imagine for themselves the harrowing ordeals he describes: "Reader! Just try – sleep like that for one night! It was five degrees Centigrade in the barracks!" Or: "There were tortures, home-made and primitive. They would crush a hand in the door, and it was all in that vein. (Try it, reader!)"[22] The "I" is omnipresent throughout *Gulag*. For Solzhenitsyn it was rendered with a mix of indignation and pity to craft a self-styled voice of authenticity that challenged and discredited the prevailing strictures of Soviet official

21 *New York Times Book Review* (16 Jun. 1974), 1.
22 Solzhenitsyn, *Gulag*, 4–5; Aleksandr I. Solzhenitsyn, *The Gulag Archipelago Two* (New York: Harper & Row, 1974), 383, 385. My reading of *Gulag* in this and the following paragraph is informed by Susan Richards, "The Gulag Archipelago as 'Literary Document,'" in John B. Dunlop, Richard Stanley Haugh and Michael A. Nicholson (eds.), *Solzhenitsyn in Exile: Critical Essays and Documentary Materials* (Stanford: Hoover Institution Press, 1985), 145–63.

speech. But readers outside the Soviet Union were also drawn into recovering the world of the Gulag with Solzhenitsyn offering them a palpable window into distant suffering and a visceral sense of the fragility of the human condition.

In what has sometimes been termed the "Gulag shock" or the "Solzhenitsyn effect," *Gulag* helped transform Western leftist perspectives on the Soviet Union and enabled new concerns with anti-totalitarianism. For the French New Left, Solzhenitsyn's insistence that repression in the Soviet Union was not an aberration but the very essence of the system provided, as one historian argues, a "nightmarish vision" that underscored the left's rejection of its former embrace of radical revolutionary movements. Emergent notions of human rights were critical to these fundamental political recalibrations, as they appeared rooted in an almost pre-political ethical sphere and promised, as one activist put it, to "resist power without imitating it."[23] Very little of this embrace of dissidents and human rights had discernable connections to the Cold War, but reflected broader intellectual changes in the 1970s. Soviet and East European dissidents were increasingly celebrated in French cultural politics for the qualities the French left believed they shared with them: a hatred of the technocracy, bureaucracy and powerful states, whether bourgeois or communist. These sensibilities would emerge most strongly in the early 1980s in French support for the Solidarity movement in Poland. Beyond France, the historian Samuel Moyn has argued that the new appeal of human rights in the 1970s marked an exhaustion with the major utopias of the twentieth century, whether international communism or radical postcolonial nationalism. The minor utopia of human rights, he suggests, offered a believable kind of anti-politics that appeared to open up a moral grounding for anti-authoritarian democratic activism.

The moral languages of the Soviet physicist and dissident Andrei Sakharov helped shape the contours of these emergent structures of global human rights thought and practice in the 1970s. Sakharov's intellectual odyssey in the late 1960s and early 1970s was instrumental in framing Soviet dissent as part of the emergent vocabulary of human rights and at the same

---

23 Robert Brier, "Beyond the 'Helsinki Effect': East European Dissent and the Western Left in the 'Long 1970s,'" in Poul Villaume, Rasmus Mariager and Helle Porsdam (eds.), *The "Long 1970s": Human Rights, East–West Détente and Transnational Relations* (London: Taylor & Francis, 2015), 777–78; Horvath, "The Solzhenitsyn Effect," 907; and Samuel Moyn, *The Last Utopia: Human Rights in History* (Cambridge, MA: Harvard University Press, 2010), ch. 5.

time remaking broader sensibilities about what human rights meant and the kinds of political work it could do. Sakharov burst onto the world stage in 1968 with the publication of "Thoughts on Progress, Coexistence and Intellectual Freedom," which argued for a "convergence" between what he saw in the socialist and capitalist worlds that transcended the political and social malaise of the West and the East. Its topical focus moved from thermonuclear extinction to ecological catastrophe, famine, uncontrolled population growth and a shared spiritual alienation across the Cold War divide. He discussed the necessity of intellectual freedom and freedom of expression as among the "rights of man" that were central to political community, raised the plight of political prisoners in the Soviet Union and argued that "[a]ll anticonstitutional laws and decrees violating human rights must be abrogated." But Sakharov did not offer human rights as a primary conceptual means for envisioning a better future both at home and in the wider world.[24]

Seven years later, in a speech titled "Peace, Progress, Human Rights" to mark his award of the Nobel Peace Prize in 1975, he did. The shift in emphasis in the title from his 1968 essay "Progress, Coexistence and Intellectual Freedom" was telling. In the years in between, as a founding member of the Committee on Human Rights in 1972, Sakharov began to take a growing interest in the rights of Soviet political prisoners and rights of ethnic and religious minorities. He undertook the first of many hunger strikes in 1974 to draw attention to the plight of political prisoners in Soviet labor camps and prisons. Increasingly, the Cold War and détente were second-order concerns for Sakharov. Pushing for the centrality of rights, reason and moral improvement in his Nobel address, he said:

> We must today fight for every individual person separately against injustice and the violation of human rights. Much of our future depends on this. In struggling to protect human rights we must, I am convinced, first and foremost[,] act as protectors of the innocent victims of regimes installed in various countries, without demanding the destruction or total condemnation of these regimes. We need reform, not revolution. We need a pliant, pluralist, tolerant community, which selectively and tentatively can bring about a free, undogmatic use of the experiences of all social systems.[25]

24 Andrei Sakharov, "Thoughts on Progress, Peaceful Coexistence and Intellectual Freedom," *New York Times* (22 Jul. 1968), 14.
25 Andrei Sakharov, "Peace, Progress, Human Rights," Nobel Lecture, 11 Dec. 1975, www.nobelprize.org/nobel_prizes/peace/laureates/1975/sakharov-lecture.html.

As Sakharov argued in *My Country and the World*, published just as his Nobel Prize was announced, human rights must be defended everywhere to exist anywhere. And, he added, violations of rights in one country threatened those rights in all other countries.[26]

It was Sakharov's capacious rendering of what human rights could mean, and the growing position of global eminence from which he spoke, that helped transform the dissident movement in the Soviet Union and Eastern Europe from a Cold War issue to a human rights cause for a variety of transnational publics. If global publics in the West could begin to better imagine what the visceral particularities of the deprivation of human rights felt like through Solzhenitsyn's more imaginative prose, Sakharov acted as a philosopher and guide through whom human rights began to acquire a global moral power. When President Carter chose to make human rights a central part of American diplomacy in the late 1970s, Carter's unprecedented and well-publicized response to a January 1979 letter from Sakharov urging him to "raise his voice" in support of human rights activists in the Soviet Union and Eastern Europe pointed toward Sakharov's transnational moral authority. Carter articulated his administration's "firm commitment to promote respect for human rights not only in our own country but also abroad," protesting to Soviet authorities their arrest of some twenty-seven members of the Moscow Helsinki Committee in 1979 and later their decision to exile Sakharov to Gorkii in 1980.[27] Sakharov's moral authority would extend to influence the Soviet leadership itself in the twilight of the Soviet Union. After Sakharov was released from seven years of internal exile by Mikhail Gorbachev in 1986, his sensibilities about human rights affected the forms of *glasnost'* and later the construction of civil society after the fall of communism.

It was not only in the Soviet Union that human rights operated in the 1970s as a local vernacular in dialogue with other political and moral languages. Somewhat later in the decade when the language of human rights came to Czechoslovakia, Poland and Hungary in the writings of dissidents such as Václav Havel, Adam Michnik and György Konrád, it operated alongside an understanding of the world informed by socialism and Eurocommunism as

---

26 Andrei Sakharov, *My Country and the World* (New York: Alfred A. Knopf, 1975), iv, 108.
27 Sakharov to Carter, 21 Jan. 1977, *New York Times* (29 Jan. 1977), 2; Carter to Sakharov, 5 Feb. 1977, *New York Times* (18 Feb. 1977), 3. See also Joshua Rubenstein and Alexander Gribanov (eds.), *The KGB File of Andrei Sakharov* (New Haven: Yale University Press, 2008), 222–24; and Andrei Sakharov, *Memoirs* (New York: Knopf, 1990), 462–70.

well as ideas drawn from phenomenology and existentialism. The vocabulary of alienation, crisis and subjectivity was just as present as rights in these new political vernaculars. Charter 77, the manifesto released in January 1977 by dissidents in Czechoslovakia including Havel, did criticize the government for failing to implement the Helsinki Accords and UN human rights covenants that it had signed, guaranteeing freedom of expression and protection for other political and civil rights. The Carter administration saw Charter 77 in this vein, very publicly protesting the Czechoslovak state's harassment and imprisonment of Havel and others as part of its broader turn to human rights diplomacy. But the larger inspiration for Charter 77 had as much or more to do with, as one scholar argues, "a sense of activity, an assertion of autonomy, a taking control of one's fate" as "with any articulated allegiance to human rights."[28]

Havel's best-known political essay, "The Power of the Powerless," suggests the ways in which human rights operated alongside other modes of political and moral thought in dissident writing. It opened with Havel asking why a greengrocer in Prague might put a placard in his shop window bearing the canonical Marxist slogan, "Workers of the world, unite!" He suggested that few shopkeepers thought much about this practice, one that formed an omnipresent "panorama of everyday life" in socialist Czechoslovakia, nor did passersby really notice the signs. The message did not matter either. It was simply how one got by in a socialist system "thoroughly permeated by hypocrisy and lies" that demanded "conformity, uniformity and discipline." For the system to work, Havel argued, individuals "need not believe" in it, "but they must behave as if they did . . . they must live within a lie." In putting his loyalty on display in the shop window, the greengrocer signaled his compliance and obedience to the regime but also his complicity in the system. He was "pulled into and ensnared by it, like Faust by Mephistopheles." Everyone, from greengrocers to prime ministers, was "in fact involved and enslaved." If one day the greengrocer "snaps and he stops putting up the slogans," Havel claimed, retribution would be swift: the loss of his position, reduced pay, the loss of special health and education benefits for his family, threats, harassment and intimidation. For the state, such an action would not have been perceived as an individual or isolated offense. Havel writes, "He has demonstrated that living a lie is living a lie . . . that the emperor is naked . . . that it *is* possible to live within the truth . . .

28 Bolton, *Worlds of Dissent*, 27.

a truth which might cause incalculable transformations in social consciousness."[29]

Living within the truth, for Havel, was the essence of dissent and what he believed the "struggle for human rights politics" ought to be about. It was an everyday politics, as suspicious of "abstract projects for an ideal political or economic order" in the democratic West as in the socialist East. Havel was also wary of the term "dissident," believing that its prevailing usage in the 1970s too often improperly lifted up prominent leaders and elided the deeper moral politics he believed necessary in a mass movement. Instead Havel reframed its meanings to argue that "the basic job of 'dissident' movements is to serve truth," in part by "defending human rights" but also by developing "parallel structures" where "a different life can be lived, a life that is in harmony with its own aims and which in turn structures itself in harmony with those aims." Through the power of the powerless, Havel argued, the "plurality, diversity, independent self-constitution and self-organization" that are the "essence of the authentic life" could flourish.[30] Havel's vision ultimately transcended human rights.

For the global left, the turn to human rights in the 1970s sometimes carried with it the kinds of ambiguities that emerged in Soviet and East European dissident discourse. Brazilian leftists, for instance, began to draw upon the language of human rights to protest the growing abuses of the military junta. They were among the victims of the regime's indiscriminate use of violence and suspension of civil liberties. Human rights came to the Brazilian left largely through their encounters with emergent human rights nongovernmental organizations and the growing exile community who had fled the country to avoid further persecution. As they appropriated and reworked the idiom of human rights, some Brazilian Marxists, one historian argues, "grafted it on top of Marxist theory and often used both idioms interchangeably." Other leftists dismissed human rights out of hand or ignored them altogether. In debates within the left over whether to launch a "Human Rights Week" in Brazil to raise awareness of the abuses by the military regime, for example, one hardline socialist group attacked human rights in good Marxist fashion as a bourgeois vision, while another more moderate group praised the language from a "tactical" perspective.[31]

29 Václav Havel, *The Power of the Powerless: Citizens Against the State in Central-Eastern Europe* (London: Hutchinson, 1985), 132, 134, 135, 136, 143, 146, 147, 150.
30 Ibid., 166, 161, 192, 194, 134.
31 Patrick William Kelly, "Sovereignty and Salvation: Transnational Human Rights Activism in the Long 1970s," Ph.D. thesis (University of Chicago, 2015), 45.

At the same time, claims to collective economic and social rights by advocates in the global South offered an alternative construction in the 1970s of what human rights might mean, one that drew upon older socialist traditions. The United Nation's General Assembly was at the center of the campaign led by the G-77, what was then termed the "developing nations" or Third World, for a "New International Economic Order," one that called for "the right to development," local control of natural resources, a global regulatory framework for multi-national corporations, and the redistribution of financial and technological resources from north to south. Over the decade, in the West these claims were largely put to the side by most self-styled transnational human rights activists, uncomfortable with the collectivist sensibilities and privileging of economic over political and civil rights that underlay what was a competing vision of global human rights.

After 1989, with the collapse of the Soviet Union and its satellite states in Eastern Europe, human rights under socialism largely became the politics of memory. Forms of transitional justice emerged over the European postsocialist landscape, including processes of lustration, or the banning of former communist officials along with secret police and their informers from holding public office, citizen access to secret police archives and trials against former officials. But in East Asia the PRC continued to navigate an international system that, at least rhetorically, put forward human rights as a common human value. The 1980s brought more official Chinese engagement in global human rights politics as the PRC first began to join a variety of international organizations. The Chinese became members of the UN Commission on Human Rights in 1982, participating in the drafting of the Convention on Torture and the Convention Relating to the Status of Refugees. By early 1998 the PRC had acceded to nine UN human rights conventions and signed the two main international covenants on human rights. This era also brought a reprise of human rights as an oppositional domestic language, first in the late 1970s Democracy Wall movement and later among figures who became known as the democracy elite, such as the astrophysicist Fang Lizhi, who drew inspiration from Sakharov. In 1987, for instance, Fang argued that all socialist countries had failed since 1945 while the success of democracies rested on their recognition of human rights. A year later, during the state-sanctioned observances for the fortieth anniversary of the Universal Declaration of Human Rights that brought official emphasis on the document's discussion of collective rights, members of the democracy elite published essays emphasizing its protections of individual and political rights. One legal scholar, Yu Haocheng, argued that the "practice of using outside interference in one's own internal affairs as an excuse to refuse to discuss human rights conditions in one's own country is no longer credible."[32]

The immediate post-Mao period was unusual in the willingness of the communist party leadership to admit its abuses of civil rights during the Cultural Revolution. Moreover, despite the continuing growth of the international human rights advocacy movement and the looming presence of human rights in American diplomacy in the 1980s, only modest criticism was directed toward China. Until Tiananmen. The democracy movement in Tiananmen Square in the spring of 1989 seldom mentioned human rights explicitly, although demands for freedom of speech were central to its aims. But in May a group of activists released a "Declaration of Human Rights" that decried the "cruel interference in and infringement of human rights by our rulers" and offered a list of sixteen political and civil rights that they insisted were essential to guarantee "social stability, people's well-being and national prosperity."[33] When the Chinese government used deadly force against peaceful protestors in Tiananmen Square in June 1989, killing thousands, and arrested tens of thousands more, its actions unleashed global attention on China's human rights policies, including international sanctions and vigorous critiques from nonstate human rights groups. The Chinese state response was a reassertion of state sovereignty and of Marx. The publication of its "White Paper" on human rights in 1991 offered an attack on Western violations of human rights in China since the Opium Wars and pushed on noninterference in domestic affairs, the centrality of the rights to subsistence and development, and a relativist conception of human rights. As Deng Xiaoping put it, "So-called 'human rights' as understood in the Western world and human rights we talk about are two different things. There are two different viewpoints in this matter."[34]

In these views the Chinese found a broader constituency with soft authoritarian states in Southeast Asia such as Singapore, in articulating what became known as the Asian-values conception of human rights.

32 Quoted in Rosemary Foot, *Rights Beyond Borders: The Global Community and the Struggle over Human Rights in China* (Oxford: Oxford University Press, 2000), 152.
33 Chinese Human Rights Movement Committee, Beijing, "Declaration of Human Rights (May 1989)," in Stephen C. Angle and Marina Svensson (eds.), *The Chinese Human Rights Reader: Documents and Commentary 1900–2000* (Armonk, NY: M. E. Sharpe, 2001), 321–22.
34 Quoted in Foot, *Rights Beyond Borders*, 147.

As the 1993 Bangkok Declaration argued, "while human rights are universal in nature, they must be considered in the context of a dynamic and evolving process of international norm-setting, bearing in mind the significance of national and regional particularities and various historical, cultural and religious backgrounds."[35] But the PRC would continue to be subject to global human rights pressures, especially in moments in which the Chinese hosted major international meetings, such as the UN's Fourth World Conference on Women in 1995, where attention turned to Tibet, family planning and female infanticide. The failure of Beijing to win the summer Olympic games in 2000 was in part about transnational advocacy against Chinese abuses of civil and political rights. In this China is not alone. Those few remaining bastions of the communist world, albeit often in market-Leninist guise, such as Vietnam, North Korea and Cuba, also remain targets of global human rights advocates.

But the broader waning of international communism in the twenty-first century is mirrored in part by a more recent decline in the use of human rights as a form of moral and political reasoning. In the United States, for instance, many of the major contemporary social movements – among them the Occupy Protests, the Fair Immigration Movement, the Fight for $15, the Marriage Equality Movement and Black Lives Matter – take primary inspiration from alternative lexicons. In their challenges to the mounting chasm in wealth and income, mass incarceration, escalating detentions and deportations of immigrants and growing racial disparities in policing, education and income, these movements might have turned to the language of the Universal Declaration of Human Rights and its promises of universal guarantees to economic and social rights, to free movement and to life without racial and gender discrimination. At times they do make rhetorical gestures to the lexicon of human rights, but their energies and tactics on the ground operate largely around a domestic space in which the global human rights imagination remains in a minor key. Elsewhere in the world, the language of human rights may be somewhat more robust but the turn to concerns about structural inequalities is also very present. Ironically, as human rights are losing some of their moral power to instruct, the critiques that shaped Marx's critique of the bourgeois rights of man continue to hover over contemporary domestic and global politics.

---

35 Bangkok Declaration on Human Rights, 1993, faculty.washington.edu/swhiting/pol s469/Bangkok_Declaration.doc.

Bibliographical Essay

Understanding the relationship between human rights and communism properly begins with Karl Marx's 1843 "On the Jewish Question," in *The Marx and Engels Reader*, ed. Robert C. Tucker (New York: Norton & Co., 1979), 26–46. Only recently have scholars of communism turned attention to the history of human rights. The Soviet Union's engagement in the UN-based human rights norm-making in the 1940s best emerges in Jennifer Amos, "Embracing and Contesting: The Soviet Union and the Universal Declaration of Human Rights, 1948–1958," in Stefan-Ludwig Hoffman (ed.), *Human Rights in the Twentieth Century* (Cambridge: Cambridge University Press, 2010), 147–65; and her "Soviet Diplomacy and the Politics on Human Rights, 1945–1964" (Ph.D. thesis, University of Chicago, 2012). On the fraught history of social and economic rights in the Soviet Union, see Mark B. Smith, "Social Rights in the Soviet Dictatorship: The Constitutional Right to Welfare from Stalin to Brezhnev," *Humanity* 3, 3 (Winter 2012), 385–406. On Soviet participation in the Nuremberg Trials, see Francine Hirsch, "The Soviets at Nuremberg: International Law, Propaganda, and the Making of the Postwar Order," *American Historical Review* 113, 3 (June 2008), 701–30.

For the making of the 1940s global human rights movement more broadly, see Samuel Moyn, *The Last Utopia: Human Rights in History* (Cambridge, MA: Harvard University Press, 2010), ch. 2; Jay Winter and Antoine Prost, *René Cassin and Human Rights: From the Great War to the Universal Declaration* (Cambridge: Cambridge University Press, 2013); and Mark Philip Bradley, *The United States and the Global Human Rights Imagination: A Twentieth-Century Transnational History* (Cambridge: Cambridge University Press, 2016), part I. The Soviet and Chinese entanglements with postcolonial state-making and human rights emerge in Roland Burke, *Decolonization and the Evolution of International Human Rights* (Philadelphia: University of Pennsylvania Press, 2010).

On Soviet dissidents, see Benjamin Nathans, "The Dictatorship of Reason: Aleksandr Vol'pin and the Idea of Rights Under 'Developed Socialism,'" *Slavic Review* 66, 4 (Winter 2007), 630–63; his "Soviet Rights-Talk in the Post-Stalin Era," in Hoffman (ed.), *Human Rights in the Twentieth Century*, 166–90; and his "The Disenchantment of Socialism: Soviet Dissidents, Human Rights and the New Global Morality," in Jan Eckel and Samuel Moyn (eds.), *The Breakthrough: Human Rights in the 1970s* (Philadelphia: University of Pennsylvania Press, 2013), 33–47. More conventional but still important narratives include Joshua Rubenstein, *Soviet Dissidents: Their Struggle for Human Rights* (Boston: Beacon Press, 1985), 30–42; and Ludmilla Alexeyeva, *Soviet Dissent: Contemporary Movements for National, Religious, and Human Rights* (Middletown, CT: Wesleyan University Press, 1985).

On Helsinki, see Sarah B. Snyder, *Human Rights Activism and the End of the Cold War: A Transnational History of the Helsinki Network* (Cambridge: Cambridge University Press, 2011); and Daniel C. Thomas, *The Helsinki Effect: International Norms, Human Rights and the Demise of Communism* (Princeton: Princeton University Press, 2001). For Czech dissent, see Jonathan Bolton, *Worlds of Dissent: Charter 77, the Plastic People of the Universe, and Czech Culture Under Communism* (Cambridge, MA: Harvard University Press, 2012).

The impact of Soviet and East European dissidents on West European leftist thought and practice in the 1970s emerges in Robert Horvath, "'The Solzhenitsyn Effect': East European Dissidents and the Demise of Revolutionary Privilege," *Human Rights Quarterly* 29, 4 (Nov. 2007), 879–907; Michael Scott Christofferson, *French Intellectuals Against the Left: The Antitotalitarian Moment of the 1970s* (New York: Berghahn Press, 2004), ch. 2; Silvio Pons, "The Rise and Fall of Eurocommunism," in Melvyn P. Leffler and Odd Arne Westad (eds.), *The Cambridge History of the Cold War*, vol. III (Cambridge: Cambridge University Press, 2010), 45–65; Robert Brier, "Beyond the 'Helsinki Effect': East European Dissent and the Western Left in the 'Long 1970s,'" in Poul Villaume, Rasmus Mariager and Helle Porsdam (eds.), *The "Long 1970s": Human Rights, East–West Détente and Transnational Relations* (London: Taylor & Francis, 2015), 71–86; and Robert Brier, "Broadening the Cultural History of the Cold War: The Emergence of the Polish Workers' Defense Committee and the Rise of Human Rights," *Journal of Cold War Studies* 15, 4 (Fall 2013), 104–27.

For Carter-era human rights diplomacy, and its connection to Soviet dissidents, see Barbara J. Keys, *Reclaiming American Virtue: The Human Rights Revolution of the 1970s* (Cambridge, MA: Harvard University Press, 2014); Kathleen Parthé, "The Politics of Détente-Era Cultural Texts, 1969–1976," *Diplomatic History* 33, 4 (Sep. 2009), 723–33; and Christian Philip Peterson, "The Carter Administration and the Promotion of Human Rights in the Soviet Union," *Diplomatic History* 38, 3 (Jun. 2014), 628–56.

On broader global concern with human rights in the 1970s, see Moyn, *Last Utopia*, ch. 4; Bradley, *United States and the Global Human Rights Imagination*, ch. 5; and contributors to Eckel and Moyn (eds.),

The Breakthrough. For the politics of postsocialist human rights memory, see Emma Gilligan, *Defending Human Rights in Russia: Sergei Kovalyov, Dissident and Human Rights Commissioner, 1969–2003* (London: Routledge Curzon, 2005); and Monika Nalepa, *Skeletons in the Closet: Transitional Justice in Post-Communist Europe* (Cambridge: Cambridge University Press, 2010).

Useful starting points for late twentieth-century Chinese human rights history include Rosemary Foot, *Rights Beyond Borders: The Global Community and the Struggle over Human Rights in China* (Oxford: Oxford University Press, 2000); Marina Svensson, *Debating Human Rights in China: A Conceptual and Political History* (Lanham, MD: Rowman & Littlefield, 2002); and Fang Lizhi, *The Most Wanted Man in China: My Journey from Scientist to Enemy of the State* (New York: Henry Holt, 2016).

7

Reform Communism

SILVIO PONS AND MICHELE DI DONATO

What Was "Reform Communism"?

Communists never used the notion of "reform communism." From World War I, their identity was built in opposition to "revisionist" tendencies among the socialist parties. They used the term "reformism" as a negative label and a synonym of right-wing "degeneration." Right up to 1989 their political culture upheld Marxist revolutionary references as a way to differentiate themselves from social democracy. Nevertheless, the lexicon and practices of a reform approach did emerge in the communist world after the death of Stalin. In the Soviet Union and in Europe, de-Stalinization and "peaceful coexistence" implied a change that could be interpreted in different ways, but clearly leaned toward gradualism and nonviolent transformation more than revolutionary thrusts. Although far-reaching ideas of reform were rapidly shelved, prospects of peaceful change still left their trace among communists, and ideas inspired by "socialist humanism" did not simply disappear.

This legacy was most evident among the Czechoslovak reformers who led the Prague Spring of 1968, which would rapidly turn into a founding myth for "socialism with a human face." Its repression after the Soviet-led intervention of August 1968 represented a lasting shock for those who held hopes of democratic renewal, leading many East European reformers to embrace dissent and opposition – even though reformist tendencies did also survive in some establishment circles. Defeated in the East, the ideas of reform communism found new focus on the other side of the Iron Curtain. In Western and Southern Europe, Eurocommunism emerged in the mid 1970s as a movement aimed at defending the legacy of the Prague Spring, assuming human rights as a component of socialist ideals, offering alternatives to the waning appeal of Soviet socialism and challenging the Cold War order both domestically and internationally. Eurocommunists tried to provide criticisms of the Soviet model that were inspired by democratic values, thus differing crucially from revolutionary Maoist and leftist critics. Theirs proved to be a lasting, if ultimately unsuccessful endeavor.

These failures and frailties notwithstanding, Mikhail Gorbachev's reforms would have been unthinkable without the legacy of the Eastern and Western communist reformers. By the late 1980s, the "new thinking" in international relations and the drive toward change in domestic affairs had established this legacy also within the Kremlin. Gorbachev's vision incorporated reform communism's appeal for the reassertion of humanistic ideals and its idea of nonviolent transformation as opposed to the Stalinist legacy. He adopted interdependence as a category for interpreting global processes, which made both "world revolution" and the Cold War obsolete. However, the new Soviet leadership also inherited all the basic contradictions of reform communism. While in the West Eurocommunism had lost momentum, crisis and collapse in Eastern Europe and the USSR sealed the fate of reform, which proved unable to sustain itself as a credible alternative path in communist history.

This chapter proposes to analyze reform communism as a historical phenomenon that cannot be equated with *perestroika* alone, even if its historical meaning should primarily be understood in light of Gorbachev's reforms. Reform communism had three distinctive features. First, it was never a consistent movement equipped with definite ideas and strategies. Rather, it was a divided and fragmented transnational set of concepts and practices aimed at reform from above. It partially emerged in the aftermath of de-Stalinization and then took shape as a form of cultural and political renewal in specific chronological and national contexts, influencing groups of intellectuals and party officials in several countries. Second, ideas of reform were formulated in terms of recovering the "original inspiration" of communism and Marxism, which they construed as a humanistic tradition. Although reform communists increasingly interacted with social democracy, they did not want to change their own identity, even when their priorities and agendas became more similar to those of social democrats than to those of other communists. Third, reform communism was essentially a European and Russian phenomenon that failed to exert substantial influence over communists outside Europe. Ideas of peaceful change were not devoid of global reflections, particularly in India and Latin America, but the violent context of the Cold War prevented their spread. This geographical

SILVIO PONS AND MICHELE DI DONATO

localization notwithstanding, reform communism captured and epitomized broader historical trends and transformations. In particular, its encounter with the issue of human rights should be understood in a global perspective, as it crucially revealed the exhaustion of the European legacy of political revolutions. Reform communism was an essential part of the metamorphosis of this tradition, which became manifest in the peaceful collapse of 1989.

Transnational Change from Above: De-Stalinization and "Socialism with a Human Face"

After the death of Stalin, ideas of reform found various advocates among the communist leaderships. In private and public discourse, uneven elements of change surfaced between 1953 and 1956 which would become archetypes for reform communists at a later stage. An entire set of measures and statements indirectly contested the Stalinist legacy of terror, forced Sovietization in Eastern Europe and even the Cold War. However, neither were these initiatives unified into a political project, nor did any single communist figure come to embrace a coherent reformist platform.

We now know that there were elements of truth in the "legend" of Lavrentii Beria as a reformer in 1953. Indeed, he and his ally Georgii Malenkov did show their readiness to undertake change in Soviet domestic and foreign policy, particularly by envisaging the rehabilitation of repressed individuals, adopting welfare measures, reducing Cold War engagements and even negotiating the reunification of Germany. Power struggles in the Soviet leadership and the upheaval in East Germany in June 1953 thwarted more significant change.[1] After Beria's arrest and execution, Malenkov tried to carry on the same agenda for some time before himself being marginalized in 1955 – as were his partners in Eastern Europe, beginning with Imre Nagy in Hungary. In the Soviet Union, many of their ideas were picked up by Malenkov's rival Nikita Khrushchev, who turned de-Stalinization into public discourse and a collective shock for all communists. The Twentieth Congress of the Communist Party of the Soviet Union in 1956 would long be regarded by many reform communists as a harbinger of unfulfilled promises of change. Yet this change from above hardly inspired a consistent shift away from the Stalinist legacy, and it again lost its hold when the perspective of liberalization began destabilizing the communist regimes. The Soviet repression in

---

1 Mark Kramer, "The Early Post-Stalin Succession Struggle and Upheavals in East-Central Europe: Internal–External Linkages in Soviet Policy Making," *Journal of Cold War Studies* 1, 1 (1999), 3–55 (part 1); 1, 2 (1999), 3–38 (part 2); 1, 3 (1999), 3–66 (part 3).

Hungary of November 1956 followed the imperatives of Cold War *Realpolitik* and destroyed new ways of political thinking within communism.[2]

The rebellions against Soviet rule in Eastern Europe took on the character of fights for national independence, but they also exhibited a transnational effect. Especially among the younger generations, hopes of democratizing socialism had taken the place of the drive for anti-fascist and socialist transformation shared by European communists at the end of World War II.[3] The communist establishments, still speaking the language of civil war inherited from the first half of the twentieth century, failed to understand the meaning of this shift from revolutionary to reform thinking and instead saw the risk of a catastrophic "domino effect" led by anti-communist forces. Even leaders such as Josip Broz Tito in Yugoslavia and Palmiro Togliatti in Italy – who, unlike Khrushchev, had both denounced the "bureaucratic degeneration" of Stalinism – perceived developments in Hungary as a threat, although they would later acknowledge the popular character of the uprising.[4] As Nagy was tragically left alone to speak the language of socialist democracy in his writings from prison, this language became a form of dissent.[5] The repression in Hungary initiated a shock wave within the communist world. The prospects of reconstructing its political culture so as to consistently include ideas of reform dissipated, while in both East and West prominent intellectuals who had believed in the "humanist potential" of communism turned into Marxist dissidents – as in the cases of Leszek Kołakowski and E. P. Thompson.

In the aftermath of the drama of 1956, de-Stalinization and "peaceful coexistence" proved to be irreversible, if ill-defined processes. The change they entailed meant different things to different people, even among communists, and the tension between conformism and dissent persisted. The establishments' adaptation measures, aimed at reconstructing the regimes' social bases, firmly excluded any far-reaching idea of political reform. Whenever these ideas emerged, they were interpreted as intolerable dissent – as was the

---

2 See Jörg Baberowski, "Nikita Khrushchev and De-Stalinization in the Soviet Union 1953–1964," in Norman Naimark, Silvio Pons and Sophie Quinn-Judge (eds.), *The Cambridge History of Communism*, 3 vols. (Cambridge: Cambridge University Press, 2017), vol. II, ch. 5; Mark Kramer, "The Changing Pattern of Soviet–East European Relations 1953–1968," ibid., ch. 6.

3 Vladislav M. Zubok, *Zhivago's Children: The Last Russian Intelligentsia* (Cambridge, MA: Belknap Press of Harvard University Press, 2009).

4 Jonathan Haslam, "I dilemmi della destalinizzazione: Togliatti, il XX Congresso del PCUS e le sue conseguenze," in Roberto Gualtieri, Carlo Spagnolo and Ermanno Taviani (eds.), *Togliatti nel suo tempo* (Rome: Carocci, 2007), 215–38.

5 Jonás M. Rainer, *Imre Nagy: A Biography* (London: I. B. Tauris, 2009).

case with Jacek Kuroń and Karol Modzelewski in Poland, who in 1965 argued from a Marxist standpoint in favor of political restructuring.[6]

The only sector in which reformist concepts could be openly debated and even experimented with, if only to a very limited extent, was that of economics – as the accomplishment of postwar reconstruction increasingly raised the problem of efficiency and productivity. The result was on the one hand the politicization of this realm, and on the other the reduction of any form of political change to administrative measures. Criticizing the Stalinist legacy of the hypercentralized command economy, reformers looked back to the NEP (New Economic Policy) and to the ideas of Nikolai Bukharin as alternative models for organizing a socialist economy. Economists such as Yevsei Liberman in the USSR and Ota Šik in Czechoslovakia translated these inspirations into schemes for adopting decentralizing measures and a regulated amount of market-inspired and efficiency-enhancing principles, while leaving in place the planned economy system. However, reform ideas and projects hit a brick wall whenever their political implications became too broad or too manifest.[7] The same was true of Yugoslav self-management, which attracted some interest especially in Poland but again encountered opposition from establishments disquieted by its potential political consequences.

In the USSR between 1957 and the mid 1960s economic reforms were mainly a question of decentralization to the regional level. This was supposed to allow more autonomy for local actors and enterprises negotiating their own interests with the central authorities. However, these measures were poorly implemented as they met with bureaucratic resistance. An intermittent restructuring practice never affected the traditional primacy given to military spending and an industrial structure dominated by large state-owned enterprises. Even the most important policy initiative in this realm – the 1965 reforms endorsed by Aleksei Kosygin – represented only a timid attempt at making the planned economy less inefficient, by promoting limited institutional devolution.[8] The political and intellectual climate would soon become even less favorable

6 Barbara J. Falk, *The Dilemmas of Dissidence in East-Central Europe: Citizen Intellectuals and Philosopher Kings* (Budapest and New York: Central European University Press, 2003), 13–18, 184–92.
7 Moshe Lewin, *Political Undercurrents in Soviet Economic Debates: From Bukharin to the Modern Reformers* (Princeton: Princeton University Press, 1974).
8 Mark Harrison, "Communism and Economic Modernization," Warwick University, Centre for Competitive Advantage in the Global Economy, Working Paper Series 92 (Jul. 2012); Pekka Sutela, *Economic Thought and Economic Reform in the Soviet Union* (Cambridge: Cambridge University Press, 1991).

to debates on economic reform. Ideas of economic renewal surfaced again briefly in Czechoslovakia and faded away in the aftermath of the crushing of the Prague Spring, out of repression or disillusionment.

The change in the communist view of international relations proved even more ambiguous. Although adopting the doctrine of "peaceful coexistence" and pursuing détente policies seemed to indicate adaptation to a polycentric world, as against uncompromising anti-imperialist positions, no common analytical revision took place, and unorthodox voices remained marginal. Malenkov and Togliatti had proposed innovative reflections on the unprecedented nature of nuclear warfare as early as 1954. Their observations were, however, never developed, since in interpreting nuclear warfare as a threat to the survival of all humanity they introduced concepts that could undermine the "two camps" doctrine and delegitimize the communist Cold War. Togliatti's vision of "polycentrism" also remained entirely theoretical as a pattern for acknowledging diversity within the socialist camp and adopting flexibility in relations among communist parties in various areas of the world. Both the Soviets and the Chinese maintained a state-centric vision of world communism. The idea of "unity in diversity" was mainly used by Western communists – though by the Italians much more than the French – as a framework within which to restore the "national roads" to socialism they had proposed at the end of World War II.[9]

In the space of a few years, the conflict between the Soviet Union and China would dwarf many other developments within the communist world as a catalyst of political and ideological concerns. Since Mao opposed both de-Stalinization and "peaceful coexistence," the unity of international communism was definitively compromised, and could not be repaired even after Khrushchev's fall from power. As a consequence, Moscow and the East European establishments placed ever-greater emphasis on the ideological cohesiveness of pro-Soviet communism, with any detachment from established dogmas becoming anathema as the Soviet leaders faced a Maoist challenge to their global ambitions.[10] Nonetheless, with all its limitations, the challenge posed by the perspective of a peaceful change in communist political culture survived and developed in the 1960s. Even if the basic assumption underpinning the concept of peaceful socialist transformation was state-centric

---

9 Carlo Spagnolo, *Sul Memoriale di Yalta. Togliatti e la crisi del movimento comunista internazionale (1956–1964)* (Rome: Carocci, 2007).
10 See Sergey Radchenko, "The Rise and Fall of the Sino-Soviet Alliance 1949–1989," in Naimark, Pons and Quinn-Judge (eds.), *The Cambridge History of Communism*, vol. II, ch. 10.

and geopolitical – the idea that a reversal in the postwar "correlation of forces" between the "two camps" was underway, which could make the world "safe for historical change"[11] – this perspective took on wide-ranging meanings that could hardly be constrained within Moscow-controlled frameworks. This was especially true of the coupling of the perspectives of peaceful transformation and practices of legality and democracy. This association was one of the threads of the experience of the communist parties in the West and was crucial to their legitimation strategies. However, its implications in terms of reform thinking remained largely ambiguous, as these parties continued to claim allegiance to their own revolutionary calling. Prospects of peaceful change also emerged in the global South in spite of the predominant influence of different approaches, such as Maoist and Castroite anti-imperialist guerrilla movements or the drive for national liberation represented by Vietnam – and also in spite of the bloody repression of an important mass party such as the Indonesian Communist Party in 1965. In 1967–68 Indian communists took over government legally as part of united front coalitions in Kerala and West Bengal. In 1969 a left alliance between reformists and revolutionaries was formed in Chile around the socialist Salvador Allende, which in 1970 became the first coalition including a strong communist party to win democratic elections in the postwar era.[12]

For a very brief moment in the late 1960s the emergence of a reform experience in the most advanced country of the socialist camp – Czechoslovakia – seemed to open up new political paths for communism, with potentially global echoes. From this point of view, the repression of the Prague Spring by the Soviet Union in August 1968 and the US-influenced *coup d'état* against Chile's Unidad Popular in September 1973 can be seen as two related events of the global Cold War that also prevented more significant change in communist history. After these defeats, peaceful perspectives of socialist democracy left the global scene, though ideas of reform communism did maintain a role in Europe.

The Legacy of the Prague Spring

The legacy of the Czechoslovak experience was crucial to the persistence of a reform communist tradition in Europe. The Prague Spring demonstrated

11 Raymond L. Garthoff, *Détente and Confrontation: American–Soviet Relations from Nixon to Reagan* (Washington, DC: Brookings Institution Press, 1994), 53.
12 See Hari Vasudevan, "Communism in India," in Naimark, Pons and Quinn-Judge (eds.), *The Cambridge History of Communism*, vol. II, ch. 20; Victor Figueroa Clark, "Latin American Communism," ibid., ch. 16.

that the incoherent post-Stalin change from above could develop into a political project. Once again, a movement that was born of national factors assumed transnational implications in Eastern Europe. Alexander Dubček kept his project within the boundaries of the Cold War divide and exercised the moral persuasion of gradual change from within the establishment. Unlike Nagy, he and his entourage avoided radical moves toward political pluralism or away from the Warsaw Pact. Their idea of one-party democracy was an incongruity and a paradox founded on a naive understanding of Leninism. But it was a paradox capable of reviving hopes and initiative from below, stimulating pluralism in society, crossing borders – especially by fueling turmoil in Poland and Yugoslavia – and obtaining the support of Italian, French and Yugoslav communists. In spite of their peaceful advancement, Dubček's reforms triggered a transnational backlash that eventually resulted in repression. For most East European leaderships, the language of socialist democracy represented a threat of contamination and dangerous subversion. From this standpoint, the division between hawks such as Władysław Gomułka of Poland and doves such as the Hungarian leader János Kádár was scarcely significant. For Brezhnev and his partners, if reform meant democratization, there could be no talk of reform at all.

The Prague Spring was part of a global movement that by 1968 brought the intersection of anti-authoritarian activism, demands for civil rights, and individual and collective protest against the Cold War order.[13] In the communist world, the Cultural Revolution in China and the Prague Spring in Europe seemingly offered two alternative transnational hubs for rethinking Marxism and the communist experience. The opposition between these two poles was never to be reconciled. Maoism was short-lived as a global phenomenon, in spite of its initial Third Worldist appeal, and soon China dropped its internationalist calling and focused on national interests. The Czechoslovak reformers originated one of the symbolic legacies that would help the peaceful reconnection of the two Europes twenty years later. Even the rediscovery of unorthodox Marxism became part of a vision that recovered a unitary concept of European civilization. Among the Czechoslovak reformers, Zdeněk Mlynář was the outstanding personality in this respect.[14] He was the exponent of an entire generation in Eastern Europe as well as in the Soviet Union that had shaped its own identity by

---

13 See Pavel Kolář, "Reform Undercurrents and the Prague Spring," ibid., ch. 7; Robert Gildea, "The Global 1968 and International Communism," in this volume.
14 Maud A. Bracke, "1968," in Stephen A. Smith (ed.), *The Oxford Handbook of the History of Communism* (Oxford and New York: Oxford University Press, 2014), 161.

trusting in de-Stalinization, overcome the shock of 1956 and found itself marginalized or forced to dissent in the aftermath of 1968.

The protagonists of the Prague Spring could hardly convey their experience to a new generation, as the massive purges of the Czechoslovak party swept away the only communist establishment in which reform attitudes were deep-rooted. Their ideas had not been fully put to the test, and their contradictions had not clearly emerged. What they left was a myth that communists could construe either as a dream or as a nightmare. The Prague Spring had a major ambivalent effect on communists on both sides of the continent. In the East, its violent crushing provoked an exacerbation of disaffection regarding the possibility of reforming Soviet-type systems. Hopes for a purified humanistic socialism melted away even in Moscow. Only limited circles of nonconformist officials and intellectuals maintained an underground sympathy for "socialism with a human face," but the realist logic of détente imposed silence on the contested implications of Dubček's reforms. Reformist foreign-policy officials (*mezhdunarodniki*) in the Soviet Union, such as Anatolii Cherniaev, could hardly exercise any influence on Brezhnev's ruling group.[15] Openly defending the Prague Spring meant joining the dissidents, as was the case with certain isolated personalities such as Roy Medvedev in the Soviet Union or Rudolf Bahro in the German Democratic Republic (GDR).[16] Even if there still was a certain ideological proximity between reform-minded people within the establishment and socialist dissidents outside it, the major trend in the networks of dissent and opposition became disillusionment with any concept of state socialism and reform from within the system. This was the path taken by exponents of 1968 countercultures such as Adam Michnik in Poland.[17] Ideas of a reformed communism increasingly yielded to different political cultures and, even more, to "nonpolitical" and postideological thinking that advanced the concept of "civil society" in a dichotomous opposition to totalitarian regimes. This was especially the case in the aftermath of the Helsinki conference of 1975 and the rise of human rights as a transnational issue. The legacy of the Prague Spring came to be transformed, reinterpreted or simply dismissed.

---

15 Anatolii Cherniaev, *Sovmestnyi iskhod. Dnevnik dvukh epokh, 1972–1991 gody* (Moscow: ROSSPEN, 2010).
16 R. Medvedev, *On Socialist Democracy* (New York: Norton, 1977); R. Bahro, *The Alternative in Eastern Europe* (New York: Verso, 1978).
17 Adam Michnik, *Letters from Prison and Other Essays* (Berkeley: University of California Press, 1985).

The Western Perspective: Eurocommunism and the Search for a New Legitimacy

It was in Western and Southern Europe that "socialism with a human face" could be openly adopted as a source of inspiration for communists. In many ways, during the 1970s reform communism in the West rediscovered the support from below that had characterized the Prague Spring and then had been lost in the East. In terms of political culture, the legacy of anti-fascism represented a key bridge between the two experiences. Anti-fascist language had been distinctive to reform-oriented criticism of the communist states in 1956 and 1968 – even if it was an ambivalent language, which was also employed by the regimes for their own legitimation. In the aftermath of 1968, anti-fascism lost any critical function in Eastern Europe.[18] However, it still represented a powerful tradition among the Western communists. While not contesting the Eastern regimes' propaganda image, they had long presented anti-fascism as a core element of European democratic identity, and thus as a source of political legitimation that went back to the pre-Cold War era.

The impulse for keeping alive the invented tradition of "socialism with a human face" came from the Italian Communist Party (Partito Comunista Italiano, PCI), the only major party to uphold the dissent originally expressed against the Soviet military intervention in Czechoslovakia. The leader of the PCI from 1972 onward, Enrico Berlinguer, followed Togliatti's legacy of polycentrism in defending the party's autonomy, but widened his criticism of the Soviet model as inadequate to Western conditions and strengthened the reference to democratic values characteristic of Italian communism. The post-1968 decay of the appeal of the Soviet Union, especially among young generations, was crucial to the development of ideas openly focused on communist renewal.

In his effort to find a key for involving communists in government and overcoming Italy's "blocked democracy," Berlinguer tried to propose a linkage between national and international change. On the one hand, he launched a strategy for a "historic compromise" with Italy's ruling Christian Democratic Party. This moderate project, inspired by the repression of Allende's government in Chile, seemed a plausible one as Italy's economic and political crisis increasingly shifted popular support in favor of the communists. On the other hand, the Italian communists supported European

---

18 James Mark, *The Unfinished Revolution: Making Sense of the Communist Past in Central-Eastern Europe* (New Haven: Yale University Press, 2010), 137–52.

détente between the blocs and definitively accepted West European integration. Their aim was to build a new Europe – one that was "neither anti-Soviet nor anti-American," as their catchphrase had it – which could become a third force in world politics. Accordingly, they supported the German Social Democrats' *Ostpolitik* – which they interpreted as a key step toward the creation of a new context for political change in Europe – and rejected the Brezhnevite dogma that the repression of the Prague Spring had been instrumental to launching détente in that it had stabilized the Soviet sphere of influence. What the Italian communists hoped for was a "dynamic" scenario that combined détente and change.[19]

Connecting the PCI's national bid for power to a transnational strategy, Berlinguer proposed Europeanism and support for "dynamic" views of détente as the cornerstones of a Western communist alliance based on democratic and pluralist approaches to socialism. Presented as the only credible proposition for social and political change in the West, this renewal was expected to boost the Western communists' standing while at the same time providing impulses for renovation in the whole of the communist world. In the aftermath of the collapse of the Bretton Woods system and the oil shock of late 1973, Berlinguer saw the emerging economic crisis as an opportunity for rethinking what socialism might mean in a setting of "advanced capitalism."

The French communists, who represented the only other mass party in Western Europe, adhered only half-heartedly to what would be later defined as the "Eurocommunist" project. Their attitude to the "founding myth" of the Prague Spring was ambiguous at best, as their dissent over the Soviet invasion of Czechoslovakia had lasted for just a few months. While affirming their "autonomy" within the communist movement, the French proposed a vision that was entrenched in the concept of national sovereignty rather than European integration, and showed little interest in détente. Nonetheless, just like the Italians, they recognized that a shared Western communist perspective could become an effective instrument for gaining legitimacy in their domestic context. No other West European communist party proved willing – or able – to participate in the Eurocommunist project, except for the Spanish Communist Party, which represented a smaller force engaged in its own country's democratic transition. Unlike France's Georges Marchais, the Spanish leader Santiago Carrillo fully supported Berlinguer's

---

19 Silvio Pons, *Berlinguer e la fine del comunismo* (Turin: Einaudi, 2006).

views, and he went even further than his Italian counterpart in criticizing the Soviet model.[20]

In fact, not all the Eurocommunists were, at the same time, reform communists convinced that socialism and democracy were inseparably linked. The Portuguese Carnation Revolution of 1974 became a key test for their attitudes. The Portuguese communist leader Álvaro Cunhal caused wide international concern as he insisted on his party's alliance with the revolutionary elements of the military and demonstrated less commitment to the defense of pluralism than to the old model of "people's democracy." Berlinguer and Carrillo criticized this stance, adopting arguments that closely resembled those of the main social-democratic parties, which were by then actively supporting their own local allies in the Portuguese and Spanish transitions.[21] This position met with negative reactions not only in Moscow, but also within the French Communist Party. Marchais sided with Cunhal and his Soviet partners, revealing how difficult it was to establish a cohesive Eurocommunist movement. Furthermore, the other Western communist parties remained predominantly pro-Soviet, sectarian and electorally insignificant. Even the British and the Belgian parties, which had opposed the repression of the Prague Spring, became mired in exhausting internecine disputes over Eurocommunism and were unable to check their historical decline. The new intellectual influence of Antonio Gramsci's thought – increasingly reinterpreted, particularly in Britain, from the perspective of a theory of "hegemony" suited to the complexity of Western societies – was of limited help to the Eurocommunist project, even if it did encourage a revival of anti-orthodox thinking in Marxist milieus.[22] The Marxist scene was mainly occupied by "New Left" groups that opposed the "revisionist" trajectory of reform communism and, in any case, experienced a rapid decline in the second half of the 1970s.

Paradoxically, Eurocommunism was altogether more popular among East European communists. Berlinguer's address to the pan-European communist conference held in Berlin in June 1976 seemingly revealed plural voices within

20 Marco Di Maggio, *Alla ricerca della terza via al socialismo. I PC italiano e francese nella crisi del comunismo (1964–1984)* (Naples: ESI, 2014); Gregorio Moràn, *Miseria y grandeza del Partido comunista de España, 1939–1985* (Barcelona: Planeta, 1986); Santiago Carrillo, *Memorias* (Barcelona: Planeta, 2006).
21 Antonio Muñoz Sánchez, *El amigo alemán. El SPD y el PSOE de la dictadura a la democracia* (Barcelona: RBA Libros, 2012); David Castaño, "'A Practical Test in the Détente': International Support for the Socialist Party in the Portuguese Revolution (1974–1975)," *Cold War History* 15, 1 (2015), 1–26.
22 Derek Boothman, Francesco Giasi and Giuseppe Vacca (eds.), *Gramsci in Gran Bretagna* (Bologna: Il Mulino, 2015).

the movement and helped expand the spaces of autonomy in the Soviet bloc. In the East, interest and sympathy with Eurocommunism grew, though they remained underground. The Hungarian establishment in particular proposed a cautiously positive reception of Eurocommunism. The Italian communists had several contacts with reform-oriented officials such as Gyula Horn and Rezső Nyers, as well as with other "moderate" officials in Poland, the GDR and even the Soviet Union.[23] The PCI also established a partnership with the Yugoslav leadership. Although Tito and his entourage were skeptical about influencing change in the Soviet bloc – and scarcely inclined to accept the democratic implications of reform thinking – this relationship reinforced the emergence of Eurocommunism as a factor in world politics, as the Yugoslavs had influence both in Eastern Europe and in the nonaligned movement in the Third World. Cultivating wide ecumenical ambitions, the Italian communists built relations with national liberation movements in the Middle East, in Africa and elsewhere – putting forward views that opposed radical attitudes, especially those held by the Cubans.[24] Nevertheless, the relevance of Eurocommunism to renewing communist political culture in non-European countries was effectively limited to Japan, where the idea of a socialist project aimed at a context of advanced capitalism exercised a certain attraction on the local communist party. In the global South, anti-imperialist traditions prevented reform communism from holding sway – with the partial exception of Brazil.[25]

Reform Communism and the European Left: Offensives and Retreats

The Eurocommunist alliance ended up gaining more foes than friends. After the movement was definitively established at the meeting of the Italian, French and Spanish communists held in Madrid in February 1977, the Soviet Union started an ideological counteroffensive that targeted Carrillo, but mainly pursued the goal of dividing the partners and preventing any spillover of their ideas in Eastern Europe. One of the most delicate aspects was the Eurocommunists' defense of human rights and dissent in the East.

---

23 Antonio Rubbi, *Il mondo di Berlinguer* (Rome: Napoleone, 1994), 93.
24 Marco Galeazzi, *Il PCI e il movimento dei paesi non allineati 1955–1975* (Milan: FrancoAngeli, 2011).
25 Peter Berton, "Japanese Communist Party: The 'Lovable' Party," in Ronald J. Hrebenar (ed.), *Japan's New Party System* (Boulder: Westview Press, 2000), 253–99; Marco Aurelio Garcia (ed.), *As esquerdas e a democracia* (Rio de Janeiro: CEDEC, 1986).

Although rather inconsistently pursued and mainly oriented to defending only socialist dissidents, this stance signaled the diminished legitimation of the Eastern bloc regimes and the growing pressure exercised, even within the communist movement, by a new universalist discourse on human rights epitomized by the Helsinki conference. However, the Eurocommunists' partial adoption of the language of human rights did not suffice to earn them political legitimation in the West. The administration of President Jimmy Carter tried to revise the USA's traditional hostility – as epitomized in previous years by the positions of Secretary of State Henry Kissinger – but continued to look at the communist parties as a potential threat to NATO, especially as the PCI had entered a "national solidarity" parliamentary majority in 1976 and drawn close to government. The governments of Western Europe, including the Social Democratic Party (SPD) in West Germany, shared these reservations.

Relations between Eurocommunists and European social democrats were problematic even in the case of the PCI. The Italian communists had initiated an informal dialogue with the SPD centered on détente as early as 1967. While undergoing many ups and downs, this relationship decisively contributed to influencing the PCI's international outlook at the moment it devised the Eurocommunist strategy. The Italian communists reconsidered their view of détente as a tool for altering the European political order in the short term and converged with the SPD position which interpreted the process as involving only a strictly gradual change. It was within this framework that the PCI came to accept Italy's membership of NATO, which was reappraised as a precondition to the maintenance of the East–West equilibrium that underpinned détente. In the same way, a positive assessment of the social democratic governments and parties' international initiatives was instrumental to fashioning the PCI's own peculiar Europeanist position. The Italian communists' network of relations with social democratic parties significantly expanded during the 1970s, and by the end of the decade it included virtually all of the European members of the Socialist International.

However, in spite of the more open attitude of a transnational faction of left-wing social democrats, the mainstream leaderships remained cautious over the ideological evolution of Eurocommunism, and generally hostile when confronted with the perspective of communist participation in any Western government. Driven as it was by a complex set of international, domestic and ideological concerns, this fundamental position – which aimed at preserving East–West equilibriums, reaffirming the ideological distinction between communism and social democracy, and containing the proponents of radical responses to the economic crisis of the 1970s within the Socialist International – saw hardly any significant evolution. For its part, the PCI had never interpreted its relations with the social democrats as a step toward the abandonment of its communist identity and criticism of the heirs of the Second International. The advocates of historicist schemes for shaping a "third way," overcoming both the orthodox communist and the social democratic traditions, the Italian communists systematically belittled the achievements of the post-1945 social democratic governments, emphasizing how they had yielded to the "logics of capitalism."[26] The Spanish Communist Party likewise tried to build up a network of relations with European social democratic parties, but it was limited in this effort by the active support the latter were providing to Felipe González's Socialists in Spain. In spite of its engagement in a formal alliance with the French Socialist Party from 1972 to 1977, the French Communist Party's international relations with European social democrats were nearly nonexistent. As the Union of the Left in France grew increasingly fractious, the communists missed hardly any opportunity to restate in ever-sharper tones their ideological distinction from social democracy and denunciation of the European social democratic govern-ments' involvement in the "international strategy of imperialism."

Eurocommunism was eventually unable to escape a defeat that depended on basic lack of cohesion as well as on shortcomings suffered by its three founding members in their national strategies. The American (and West European) veto on communist participation in Western governments, on the one hand, and Soviet ideological hostility, on the other hand, were strong enough to contain the PCI. As détente waned and the most important Western communist party went back to opposition in early 1979, the entire transnational strategy fell apart. Moscow's harsh reaction against Eurocommunism was effective in forcing the French communists to step back from their vague dissent stances, and all the more so since they were affected domestically by the rise of the socialists. The Spanish Communist Party was unable to challenge the socialists and suffered from internal splits, also fueled by the Soviets. Not only was the movement defeated, but within a few years all Western parties were greatly reduced in their membership and electoral support. Having been contained in its national challenge, the PCI lost the international resonance it had gained in the previous years. The "second Cold War" brought about by the Euromissile crisis and the

---

26 Michele Di Donato, *I comunisti italiani e la sinistra europea. Il PCI e i rapporti con le socialdemocrazie (1964–1984)* (Rome: Carocci, 2015).

Soviet invasion of Afghanistan was hardly a favorable environment for its projects. Eurocommunism had exposed the exhaustion of international communism, but failed the test of trying to bring about a new pole.[27]

Nevertheless, although the Italian communists had to renounce the perspective of building a new movement, they still represented a major national force – as well as the only mass communist party in Western Europe. The PCI leadership defended their party's evolution by condemning the Afghan war in 1980 and Wojciech Jaruzelski's 1981 coup in Poland. It was this latter event that provoked Berlinguer's famous declaration that "the propulsive capacity for the renewal of the societies – or at least of some of the societies – that have been created in Eastern Europe has been exhausted."[28] The implications for political culture were important, as Berlinguer and other Italian communist leaders – particularly Giorgio Napolitano – rejected both appeals to loyalty to the Soviet Union based on "class" principles and any accusation of "counterrevolution" leveled against Solidarność in Poland. They knew that in Moscow people like Cherniaev spoke a very similar language, even though they were cut off from decision-making. In any case, the Polish crisis of 1980–81 represented the historical moment when some of the crucial dilemmas of reform communism came to light, even before Gorbachev. The Italian communists still hoped for some time that Stanisław Kania could undertake "reform from above," but they eventually had to concede that the pattern of change from below represented by Lech Wałęsa had prevailed. The reference to the myth of the Prague Spring came into question, while for the first time since Stalin's death reform ideas had apparently lost their transnational character.

It was precisely in the early 1980s that the Italian communists intensified their dialogue and exchanges with left-wing social democratic forces. They showed their common attention toward the new issues emerging in the political culture of the European left, such as the dismissal of bipolarism as an outdated order; the idea of an increasing centrality of North–South relations; and interest in themes advanced by the environmentalist and feminist movements. In many ways, this encounter with social democrats epitomized a significant transition for the reform communists. Some of the traditional distinctions between the two groups were losing their significance: In spite of their differences, both stood for détente, the mixed economy and the state's

27 Silvio Pons, "The Rise and Fall of Eurocommunism," in Melvyn P. Leffler and Odd Arne Westad (eds.), *The Cambridge History of the Cold War,* vol. III, *Endings* (Cambridge: Cambridge University Press, 2010), 45–65.
28 Antonio Tatò (ed.), *Conversazioni con Berlinguer* (Rome: Editori Riuniti, 1985), 271.

active role in society and the economy, as well as the need for a politically led restructuring of the international economic order. Specific themes of their dialogue would soon demonstrate their crucial significance – for instance, the ideas of "common security" and "nonoffensive defense" advocated by the German and Swedish social democrats and endorsed by the Italian communists would have a decisive impact on Gorbachev.[29] However, both social democrats and Eurocommunists were now forced into a defensive position. They both suffered the impact of the emerging globalization process, which required a rethinking of the most successful aspects of their national political experiences and economic recipes, and hence limited their ability to rally consensus support.

Eurocommunism had failed both as a tool for political legitimation and as a pole of attraction, and by the early 1980s even the Italian communists ceased using the term. Still, they maintained reform communism as a discursive framework, allowing them to break out of Cold War constraints and as a way to modernize communist culture and practices by restoring a link between socialism and democracy. The notion of a "third way" between social democracy and Soviet socialism became central to Berlinguer's political discourse. Aiming at preserving the revolutionary tradition while at the same time opening the way to integration into the European left, this idea entailed both criticism of social democracy and an enduring trust in the possibility of peaceful structural changes in the West. At the same time, although they criticized Soviet-type socialism as "backward," Italian communists considered it still capable of maintaining its place in late twentieth-century modernity, by virtue of its anti-consumerist qualities and potential for self-renewal. They refused to acknowledge the depth of the crisis of communism and kept faith in the "reformability" of the system. Their discourse and testimony were marginal in the context of 1980s Western Europe, but still resonated among what was left of reform-oriented officials and thinkers in the East as signposts of a political culture that could provide an effective alternative to worn-out revolutionary rhetoric.

In the West, the 1960s and 1970s Marxist projects of radical transformation had dissolved, and while the PCI rejected the spectre of "social-democratization" it followed longstanding reformist practices in its local administrations. In this respect, post-1968 reform communists experienced from within the contradictory transformation of the key revolutionary

29 Matthew Evangelista, *Unarmed Forces: The Transnational Movement to End the Cold War* (Ithaca: Cornell University Press, 1999), 160–62, 184–87.

tradition of the twentieth century, as the changes made in their political culture increasingly conflicted with their defense of their identity.

"New Thinking" and the Path Not Taken

When he came to power in March 1985, Gorbachev did not hold coherent reform ideas, let alone a clear-cut political strategy. Historians have probably overestimated the coherence of his ideas and the extent of consensus within the Soviet ruling class on projects for change. However, a significant elite of reform-oriented officials, representing the de-Stalinization generation, did emerge around him. They shared common ideals of openness, liberalization and transformation from above. Many of them had an important international background of relations, thinking or diplomatic activity, and this in itself formed an experience completely different from those of the older political elites.[30] In a short time, Gorbachev and his leading group were ready to launch a radical attack on the main domestic and international categories of the Soviet Cold War, such as the application of class principles to international relations, the perception of permanent Western hostility, the preeminence of military defense over any political concept of security, and the "Brezhnev doctrine" of limited sovereignty in Eastern Europe. In this respect, Gorbachev was a child of "new thinking" much more than its creator – although the role of his personality in the rapid development of the concepts and practices of reform was crucial.

The genealogy of "new thinking" depended on various sources and experiences. It was a heterogeneous set of ideas accumulated over three decades, some of which were borrowed from the West, interlaced with Soviet peace rhetoric. The Soviet reformers looked to "purified" Marxist inspirations – believing in the myth of Leninism and the NEP as an alternative to Stalinism – as well as ideas of interdependence debated in Western political and intellectual circles, social democratic notions of common security for Europe and even critiques of "actually existing socialism."[31] However, there were hierarchies of sense among their sources. Their most direct inspiration came from "socialism with a human face" and Eurocommunism. In fact, the

---

30 Robert D. English, *Russia and the Idea of the West: Gorbachev, Intellectuals, and the End of the Cold War* (New York: Columbia University Press, 2000).
31 Robert D. English, "Ideas and the End of the Cold War: Rethinking Intellectual and Political Change," in Silvio Pons and Federico Romero (eds.), *Reinterpreting the End of the Cold War: Issues, Interpretations, Periodizations* (London and New York: Frank Cass, 2005), 117–36.

transnational legacy of the Czechoslovak and West European communist reformers represented the only model they had for translating intellectual and political visions into concrete projects and policymaking. The repression of the Prague Spring and the condemnation of Eurocommunism were touchstones of an underlying conflict with the older generation of Soviet leaders. In this respect, the symbolic meaning of Gorbachev's personal attendance at Berlinguer's funeral in June 1984 can hardly be overestimated. The authentic popular participation demonstrated a deep-rooted PCI influence that was unimaginable for communists in power, and which made a strong impression upon Gorbachev.[32]

The reform communist tradition's influence on Gorbachev and his leading group can be detected in the memoirs of protagonists such as Mlynář and Cherniaev.[33] What is less well known is that personal encounters with Italian communist leaders were also significant for the evolution of the Soviet reformers' ideas. Even after Berlinguer's death, the Italian communist leaders acted as a cosmopolitan group who still had a mass influence in their own country. They had come to the conclusion that communist internationalism no longer made sense, as only the ideas of a "third way," Europeanism and "humanistic socialism" could offer viable renewal. Theirs was the only discourse Gorbachev could hear within the communist movement that sounded consistent with his own concern for change and innovation. Not by chance, his relationship with the Italian communists became stronger from mid 1987 onward, in parallel with the radicalization of his reform attempts – whereas he instead experienced increasingly icy relations with most other parties, including the French Communist Party.[34]

Gorbachev's project to put an end to the Cold War in order to liberate resources for domestic reform was closely connected with an ideal relegitimation of the Soviet Union and communism. Not only did his initial view of *perestroika* seeking to prevent decline evolve into radical reform, as he perceived conservative resistance at home and in Eastern Europe. In his view the very notion of reforming the Soviet system was also always linked to the perspective of recovering a mission that could be said to represent

32 Cherniaev, *Sovmestnyi iskhod*, 566.
33 Mikhail Gorbachev and Zdenek Mlynář, *Conversations with Gorbachev: On Perestroika, the Prague Spring, and the Crossroads of Socialism* (New York: Columbia University Press, 2002); Anatoly Cherniaev, *Shest' let s Gorbachevym* (Moscow: Progress, 1993; available in English translation as Anatoly Chernyaev, *My Six Years with Gorbachev* [University Park: Pennsylvania State University Press, 2000]).
34 Silvio Pons, "Western Communists, Mikhail Gorbachev and the 1989 Revolutions," *Contemporary European History* 18, 3 (Aug. 2009), 349–62.

universal aims. The two plans clearly came to interact in late 1987. The turning point was Gorbachev's speech made in November 1987 upon the seventieth anniversary of the October Revolution, in which he declared that "it is now impossible to examine global developments exclusively from the point of view of the struggle between two opposing social systems." He thus dropped the "two camps" theory that was central to the Soviet Cold War, and instead embraced the perspective of interdependence. This was something that Eastern reformers had imagined and Eurocommunists had to some extent theorized. This was a move away from the dichotomous communist worldview that had shaped revolutionary identity for decades, and that dated back to the 1920s. Gorbachev's stance implied increasing attention toward social democracy as well as a mounting discontent with the state of the communist movement. He emphasized the crucial importance of social democratic delegations' participation in a Moscow meeting of November 1987.[35] However, the encounter and exchange with social democratic languages did not mean transformation of communism into social democracy.[36] It was, rather, an attempt at imagining a postrevolutionary identity for communists and at founding a new pluralist left in Europe. Gorbachev's "common European home" was designed not only to claim Russia's place within this home, but also to open the way for socialist renewal.

It can be said that during 1988 Gorbachev and his leading group implemented domestic reforms inspired by "socialism with a human face" – basically aiming at expanding the post-Chernobyl campaign for "transparency" (*glasnost'*) into full acceptance of the concept of human rights, while defining plans to abolish ideological censorship, separate the party from the state and launch market-oriented transition. At the same time, they carried out in their own way suggestions that Western reformers had made – particularly the idea of the "third way" and the definitive shift from class-based "peaceful coexistence" to a new concept of interdependence that made communist internationalism a historical relic. In July 1988, Cherniaev wrote a note to Gorbachev stating that after many years of inertia the time had come to get rid of international communism "as a political category."[37] Gorbachev's leitmotif now still further insisted on the idea that the failure

35 *V Politbiuro TsK KPSS. Po zapisami Anatoliia Cherniaeva, Vadima Medvedeva, Georgiia Shakhnazarova (1985–1991)* (Moscow: Al'pina Biznes Books, 2006), 273.
36 For a different view, see Archie Brown, *The Gorbachev Factor* (Oxford: Oxford University Press, 1996), 175, 248.
37 Pons, "Western Communism," 355.

of *perestroika* would mean not only Soviet decline but also a predicament for socialism worldwide. This argument was a vital motivation – if one posed in implicit terms – for the speech he gave at the United Nations in December 1988, intended as an attack on "the foundations of the Cold War."[38] The virtual end of the Cold War and the promise to abandon the use of violence in Soviet relations with Eastern Europe deprived conservative communist establishments of the main protective umbrella Moscow provided, and exposed them to the alternative between sudden change or inexorable crisis.

However, there was no way to renewal. Change in Eastern Europe came mainly from below, while the paralysis of the establishments led to their collapse. As it turned out, Gorbachev's reforms made this collapse peaceful but could not ultimately prevent it. An irresolvable contradiction emerged between his visions of reform and their compatibility with Soviet-type systems. Gorbachev demonstrated that he was ready to pay the highest price in terms of power – giving up the European sphere of influence established by Stalin – in order to avoid the use of violence from above. He rejected Deng Xiaoping's Tiananmen model of bloody repression, such as Erich Honecker might have imported to Europe in 1989. By remaining committed to peaceful conduct inspired by "humanistic socialism," he provided a decisive contribution to deterring any apocalyptic outcomes. He consistently ensured that resorting to force would be a senseless choice.[39]

Such consistency waned when it came to sustainable political projects. Even in the Soviet Union, by late 1989 the wave of liberalization had gone well beyond the bounds of one-party democracy, with a polarization between radicalized democratic reformers increasingly distrustful of Gorbachev's caution, and the blind resistance of an establishment frustrated by the "loss" of the European sphere of influence. In the aftermath of the fall of the East European regimes, the Soviet reformers' plan to separate the party from the state came to look old-fashioned and delegitimized. The same went for economic reform measures. Although Gorbachev's plans went far beyond the failed pattern of 1965, at the same time they were hardly realistic – and unsuitable for facing the mounting crisis – given that direction and enforcement still relied on centralized institutions.[40] The Soviet reformers were

---

38 *V Politbiuro TsK KPSS*, 426.
39 Stephen Kotkin, *Armageddon Averted: The Soviet Collapse, 1970–2000* (Oxford: Oxford University Press, 2001).
40 Mark Harrison, "Coercion, Compliance, and the Collapse of the Soviet Command Economy," *Economic History Review* 55, 33 (2002), 397–433.

isolated. Even before 1989, not only communist establishments in Eastern Europe, but also almost all the other communist parties opposed *perestroika*, with the PCI being the only major exception. This was particularly true in the Third World: Castro's manifest hostility when Gorbachev visited Cuba in April 1989 epitomized a longstanding aversion toward the European reform communists.[41] Projects for cultural rapprochement with social democracy had not produced an alternative set of political alliances. The landscape was no better after 1989, in spite of Gorbachev's illusory view that the postcommunist regimes would maintain some kind of socialist orientation and friendly relations with Moscow. In fact, the pattern of change in Eastern Europe ruled out any socialist perspectives, and paved the way for a European order that marginalized the Soviet Union. The West did nothing to support the Soviet reformers' agenda and contributed to undermining them.[42]

Destabilization, however, came essentially from within, and radical reform was its key driver. Gorbachev's reforms proved to be unsustainable for the system – all the more so as he declared in February 1990, before being elected head of state, that the monopoly of the communist party should be removed from the Soviet constitution. In many ways, the end of the Cold War deprived the Soviet system of a fundamental cohesive factor, while "humanistic socialism" was insufficient for building a new legitimacy. This problem was understood by conservative opponents of "new thinking" both in Eastern Europe and the Soviet Union, where they increasingly tried to influence Gorbachev and then opted to get rid of him. The Soviet reformers feared the menace of an authoritarian *coup d'état* but did not really consider the scenario of collapse on the pattern of the East European regimes.

Conclusion

The fatal failure of the Soviet reformers evidenced underlying contradictions. Reform communism had never defined the balance between visions of change and the preservation of a specific political identity. The problem was that "humanistic socialism" could lead to a fundamental alteration of the revolutionary identity and, consequently, delegitimize the very sources of the communist experience. By the end of the 1980s, the idea of recovering the purity of Leninism, characteristic of reform communism's invented tradition

---

41 *V Politbiuro TsK KPSS*, 468–69.
42 Archie Brown, *Seven Years That Changed the World: Perestroika in Perspective* (Oxford: Oxford University Press, 2007).

and its anti-Stalinist narrative of history, was no longer plausible. Gorbachev understood this problem. In November 1990, he told Cherniaev that, for all its historical meaning, the October Revolution had "divided the world" while "our current revolution unifies it, opening up an era of a great and real common civilization."[43] In other words, he imagined a post-Leninist scenario and, at the same time, could not help portraying himself as a revolutionary. He and his leading group represented the ultimate evolution of reform communism, and came to see how "new thinking" meant change not only for political ideas and projects, but also for communist identity as such.

As the final expression of reform communism, the Soviet reformers' "new thinking" also symbolized the exhaustion from within of the twentieth-century revolutionary tradition in Europe and Russia. From their own experience they drew the lesson that state violence had hardly served any cause of social progress. Even if Marxism's legacy was still important for them in terms of devising grand designs drawing on an elevated idea of politics as the crucial transformative force of society, they acknowledged the importance of human rights to global civilization and tried to embed it into a vision of universalist socialist politics. However, they failed to see that human rights marked a fundamental rupture in the continuity of modern revolutionary thinking and served to displace declining utopian ideas.[44] Particularly in Eastern Europe, human rights were associated with disbelief in politics and new ideas of moral and "apolitical" transformation. It was the latter that emerged as the main discourses in 1989 and its aftermath. The reform communists and their language of "socialist humanism," conversely, epitomized the fading away of any vision of modernity influenced by the Marxist revolutionary tradition.

Bibliographical Essay

For histories of twentieth-century communism providing analysis on the problem of reform in communist political culture, see notably Archie Brown, *The Rise and Fall of Communism* (New York: HarperCollins, 2009); Silvio Pons, *The Global Revolution: A History of International Communism 1917–1991* (Oxford and New York: Oxford University Press, 2014). On revolution and reform in world politics, see Fred Halliday, *Revolution*

---

43 Cherniaev, *Shest' let s Gorbachevym*, 379.
44 Samuel Moyn, *The Last Utopia: Human Rights in History* (Cambridge, MA: Belknap Press of Harvard University Press, 2010).

and World Politics: The Rise and Fall of the Sixth Great Power (London: Macmillan, 1999).

Post-Stalin reforms in the Soviet Union are best analyzed by William Taubman, *Khrushchev: The Man and His Era* (London: Free Press, 2003). On the survival of reform ideas in the USSR and Eastern Europe after 1956, see Barbara J. Falk, *The Dilemmas of Dissidence in East-Central Europe: Citizen Intellectuals and Philosopher Kings* (Budapest and New York: Central European University Press, 2003); and Vladislav M. Zubok, *Zhivago's Children: The Last Russian Intelligentsia* (Cambridge, MA: Belknap Press of Harvard University Press, 2009). On the implications of economic reforms in the 1960s, Moshe Lewin, *Political Undercurrents in Soviet Economic Debates: From Bukharin to the Modern Reformers* (Princeton: Princeton University Press, 1974), still offers precious insights. An archetypal testimony of the post-1956 trajectory of Western Marxist intellectuals influenced by the ideals of "humanistic socialism" is Edward P. Thompson, "An Open Letter to Leszek Kolakowski," in Edward P. Thompson, *The Poverty of Theory and Other Essays* (London: Merlin Press, 1978), 303–97.

For an overview of the literature on the Prague Spring, see the bibliographical essay related to Pavel Kolář, "Reform Undercurrents and the Prague Spring," in Norman Naimark, Silvio Pons and Sophie Quinn-Judge (eds.), *The Cambridge History of Communism*, 3 vols. (Cambridge: Cambridge University Press, 2017), vol. II, ch. 7. Maud A. Bracke, *Which Socialism, Whose Détente? West European Communism and the Czechoslovak Crisis of 1968* (Budapest: Central European University Press, 2007), analyzes the impact of the Czechoslovak experience on Western communists. For a concise overview of Eurocommunism, see Silvio Pons, "The Rise and Fall of Eurocommunism," in Melvyn P. Leffler and Odd Arne Westad (eds.), *The Cambridge History of the Cold War*, vol. III, *Endings* (Cambridge: Cambridge University Press, 2010), 45–65. By the same author, *Berlinguer e la fine del comunismo* (Turin: Einaudi, 2006) focuses on the Italian communist leadership as the main protagonist of the Eurocommunist experience. Michele Di Donato, *I comunisti italiani e la sinistra europea. Il PCI e i rapporti con le socialdemocrazie (1964–1984)* (Rome: Carocci, 2015), investigates the relationship between Eurocommunists and social democrats. For a focus on relations between the Italian and French communists, see Marco Di Maggio, *Alla ricerca della terza via al socialismo. I PC italiano e francese nella crisi del comunismo (1964–1984)* (Naples: ESI, 2014). The most recent study of the US response to Eurocommunism is Frédéric Heurtebize, *Le Péril Rouge. Washington face à l'eurocommunisme* (Paris: Presses Universitaires de France,

2014). On Eurocommunism and human rights, see Valentine Lomellini, *L'appuntamento mancato. La sinistra italiana e il dissenso nei regimi comunisti (1968–1989)* (Florence: Le Monnier, 2010), and Valentine Lomellini, *Les relations dangereuses. French Socialists, Communists, and the Human Rights Issue in the Soviet Bloc* (Brussels: Peter Lang, 2012). Among several prominent Eurocommunist leaders who have written memoirs, the most significant is Giorgio Napolitano, *Dal PCI al socialismo europeo. Un'autobiografia politica* (Rome and Bari: Laterza, 2005).

For coeval literature and memoirs witness to reform communism's endurance after the repression of the Prague Spring, as an underground current within the establishment in the Soviet Union, see particularly the diary of Anatolii Cherniaev, *Sovmestnyi iskhod. Dnevnik dvukh epokh, 1972–1991 gody* [Joint Exodus: A Diary of Two Epochs, 1972–1991] (Moscow: ROSSPEN, 2010); and also his memoirs: Anatoly Chernyaev, *My Six Years with Gorbachev* (University Park: Pennsylvania State University Press, 2000). On reform communism as a component of left-wing dissent, see as prominent examples Roy Medvedev, *On Socialist Democracy* (Basingstoke: Macmillan, 1975), and Rudolph Bahro, *The Alternative in Eastern Europe* (New York: Verso, 1978). The influence of cosmopolitan reformist officials on the making of Gorbachev's "new thinking" is analyzed by Robert D. English, *Russia and the Idea of the West: Gorbachev, Intellectuals, and the End of the Cold War* (New York: Columbia University Press, 2000); see also Robert D. English and Ekaterina Svyatets, "Soviet Élites and European Integration: From Stalin to Gorbachev," *European Review of History – Revue européenne d'histoire* 21, 2 (2014), 219–33. For a personal account of the tradition of reform communism and Gorbachev's political culture, see Mikhail Gorbachev and Zdeněk Mlynář, *Conversations with Gorbachev: On Perestroika, the Prague Spring, and the Crossroads of Socialism* (New York: Columbia University Press, 2002). More broadly, see also Archie Brown, *The Gorbachev Factor* (Oxford: Oxford University Press, 1996), and Stephen Kotkin, *Armageddon Averted: The Soviet Collapse, 1970–2000* (Oxford: Oxford University Press, 2001). On the Soviet leader's interactions with the Western left, see Silvio Pons, "Western Communists, Mikhail Gorbachev and the 1989 Revolutions," *Contemporary European History* 18, 3 (Aug. 2009), 349–62; and also, though with an excessive tilt toward "social-democratizing" Gorbachev, Archie Brown, "Did Gorbachev as General Secretary Become a Social Democrat?," *Europe-Asia Studies* 65, 2 (2013), 198–220.

8

The Decline of Soviet-Type Economies

ANDRÉ STEINER

One of the starting points for the decline of Soviet-type economies was the suppression of the Prague Spring in 1968 and the concomitant disconti-nuation of the first wave of economic reforms within Eastern bloc states in the 1960s. The system then finally collapsed in the late 1980s and early 1990s, the causes of which are explored here. The initial focus is on the repeated changes in economic control within the countries examined, Czechoslovakia, East Germany (German Democratic Republic, or GDR), Hungary, Poland and the Soviet Union, as well as on their fundamental problems and the solutions suggested during the 1970s and 1980s, before then considering the economic policies pursued by the communist parties in power within these countries. In a third step, the focus shifts to changes in the world economy and their consequences for Eastern bloc states. On this basis, some light can be shed on the resulting development of consumption and growth before finally turning to the process of the dissolution of Soviet-type economies.

Economic Control

With the economic reforms of the 1960s, party leaders within the Eastern bloc tried to respond to the fundamental problems of the Soviet-type planned economy. These were supposed to accelerate economic growth now that the production factors available had been widely exhausted and the extensive sources of growth had thus reached their limits. The reforms were based on the idea that planning and the market could be connected so as to allow mutual complementation and correction, albeit that the "mar-ket" was to remain an instrument of central economic control. Essentially, market mechanisms were to be simulated within the framework of the

Translated by Kirsten Petrak-Jones.

planned economy without introducing the fundamentals of a market economy.[1] Yet, for various reasons, the reforms proved to be only partially successful. The violent suppression of the Prague Spring in 1968 suffocated ideas of reform and brought them to an end. Their internal contradictions and disputes over which course to take, Soviet pressure and the influence of other more conservative party leaders, as well as a sensed threat to the maintenance of power, ultimately brought all rulers to retreat from the risky reform policy.[2] There was a departure from monetary and decentralized instruments, and direct planning of production and distribution of certain goods was now practiced more than before. So central economic control as defined by the classical model of the Soviet-type economy was reestablished to varying degrees within the individual states.

Yet the fundamental problems of Soviet-type economies were thus exacerbated: especially the problems of information and of incentives. As this system was supposed to do without prices as an independent source of information, central office – in the form of the central economic agencies and the economic departments within party headquarters – could draw the necessary information for economic decisions only from the planning process itself. However, within this bureaucratic and hierarchical process, information was falsified due to the different interests of subordinate and superior levels. In addition, the variety and complexity of the economic process made it impossible for all the appropriate information to be gathered centrally in the necessary quality and to make optimal economic decisions. As a result, those in charge of the economy focused mainly on political priorities in accordance with their claim to leadership.

Beyond this aspect, it proved difficult to motivate enterprises and employees to achieve the highest performance. The state ownership of machines and factories – under the ideological gloss of being the property of workers and farmers, or of the people – was no guarantee of higher work motivation and work performance. At the same time, communist regimes also required economic growth to satisfy the expanding needs of their populations and to stand up to competition with the West. However, the pressure to perform, which was necessary in economic terms, was inconsistent with the system's legitimacy – based as it was, for example, on the claim of guaranteeing full

---

1 János Kornai, "The Hungarian Reform Process: Visions, Hopes, and Reality," *Journal of Economic Literature* 24, 4 (1986), 1728–30.

2 Rudolf L. Tőkés, *Hungary's Negotiated Revolution: Economic Reform, Social Change and Political Succession 1957–1990* (Cambridge: Cambridge University Press, 1996), 102–05; André Steiner, *The Plans That Failed: An Economic History of the GDR* (New York: Berghahn, 2010), 134–36.

employment. This goal, though, was an obstacle to the implementation of the *ultima ratio* – i.e. the bankruptcy of enterprises and the dismissal of employees – when economic results proved insufficient. So additional pressure to perform was a potential threat to the legitimacy of power held by the communist parties; but its renunciation was an equal threat due to the decline in economic efficiency.

In addition to the problems of information and of incentives, there was also a widespread lack of innovation that was caused by the system itself. It was the result of enterprises being fixed to the (quantitative) fulfillment of the plan, which made any innovation a disruption. This was one of the fundamental reasons why technological developments and the efficiency of Soviet-type economies increasingly lagged behind those of developed industrial states in the West.[3]

In order to reduce the complexity of economic control from the perspective of central office, from the 1970s bigger economic units – industrial combines or industrial associations – were set up within all the states examined here, and were granted greater rights, but these only partially came into effect. As a result, the average size of industrial units was larger than in the West. While this met economic requirements in some ways, these combines often proved to be unwieldy and risk-averse. In consequence they tended to develop into autarkic economic units. A reduction in the division of labor also ensued, which led to a substantial loss of efficiency.[4]

Aside from what were essentially organizational changes, the GDR and Czechoslovakia avoided further comprehensive reform of the planned economy during their last two decades, as did the Soviet Union up to the mid 1980s. At the same time, attempts were made to improve the system of control by tinkering with the basic targets and incentives for enterprises and their employees. But such a piecemeal approach did not solve existing problems.[5] In Poland too it remained the case that – driven by acute crises and worker unrest – reform attempts were initially half-hearted. Not until the latter half of the 1980s did the impetus for a liberalization process emerge, to which we will return later. It was only in Hungary after 1978

3 On the problems inherent to the system's structure, see János Kornai, *The Socialist System: The Political Economy of Communism* (Oxford: Oxford University Press, 1992).
4 Robert Bideleux and Ian Jeffries, *A History of Eastern Europe: Crisis and Change* (2nd edn., London: Routledge, 2007), 568–70.
5 Philip Hanson, *The Rise and Fall of the Soviet Economy: An Economic History of the USSR from 1945* (London: Longman, 2003), 143–48; Martin R. Myant, *The Czechoslovak Economy 1948–1988: The Battle for Economic Reform* (Cambridge: Cambridge University Press, 1989), 209–13; Steiner, *Plans That Failed*, 176–78.

that the party leadership reacted to growing foreign debts, and to the increasing dissatisfaction of its population with living standards, by returning to the reform process. While this proved more and more to be "a set of improvised political fire-fighting measures," the genie of reform had been let out of the bottle again, and it then increasingly developed a liberal dynamic of its own. So even large economic units were partially decentralized, and small private companies were permitted. A two-tier banking system – with separation between the issuing bank and commercial banks now operating according to market principles – and the first companies with a foreign majority holding pointed to the path ahead. However, the biggest achievement of Hungarian reform was "the unintended restoration of individual initiative."[6] Hungary also thus became the model for later reform processes in Poland.

Economic Policy

In December 1970, workers in Poland reacted to an austerity program with strikes, which were then bloodily suppressed. They were a reflection of the widespread dissatisfaction with living conditions in the Eastern bloc. This triggered an about-turn in economic and social policies in 1971 across all Eastern bloc countries aside from Romania. The course of modernization previously introduced in several countries, which had been linked to economic reform to the detriment of the consumer goods industry, was now to be replaced by a policy that aimed to improve the situation of workers, with a comprehensive package of welfare measures and a better supply of consumer goods. The party leaderships' prime aim was to pacify the workers while securing their own power. This policy clearly followed the Hungarian model where this barter had long been established: political calm in return for relative affluence and social security.[7]

Given the strained supply situation and a limited production capacity for consumer goods, this strategy meant that additional imports were required in most countries. As the possibilities of exporting had an overall limit, however, this involved the necessity of borrowing – mostly from the West. Another fundamental problem within this context was the fact that consumer goods and social benefits were not linked to incentives for employees. This established an economic discrepancy between low productivity and the promise of growing consumption. Moreover, the increasing expenditure on

6 Tökés, *Hungary's Negotiated Revolution*, 115–16.   7 Steiner, *Plans That Failed*, 143–44.

consumption limited the means available for the development of technological innovation and investment.

As a way out of this conundrum, several countries turned to an import-led growth strategy: Not only various supplies and materials were imported from the West but also machinery and plant equipment in order to increase growth. The money borrowed for these imports was supposed to be covered by the additional returns expected from the modern technologies. Yet this calculation proved to be flawed because actual returns were less than those expected: On the one hand, the imported technologies failed to lead to the anticipated jump in productivity because they were often applied in isolation. On the other, the competitiveness of export goods was not increased to the extent necessary to allow their export to the West in substantial quantities. In sum, this strategy led to a spiral of growing imports from the West and sinking returns from exports, which increased the level of debt to the West while economic substance at home was increasingly drained. Such a policy was broadly followed by the GDR and Hungary while Czechoslovakia and the Soviet Union were more reserved in this respect. The strategy was, however, most pronounced in Poland, where during the first half of the 1970s an unprecedented investment boom was set off, but this was in itself unbalanced and then led to a growing dependence of production and investments on imports from the West. When in 1976 debts and debt servicing reached a critical level, investments were cut arbitrarily. As a result, projects were left unfinished and substantial losses were incurred.[8]

All in all, debt service and expenditure on consumption were growing, which reduced the scope for investment even more. Within the individual states, the increases in investment were cut to varying degrees or had to be cut back absolutely. This led to a growing number of unfinished projects which did not come into operation, straining the efficiency of the funds thus employed. Moreover, even the replacement of worn-out machinery was not guaranteed, so that the proportion of run-down facilities still operating rapidly increased. Nevertheless, in order to achieve the most possible with more and more limited investment funds, the party leaderships in some countries concentrated these on certain priorities. This involved mainly parts of the arms industry in the case of the Soviet Union; in other countries power generation remained a priority. In contrast, a program to promote the development of microelectronics was launched in the latter half of the 1970s

8 Batara Simatupang, *The Polish Economic Crisis: Background, Causes, Aftermath* (London: Routledge, 1994), 211–13.

in the GDR as this field had increasingly emerged worldwide as the key innovation.

Yet such programs failed to solve existing problems. To the contrary, in the sectors that were not especially promoted, these were even strengthened. In particular, the monopoly enjoyed by the combines or associations, the relatively low qualitative demands of trade within the Eastern economic alliance (the Council for Mutual Economic Assistance or Comecon) and a control mechanism that still continued to reward mainly quantitative growth prevented a successful renewal of production. Isolation from the international division of labor and the resulting relatively broad range of goods both had the same effect. They dissipated research and development activities and thus produced only few results. This was also one reason why the provision of industry with modern equipment was poor by international standards; in the case of the latest developments, such as in computing and information technology, the Eastern bloc countries increasingly fell behind.[9]

At the same time, the growing imports of Western technology and consumer goods worsened – to differing degrees – the debt level of Eastern bloc countries to the West. The political fear of thus becoming dependent on the competitor's system was overcome, on the one hand, by East–West détente. On the other, it was believed that, given the high rate of inflation in the West in the 1970s and initially low nominal interest, the real costs of the debts would be very low or even negative, which encouraged borrowing all the more. In the West, the latter was supported because of its own economic crisis of 1973–75, the liquidity of its banks, the petrodollar surplus and the belief of the West in the Soviet financial umbrella. By the latter half of the 1970s, the debts of some of the Eastern bloc countries, especially Poland, Hungary and the GDR, had already increased so strongly that a growing part of new loans had to be used to service existing debts.[10]

At the end of the 1970s, the majority of Eastern bloc states were already in massive economic difficulties, determined not only by domestic developments as outlined above but also by changes in the external economic environment.

9 James W. Cortada, *The Digital Flood: The Diffusion of Information Technology Across the US, Europe, and Asia* (Oxford: Oxford University Press, 2012), 238–99.
10 Stephen Kotkin, "The Kiss of Debt: The East Bloc Goes Borrowing," in Niall Ferguson, Charles S. Maier, Erez Manela and Daniel S. Sargent (eds.), *The Shock of the Global: The 1970s in Perspective* (Cambridge, MA: Belknap Press of Harvard University Press, 2010), 80–94.

International Interdependencies

In the 1950s and 1960s, world market prices for raw materials increased only slowly at first but the boom in the developed industrial states and the economic rise of some Asian countries had already gradually strengthened the price increase prior to the oil price shock of 1973. Although the causes were diverse, this marked the end of the boom, and the capitalist world economy fell into a deep recession. These developments seemed at first not to concern Eastern bloc states as they imported most raw materials they required from the Soviet Union at prices that noticeably lagged behind world market prices. However, following the increase in prices for raw materials, the prices for semi-finished and finished products also increased on the world markets; these had to be paid by the USSR too for corresponding imports. The Soviet Union thus pressed the other Comecon members for changes to the existing price mechanism within the economic alliance. So, after 1975, prices for raw material supplies within Comecon responded to price movements on the world market more quickly and decisively than before.

Thus the prices to be paid by Eastern bloc states increased more rapidly, and a further upward development was foreseeable: Between 1971 and 1978 the price for raw oil within Comecon increased fourfold and on the world markets sixfold. These price increases for raw oil in particular forced Eastern bloc states, depending on their own resources, to introduce radical cuts, comprehensive measures of substitution and corresponding structural changes in raw-material consumption and power generation. They were immensely expensive and had a number of negative consequences – such as for the environment, for example – but these were taken into account in order to improve domestic reserves of hard currencies. Suggestions that the expenditures for consumption and the welfare policy should be cut back in light of the new burdens were mostly not voiced for fear of threatening political stability.[11] Hungary, by contrast, did allow reductions in the standard of living under the pressure of economic realities.[12]

That prices for raw materials rose while the competitiveness of Eastern bloc export products on the world market failed to improve worsened the

---

11 For the GDR, see André Steiner, "'Common Sense Is Necessary': East German Reactions to the Oil Crises of the 1970s," in Frank Bösch and Rüdiger Graf (eds.), *The Energy Crises of the 1970s: Anticipations and Reactions in the Industrialized World* (Cologne: GESIS, 2014), 231–50.

12 Pál Germuska, "Failed Eastern Integration and a Partly Successful Opening Up to the West: The Economic Re-orientation of Hungary During the 1970s," *European Review of History* 21, 2 (2014), 280–82.

terms of trade of those Comecon states that lacked raw materials. For example, "in 1974, the Soviets accepted 800 units of Hungary's Ikarus bus in exchange for 1 million tons of oil, but by 1981 that same quantity of oil required 2300 buses, and by the mid 1980s 4000 buses."[13] Nevertheless, the oil price which the Comecon states had to pay the USSR was still below the world market price of the day. This ratio also created the implicit subsidies which the Soviet Union effectively granted the Eastern bloc states to varying degrees. These probably had their origins in the late 1950s and early 1960s and resulted from the fact that the Soviet Union supplied its raw materials to the other states at prices below world market levels; in addition, it imported industrial products from the other states at prices that were above those attainable on the world market for the same products. These indirect forms of support were not, however, based on political considerations, but resulted from the fact that, within the restricted trading area of Comecon, prices systematically deviated from world market prices – one could say in correspondence to the existing relations of scarcity.[14] Nevertheless, prices for raw materials continued to rise here during the latter half of the 1980s due to the mechanics of the Comecon price-fixing mechanism, while world market prices, especially for raw oil, fell. So the implicit subsidies for the countries involved were lost to varying degrees from the mid 1980s. In consequence, the value of Comecon for its member states also continued to dwindle.

Established in 1949, the Eastern economic alliance was, from the 1960s, primarily supposed to promote the economic division of labor within the Eastern bloc. As currencies were not convertible, however, the mechanisms of the planned economy meant that – despite all the reform discussions already held in the 1960s – no more was achieved than a bilateral exchange of goods, and the integration of the national economies into one economic area remained out of reach. But this was also a result of the rather disparate development levels of the countries involved – with the more highly developed industrial states Czechoslovakia and the GDR facing still basically agrarian states such as Bulgaria and Romania – which fueled national egoisms. In order to reduce obstacles to economic integration within Comecon, some countries again attempted during the latter half of the 1980s to mold the alliance more strongly as a common market with convertible currencies and a certain openness to world markets. The GDR and Bulgaria were most

---

13 Stephen Kotkin, *Uncivil Society: 1989 and the Implosion of the Communist Establishment* (New York: Modern Library, 2009), 26.
14 For a summary, see Bideleux and Jeffries, *History of Eastern Europe*, 570.

strongly opposed to these suggestions, already recognizing their potentially explosive threat to the system.[15]

In addition, given the lack of integrative effects within Comecon, East–West trade grew significantly more quickly than trade within Comecon from the 1970s onward. In the cases of Poland, Hungary, Romania, Czechoslovakia and the GDR at least, the proportion of intra-bloc trade fell in the long term, so that by the end of the 1980s it no longer dominated the foreign trade of these countries. This also meant, however, that the share of the "capitalist world" in the foreign trade of Eastern bloc states markedly increased too. Paradoxically this was a reflection of the falling competitiveness of its products, as more and more exports were thus necessary in order to pay for the imports required, irrespective of the question of whether or not they ran up further debt.[16]

Yet the growing trade between the East and West was – as already illustrated – linked to initially favorable borrowing terms and East–West détente, which facilitated trade, but this came to a close at the end of the 1970s: A further round of the arms race took its economic toll on the Soviet Union too, and from the early 1980s the USA worked on fighting the Eastern bloc economically. This also involved the CoCom (Coordination Committee for Multilateral Export Controls) list for the control of technology exports to the Eastern bloc being applied more strictly again after the more relaxed approach of the 1970s. Moreover, the debtor nations of the Eastern bloc increasingly met with difficulties as interest rates had already been rising since the late 1970s and, under pressure from the USA, the readiness of the banks to reschedule debts also became more limited. The situation worsened with the second oil-price shock of 1979–80 which again made world market prices for raw materials soar. Furthermore, in 1981, burdened by its own increasing economic difficulties, the Soviet Union cut its supplies of raw oil to the Comecon states which had paid lower prices than on the world market and in transferable rubles. As a result, these now had to buy a growing part of their raw oil – now at higher prices and in US dollars – on the world market, which represented a further strain for these states.[17]

15 Randall W. Stone, *Satellites and Commissars: Strategy and Conflict in the Politics of Soviet-Bloc Trade* (Princeton: Princeton University Press, 1996), 212–14.
16 Ralf Ahrens, "Debt, Cooperation, and Collapse: East German Foreign Trade in the Honecker Years," in Hartmut Berghoff and Uta Andrea Balbier (eds.), *The East German Economy, 1945–2010: Falling Behind or Catching Up?* (New York: Cambridge University Press, 2013), 164.
17 For a summary, see André Steiner, "The Globalisation Process and the Eastern Bloc Countries in the 1970s and 1980s," *European Review of History* 21, 2 (2014), 169.

At the beginning of the 1980s, a debt crisis emerged in Eastern Europe, and Poland proved to be the focal point. The particular issue within this country was rooted in the interlinked economic and political crises between 1979 and 1982. The conflicts between workers and the regime, which cannot be dealt with in detail here, were primarily the result of social and economic difficulties and thus worsened not only the political but also the economic situation.[18] So, by the spring of 1981, Poland was practically bankrupt, and at the same time the Soviet Union declared that there would be no financial umbrella for Eastern bloc states. In addition, Romania not only had liquidity problems but also failed to inform its creditors of this and omitted to pay for received goods.[19] Taken together, these developments damaged the creditworthiness of other Eastern bloc states too and exacerbated their situation.

When at the end of 1981 martial law was declared in Poland, Western states imposed credit sanctions on all Eastern bloc countries, which worsened the situation throughout the bloc and especially in Poland. Subsequently the country had to generate a trade surplus: Imports were cut even more and exports, especially of coal and food, were slowly increased. With the trade surplus thus achieved, Poland was able to service the loans from commercial banks while the (far greater) obligations to Western states were still neglected, so total debts continued to grow. Overall, this policy withdrew from the Polish national economy resources that would have been necessary for any forward-looking investments.[20]

Other Eastern bloc states, such as the GDR and Czechoslovakia, also reacted to the credit ban imposed by the West with import reductions and export campaigns in order to reduce debts (which in the case of Czechoslovakia were lower anyway). Here East Germany received – with bankruptcy imminent – indirect support not just from West Germany but from the Soviet Union too. Given the lower competitiveness of its products, however, increases in exports were solely possible at dumping prices which diminished economic assets.[21] Hungary was able to solve its acute balance-of-payments crisis in 1982 only by joining the International Monetary Fund (IMF) and the World Bank. Nevertheless, attempts were also made in this situation to increase exports in

18 Kazimierz Z. Poznanski, *Poland's Protracted Transition: Institutional Change and Economic Growth 1970–1994* (Cambridge: Cambridge University Press, 1997), 26–29.
19 Harold James, *International Monetary Cooperation Since Bretton Woods* (Washington, DC: International Monetary Fund, 1996), 361, 561–62.
20 Poznanski, *Poland's Protracted Transition*, 92–93.
21 Myant, *Czechoslovak Economy*, 192–93; Steiner, *Plans That Failed*, 172–74.

order to reduce the debt burden. Moreover, the party leadership saw no option other than to lower the living standards of its own population too.[22] Romania sought a more drastic solution: A radical program of austerity, with electricity cuts and food rationing which primarily burdened its own people, was supposed to secure a total reduction of debts issued by Western creditors.[23] Such a price was out of the question for the party leaderships of the other countries for fear of political instability and the loss of their own power. So political considerations provided the criteria that determined to what extent and with which means the reduction of the debt level was to be achieved.

The case of the Soviet Union regarding the question of debts deserves to be examined in its own right: While it profited from the worldwide increase in oil and gas prices, this was counteracted by years of crop failure and the concomitant import demands. At the same time, as a result of the oil price increases, it also suffered from a drop in imports from the West in terms of real prices. The end of détente and the sanctions by the West which followed the invasion of Afghanistan in 1979 were also not without effect. As a result, the Soviet Union also developed a tendency toward trade deficits with the West, although these were initially covered by the sale of gold and weapons and only then through borrowing, to which the Soviets had also maintained a more cautious approach. In line with this, they reduced imports of machinery and technology as more grain imports became necessary.[24] Even so, in 1982 they were also hit by the credit ban imposed by the West.

It was not until 1984 that this situation changed, once the Eastern bloc states had reduced their debts and had again received bigger loans. The external liabilities of the Eastern bloc fell markedly between 1981 and 1984. Nonetheless, after 1984 they increased significantly again, and by the end of 1987 they exceeded the maximum level of 1981. However, the rise in debt levels prior to 1981 had been linked to a strong growth in East–West trade, while after 1984 Eastern bloc exports to the West dwindled. So the ratio between gross liabilities in the West and exports in the same direction had improved for the Eastern bloc countries from 100 percent in 1981 to 75 percent in 1984, but by the end of 1986 it had already risen again to 130 percent. The structural dilemma faced by Eastern bloc states was that on the one hand

22 Sándor Szakács, "From 'Goulash Communism' to Breakdown," in Lee W. Congdon and Béla K. Király (eds.), *The Ideas of the Hungarian Revolution, Suppressed and Victorious: 1956–1999* (New York: Columbia University Press, 2003), 211; Germuska, "Failed Eastern Integration," 283–84.
23 Ivan T. Berend, *Central and Eastern Europe 1944–1993: Detour from the Periphery to the Periphery* (Cambridge: Cambridge University Press, 1996), 231–32.
24 Hanson, *Rise and Fall*, 155–56.

they required more imports and thus more borrowing. On the other, they were not able to sell their products on the Western markets to a sufficient degree as these products were not competitive. In this situation, it was not surprising that the level of debts escalated again by the end of the 1980s and that a growing proportion of returns from exports had to be reserved for debt servicing.[25]

As the explosion in world market prices for raw materials was keenly felt in the Eastern bloc too, even the last of the communist leaders began to falter in their conviction, established by Stalin, that there were two separate – one capitalist and one socialist – world markets. Facing increasing economic problems at home, stronger attempts were made to do business with the West beyond foreign trade alone. The Eastern bloc states had already agreed on so-called compensation agreements since the 1970s. These involved investment goods from the West being supplied on credit over several years, and these loans were in turn refinanced with countersupplies of those products which were produced with the machinery and plant equipment that had been imported in this way. In this manner, companies in the West employed the Eastern bloc as their "extended workbench" in reaction to the rising costs (prices for raw materials, lending rates). These transactions can indeed be understood as the functional equivalent of direct foreign investments under the particular conditions of the Eastern bloc. Direct foreign investments in their classical form remained relatively small within Eastern bloc states but increased at this low level over the course of the 1980s, a development in which Hungary played a pioneering role.[26]

A further instrument of cooperation was perceived in East–West joint ventures for which in the latter half of the 1980s not only Hungary and Poland, but also the Soviet Union and Czechoslovakia, established a legal framework. However, this form of company initially remained an isolated phenomenon within Eastern bloc countries. Not until 1988, when it became permissible for foreign investors to hold the majority interest in joint ventures in the USSR, Hungary, Poland and Czechoslovakia, did the number of East–West joint ventures multiply in these states and especially in the Soviet Union.[27]

Beyond this, most Eastern bloc states drew closer to the international financial institutions – the IMF and World Bank – in the latter half of the

25 Steiner, "Globalisation Process," 172.   26 Ibid., 170–71.
27 Patrick Gutman, "Joint Ventures in Eastern Europe and the Dynamics of Reciprocal Flows in East–West Direct Investments: Some New Perspectives," in Patrick Artisien, Matija Rojec and Marjan Svetličić (eds.), *Foreign Investment in Central and Eastern Europe* (Basingstoke: Macmillan, 1993), 54–81.

1980s, after Romania had become a member of the IMF in 1972 and Hungary in 1982. These institutions were of interest to Eastern bloc states primarily because of the promise of access to new loans. In addition, these institutions were later instrumentalized in some of these countries as a forceful embodiment of market principles.[28] This took place in the context of efforts to reform the existing system in the late 1980s, which heralded the path ahead of transformation into a market economy. Yet it was probably the ever-faster spread of consumer wishes and consumption patterns in the context of globalization that made a substantial contribution to the dissolution of the planned economy and the end of the Eastern bloc.

The Development of Consumption and Growth

In the West, mass consumer society had been established by the 1970s, at the latest, and consumer demands developed in ever-greater variety, becoming more and more refined. This development represented a real problem for the leaderships of the communist parties within the Eastern bloc – and all the more so the closer the country in question was to the western border of the bloc and the greater the opportunities of its citizens to travel as well as the greater number of visitors from the West. The people living within the Eastern bloc states learnt via TV and radio, from visitors and their own visits about the consumer possibilities now available in the West. There it was no longer a question of satisfying simple consumer needs but increasingly about certain types of clothes or brands of car. Within Eastern bloc states, the younger generations in particular expected a corresponding range of goods within their own country. But, at best, the communist party leaders could, and wanted to, meet these demands only in a limited way. By the 1970s and 1980s, the – never to be fulfilled – claim of socialism to be an alternative to capitalism with its own consumer patterns and goods supply was no longer the issue.[29]

The supply of consumer goods also remained restricted because their production was always neglected with regard to the allocation of finite resources – apart from some short-term exceptions. The relevant imports were in turn limited by the availability of hard currency. Aside from the conditions of general shortage and backwardness when compared to the

---

28 James, *International Monetary Cooperation*, 558–82.
29 Judd Stitziel, *Fashioning Socialism: Clothing, Politics, and Consumer Culture in East Germany* (Oxford: Berg, 2005), 166–68.

West, there were not insignificant differences in living standards between the individual states of the Eastern bloc.

Notably, the insufficient goods supply was faced with more or less continually rising nominal incomes. On the one hand, the issue of incentives described earlier made it difficult for company management to adapt performance norms to new technological conditions, so that these norms were rather "soft." On the other, the party leaderships repeatedly resorted to placating the workers with income increases. What these workers could actually buy with their growing income was then a question not only of what was on offer but also of price developments. Since prices were not determined by the market but by the state, the latter had to take the rising costs into account. The driving forces here were wages and above all the prices for raw materials. In order to counter higher costs, either the supply of consumer goods could be subsidized or prices needed to be pushed up accordingly. For political reasons, the party leaderships shied away from the latter.

In general, the prices for basic needs – essential foods and housing as well as energy and public transport – were kept at artificially low levels in order to keep them affordable for everybody and thus to achieve one goal of socialism. The necessary subsidies these entailed used up a growing proportion of budget expenditure: In the Soviet Union this increased between 1965 and 1989 from 4 percent to 20 percent. In the GDR the proportion was similar.[30] As a result, the financial resources available for other expenditures such as investments were restricted. Moreover, these subsidies led to abuse and waste.

If, however, these overstretched the financial options of the state, the party leaderships also attempted to increase prices directly, as was repeatedly the case in Poland where it provoked worker unrest. The wage drift inherent in the system, reinforced by the weakness of the regime and the necessity of pacifying the workers, led, in conjunction with the shortage of goods and increases in costs, to an inflationary wage–price spiral. In Poland this constellation became extremely explosive, thus playing its part in the political instability of the country in the 1970s and 1980s, and finally in the path to the transformation process that emerged in the late 1980s.[31]

30 Byung-Yeon Kim, "Causes of Repressed Inflation in the Soviet Consumer Market, 1965–1989: Retail Price Subsidies, the Siphoning Effect, and the Budget Deficit," *Economic History Review* 55, 1 (2002), 105–27; Steiner, *Plans That Failed*, 185–86.
31 Simatupang, *Polish Economic Crisis*, 215–16.

Furthermore, the subsidies increased the permanent and growing surplus of purchasing power that was created by the imbalance between growing demand and restricted supply. Assuming a constant propensity to save, this would normally have led to inflation, but was (to a great extent) suppressed by the state administration of prices. At the same time, enterprises always had scope to push up prices for their products which, as was often criticized, led to creeping inflation. Indeed, given the shortages in supply, the surplus in purchasing power and the suppressed inflation, a second economy and black markets inevitably developed. The first provided goods and services otherwise in short supply and served as an additional source of income. There also evolved signs of a new, private entrepreneurship. In the case of the black market, goods and services could be obtained – often for hard currencies which practically emerged as an additional currency – which were otherwise totally out of reach. The second economy was most advanced (and also legal) in Hungary, where estimates suggest that in the mid 1980s two-thirds to three-quarters of households were involved in this sector.[32] In the case of the other countries – regardless of the variation that can be assumed – at least one general point of reference is provided by an estimate for the Soviet Union. According to this estimate, 16.3 percent of household income was generated in the second economy and 22.9 percent of spending was carried out in this sector in the 1970s and 1980s, which represented a contribution of 6–7 percent to the GDP.[33] This was a dimension not to be ignored.

The real incomes within the countries examined here increased in the 1970s and decreased in the 1980s. Compared to the industrial states of the West, however, they lost ground throughout the whole period, while the GDR and Czechoslovakia displayed the highest incomes. The real income of Polish employees rose markedly during the first half of the 1970s and then stagnated, falling drastically in 1978 and again in 1982, so that by the 1980s it probably fell to the lowest level within the group of countries in question here. In Hungary, it increased up to 1978 before then steadily falling. In the Soviet Union, real income remained at the lowest level of all states until 1982 but increased up to the end of the 1970s before then moderately falling.[34]

32 Ignác Romsics, *Hungary in the Twentieth Century* (2nd edn., Budapest: Corvina, 2010), 357.
33 Byung-Yeon Kim, "Informal Economy Activities of Soviet Households: Size and Dynamics," *Journal of Comparative Economics* 31, 3 (2003), 548.
34 These figures can provide only a general picture. See Benedykt Askanas, *Niveau und Entwicklung der Reallöhne in den RGW-Ländern im Vergleich mit Österreich* (Vienna: Wiener Institut für Internationale Wirtschaftsvergleiche, 1985).

Economic growth had a tendency to decline throughout the whole period across all countries examined here, although this included quite some variation between the individual states.[35] In particular, developments in Poland deviated somewhat from this pattern: During the first half of the 1970s, the import-led growth strategy was still generating marked growth. After 1978, though, strikes, the related chaos in production, foreign trade difficulties and political conflicts brought about a drastic drop in production. In 1989 economic performance finally fell below that of 1978.[36]

This general pattern of growth can primarily be explained by the fact that the extensive sources of growth were more or less exhausted in most countries, while there was a failure to increase economic efficiency anywhere in such a way as to reach earlier growth rates. In other words, the extensive model of development was maintained. Beyond this, there were also a number of contingent factors involved: The political decision to expand consumption in addition to the explosion in energy costs limited the means available for investment. This problem was to be bypassed through more borrowing. Although the funds acquired in this manner – insofar as these were not used for consumption – were employed in modern technologies, they failed to result in the returns hoped for, as investment in general failed to do so. The overall decline in investment efficiency increasingly proved to be a key problem as it also failed to improve the already low level of competitiveness and productivity. With the costs of debt out of control, import cuts and export increases finally became necessary. As a result, the disposable national product fell or stagnated, which was again to the detriment of investment and of modern machinery in particular. Moreover, the strategy of exporting as much as possible at all costs meant that those sectors with products that were significant as exports but that could only be sold at dumping prices on the world market were allocated substantially more resources. The consequence was that the structure shifted in favor of sectors of low productivity. All in all, the Eastern bloc states had maneuvered

---

35 For an overview, see David F. Good and Tongshu Ma, "The Economic Growth of Central and Eastern Europe in Comparative Perspective 1870–1989," *European Review of Economic History* 3, 2 (1999), 103–37. On individual countries, see Mark Harrison, "Trends in Soviet Labour Productivity, 1928–1985: War, Postwar Recovery, and Slowdown," *European Review of Economic History* 2, 2 (1998), 171–200; Nigel Swain, *Hungary: The Rise and Fall of Feasible Socialism* (London: Verso, 1992), 146; Stephen Broadberry and Alexander Klein, "When and Why Did Eastern European Economies Begin to Fail? Lessons from a Czechoslovak/UK Productivity Comparison, 1921–1991," *Explorations in Economic History* 48, 1 (2011), 37–52; Steiner, *Plans That Failed*, 160, 178.

36 Simatupang, *Polish Economic Crisis*, 219.

themselves into a vicious circle which led to a further draining of economic substance.

Furthermore, against the background of the promise and the claim of economic and technological modernization – which were obviously not being fulfilled – and the accompanying dependence on the West – and inability to outdo the latter – the planners increasingly lost their authority. During the 1980s, managers of enterprises, combines and associations, but also the central economic actors of state, were mainly involved in somehow dealing with the smaller and bigger crises alternatively provoked by the domestic economy and by foreign economic developments. A form of muddling through became increasingly widespread, and the power of the plan became more and more watered down.[37] Moreover, this also under-mined the legitimacy of the system.

Processes of Dissolution

These Soviet-type economies could nevertheless have continued to exist. Mostly political decisions sparked off the process of dissolution of this economic system against the background of economic weakness. The party leaderships reacted to the economic problems in different ways within their individual countries, while neither the reformers nor the "conservatives" wanted to abolish socialism; both wanted to make it feasible. Party leaders in the GDR and Czechoslovakia chose to continue the existing system and merely to "make it more perfect." Indeed, the economy and living standards of both these countries were clearly on a higher level than in other Eastern bloc states and so, in their eyes, the variant of the system they represented was tried and tested – at least by comparison to the other Eastern bloc countries.

Hungary, on the other hand, continued its reform program – as described above – and its communist leadership, even once the privatization of state property had begun, remained convinced that it was introducing a new model of socialism and not another system, although it was already in the process of doing so.[38] In Poland, communist party leaders wanted stronger reform of the existing economic system in 1986–87, following the example of Hungary in some respects: Commercial banks were set up and the number of ministries reduced. In addition, the numbers of targets set and distributive

---

37 Harrison, "Trends in Soviet Labour Productivity," 196–97; Steiner, *Plans That Failed*, 178.
38 Szakács, "From 'Goulash Communism' to Breakdown," 212–13.

decisions made by central office were diminished. Changes to the structure of ownership were also addressed but remained piecemeal. Not until the reform-oriented government of Mieczysław Rakowski came to office, in mid 1988, did these ideas for reorganization become radicalized – promoted by a wave of strikes provoked by a further worsening of living conditions – no longer aiming at a mixed economy as before but at a consolidation of market powers. Controls on prices were lifted step by step, the subsidization of industrial combines and employment guarantees abolished and thus bankruptcy and unemployment made permissible. Moreover, the private sector was now sponsored more than the state sector. In effect, the communist party itself abolished the centrally planned economy.[39]

However, all this was only possible because of the developments in the Soviet Union from the mid 1980s, which had accelerated events in other Eastern bloc states as well. When Mikhail Gorbachev became general secretary of the Communist Party of the Soviet Union in 1985, the Soviet Union had also reached its limits: Crop failure and the increasing costs of extracting raw materials against the background of an increasing arms burden, in addition to a falling world market price for oil, all restricted its scope for action.[40] In consequence, the Soviets could and would no longer support other Eastern bloc states, neither explicitly nor implicitly, albeit that the reduction in implicit subsidies was probably more unintentional. Gorbachev initially remained hesitant with regard to reform because neither the required extent nor the goal seemed clear, and there was substantial opposition to reform within the state bureaucracy. As he then became aware of the extent of the country's economic difficulties, he attempted to find ways to end the arms race and to make the Soviet Union viable.

Nevertheless, when in 1987 those in power decided to endorse economic reform, the necessary preparations had not been made, so reform was initially limited to organizational changes. The Enterprise Law of 1987 deprived the ministries of their powers, and the managers of industrial combines were given more scope for action. But up to this point, the ministries had been responsible for the allocation of resources. In 1988 even the economic departments within party central office, which had formerly represented central state control and intervention, were abolished. This not only weakened the centrally planned economy but also dismantled two of its decisive pillars – the allocation of resources through

39 Poznanski, *Poland's Protracted Transition*, 88–89, 100–01, 106–08.
40 Hanson, *Rise and Fall*, 132–40.

the ministries and the freedom of the party to intervene – without establishing a new system of allocation. At the same time, the central state authorities were thus deprived of more of their authority and credibility. Gorbachev was convinced that, if controls were reduced, producers would multiply their efforts, but in fact the opposite happened: Production collapsed, which promoted regional particularism, tore apart supply networks and in consequence further accelerated the decline in production. Finally, after 1991, the transition to the market economy occurred incrementally.[41]

Prior to this, the Soviet Union had already announced in June 1990 that from 1991 onward trade with Comecon partners would be possible only in convertible currencies and at current world market prices. This adoption of free-market trade practices marked the end of the Eastern economic alliance, which was accelerated by the departure of the GDR after German reunification, just as by the radical political changes in other Eastern bloc states. Comecon formally dissolved itself in June 1991 at a council meeting in Budapest.[42]

It was an unintended consequence of the communist leaderships' own reforms that they furthered the dismantlement of the planned economy and abolition of socialism in general. The decisive cause of the economic weakness of the Eastern bloc states was, however, the inability of the socialist economic system to bring about structural as well as technological change from within when faced by the exhaustion of extensive sources of growth. The system was not able to react effectually to the new basic conditions – globally changing prices for important resources and the international spread of a post-Fordist production regime based on flexible technologies – and to adapt to them. While developments in foreign trade did make these problems worse, they were not the actual root cause. These were primarily linked to the inflexibility and the insufficient incentive structures of the control mechanisms as well as to basic economic–political decisions which eroded the substance of these economies. The Eastern bloc states had – some more and others less – lived beyond their means for many years, as is documented by the level of debt and the deterioration of the capital stock. The inability to meet the growing consumer demands of their own populations, in either quantitative or qualitative terms, accelerated the decline and contributed to the political upheaval of 1989–90.

41 Alec Nove, *An Economic History of the USSR: 1917–1991* (London: Penguin, 1992), 395–401, 418–19; Mark Harrison, "Coercion, Compliance, and the Collapse of the Soviet Command Economy," *Economic History Review* 55, 3 (2002), 397–433.
42 Stone, *Satellites and Commissars*, 204–27.

Ultimately, the Soviet-type planned economies failed because they could not live up to their own claim of being superior to the capitalist system in economic terms too – which served to legitimate communist rule – because of problems inherent to the system: Neither in terms of technology or productivity, nor in consumption, could they provide real alternatives to the capitalist West, quite aside from the question of whether they achieved its level.

Bibliographical Essay

The economic decline of the Eastern bloc has been examined in various perspectives. The multitude of economic analyses on how Soviet-type economies functioned and their fundamental defects has been expertly summarized by János Kornai, *The Socialist System: The Political Economy of Communism* (Oxford: Oxford University Press, 1992). Overviews from a general historical perspective which also provide insights into economic processes need not be referred to here as these are already cited in other chapters within this book. For an examination of the long lines of economic change, see Derek H. Aldcroft and Steven Morewood, *Economic Change in Eastern Europe Since 1918* (Aldershot, UK: Edward Elgar, 1995). A greater emphasis on economic history is also provided by Ivan T. Berend, *Central and Eastern Europe 1944–1993: Detour from the Periphery to the Periphery* (Cambridge: Cambridge University Press, 1996), and *From the Soviet Bloc to the European Union: The Economic and Social Transformation of Central and Eastern Europe Since 1973* (Cambridge: Cambridge University Press, 2009). As both historian and participator in the processes described, the author provides a more essayistic account of economic developments in Central Eastern and Eastern Europe, with the exemption of the case of the GDR. For a more analytical approach, see Steven Morewood, "The Demise of the Command Economies in the Soviet Union and Its Outer Empire," in Derek H. Aldcroft and Michael J. Oliver (eds.), *Economic Disasters of the Twentieth Century* (Cheltenham, UK: Edward Elgar, 2007), 258–311.

To date, only one publication on Comecon also draws on documents from its internal archives: Randall W. Stone, *Satellites and Commissars: Strategy and Conflict in the Politics of Soviet-Bloc Trade* (Princeton: Princeton University Press, 1996). Also worthwhile here is Jozef M. van Brabant, *Economic Integration in Eastern Europe: A Handbook* (New York, Routledge, 1989). The more recent increase in interest in the foreign relations of Soviet-type economies is particularly reflected in Angela Romano and Federico Romero (eds.), "European Socialist Regimes Facing Globalisation and European Cooperation: Dilemmas and Responses," *European Review of History* 21, 2 (2014) (special issue).

The comprehensiveness of English-language publications on the economic developments in individual countries varies, as does the access to internal documents in the archives. So the literature listed below includes different approaches. For Czechoslovakia, see Martin R. Myant, *The Czechoslovak Economy 1948–1988: The Battle for Economic Reform* (Cambridge: Cambridge University Press, 1989). The East German economy is examined in André Steiner, *The Plans That Failed: An Economic History of the GDR* (New York: Berghahn, 2010). Beyond these, various aspects find analysis in Hartmut Berghoff and Uta Andrea Balbier (eds.), *The East German Economy, 1945–2010: Falling Behind or Catching Up?* (New York: Cambridge University Press, 2013). For the case of Hungary, see mainly Ivan T. Berend, *The Hungarian Economic Reforms 1953–1988* (Cambridge: Cambridge University Press, 1990), as well as Gábor Révész, *Perestroika in Eastern Europe: Hungary's Economic Transformation 1945–1988* (Boulder: Westview Press, 1990). Given its marked significance for the overall collapse of the Eastern bloc, economic development in Poland has received more attention. In particular, see Kazimierz Z. Poznanski, *Poland's Protracted Transition: Institutional Change and Economic Growth 1970–1994* (Cambridge: Cambridge University Press, 1996), Batara Simatupang, *The Polish Economic Crisis: Background, Causes, Aftermath* (London: Routledge, 1994), and Ben Slay, *The Polish Economy: Crisis, Reform, and Transformation* (Princeton: Princeton University Press, 1994). Finally, for the Soviet Union, Alec Nove's classic publication, *An Economic History of the USSR: 1917–1991*, 3rd edn. (London: Penguin Books, 1992), is still relevant. Contemporary insider reports now available have been summarized by Michael Ellman and Vladimir Kontorovich (eds.), *The Destruction of the Soviet Economic System: An Insiders' History* (Armonk, NY: M. E. Sharpe, 1998). This and other more recent studies are drawn on in Philip Hanson, *The Rise and Fall of the Soviet Economy: An Economic History of the USSR from 1945* (London: Longman, 2003).

9

Europe's "1989" in Global Context

JAMES MARK AND TOBIAS RUPPRECHT

The collapse of socialist regimes across Central and Eastern Europe was a turning point in European history. What is often referred to by the shorthand "1989" significantly accelerated a process of the reintegration of a continent divided by the Cold War. Yet this regional transformation was also part of larger world-historical developments. Europe's "1989" extended the processes of democratization that had taken place in Southern Europe in the 1970s, and in Southeast Asia and Latin America in the 1980s; it marked an acceleration of globalization and the neoliberal restructuring of economies that had begun just over a decade earlier; and it was the end of a longer-term process of imperial disintegration that stretched across the twentieth century. From a global vantage point, "1989" appears less a revolutionary watershed than an important regional manifestation of changes that already had momentum. This is not the whole story, however. The engineers of change from within the region were not only recipients of ideas produced elsewhere. Central and East European economists, politicians and opposition movements were both influenced by and contributed to these global developments. Indeed, the fall of the communist alternative in Eastern Europe provoked powerful reactions across the world.

"1989" as a Neoliberal Revolution

The communist states of Central and Eastern Europe collapsed at a moment of high faith in the efficacy of privatized economies and an ever more integrated world economy. Over the course of the 1980s, newly influential neoliberal reformers helped implement what became known as the "Washington Consensus" around the world. High levels of debt in Africa and Latin America gave leverage to the increasingly powerful

World Bank and the International Monetary Fund (IMF) to insist on so-called structural adjustment – usually meaning privatization, deregulation and open economies – in return for the easing of repayment terms. East European countries faced similar conditions: The model of extensive growth that had guaranteed high increases in GDP in the postwar period had been exhausted by the early 1970s. In order to satisfy domestic consumer demand, and with a view to modernizing their industries to be competitive on the world market, East European states started to borrow the so-called petrodollars that had flowed out of energy-producing states at low rates of interest in the wake of the oil crisis. Yet the expected revolution in productivity and quality never occurred. From Poland to Bulgaria, states became more and more indebted, increasingly borrowing simply to maintain standards of living necessary to secure the communist parties' short-term legitimacy.[1]

This indebtedness increased the leverage that international financial institutions had over East European states. The structural adjustment policies enforced on Yugoslavia by the IMF disrupted the economic cooperation between its republics, helping accelerate the centrifugal forces which led to its disintegration.[2] Long before the system's collapse, in order to access further credit, Hungary (1982) and Poland (1986) joined the IMF. As communist parties fell in 1989, global financial institutions were able to insist on particular economic prescriptions in return for substantial debt forgiveness. Latin America, the most recent region to undergo democratization and bouts of neoliberal reform, became a rich source of inspiration.[3] Advisors such as Jeffrey Sachs and Arnold Harberger as well as many World Bank experts looked to Chilean, Bolivian and Mexican privatization for their

1 Of Hungary's US$ 20 billion debt, only US$ 4–5 billion was invested in increasing productivity: Ivan T. Berend, "Global Financial Architecture and East Central Europe Before and After 1989," in Ulf Engel, Frank Hadler and Matthias Middell (eds.), *1989 in a Global Perspective* (Leipzig: Leipziger Universitätsverlag, 2015), 56–57; Stephen Kotkin, "The Kiss of Debt: The East Bloc Goes Borrowing," in Niall Ferguson, Charles S. Maier, Erez Manela and Daniel S. Sargent (eds.), *The Shock of the Global: The 1970s in Perspective* (Cambridge, MA: Harvard University Press, 2010), 80–93.

2 Susan Woodward, *Balkan Tragedy: Chaos and Dissolution After the Cold War* (Washington, DC: Brookings Institute, 1995), esp. ch. 3.

3 Werner Baer and Joseph Love, "Introduction," in Werner Baer and Joseph Love (eds.), *Liberalization and Its Consequences: A Comparative Perspective on Latin America and Eastern Europe* (Cheltenham: Edward Elgar, 2000), 4. Influential Hungarian economists advised their government to replicate the *maquiladora* system to attract investments from Western Europe, as Mexico had done from the United States. For contemporary fears that Eastern Europe would become an impoverished Latin America, see e.g. Adam Przeworski, *Democracy and the Market: Political and Economic Reforms in Eastern Europe and Latin America* (Cambridge: Cambridge University Press, 1991), 191–92.

postcommunist economic experiment.[4] Poland was targeted as the first key country for reformers: If neoliberal "shock therapies" succeeded in the region's largest economy, they thought, they would be imitated across Eastern Europe.[5]

GDP declined 25–30 percent across the region between 1990 and 1993, leading to high levels of unemployment and falling wages. The economic gap between Western and Eastern Europe widened during the 1990s.[6] Nevertheless, there was remarkably little protest either from the new establishment or from society. The fact that the massive dislocation that accompanied reforms was tolerated, or even welcomed, was partly the result of a neoliberal consensus that had been growing within sections of East European elites before 1989.[7] Reforming economists in particular, despite constituting only a thin intellectual stratum within East European societies, would play a large role in shaping the "transition" – a term derived from the Spanish *"transición"* which usually refers to the postauthoritarian period in Spain from 1975 and in Chile from 1988.[8]

Their embrace of variants of neoliberalism after 1989 resulted from the fact that they had been able to adapt its ideas to many different political projects – even before the political collapse. Before 1989, marketization and global integration were not necessarily linked with the end of one-party

4 On this fascination with Latin American transition as model, see Duccio Basosi, "An Economic Lens on Global Transformations: The Foreign Debt Crisis of the 1980s in the Soviet Bloc and Latin America," in Piotr H. Kosicki and Kyrill Kunakhovich (eds.), *The Legacy of 1989: Continuity and Discontinuity in a Quarter-Century of Global Revolution* (forthcoming). Other "maverick" advisors such as Victor Huaco and Boris Jordan had worked in Latin America before they came to Eastern Europe; see David E. Hoffman, *The Oligarchs: Wealth and Power in the New Russia* (New York: Public Affairs, 2002), 198; Philipp Ther, *Die neue Ordnung auf dem alten Kontinent. Eine Geschichte des neoliberalen Europa* (Berlin: Suhrkamp, 2014), 51.

5 Anders Åslund and Simeon Djankov, *The Great Rebirth: Lessons from the Victory of Capitalism over Communism* (Washington, DC: Peterson Institute for International Economics, 2014); Ther, *Die neue Ordnung*, 90–93. On Eastern Europe as a testing ground for neoliberalism, see Peter Gowan, "Neo-Liberal Theory and Practice for Eastern Europe," *New Left Review* 213, 1 (1995), 3–60; Naomi Klein, *The Shock Doctrine: The Rise of Disaster Capitalism* (London: Penguin Books, 2007), 169. On Poland's influence on Russian liberalization under Gaidar, see Hoffman, *Oligarchs*, 184.

6 Berend, "Global Financial Architecture," 58.

7 For this approach, see János Mátyás Kovács and Violetta Zentai, "Prologue," in János Mátyás Kovács and Violetta Zentai (eds.), *Capitalism from Outside? Economic Cultures in Eastern Europe After 1989* (Budapest: Central European University Press, 2012), 3–7. On the role of regional economists in transnational debates since the 1960s, see Johanna Bockman, *Markets in the Name of Socialism: The Left-Wing Origins of Neoliberalism* (Stanford: Stanford University Press, 2011).

8 Ther, *Die neue Ordnung*, 32.

rule. The socialist states of East Asia were already abandoning central planning and autarky but retaining their authoritarian political structures. China's embrace of entrepreneurship, marketization and openness to world trade was a key moment in the erosion of faith in the Soviet model of planning.[9] Vietnam had rejected regulated prices and was encouraging individual entrepreneurship in key areas of the economy. Nor was the world short of authoritarian states of the political right that were shepherding market transition and integration into the world market, while enjoying the support of Western democracies.[10] When the communist Károly Grósz became prime minister of Hungary in 1987, he looked to the authoritarian model of integration into the world economy exemplified by Park Chung Hee's South Korea.[11] In Poland, so-called Kraków liberals rejected the trade union Solidarność's social-democratic welfarism and called for General Wojciech Jaruzelski to turn himself into a "Polish Pinochet" and carry out the necessary neoliberal reforms himself.[12] Others did challenge such authoritarianism: In Hungary, Poland and Czechoslovakia, economic experts and dissidents, both of whom recognized the potential for the market and privatization to destabilize the *nomenklatura*'s grasp on power, entered into strategic alliances to defeat the party-state.[13] Yet even here it was not clear that such reforms would lead either to capitalism or to a multiparty system. Right up until the collapse, some prominent East European economists advocated a market economy and enterprise autonomy to save socialism from the overly centralized and unwieldy planning state and hoped that Western neoliberals such as Jeffrey Sachs would be

9 Ibid., 48, 51; Odd Arne Westad, "Conclusion," in George Lawson et al. (eds.), *The Global 1989: Continuity and Change in World Politics* (Cambridge: Cambridge University Press, 2010), 273.
10 On the unusual combination in Eastern Europe of democracy followed by marketization, see Leszek Balcerowicz, "Understanding Postcommunist Transitions," *Journal of Democracy* 5, 4 (1994), 76.
11 Stephen Kotkin, *Uncivil Society: 1989 and the Implosion of the Communist Establishment* (New York: Modern Library, 2009), 33.
12 On Franco and Pinochet as models, see Mirosław Dzielski, "Potrzeba twórczego antykomunizmu," *13 Grudnia* 11 (1987), 7; Adam Michnik, *Letters from Freedom: Post-Cold War Realities and Perspectives* (Berkeley: University of California Press, 1998), 99; Tobias Rupprecht, "Formula Pinochet: Chilean Lessons for Russian Liberal Reformers During the Soviet Collapse, 1970–2000," *Journal of Contemporary History* 51, 1 (2016), 165–86.
13 On Czechoslovakia, see Petr Roubal, "Anti-Communism of the Future: Czech Post-Dissident Neoconservatives in Post-Communist Transformation," in Michal Kopeček and Piotr Wciślik (eds.), *Thinking Through Transition: Liberal Democracy, Authoritarian Pasts, and Intellectual History in East Central Europe After 1989* (Budapest and New York: Central European University Press, 2015), 188–89.

supporters of their reforms. They were shocked when he declared that his aim was to destroy socialism.[14]

Thus even within parts of Eastern Europe the preconditions for a powerful neoliberal elite consensus already existed before 1989. As communist power collapsed, many reformers of socialism did not find their transformation into cheerleaders for capitalism overly taxing. Leszek Balcerowicz, who had studied economics in the United States in the 1970s and been a communist party member until 1981, became an economic advisor to the Polish opposition in Solidarność and advocate of (socialist) marketization in the 1980s. He then established himself as *the* domestic architect of so-called shock therapy in postcommunist Poland. Others who had earlier recognized neoliberalism's capacities in the struggle against bureaucratic socialism, but had remained in "internal exile" within the state apparatus, came to the political fore. In Prague, Václav Klaus, a member of the Friedrich Hayek Society and an admirer of Margaret Thatcher and Ronald Reagan, was prime minister for most of the 1990s, and from this position acted as one of the most effective cheerleaders in the region for a "market without adjectives."[15] The group that in the 1980s was called "Gdańsk liberals" would produce a Polish prime minister, Jan Bielecki, and a minister for privatization, Janusz Lewandowski.[16]

In those places where internal neoliberal oppositions had not developed, such as Bulgaria and Romania, the "Washington Consensus" was much slower to arrive.[17] Romania had in fact been one of the first countries to open to the West. It had imported Western technology from the late 1960s, had joined the IMF in 1972 and had been one of the first Comecon (Council of Mutual Economic Assistance) countries to embrace East–West joint ventures. However, from 1981, Romania had decided to pay off all its national debt. The country was thus removed from the reach of Western finance and was ruled with a far greater degree of surveillance and violence

14 On the revival of interest in market socialism in the late 1980s, see Johanna Bockman, "The Long Road to 1989: Neoclassical Economics, Alternative Socialisms, and the Advent of Neoliberalism," *Radical History Review* 112 (2012), 25–30; Agnieszka Paczynska, *State, Labor, and the Transition to a Market Economy: Egypt, Poland, Mexico, and the Czech Republic* (University Park: Pennsylvania State University Press, 2009), 135.
15 Milan Znoj, "Václav Havel: His Idea of Civil Society," in Kopeček and Wciślik (eds.), *Thinking Through Transition*, 112–13; Gil Eyal, *The Origins of Post-Communist Elites: From the Prague Spring to the Breakup of Czechoslovakia* (Minneapolis: University of Minnesota Press, 2003), ch. 3.
16 Kochanowicz, "Have Polish Economists Noticed New Institutionalism?," in Kovács and Zentai (eds.), *Capitalism from Outside?*, 205–06.
17 For Bulgaria, see Venelin I. Ganev, *Preying on the State: The Transformation of Bulgaria After 1989* (Ithaca: Cornell University Press, 2007), 30, 71–72.

than any other bloc country.[18] With neither the internal development of neoliberalism nor the emergence of a democratic opposition, the domestic basis for a rapid rupture during transition did not exist. The first transitional governments consisted of former communists who followed Moscow's attempts at restructuring a command economy until the Soviet Union's collapse in 1991, and fought to keep workers' social protections in the face of external pressure. In Bulgaria, the former *nomenklatura* dominated the immediate postcommunist political system – keeping neoliberals out of power until 1997.

Levels of social protest in the region were also low. Although surveys in the early 1990s noted the survival of "socialist values" and a skepticism about privatization and foreign investment, the economic and social disruption caused by transition did not come under organized attack.[19] Labor unions were weak, faced a collapsing membership and were unable to expand into new capitalist workplaces, and were easily demonized through their association with the communist era.[20] There was also a widespread faith in the long-term potential of Westernization. Since the 1960s, many communist elites had nurtured a faith in an individualistic consumerism which their own system had been unable to fulfill – the new capitalism appeared to offer the future possibility of its realization.[21] In Poland, Hungary and Czechoslovakia, elites built these expectations into what has been termed "market populism" – a socially resonant morality tale of the good capitalists pitted against the evil communists.[22] Only in Vladimír Mečiar's Slovakia and Ion Iliescu's Romania did resistance show itself: Here governments encouraged opposition to neoliberalism as an essentially foreign imposition, in order to bolster their credentials as protectors of the working class or the nation. Even here, however, privatization would eventually arrive in the late 1990s.

18 Cornel Ban, "Sovereign Debt, Austerity, and Regime Change: The Case of Nicolae Ceauşescu's Romania," *East European Politics and Societies* 26, 4 (2012), 743–76.
19 Jan Drahokoupil, *Globalization and the State in Central and Eastern Europe: The Politics of Foreign Direct Investment* (London: Routledge, 2009), 97.
20 David Ost, "The Consequences of Postcommunism: Trade Unions in Eastern Europe's Future," *East European Politics and Societies* 23, 1 (2009), 14–19.
21 Paulina Bren and Mary Neuberger, "Introduction," in Paulina Bren and Mary Neuberger (eds.), *Communism Unwrapped: Consumption in Cold War Eastern Europe* (New York: Oxford University Press, 2012), 12–13; György Péteri, "Introduction," in György Péteri (ed.), *Imagining the West in Eastern Europe and the Soviet Union* (Pittsburgh: University of Pittsburgh Press, 2010), 8–12.
22 David Ost, *The Defeat of Solidarity: Anger and Politics in Postcommunist Europe* (Ithaca: Cornell University Press, 2005), 155–56.

"1989" as a Democratic Awakening

Europe's "1989" became the poster child for the idea that democracy was naturally equated with the market – evidence of a natural order toward which regions across the world were converging.[23] With the exception of Belarus, a democratic settlement prevailed across the region. Romania aside, this change was peacefully enacted in that year. These processes were later harshly criticized by those who believed that justice for the crimes of communism had been sacrificed on the altar of superficially civilized change.[24] Nevertheless, "1989" was a high-water moment for peaceful democratization, and the end point of a series of transformations in the techniques of opposition and in the worldviews of communists that reflected changes in political practices both regionally and globally.

The largest and most influential opposition movement was the Polish trade union Solidarność (Solidarity), which, at its peak in 1981, had more than 10 million members. It was not only the greatest organized challenge to the authority of any regime in the bloc, but also developed forms of opposition that became influential among other East European dissidents and even democracy campaigners in China.[25] Its overwhelming victory in the limited number of seats it was allowed to contest in the June 1989 elections in Poland sparked the first negotiated exit out of communism, providing a model to be followed, domino-like, by a series of national transformations across the region.

At the heart of the movement's strategy lay peaceful, evolutionary change. This was partly a result of regional experiences: The 1960s reformist opposition movements had challenged the policies of the ruling elites and had been met with force – either through internal repression, as in Poland and Yugoslavia, or through Soviet intervention, as in Czechoslovakia and Hungary. The founders of Solidarność came from a generation which knew, following the defeat and then the suppression of workers' strikes in Poland in 1970 and 1976, that little could be achieved through direct political confrontation with the state.[26] The model of Spanish transition of

23 This is most famously articulated in Francis Fukuyama, *The End of History and the Last Man* (New York: Free Press, 1992).
24 James Mark et al., "1989 After 1989: Remembering the End of State Socialism in East-Central Europe," in Kopeček and Wciślik (eds.), *Thinking Through Transition*, 498–99.
25 Padraic Kenney, *A Carnival of Revolution: Central Europe 1989* (Princeton: Princeton University Press, 2002), 136.
26 On links between March 1968 and later dissidence, see Robert Gildea, James Mark and Anette Warring (eds.), *Europe's 1968: Voices of Revolt* (Oxford: Oxford University Press, 2013), 128–29.

compromise between regime and society, which Solidarność leader Adam Michnik termed in the mid 1970s the "New Evolutionism," was seen as a possible way forward for the Eastern bloc, too.[27] This approach would eventually help to create the political conditions in which communist regimes were prepared to embrace a nonviolent exit out of dictatorship.

Solidarność was able to grow in the late 1970s partly because of the communist state's own (rhetorical) commitment to the idea of citizens' rights. In the 1960s, the Eastern bloc, in alliance with states from the global South, had been at the forefront of the global promotion of rights – particularly to combat racial and religious discrimination, and threats to national sovereignty. Yet by establishing rights as an accepted part of international law – a strategy that was designed to shame Western capitalism and colonialism – they created norms that would eventually disrupt their own authority. In the context of détente, these ideas were now retooled in the Helsinki Accords of 1975.[28] Communist states had initially viewed this agreement as a victory: Its first part had ensured Western recognition for their previously contested borders and thus guaranteed their right to sovereignty. The Accords' protection of other types of rights – notably to free assembly and expression – did not initially appear to threaten states that claimed to be the true bearer of these ideals.[29] Nevertheless, over the next decade, dissident groups, and the transnational networks of human rights advocates that supported them, would make effective appeals to these legal frameworks to eke out spaces that became crucial for the expression of opposition.

The growth of Solidarność was also made possible by its political restraint, the so-called self-limiting revolution.[30] Until the very last years of the 1980s, its leaders did not embrace liberalism or multiparty democracy. This was not merely a matter of tactics under an unreformable state, but was also a reflection of its status as a trade union founded to defend the rights to work

27 Dominik Trutowski, "Poland and Spain 'Entangled': Political Learning in Transitions to Democracy" (forthcoming). On the influence of Mohandas Gandhi and Martin Luther King, Jr., on Michnik, see also Jeffrey Stout, "Between Secularism and Theocracy: King, Michnik, and the American Culture Wars," in Kosicki and Kunakhovich (eds.), *Legacy of 1989* (forthcoming).

28 Steven L. B. Jensen, *The Making of International Human Rights: The 1960s, Decolonization, and the Reconstruction of Global Values* (New York: Cambridge University Press, 2016), 217–18, 235.

29 Ned Richardson-Little, "Dictatorship and Dissent: Human Rights in East Germany in the 1970s," in Jan Eckel and Samuel Moyn (eds.), *The Breakthrough: Human Rights in the 1970s* (Philadelphia: University of Pennsylvania Press, 2014), 59.

30 Jadwiga Staniszkis, *Poland's Self-Limiting Revolution* (Princeton: Princeton University Press, 1984).

and welfare which communist states themselves had long claimed to nurture.[31] Solidarność was committed to an alternative democratic socialism, based around the dignity of the individual and social justice.[32] Following the visit of the Polish pope John Paul II in 1979, the movement incorporated specifically Catholic notions of dignity into its agenda, a development that helped unite the conservative and liberal-left wings of the opposition. Its leaders also framed Solidarność as part of a global rights movement that fought against abuses of power that emanated from regimes of either the right or the left. In doing so, they aimed to present themselves to an international audience as a modern political force that transcended the now-outdated divides of the Cold War.[33] Nevertheless, in Poland in December 1981, it appeared that Solidarność's opposition had not been limited enough: Threatened by the spread of the movement, the communist state imposed martial law. Solidarność did not regain its standing until the late 1980s. A now-dominant liberal-left leadership very quickly moved from its earlier focus on workers' rights to embrace multiparty democracy, constitutionalism and the rule of law, joining forces with economic neoliberals. According to later leftist critiques, this alliance marked the moment at which the vision of Solidarity as an economically and democratically inclusive movement was defeated.[34]

East European communist elites, too, played a central role in 1989. In Hungary and Poland, they helped usher in multiparty democracy at roundtable talks; in Czechoslovakia and the German Democratic Republic (GDR), they gave up power following a minimum of social pressure. Only in Romania was a violent revolution necessary to remove a dictator from power.[35] The story of "1989" also needs to explain how elites across the region came to embrace, tolerate or reluctantly accept peaceful, democratic change. By 1989, growing numbers in the smaller countries of Eastern Europe

---

31 Maciej Gdula, "The Architecture of Revival: Left-Wing Ideas and Politics in Poland After 2002," in Kopeček and Wciślik (eds.), *Thinking Through Transition*, 372.

32 Jerzy Szacki considered Solidarność at best "proto-liberal"; see his *Liberalism After Communism* (Budapest: Central European University Press, 1995), 173.

33 Kim Christiaens and Idesbald Goddeeris, "Entangled Solidarities? Solidarność and the Global South During the 1980s," in Artemy Kalinovsky, James Mark and Steffi Marung (eds.), *Alternative Globalisations: Encounters Between the Eastern Bloc and the Postcolonial World* (Bloomington: Indiana University Press, forthcoming); Kacper Szulecki, "Hijacked Ideas: Human Rights, Peace, and Environmentalism in Czechoslovak and Polish Dissident Discourses," *East European Politics and Societies* 25, 2 (2011), 272–95.

34 Ost, *Defeat of Solidarity*.

35 On the importance of elites, see Kotkin, *Uncivil Society*. For a critique, see Konrad H. Jarausch, "People Power? Towards a Historical Explanation of 1989," in Vladimir Tismaneanu and Bogdan C. Iacob (eds.), *The End and the Beginning: The Revolutions of 1989 and the Resurgence of History* (Budapest and New York: Central European University Press, 2012), 109–25.

were questioning the viability of state socialism, envisioning their countries' futures as part of a broader European community that transcended the Iron Curtain, and envisaging a life for themselves beyond a one-party system and socialist scarcity.

In the early 1970s, the traditional claims of communist elites that they were part of an expanding global system and an important bulwark against reactionary imperialism had not yet become entirely implausible. Outside Europe, decolonization had, in recent decades, brought socialist – or at least noncapitalist – projects to many countries in Africa and Asia. What communists portrayed as fascism seemed to be on the rise too: Elites often noted the renewed importance of communist solidarity in the 1960s and 1970s given the ever-widening presence of right-wing authoritarianism in Latin America, Africa and Southern Europe. Where such right-wing authoritarian regimes were in a state of decay – as with the end of the Franco and Salazar regimes in the mid 1970s – it was still possible to believe that a democratic socialism might take root. Even Henry Kissinger believed the Portuguese "Carnation Revolution" in spring 1974 might be a replay of the Russian Revolution, with Mário Soares playing the role of Aleksandr Kerenskii and paving the way for a radical or Bolshevik takeover.[36] In a speech given in September that year, Hungary's leader János Kádár still had confidence that, just as socialists would eventually oust Augusto Pinochet in Chile, so their comrades would overthrow right-wing dictatorship on the Iberian peninsula and take power.[37]

Yet over the course of the 1970s this worldview was significantly eroded. First, it was increasingly unclear if the world was "going their way." Many East European regimes became ever more distanced from those progressive experiments in the global South which had in some cases turned to radical authoritarianism and, in others, declared allegiance to a campaign for the radical redistribution of wealth from North to South, the so-called New International Economic Order. Only Romania and Yugoslavia joined the club of these states – the G77. The world debt crisis, which forced countries in both regions to prioritize debt payments to the West over older socialist solidarities, further cemented the rift.[38] It was also becoming plain that state

---

36 This account opens Samuel P. Huntington's *The Third Wave: Democratization in the Late Twentieth Century* (Norman: University of Oklahoma Press, 1993), 4–5.

37 See János Kádár's speech, 2 Sep. 1974: "Beszéd a Politikai Főiskola Fennállásának 25. Évfordulója alkalmából rendezett ünnepségen," reproduced in János Kádár, *A fejlett szocialista társadalom építésének utján* (Budapest: Kossuth, 1975), 14–15.

38 Johanna Bockman, Iakov Feygin and James Mark, "The Soviet Union, Eastern Europe and Alternative Globalisations," in Kalinovsky, Mark and Marung (eds.), *Alternative Globalisations*.

socialism was unlikely to spread within Europe: The Southern European transitions saw the advent of liberal democracy, with Spanish Eurocommunists breaking with the Soviet (and Portuguese) traditions of popular workers' democracy, and embracing the liberal-democratic multi-party system. By the late 1970s, the idea of Europe itself was firmly associated with liberal democracy and with the "politics of moderation."[39]

Second, it was increasingly difficult to view the West simply as the enemy. In the early 1970s, West German leaders abandoned confrontation, reached out to the East and promised to guarantee previously contested borders with Poland. With the fear of Western revanchism much diminished, the claims that communist regimes were protectors of the nation from Western imperialism lost their meaning.[40] Links between East and West European economies increased, too: Central European countries began to privilege export to West European markets and to engage in joint ventures. So-called tripartite industrial projects brought together West and East European firms in development projects in Africa and elsewhere.[41] Comecon and the European Community strengthened their ties in the 1970s and 1980s.[42] Claims that Eastern bloc countries were threatened by a predatory Western imperialism were increasingly difficult to sustain.

Nonetheless, this did not mean that communists were ready to give up power. The imposition of martial law in Poland in December 1981 demonstrated the limits of such flexibility when the authority of regimes was threatened. In the late 1980s, elites in the GDR and Czechoslovakia had not opened themselves up to the West or to reform at home. Mikhail Gorbachev's socialist campaigns for *glasnost'* (openness) and new economic thinking left them unmoved. Even in 1988 and 1989, it was not certain they would not resort to force to stay in power. However, after seeing the violent repression of dissent around Tiananmen Square in June 1989, fewer East

39 On the lesson of Portugal as a turn to moderate solutions, see Kenneth Maxwell, "Portugal's Revolution of the Carnations, 1974–1975," in Adam Roberts and Timothy Garton-Ash (eds.), *Civil Resistance and Power Politics: The Experience of Non-Violent Action from Gandhi to the Present* (Oxford: Oxford University Press, 2009), 161.
40 This was particularly the case in Poland. See also Charles Maier, "What Have We Learned," *Contemporary European History* 18, 3 (2009), 261.
41 Patrick Gutman, "West-östliche Wirtschaftskooperationen in der Dritten Welt," in Bernd Greiner, Christian Müller and Claudia Weber (eds.), *Ökonomie im Kalten Krieg* (Hamburg: Hamburger Edition, 2010), 395–414.
42 Angela Romano and Federico Romero, "European Socialist Regimes Facing Globalisation and European Co-operation: Dilemmas and Responses – Introduction," *European Review of History* 21, 2 (2014), 157–64; Suvi Kansikas, *Socialist Countries Face the European Community: Soviet-Bloc Controversies over East–West Trade* (Frankfurt am Main: Peter Lang, 2014).

European elites were attracted to what became known as the "Chinese solution."[43]

The collapse of state socialism in the region eventually occurred through a series of national, albeit interconnected settlements that reflected the assumptions of all participants that the nation-state was the natural vehicle for transformation.[44] It was Poland and Hungary that led the charge in negotiated round-table talks between regime and opposition. For communists, the advantage was obvious: It allowed them to retain a degree of economic and political power. In the years before the political collapse, in Hungary, Poland, Bulgaria and elsewhere, state managers had already spontaneously taken control of their enterprises and turned them into private companies – often in suspicious circumstances.[45] Bureaucrats in education, military and the Communist Youth had already appropriated the assets of the institutions they controlled.[46] Round-table talks, which were essentially negotiations about politics, left the foundations of former functionaries' new economic power unchallenged. Western leaders encouraged their participation, too: The Spanish prime minister Felipe González provided "sensible communists" with advice about survival derived from his experience of the Spanish transition, and encouraged them to envisage a role for themselves building a socialist Europe in the 1990s. Washington, too, made it clear that it valued the role of reformist communists in ensuring peaceful and predictable change.[47] These roles also allowed them to build new forms of political capital as the cofounders of democracy: In Hungary and Poland, where communists committed to negotiated settlements, they returned to power, recast as economically liberal social democrats.[48]

43 Péter Vámos, "The Tiananmen Square 'Incident' in China and the East Central European Revolutions," in Wolfgang Mueller, Michael Gehler and Arnold Suppan (eds.), *The Revolutions of 1989: A Handbook* (Vienna: Austrian Academy of Sciences Press, 2014), 106–11.

44 Chris Armbruster, "The Revolutions of 1989," in Lawson et al. (eds.), *Global 1989*, 210–13; Gregor Feindt, *Auf der Suche nach politischer Gemeinschaft. Oppositionelles Denken zur Nation im ostmitteleuropäischen Samizdat 1976–1992* (Berlin and Boston: De Gruyter Oldenbourg, 2015).

45 Eric Hanley, "Cadre Capitalism in Hungary and Poland: Property Accumulation Among Communist-Era Elites," *East European Politics and Societies* 14, 1 (1999), 143–78; Ganev, *Preying on the State*, 50–55, 57; Jadwiga Staniszkis, *The Dynamics of Breakthrough in Eastern Europe: The Polish Experience* (Berkeley: University of California Press, 1991).

46 Steven Lee Solnick, *Stealing the State: Control and Collapse in Soviet Institutions* (Cambridge, MA: Harvard University Press, 1998).

47 László Borhi, "Domestic Change, International Transformation: Hungary's Role in Ending the Bipolar System in 1989," in Engel, Hadler and Middell (eds.), *1989 in a Global Perspective*, 88–89, 95–96.

48 James Mark, *The Unfinished Revolution: Making Sense of the Communist Past in Central-Eastern Europe* (New Haven: Yale University Press, 2010), ch. 1; Anna M. Grzymała-Busse,

The dismantling of the system in Poland and Hungary without Soviet intervention made it plain to those elites who wanted to cling to power that their days were numbered. It still took a modicum of "people power," however. The opening of Hungary's border in May 1989 enabled large numbers of GDR citizens to cross to Austria – leaving their regime increasingly isolated, and its hold on power weakened. The Monday demonstrations in Leipzig, which grew out of the oppositional work of the Protestant Church and the mass protests on Wenceslas Square in Prague, were crucial final steps in pressuring their harder-line regimes to relinquish power. In Romania alone did the regime resort to the use of force, and only here did the world see scenes of violent revolution and the crushing of defeated communists. A repressive state had ensured that there was no organized opposition with whom to negotiate a settlement. A revolution that was started by the protests of a Hungarian reformed church priest in Timișoara led to brutal repression, and more than 1,100 dead, before the army withdrew its support for the regime and summarily executed the leader Nicolae Ceaușescu and his wife Elena.

Yet for the most part "1989" in Europe was a year of elite-guided transitions – indeed, even in Romania the popular revolutionary process was coopted by a newly formed organization, the National Salvation Front – which was in essence a reformed wing of the communist party.[49] Even oppositions were fearful of excessive democratic sentiment. In Poland, liberal-left elites in Solidarność dreaded potentially destabilizing excessive religious, nationalist and moralistic sentiments that the collapse of authoritarianism might release.[50] In Hungary, the designers of the Round Table feared a return to the violence of 1956 without a managed process that would keep the radical anti-communist forces on the political margins.[51] A wide variety of human rights, anti-militaristic, religious and ecological groups had mobilized in the years leading up to 1989. Their activities provided a context in which swift and large-scale protest against one-party states became feasible in late 1989. Yet the expressions of direct democracy and radical change that

Redeeming the Communist Past: The Regeneration of Communist Parties in East Central Europe After 1989 (Cambridge: Cambridge University Press, 2002).

49 Peter Siani-Davies, *The Romanian Revolution of December 1989* (Ithaca: Cornell University Press, 2005), ch. 7.
50 Adam Michnik, *Takie czasy ... rzecz o kompromisie* (London: Aneks, 1985); Adam Michnik, "Three Kinds of Fundamentalism," in Michnik, *Letters from Freedom*, 178–84; Hella Dietz, *Polnischer Protest. Zur pragmatistischen Fundierung von Theorien sozialen Wandels* (Frankfurt am Main and New York: Campus, 2015), 281–91.
51 Mark, *Unfinished Revolution*, 5–6.

groups such as Poland's Freedom and Peace movement, Hungary's Orange Alternative and Czechoslovakia's Independent Peace Association represented were quickly sidelined in the settlement itself.[52]

For Václav Klaus, who would become prime minister of the Czech Republic (1993–98) and then its president (2003–13), the collective and populist impulses which had been nurtured under communism would, if not checked, lead to a directionless popular democracy outside a party system that would result "not in freedom, the market and democracy, but in nonpolitical politics; a dependence on vaguely defined civic movements, forums and impulses; the promotion of ambiguous utopian projects by intellectuals [and] new collectivisms."[53] For Klaus, consolidated indirect party politics and market capitalism were the disciplining tools to build a new society; "the third way," by contrast, was "the fastest way to the Third World."[54] In this sense, "1989" was not only a triumph of a peaceful and civilized settlement – an image that was later assiduously cultivated by its participants – but was also a managed road to a parliamentary system led by former elites and oppositionists both of whom were skeptical about their own societies' capacity to cope with the challenges of freedom after decades of dictatorship.[55]

"1989" as the End of Empire

It was at the western borders of the Moscow-led bloc that authoritarian rule first started to crumble in 1989, a process in which all European communist parties would lose their power and which eventually led to the disintegration of the Soviet Union itself within two years. But democratization was the result of, not the trigger for, this retreat of the last European empire in the twentieth century. At the moment when Gorbachev had taken over in the Kremlin four years earlier, national democratic movements in Eastern Europe as well as human rights activists in the Soviet Union were being firmly held at bay by authoritarian political rulers.[56] It was an impulse from

---

52 Kenney, *A Carnival of Revolution*, 299.

53 Václav Klaus, speech at the 10th Party Conference, Občanská demokratická strana (Civic Democratic Party), Dec. 1999, quoted in Znoj, "Václav Havel," 127.

54 Václav Klaus, speech at the World Economic Forum, Davos, Jan. 1990.

55 On the link between managed transition and later illiberalism, see Ivan Krastev, "The Strange Death of the Liberal Consensus," *Journal of Democracy* 18, 4 (2007), 58–60.

56 Robert Brier, "Entangled Protest: Dissent and the Transnational History of the 1970s and 1980s," in Robert Brier (ed.), *Transnational Approaches to the History of Dissent in Eastern Europe and the Soviet Union* (Osnabrück: Fibre, 2013), 25; Kotkin, *Uncivil Society*, 122–23.

Moscow, an act of voluntary withdrawal from imperial control, that allowed popular movements to regain influence in the periphery and that enabled their assertive claims to national independence. While Western political leaders including US president George Bush had long supported the territorial integrity of the Soviet Union (without the Baltic states), these reinvigorated East European independence movements, in turn, inspired and supported nationalists in some of the Soviet republics. Eastern Europe's "1989" thus strengthened the centrifugal forces in the Soviet Union and contributed to its collapse in 1991.

Ironically, the imperial retreat during *perestroika*, which finally led to the end of state socialism in Europe, had begun as an attempt to revive socialist ideology.[57] Under Leonid Brezhnev's and Yurii Andropov's leadership, the capacity to enact authoritarian control had often been more important than the belief in the socialist cause. In Eastern Europe, the Soviets had acclaimed the rule of a nationalist military leader, General Wojciech Jaruzelski, who had suppressed the socialist trade union movement Solidarność. A new type of pragmatist imperialism had dominated in relations with Third World allies, too: No longer was it apparently idealistic socialist liberation heroes who enjoyed most Soviet support, but hard-boiled military regimes such as those in Ethiopia, South Yemen, Libya and Peru.[58] The Soviet Union had also revised earlier socialist economic visions abroad: In the case of Vietnam, a member of Comecon, the Kremlin terminated its support of failed industrialization projects and advocated an adjustment to world market demands instead.[59]

Gorbachev, by contrast, referred to an idealized notion of Leninism in foreign as in domestic politics and often used the old Prague Spring catchphrase of "socialism with a human face." His worldview had been shaped by his career in the provincial ranks of the Communist Party of the Soviet Union (CPSU), far from the cynicism and pragmatism in the imperial center. It was informed by an early encounter with Jawaharlal Nehru's political philosophy during his student years in 1950s Moscow and by the idealist socialism of the Soviet 1960s generation; and was influenced by

---

57 Stephen Kotkin, *Armageddon Averted: The Soviet Collapse 1970–2000* (New York: Oxford University Press, 2008), 29–30; Michail Gorbatschow, *Perestroika. Die zweite Russische Revolution* (Munich: Droemer Knaur 1987), 27–29, 207–09.
58 Tobias Rupprecht, *Soviet Internationalism After Stalin: Interaction and Exchange between the USSR and Latin America During the Cold War* (Cambridge: Cambridge University Press, 2015), 231–32.
59 Chris Miller, *The Struggle to Save the Soviet Economy: Mikhail Gorbachev and the Collapse of the USSR* (Chapel Hill: University of North Carolina Press, 2016).

Italian and French Eurocommunism, which he got to know during his many trips across Europe in the 1960s and 1970s.[60] Holding on to an idealized version of socialist internationalism, Gorbachev and his foreign-policy advisors Anatolii Cherniaev and Aleksandr Yakovlev ended this imperialist pragmatism toward pro-Soviet dictators, and strengthened contacts with those whom they considered true socialists. In the Third World, they increased support for leftists such as the Nicaraguan Sandinistas.[61] In the West, Gorbachev reached out to the leading representatives of the Socialist International such as Willy Brandt and Pierre Mauroy. He became a close friend of Felipe González, head of the Spanish Socialist Workers' Party, and he admired the Swedish socialist Olof Palme.[62]

Soviet policies toward the East European satellite states during *perestroika* wavered between pressure for change and fears of destabilization. Once Gorbachev had consolidated his power, the highly centralized decision-making processes of Soviet foreign policy allowed him to pursue his idealistic idea that freeing states from the Kremlin's control would liberate them to opt for reformed socialism and more amicable relations with Moscow. In early 1989, he ordered the withdrawal of Soviet troops from Afghanistan and later that year from most of Eastern Europe. The "Sinatra doctrine," announced by his foreign affairs spokesman Gennadii Gerasimov in Helsinki in October 1989, enabled the states of the Soviet empire to "do it their way." Yet the reformers of *perestroika*, initially, had not expected a Westernization of the socialist world, but rather multiple freely chosen paths to a reformed socialism. The rhetoric of a "common European home," a phrase already used by Brezhnev during his 1981 visit to Bonn, and by Gorbachev in London in 1984, replaced the theory of two ideologically opposed camps which had perpetuated a divided Europe. Nevertheless, this "new thinking" in foreign policy still had an anti-American thrust, and was contained within broadly socialist categories, though they were ill defined and in the process of change.[63]

60 Michail Gorbatschow, *Erinnerungen* (Berlin: Siedler, 1995), 80, 147, 247, 759–61, 988; Archie Brown, *The Gorbachev Factor* (Oxford: Oxford University Press, 1996), 116.
61 Gorbatschow, *Perestroika*, 221–46.   62 Gorbatschow, *Erinnerungen*, 752, 760–67.
63 Helmut Altrichter, *Russland 1989. Der Untergang des sowjetischen Imperiums* (Munich: C. H. Beck, 2009), 327–28; Dietrich Beyrau, "Das sowjetische Modell. Über Fiktionen zu den Realitäten," in Peter Hübner, Christoph Kleßmann and Klaus Tenfelde (eds.), *Arbeiter im Staatssozialismus. Ideologischer Anspruch und soziale Wirklichkeit* (Vienna: Böhlau, 2005), 47–70; Archie Brown, "Did Gorbachev as General Secretary Become a Social Democrat?," *Europe–Asia Studies* 65, 2 (Mar. 2013), 198–220.

Gorbachev's tragedy was that few people inside or outside the Soviet Union around 1989 still shared his idealist socialism. The conservatives in the CPSU were more interested in the retention of power, or sympathized with Slavic nationalism. For the bulk of the Soviet population, the economic situation had worsened dramatically by 1989, and they did not care much about ideology and foreign affairs: In a review of the past year's events, the press agency Novosti discussed the ten topics that concerned citizens most; none referred to anything beyond the Soviet Union. The popular journal *Ogonek* reported in October 1989 that only 12 percent of Soviet citizens expected a significant improvement in their lives thanks to Gorbachev's reforms.[64] The Soviet empire was associated with socialist internationalism and was thus now mostly seen as a waste of the people's scarce resources.[65] The idea that the union and the bloc were a financial burden also led Russian nationalists to demand an end to empire: Valentin Rasputin, one of the most popular Russian novelists at the time, addressed the Soviet People's Congress in early 1989 and, in a philippic against moral decline and Western pluralism, suggested that Russia leave the union.[66] In this spirit, the populist Boris Yeltsin, as president of the Russian People's Congress, declared secession a year later – an event subsequently celebrated annually in Russia as Independence Day.

In the East European "outer empire," the Soviet retreat in the late 1980s provoked different reactions. Those conservative political elites who were hoping to ride out *perestroika*, such as Erich Honecker in the GDR, Nicolae Ceauşescu in Romania and Todor Zhivkov in Bulgaria, were eventually toppled in palace coups by more reform-oriented circles of their own parties, who had support from Moscow. But political leaders who, inspired by *perestroika*, supported reforms within the socialist system, such as General Jaruzelski in Poland and Alexander Dubček in Czechoslovakia, were soon overruled too. Dissident movements gained confidence from Gorbachev's renouncing of Soviet imperialist ambitions: Poland's Adam Michnik believed that the Soviet leader viewed Solidarność as the realization of his "Reformation" in Central Europe, and such groups were emboldened in their struggle against hardline elites.[67] Some, particularly in the two Germanys, enthusiastically hailed Gorbachev as liberator and idealized him – in a productive misunderstanding – as a Westernizer. Economic liberals,

---

64 Altrichter, *Russland 1989*, 39–40.
65 Rupprecht, *Soviet Internationalism After Stalin*, 281–83. 66 Altrichter, *Russland 1989*, 37.
67 Adam Michnik, "1989, from Poland to the World," in Kosicki and Kunakhovich (eds.), *Legacy of 1989* (forthcoming).

nationalists and anti-socialist intellectuals all over Central and Eastern Europe, by contrast, took heart from their perception of Gorbachev's reformed socialist project as a failure, a development they considered to herald the end of the Soviet-dominated system as a whole.

While Gorbachev's voluntary retreat from imperial control is a textbook case of historical contingency and of the role of the individual in history, the end of the Soviet empire, from a world-historical perspective, can be viewed as the final stage of the European age of imperialism after the disintegration of the Austro-Hungarian and Ottoman Empires after World War I, the end of the Nazi Empire in World War II and of the French, British and Portuguese Empires after that. In 1960s Eastern Europe, this connection had commonly been made: Both anti-communists who wished to throw off Soviet control, and leftist critics of communist authoritarianism, took inspiration from the postwar decolonization of Africa and Asia and its socialist liberation movements. Nevertheless, by the 1980s, few saw themselves as part of this tradition. An increasingly assertive nationalism, bare of socialist anti-imperialist rhetoric, and often explicitly anti-socialist, predominated, which called for a re-creation of national culture and a "return to Europe."

This East European nationalism reverberated in the western parts of the Soviet Union. The political liberalization under Gorbachev in the late 1980s had allowed nationalist sentiments to develop rapidly; the end of communist rule in Eastern Europe further emboldened those who challenged the Soviet regime from within. Popular fronts and human rights movements in the Baltic states demanded political autonomy: Estonian elites, for instance, called for a "Hungarian model." Following Ceaușescu's execution, the new Romanian government stoked pan-Romanian anti-Soviet nationalist sentiment in the Soviet republic of Moldova.[68] Polish actors were the most active in promoting their country as a role model of transition for Soviet republics, and they helped to inspire a reinvigorated nationalism in the Baltic states, Belarus, Ukraine and Moldova.[69] Polish tourists and organizations smuggled pro-independence literature into the Soviet Union; Polish television was an important source of information during the independence struggle in Latvia and Lithuania. Solidarność developed particularly close ties with pro-independence groups in Ukraine and Lithuania: Political leaders in Vilnius declared their "readiness to follow Poland's own path away from

68 Mark Kramer, "The Collapse of East European Communism and the Repercussions Within the Soviet Union (Part 1)," *Journal of Cold War Studies* 5, 4 (2003), 238–42.
69 Kotkin, *Uncivil Society*, 138–39.

Communism";[70] and in the Donbass striking coalminers took their inspiration from the Polish trade union movement.[71] Intellectual movements in Central Asia such as Rastokhez (Revival) in Tajikistan and Birlik (Unity) in Uzbekistan in turn modeled themselves on Baltic popular front movements like Sajudis, and received assistance from them in their political work.[72]

Gorbachev's attempts to contain this spillover from Eastern Europe into the western parts of the Soviet Union proved futile. After a brief recourse to violence in Vilnius, the Soviet army was called off, and all Soviet republics declared their independence after the August 1991 putsch in Moscow. In the Central Asian republics, by contrast, populations voted to remain part of a reformed union. Here, Eastern Europe's "1989" had the reverse effect: Communist party bosses such as Nursultan Nazarbaev in Kazakhstan and Islam Karimov in Uzbekistan observed the democratic awakening in the western Soviet Union warily and looked to preserve their power by managing independence from above and rebranding themselves as nationalist leaders.

The Global Impact of Europe's "1989"

The events of Europe's 1989 resonated in most parts of the world. Hitherto-influential communist parties disbanded or sank into irrelevance once support from Moscow was cut. Gorbachev's socialist ideas of a "common European home" were superseded by a neoliberal Europe from Galicia to Galicia. The Russian world, where political and economic reforms soon stagnated, was left beyond the walls of this home, where many new inhabitants rejected the idea of being "eastern" and revived the westward-facing concept of Central Europe. For the old "Western" Europe of the Cold War, "1989" was a historical watershed, too. Social democrats, who implemented privatization schemes and a deregulation of the labor market in the course of the following decade, repositioned themselves alongside their East European counterparts. After the end of the communist threat from the East, neoliberalism also gained further momentum in the West and the South.[73]

The end of state socialism also encouraged the assertion of ethnic nationalisms, which had been simmering within European polities, irrespective of

---

70 Kramer, "The Collapse of East European Communism," 204–12.   71 Ibid., 216–37.
72 Isaac Scarborough, "From February to February and from Ru ba Ru to Rastokhez: Political Mobilisation in Late Soviet Tajikistan (1989–1990)," *Cahiers d'Asia Centrale* 26 (2016), 143–71.
73 Ther, *Die neue Ordnung*, 281.

their ideological orientation, since the late 1970s. As the Soviet Union headed toward collapse, conflicts broke out in Transnistria, Nagorno-Karabakh, South Ossetia, Abkhazia, Chechnya and the Fergana Valley, which remain unsettled to this day.[74] The nationalist Slobodan Milošević took over the presidency in the Republic of Serbia in May 1989, and Yugoslavia drifted toward a bloody conflict that broke the country apart. The revival of minority nationalisms did not stop at the former Iron Curtain. Radical anti-imperialist movements with a socialist bent, from Northern Ireland to West Germany and from the Basque country to Kurdistan, having lost the support of East European secret services, sometimes disbanded, but more often just toned down the socialist element in their nationalist rhetoric. At the same time, a number of right-wing separatist-nationalist movements gained influence all over the continent. In May 1989, all major Belgian parties agreed on the political isolation of the Vlaams Belang (the Flemish nationalist party), whose support was growing. Separatists in northern Italy founded the Lega Nord in December 1989. Spanish prime minister Felipe González, confronted with Catalan and Basque separatism, was well aware of the contagiousness of this reinvigorated nationalism from the East. More than any other Western political figure, he encouraged Gorbachev to keep the Soviet Union together; Spain later refused to recognize the independence of Kosovo.[75]

Beyond Europe, the transformations of 1989 contributed to the fall of other authoritarian-socialist regimes, particularly in Africa. The televised execution in December 1989 of Romanian ruler Nicolae Ceauşescu, a frequent visitor to the continent since the 1970s, shocked many a dictator. In the months that followed the "fall" in Eastern Europe, most governments made gestures toward multiparty rule. Marxism-Leninism was abandoned as official state philosophy by ideologically flexible leaders in Angola, Mozambique, the Republic of the Congo, Cape Verde, Guinea-Bissau, Benin, Zambia, Mali and Madagascar.[76] Several countries adapted to the demands of the thoroughly "neoliberalized" IMF. In Somalia and Ethiopia, socialist autocrats were overthrown.[77] While rulers in most other countries managed to stay in power by rigging elections, Botswana, Gambia, Mauritius, Namibia and Senegal preserved democracy – and

74 Fred Halliday, "Third World Socialism: 1989 and After," in Lawson et al. (eds.), *Global 1989*, 132.
75 Gorbatschow, *Erinnerungen*, 763.
76 Richard Banégas, "Tropical Democracy," in Jacques Rupnik (ed.), *1989 as a World Event: Democracy, Europe and the New International System in the Age of Globalization* (London: Routledge, 2007), 101–10.
77 Halliday, "Third World Socialism," 123.

political figures all over the continent showed interest in learning from Eastern Europe's transition: The 1990 Africa Leadership Forum conference on the implications for Africa of changes in Eastern Europe attracted some fifty political leaders from across Africa.[78]

In southern Africa, superpower rapprochement allowed for a settlement of the war in what became Namibia; both Cuba and South Africa withdrew their troops. Within the now ruling South West Africa People's Organization (SWAPO), liberal forces gained the upper hand over the Marxist wing. No longer fearing the pro-Moscow strand in the African National Congress (ANC), the United States pressured the South African government to end the ban on the organization and release Nelson Mandela from prison.[79] By the early 1990s, the ANC, which had abandoned armed struggle in favor of negotiation, and Marxism in favor of the market economy, looked to the peaceful settlement in Eastern Europe for inspiration through what they, alongside the South African Communist Party, termed the "Leipzig option" of peaceful mass action.[80] Participants in the Polish Round Table discussions were invited to South Africa to share their experience of negotiated settlements.[81]

Latin American popular movements and authoritarian political rulers of the left and the right reacted differently to the winds of change. Inspired by Gorbachev's reforms, Mexican pundits, around 1989, called for a PRIstroika, a democratization of the country's political institutions following the decades-long one-party rule of the Partido Revolucionario Institucional (PRI).[82] Paying close attention to the democratic changes already under way in Poland and Hungary, 91 percent of Chilean voters opted for a return to political pluralism and democracy in a June 1989 referendum, which the military junta had considered acceptable after the end of the perceived threat of international communism. Socialists returning from their exile in Eastern Europe had no desire to implement centralized planning as they had seen it and thus more readily acceded to the neoliberal consensus. In Paraguay,

78 Ulf Engel, "Africa's '1989,'" in Engel, Hadler and Middell (eds.), *1989 in a Global Perspective*, 331–48; Fukuyama, *The End of History*, 35; Jorge Braga de Macedo, Foy Colm and Charles Oman (eds.), *Development Is Back* (Paris: OECD Development Studies, 2002), 270.
79 Chris Saunders, "'1989' and Southern Africa," in Engel, Hadler and Middell (eds.), *1989 in a Global Perspective*, 349–61.
80 Ibid., 358.
81 Padraic Kenney, "Electromagnetic Forces and Radio Waves or Does Transnational History Really Happen?," in Brier (ed.), *Transnational Approaches*, 50.
82 Russell H. Bartley and Sylvia Erickson Bartley, *Eclipse of the Assassins: The CIA, Imperial Politics, and the Slaying of Mexican Journalist Manuel Buendía* (Madison: University of Wisconsin Press, 2015), 63.

a palace coup ended Alfredo Stroessner's dictatorship in February 1989. Brazil, in November that year, held its first democratic presidential elections since 1960. Democratic elections were announced in Nicaragua in 1989, which the socialist Sandinistas lost the year after, when the return to democracy also paved the way for the later settlements of the Guatemalan and Salvadoran civil wars. Cuba remained an exception in the Americas: Now cut off from Soviet economic aid, the country experienced harsh economic decline, but Fidel Castro initially refused any political reforms. Only in the mid 1990s would he grudgingly legalize a small degree of private farming to tackle widespread undernourishment. The rest of Latin America, by that time, had entered a phase of neoliberal economic reforms that, in turn, informed similar policies back in Eastern Europe: Balcerowicz had drawn inspiration from the successful Bolivian struggle against inflation and for fiscal stabilization in the mid 1980s; as Polish finance minister around 1990, he was closely monitoring the parallel reforms in Argentina under President Carlos Menem.[83]

The transformation of Eastern Europe did not help the cause of democracy elsewhere. In the People's Republic of China, many of the factors that had led to the disintegration of one-party rule had not pertained: The country had avoided significant indebtedness and had overseas communities prepared to invest; reform had been confined to the economic sphere and had – through the liberalization of agriculture in a country with lower levels of development – created dynamic growth in the 1980s that had not simultaneously stoked societal demands for Western levels of consumption. Foreign models had not been democratic: The East Asian tigers provided a template for development that retained strong state control.[84] Indeed, the political collapse in the Soviet Union and Eastern Europe may have helped the Chinese communists avoid a similar fate. Gorbachev, whose reforms, alongside Václav Havel's writings, had inspired a young protest movement in China, visited Beijing in May 1989. But the lessons his official hosts drew from the Soviets was that excessive criticism undermined faith in the party and that

---

83 Interview with Balcerowicz in *Der Spiegel* 5 (1990); see also Rupprecht, "Formula Pinochet", Basosi, "An Economic Lens" and the interviews with economic decision-makers at www.pbs.org/wgbh/commandingheights/lo/index.html.
84 Martin Dimitrov, "Understanding Communist Collapse and Resilience," in Martin Dimitrov (ed.), *Why Communism Did Not Collapse: Understanding Authoritarian Regime Resilience in Asia and Europe* (Cambridge: Cambridge University Press, 2013), 20–24; Christoph Boyer, "Big '1989,' Small '1989': A Comparative View," in Engel, Hadler and Middell (eds.), *1989 in a Global Perspective*, 193–202.

democratization would lead to social and economic chaos.[85] They also drew similar lessons from Jaruzelski's Poland: Martial law was introduced in China, too, just after Gorbachev left the country. And two weeks later Deng Xiaoping ordered the violent suppression of the ideologically diverse student protests around Tiananmen Square, with units that had been sent to Poland for anti-riot training.[86] The Chinese crackdown on dissent helped to prevent further change in the broader region, and communist parties in Vietnam, Laos and North Korea held onto political power. Democratization was limited to Taiwan, South Korea and the Philippines. In much of Asia around 1989, economic policies changed more than political systems did. Countries from Indonesia to India gave up their state-developmentalist policies, deregulated their economies and opened to the world market.[87]

The geopolitical effects of "1989" were felt in the Middle East, too, but, as in China, the wave of democratization petered out before it hit the region. Deprived of a powerful external counterweight, Arab states' willingness to negotiate with the West over the Israeli–Palestinian conflict increased. Palestinians, bereft of Soviet support, were prepared to make concessions that eventually led to the Oslo Accords. Yet, unlike in Latin America or southern Africa, urban elites in the region clung to secular and protectionist authoritarian dictators, often out of fear of radical Islam, which had also profited from the Soviet retreat. But among some Western elites, "1989" as a self-congratulatory story of the victory of market capitalism, and of the demise of communism, increased confidence that they could liberate countries of autocratic systems from the outside.[88] Former Cold War security specialists of the "neoconservative" and "liberal-interventionist" schools became

85 David L. Shambaugh, *China's Communist Party: Atrophy and Adaptation* (Washington, DC: Woodrow Wilson Center Press, 2008); Václav Havel's 1979 samizdat essay "The Power of the Powerless" was translated into dozens of languages and became a popular reference for anti-authoritarian political movements worldwide: Václav Havel, *The Power of the Powerless: Citizens Against the State in Central-Eastern Europe* (London: Hutchinson, 1985).
86 Jean-Philipp Béja, "China and the End of Socialism in Europe: A Godsend for Beijing Communists," in Rupnik (ed.), *1989 as a World Event*, 214–15; Maurice Meisner, *The Deng Xiaoping Era: An Inquiry into the Fate of Chinese Socialism, 1978–1994* (New York: Hill & Wang, 1996), 455.
87 David Harvey, *A Brief History of Neoliberalism* (New York: Oxford University Press, 2005), 118.
88 Barbara J. Falk, "From Berlin to Baghdad: Learning the 'Wrong Lessons' from the Collapse of Communism," in Lawson et al. (eds.), *Global 1989*, 244–46; see also Ellen Schrecker (ed.), *Cold War Triumphalism: The Misuse of History After the Fall of Communism* (New York: New Press, 2004).

influentiol foreign-policy advisors, and Western coalitions toppled those left-wing revolutionary autocrats in the Islamic world whom they regarded as Cold War hangovers, from Saddam Hussein in 2003 to Muammar Gaddafi in 2011. Interpreting the assistance of Western anti-communists during the Cold War for Eastern Europe's "liberation" as a source of moral obligation, and viewing support for democracy as an important demonstration of their newly cemented Western identity, many East and Central European elites supported such interventions too.[89] Leszek Balcerowicz and Yegor Gaidar shared their expertise from the Polish and Russian privatization and deregulation programs for the transformation of Iraq.[90] And, during the so-called Arab Awakening, Polish and Bulgarian elites took this message of peaceful transition to Egypt, Libya and Tunisia.[91]

None of the major shifts in global geopolitics and economic reforms after 1989 were caused by the end of state socialism in Eastern Europe alone. But the events in Moscow, Warsaw, Budapest and Berlin were one factor that contributed to political and economic changes across Asia, Africa and Latin America. The demise of the communist alternative in Eastern Europe helped resolve Cold War conflicts; it contributed to the collapse, and in other places to the survival of, authoritarian regimes, provided an important exemplar of negotiated transition, and contributed to the ongoing circulation and political implementation of neoliberal economic ideas. Democratization, very much dominant in the Western perception of "1989," proved less successful on a global scale, and has lately experienced setbacks in several parts of the post-Soviet sphere as well. New forms of cultural and economic globalization after 1989 meant that not only the former Soviet bloc, but soon also Western Europe, and with it its concept of modern democratic society, lost some of its political leverage on the global scale:[92] "1989" may have been the last European event to have truly global resonance.[93]

---

89 Maria Mälksoo, *The Politics of Becoming European: A Study of Polish and Baltic Post-Cold War Security Imaginaries* (London: Routledge, 2010), 125, 128–30.

90 Leszek Balcerowicz, "Economic Reform: Lessons for Post-Saddam Iraq from Post-Soviet Europe," working paper for the American Enterprise Institute, 24 Mar. 2005; "Ein 'Balcerowicz-Plan' für den irakischen Wiederaufbau. Was der Irak von Polen lernen kann," *Neue Zürcher Zeitung* (14 Jun. 2005); Oksana Yablokova and Catherine Belton, "Gaidar Invited to Shock, Awe Iraq," *Moscow Times* (9 Sep. 2003).

91 Mark et al., "1989 After 1989," 498–99.

92 Matthias Middell, Frank Hadler and Ulf Engel, "Introduction," in Engel, Hadler and Middell (eds.), *1989 in a Global Perspective*, 10.

93 Jacques Rupnik, "The World After 1989 and the Exhaustion of Three Cycles," in Rupnik (ed.), *1989 as a World Event*, 7.

Bibliographical Essay

For contemporary accounts, see Timothy Garton Ash, *The Magic Lantern: The Revolution of '89 Witnessed in Warsaw, Budapest, Berlin, and Prague* (New York: Random House, 1990); Ralf Dahrendorf, *Reflections on the Revolution in Europe: In a Letter Intended to Have Been Sent to a Gentleman in Warsaw* (London: Chatto & Windus, 1990).

For 1989 in broader transnational or global context, see Ulf Engel, Frank Hadler and Matthias Middell (eds.), *1989 in a Global Perspective* (Leipzig: Leipziger Universitätsverlag, 2015); Piotr H. Kosicki and Kyrill Kunakhovich (eds.), *The Legacy of 1989: Continuity and Discontinuity in a Quarter-Century of Global Revolution* (forthcoming); George Lawson et al. (ed.), *The Global 1989: Continuity and Change in World Politics* (Cambridge: Cambridge University Press, 2010); Jacques Rupnik (ed.), *1989 as a World Event: Democracy, Europe and the New International System in the Age of Globalization* (London: Routledge, 2007). For "1989" as part of the rise of neoliberalism, see Philipp Ther, *Europe Since 1989: A History* (Princeton: Princeton University Press, 2015).

There are many works on the perspective of different actors. On the importance of communists dismantling their own systems, see Stephen Kotkin, *Uncivil Society: 1989 and the Implosion of the Communist Establishment* (New York: Modern Library, 2009). On the role of Gorbachev, see Archie Brown, *The Gorbachev Factor* (Oxford: Oxford University Press 1996). On the rise of the "oligarchs," see David E. Hoffman, *The Oligarchs: Wealth and Power in the New Russia* (New York: Public Affairs, 2002). On "1989" from below, see Padraic Kenney, *Carnival of Revolution: Central Europe 1989* (Princeton: Princeton University Press, 2002); Robert Brier (ed.), *Transnational Approaches to the History of Dissent in Eastern Europe and the Soviet Union* (Osnabrück, Germany: Fibre, 2013).

There are excellent collections that address the causes and meanings of "1989" from multiple perspectives. See Vladimir Tismaneanu (ed.), *The Revolutions of 1989* (London: Routledge, 1999). For the most comprehensive intellectual history of the shifts "around 1989," see Michal Kopeček and Piotr Wciślik (eds.), *Thinking Through Transition: Liberal Democracy, Authoritarian Pasts, and Intellectual History in East Central Europe After 1989* (Budapest and New York: Central European University Press, 2015); Wolfgang Mueller, Michael Gehler and Arnold Suppan (eds.), *The Revolutions of 1989: A Handbook* (Vienna: Austrian Academy of Sciences Press, 2014).

For a revisionist account that is aware of alternatives, see Johanna Bockman, "The Long Road to 1989: Neoclassical Economics, Alternative Socialisms, and the Advent of Neoliberalism," *Radical History Review* 112 (2012), 9–42. For the "disappointments of 1989," see David Ost, *The Defeat of Solidarity: Anger and Politics in Postcommunist Europe* (Ithaca: Cornell University Press, 2005); and James Mark, *The Unfinished Revolution: Making Sense of the Communist Past in Central-Eastern Europe* (New Haven: Yale University Press, 2010).

The Collapse of the Soviet Union

VLADISLAV M. ZUBOK

The endgame of the history of international communism was highlighted by two events: the dissolution in rapid succession of all communist regimes in Eastern Europe in 1989, and the rapid collapse of Soviet Union two years later. These two events irrevocably changed the political and economic map of Europe; they also demonstrated to the entire world, with the help of satellite television news, the inability of Soviet-type regimes in Europe (unlike in Asia) to adapt to the new challenges of modernization and globalization, or to overcome old ones such as nationalism. In 1989–91, the leadership of the Soviet Union and many of its constituent republics repudiated all ideological, political and economic tenets that underlined the practical foundations of the Soviet communist model. Gorbachev declared a new goal of moving to a "mixed economy," inspired by the social-economic thinking of the 1960s, and of integrating the country's economy with global markets. The Soviet leader also refused to use force to stop the de facto secession of six of fifteen Soviet republics and negotiated with the rest on a new voluntary treaty.

After the failed attempt at dictatorship by the State Committee on the Emergency Situation (Gosudarstvennyi komitet no chrezvychainomy polozheniiu, GKChP), formed primarily by the KGB and army leaders in August 1991, the political initiative passed to radical anti-communist forces, led by Boris Yeltsin. These forces seized power in the Russian Federation, the key constituent republic of the USSR. In the spirit of anti-communist "revolution," Yeltsin adopted an International Monetary Fund (IMF)-style program of shock therapy and privatization for Russia, which meant its economic and financial secession from the union. Mikhail Gorbachev's

Research for this chapter has been facilitated by the W. Glenn Campbell and Rita Ricardo-Campbell National Fellowship Program by the Hoover Institution and Stanford University (2013) and a fellowship at the Woodrow Wilson International Center for Scholars (2015).

last-minute attempt to patch up the disintegrating common economic and political space, in a form of a confederation of sovereign republics, was an exercise in illusion. On 8 December 1991 the leaders of three republics, the Russian Federation, Ukraine and Belarus, dissolved the union and agreed to form a nebulous Commonwealth of Independent States.

This chapter argues that Gorbachev's reforms set in motion the decomposition of Soviet-style structures, and produced powerful dynamics and forces that tore the Soviet Union apart. First, this was the unraveling of the Soviet economic-financial system, unintentionally triggered by the transition to a "mixed economy." Second, it was *glasnost'* and Gorbachev's political liberalization, which led to the removal of the communist party from management of economic and political affairs. These reforms, accompanied by relative freedom of speech and conscience, produced unintended destabilizing effects for the Soviet Union, such as further disorganization of economy and finances, the anti-communist revolt of the Soviet intelligentsia against the "totalitarian center," and the collapse of political legitimacy of the central ("union") government. Third, it was the rapidly dwindling popular support for Gorbachev, the rise of anti-communist feelings and, above all, the rise of national separatism, conditioned by the federated construction of the Soviet Union, where Soviet-built "nationalities" had instruments and incentives for secession. Fourth, there were choices for and limitations on the Soviet leadership, most notably Gorbachev, whose strategy failed to tame the destructive tide of anti-communism and national separatism.

The international context was also crucial for understanding the reasons for the Soviet demise. The pressures of the global economy and the need for foreign capital, the sudden collapse of trade between the Soviet Union and East European countries after the decision to use hard currency as the only form of payment, and the persistent clash between Soviet domestic pressures and international commitments, the stance of the United States and the institutional demands of the international financial system, represented by the IMF, all contributed powerfully to the sense of urgency, the debates and the choices within the Soviet leadership, between Gorbachev and the anti-communist opposition, and between the center and the republics. In a sense, the end of the Soviet Union indeed can be conceptualized not only as a farewell to global communism, but also as the first major casualty of the new era of capitalist liberal globalization.

The collapse of the Soviet Union remains a subject of intense curiosity, fears, hopes and politics on the territory of the former Soviet republics and elsewhere, particularly in China and other countries still ruled by communist parties. Like other milestones of global communism, the end of the USSR would remain in the focus of "politics of history" with considerable implications for the legitimacy, strategic choices and international behavior of Russia and other countries of Eurasia and Eastern Europe.

Unintended Economic Crisis

The Soviet economic crisis and financial troubles began in the 1970s, when the militarized model of the Soviet economy, built in the 1930s, came into conflict with new social realities that emerged in the 1960s: the exhaustion of the cheap pool of peasant labor; the growth of state-funded social programs; the empowerment of trade unions and workers' collectives; and the rise of urban and educated groups that lacked incentives for productive labor. From sociological works, inside the USSR and then by émigré sociologists, it became clear that all major groups of Soviet society resisted economic reforms pushed by reform-minded technocrats from above. A number of studies abroad, e.g. by János Kornai, revealed severe contradictions in "reformed" East European economies, with their inability to meet the requirements of a postindustrial, consumerist society.

From the time of Stalin, the stability of the state-run centralized economy rested on three pillars: the state's near-monopoly on economic assets and profits, its tight control over wages and consumption, and severe restrictions on liquid capital in private hands. From time to time, the Soviet state had to announce "financial reform," to confiscate billions of rubles that people had accumulated, in order to restore the monetary balance. The end of this system, just like its construction, was the result of the Politburo's decisions. In 1983, the Politburo created a special commission on reforms headed by Nikolai Ryzhkov; the top economist there was deputy minister of finances Stepan Sitarian. Soviet economists returned to the unrealized ideas and concepts of the 1960s, without grasping why the early attempts to move to a "mixed economy" had failed.[1]

In the summer of 1987, on the basis of the work of Ryzhkov's commission, Gorbachev's Politburo and the Council of Ministers approved the decree "On State Enterprises"; in 1988 a second important decree was passed "On Cooperatives." The first decree authorized directors of plants and factories to retain profits that had previously been transferred to the state. The idea was that "state enterprises" ("socialist enterprises" in the original draft) would start functioning like Western corporations, investing in

1 Michael Ellman and Vladimir Kontorovich (eds.), *The Disintegration of the Soviet Economic System* (New York: Routledge, 1992), 26.

production and improving their own economic performance. Directors, who had no owners' responsibilities, but had access to profits, only looked for opportunities to transfer these profits into money in the form of salaries. They had no incentive to invest and perform. The creation of cooperatives, Sitarian's pet project, allowed them and union leaders to funnel "black cash" from the enterprises into their pockets: These cooperatives became the vehicles for privatizing state funds without contributing to productive sectors. The rapid accumulation of cash produced inflation that the Soviet economy could not absorb. Then, in 1988, when Gorbachev began political liberalization, the Soviet leadership began to remove wage controls, to purchase political support among workers. Thus, control over inflation was lost; the old financial system that had existed since Stalin's time was doomed. The State Bank began to issue more and more rubles to match the runaway growth of salaries. In turn, inflation led to the crisis of consumption: Tens of millions of people across the Soviet Union stood in endless lines, in order to buy food and consumer goods that were disappearing from state stores.[2]

Neither Gorbachev and Ryzhkov, nor reform-minded economists, understood the reasons for the disaster. They shared the generational optimism and beliefs of the 1960s: They believed that once "the mechanism of stagnation," e.g. ignorant and reactionary apparatchiks, was replaced by "progressive" managers, and once workers received more material incentives, the Soviet economy would resume its growth. They overlooked the fact that workers and managers alike were part of the mechanism of stagnation; the more they were empowered, the worse off the Soviet economy and finances became. Every round of economic reforms merely aggravated the situation. In the end, Gorbachev's economists resembled the crew of the RMS *Titanic*: They directed the Soviet economy from one iceberg to another, until it began to leak from all sides and sank.

In 1986–89 international factors added to the negative effects of misguided reforms. The oil price plummeted from more than US$ 35 per barrel to less than US$ 12. During the previous year, because of windfall oil profits in hard currency, the problems of stagflation and finding currency for imports were mitigated and concealed; now they broke out of control, aggravating trade balance and credit payments, and exacerbating shortages of consumer goods and those endless lines in front of state stores.

2 David Woodruff, *Money Unmade: Barter and the Fate of Russian Capitalism* (Ithaca: Cornell University Press, 1999), 45–55.

In addition, Gorbachev also launched a well-intentioned anti-alcohol campaign, an Andropov-style measure "to improve workers' discipline." The Chernobyl nuclear power plant disaster blasted another enormous hole in Soviet budget revenues.

The Soviet economic demise took place in the context of rapid globalization, an information revolution and postindustrialization. This added to Soviet problems, yet does not necessarily explain the Soviet collapse. True, in the United States the regions of the industrial giants, models for Soviet industrialization of the 1930s–1950s, turned into "rust-belts." But this was only because production began to move to China. In Germany, before and after unification, a successful (if expensive) modernization of industry took place. The Soviet Union, theoretically, could have followed the same path. It had an advanced technological-scientific-industrial complex, second to none. There were strong hopes in the 1980s that, given its proper "conversion," this complex could provide an engine for Soviet reindustrialization and a counterweight to economic disintegration. The fact that this did not happen can be ascribed to the badly designed reforms and the political dynamics in the USSR. Scholars who describe the story of Soviet demise as bizarre self-destruction make a valid point.[3]

The Soviet military-industrial complex is usually regarded as a problem and an obstacle to reform. How important was the burden of militarization on the Soviet economy? Some American authors claim that Ronald Reagan's round of arms control "bankrupted" the Soviets. Various statements by Gorbachev and Soviet officials lend credibility to this thesis. Certainly, this burden was excessive and consumed the best resources and most skillful labor. Still, the impact of this factor on the Soviet crisis of 1985–90 is hard to measure. For a long time even Soviet leaders did not know how much went on military spending. When the quality of statistics improved in 1990–91, direct defense expenditures stood at 8–10 percent of the Soviet budget; with indirect expenses, to finance the 10-million-strong military-industrial complex, the costs probably went up to 20 percent. Still, it was much less than the figure of 40 percent that Gorbachev and some Western sources cited. And we still need more credible evidence to conclude that this burden disrupted macroeconomic stability and caused a crisis of payments in the USSR.

---

3 Steven L. Solnick, *Stealing the State: Control and Collapse in Soviet Institutions* (Cambridge, MA: Harvard University Press, 1998); Stephen Kotkin, *Armageddon Averted: The Soviet Collapse 1970–2000* (New York: Oxford University Press, 2001).

Another unconvincing argument is that the military-industrial complex was a major "mechanism of stagnation," a lobby that allegedly blocked economic reforms. In fact, many people from the military-industrial complex were part of the "progressive" technocratic cadres who in 1985–89 supported Gorbachev's course of reforms. Engineers and scientists from defense institutes and labs went in droves to take part in pro-Yeltsin rallies in Moscow, Sverdlovsk and other cities. In 1990 the leaders of military industries, as well as the scientific-technical personnel, became convinced that market reforms were inevitable. The military-industrial complex began to shrink: In 1990 alone, about 300,000 workers, engineers and scientists left for other sectors of the economy. The military budget prepared by the General Staff for 1991 envisaged a reduction in expenses, after inflation, and a sharp cut in the purchases of new military equipment.[4]

At the same time, Gorbachev, Soviet economists and leaders of military industries could not and did not want to trigger the chaotic destruction of the militarized economy. Historically, the defense sectors of the economy had accumulated the most skilled labor, the best knowhow and the most advanced equipment. In internal debates, at parliamentary hearings and in discussions of economic programs, the leaders of military industries warned that unregulated privatization and liberalization would deindustrialize the Soviet Union, squandering its scientific-technological potential. In late 1990, when liberalization and national separatism began to threaten the integrity of the military-industrial complex, the Soviet military, as well as directors of defense-related plants and labs, pushed Gorbachev to introduce authoritarian rule, in order to carry out a managed transition to the market. Oleg Baklanov, the head of the military-industrial commission, one proponent of this option, became a co-organizer of the GKChP, which failed in August 1991.

The Effects of Liberalization

In 1988, facing the failure of economic reforms, Gorbachev drew a "neo-Leninist" conclusion from this failure: that the Communist Party of the Soviet Union (CPSU) was at the core of the problem. One needed "to unlock the initiative from below" against the bureaucratized party-state structures. Gorbachev's idea, alongside liberating reformist energy from Soviet society,

4 See O. D. Baklanov, *Kosmos – sud'ba moia. Zapiski iz "Matrosskoi tishiny,"* vol. I (Moscow: Obshchestvo sokhraneniia literaturnogo naslediia, 2014); see also the Kataev Papers, box 3, folder 1, Archive of the Hoover Institute of War, Revolution, and Peace.

was to create a "normal" state, in which the communist party would no longer perform its dictatorial functions, but would cede them, step by step, to the government ministries and, in the constitutional sense, to the soviets, the representative councils of "socialist democracy" that had been touted by Lenin and the old Bolsheviks. This neo-Leninist conclusion could as well be called neo-Trotskyism. It was a remarkable turn for the general secretary, who owed his whole career to the party apparatus.

At the end of the year, Gorbachev obtained the Politburo's approval of his proposal to reduce the size and functions of the party apparatus. The Secretariat and the central party apparatus lost absolute control over many segments of the Soviet economy, and paid party positions on all levels were supposed to be cut by between 500,000 and 700,000 jobs. One Russian historian concluded that, with this reform, Gorbachev "was destroying the foundations and stability" of the whole political system.[5] Gorbachev's idea of transforming the CPSU into a "normal" political party turned out to be utopian. The communist party, after so many decades of dictatorial power, stood no chance, at least for a while, of gaining any popular support.

Gorbachev advanced a neo-Leninist project of reviving the government of soviets. With the consent of his colleagues, he changed (in a completely authoritarian way) the Soviet constitution, to convene a Congress of People's Deputies: Two-thirds of its 2,250 members were elected according to the majoritarian system. The CPSU and other "public organizations" (e.g. the Academy of Sciences, trade unions, etc.) nominated one-third. The party secretaries, who did not get secure nominations, were encouraged "to run" like everyone else in contested elections. The old methods of ballot-stuffing, as well as new public relations technologies, were not used; as a result the elections in March 1989 ended in humiliating defeat for many senior party officials. The Congress that opened at the end of May became a televised "feast" of free speech, which shocked the country.

At this very time, in China, the political leadership suppressed a "democratic revolution" of students and reaffirmed the Chinese Communist Party (CCP) as an authoritarian tool of power, while developing a new market economy under tight controls. Gorbachev followed his own logic; he consciously opposed the type of violence practiced by Deng Xiaoping. He began to dismantle the CPSU as the only instrument of

---

5 Rudolf Pikhoia, *Sovetskii soiuz. Istoriia vlasti* (Novosibirsk: Sibirskii Chronograf, 2000), 543.

governance that was allowed to control the entire Soviet Union, while at the same time loosening controls over the existing state-funded economy. This fateful liberalization had nothing to do with creating new market institutions. There were no attempts to create self-funded corporations under central control and regulation. The ministers and top managers of major industries, which used to be under strict party control, realized that they could take advantage of enormous state assets for self-enrichment, without any incentives to increase their productivity. This added to the negative synergy of Soviet economic disorganization and decline.

Many in the Soviet government would have supported the Chinese path, but political liberalization in 1989 shrank the government's controls rapidly. During the summer of that year, a wave of miners' strikes shook the Soviet economy. Workers acted as a potential analogue of Poland's Solidarity; their strikes damaged the Soviet economy. Hundreds of thousands of miners in Russia and Ukraine began to use political slogans, demanding more control over profits and enterprises and chanting, "Power to the soviets! Factories to workers!" About the same time, another analogue of Solidarity entered the Soviet scene: an anti-communist opposition. Its nucleus emerged at the Congress of People's Deputies, as the "Interregional Deputies' Group." Nobel physicist and human rights defender Andrei Sakharov became its informal leader. The majority were, paradoxically, long-time members of the communist party. In 1990 many of them were still searching for "socialism with a human face," like Gorbachev, but some of them began to switch to anti-communism. Soon these people developed an ardent mass following, mostly at institutions of culture, education and science, as well as the laboratories of science, engineering and technology linked to the military-industrial complex. Over the next year and a half, this force would seek to guide and politicize the workers' movement and would turn against the Soviet central government structures, associating them with "totalitarianism."

The leading intellectuals of this movement quickly abandoned the slogans of third way "socialism" espoused by Gorbachev. Yurii Afanasev, Yelena Bonner, Sergei Stankevich, Galina Starovoitova and other leaders of Democratic Russia, many of them ex-communists, quickly shifted to a radical liberal platform, declared that not only Stalinism, but also the Bolshevik Revolution, Lenin and early Bolshevik history were part of "seventy years of tragedy and crimes." Some of Gorbachev's associates (e.g. Aleksandr Yakovlev) joined this movement. *Glasnost'* gave powerful tools to this deconstruction of the mythological foundations of the Soviet communist regime. The legitimacy of all existing power structures in the USSR was undermined in one fell swoop.

Why did many in the Soviet intelligentsia, who embraced "communism with human face" in the early 1960s, fail to move to social democracy or leftist statism? And why did so many adopt ideas and language from right-wing libertarians and anti-communists in the West, rejecting the entire legacy of Russian socialism? These are big questions for historical and sociological research. Soviet scholar Dmitry Furman described it as "a revolution of people, who used to sit quietly in their scientific labs and in their kitchens, and were predominantly party members. Now these people have lost their fear, and have begun to compensate feverishly for their passivity in the past, for their lies and conformism." During the 1970s, many party members who worked inside scientific labs and were members of creative unions, increasingly frustrated by the limitations of Soviet life, developed uncritical and passionate forms of Westernism. They argued for the importation of Western models without admitting their social costs for the country and the people. They attacked the Soviet leader, while posing as radical, uncompromising fighters against "Soviet totalitarianism."[6] After Sakharov's death in December 1989, the mantle of leadership in the anti-communist opposition passed to Boris Yeltsin, a former Politburo member turned party apostate and populist politician, with a strong authoritarian bent.

By launching political liberalization, Gorbachev put the cart before the horse (the economy). Incidentally, this overlapped with a general dissident belief in the primacy of politics and political culture over economics. The result was the political mobilization of workers, organized in Soviet-style trade unions: While demanding more power and more money, these unions continued to undermine the Soviet economy with their strikes. The Soviet leader had to make more economic concessions to workers, but the radical opposition offered even more. Eventually, Gorbachev gave up on economic reforms and had to focus all his energy on the construction of new institutions and constitutional foundations for Soviet statehood. Pressed by the growing anti-communist momentum, in February 1990, the general secretary forced the CPSU to accept the end of its constitutional political monopoly. The extraordinary Third Congress of People's

---

6 Dmitirii Furman, "Perestroika glazami moskovskogo gumanitariia," www.congress-st .ru/post/dmitirii-furman-perestroika-glazami-moskovskogo-gu/. I can attest from my own experience that Furman's scathing analysis draws on profound insights.

Deputies in March 1990 approved constitutional changes: Instead of the Politburo, it sanctioned the new executive institution of the presidency. After intense debates, the same Congress elected Gorbachev as president of the USSR. Gorbachev and his associates believed that he was now immune to the danger of a coup like the one that had deposed Nikita Khrushchev in 1964. Yet the presidency did not get the imprimatur of a universal ballot and was a weak institution. The army, the KGB and the police forces were under direct control of the president. At the same time, Gorbachev had to rule with the consent of a huge and inherently fractured parliamentary assembly.

In addition, Gorbachev began to lose control over economic and financial processes. In the Soviet system, the Politburo and ultimately the general secretary controlled the State Bank, its financial transactions and its issuing of currency, as well as caps on the state budget, foreign credits and domestic prices. In 1989, the Supreme Soviet assumed political control over the State Bank, and could now order new money to be issued, in competition with Gorbachev. Soviet bankers, who had been subject to Politburo pressure, now faced greater pressure from populist deputies, who demanded larger social payments to their constituencies and toyed irresponsibly with the slogans of demonopolization and deregulation of Soviet finances, in the false belief that these policies would bring freedom and prosperity for all.[7]

Rule by Congress and the Supreme Soviet undermined the union's executive powers and unleashed centrifugal and destructive forces. The Soviet legislature, ironically, became the platform not so much for anti-Soviet socialists, but rather for anti-communist and national-separatist factions. Soon this process moved with much greater intensity to the level of the republics: The institutions built by Stalin under tight party control turned into vehicles of national mobilization.

The "Inevitability" of National Separatism

The Soviet Union, constructed by the Bolsheviks as "anti-empire," was more vulnerable to fragmentation than even tsarist Russia. Constitutionally, it was a federation, a "voluntary alliance" of four original republics: the Russian Federation, Ukraine, Belarus and the Trans-Caucasian Federation.

7 N. I. Krotov, *Istoriia sovetskoi bankovskoi sistemy. Spetsbanki* (Moscow: ANO Ekonomicheskaia letopis, 2008), vol. I, 400–02.

All constituent republics of the Soviet Union had the right of "self-determination, including secession." Some scholars of Soviet society and nationalities had long forecast that Soviet breakdown, if it started, would proceed along republican lines. They claimed that ethnic mobilization was a universal and inevitable reaction to the crisis of any Soviet-type society and economy. They also wrote about the stabilization of nationalist clienteles in Soviet republics during the reign of Leonid Brezhnev. The Leninist-Stalinist model of the state, sometimes called the "affirmative action empire," could not sustain the twin pressures of economic crisis and political liberalization.[8]

This line of argument has much merit and stands up well to scrutiny. Did Gorbachev and the Soviet leadership underestimate the danger of national separatism? The evidence shows the opposite: Very early on the Soviet leadership feared triggering national conflicts on Soviet territory.[9] Gorbachev's choice of political liberalization was guided, in part, by his illusion that representative institutions would help to channel and mitigate the forces of ethnic hostility and nationalist hatred. This turned out to be another "neo-Leninist" recipe: Instead of preventing conflicts, it poured oil on the fire. From 1988 onward ethnic tensions, violence and territorial disputes swept through the south Caucasus. The greatest challenge for Soviet statehood, however, were the strong national movements in the Baltic republics, demanding the acknowledgement and annulment of their forced annexation by Stalin in 1940. In 1989, with the creation of new representative institutions, national separatism in Lithuania, Latvia and Estonia became institutionalized. The majority of ethnic communists joined the movement toward secession, still masked by the slogans of greater economic and political autonomy. From the end of 1989 onward, the seces-sionist momentum in the Baltic states became an overt challenge to Soviet statehood and Gorbachev's political authority.

The literature on Soviet nationalism speaks about the inevitability of Soviet breakup. American political scientist Mark Beissinger put it more elegantly: The synchronization of tides of "national liberation" movements,

---

8 Victor Zaslavsky, *The Neo-Stalinist State: Class, Ethnicity, and Consensus in Soviet Society* (Armonk, NY: M. E. Sharpe, 1994); Roman Szporluk, "The National Question," in Timothy J. Colton and Robert Legvold (eds.), *After the Soviet Union: From Empire to Nations* (New York: W. W. Norton, 1992), 84–112.
9 A. B. Veber, V. T. Loginov, G. S. Ostroiumov and A. S. Cherniaev (eds.), *Soiuz mozhno bylo sokhranit. Dokumenty i fakty o politike M. S. Gorbacheva po reformirovaniiu i sokhraneniii mnogonatsional'nogo gosudarstva* (Moscow: Gorbachev Fond, Aprel-85, 1995).

first in Eastern Europe, and then within the Soviet Union, created a perception of inevitability. Eventually, this perception became a near-consensus that empowered separatists and paralyzed supporters of the union.[10] The crucial – and the least understood – part of this story is the rise of a separatist movement in the Russian Federation, the largest of the union's republics. In the Leninist-Stalinist design, this republic was to be permanently weakened, and at the same time serve as a backbone of the federated state. Stalin, especially after World War II, succeeded in convincing the Russians that they should play the role of an imperial "senior brother" and channel their resources into the construction of a superpower. Ethnic Russians (and other Slavs) became the main pool for the union *nomenklatura*, economic ministries and scientific-technical intelligentsia. Russian language and culture became, despite official promotion of "national cultures," the glue of the Soviet Union's common identity.

It would be logical to assume, in accordance with classical theories of empire, that a growing Russian nationalism caused the Soviet empire to collapse. In reality, these theories are not applicable to the case of Soviet collapse. As the Russian Federation declared its "sovereignty" and its drift toward separatism began, Russian nationalists remained on the margins of this process. Indeed, many of them remained supporters of the Soviet Union, if only because 25 million ethnic Russians lived outside the boundaries of the Russian Federation, and these boundaries had never been recognized by most Russian nationalists as the confines of the "Russian nation-state." How could Russian nationalists end up impotent? Why did the Russians, instead of mobilizing like the Serbs for a nationalist cause, turn their back not only on their "empire," but also on ethnic Russians in the Baltic states, Ukraine, Central Asia and elsewhere? According to Beissinger, the alliance between Russian liberals and non-Russian separatists against the Soviet regime and subsequently against the Soviet state became "key to the eventual outcome of Soviet collapse."[11]

The process of subtle interception of Russian national discourse by anti-communist liberal radicals was indeed the key to the story of the center's destabilization and the emergence of dual power in Moscow in 1990. The second year of political liberalization was the time when every political radicalization and mobilization took the form of ethnic autonomism and national separatism. The "democrats" in the anti-communist opposition

10 Mark R. Beissinger, *Nationalist Mobilization and the Collapse of the Soviet State* (New York: Cambridge University Press, 2002).
11 Ibid., 389.

shared Gorbachev's fear of Russian nationalism. In November 1989, Andrei Sakharov and other leaders of the "Interregional Deputies' Group," concerned with the danger of a Russian nationalist backlash, sent Gorbachev a proposal for a fundamental reform of the Soviet Union, to transform it into "a voluntary union of sovereign republics of Europe and Asia." Sakharov and ethnographer Galina Starovoitova feared that the Russian Federation was too large to fit into this new union. Its sovereignty would inevitably produce an imbalance and problems with other, much smaller republics, including Ukraine, Belarus and Kazakhstan. They suggested that perhaps Russian territory should be divided into several parts, including non-Russian national autonomies on its territory.

These forecasts turned upside down after the unexpected success of candidates with liberal-democratic and radical populist views in the elections of March 1990, remarkably free and contested, to the Congress of the Russian Federation. All Russian nationalist advocates failed to seize the moment; their message was to defend the Soviet Union as an analogue of Russia, and this did not cut the ice with the electorate. At the Congress, in late May, with a tiny margin, Boris Yeltsin was elected as the chairman of the Russian legislature. This rapid ascendancy of the former Politburo member meant a fantastic boost for the liberal anti-communists. At the same time, this was a step toward dual power in Moscow, because Yeltsin and Gorbachev were political enemies, divided by mutual hatred and contempt.

Just as Lenin and Stalin had warned, the "Russification" of Soviet politics created new alignments that presented a mortal threat to unitary state structures. The next development was the constituent congress of the "Russian" Communist Party, which automatically made the majority of CPSU members "Russian communists." It hastened both the fragmentation of the communist *nomenklatura* along republican lines, and the transformation of communism into another version of nationalism. On 12 June the Russian legislature, communists and anti-communists, voted almost unanimously for the republic's declaration of sovereignty. They decreed that the Russian republican laws should have precedence over the union's laws, and that Russia take control of most economic assets on its territory (aside from the vital defense plants, the electricity grid and communications) as well as of tax revenues, and set up an "independent" Russian Bank. This was a temporary confluence of liberal anti-communism with national communism, and a revolt of provincial party and economic elites, who were dissatisfied with Gorbachev's center and emboldened by the impotence of the union *nomenklatura*.

Gorbachev did not know how to behave in the new situation. He might have hoped that the "Russian" communist party would become a counterbalance to the Russian legislature and Boris Yeltsin, a new focal point for liberal-democratic forces. Yeltsin, however, upped the ante: He renounced his party membership and posed as a politician who represented "all people of Russia." He no longer concealed his anti-communism and declared that his goal was an "independent Russia." The "war of laws" between "Russia" and the center contributed to the havoc in the Soviet economy: Yeltsin and Russian deputies encouraged state enterprises in the Russian Federation not to pay taxes and to withhold their profits from the union center. They also made populist promises of higher wages and greater cuts in profits to state enterprises if they "passed" from union jurisdiction to the jurisdiction of the Russian Federation and its "sovereign" government.

In the glasnost' publications, the history of 1917 and dual power (the Provisional Government and the soviets) that had emerged then was presented as the main cause of chaos and collapse. Millions of readers read and compared it to the dual power in 1990 (Gorbachev's Soviet government and Yeltsin's Russian Supreme Soviet). Reflecting public fears of a new Time of Troubles, Yeltsin claimed, without any concern for consistency, that he stood for preservation of the union. Gorbachev was also not consistent: He was torn between his contempt for Yeltsin as irresponsible demagogue, and attempts at a constructive coexistence with him, in the name of political and economic stability. In July 1990, the young economist Grigorii Yavlinskii, with a group of other economists, proposed a program of radical transition to a market economy in "500 days." It was based on the IMF model of liberalization and monetary austerity, recently tried in Poland. Gorbachev embraced the "500 days" as a new chance for the Soviet Union, and Yeltsin backed it as a movement toward a market economy and an opportunity to redistribute economic power in favor of the Russian Federation. After two months of work, excitement and hope, the "500 days" fell victim to the Yeltsin–Gorbachev rivalry and chaotic Soviet politics. Radical liberal critics blamed this failure on Gorbachev and the "conservative" union government, particularly the military-industrial complex. In reality, the program of economic "shock therapy" entailed huge political risks and uncertainty for all sides. Gorbachev, pressed by his government ministers, realized that this move might result in his loss of power. A year later, another group of radical anti-communist economists, headed by Yegor Gaidar, implemented a modified version of this program, but only for the Russian Federation, and with highly traumatic results for the Russian economy and society.

The Russian declaration of sovereignty and "war of laws" accelerated and empowered national separatism in the non-Russian republics. Yeltsin initiated a coalition against the union government with the leaders of Ukraine, Belarus and Kazakhstan. The spectacle of Russian radical democrats openly assailing Gorbachev in Moscow, in total defiance of the Soviet constitution, radicalized Baltic separatists: They began a campaign of civic resistance to the Soviet military, disrupted the military draft and demanded immediate independence. The anti-communist opposition in Moscow sided with Baltic nationalists, ignoring dangers of violence and the existence of Russian ethnic minorities in Baltic republics. One by one, Gorbachev's associates abandoned him and voiced their support for the liberal anti-communist movement and national separatists.

At the end of 1990 about one-fourth of the population in the Russian Federation began to think that the end of the union was "likely" and even "inevitable." Frustrated by growing shortages of goods and by economic deterioration, an increasing number of people became convinced that dissolving the USSR and establishing the "independence of Russia" would be preconditions for economic reforms and recovery. As 1991 started, the KGB and other Soviet forces of "law and order" used force in Vilnius, and then in Riga, seizing government buildings and television stations. Yeltsin seized the political moment, accusing Gorbachev of "bloodshed" and calling for his resignation. February–March was the time when a descent into chaos and perhaps even a civil war became possibilities. The radical opposition also called for massive workers' strikes, which paralyzed the coal industry of the Russian Federation and Ukraine.

Struggling to boost the center's political legitimacy, Gorbachev pushed through the Congress of People's Deputies of the USSR a bill to hold an all-union referendum on the future of the Soviet Union. The reformed USSR was defined as "a renovated federation of equal sovereign republics where the rights and freedoms of a person of any nationality will be fully guaranteed." Gorbachev defended "the socialist choice" and sharply criticized "so-called democrats" as "neo-Bolsheviks," who wanted to bury the heritage of the Russian Revolution and restore capitalism in the country.

On 17 March 1991, 113.5 million people cast their vote, and 77.85 percent supported the idea of a reformed union; 22 percent voted against it. Gorbachev viewed the results as his victory, yet the referendum proved to be another of his miscalculations. The three Baltic republics, plus Georgia, Armenia and Moldova, boycotted the referendum. Introducing the practice of national referendums in a situation when the old constitutional order was shaken to the core meant only an invitation to greater political chaos. The republican elites and opposition used this powerful tool of "direct democracy" for their own political needs. In Ukraine, the referendum included a question about Ukrainian independence, and many people in western parts of the republic voted in favor. And the Russian Supreme Soviet decreed another referendum, also on 17 March, to create a new post of the president of the Russian Federation, elected by a direct national ballot within the RSFSR. The overwhelming majority of voters approved it. It was obvious that in open elections Yeltsin would have a good chance of winning. Jack Matlock, the US ambassador in Moscow, recorded his verdict: "Gorbachev had unwittingly set a trap for himself" and Yeltsin "sprang it."[12]

Gorbachev and the Politics of Disintegration

The nature and limitations of Gorbachev's leadership in 1990–91 were, to a great extent, an extension of his unique personality. This personality included features such as a remarkably optimistic ego, a penchant for ad hoc reformism, a deep aversion to the use of force, and idealistic Westernism.[13] While repudiating and dismantling the traditional foundations of Soviet power, Gorbachev proclaimed "new thinking": an idealistic approach to domestic and international politics, based on voluntary consensus, interdependence and common human interests.

Almost to the end of his rule, Gorbachev remained a proponent of two myths: one of the Russian Revolution as a great progressive act of history, and the other of humane Leninism, allegedly aborted by the civil war, terror and the Stalinist dictatorship. Gorbachev's neo-Leninist utopia gave the Soviet leader a powerful sense of revolutionary mission, but also made him amazingly prone to taking the risks of political liberalization. Had he been a cynical apparatchik, Gorbachev probably would have preferred to preserve

---

12 Pikhoia, *Sovetskii soiuz*, 621; Jack Matlock, *The Autopsy on an Empire: The American Ambassador's Account of the Collapse of the Soviet Union* (New York: Random House, 1995), 478, 480.

13 On Gorbachev's personality, see more in Vladislav Zubok, *A Failed Empire: The Soviet Union in the Cold War from Stalin to Gorbachev* (Chapel Hill: University of North Carolina Press, 2007), 311–21.

the monopoly of the communist party, and perhaps would have cautiously tried to introduce authoritarian reforms, possibly borrowing some of China's experience. Instead, Gorbachev willingly dismantled, step by step, the political dictatorship of the communist party, the main system of power in the Soviet Union. Deng Xiaoping in China called Gorbachev "a fool," yet such a choice appealed to Gorbachev's messianic, idealistic self. He viewed his *perestroika* as an example to the world, as the return of the Soviet Union to the central stage of world affairs. In 1989 he advanced an ambitious project of a "common European home"; it had some geopolitical elements, but above all it was an idealistic vision of a reformed Soviet Union accepted by the United States and other Western powers as an equal, and participating on respectable terms in the global economic system. To the end of his days in the Kremlin and many years later, Gorbachev claimed that *perestroika* was a unique historical chance to build a fair and peaceful global order, based on social-democratic and other "all-human" values; he subsequently reproached the United States for missing this chance and pursuing other priorities, at the expense of the Soviet Union and later Russia.[14]

Some would say that, without his optimistic ego and supreme self-confidence, Gorbachev would have given up psychologically much earlier, under the pressure of the hardliners or the separatists in the republics. At the same time, Gorbachev's personality, with his preference for consensus over authoritarian rule, as well as his loyalty to the "socialist choice" made him cling to the illusion that the CPSU could be reformed into some kind of social-democratic party, a vehicle for electoral politics. This romantic misperception did great damage to Gorbachev's authority, and made him lose his political battle against Yeltsin and the anti-communist opposition.

Rapidly, Gorbachev's choices created a new political situation that put severe limits on his room for maneuver. The anti-communist opposition falsely accused him of having an insatiable hunger for power – a blatant misreading of his personality and intentions. In early 1991, while holding two posts, general secretary and president, Gorbachev was already

---

14 On Gorbachev's peculiar neo-Leninism that led him to social democracy, see Steven Hanson, "Gorbachev: The Last True Leninist Believer?," in Daniel Chirot (ed.), *The Crisis of Leninism and the Decline of the Left: The Revolutions of 1989* (Seattle: University of Washington Press, 1991), 33–59; Silvio Pons, *The Global Revolution: A History of International Communism, 1917–1991* (Oxford: Oxford University Press, 2014), 306.

hemmed in and hugely unpopular; short of a brutal use of force, he had no political capacity to act decisively. Some scholars, then and later, argued that Gorbachev made a mistake in not breaking with the party and in not running for presidency in open elections. Such a proposition, however, would have carried enormous risks, and not just to Gorbachev himself; moderate liberal reformers felt this could end up in a violent disintegration.[15] Gorbachev's domestic popularity was already in drastic decline, and there was no guarantee that he would be elected, particularly against Boris Yeltsin.

In the spring of 1991, the personal duel between Yeltsin and Gorbachev embodied a profound realignment in the Russian Federation; the outcome of this realignment, as everyone recognized, would be either prolonging the life of the Soviet Union or ending it. Many of Yeltsin's supporters, among them a great number of intellectuals and people working for the media, imagined what happened as a struggle between "forces of freedom and democracy" on the one hand, and "the totalitarian state" on the other. This was the core of the movement. In reality, the deepening economic crisis created a strong countercurrent: An increasing number of people began to turn away from parliamentary institutions and pinned their hopes on a future strong, authoritarian leader who would fix the catastrophic economic situation. Both currents favored Yeltsin and disadvantaged Gorbachev. While anti-communism, in its liberal and authoritarian facets, kept growing, the communist party began to disintegrate and break up into factions. Smarter apparatchiks realized that the game was up and made strategic choices. Instead of waging a political struggle for power, they defected from it into business and other activities. They became engaged in what Steven L. Solnick defined as a "run on the bank": to steal the state assets through existing loopholes, such as cooperatives, commercial banks and other venues of "socialist" and then "market entrepreneurship" legalized in 1987–90.[16]

Archie Brown was the first to argue that by 1991 Gorbachev had evolved from a reform communist to a social democrat. Gorbachev's assistants, however, could not pinpoint the moment when Gorbachev abandoned the vestiges of his neo-Leninism: Was it in February, when he compared anti-communist opposition to "neo-Bolsheviks"? Or in June, when he finally agreed to privatization and dropped "Soviet and socialist" from the name

---

15 Timothy Colton, *Yeltsin: A Life* (New York: Basic Books, 2008), 180; Anatolii Sobchak, *Khozhdeniie vo vlast* (Moscow: Novosti, 1991), 167–84.
16 Solnick, *Stealing the State*.

of a proposed union treaty? Brown himself points to July 1991, when Gorbachev signed a draft party program for the next CPSU congress, one that abandoned all Leninist tenets.[17] For the anti-communist opposition, Gorbachev's evolution evoked no sympathy: They continued to view him as clinging to the old communist establishment. And the average Russian regarded him simply as a weak, inept leader.

Seeking to protect himself against a potential revolt of the hardliners at the April plenum of the CPSU, Gorbachev made a sudden move in the opposite direction: He invited Yeltsin and the leaders of eight other republics (with six republics abstaining) to agree on the terms of a new union treaty. This move caught the hardliners by surprise: They did not dare to get rid of Gorbachev as their leader, which would have left them face to face with Yeltsin and the awful economic legacy of Gorbachev's reforms. At the same time, it was another step in the dismantling of the union. Gorbachev renounced both the option of presidential rule and the center's legal supremacy. He also, for the first time, accepted the republican leaders as equal parties in the reform process. Liberal Russian parliamentarian Viktor Sheinis aptly noted that "nine-plus-one" talks brought the Soviet Union back to the initial drawing table, by implicitly acknowledging that the USSR formed by the treaty of 1922 was no longer viable.[18]

After a month-long campaign, Yeltsin scored a landslide victory, becoming the first popularly elected president of the Russian Federation: 57 percent of voters chose him over four other candidates, all of them members of the communist party. Yeltsin's inauguration in the Kremlin was, in form and in substance, a clear break with communist and socialist traditions. At this point, Gorbachev decided on his biggest gamble: He made key concessions to Yeltsin and the Russian Federation in the draft union treaty, in exchange for Yeltsin's consent to sign it and to support Gorbachev in the forthcoming elections for the presidency of the union. Gorbachev set the date for the treaty's signing on 20 August, without even waiting for Ukraine to agree to it.

On 18 August, a conspiracy of senior government officials, led by KGB head Vladimir Kriuchkov, moved to prevent the signing of the treaty. On 19 August, they proclaimed the establishment of the State Committee on the Emergency Situation and introduced troops to Moscow. The so-called

17 Archie Brown, "Did Gorbachev as General Secretary Become a Social Democrat?," *Europe–Asia Studies* 65, 2 (Mar. 2013), 198–220.
18 Viktor Sheinis, *Vlast' i zakon: politika i konstitutsii v Rossii v XX–XXI vekakh* (Moscow: Mysl', 2014), 463.

coup was a half-hearted affair, and none of its participants had the guts to use force and shed blood. They left Gorbachev, vacationing in Crimea, under house arrest, but did not even try to detain Yeltsin. In the absence of political legitimacy (the formal leader of the GKChP, Vice-President Gennadii Yanaev, was a political lightweight), they probably hoped to work out a deal with Yeltsin and counted on his hatred of Gorbachev.[19]

Yeltsin snatched victory from the jaws of defeat. He appealed to the nation and the world, declaring the GKChP to be "a reactionary anti-constitutional coup" and called its members "criminals." He posed as a defender of "freedom and democracy" and vowed to return Gorbachev to power. The CNN images of Yeltsin resisting the coup from the top of the tank made him a hero for Russians and in Western public opinion. The Russian president assumed, in Gorbachev's absence, the functions of the commander-in-chief and proclaimed himself de facto a supreme leader of the Soviet Union as well as Russia.

The leaders of the GKChP were dedicated communists, yet even they had no will to do what Lenin would have done without blinking an eye: They never dared to use force and spill blood. The denouement of the coup meant the collapse of the center and its governmental structures. The "anti-communist revolution" reigned in the streets of Moscow, Leningrad and some other Russian cities. For the first time, youth made itself visible in those days; three young men died on the night of 20 August in a clash with the military. It was Yeltsin, however, who called the shots: On 23 August, he forced the reluctant and shocked Gorbachev to sign a ban on the CPSU. He also announced Russia's immediate recognition of independence of the Baltic states. Gorbachev concurred. The Russian government took over the union's finances.

The replacement of the weak union center by Yeltsin's "Russia" produced an avalanche of republican separatism. Communist elites in Ukraine and Kazakhstan rushed to "nationalize" union property and rallied around national-separatist banners. On 28 October, Yeltsin announced that the Russian Republic would move separately to enact radical economic reforms, according to IMF guidelines. And on 1 December the population of Ukraine voted in a republican referendum, by an overwhelming majority, in favor of leaving the Soviet Union.[20]

19 Ignaz Lozo, *Der Putsch gegen Gorbatschow und das Ende der Sowjetunion* (Cologne: Boehlau Verlag, 2014).
20 On these events, especially in Ukraine, see Serhii Plokhy, *The Last Empire: The Final Days of the Soviet Union* (New York: Basic Books, 2014).

On 8 December 1991, in an impromptu meeting in a Belarusian resort, Yeltsin, the president-elect of Ukraine, Leonid Kravchuk, and the head of the Belarus Supreme Soviet, Stanislav Shushkevich, signed a declaration that the Soviet Union no longer existed "as the geopolitical reality and a subject of international law." They agreed to create a "Commonwealth of Independent States," an umbrella for the complete dissolution of unitary statehood. Yeltsin assumed de facto control over the Soviet army, Soviet finances and the Soviet nuclear arsenal. Gorbachev did not offer any resistance and formally resigned on 24 December 1991.

Whatever the structural causes and dynamics behind the Soviet disintegration, the observers were stunned that the superpower broke up with so little resistance (aside from the operatic "coup"). The combination of institutional degradation, economic catastrophe and national separatism serve as a partial explanation for this outcome. Even before the August events, the vast majority of Russians and non-Russians had lost faith in Gorbachev's leadership. Yeltsin, with his enormous populist appeal among Russians, became another crucial factor in the drama of Soviet collapse. One could imagine a Yugoslav scenario, if a nationalist leader, like Slobodan Milošević, had come to power riding the wave of mass discontent. Some analysts assume that, without Yeltsin's passionate anti-communism and his abiding hatred for Gorbachev, the center might have been transformed into a confederation, including Russia, Ukraine, Belarus and Kazakhstan. This purely hypothetical scenario appears even more unlikely if we consider the natural imbalance between Russia and the other republics, and the collapse of the central structures that could have balanced the ambitions of the largest republic of the union.

The International Context and the "American Factor"

Gorbachev prioritized foreign policy over domestic reforms in 1986–88, in the belief that only the end of the Cold War would make Soviet transformation possible. He used the need for rapprochement with the West and observation of international commitments, such as the Helsinki Accords, as an additional powerful reason to justify political liberalization. Yet the Cold War ended not on Gorbachev's terms, but on the terms of the West. After the democratic revolutions in Eastern Europe, all former Soviet allies shifted their allegiance to the United States, NATO and the European community, in the desire to join the Western world. The Soviet initial response to this inevitable geopolitical shift was inept, to say the least. The Soviet government trans-ferred intra-bloc trade within Eastern Europe to hard currency; as a result, the bulk of Soviet import and export trade with its former allies collapsed, and this further exacerbated the economic and financial problems of the USSR.

In effect, as scholars noted, the end of the communist regimes in Europe and the end of the Cold War did not assist the reform of the Soviet Union.[21] Gorbachev and the Soviet government discovered that, in the post-Cold War situation, they became dependent on the advice and consent of the United States, the new uncontested superpower and a hegemon in Europe. The process of German reunification in the first half of 1990 revealed this new fact; Gorbachev, after long hesitation, was forced to accept Germany's membership in NATO.

Germany, specifically Chancellor Helmut Kohl, did provide substan-tial credits and financial assistance to the USSR, mainly to secure the smooth withdrawal of Soviet troops from East German lands. As the Soviet Union careened toward its fatal crisis, however, the position of the Western community toward the process of Soviet reforms and the preservation of the Soviet Union remained ambiguous. The administra-tion of George Bush (1989–93) consisted of Cold War veterans, who supported Gorbachev in power as long as this helped to achieve American pragmatic interests, especially to reduce the most dangerous Soviet nuclear arsenals and to remove Soviet military power from Central and Eastern Europe. This first Bush administration egged Gorbachev and his liberal advisors on toward greater political liberal-ization, independence for the Baltic republics and the rapid conversion of the Soviet military-industrial complex.

The US Congress, media, ethnic lobbies, nongovernmental organizations and other nongovernmental networks and associations were also part of the "American factor" that affected the precarious balance of conflicting forces inside the Soviet Union. Congress opposed helping Gorbachev, viewing him as a hostage of the communist hardliners; in contrast, Yeltsin won numerous friends in the United States. In June 1991 the KGB chief, Kriuchkov, spoke about the sinister work of "destructive forces," which included "American agents of influence" allegedly directed from Washington. In reality "the American impact" on the Soviet endgame was not a malevolent conspiracy. Rather, it was an expression of the enormous "soft power" of the United

---

21 Jacques Levesque, *The Enigma of 1989: The USSR and the Liberation of Eastern Europe* (Berkeley: University of California Press, 1998), 162–65, 210–11; Pons, *The Global Revolution*, 311.

States in the Soviet Union, particularly in the ranks of Westernized and politically mobilized intelligentsia. The Westernism of the anti-communist Soviet intelligentsia went back much further than *perestroika*; in the late 1980s the Russian liberal ethos was infused with American imagery, culture and the example of great success, as opposed to Soviet failure. American anti-communism found eager followers in Russia, while West European social democracy, not to mention "Eurocommunism," had minimal impact on the Russian "democrats." Yeltsin and activists of liberal anti-communist opposition began to view the United States, its administration and the right-wing Republican elite as their allies in the struggle against "the totalitarian center." Under pressure from the US Congress and public opinion, and after Yeltsin's election as Russian president, the Bush administration had to adopt a policy of dealing with Yeltsin and Gorbachev simultaneously.

Western financial power, coordinated from the United States, exercised powerful influence in the debates in the Soviet Union about economic and political reforms. When Chancellor Kohl negotiated with Gorbachev on German reunification and NATO membership for a reunited Germany, the Bush administration encouraged him to use "the power of the purse" to facilitate Soviet agreement to withdraw from Central Europe. After this, the US priority was "to lock in" the new realities in Eastern Europe, to help integrate the region with the Western community and NATO. The IMF and its American advisors helped the Polish government carry out economic liberalization. The model of radical reforms launched in Poland became a standard by which to measure economic reforms in the Soviet Union. An IMF study of the Soviet economy in January 1991 suggested a reduction in and the "marketization" of the universal pension system; the "absorption" of family savings through freed prices; the end of fixed rents; and "downsizing" (i.e. liquidation) of military industries, petrochemicals and machine-building plants. Foreign investments into the Soviet oil, gas and coal sectors should be subject to "international arbitration." The IMF imposed similar conditions on Latin American countries. Their acceptance was not only humiliating for a superpower, but also politically unfeasible for Gorbachev and his government.[22]

The same approach – reforms and monetary stabilization first, Western assistance next – remained the official US position in June 1991, at the G-7

22 Peter Reddaway and Dmitri Glinsky, *The Tragedy of Russia's Reforms: Market Bolshevism Against Democracy* (Washington, DC: United States Institute of Peace Press, 2001), 176, 178–80.

summit in London. The Bush administration, despite some lobbying by Giulio Andreotti and François Mitterrand, flatly refused to consider any "Marshall Plan" to help Soviet economic reforms. American policy was dictated by "market fundamentalism," but also by geopolitical calculations and unwillingness to get "entangled" in the process of Soviet disintegration. Western leaders even refused to restructure Soviet foreign debts.[23]

American policy continued to set parameters for Soviet devolution: radical economic reforms, but without use of force; respect by the center for national self-determination and democracy in the republics, but not aggressive nationalism. After the failure of the August "coup," the US government took a more proactive stance. It presented all Soviet republics, vying for American recognition, with conditions based on the norms of the international liberal order. In doing this, Americans wanted to avoid the violent breakup of the country and pursued their primary goal: the safe control of nuclear weapons.[24]

Earlier, I analyzed how international factors encouraged Gorbachev to dismantle communist institutions, in the hope of integrating the reformed Soviet Union into a "common European home" and world economy. A more detailed look, however, reveals that the international context accelerated the Soviet crisis and disintegration. In particular, the "American factor," especially the actions of nongovernment institutions and American media, emboldened the forces of national separatism, as well as the liberal anti-communist movement in the Russian Federation. Overall, the Bush administration, as the leader of the anti-communist world, acted subtly and prudently in dealing with its "defeated" and tottering communist rival. At the same time, US policies created ambiguous memories: instead of a display of generosity and acceptance of the former foe into the new global order, the Bush administration locked in its gains and secured the ground for the continuation of American liberal hegemony in Europe.

Conclusion

The end of the communist regime and the collapse of the Soviet Union were not the same thing. Gorbachev's reforms had largely dismantled

---

23 James M. Goldgeier and Michael McFaul, *Power and Purpose: US Policy Towards Russia After the Cold War* (Washington, DC: Brookings Institution Press, 2003).
24 James Baker, with Thomas M. Defrank, *Politics of Diplomacy: Revolution, War and Peace, 1989–1992* (New York: Putnam, 1995), 525.

and disempowered communist institutions, above all the party; free, contested elections gave birth to legitimate representative institutions; the "nine-
plus-one" talks prepared the legal ground for transformation of the existing
state into a voluntary federation or confederation. Gorbachev's reformism
stumbled only at the huge task of creating a market economy, next to or
within the state-funded industrial mammoth built over decades of communist rule.

Unfortunately, the history of Soviet collapse continued to be influenced
by politics; reassessments of recent events became an exercise in crafting
a past usable for purposes of current politics. During Yeltsin's first state visit
to the United States, speaking at a joint session of the US Congress
in June 1992, the Russian leader praised the people of Russia, who had
found the strength "to shake off the burden of the totalitarian system," and
praised President Bush and the American people "for their invaluable moral
support."[25] This interpretation of the Soviet collapse, however, did not
remain dominant for long.

The primary reason for this change was the series of radical economic
reforms after January 1991, called "the Gaidar revolution." Its designers
claimed that the main political purpose of reforms was to prevent a return
to power of communism and its agents by creating a financial and economic
oligarchy. The argument that the Gaidar reforms were the only way to make
a comeback of communist dictatorship impossible is a counterfactual
that one cannot prove or refute. It is evident, however, that the transition
undermined the financial and social bases for liberal reforms in Russia –
privatization and the destruction of state programs weakened the same
state-funded "Soviet intelligentsia" that had backed Yeltsin and the liberal
anti-communist opposition against Gorbachev in 1991.

At the same time, the conservative-nationalist opposition emerged, sometimes drawn from the same social groups. In October 1993, Yeltsin had to use
tanks against this opposition and its institutional center, the Supreme Soviet
of the Russian Federation. Yeltsin's political ratings continued to plummet
to single-digit numbers. The war in Chechnya he launched in December 1994
did not help him either. He was reelected in 1996 due only to massive use
of money, political manipulation and skillful political maneuvering.
The elections showed that the majority of Russian people were bitterly
disillusioned with the "democratic regime."

25 Yeltsin's address to Joint Session of Congress, 17 Jun. 1992, www.speeches-usa.com/
Transcripts/047_yeltsin.html.

The majority did not want to return to the communist past and did not subscribe to any kind of Marxism-Leninism. Still, enormous nostalgia for Soviet times spread. Memories about the Soviet collapse changed rapidly with post-Soviet economic and political realities. In Russia, the communist party quickly recovered and received impressive support from voters in the Duma elections of 1993; a communist candidate competed against Yeltsin in the presidential elections of 1996.

International developments contributed to the reassessment of Soviet collapse inside Russia. The Yeltsin government proclaimed the Russian Federation to be the legal successor of the Soviet Union and accepted all Soviet international obligations. The United States and other Western countries urged the Russian leadership to do so for their own reasons, because of their concern about international treaties signed by Gorbachev, Soviet-era debts, nuclear weapons and the stability of international institutions, such as the UN Supreme Council. In the second half of the 2000s, however, the Russian government and public opinion became frustrated with the post-Cold War architecture of European security and politics. Gorbachev's "common European home" and Yeltsin's scheme for US–Russian partnerships came to naught. NATO's enlargement into Eastern Europe, its bombing in Yugoslavia and finally the US invitation to Ukraine to join NATO eroded support for pro-Western foreign policy in Russia. The fringe opinion that the United States always wanted to destroy the Soviet Union and sought to weaken Russia became dominant under the administration of Vladimir Putin. The second Russian president publicly declared that the Soviet collapse was "the greatest geopolitical catastrophe" of the past century.[26]

The politics of history is not limited to the former protagonists in the Cold War. In China, scholars of the Soviet Union, mostly working in the party-related institutes, studied the Soviet collapse carefully and drew lessons that pointed to the dangers of political liberalization. Most certainly the impact of Soviet events remains a potent reason why the CCP leadership keeps under tight control all instruments of repression, especially the army.

It would be not too pretentious to suggest that the Soviet collapse and its relationship with the end of communism will remain a pivot of historical controversy and debates, attracting the attention not only of

26 Vladislav Zubok, "Russia and the West: Twenty Difficult Years," in Geir Lundestad (ed.), *International Relations Since the End of the Cold War: New and Old Dimensions* (Oxford: Oxford University Press, 2013), 209–28.

professional historians, but also of a broad spectrum of politicians and the general public.

Bibliographical Essay

Almost nobody, at least until 1990, predicted that reforms and instability could lead to the collapse of the Soviet Union. When the Soviet Union ceased to exist, however, there were suddenly many confident explanations of its denouement. The discussion of why the communist regime ended became a contested concept, with many competing claims. In Western historiography, the dominant approach draws on the theories of nationalism and decolonization, and this chapter addresses the arguments of this approach, especially in the work of Mark Beissinger. Another approach, one that focuses on the evolution and decomposition of communism per se, its ideology, political and cultural institutions, trails behind in importance, and focuses primarily on the personality of Mikhail Gorbachev and his reforms. It is pioneered by the work of Archie Brown, such as "Did Gorbachev as General Secretary Become a Social Democrat?," *Europe–Asia Studies* 65, 2 (Mar. 2013), 198–220. Finally, a relatively new approach, crosscutting cultural history and social anthropology, deemphasizes the political and ideological binaries of communism and anti-communism, and draws on postmodernist theories to explain the sudden dissolution of Soviet power. This approach can be found in Berkeley anthropologist Alexei Yurchak's book *Everything Was Forever, Until It Was No More: The Last Soviet Generation* (Princeton: Princeton University Press, 2006).

Many authors argue that the Soviet Union could not be reformed and "saved" once the communist system and communist political regime were gone. A skeptic can and should challenge this approach. See Stephen F. Cohen, "Was the Soviet System Reformable?," *Slavic Review* 63, 3 (Autumn 2004), 459–88.

The social history of the Soviet collapse still has to be written. The focus is on the behavior of Soviet communist elites (party *nomenklatura*) and their role. The dominant argument is that they had "a run on the bank": abandoning the Soviet communist regime and leaving its institutions crumbling. See Steven L. Solnick, *Stealing the State: Control and Collapse in Soviet Institutions* (Cambridge, MA: Harvard University Press, 1998); Stephen Kotkin, *Armageddon Averted: The Soviet Collapse 1970–2000* (New York: Oxford University Press, 2001). Relatively little is done to explore the role of unionized workers, the divisions within the Soviet military-industrial complex, the KGB, the army and other state institutions. There was a pioneering study of ideational changes within the party elites: Robert English, *Russia and the Idea of the West: Gorbachev, Intellectuals, and the End of the Cold War* (New York: Columbia University Press, 2000), but very little has been done to study regional and local dimensions of this problem. The study of elite politics remains dominant in the historiography; one recent example is a study of the "coup" in August 1991: Ignaz Lozo, *Der Putsch gegen Gorbatschow und das Ende der Sowjetunion* (Cologne: Boehlau Verlag, 2014).

In post-Soviet countries, the historiography of the Soviet collapse has been shaped by politics. Mikhail Gorbachev and his liberal associates and advisors presented their narrative, one of evolutionary and peaceful transition to social democracy and integration into global liberal order, abrogated by the August coup and Yeltsin's radicalism. The Gorbachev camp published an impressive assortment of accounts and documentary collections. In particular, see Anatolii Cherniaev, *Sovmestnyi iskhod. Dnevnik dvukh epokh, 1972–1991 gody* [Joint Exodus: A Diary of Two Epochs, 1972–1991] (Moscow: ROSSPEN, 2008); Georgii Shakhnazarov, *Tsena svobody. Reformatsiia Gorbacheva glazami ego pomoshchnika* [The Price of Freedom: Gorbachev's Reforms Through the Eyes of His Aide] (Moscow: Rossika, Zevs, 1993); Anatolii Cherniaev, *V Politbiuro TsK KPSS* (Moscow: Al'pina Biznes Buks, 2006). The Yeltsin camp came up with its own interpretation, one not generous to Gorbachev. Separately, Yegor Gaidar and his colleagues were the first to explore the collapse from the economic-financial angle: Yegor Gaidar, *Collapse of an Empire: Lessons for Modern Russia* (Washington, DC: Brookings Institution Press, 2007). In some other post-Soviet states, most notably Ukraine, the events of 1990–91 became part of the narrative of national tragedy, revival, and destruction of the "empire."

The end of the Soviet Union does not end the international history of communism. How could it be written without taking China's evolution into account? The task for future scholarship is to place the Soviet developments of 1989–91 into a broader historical and international context. Among promising ways to do this is to study the impact of global consumerism on communist societies and to study economic transition from the centralized communist-type economies to market economies.

PART II

*

EVERYDAY SOCIALISM
AND LIVED EXPERIENCES

The Aging Pioneer: Late Soviet Socialist Society, Its Challenges and Challengers

JULIANE FÜRST AND STEPHEN V. BITTNER

Once the Soviet Union was a beacon of light for communists the world over. It was the first and for a long time the only country that was governed by a communist party. To many European, Asian and Latin American intellectuals, such as Sidney and Beatrice Webb, Bernard Shaw, Leon Feuchtwanger, Mao Zedong and Pablo Neruda, the Soviet Union embodied the hope that societal relations could be changed for the better and capitalism defeated. Hidden away from the view of most who supported its ideas, the Soviet Union was seen as more just, free and progressive than anywhere else. (Ironically, in this regard, the Soviet Union was rivaled only by the pioneer image that clung to the United States until the Great Depression.) The Soviet Union carefully cultivated this image even when disturbing reports of violence, famine and terror reached the ears of outsiders. Yet within the Soviet Union, the light began to pale the moment the *bolsheviki* became the hegemonic power – the establishment – and revolutionary fervor began to slip away. The Great Fatherland War stoked the last burning fires of devotion, because everything was at stake. Yet once the upheaval of World War II had subsided and normality returned, there was no hiding from the fact that the Soviet Union was an aging pioneer.

In 1967 the Russian Revolution was a half-century old. Its veterans, as much as they were still alive, represented not the parents but the grandparents of the current generation of youth. The Soviet project had seen every mode of politics, from reform to radical purge, from New Economic Policy (NEP) compromise to a desperate fight for survival in the struggle against Nazi Germany. Yet by the late 1960s it appeared to many to have come to a curious halting point. The era of the Thaw, which had generated so much hope as well as anxiety, had ended. The forceful crackdown on the Prague Spring in 1968 and the arrest of a number of prominent dissidents during that year – most notably those who had gone onto Red Square out of a sense of solidarity with the Czechoslovak reformists, with banners reading "For Your Freedom and Ours" – left little doubt about the current state of things. While during the previous fifteen years there had been ups and downs in Soviet policy vis-à-vis cultural freedom, individual and human rights, and official acknowledgements of the Stalinist past, in the wake of Prague Spring even the most hopeful Soviet *shestidesiatnik*, or person of the 1960s generation, did not expect that the Soviet Union was going to reform itself. Stagnation, which was to give the following years its epitaph, was present first and foremost in the mind of the Soviet citizens. And paradoxically, it was the mind, not reality, that was crucial to the existence, survival and development of the Soviet project during its final decades.

In retrospect Soviet society was a happening place in the 1970s. From holidays on the Baltic Sea to nonconformist art performances, from building the Baikal–Amur Mainline (a railway through the taiga, north of Lake Baikal) to refusenik sit-ins, the decade was saturated with events that defined and redefined the relationship between Soviet state and individual, on the one hand, and the nature of the Soviet project, on the other. In terms of creating a new Soviet person this period was no less instrumental than the preceding decade. Yet neither Thaw nor stagnation produced the long-awaited and repeatedly announced arrival of communism, opening up an ever-increasing challenge to the Soviet project's legitimacy and hence to the legitimacy of communism the world over. The image of *Homo sovieticus* mutated from the heroic and devoted builder of communism to the caricature created by writer and dissident Aleksandr Zinoviev, who painted the new Soviet person as obedient to the norm, corrupt when possible and caught in fantasies about Western materialism. In parallel with this trajectory, the Soviet Union itself became an ailing colossus, prone to resort to repression when challenged, lacking ideas of renewal and dynamism in the eyes of both East and West. The latter was especially true in comparison to the other communist megalith, China, which began to open itself to economic reform in the years following Mao's death.[1]

This chapter will outline the various official and unofficial attempts to return credibility to the Soviet project, which in the postwar years seemed dangerously stuck in a state of "actually existing socialism" rather than marching forward toward utopian communism.[2] It will show that the aging, once pioneering

[1] Alexander Zinoviev, *Homo Sovieticus* (London: Gollancz, 1985).
[2] This term was coined by Rudolf Bahro with reference to East Germany, but holds true for all the East European states in this period: Rudolf Bahro, *Die Alternative: zur Kritik des real existierenden Sozialismus* (Cologne: Europäische Verlagsanstalt, 1979).

Soviet Union struggled to reform its structures without endangering its *raison d'être*: the creation of communism. The West was a permanent presence, both as a fascinating provider of all things desirable and as a constantly goading competitor, leading the Soviet state to devote considerable sums to its military-industrial complex. While structural and cultural challenges were numerous, the Soviet Union's largest problem was its own citizens, whose participation and mobilization were supposed to form the backbone of the Soviet project. Yet the late Soviet subject was a complex construct who responded to the realities of the surroundings, who adapted to necessity as well as ideology and who defied easy classification into categories of support or resistance.[3] For the most part, and for different reasons, the late Soviet citizen did little to advance the country's progress toward communism. Indeed, such citizens had adapted so well to the current reality that the previous decade's relentless hope for systemic change seemed to belong to a different world altogether. The Soviet state responded to this part-cynical, part-compliant, part-recalcitrant citizen with carrot and stick, depending on the time, circumstance and type of transgression. Leonid Brezhnev's state provided Soviet citizens with comforts they had not experienced before. But it was still merciless in clamping down on those it perceived to be harmful to its character and survival. Ultimately, the Soviet project started to falter in the face of a Soviet reality that had long stopped being shaped by communist ideology – or by any realistic belief that communism could be achieved. "Developed socialism" was increasingly a set of "lived practices" rather than ideologically infused norms. The story of the late Soviet Union is the story of a system that found a stable, if not always happy equilibrium in lived socialism and, in the process, drained itself of hope for communism.

Saving the Soviet Project in the Post-Stalin Period

In the 1950s and 1960s, efforts to save the Soviet project were closely linked with overcoming the legacy of Stalinism, and with the ideological optimism of Nikita Khrushchev, who as First Secretary of the Communist Party of the Soviet Union was Stalin's principal successor. Famously predicting that communism would be achieved "in the main" by 1980, Khrushchev

---

3 For state–subject relations in the late Soviet Union, see among others Alexei Yurchak, *Everything Was Forever, Until It Was No More: The Last Soviet Generation* (Princeton: Princeton University Press, 2006); Donald Raleigh, *Soviet Baby Boomers: An Oral History of Russia's Cold War Generation* (Oxford: Oxford University Press, 2011); Petr Vail' and Aleksandr Genis, *Mir sovetskogo cheloveka 60-e* (Moscow: Novoe literaturnoe obozrenie, 2001); and Juliane Fürst, "Where Did All the Normal People Go? Another Look at the Soviet 1970s," *Kritika* 14, 3 (Summer 2013), 621–40.

envisioned a Soviet Union that was more beneficent and less repressive than Stalinism, a Soviet Union that was truer to its original emancipatory promise. Consequently, following Stalin's death came a decade of concerted reform – de-Stalinization – that affected the lives of nearly every Soviet citizen and that created relative security and prosperity – in short, the aging pioneer's habitat.

De-Stalinization's initial beneficiaries were a group of mostly Jewish doctors, supposed conspirators in a plot to murder Kremlin leaders with bad medicine. Charges against them were dismissed almost before Stalin's body had grown cold in the mausoleum. By early summer, former *zeki* – Gulag prisoners – could be found in train stations across the Soviet Union, slowly making their way back to lives long interrupted. At the beginning of 1953, the total camp population stood at about 2.5 million people; on 27 March, roughly half of these people were amnestied. By 1960, the total camp population had fallen by 80 percent. As events of 1954 in Kazakhstan would show, when a Gulag revolt was put down with military force, the emptying of the camps was not simply a matter of doing what was right. The Gulag had become a tinderbox of national and political grievances that threatened to spill beyond the fence.[4]

It was no easy task to reincorporate in short order so many people into the "big zone" of Soviet civilian society; only postwar demobilization stood as a precedent. As newly released inmates made their way back to former lives, a crime wave engulfed railroad lines, train stations and cities along the way. Once settled, former inmates encountered widespread fears of social contagion, and skepticism from neighbors and work colleagues that so many people could be innocent of the crimes for which they had been convicted. Insofar as many inmates had been socialized by their time in camp to excel at lives of criminality, the former, at least, was not unjustified. Soviet officials responded by offering a pathway to "rehabilitation" for those who had been wrongly convicted; of course, many tens of thousands of people could be rehabilitated only posthumously.

With the removal of terror from the political quiver, Soviet leaders lost one of their most effective tools for ensuring popular compliance. In its stead, they enacted a patchwork of repressive measures that tried to mimic in effect – if not in scale and intensity – what had been lost with Stalin's

4 Miriam Dobson, *Khrushchev's Cold Summer: Gulag Returnees, Crime, and the Fate of Reform After Stalin* (Ithaca: Cornell University Press, 2009), 2; and Steven A. Barnes, *Death and Redemption: The Gulag and the Shaping of Soviet Society* (Princeton: Princeton University Press, 2011), 201–53.

death. After 1953, for instance, millions of Soviet citizens were brought up on the administrative (noncriminal) charge of "hooliganism," a catchall term for petty offenses that ranged from domestic violence to drunken vandalism. People convicted of hooliganism tended to be overwhelmingly male, middle-aged and proletarian. As Brian LaPierre has argued, "the Soviet state found itself . . . at war with the existing lifeways of a working class that it claimed to champion, but that it could neither understand nor esteem." Concern about hooligans was paired with broader efforts to harness the capacity of nonstate actors to patrol public behavior. So-called *druzhiniki*, typically Komsomol members, were common sights in big Soviet cities in the late 1950s and early 1960s and beyond. They kept vigilant watch over the ideological mistakes young people were prone to make: excessive amorousness, inappropriate fashion and hairstyles, and public consumption of alcohol. Similar types of nonstate policing were so common during the 1950s and 1960s that one scholar has argued, to considerable controversy, that one of the defining characteristics of the Khrushchev years was the development of more invasive forms of social control and surveillance.[5]

Members of the intelligentsia were kept in line with similar measures of soft repression. For most, the risk of not being published, of being denied the ability to exhibit or to travel abroad, of a professional and material life made more difficult, was enough to induce acquiescence to what Václav Havel termed "the way it has to be . . . if one is to get on in life."[6] But, for the intrepid few, the Soviet state had more stringent measures. The early 1960s saw an official campaign against "social parasitism," in short, having no legally recognized job. Its most famous victim was the poet Joseph Brodsky, then a young disciple of Anna Akhmatova in Leningrad. In 1964, Brodsky was sentenced to five years' hard labor in a trial that many contemporaries saw as the beginning of the end of Khrushchev's Thaw, and the opening salvo in the campaign against dissidents. In 1958, Boris Pasternak was subjected to a lengthy campaign of harassment in the press, after he published *Doctor Zhivago* abroad without permission. He was later forced to decline the Nobel Prize for Literature. In 1965, Andrei Siniavskii and Yulii Daniel were sentenced to prison for similar offenses. The public outcry surrounding their

---

5 Brian LaPierre, *Hooligans in Khrushchev's Russia: Defining, Policing, and Producing Deviance During the Thaw* (Madison: University of Wisconsin Press, 2012), 13; and Oleg Kharkhordin, *The Collective and the Individual in Russia: A Study in Practices* (Berkeley: University of California Press, 1999).
6 Václav Havel, *Open Letters: Selected Writings, 1965–1990* (New York: Vintage Books, 1992), 132.

trial was so immense that Soviet leaders backtracked. Thereafter, many dissidents and nonconformists were quietly committed to psychiatric hospitals. Some were given a choice between exile abroad or imprisonment at home.

With the end of Stalinist terror came reforms that sought to improve living standards and promote greater egalitarianism. Urban housing designs were less ornate and more cost-conscious, as the five-story apartment building, made from prefabricated concrete slabs, became a ubiquitous feature of the Soviet cityscape. The crumbling shells of these buildings, the vast majority of which are still inhabited, remain Khrushchev's most evident legacy. Millions of urban residents moved from crowded communal apartments to single-family apartments, igniting society-wide discussions about home and hearth, privacy, gender, family life and domesticity.[7] Reforms of university curricula emphasized practical work on the jobsite, and sought to tear down long-standing hierarchies of status between blue- and white-collar workers. So-called Virgin Lands in Kazakhstan and Siberia were brought into cultivation to boost agricultural yields, often with the sweat and toil of Komsomol brigades from distant cities. Some of this land was planted with the American staple, corn, which Khrushchev embraced as the most effective way to fatten cows and pigs, and thus enrich Soviet diets. Regional party secretaries, who in the absence of Stalinist terror had become an almost permanent elite, found limits placed on their tenure. They thus became a natural constituency – one among several, as it turned out – in the efforts to remove Khrushchev in October 1964 by a clique of conservative nationalists headed by former and current Komsomol and KGB functionaries. And, in 1957, the Soviet Union beat the United States into space with the launch of Sputnik. Four years later, Yurii Gagarin would trace a similar path across the heavens. Few events better captured the optimism of that first post-Stalinist decade.

Behind all of these reforms was a succession struggle, first between Khrushchev, Georgii Malenkov, the nominal head of state, and their principal rival and threat, Lavrentii Beria, the head of the NKVD (Narodnyi komissariat vnutrennikh del, or People's Commissariat for Internal Affairs), who was executed at the end of 1953 on trumped-up charges of being a foreign spy, and

---

7 See, for instance, Steven E. Harris, *Communism on Tomorrow Street: Mass Housing and Everyday Life After Stalin* (Washington, DC, and Baltimore: Woodrow Wilson Center Press and Johns Hopkins University Press, 2012); and Christine Varga-Harris, *Stories of House and Home: Soviet Apartment Life During the Khrushchev Years* (Ithaca: Cornell University Press, 2015).

then between Khrushchev and the so-called Anti-Party Group of 1957, Malenkov, Viacheslav Molotov and Lazar Kaganovich, who felt that Khrushchev had pushed reforms dangerously far and betrayed the oligarchical rule that had been agreed upon during those first post-Stalinist hours. Between these two moments of intra-leadership strife was the most important event of that first post-Stalinist decade: the Twentieth Congress of the Communist Party of the Soviet Union in February 1956. There Khrushchev denounced Stalin for bungling the war, orchestrating his own cult of personality and overseeing the persecution of party members he knew to be innocent. It is nearly impossible to overstate the significance of this event. While Khrushchev's speech marked the Soviet Union's first experiment with *glasnost'* – openness about things already known, but rarely spoken of – few of the shocked delegates in the congress hall, much less in the streets of Moscow where rumors quickly began to circulate that something extraordinary had happened, could have imagined such an event. Khrushchev's un-deification of Stalin provoked months of nervous handwringing in party cells across the country, as party members denounced the little Stalins in their private and professional lives, and sought to eliminate the behaviors and iconography of the cult of personality. In Gori and Tbilisi, the sudden fall of Georgia's most famous son provoked unrest that was put down only by force. And in Eastern Europe Khrushchev's speech was linked with protests in Poznań and violence in Budapest. Within months of the Twentieth Party Congress, party leaders in Moscow were backtracking and, by the end of the year, they had identified young people as a group especially at risk of misinterpreting Khrushchev's speech.[8]

Because de-Stalinization was so often caught up in the leadership struggle, it is reasonable to question the sincerity of Soviet leaders, who were constantly trying to outmaneuver their rivals and solidify their own claim to the mantle of reform. Beria, for instance, proposed the most far-reaching amnesties in 1953, despite having hands that were drenched in blood. Khrushchev similarly ignored the reservations of top leaders in 1962, when he authorized the publication of Solzhenitsyn's *One Day in the Life of Ivan Denisovich*, with its revelations about camp life that were consonant with his public denunciation of Stalin at the Twenty-Second Party Congress in 1961. Yet grandstanding does not explain all. As Khrushchev and others in leadership circles noted in their autobiographical writings, there was genuine fear among Stalin's

---

8 Polly Jones, *Myth, Memory, Trauma: Rethinking the Stalinist Past in the Soviet Union, 1953–1970* (New Haven: Yale University Press, 2013), 17–56.

successors that the Soviet Union was in a precarious state. It could easily spin out of control, as people grew weary of continued sacrifice and hardship after victory in war. Moreover, there was genuine embarrassment about the miserable conditions in which ordinary working people lived, which paled by the standards of both tsarist Russia and the capitalist West.[9] Consequently, many of Khrushchev's public appearances – from his denunciation of Stalinist architectural styles in December 1954, to his penchant for colorful and profane folk aphorisms and threats (which were directed not only at the capitalist West, but also at many of the Soviet Union's prominent artists and writers, such as Ilia Ehrenburg and Yevgeny Yevtushenko) – were saturated with a populist anti-elitism.

Khrushchev's unpredictable and profane outbursts were almost certainly the reason that so many people in the intelligentsia responded enthusiastically to his ouster in October 1964, despite the fact that Khrushchev could take principal credit for the more tolerant and pluralistic cultural atmosphere of the post-Stalin years. Aleksei Rumiantsev, the editor of *Pravda* and an important figure in 1960s party intellectual circles, reinforced the general good cheer by writing in February 1965 that, "It was not surprising that an individual 'boss,' certain of his own righteousness, considered himself to be the final arbiter in all spheres of human activity, but most of all in the realm of intellectual work."[10] Yet the change of leadership appeared to spell the beginning of the end of concerted reform in the Soviet Union. While the intelligentsia's oft-stated fears in 1966 and beyond of a return to Stalinism were nearly as hysterical as Khrushchev's former diatribes against them, something ineffable was changing. The year 1965 was a good one, characterized by Leonid Brezhnev's staid leadership style, a return to the principles of oligarchy that Khrushchev had betrayed, and talk of market incentives to spur the economy, the so-called Kosygin reforms. Yet, by the end of the year, Siniavskii and Daniel were behind bars for publishing anti-Soviet materials abroad. Their trial marked the beginning of a campaign against dissidence, which would last until Mikhail Gorbachev called a halt to it in the late 1980s. Events in 1968 in Prague drove home the fact that reform communism, "socialism with a human face" or anything that threatened the supremacy of Soviet communist rule could not be tolerated at home or abroad.

This is not to say that the Brezhnev years were devoid of reform. Indeed, Kosygin's efforts to reorganize the way enterprises interacted with each other

---

9 See, for instance, Nikita Khrushchev, *Khrushchev Remembers: The Last Testament*, trans. and ed. Strobe Talbott (Boston: Little, Brown & Co., 1974), 87.
10 A. Rumiantsev, "Partiia i intelligentsia," *Pravda* (21 Feb. 1965), 2.

and with the state formed the most far-reaching attempt to alter the fundamentals of the Soviet economy since the NEP period. Yet the Kosygin reforms mainly drove home Leszek Kołakowski's point about the impossible antinomies of reform socialism: Market incentives in the Soviet economy were just another "fried snowball." By the 1970s, Brezhnev began to pursue subtle methods to reinvigorate socialism, such as reining in alcohol production and sales, which would become a leitmotif of the final Soviet decades. Many of Brezhnev's initiatives mirrored previous campaigns, which was precisely the point for a political leadership profoundly skeptical and fearful of the "adventurism" of the Khrushchev years. Two projects stand out: the construction of the Baikal–Amur Mainline (BAM) and the promulgation of a new constitution in 1977. BAM was to the Brezhnev years as the Virgin Lands were to the Khrushchev ones: a project to harness the enthusiasm and energy of youth to achieve economic goals. It was supposed to inculcate a new Soviet generation with the ideals of socialism while producing the economic infrastructure necessary for communism. BAM's success mirrored that of previous large-scale projects. It forged communities of shared sacrifice and political enthusiasm, and it did achieve some short-term economic successes. Yet it also created a whole host of social and economic problems among indigenous peoples and prison workers, and environmental damage to a Siberian taiga that was still mostly pristine. Similar to the Virgin Lands, BAM's boomtowns were quickly abandoned with the collapse of communism.[11] The 1977 constitution also had several precursors, most notably the Stalin Constitution of 1936. Like Stalin, Brezhnev confirmed that socialism had been achieved, imbuing optimism into times that were not so revolutionary anymore. Echoing Khrushchev's new party program, which proclaimed the formation of an "all-people's state," Brezhnev's constitution abolished class struggle, and indeed the notion of class as a defining feature of the Soviet state overall. In 1977 there were only Soviet citizens, all equal in their rights and duties. What this meant in the world of "actually existing socialism" was left open to the interpretation of state and people.

The Brezhnev years were not Stalinism, to be sure. With the influx of oil money, living standards continued to improve in the late 1960s, albeit at slowing rates. Soviet society became more consumption-oriented than ever before, as televisions, automobiles, electric razors, washing machines and

---

11 Christopher J. Ward, *Brezhnev's Folly: The Building of BAM and Late-Soviet Socialism* (Pittsburgh: University of Pittsburgh Press, 2009); Johannes Grützmacher, *Die Baikal-Amur-Magistrale. Vom stalinistischen Lager zum Mobilisierungsprojekt unter Brežnev* (Munich: Oldenbourg Verlag, 2012).

holidays on the Black Sea became coveted staples of urban life. For arguably the first time since the 1920s, private life blossomed, which was made possible by the hallowing of ideological rituals, and by a state that exercised its power with all the swiftness and deliberation of a hippopotamus out of water. In this context, cynicism became the reigning ideology, and humor a safety valve for popular derision. For the vast majority of Soviet citizens, life after Khrushchev was neither uncomfortable nor unhappy. But the ideological optimism that had characterized so much of the Khrushchev years was gone.[12] Paradoxically, the good life of the present was transforming the utopia of the future into an object of ridicule.

The Shadow on the Wall: The West in Soviet Life and Mind

Soviet foreign relations in the post-Stalin years were a complex stew of heightened international tension and belligerence on the one hand, and increased interaction and cooperation on the other. Almost immediately after Stalin's death, Soviet leaders moved to end the Korean War, where North Korean communists had been fighting UN-flagged troops since 1950, despite the Soviet presence on the Security Council. Yet at virtually the same moment, Khrushchev ordered Soviet forces to put down a popular uprising in East Berlin, and later encouraged Walter Ulbricht to halt movement into Berlin's western sectors by constructing a wall. The latter events reflected the special status of Eastern Europe as war booty and guarantor of Soviet security. Paradoxically, in many East European countries, Stalinism survived long after Soviet leaders began to embrace de-Stalinization at home. Thus, one of the most important tasks was to remove from power the old guard – Bolesław Bierut in Poland and Mátyás Rákosi in Hungary. In Poland, at least, this helped quell the protests that the Twentieth Party Congress had precipitated. Traveling to Belgrade in 1955, Khrushchev patched up relations with Yugoslavia, which had been strained since the anti-Titoist trial of László Rajk in 1949. Yet Khrushchev also bore outsized responsibility for the Sino-Soviet split, which occurred in large part because of Chinese concerns about the loss of ideological stridency and growing complacency of Soviet leaders.

---

12 See, among others, Benjamin Nathans and Kevin Platt, "Socialist in Form, Indeterminate in Content: The Ins and Outs of Late Soviet Culture," *Ab Imperio* 2 (2011), 301–24; and Amir Weiner, "Robust Revolution to Retiring Revolution: The Life Cycle of the Soviet Revolution, 1945–1968," *Slavonic and East European Review* 86, 2 (Apr. 2008), 208–31.

"Peaceful coexistence," the diplomatic slogan of the 1950s and early 1960s, the Soviet refusal to share atomic weapons technology with China, and capitulation in the Cuban Missile Crisis in 1962 seemed to be proof of both in Beijing's eyes.

By the standards of Stalin, who rarely left Moscow, Khrushchev was an unusually adept global traveler. From Beijing to Oxford, Vienna to Disneyland, Iowa to Indonesia, Khrushchev led official delegations to summit meetings and on fact-finding trips, where his immense curiosity and braggadocio bore some resemblance to Peter the Great's. Khrushchev's initiatives and example paved the way for thousands of Soviet specialists to work abroad in the communist and developing worlds, where among other things they helped build the Aswan High Dam in Egypt. By the late 1960s, representatives of the Soviet friendship societies (a quasi-Peace Corps) could be found throughout the developing world. The Soviet Union couched itself as friend to anti-colonial, liberation movements in Africa and Asia, and attracted students from across the developing world to its universities. Yet, closer to home, it sought the preservation of empire and the maintenance of the status quo, even at the cost of ideological militancy. Thus, the Brezhnev Doctrine coexisted with détente, the crushing of the Prague Spring with growing Soviet involvement in a web of international arrangements that governed everything from intellectual copyright (which had the unexpected upshot of helping rein in so-called *tamizdat* literature) to commerce and sport. In the 1920s and 1930s, the Soviet Union subverted the capitalist world and even its left-wing political parties through the Communist International. A half-century later, it cooperated with its capitalist adversaries in ways once unimaginable. Being a superpower and wanting the trappings of success on the international stage came at a high price to revolutionary fervor.

Much more powerful than the existing West on the international scene was the imaginary West in the minds of Soviet citizens. While only a few Soviet citizens were granted permission to travel to capitalist countries, the West had a ubiquitous presence in the collective consciousness. That was true in the negative as well as the positive, even though the latter undoubtedly was predominant. It was perfectly possible for Soviet individuals to accommodate a whole variety of perceptions of the West, which were often mutually contradictory.[13] A surprising number of Soviet citizens agreed with their government's dictum that life under socialism was preferable to life under capitalism at the same time as they hankered for Western consumer

---

13 Yurchak, *Everything Was Forever*, 158–206.

items. They decried Western policy in Vietnam and elsewhere, and lapped up news from Radio Liberty and the BBC as more "true" than what their own media told them.[14]

For the most part, the West was encountered and consumed in what people would have called "apolitical" circumstances. One of the most powerful Western presences was rock-and-roll. Much has been said and written about the incredible impact that the Beatles had on Soviet youth and culture.[15] While jazz, transmitted via the Voice of America and in particular Willie Conover's Jazz Hour, spawned the subculture of the *stiliagi*, the Beatles influenced a whole generation, setting off a wave of Beatlemania and fostering the rise of unofficial amateur bands, which covered their favorite songs at school and university concerts. The repercussions of this new phenomenon were visible in youth fashion (ultimately creating a vivid and long-lived hippie subculture), and in the rise of a powerful domestic rock music scene.[16] Bands such as Time Machine and Aquarium soon abandoned Western cover songs, and started writing their own lyrics and music, tapping into the legacy of the 1960s bards and expressing the specific concerns of their generation. While Time Machine was coopted into the official fold in the 1980s, many bands, most notably Aquarium and its legendary lead singer Boris Grebenshikov, remained in the underground until the late 1980s, automatically pitching their large fan base against Soviet rule. For the party, of course, neither the Beatles (who were banned) nor Russian rock bands (which were eyed with extreme suspicion) were apolitical. Every aspect about them was a challenge to the party's stewardship of politics and culture. Their youthful spontaneity and independence flew in the face of young people respecting their party elders and supporting revolutionary myths. Their personal and often critical lyrics broke with an ideology that emphasized collective optimism. Their fashion and behavior did not conform to Soviet standards of decency and decorum, which still championed the tidily dressed Komsomol leader with a neat haircut. At a 1980s rock music competition in Tbilisi, Grebenshikov famously sported sunglasses in a dark

14 Vladimir Shlapentokh, *Strakh i druzhba v nashem totalitarnom proshlom* (St. Petersburg: Izd. zhurnala Zvezda, 2003).
15 Leslie Woodhead, *How the Beatles Rocked the Kremlin: The Untold Story of a Noisy Revolution* (London: Bloomsbury, 2013).
16 Juliane Fürst, "If You Are Going to Moscow, Be Sure to Wear Some Flowers in Your Hair (and Bring a Bottle of Port Wine in Your Pocket): The Soviet Hippie 'Sistema' and Its Life in, Despite and with 'Stagnation,'" in Dina Fainberg and Artemy Kalinovsky (eds.), *Reconsidering Stagnation in the Brezhnev Era: Ideology and Exchange* (Lanham, MD: Lexington Books, 2016), 123–46.

indoor room, wore his shirt unbuttoned to the stomach and pretended to make love to his guitar on stage.[17]

With music came fashion. While few Soviet citizens bought into the full-scale rock-and-roll look that Grebenshikov sported, a very large number were prepared to spend a full month's salary on a pair of jeans. Ideally, these were not just any pair of jeans manufactured in the Soviet Union. Products from the people's republics, such as Poland and Czechoslovakia, ranged higher in the pecking order and were more desirable. But at the top were real American blue jeans, such as Levi's and Wranglers. There was a booming black market in American jeans, which was spearheaded by a cohort of speculators operating around Moscow's international hotels. They would buy clothing off the backs of Western tourists and businessmen. All of this was, of course, very much against the spirit of communism, which eschewed fashion as bourgeois and individualistic. It was also humiliating for a Soviet state whose products were derided by its own people as inferior, and not only in the jeans department.[18]

In reality the Soviet state too had long ago succumbed to the notion of the West's superiority in trendsetting and style. The state-run houses of fashion, for instance, looked to Paris and Milan for inspiration. It was no coincidence that one of the major events of Khrushchev's Thaw was Christian Dior's visit to Moscow, which drew huge crowds and much admiration. The Soviet Union continued to compete with the USA in matters of lifestyle and consumer culture, which proved to be a pointless and ultimately damaging game. Khrushchev had been taken by his encounters with the United States, as had several people in his entourage, such as Anastas Mikoian, who worked hard to bring refrigeration to the Soviet apartment.[19] Of course, the Americans were happy to advertise for Khrushchev the material benefits of free-market capitalism. Khrushchev engaged Richard Nixon about the merits of communism and capitalism at the American National Exhibition in 1959. While Khrushchev held his own in debate, the fact that it occurred in Moscow only underscored the Soviet Union's considerable failings in alleviating the daily lives of its citizens. Soviet rule may have produced greater equality than American capitalism, but it was an

---

17 Artemy Troitsky, *Back in the USSR: The True Story of Rock in Russia* (London: Omnibus, 1987), 47–48.

18 Natalya Chernyshova, *Soviet Consumer Culture in the Brezhnev Era* (London: Routledge, 2013), 133–61; and Sergei Zhuravlev and Yukka Gronov, *Moda po planu. Istoriia modi i modelirovanie odezhdy v SSSR 1917–1991* (Moscow: IRI RAN, 2013), 345–408.

19 Weiner, "Robust Revolution to Retiring Revolution," 230.

equality of relative impoverishment.[20] Brezhnev was not prone to these kinds of public stunts, but under his direction the Soviet Union continued to benchmark itself against Western achievements in the lifestyle sector. US trade shows were allowed to go as far as Siberia to showcase the American way of life, and Soviet amenities were quick to reference themselves against Western models. Thus, Crimea became the Soviet Riviera and the Baltic countries the Soviet Union's little Europe. Even jeans started to be produced in large quantities, which significantly dropped their black-market price, but ultimately did little to take away their American cachet.[21]

Most Soviet citizens sensed rather than believed in Western economic superiority. Information about life in the West was hard to come by, even though a surprising amount of Western topics were covered by official publications. People learned to read "the opposite" of critical articles and pick out the interesting and informative bits in ideologically infused reportage. The West became the bearer of "truth," while for many everything Soviet was a lie. This attitude went far beyond dissident circles and permeated large segments of society – even the ranks of party and Komsomol officials. Late Soviet people trusted rumors more than *Pravda* or *Izvestiia* (which might explain the high esteem conspiracy theories still enjoy in Russia). Rumors often originated with broadcasts on foreign radio such as Radio Free Europe / Radio Liberty, Voice of America, the BBC and German Wave. It is not clear how many people actively listened to these stations, but it is apparent that a large number of people knew about their broadcasts and individual news items.[22] Dissident publications, especially the Moscow-based *Chronicle of Current Events*, attempted to counter the information vacuum with their own news services. In the 1960s it was customary for dissidents to travel to far-flung factory towns to verify hearsay about strikes and demonstrations. Doing so was dangerous, and the resulting stories often had little impact in a country the size of the

20 Susan Reid, "Cold War in the Kitchen: Gender and the De-Stalinization of Consumer Taste in the Soviet Union Under Khrushchev," *Slavic Review* 61, 2 (Summer 2001), 212–52.
21 Leonid Parfenov, "Dzhinsy za 150 rub.," in Leonid Parfenov (ed.), *Namedni: nasha era 1971–1980* (Moscow: KoLibri, 2009), 194.
22 Since no statistical data can be established on who read and listened to what, the evidence is mainly anecdotal. See among others William Taubman, *The View from Lenin Hills: An American Student's Report on Soviet Youth in Ferment* (London: Hamilton, 1968); Igor' Makarevich, "Dialogicheskii monolog 'Pro eto,'" in Georgii Kizelvalter (ed.), *Eti strannye semidesiatye ili poteriia nevinnosti* (Moscow: Novoe literaturnoe obozrenie, 2010), 68; Yurchak, *Everything Was Forever*, 175–81; Georgie Anne Geyer, *The Young Russians* (Homewood, IL: ETC, 1975), 156–57.

Soviet Union.[23] Yet the acute desire, widespread among Soviet citizens, for more and better information shaped to no small extent the forces of Gorbachev's reforms, which started out as an attempt to achieve more *glasnost'* – greater transparency – and spiraled from there.[24]

Very few Soviet citizens equated a love for jeans or a desire to own the newest Beatles album with an anti-communist attitude. Soviet officials, however, recognized much earlier the corrosive potential of the fascination with all things Western. Yet they had little substantive response to it, repeating instead the same old rhetoric of bourgeois corruption and Western infiltration. They also attempted to replicate the thrill of Western consumption with Soviet products, which generally did not live up to consumer expectations. The real problem, of course, was not that wearing jeans and listening to Western rock-and-roll were dissident activities, but that they were apolitical, which was contrary to the core principles of the Soviet project. There were moments when it became apparent that this cocktail of Western music, youthful thrill-seeking and disdain for Soviet reality could prove explosive. In 1978 *Leningradskaia Pravda* announced a concert, headlined by the Beach Boys, Santana and Joan Baez. It drew several thousand youngsters to Palace Square on the appointed date. Yet Leningrad party officials had canceled the concert long before, and failed to convey their decision to the public. Disappointed youngsters began to riot and clash with the hastily summoned police. According to testimony from eyewitnesses, people shouted anti-Soviet slogans, and street fighting continued for several hours.[25]

The Late Soviet Citizen: A Story of Adaptation

For many years the story of late socialism was, for Western ears, intimately connected to that of the Soviet dissidents. Aleksandr Solzhenitsyn, Natan Sharanskii and Yurii Orlov were household names, whose tales of resistance and repression captured the imagination of a West that knew the Soviet Union best via the novels of John le Carré and Martin Cruz Smith. In the Western imagination the Soviet Union was a grim, frosty place full of KGB agents, who suppressed a small band of people bravely fighting for freedom and democracy.

23 Liudmila Ya. Alexeeva, *Istoriia inakomysliia v SSSR* (Moscow: ZAO RITS Zatsepa, 2001), 224–27.
24 Robert Horvath, *The Legacy of Soviet Dissent: Dissidents, Democratization and Radical Nationalism in Russia* (London: RoutledgeCurzon, 2005), 50–80.
25 Nika Strizhak, *Zapreshchennyi kontsert. Nemusikal'naia istoriia*, documentary film (2006).

In fact, everything about this story was more complicated in real life. The Soviet Union was not a free country in the 1960s and 1970s but, in contrast to the Stalinist decades, when arrests were capricious, one generally had to court trouble to get into it. The system was unforgiving of those who transgressed sometimes ill-defined norms. Yet it was no longer randomly repressive, and its power was only rarely directed against large segments of the population. The nature of Soviet dissidence was also more complicated than was commonly perceived in the West. Almost all major dissidents who were active in the human rights movement of the 1970s and 1980s came from the so-called *shestidesiatnik* generation, a term that located them not only as an age cohort ("people of the Sixties") socialized in the early post-Stalin years, but also as part of a generation that believed the Soviet Union and its communist system capable of reform. Initially their hopes and energy were directed toward Khrushchev's Thaw. At least at the beginning of their careers, many of these dissidents spouted various forms of reform socialism and neo-Leninism. In general, they believed that a more accurate reading of Marx and Lenin would lead to a better version of socialism, which had to be awakened from its Stalinist petrification. The 1968 invasion of Czechoslovakia put an end to the rejuvenation brand of dissidence.[26]

In the 1970s, outspoken critics of Soviet socialism began to fragment along political and identity lines. Yet nonconformists and dissidents – and indeed large swathes of the intelligentsia – shared one important conviction: They had largely lost faith in the idea that Soviet-style socialism was the ideal future.[27] Alternatives, however, were as yet ill defined and differed widely among dissidents, even among those who were in the same networks. The most vocal challenge – and the one that was most reported in the West, since it conformed to Western expectations – came from so-called human-rights activists, who used the Soviet Union's signature of the Helsinki Accords to demand greater freedoms of speech, assembly and artistic expression, and more transparency. On the other end of the dissident spectrum were people who in later years came to be seen as the "New Left." These mostly young people critiqued Soviet reality from a radical socialist perspective, drawing on Marx, Mao and contemporary leftist thinkers such as Albert Camus and Jean-Paul Sartre. (The extent to which people were aware of this literature varied.)[28] The 1970s were also the heyday of nonconformist artists

26 Veniamin Yoffe, *Novye etiudy ob optimizme* (St. Petersburg: Memorial, 1998).
27 Platt and Nathans, "Socialist in Form, Indeterminate in Content," 301–24.
28 Dmitrii Rubliov, "Novye levye v SSSR," *Alternativy* 2 (2012), 141–55; Aleksandr Skobov, "Perspektiva – DieZeitschrift der Neuen Linken," in Viacheslav Dolinin and

who challenged the Soviet establishment by painting and exhibiting outside official institutions and in styles that ran counter to the dictates of Socialist Realism. Artists working outside Socialist Realism enjoyed unprecedented public exposure with numerous illegal apartment-based and open-air exhibitions and even some officially sanctioned events, which drew thousands of people.[29] Underground writers and political commentators also used the sophisticated samizdat distribution networks to channel forbidden literature to people far from the dissident milieu. Yet these alternative thinkers were not entirely divorced from society. Rather, the lines between those who worked officially and who worked underground were blurred, just as the point where nonconformism departed from official Soviet norms was not absolute.[30]

In retrospect it is clear that the greatest challenge to Soviet ideology came from the nationalist corner. This had been quite evident in the case of the rising nationalist challenges in the republics, all of which to a greater or lesser extent sported a national opposition. Yet they were more pronounced in the Baltic countries and the Caucasus. In 1977 a bomb explosion in the Moscow metro, supposedly the work of Armenian nationalists, brought modern-style terrorism to the Soviet capital, just as the West was rocked by left-wing extremist actions, some of which occurred with the backing of Soviet bloc states. A number of plane hijackings took place in the Soviet Union in the 1970s and 1980s, mostly by people trying to exit Soviet territory. The most famous incident catapulted the cause of Soviet Zionists to world attention. Nine Jews from Riga planned to take control of a plane at Leningrad airport and divert it to Stockholm from where they planned to emigrate to Israel. Their conspiratorial effort was badly compromised. The KGB foiled the hijacking, and all nine perpetrators were sentenced to long prison terms, including a young pregnant woman. The two ringleaders, Mark Dimshitz and Eduard Kuznetsov, once a participant in the famous Thaw-era poetry readings on Moscow's Maiakovskii Square, were sentenced to death. The severity of their sentence caused an outcry in the Western world and helped give rise to the international refusenik movement, which demanded free exit for Soviet Jews. While only a fraction of the Jews who emigrated in

Boris Ivanov (ed.), *Samizdat. Po Materialien der Konferenz "30 Jahre unabhängige Presse," 1950–80er Jahre* (Moscow: Memorial, 1992), 117–22.
29 Kizelvalter (ed.), *Eti strannye*; Matthew Jesse Jackson, *The Experimental Group: Ilya Kabakov, Moscow Conceptualism, Soviet Avant-Gardes* (Chicago: University of Chicago Press, 2010).
30 See Polly Jones, "The Zones of Late Socialist Literature," in this volume.

the following two decades in fact went to Israel, the underlying sentiment that supported the refusenik and Jewish emigration movement both inside and outside the Soviet Union was a new kind of Jewish nationalism, fueled and supported by the successes of the state of Israel, by US policy and by the semi-official anti-Semitism that was rampant in the Soviet Union.[31]

Interestingly, the nationalist sentiment that received the least public attention was arguably the one that had, and continues to have, the largest impact. Kuznetsov's former co-conspirator from Maiakovskii Square, Vladimir Osipov, also found his national roots – Russian in this case – and became the founder and publisher of the nationalist and often anti-Semitic journal *Veche*. With this he tapped into a sentiment that had been percolating underneath the veneer of Soviet patriotism since the Great Fatherland War, whose commemoration unashamedly privileged the Russian nation over other Soviet nationalities. Russian nationalism grew within the party and Komsomol leadership as well as in the Soviet Union of Writers.[32] It came in various guises, from anti-Semitic policies to the rebirth of Russian village prose, an interest in the ethnography of rural peasant populations and a growing popular disgruntlement over the perception that Russia was sustaining the communist empire economically. Russian nationalism rose not so much in opposition to Soviet communism, but in tandem with it, and interlaced with it, as a logical consequence of Soviet communism's failures. Brezhnev in particular made use of the relatively easy appeal to Russian national sentiment when he implemented comprehensive ritualistic practices to venerate victory in the Great Fatherland War, while downplaying the communist revolutionary legacy even during the extensive festivities for the sixtieth anniversary of the Russian Revolution in 1977.[33]

Only a tiny minority of Soviet citizens engaged consciously with questions of ideological substance, resistance and alternatives to socialism. The vast majority thought of their lives with and within the Soviet state, while safeguarding personal desires and preferences that were apolitical. Indeed, it would be wrong to assume that there were two distinct entities at play here: the state's demands and citizens' interests. Rather the lines were blurred, since Soviet socialization ensured that people's personal worlds

31 Yaacov Roi, *The Jewish Movement in the Soviet Union* (Washington, DC, and Baltimore: Woodrow Wilson Center Press and Johns Hopkins University Press, 2012).
32 Nikolai Mitrokhin, *Russkaia partiia: dvizhenie russkikh natsionalistov 1953–1985 gg.* (Moscow: Novoe literaturnoe obozrenie, 2003).
33 Nina Tumarkin, *The Living and the Dead: The Rise and Fall of the Cult of World War II in Russia* (New York: Basic Books, 1995).

constantly reflected Soviet norms and values. The Soviet state also made popular satisfaction part of its *raison d'être* and official program.

Nonetheless, the gap between what people did and felt and what the state wanted them to do and feel widened in the Brezhnev period. Most damagingly, many people found it increasingly difficult to take the Soviet project seriously. Brezhnev-era pomposity, repetitiveness and love for rhetorical monotony and the spectacular failure to deliver what was promised in many sectors undermined the Soviet state's claim on popular devotion. A complicated set of ironies, ridicule and nonattention defined many people's daily relationship with official structures. This, however, did not mean that these very same people were divorced from official structures themselves, but that they performed in them. This performance mutated more often than not into actions that were characterized by insincerity, or was transformed into practices beneficial to the individual and small personal collectives, not necessarily to the Soviet project *in toto*. "We pretend to work and they pretend to pay us," was a favorite saying of the Brezhnev years. The work collective became, and indeed was often portrayed in Soviet media as, a jovial community of moderately industrious friends and acquaintances, who spent weekends at their dachas, where they devoted their labor to tending the vegetable garden. The latter they did with a great deal more gusto and efficiency than was extended to their official workspaces.

Alexei Yurchak has analyzed the "performative shifts" Soviet people executed in order to participate in the different levels of late Soviet life. These shifts covered and bridged the inherent contradictions of late socialism, yet they also created "deterritorialized milieus," which were ideologically hollow spaces that were nevertheless laden with personal meaning for their creators and participants.[34] A large proportion of Soviet people were "Soviet" not by ideology, but because they had mastered nuanced practices of limited engagement and limited dissent, and indeed continued to refine and adapt these practices to accommodate their simultaneous need to belong to Soviet socialism while distancing themselves from it.

Certain aspects seemed more stable and promising than others and for a while took precedence over attempts to change. In particular Soviet patriotism, which translated into a general acceptance of Soviet foreign policy and pride in Soviet sporting achievements, was one of the last areas of congruence between official ideology and popular sentiment. It is thus not surprising that the Moscow Olympic Games in 1980 did not result in a relaxation of Soviet

---

34 Yurchak, *Everything Was Forever*, 126–57.

policies, but ushered in a period of hardline measures designed to rein in the excesses of alienated citizens. The fact that the restraint of unruly Soviet citizens required not insubstantial manpower – ranging from police to judiciary, from party and Komsomol functionaries to neighbourhood watchdogs – proves that even at this stage many people were invested enough in the system to ensure the continuation of its repressive function and survival. Indeed, to most people – no matter if they were dissidents, careerists or conformists – the Soviet state and the socialist state of things seemed destined to exist forever and change very little. It was from this perception that the term "stagnation" has its justification – and its limits. It was in the shadow of a conviction that nothing was and would be changing that people began to arrange their lives in ways that minimally passed official demands, ironically making the late Soviet Union a happening, if not exactly a very communist place.

Dachas and Madhouses: Late Socialism Between Consumption and Repression

The watering down of socialist ideology as a basis for everyday life was a process that was not driven merely by Soviet citizens' desire to establish livable mental and physical spaces. The Soviet state, too, had been experimenting with new forms of translating socialism into lived life, and in the process encouraged practices that redefined the meaning of "everyday socialism." They stood in stark contrast to earlier revolutionary ideals such as austerity and primacy of the collective over individual comforts. While even in the 1930s there had been attempts to make socialist life more livable by broadening the definition of what was called Soviet, it was under Khrushchev that real commitment to consumption as a socialist practice took root.[35] Fueled by Cold War competition, the Soviet Union tried to match Western consumer culture with homemade products designed to give customer satisfaction without stratifying society along consumerist lines. In 1961 a new party program linked material abundance with communism. Gradually in the press the consumer took shape as an individual who could make choices; yet he, or more often she, was not viewed as an independent agent. Rather, the

35 In the 1930s Soviet norms shifted toward the conservative, but were also defined as including formerly bourgeois occupations such as (where appropriate) dancing, comedy, veneration of traditional Russian culture and so on. See, for instance, David L. Hoffmann, *Stalinist Values: The Cultural Norms of Soviet Modernity, 1917–1941* (Ithaca: Cornell University Press, 2003); and Karen Petrone, *Life Has Become More Joyous, Comrades: Celebrations in the Time of Stalin* (Bloomington: University of Indiana Press, 2000).

abundance of Khrushchev-era consumption advice was geared toward replacing violent coercion with systemic soft power, which had the same claim over the private life and the privacy of Soviet citizens as in Stalin's era.[36]

At the same time Khrushchev identified consumption – and especially the hierarchies created by consumption – as a battlefield of the Cold War. His debate with Nixon in front of a model kitchen at the American National Exhibition demonstrated all the idiosyncrasies and contradictions in the Soviet relationship with consumption: No Soviet consumer could afford or hope to buy an American kitchen, yet American consumer products were regularly shown in special exhibitions not only in Moscow but also in the provinces. The individual kitchen itself was a capitulation of the early Soviet ideal of mass catering and freeing women from domestic work – an idea that was now replaced by the Western concept of liberating women by easing their work through technological progress and consumption of its fruits. That indeed was a pact with the devil. The Soviet Union sought to harness Western ideas to achieve the communist utopia, thus toeing a precarious line between selling out and staying true to the final goal of creating communism. Socialist consumption was supposed to look the same as Western consumption but work toward a very different goal. Thus to Khrushchev, the modern, private kitchen would achieve what the communal kitchen had failed to do: socialist equality and abundance for the masses – the very opposite of what the luxury American kitchen promised its users, which was differentiation and exclusivity.

Socialist consumption policies continued to be a precarious balancing act, especially once consumerism became a reality for Soviet citizens and not a promise for the future. At the same time the economy was understood to have real and fundamental problems that stemmed from the command system. This called for an overhaul, especially in the consumer industries. While the Kosygin reforms of 1965 were short-lived, they took the first steps toward a system that was driven by consumer demand, albeit one with a huge military-industrial complex. The latter idea survived even the reforms. The Soviet press devoted more and more coverage to consumer complaints in the 1970s. The consumption practices of Soviet citizens suggested that they had become more discriminating in their shopping. Items of low quality were now left in the shops, creating backlogs as well as deficits. Widespread official lambasting of consumerist behavior and attitudes suggest that Soviet people

---

36 Victor Buchli, *An Archeology of Socialism* (Oxford: Berg, 1999); Kharkhordin, *The Collective and the Individual.*

were keenly aware that overt consumerism was supposed to be condemned as materialistic, but they engaged in it nonetheless, with great devotion and determination. Precisely because so many items were rare, their attainment became a preoccupation, even an obsession.[37]

In comparison to earlier decades, Soviet citizens lived better in the 1970s, had wider consumption choices and enjoyed luxuries on a scale that had been unthinkable for the average Soviet person of the 1930s. Private dwellings and travel to interesting parts of the Soviet Union became the norm in the 1970s. People bought into the "little deal" offered by the Brezhnev system: outward compliance in return for modest prosperity.[38] However, this did not mean that they subverted the kind of "wealth" the system offered them, pushing the boundaries of what was permitted both ideologically and, even more often, economically. Tourism went increasingly wild, with people setting out in their cars rather than with prebooked holiday vouchers. They camped or relied on renting private homes and apartments.[39] The same kind of spirit informed the growing small-scale commercial arbitrage, which saw people buy goods in one part of the country and sell them for more in another, using and abusing the shortages that plagued Soviet society. The so-called *fartsovsh-chiki* had been part of the urban landscape for decades. They sold everything from books to *valiuta* – foreign currency. With them the Soviet state had no mercy. Trading *valiuta* was punishable by death – a sentence that was indeed enforced in the late Soviet Union, demonstrating that Soviet power had by no means lost its teeth.[40]

Indeed, for those who stepped across the line of the "little deal," the Soviet Union drew on an entirely new repertoire of repressive measures, which were not as deadly as Stalin's but nonetheless terrifying enough and astonishingly perfidious. There were still plenty of camps and prisons holding political prisoners of all kinds: dissidents, Zionists, religious dissenters and those who had been framed as criminals, mostly through the planting of drugs or by provoking violent situations which allowed prosecution. Exile and banishment were also in the state arsenal. The Soviet Union's most famous exile was its former scientific superstar Andrei Sakharov, who was banished to

37 Chernyshova, *Soviet Consumer Culture*.
38 James R. Millar, "The Little Deal: Brezhnev's Contribution to Acquisitive Socialism," *Slavic Review* 44, 4 (1985), 694–706.
39 Christian Noack, "Brezhnev's 'Little Freedoms': Tourism, Individuality, and Mobility in the Late Soviet Period," in Fainberg and Kalinovsky (eds.), *Reconsidering Stagnation in the Brezhnev Era*, 59–76.
40 Dmitrii Vasil'ev, *Fartsovshchiki. Kak delalis' sostoianiia* (St. Petersburg: Nevskii prospekt, 2007).

a "gilded cage" in the closed city of Gorkii in 1980, primarily to keep him away from Western reporters in Moscow. He was released only at Gorbachev's insistence in 1986. Many others, who were not protected by fame, fared worse. Forced abortions for female prisoners and terrible death-inducing conditions in camps and prisons were not unknown in the post-Stalin years.

The most noted, and probably the most characteristic, form of late socialist repression, however, was the use of psychiatry and psychiatric institutions. Like so many things in the last Soviet decades, the abuse of mental hospitals as places of detainment for nonconformists straddled the border between blatant cynicism and sincere conviction. While the world renounced Professor Andrei Snezhnevskii's Serbskii Institute, which was the forerunner and trendsetter in the diagnosis of "sluggish schizophrenia," many Soviet psychiatrists worked in good faith. Their assessment of dissidents as "mad" was shared by large numbers of the Soviet population, who viewed outright opposition as both pointless and abnormal.[41] For the state, the classification of many dissidents as "schizophrenic" and hence incurably ill allowed a facade of legality and mercy while permitting ruthless cleansings of unwanted elements. Once they were diagnosed with mental disorders, no incident was needed to allow renewed detainment of uncomfortable citizens. Nonconformist Soviet subjects thus found themselves confined every time the state wanted to celebrate its achievements. The largest cleansing operation was conducted before the Moscow Olympics in 1980, when not only dissidents but also hippies, punks, homeless people and other nonconformists found themselves locked away in order to portray the perfect society the Soviet Union had failed to achieve.

Ironically, most of the intended audience for this vision of good socialist order did not even turn up to the event. In response to the Soviet invasion of Afghanistan, most Western nations refused to travel to the Moscow Olympics. Yet the image of the Soviet Union as a model solution to societal problems was even more important when directed toward the developing world, whose alignment with either East or West was up for grabs. The West had long ceased to harbor an existential fear of the appeal of Soviet communism or its scientific achievements. It was now the possibility of mutual annihilation that was uppermost in people's minds and informed a large peace movement, which, significantly, did not see its mission as connected to supporting communist ideas. In the developing world, to the contrary,

---

41 Sidney Block and Peter Reddaway, *Russia's Political Hospitals* (London: Gollancz, 1977), 227–30; Yurchak, *Everything Was Forever*, 102–03.

promises of Soviet support could still ring bells, at least until the latter half of the 1980s. In competition with China the Soviet government aggressively courted the developing world through soft-power tools such as youth exchanges, cultural and economic relations, and generous disbursements of financial aid that often went into military rather than civil projects.[42] It was partly because of this that the conviction arose among many Soviet citizens, particularly its Russian ones, that the empire and its extensions did not serve them but cost them dearly. Since most spiritual ties to the Soviet project had been replaced by performative ritual, which signified Soviet loyalty but also felt quite meaningless, the sense of betrayal was swift and damaging. By the late 1980s there was a growing consensus that the Soviet Union had grown old and cumbersome. When death came in 1991, few mourned.[43] Yet there was more Sovietness left in the Soviet Union than people thought at the time. In memory the Soviet Union shines on much brighter than it ever did in its last few decades of life.

Bibliographical Essay

In recent years, historical scholarship on post-Stalinist society has been in full bloom. Compared to the Stalin years, however, it is still underresearched and relies heavily on memoirs and autobiographies.

The era began with one of Khrushchev's cardinal achievements: the emptying of the Gulag, which is the topic of Miriam Dobson's *Khrushchev's Cold Summer: Gulag Returnees, Crime, and the Fate of Reform after Stalin* (Ithaca: Cornell University Press, 2009). Alan Barenberg describes the transformation of Vorkuta from camp to factory town after Stalin's death in *Gulag Town, Company Town: Forced Labor and Its Legacy in Vorkuta* (New Haven: Yale University Press, 2014), highlighting one of the many structural consequences of the end of terror. Perhaps no topic in the 1950s and 1960s has received more attention than the intelligentsia and the Thaw, particularly official and popular efforts to make sense of Stalinism. Denis Kozlov's *The Readers of Novyi Mir: Coming to Terms with the Stalinist Past* (Cambridge, MA: Harvard University Press, 2013), Stephen V. Bittner's *The Many Lives of Khrushchev's Thaw: Experience and Memory in Moscow's Arbat* (Ithaca: Cornell University Press, 2008), Polly Jones's *Myth, Memory, Trauma: Rethinking the Stalinist Past in the Soviet Union, 1953–1970* (New Haven: Yale University Press, 2013) and

---

42 Jeremy Friedman, *Shadow Cold War: The Sino-Soviet Split and the Third World* (Chapel Hill: University of North Carolina Press, 2015).
43 See Vladislav Zubok, "The Collapse of the Soviet Union," in this volume.

many of the essays in Denis Kozlov and Eleonory Gilburd's *The Thaw: Soviet Society and Culture in the 1950s and 1960s* (Toronto: University of Toronto Press, 2013) deal with important aspects of this question. An interesting exploration of the world of the 1960s intellectual from within can be found in Petr Vail' and Aleksandr Genis, *Mir sovetskogo cheloveka 60-e* [The World of the Soviet Man of the 1960s] (Moscow: Novoe literaturnoe obozrenie, 2001). Oleg Khakhordin's *The Collective and the Individual in Russia: A Study in Practices* (Berkeley: University of California Press, 1999) asks similar questions and forms part of a number of scholarly attempts to draw parallels between the pre- and post-Stalinist periods. Official efforts after Stalin's death to bolster living standards and consumption in the context of the Cold War, and popular responses to them, are the topic of a number of seminal essays by Susan E. Reid. Especially notable is "Cold War in the Kitchen: Gender and the De-Stalinization of Consumer Taste in the Soviet Union Under Khrushchev," *Slavic Review* 61, 2 (Summer 2001), 212–52. Housing, the focus of the greatest investment and arguably the most life-changing project for the average Soviet citizen, is the central concern in Steven E. Harris's *Communism on Tomorrow Street: Mass Housing and Everyday Life After Stalin* (Washington, DC, and Baltimore: Woodrow Wilson Center Press and Johns Hopkins University Press, 2012) and Christine Varga-Harris's *Stories of House and Home: Soviet Apartment Life During the Khrushchev Years* (Ithaca: Cornell University Press, 2015).

Soviet society in the Brezhnev years is less well documented, even though it should be noted that there is an extraordinary amount of work in progress. Donald Raleigh's *Soviet Baby Boomers: An Oral History of Russia's Cold War Generation* (Oxford: Oxford University Press, 2011) follows a cohort of so-called *shestidesiatniki* into the "stagnation" of the Brezhnev years. The epitaph "stagnation" finds itself under fire, yet not replaced by a more suitable paradigm, by a number of authors who are published in Dina Fainberg and Artemy Kalinovsky (eds.), *Reconsidering Stagnation in the Brezhnev Era: Ideology and Exchange* (Lanham, MD: Lexington Books, 2016). The most influential analysis of the late Soviet citizen comes from Alexei Yurchak's *Everything Was Forever, Until It Was No More: The Last Soviet Generation* (Princeton: Princeton University Press, 2006). Yurchak's concentration on those who lived in the liminal space that was part of the Soviet system, as well as outside it, suggests that Soviet "normality" became a highly complex and subjective concept in this period. The thesis of the disintegration of the Soviet "norm" is borne out in works as diverse as Chris Ward's study of the Baikal–Amur Mainline railway, *Brezhnev's Folly: The Building of BAM and Late Soviet Socialism*

(Pittsburgh: University of Pittsburgh Press, 2009) and Michael Jesse Jackson's study of the Moscow conceptual group, *The Experimental Group: Ilya Kabakov, Moscow Conceptualism, Soviet Avant-Gardes* (Chicago: University of Chicago Press, 2010). The borders of late Soviet normality are also investigated in V. A. Kozlov's *Massovye besporiadki v SSSR pri Khrushcheve i Brezhneve* [Mass Riots in the USSR Under Khrushchev and Brezhnev] (Moscow: ROSSPEN, 1999), which explores the state's response to social unrest after Stalin's death, as well as in the essays presented in Juliane Fürst and Josie McLellan (eds.), *Dropping Out of Socialism: The Creation of Alternative Spheres in the Soviet Bloc* (Lanham, MD: Lexington Books, 2016), which looks at subcultural and marginal phenomena across the Soviet bloc. There has been a certain reluctance by scholars of this period to draw conclusions about the peculiarities of late Soviet society and its ultimate demise, as noted by Kevin Platt and Benjamin Nathans in "Socialist in Form, Indeterminate in Content: The Ins and Outs of Late Soviet Culture," *Ab Imperio* 2 (2011), 301–24. Whether it is methodologically improper to interpret late Soviet history backwards, from the vantage point of its collapse in 1991, or whether the historian of this period has indeed a duty to explain as well as chronicle this collapse, remains an open question among scholars of late Soviet society.

12

Communism and Religion

STEPHEN A. SMITH

In an essay of 1844 Karl Marx famously postulated:

> *Religious* suffering is, at one and the same time, the *expression* of real suffering
> and a *protest* against real suffering. Religion is the sigh of the oppressed
> creature, the heart of a heartless world, and the soul of soulless conditions.
> It is the *opium* of the people ... To call on them to give up their illusions
> about their condition is to call on them to *give up a condition that requires
> illusions*.[1]

When Marx wrote this, he was still a left neo-Hegelian, who saw religion as
the alienation of human essence rather than as the product of social relations.
It was only in *The German Ideology* (1846) that he began to conceptualize
religion in recognizably "Marxist" terms, i.e. as a form of ideology conditioned by material production and corresponding social relations.
Nevertheless this "pre-Marxist" characterization affirmed the dialectical character of religion both as a legitimation of existing social conditions and as
a protest against them – something the Marxist regimes of the twentieth
century would largely forget.[2] It was Friedrich Engels, his collaborator,
who put historical flesh on Marx's skeletal conception by investigating the
relationship of Christianity to changes in the mode of production and social
formation, demonstrating, for example, that in sixteenth-century Germany
different forms of Christianity – "feudal" Catholicism, "bourgeois"
Protestantism and plebeian heresies – were fought over by antagonistic social
forces.[3] Both Marx and Engels were antipathetic to religion as an organized

---

1 Karl Marx, "A Contribution to the Critique of Hegel's Philosophy of Right," www
.marxists.org/archive/marx/works/1843/critique-hpr/intro.htm (emphasis in original).
2 Michel Löwy, "Marxism and Religion," www.internationalviewpoint.org/article.php3?
id_article=807.
3 Friedrich Engels, "The Peasant War in Germany" (1850), www.marxists.org/archive/
marx/works/1850/peasant-war-germany/.

force, yet Marx, in particular, stood at some distance from the Enlightenment tradition that saw religion merely as an instrument of obscurantism and oppression, one that could be countered by "reason." Within the German Social Democratic Party (SDP, founded in 1875), the main political party inspired by the ideas of Marx and Engels, Marx's dialectical understanding of religion persisted, yet currents within the party stood closer to the Enlightenment tradition, stressing the capacity of science to bring intellectual emancipation from religious belief. Worker activists, for example, were urged to read classic materialist texts such as Ludwig Büchner's *Kraft und Stoff. Empirisch-naturphilosophische Studien* (1855) (Force and Matter: Empirico-philosophical Studies) or Ernst Haeckel's *Die Welträtsel* (1895–1899) (published as *The Riddle of the Universe* in 1901). The SDP avoided shrill anti-religious rhetoric in favor of a generalized secular humanism; in its propaganda, it placed the accent on its commitment to freedom of religious belief.[4] Vladimir Lenin would see in this a tendency to "opportunism" and claim to recuperate an orthodox Marxist position: "Marxism has always regarded all modern religions and churches ... as instruments of bourgeois reaction that serve to defend exploitation and befuddle the working class." He insisted that Russian Social Democrats must intransigently expose the "class role of the church and the clergy in supporting the Black-Hundred government and the bourgeoisie in its fight against the working class."[5] Even more than their German comrades, the Russian Social Democrats were shaped by an Enlightenment tradition, reinforced by nineteenth-century philosophical materialism, that championed reason and looked to the application of scientific knowledge to nature and society as the key to social progress. Their hostility to religion doubtless reflected the fact that they were a product of a society in which the culture of the intelligentsia was strongly secular and in which the Russian Orthodox Church was a pillar of the tsarist state, organizationally subordinate to and financially dependent upon it.

Following their seizure of power in October 1917, the Bolsheviks determined not only to institute the separation of church and state that had become standard in Europe but also to carry out a policy of attacking the Orthodox Church and of opposing religion in all its forms. The Decree on

4 Sebastian Prüfer, *Sozialismus statt Religion. Dei deutsche Sozialdemokratie vor der religiösen Frage 1863–1890* (Göttingen: Vandenhoeck & Ruprecht, 2002); T. H. Weir, *Secularism and Religion in Nineteenth-Century Germany* (Cambridge: Cambridge University Press, 2014).
5 V. I. Lenin, "The Attitude of the Workers' Party to Religion" (1909), www.marxists.org/archive/lenin/works/1909/may/13.htm.

Separation of Church and State, issued on 20 January 1918, proclaimed freedom of conscience and the right to profess any religion or none. It nationalized the property of the church, deprived religious bodies of recognition as legal entities, forbade religious education in schools and made the registration of births, marriages and deaths a civil matter. It also ordered the removal of religious symbols and rituals from public places, although religious processions and services in the open air were tolerated until the late 1920s.[6] Although the decree forbade persecution of believers, the Soviet constitution of 1918 deprived priests of voting rights, restricted their entitlement to rations and housing, and required them to pay higher taxes. The response of the new patriarch, Tikhon, was swift: In January 1918 he pronounced an anathema on the Bolsheviks, warning that they would "burn in hell in the life hereafter and be cursed for generations." During the civil war from 1918 to 1921, he urged the faithful to resist the godless regime by spiritual means alone, but after the emergence of White-controlled territories in autumn 1918, many senior clergy openly sided with the Whites, and some priests even fought in the armies of General Anton Denikin and Admiral Aleksandr Kolchak. Twenty-eight bishops and possibly up to several thousand clergy were killed by the Cheka and Red Army soldiers in the course of this often-barbaric conflict.[7] The church had not been unaffected by the revolution. The authority of senior clergy was significantly weakened as a result of the collapse of the bureaucratic structure through which the tsarist state controlled the church, and the Church Council of 1917–18 authorized greater lay involvement in ecclesiastical affairs. At parish level, lay activists formed "groups of twenty," which were responsible for various aspects of parish life, including the maintenance of property that the new government had nationalized.[8] In addition, there was a resurgence of semi-monastic brotherhoods that took on works of charity and religious instruction, and later these would serve as a nucleus of resistance to the regime's anti-religious policies and be crushed during Stalin's "revolution from above" in 1928–32.

6 W. B. Husband, *"Godless Communists": Atheism and Society in Soviet Russia, 1917–1932* (DeKalb: Northern Illinois University Press, 2000), ch. 2.
7 Vladimir Vorob'ev (ed.), *Sledstvennoe delo Patriarkha Tikhona* (Moscow: Pamiatniki istoricheskoi mysli, 2000), 15. The Cheka was the Bolshevik political police, created in December 1917.
8 Glennys Young, *Power and the Sacred in Revolutionary Russia: Religious Activists in the Village* (University Park: Pennsylvania State University Press, 1995).

During the civil war the battle against religion came low on the list of Bolshevik priorities. Efforts to enforce the Decree on Separation of Church and State sometimes provoked popular opposition, as when icons were removed from schools or people were forced to register births with the local soviets, but even pious believers supported the expropriation of church lands, although rural priests were usually given a plot of land to support their families. There was no attempt to close churches at this stage, although monasteries, a few of which had extensive land holdings, did come under attack: By 1921, 673 of 1,253 monasteries and convents had passed into state ownership.[9] The 1918 program of the Bolshevik Party called for "systematic antireligious propaganda to free the masses from their prejudices but without irritating the feelings of others." Yet relatively little was done in this regard. Significantly, there was no attempt at anti-religious propaganda in the Red Army. The one curious and largely counterproductive exception to this was the campaign to expose fake relics by opening up the tombs of saints.[10]

Following victory in the civil war, the Bolsheviks determined to crush the one institution from the old regime that still stood as a challenge to its attempts to achieve a monopoly of power. In February 1922, against the background of a massive famine in the Volga region, the Politburo ordered the church to give up ecclesiastical treasures to aid famine victims. In the previous year Patriarch Tikhon had called on clergy to donate valuables to the starving but had exempted consecrated vessels. In March in Shuia, a textile town to the northeast of Moscow, a bloody clash erupted when believers tried to stop police and soldiers seizing such items. Lenin ordered that the Shuia "insurrectionists" be put on trial, and proposed that the trial culminate in the "shooting of a very large number of the most influential and dangerous of Black Hundreds." A trial duly took place, resulting in the execution of eight priests, two laymen and a laywoman, and the imprisonment of twenty-five others. In Petrograd, where popular agitation took on an anti-Semitic coloration, Metropolitan Veniamin and three others were tried and executed.[11]

9 M. V. Shkarovskii, "Monastyri severo-zapada Rossii v 1920–1930-e gody," in *Tserkov' v istorii Rossii*, vol. I (Moscow: Institut rossiiskoi istorii RAN, 1997), 18.

10 S. A. Smith, "Bones of Contention: Bolsheviks and the Exposure of Saints' Relics, 1918–1930," *Past & Present*. 204 (Aug. 2009), 155–94.

11 N. A. Krivova, "The Events in Shuia: A Turning Point in the Assault on the Church," *Russian Studies in History* 46, 2 (2007), 8–38.

This was an extremely painful time for the Orthodox Church, which up to the revolution had embraced around 70 percent of the population. The identification of the church with the White cause had estranged not insignificant numbers of the lower clergy and laity who looked on the revolution with hope, and the church valuables crisis helped in 1922 to precipitate a left-wing movement known as the "Living Church." This campaigned for liturgical reform (services in modern Russian and use of the new calendar), structural reform (the election of senior clergy and married clergy to be allowed to become bishops) and affirmed the compatibility of Christianity and socialism, hailing Lenin as a "great fighter for truth." The Soviet political police sought to use the Living Church to undermine the official hierarchy, but when Tikhon showed willingness to recognize the Soviet regime in 1923, the Bolsheviks began to withdraw support from the movement. By the late 1920s, the Living Church was routed. This did little to ease the plight of the church, however, since schisms had emerged on the right wing following the death of Tikhon in April 1925. Conservatives, outraged when Metropolitan Sergii swore fealty to the Soviet regime in May 1927, formed congregations deep in the underground that sought to keep contact with the godless regime to a minimum. Some survived right through the Soviet era.

Until the mid 1920s official policy toward Protestant denominations and indigenous faith communities, such as the Old Believers (who had separated from the Orthodox Church in the mid seventeenth century), was more conciliatory, since these groups had suffered under the old regime and their commitment to hard work, sobriety, strict moral standards and communal forms of organization was seen as facilitating work discipline and the growth of agricultural communes. Even in the early 1920s, however, the political police kept a strict eye on what they called "sects," and there were conflicts over the refusal of certain groups to do military service. From April 1926 official policy toward them hardened. This was the moment when policy toward Islam also toughened. The 1922–23 constitutions of the soviet republics in Central Asia and the Caucasus had allowed considerable scope for the practice of Islam, including *shariʿah* law, but the number of Islamic schools steadily declined, so that by 1926 only 969 existed in the 13,650 districts in the Volga–Urals region where a mosque existed.[12] From mid 1926 a more frontal assault on Islamic institutions commenced, with mullahs depicted as

12 Mustafa Tuna, *Imperial Russia's Muslims: Islam, Empire, and European Modernity, 1788–1914* (Cambridge: Cambridge University Press, 2015), 237.

obscurantist and oppressive. In respect of Judaism, too, policy was tightened. Initially, the Bolsheviks had acted cautiously, fearing to fan popular anti-Semitism. In Petrograd the number of synagogues and prayer-houses actually increased to seventeen after October. However, the Jewish sections of the party vehemently opposed Yiddish secular culture to Hebrew religious culture, and from the mid 1920s the political police began to close down synagogues and religious schools and to hound rabbis. In sum, as the policy toward the Orthodox Church eased briefly in the mid 1920s, that toward other faiths hardened.

Behind the twists and turns of official policy lay fundamental disagreements about how the state should seek to extirpate religious belief. There was general agreement that religion instilled values at odds with the activism and collectivism required of the socialist citizen, encouraging fatalism and humility, fostering acquiescence in the status quo, promoting an individualistic concern with personal salvation and orienting believers toward the supernatural rather than the secular world. Above all, religion was seen as a weapon used by the ruling classes to keep the masses in thrall. So far as crafting an anti-religious policy was concerned, there was little consensus. Some Bolsheviks argued, in the spirit of Marx, that religion would wither away of its own accord as the social conditions that underpinned it were transformed. Others argued that the state should use its panoply of ideological, pedagogical, legal and repressive powers vigorously to eliminate religion. Others argued that such "administrative methods" were unacceptable and that the struggle against religion was a matter of long-term education. Finally, some argued that the positive promotion of scientific knowledge and rationality should predominate. Such differences of opinion – which became caught up in the intra-party struggle between Stalin and the "Right Opposition" of Nikolai Bukharin and Aleksei Rykov – were compounded by the fact that there was no single organization responsible for anti-religious policy and propaganda. The Anti-Religious Commission of the Central Committee (active from 1922), the political police, the Permanent Cult Commission of the Central Executive Committee of the Soviets (set up in 1929), together with its inspectors of religious affairs in local soviets, the Commissariat of Justice, the Commissariat of Enlightenment, the Komsomol and the League of Godless all competed in this area. Initially, the League of Godless, founded in 1925 as a nonofficial body, was distinguished by its advocacy of propaganda and education – against the so-called priest-eaters of the Komsomol, who favored a confrontational approach to religion and who reveled in antics such as setting pigs loose in church and staging "anti-festivals" at Easter and Christmas. The league itself, however, was split between a majority of *Kulturträger* and a minority that favored a "class struggle" approach to religion. Despite occupying a "prominent and even noisy position within the Bolshevik propaganda apparatus," the League of Godless was in almost constant crisis, its obsession with recruitment, training cadres and selling magazines leaving little time to engage seriously with the existential concerns of believers. It clung on into the 1930s but was wound down with the outbreak of war.[13]

From 1928 the class-struggle approach to religion came to predominate, as Stalin launched what has been called a "cultural revolution" (in recognition of its similarity to events in the People's Republic of China from 1966 to 1976). This saw a vociferous campaign launched to push a "proletarian" line in all branches of cultural production. On 8 April 1929 a Law on Religious Associations was enacted, which banned public worship, closed most places of worship, removed church bells, authorized the mass arrest of clergy and imposed burdensome taxes and insurance fees on functioning congregations. The leitmotif of official discourse was that the "class enemy is carrying out its work under the cover of religion."[14] The campaign was tempered slightly in the early 1930s but was resumed with a vengeance with the great terror of 1937–38. Order 00447 of July 1937 set target numbers for the imprisonment or execution of key social groups, including clergy and religious activists and, according to church sources, 137,000 clergy and laity were repressed, of whom 85,000 were shot.[15]

World War II marked a watershed in the development of Soviet society. The Nazi invasion triggered a wave of patriotism in Orthodox clergy and laity alike. German occupying forces in Ukraine and the western borderlands, however, encouraged the revival of church life, at least initially, as a way of undermining the Soviet regime. In summer 1941 there were only a few hundred churches operating in Ukraine, Belorussia and the occupied parts of the RSFSR; by 1944 there were about 10,000.[16] Following the Battle of

13 D. Peris, *Storming the Heavens: The Soviet League of the Militant Godless* (Ithaca: Cornell University Press, 1998), 226.
14 A. Luukkanen, *The Religious Policy of the Stalinist State* (Tampere: Tammer-Paino Oy, 1997), 66.
15 V. Kudriavtzev and A. Trusov, *Politicheskaia iustitsiia v SSSR* (Moscow: Nauka, 2000), 111.
16 A. L. Beglov, "Ob"edineniia pravoslavnykh veruiushchikh v SSSR v 1920–1930-e gody. Prichiny vozniknoveniia, tipologiia, i napravleniia razvitiia," *Rossiiskaia istoriia* 3 (2012), 99. For a more skeptical view of religious revival in Ukraine, see Karel S. Berkhoff, "Was There a Religious Revival in Soviet Ukraine Under the Nazi Regime?," *Slavonic and East European Review* 78, 3 (2000), 536–67.

Kursk in July 1943, Stalin summoned Metropolitan Sergii to announce that he was to be made patriarch. This was a calculated strategy to tap into the wellspring of Russian national identity – the idea that to be Russian was to be Orthodox – but it was also motivated by a desire to counter the threat from the Uniates (i.e. Orthodox Christians who recognized the authority of Rome, in the areas under German occupation) and to undermine the influence of religion on local nationalisms and partisan resistance to the Red Army.[17] This proved to be the start of a period of uneasy cooperation between the Orthodox Church and the Soviet state that would last, with some hiccups, until 1958. In these years, the number of clergy and parishes grew, although usually only after persistent petitioning by the laity; a few monasteries and theological schools reopened; and the church was allowed to raise income and to rent and build property. There were even reports that local soviets made use of priests to promote economic and political campaigns, such as timely delivery of grain, subscription to state loans and participation in soviet elections. The church, however, was not allowed to resume activities in the spheres of education or social welfare. From 1947, hardliners in the party regularly expressed disquiet at the extent to which the church (and certain Protestant confessions) had regained the ground they had lost during the 1920s and 1930s.[18] Church attendance especially on feast days had increased, more children were being baptized (at least one-fifth of infants in the RSFSR in the 1950s), more people were marrying in church and pilgrimages to sacred shrines were popular.[19]

With the death of Stalin in 1953 and the accession to power of Nikita Khrushchev, many of Stalin's policies were reversed, but Khrushchev's desire to revitalize the drive to create a communist society entailed a reinvigoration of efforts to create the world's first atheist society. On 7 July 1954, against a background of agricultural crisis and religious revival in the countryside, the Central Committee of the Communist Party of the Soviet Union (CPSU) issued a decree which threatened to revive the *Sturm und Drang* policies of the prewar era: "Churchmen and sectarians are seeking different methods to poison the consciousness of the people with the drug of religion." Almost immediately, however, it was brought to a halt, proving divisive in a society

17 S. M. Miner, *Stalin's Holy War: Religion, Nationalism, and Alliance Politics, 1941–1945* (Chapel Hill: University of North Carolina Press, 2003).
18 E. Zubkova, *Russia After the War: Hopes, Illusions and Disappointments, 1945–1957*, trans. and ed. H. Ragsdale (Armonk, NY: M. E. Sharpe, 1998), 69–70.
19 M. V. Shkarovskii, *Russkaia pravoslavnaia tserkov' pri Staline i Khrushcheve* (Moscow: Krutitkoe Patriarshee Podvor'e, 1999), 357.

still coming to terms with the trauma of World War II and the legacy of Stalinism.[20] For the next few years, a tussle went on behind the scenes between hardliners, led by M. A. Suslov, Second Secretary of the CPSU, and the Council for the Affairs of the Russian Orthodox Church, the body charged with overseeing the hierarchy, handling complaints and informing party leaders of developments on the ground.[21] In 1958 the hardliners won out, and a campaign against religion was launched that would last until 1965. Although there was no mass terror, the campaign saw more than 6,000 churches and over 1,000 non-Orthodox places of worship shut down, monastic communities disbanded, restrictions placed on parents' right to teach their children religion, and a ban enforced on the attendance of children at church services (directed against Baptists in 1961 and extended to Orthodox in 1963).[22]

Since the 1930s little finance or energy had been put into anti-religious propaganda, but in 1954 the Znanie (Knowledge) Society – the organization tasked with popular enlightenment – called for the creation of a special journal to propagate atheism. In the same year, "scientific atheism" – tacitly distinguished from the "militant atheism" of the 1920s – was formally consecrated as a dimension of Marxism-Leninism, construed as "integral yet relatively independent."[23] In 1959, institutions of higher education were required to teach a course on "The Foundations of Scientific Atheism," although it became mandatory for students only in 1964; and in secondary schools evolution and the origins of life began to be taught intensively. Yurii Gagarin's failure to discover God on his orbit of the earth in 1961 was milked to the full in anti-religious propaganda. With the end of Khrushchev's anti-religious campaign in 1964, however, the new Council on Religious Affairs immediately softened its propaganda against the Orthodox Church, reserving its opprobrium for so-called sectarians, particularly unregistered religious groups such as Baptists, Jehovah's Witnesses and Seventh-Day Adventists. Anti-religious propaganda continued, but a climate steadily developed in which church architecture and religious art were more likely to be seen as

20 M. V. Shkarovskii, *Russkaia pravoslavnaia tserkov' v XX veke* (Moscow: Veche, 2010), 350–53; J. D. Grossman, "Khrushchev's Anti-Religious Policy and the Campaign of 1954," *Soviet Studies* 24, 3 (1973), 374–86.
21 T. A. Chumachenko, *Church and State in Soviet Russia: Russian Orthodoxy from World War II to the Khrushchev Years*, ed. and trans. E. E. Roslof (Armonk, NY: M. E. Sharpe, 2002), 3.
22 John Anderson, *Religion, State and Politics in the Soviet Union and the Successor States* (Cambridge: Cambridge University Press, 1994), chs. 2 and 3.
23 J. Thrower, *Marxist-Leninist "Scientific Atheism" and the Study of Religion in the USSR* (Berlin: Mouton, 1983), 149.

expressions of the spirituality innate to the Russian people than as symbols of obscurantism and reaction.[24]

The price the church paid for greater toleration was carefully to toe the party line in politics, playing a central role, for example, in the officially sponsored peace movement. The deal was mutually advantageous. On 23 June 1975 the 1929 Law on Religious Organizations was revised, and in 1982 the Council on Religious Affairs further liberalized the rights enjoyed by the church (allowing parish councils, for example, to meet without prior authorization). Memoirs suggest that in this period many of the laity came to believe that there was no contradiction between being a believer and being a good Soviet citizen.[25] Yet the 1970s also witnessed a reaction among some clerics against what was perceived as the stifling conformism of the hierarchy – a conformism dictated, it should be said, by knowledge that there were KGB informers in its ranks. Charismatic priests, such as Dmitrii Dudko, Aleksandr Ogorodnikov and Aleksandr Men, won followings for their defense of human rights and were drawn into the burgeoning dissident movement, to the embarrassment of Patriarch Pimen (1970–90). By the 1980s, however, relations between church and state were more cordial than they had ever been. In preparation for the millennium of the arrival of Christianity in Russia, some churches were handed back, notably the Danilov monastery in Moscow in 1983. In April 1988, months prior to the millennium celebrations, Mikhail Gorbachev, general secretary of the CPSU, met the patriarch. In June a Church Council was held for the first time since 1917–18. Between 1985 and 1989 the number of registered Orthodox congregations in the USSR rose from 6,806 to 10,110 and the number of Muslim congregations from 392 to 773.[26] In 1990, just before the collapse of the Soviet Union, a decree on freedom of conscience finally restored the conditions that had appertained in 1917.

The Eastern Bloc

In the late 1940s, the newly established socialist states of Central, Eastern and Southeastern Europe were required by the Soviet Union to adopt the

---

24 Catriona Kelly, "From 'Counter-Revolutionary Monuments' to 'National Heritage': The Preservation of Leningrad Churches, 1964–1982," *Cahiers du monde russe* 54, 1–2 (2013), 1–34.

25 Catriona Kelly, *Socialist Churches: Radical Secularization and the Preservation of the Past in Petrograd and Leningrad, 1918–1988* (DeKalb: Northern Illinois University Press, 2016), 236–37, 253–54.

26 See www.pravoslavie.ru/60168.html.

anti-religious policies it had pioneered. Church and state were separated in countries where this had not already happened (although doubtfully in the case of Czechoslovakia); ecclesiastical property was nationalized; religious instruction in schools was banned and the public activities of religious institutions were severely curbed. Although some priests and laity viewed the prospect of socialism positively, senior clerics were almost universally hostile to the communist takeovers. This precipitated the arrest and imprisonment of the most vocal ecclesiastical critics, notably in Hungary where the trial of Cardinal József Mindszenty in February 1949 became a *cause célèbre* of religious persecution. In its wake the Vatican advised Catholic bishops to pursue a nonconfrontational course but not to collaborate actively with the communist authorities. As they consolidated their power, the new states tended to pursue a policy of divide and rule, favoring certain confessions while treating others harshly. Over time, however, a *modus vivendi* was reached between church and state, some clerics accepting that a degree of cooperation with the state was inevitable if resources were to be accessed, and others endorsing the regimes more positively for nationalist, social justice or opportunistic reasons.

During the Cold War the churches were pressed into service, particularly in support of the Soviet-backed peace movement. The Christian Peace Conference, founded in 1958 by the Czech pastor Josef Hromádka, is said to have received Soviet funding. And the involvement of the Russian and Romanian Orthodox Churches in the World Council of Churches from 1961 may have helped ensure that that body never united to condemn religious persecution behind the Iron Curtain.[27] During the 1960s, however, the specifically religious dimension of the Cold War eased as the World Council of Churches, and then the Roman Catholic Church following the Second Vatican Council (1962–65), took an increasingly progressive stance on peace and justice issues. By the 1960s overt conflict between state and religious organizations had diminished in most countries, in part a reflection of the fact that the Eastern bloc governments were increasingly pursuing courses independent of Moscow. One sign of the general easing of church–state tension was Christian–Marxist dialogue, which had its heyday between 1966 and 1971. Finally, we should note – although the effect is hard to measure – that rapid modernization in many socialist countries from the late 1950s

---

27 Lucian Leuştean, *Orthodoxy and Cold War: Religion and Political Power in Romania, 1947–1965* (London: Palgrave, 2009), 8.

served to erode the high levels of religiosity that had been evident at the end of World War II.

These commonalities aside, what is striking is the diversity that characterized the religious fields of the socialist bloc countries, a variety that came to be reflected in the religious policies practiced by the different governments. The diversity of national religious landscapes was manifest, first, in the historic divide between Western Christian confessions and Eastern Orthodox Churches, the latter being institutionally autocephalous, essentially organized along ethnonational lines. Second, there were countries that were largely monoconfessional, notably the overwhelmingly Roman Catholic countries of Poland, Croatia and Lithuania, and on the Orthodox side, Bulgaria and Romania. In these countries, religion served to underpin national identity, as had become steadily apparent in the late Soviet Union. Third, and more commonly, there were countries that were religiously mixed where one confession might have a plurality of adherents yet exist alongside other confessions with a significant membership. In Hungary, for example, Roman Catholics were the largest denomination but existed alongside a sizeable Reformed confession and a small Lutheran minority. In Albania Sunni Islam (but with a Bektashi minority) was dominant, but there was an Orthodox minority and a small but influential Catholic minority in the north.[28]

Following the death of Stalin in 1953, religious policies began to diversify in ways that reflected the variegation of the religious fields. In Poland the authorities initially sought to contain the influence of the Catholic Church in public life, but after 1956 restrictions on religious education, the press, seminaries and monasteries were lifted, and in Lublin the only Catholic university in the Eastern bloc functioned. In East Germany, the only country in the socialist bloc where Protestantism was dominant, state policy toward the Evangelical Church went from being repressive in the first couple of decades to being one of the most liberal after 1969, when the Evangelical Church broke ties with its counterpart in West Germany and declared "critical solidarity" with the regime. In return, the government made

28 Sabrina P. Ramet, *Nihil Obstat: Religion, Politics, and Social Change in East-Central Europe and Russia* (Durham, NC: Duke University Press, 1998); P. Walters, "The Revolutions in Eastern Europe and the Beginning of the Post-Communist Era," in H. McLeod (ed.), *The Cambridge History of Christianity*, vol. IX, *World Christianities, c. 1914–c. 2000* (Cambridge: Cambridge University Press, 2006), 348–65; and Lucian Leuştean (ed.), *Eastern Christianity and the Cold War, 1945–1991* (London: Routledge, 2010).

concessions with regard to church property, tempered atheist propaganda and, by the mid 1970s, allowed the Lutheran churches to appoint bishops without state interference and made provision for an alternative to military conscription.[29] In Yugoslavia, too, the authorities pursued a relatively liberal course, while remaining vigilant about the association of different confessions with different ethnic groups (the Serbian Orthodox Church with Serbia, the Catholic Church with Croatia and Slovenia, and Islam with Bosnia). By the 1960s religious orders and welfare organizations operated freely, large religious gatherings were permitted, and the state did not interfere in seminaries and church life.

In Romania the Eastern Rite Uniate Church, in communion with Rome, was forcibly incorporated in 1948 into the Romanian Orthodox Church, which became almost completely coopted by the government. It suited the Romanian Communist Party – bereft of nationalist credentials – to court the church while clamping down on other confessions, such as the now illegal Uniates. Orthodox clergy were paid a salary by the state (something that did not happen in the Soviet Union or Bulgaria), churches were restored and religious publications were fairly free to publish. Following the "divorce" from Moscow in 1964, Nicolae Ceaușescu set about creating an autarkic, militaristic form of "national Stalinism" but did not balk at appropriating religious symbols to bolster his legitimacy.[30] He oversaw the restoration of many churches, tolerated Orthodox baptisms, marriages and funerals, and even publicized his father's burial with Orthodox rites in 1972. From this time on, however, his regime became steadily more repressive, churches were closed and atheist propaganda was stepped up. In a religiously diverse country such as Czechoslovakia, where peasant Slovakia was largely Catholic and the Czech lands Catholic, Hussite, Evangelical and Uniate, the government was inclined to a policy of divide and rule. With the brief exception of the Prague Spring in 1968, the Czechoslovak authorities clamped down on all religion, but especially on the Catholic Church, whose clergy were licensed by the state and were paid official salaries and whose bishops were subject to government approval. Similar to China (see below) an attempt was made to split the church by creating a pro-regime church.

29 Paul Betts, *Within Walls: Private Life in the German Democratic Republic* (Oxford: Oxford University Press, 2010), 77–78.
30 V. Tismaneanu, *Stalinism for All Seasons: A Political History of Romanian Communism* (Berkeley: University of California Press, 2003).

By the early 1980s, eight of the thirteen Catholic dioceses had no bishop, and more than one-third of Catholic parishes had no priest.[31]

All the regimes of the socialist bloc espoused scientific atheism, yet the energy invested in this varied from state to state. In 1954 Walter Ulbricht declared that East Germany would "carry on its campaign against super-stition, mysticism, idealism and all other unscientific worldviews," and the launch of Sputnik in 1957 encouraged his government to step up atheist education in schools.[32] In Romania a Society for the Popularization of Science and Culture was established in 1949 to "propagate among the labour-ing masses political and scientific knowledge to fight obscurantism, super-stition and mysticism and all other influences of bourgeois ideologies," but the resources devoted to this were paltry.[33] Albania was the only state in the socialist bloc to declare itself atheist, the Hoxha regime unleashing a drive in 1967 to close every mosque, church and monastery in the country. Article 37 of the 1976 constitution proclaimed: "The state recognizes no religion and supports atheistic propaganda in order to implant a scientific materialistic world outlook in the people." The following year the penal code imposed terms of three to ten years' imprisonment for religious propaganda. Interestingly, the motivation seems largely to have been nationalistic, with the Albanian Party of Labor claiming that the country's three confessions were destroying the "national uniqueness" of Albania. In Czechoslovakia, atheist education was pursued with rigor although, unusually, the govern-ment allowed clergy into primary schools after school hours to give religious education. In December 1957, the Czechoslovak Society for the Dissemination of Political and Scientific Knowledge organized a conference to discuss the poor state of anti-religious work in the country's schools. In 1958 and 1959 mandatory courses in atheism were introduced in all institutions of higher education. In 1960 the new constitution laid down that education should be conducted "in the spirit of the scientific worldview of Marxism-Leninism."[34]

In many parts of the socialist bloc, from the 1960s regimes still formally loyal to Moscow began to pursue a more nationalistic course. Communist states, like all twentieth-century polities, based themselves on the territorial

31 Steve Bruce, *Choice and Religion: A Critique of Rational Choice Theory* (Oxford: Oxford University Press, 1999), 102.
32 Betts, *Within Walls*, 59, 66.
33 L. N. Leuştean, "Constructing Communism in the Romanian People's Republic: Orthodoxy and State, 1948–1949," *Europe-Asia Studies* 59, 2 (2007), 303–29.
34 Ramet, *Nihil Obstat*, 125, 129, 130.

and social space of the nation-state, and one of the most effective ways in which these sometimes deeply unpopular regimes could build their legitimacy was to focus the identities of their citizens around the nation (often defined in ethnic rather than civic terms) and to present the state as the institutional repository of the nation. This was especially true in the Orthodox countries, where the autocephalous churches possessed symbolic capital that communist states sought to appropriate. In Bulgaria Liudmila Zhivkova, daughter of Todor Zhikov, the First Secretary of the Bulgarian party from 1954 to 1989, created a permanent exhibition of Bulgarian medieval religious icons in the crypt of Aleksandar Nevski Cathedral in Sofia, and Saints Cyril and Methodius, who had brought Christianity to the Bulgarian people, were promoted to the status of icons of Bulgarian nationhood.[35] Even regimes that were hypersensitive to the danger of playing the nationalist card, such as East Germany, could by the 1960s celebrate Martin Luther as a national hero rather than as the "traitor against the peasants" that he had been portrayed as in the 1950s.

By the 1980s most churches had long come to an uneasy accommodation with communist regimes, although those confessions singled out for persecution persisted in the underground. This meant that generally the churches were not in the forefront of the civic movements that helped to bring about the demise of communism, although there, too, the picture was mixed. Poland was the great exception. In 1978 mounting intellectual and working-class opposition to the regime was given impetus by the election of Archbishop Karol Wojtyła of Kraków to the papal throne. His return as Pope John Paul II the following year firmed up anti-communist sentiment and catalyzed the events that would lead ten years later to the fall of the regime. His defense of human rights also helped to galvanize Catholic opposition in Czechoslovakia, albeit not on the same scale, with underground groups crystallizing into an opposition movement in the 1980s. In Romania, too, the events that led to the toppling of Ceaușescu were sparked by the arrest of a Calvinist pastor, Laszlo Tokes. More typical, however, was the situation in East Germany, where the Protestant Church, which had long accommodated to the regime out of a desire for self-preservation, served as an arena in which nonconformists, some of whom went on to play an active part in the movement for democratic reform, could find refuge.[36] In the predominantly Orthodox

35 I. N. Atanasova, "Ljudmila Zhivkova and the Paradox of Ideology and Identity in Communist Bulgaria," *East European Politics and Societies* 18, 2 (2004), 291.
36 Corey Ross, *The East German Dictatorship* (London: Arnold, 2002), 118.

countries, by contrast, the national churches played little if any role in bringing about the end of communism, ultimately because of the historical closeness of church and state.

The People's Republic of China

The religious field in China was very different from that in the Soviet Union and the Eastern bloc. When the Chinese Communist Party (CCP) came to power in 1949 it did not face opposition from mighty religious organizations such as the Orthodox and Catholic Churches. Daoism and Buddhism had enjoyed imperial patronage at various times across the centuries, but they had never received endorsement as religions of state. Confucianism, which was more the ideology of statecraft than a religion, had been propagated in the mid Ming and early Qing dynasties via the local gentry, especially through the promotion of ancestor worship, but the overthrow of the Qing dynasty in 1911 deprived it of its symbolic center, and it went into uncertain decline. The religion of the overwhelming majority of the Han population was neither Buddhist, Daoist nor Confucian, but drew selectively on all three traditions and combined these with elements of local ritual and belief. Popular religion was *par excellence* local, rooted in networks of cults, festivals and ancestor worship based on the household, territorial communities, guilds and other associations. Diffuse in character, it lacked many of the features associated with the modern conception of religion, such as institutionalized structures, trained personnel and a coherent belief system. For that reason, popular religion was not recognized as a religion at all by either the Nationalists or the CCP, but dismissed as "feudal superstition."

To a surprising extent, the religious policy of the CCP government was a continuation of that pioneered by the Nationalists. The 1912 constitution of the new republic separated state and religion and proclaimed freedom of religion. However, the latter applied only to those religions deemed to meet the criteria of a modern religion, namely, the five "world" religions of Buddhism, Daoism, Islam, Catholicism and Protestantism. These had clergy, bodies of doctrine, places of worship and training centers, and thus accorded with an essentially Western notion of what religion was. Nevertheless, the Nationalist government required Buddhism and Daoism to meet these criteria more closely by creating national bureaucratic structures and formalizing their procedures. The communist government largely operated within this framework, establishing national "patriotic" associations to represent each of the five recognized religions. These associations – such as the Islamic Association or the Three-Self Movement, which represented Protestants – were funded by government, and their task was to communicate state policies to their members, to ensure that local congregations registered with the authorities, to report on their activities and to mobilize their members in campaigns such as those to eliminate corruption, increase production and support the war effort in Korea.

Unlike religious policy in the Eastern bloc, the religious policy of the CCP was not closely modeled on that of the Soviet Union. The Jiangxi Soviet republic (1931–34) had followed the Soviet constitution of 1918 by depriving religious personnel of political rights. Yet in 1937, with the creation of the Second United Front with the Nationalists to fight the Japanese, the CCP shifted from an anti-religious policy to a positive religious policy suited to the needs of the united front and the maintenance of good relations with ethnic minorities. Following the CCP victory in 1949, Zhou Enlai made it clear that the new government did not intend slavishly to follow Soviet policy in the religious sphere. On 25 June 1950, in a report to the party cell of the Chinese People's Political Consultative Conference, he explained that there were two facets of religion in China that made it distinctive: One was its connection to ethnic minorities – through Islam and Mongolian and Tibetan Buddhism; the other was its connection to imperialism – through Christianity – both facets requiring that religion be handled with great care. Where a minority of hardened reactionaries sought to exploit religion for political ends, this should be treated as a political and not a religious offense. However, Zhou commented that, while Lenin's statement of 1909 that religion was an instrument of bourgeois reaction was appropriate for a period of revolution, it was not a suitable slogan for a government in power.[37] Such an opinion, mildly distancing him from Lenin, was highly unusual for a communist leader at this time. The previous month he had elaborated on this in a speech to Christian leaders: "Whoever tries to abolish religion artificially will find it impossible. The Soviet Union is a socialist country but it still has religion. We emphatically do not intend to do this. If we imagine that things we do not like will simply cease to exist, then that is not in accordance with objective reality."[38]

---

37 *Zhou Enlai nianpu, 1949–1976* [A Chronological Record of Zhou Enlai, 1949–1976], vol. I (Beijing: Zhongyang wenxian chubanshe, 1997), 49–50.
38 *Zhou Enlai tongyi zhanxian wenxuan* [Selected Works of Zhou Enlai on the United Front] (Beijing: Renmin chubanshe, 1984), 185.

In 1953 Li Weihan, head of the United Front Work Department of the Central Committee, outlined what was to become the crucial formula summarizing the CCP perspective on religion, a formula that would come to be much quoted in the post-Mao era: Religion in China, he said, has "five characteristics" – namely, longevity, a mass character, a link with ethnic minorities, international connections and innate complexity.[39] Party ideologists argued that religion would die away as the country advanced toward socialism, as economic wellbeing increased and as the Chinese people became more educated and more scientific in their understanding of the natural and social worlds. The elimination of religion would thus be a long-term process, so "any idea about taking coercive action is useless and positively harmful."[40] One consequence was that far fewer resources were put into atheist propaganda than in the Soviet Union or Czechoslovakia: There was, for example, no journal propagating atheism until the turn of the twenty-first century. For CCP members, of course, "scientific atheism" was a compulsory element in their political education.[41]

In theory, this noncoercive religious policy was framed by the requirements of the united front and the need for good relations with ethnic minorities. This was manifest, for example, in the fact that religious leaders were appointed to government bodies such as the People's Congress and the People's Consultative Conference at local, provincial and national levels (something that would have been unthinkable in the Soviet Union).[42] Yet if repression of religion was decried, its strict regulation was the order of the day. In addition to the aforementioned "patriotic" organizations that regulated the affairs of the five recognized religions, the Religious Affairs Bureau, under the State Council from 1954, took political direction from the United Front Work Department, and its regional offices monitored what was going on in the localities. Moreover, the freedom to practice religion was absolutely conditional on broad conformity with government policy. As Venerable Juzan, who founded the New Buddhist Movement in the mid 1940s to campaign against the corruption of the monastic estate, explained: "New Democracy takes as its premises the struggle against imperialism,

39 Chen Jinlong, *Zhongguo gongchandang yu Zhongguo de zongjiao wenti* [The Chinese Communist Party and Chinese Religious Issues] (Guangzhou: Guangdong renmin chubanshe, 2006), 128.
40 *Renmin ribao*, 23 Sep. 1950, 4.
41 Christopher Marsh, *Religion and the State in Russia and China* (New York: Continuum, 2011), 173.
42 Vincent Goossaert and David Palmer, *The Religious Question in Modern China* (Chicago: University of Chicago Press, 2011), 153.

feudalism, and bureaucratic capitalism, the overthrow of the reactionary power of the Nationalists and the purge of open and hidden counter-revolutionary forces. Buddhists who do not accept these premises are either reactionaries or backward elements. Reactionaries have no political rights."[43] Leaders of the five recognized religions who refused to cooperate with the authorities came in for outright repression. Catholic clergy, for example, put up considerable resistance to the demand that they renounce obedience to the Vatican, and in 1951 two archbishops, two bishops and fifteen priests were killed or died in prison.[44] Apolitical Evangelicals, such as Ni Tuosheng, were alienated by the Three-Self Movement, which was led by progressive Protestants. In 1956, Ni was condemned as the head of a "counterrevolutionary clique" and sentenced to fifteen years in prison. In particular, no quarter was shown toward the homegrown redemptive sects (*huidaomen*), which were voluntary congregations that had flourished in the unstable socioeconomic conditions that had appertained since the 1920s. They preached a message of universal salvation in the expectation of the coming of the Maitreya Buddha. Their apocalyptic orientation, combined with the fact that some had enjoyed an unduly cosy relationship with the Japanese occupation regime, put them beyond the pale so far as the new communist government was concerned, and they were vigorously persecuted.[45]

In the course of land reform (1947–51), land belonging to temples and monasteries was confiscated and landlords and those elite members who were informal leaders of temple associations were attacked. There were a few very wealthy Buddhist and Daoist temples, but most monasteries had relatively little land, and such land as they did have was worked by the monks and nuns. The exception was Tibet, where monasteries owned more than a third of the country's land, property and livestock.[46] Religious personnel who were willing and able to work were given a share of land, but monks and nuns came under pressure to abandon their vocations, and it is reckoned that in the course of the 1950s the number of Buddhist monks fell from around

43 Holmes Welch, *Buddhism Under Mao* (Cambridge, MA: Harvard University Press, 1972), 6.
44 David Aikman, *Jesus in Beijing: How Christianity Is Transforming and Changing the Global Balance of Power* (Washington DC: Regnery, 2006), 208.
45 S. A. Smith, "Redemptive Societies and the Communist State, 1949 to the 1980s," in Jeremy Brown and Matthew D. Johnson (eds.), *Maoism at the Grassroots: Everyday Life in China's Era of High Socialism* (Cambridge, MA: Harvard University Press, 2015), 340–64.
46 Vincent Goossaert, *Dans les temples de la Chine. Histoire des cultes, Vie des communautés* (Paris: Albin Michel, 2000), 148; Chen Jinlong, *Zhongguo gongchandang*, 188.

500,000 to just over 100,000.[47] The CCP accelerated the policy that had been in operation since the early twentieth century of converting temples to schools, granaries and government offices. In some areas, however, the restoration of order after more than a decade of war enabled villagers to restore destroyed temples, often with the connivance of local officials. Indeed the government itself restored more than a hundred showcase temples and monasteries in the period up to 1958 as a way of demonstrating goodwill toward Buddhists outside China (again, an action unthinkable in the Soviet Union).

As in Soviet Russia, however, the temptation to use "administrative methods" to overcome religion ultimately proved irresistible, especially when the Great Leap Forward was launched in 1958. In March of that year, *Red Flag* carried an article entitled "A Major Victory for Atheism," which deprecated the waste of valuable resources on superstitious activity and claimed that the campaign to "smash gods and spirits" and obliterate super-stitious beliefs in the villages was emanating from the "basic desire of the masses ... to raise production and improve livelihood."[48] In Beijing more than 2,000 temples, mostly very small, were confiscated or demolished.[49] Clergy began to be "targets of dictatorship," and many were packed off to labor camps. Chen Jinlong cites an astonishing statistic that, by the end of 1961, only 8 percent of places of worship that had existed in 1949 were still operational; and in some areas the percentage was as low as 1 to 2 percent.[50] Despite *Red Flag*'s talk of an "all-out campaign," however, the extent to which the anti-religious campaign was actually implemented varied, being heavily dependent on the initiative of local cadres, for whom the elimination of religion was usually a low priority compared with the requirement to increase grain production.

As is well known, the Great Leap Forward led to a ghastly famine that killed millions of peasants. What is less well known is that in the aftermath of the famine there was a vast and spontaneous upsurge in religious activity of all kinds. The 1 million plus members of the work teams sent into the villages as part of the Socialist Education Movement (1963–66) were horrified to discover the scale of the revival. Money, they reported, was being "wasted" on temple reconstruction, on extravagant temple festivals and on lavish

47 Goossaert and Palmer, *Religious Question*, 160.
48 *Hongqi*, Mar. 1958, *Selections from China Mainland Magazines* 138 (1958), 5–17.
49 "Beijing: The Fate of the Old," www.chinaheritagenewsletter.org/features.php?search term=001_beijing.inc&issu e=001.
50 Chen Jinlong, *Zhongguo gongchandang*, 233.

marriage and funeral rituals. The religious revival was particularly marked in the coastal regions of the south. In 17 counties and cities of Zhanjiang in southwest Guangdong, 2,173 temples were rebuilt in 1963.[51] In Liaoning the provincial public security bureau announced in August 1963 that, according to incomplete statistics from 22 counties, 4,182 practitioners of superstition were active, among whom the most numerous were the 3,400 female and male spirit mediums. It noted with alarm that around a quarter of these had taken up this activity only recently: "Some young people, with no care for expense, become apprentices of masters."[52] What was new in official discourse in the early 1960s was the claim that the religious revival was being stirred up by landlords, rich peasants, counterrevolutionaries and "bad elements" in order to sabotage socialist construction. This echoed the emphasis in Stalinist discourse during the "revolution from above" that religion was being used by class enemies to undermine the revolution. Anti-religious rhetoric was steadily cranked up: In 1965 the magazine *New Construction* called for "a rigorous struggle against religion on all fronts, the pulling up and destruction of its poisonous roots."[53]

The resurgence of popular religion may have been an indirect cause of the assault on the "four olds" that became a defining feature of the Cultural Revolution. When Mao called for a struggle against religion, old ideas, old culture and old customs on 20 August 1966, Red Guards responded with alacrity, although the chairman's intentions were far from clear. On Mount Wutai in Shanxi twenty-four of sixty-two temples were destroyed and the rest were turned into offices.[54] On Putuo island in Zhejiang forty-eight of the huge complex of Buddhist monasteries were wrecked.[55] The Religious Affairs Bureau was dissolved, and Red Guards occupied the headquarters of the Three-Self Movement and the Patriotic Catholic Church. For the first time since 845 CE, barely a single monastery functioned in China (although away from prying eyes clandestine ritual activity continued). Nor were village temples immune. Statues, wood carvings, stone inscriptions and scrolls were smashed or effaced, and revolutionary slogans daubed on them, a symbolic assertion of red values over feudalism and capitalism. In Qufu, the ancient seat of Confucius, a statue of the sage was toppled and paraded through the town, and some 2,000 graves in the Kong family cemetery were

51 Guangdong Provincial Archive, 217–1–133.   52 *Neibu cankao*, 15 Aug. 1963.
53 *Xin Jianshe*, 10, 3 (20 Oct. 1965).   54 Chen Jinlong, *Zhongguo gongchandang*, 235.
55 Jocelyne Fresnais, *La protection du patrimoine en République populaire de Chine, 1949–1999* (Paris: Éditions du CTHS, 2001), 100.

desecrated. All public manifestations of religion disappeared completely at least until the early 1970s, when they began to resurface.

Following the death of Mao Zedong in 1976 and the beginning of the era of reform in 1978, the CCP's religious policy liberalized dramatically. In 1980 the State Council decreed that all religious property confiscated since 1949 – i.e. not just property seized during the Cultural Revolution – should be returned. In 1982 the Central Committee issued what is known as Document 19, which condemned leftist errors in religious policy that had reached their apogee in the Cultural Revolution. Religious personnel were released from prison; monasteries, churches and mosques were reopened. Official policy continues to be one of regulation, requiring congregations to register with the authorities and to abide by what the state considers acceptable religious practice. The unofficial Catholic Church – i.e. those priests and congregations who recognize the authority of the Vatican – and the redemptive sects continue to be proscribed. Indeed the activities of Falungong, a sect founded in 1992 which combines bodily cultivation practices with a Buddhist-inspired cosmological system, so alarmed the authorities when some 10,000 practitioners gathered in Beijing on 25 April 1999 that it unleashed an onslaught against "evil cults." Yet such measures have not prevented a massive revival of religion. This is evinced in a huge expansion of the five officially recognized religions – the numbers in Protestant congregations have soared, and in 2014 it was claimed that 18 percent (240 million) of the population consider themselves Buddhists.[56] But popular religion, too – now less likely to be dismissed as "feudal superstition" – has undergone a spectacular resurgence, sometimes in new or reinvented forms that express local identity. As government has withdrawn from ensuring guaranteed jobs, housing and medical care, the temple and the ancestral hall have become foci of moral order, and Buddhist and Christian congregations offer welfare services as well as social contact at a time when traditional communities are hemorrhaging young people.

Conclusion

The drive by communist regimes to extirpate religious belief and practice was clearly a failure. The major religious organizations that threatened the communist monopoly of power were never rendered impotent,

---

56 See www.mzb.com.cn/html/report/1512367452–1.htm.

though in certain times and places they were bludgeoned into submission; and the wider effort to eliminate popular forms of religiosity by disseminating science and rationality never uprooted religious faith among significant (though not necessarily majority) sections of the population. These managed to maintain their faith away from the eyes of authority, through family, kin and community networks. If, given the ambition of the anti-religious project, it must be deemed a failure, secularization nevertheless was a major feature of communist modernization. Leaving aside the current debates about the extent to which secularization is an inevitable component of modernization, it is clear that in all the societies discussed above religion came to hold a less central place in social life than it had at the time the communist regimes were established. Religion by no means disappeared, but it became a matter of individual choice rather than an expression of communal solidarity and ideological conformity. How far the anti-religious policies of communist regimes abetted this process is hard to tell. Certainly, key arenas of social life – the schoolroom, the army barracks, the factory and office, public holidays and public spaces – were notable for their resolutely secular character. Yet, allowing for the fact that the generally hostile atmosphere helped to discredit religion, especially among those who were born under communist regimes, the essentially Enlightenment view of the regimes themselves – that the ideological and material promotion of science and rationality would steadily conquer territory from religion and superstition – disabled them from understanding why religious faith persisted.

The assumption of Marx and Engels that the abolition of capitalism would lead to the disappearance of religious belief was hardly borne out by the communist experience. Nevertheless, their insight that it is insufficient simply to "call on" people to give up religious "illusion" – i.e. their recognition that religious belief is not primarily a matter of intellectual error but of social existence – was certainly vindicated, though we may argue about whether the persistence of religion was a reflection of the continuance of social oppression or of the failure of communism to offer answers to the existential questions that concern human purposes, meanings and values. Engels's emphasis on the variety of political purposes that religion can serve was certainly borne out: Religious establishments generally stood in defense of the old order, yet in all major confessions there were breakaway movements that identified with the communist revolution. Indeed, what is striking is the diversity of religious responses to communism and, even more perhaps, the diversity (and mutability) of the responses of communist regimes themselves to religion, across both space and time. In China today a still communist government continues to maintain that religious belief is incompatible in the long run with a modern socialist society, yet President Hu Jintao (2003–13) declared on a number of occasions that religion could contribute to the creation of a "harmonious society," a reflection perhaps of the fact that communist regimes learned through bitter experience that religion is far more than an instrument of bourgeois reaction.

Bibliographical Essay

Since the fall of communism there has been an outpouring of writing on the Russian Orthodox Church in the communist period, but most of it is in Russian, and most is cast within the framework of relations between church and state. The works of Dimitry Pospielovsky are still useful: *A History of Marxist-Leninist Atheism and Soviet Antireligious Policies* (New York: St Martin's Press, 1987) and *Soviet Antireligious Campaigns and Persecutions* (New York: St Martin's Press, 1988). Post-Soviet studies that seek to look at religion as it was practiced and experienced on the ground have developed apace, but mainly for the 1920s. They include William Husband, *"Godless Communists": Atheism and Society in Soviet Russia, 1917–1932* (De Kalb: Northern Illinois University Press, 2000); Glennys Young, *Power and the Sacred in Revolutionary Russia: Religious Activists in the Village* (University Park: Pennsylvania State University Press, 1997); Heather J. Coleman, *Russian Baptists and Spiritual Revolution, 1905–1929* (Bloomington: Indiana University Press, 2005); Edward E. Roslof, *Red Priests: Renovationism, Russian Orthodoxy and Revolution, 1905–1946* (Bloomington: Indiana University Press, 2002); and Daniel Peris, *Storming the Heavens: The Soviet League of the Militant Godless* (Ithaca: Cornell University Press, 1998). There is a lively collection of essays in Catherine Wanner (ed.), *State Secularism and Lived Religion in Russia and Ukraine* (Oxford: Oxford University Press, 2012). Gregory L. Freeze, the leading historian of Russian religion in the West, ranges over the centuries; for the Soviet period see, in particular, his "The Stalinist Assault on the Parish, 1929–1941," in Manfred Hildermeier (ed.), *Stalinismus vor dem Zweiten Weltkrieg: Neue Wege der Forschung* (Munich: Oldenbourg, 1998), 209–32. The postwar period is covered by T. A. Chumachenko, *Church and State in Soviet Russia: Russian Orthodoxy from World War II to the Khrushchev Years* (Armonk, NY: M. E. Sharpe, 2002), and John Anderson, *Religion, State* and Politics in the Soviet Union and the Successor States (Cambridge: Cambridge University Press, 1994).

The historiography on communism and religion in the Eastern bloc has mainly focused on state repression, on the official promotion of "scientific atheism," on the collaboration of the churches with the state, on the role of religion in fostering political resistance and on the emergence of civil society in Eastern Europe. See B. Berglund and B. Porter-Szucs (eds.), *Christianity and Modernity in Eastern Europe* (Budapest: Central European University Press, 2010); Sabrina P. Ramet, *Nihil Obstat: Religion, Politics and Social Change in East-Central Europe and Russia* (Durham, NC: Duke University Press, 1998); George Weigel, *The Final Revolution: The Resistance Church and the Collapse of Communism* (New York: Oxford University Press, 2003); B. von der Heydt, *Candles Behind the Wall: Heroes of the Peaceful Revolution That Shattered Communism* (London: Mowbray, 1993). Relatively little work has been done on the lived experience of believers, although that is now changing. See Paul Betts and S. A. Smith (eds.) *Science, Religion and Communism in Cold War Europe* (London: Palgrave Macmillan, 2016).

There has been interesting recent work on the nature of religion in modern China, represented in David A. Palmer and Vincent Goossaert, *The Religious Question in Modern China* (Chicago: University of Chicago Press, 2010), and Paul R. Katz, *Religion in China and Its Modern Fate* (Waltham, MA: Brandeis University Press, 2014) (dealing with the period up to 1949). Excellent on the republican period is Rebecca Nedostup, *Superstitious Regimes: Religion and the Politics of Chinese Modernity* (Cambridge, MA: Harvard University Press, 2010). There is very little work on religion in the Mao era, but some of the many studies of the resurgence of religion in the post-Mao era look backwards. For wide-ranging collections on religion in the reform era, see Yoshiko Ashiwa and David. L. Wank (eds.), *Making Religion, Making the State: The Politics of Religion in Modern China* (Stanford: Stanford University Press, 2009), and Mayfair Mei-Hui Yang (ed.), *Chinese Religiosities: Afflictions of Modernity and State Formation* (Berkeley: University of California Press, 2008). For local studies that touch on the Mao era, see Thomas D. DuBois, *The Sacred Village: Social Change and Religious Life in North China* (Honolulu: University of Hawaii Press, 2005); Adam Yuet Chau, *Miraculous Response: Doing Popular Religion in Contemporary China* (Stanford: Stanford University Press, 2016); Henrietta Harrison, *The Missionary's Curse and Other Tales from a Chinese Catholic Village* (Berkeley: University of California

Press, 2013). A general study of Catholics is Richard Madsen, *China's Catholics: Tragedy and Hope in an Emerging Civil Society* (Berkeley: University of California Press, 1998); and on new religious movements see David A. Palmer, *Qigong Fever: Body, Science and Utopia in China, 1949–1999* (London: Hurst & Co., 2007).

Recent comparative treatments of religion under communism are few, but see Christopher Marsh, *Religion and the State in Russia and China: Suppression, Survival, and Renewal* (New York: Continuum International, 2011); Richard Madsen, "Religion Under Communism," in S. A. Smith (ed.), *The Oxford Handbook of the History of Communism* (Oxford: Oxford University Press, 2014), 588–604; and S. A. Smith, "On Not Learning from the Soviet Union: Religious Policy in China, 1949–1965," *Modern China Studies* 22, 1 (2015), 70–97.

13

Visualizing the Socialist Public Sphere

REUBEN FOWKES

The amorphous art, design and architecture that filled the public space of socialist countries from the 1960s to the 1980s lie sandwiched between the sharply defined visual codes of the preceding and subsequent eras. On the one hand, the short-lived but highly influential style and method of Socialist Realism, which had transformed the visual landscape and shaped artistic expression under Joseph Stalin, remained an inevitable point of reference for state-funded artistic production, even where the model was deliberately rejected. Consequently, the journey from the closely controlled aesthetic order of high Socialist Realism, with its ambition to encode a precise, literal, concrete utopia, to the more open-ended and ambivalent public art of the later period is a story of the testing of ideological boundaries and loosening of political control of art. However, as this chapter shows, changes in public art were not just a function of the dissipation of political ideology, but also a response to global transformations in the spheres of technology, culture and lifestyles refracted through the specific conditions of "actually existing socialism."

To the same extent that the monumentality of Socialist Realism tends to overshadow the often less spectacular achievements of official art and urbanism in the post-Stalinist era, the drama of the fall of communism and the triumphalism of neoliberal transition color our appreciation of the artistic products of "late socialism." The temptation to read the visual culture of the period as a premonition of impending doom, such as by overstressing the significance of artworks that appear to point to the eventual dissolution of the system, has worked against the creation of a balanced picture of the era's heterogeneous artistic production and obscured a more nuanced understanding of the role of the visual arts in shaping the lived experience of socialism. Instead, monuments that today appear tragically flawed or ironic may be more usefully approached in terms of their original intentions and desired function in their specific social and spatial settings. The key question for the visual culture of a period heavily bracketed by Stalinism and the fall of communism is to understand how artistic production contributed to creating the particular atmosphere of a now-lost era and the extent to which this lived socialist aesthetic expressed the ideals and reality of socialism.

Judgements about the visual culture of socialism and its role in creating the identity of socialist societies are closely related to terminological choices that on the one hand risk erasing the particularities of the art system of the Eastern bloc by uncritically applying categories developed in a nonsocialist context, and on the other of overpoliticizing accounts of cultural and artistic phenomena by favoring a strictly ideological interpretation. In this sense, public space was both more and less "public" in societies that had taken significant steps toward the abolition of private property, making the binary division between the public and the private a less pressing concern for artists than the possibility of free public expression as such. Artists working under socialism, in contrast to their colleagues in the capitalist world, were therefore concerned with navigating not so much the divide between public institutions and commercial galleries as the one between the "first" and "second" public spheres, with the former referring to the official infrastructure of state-run museums, journals and artist unions, and the latter to the unofficial circuit of apartment galleries, samizdat publications and social networks of the alternative scene. This essential difference has implications, for example, for the notion of public art, in that there was practically no privately commissioned public art under socialism, with the result that all the monuments and public sculpture erected in public space were designed to serve social and political goals defined by the state, rather than the interests of private companies or individuals. Equally, it was very often competing notions of public space and attempts to free it from state control that lay behind intrinsically risky artistic interventions in socialist public space from the 1960s onwards, rather than a desire to extend the private space of the artist's studio into the public space of the city. The blurring of the divide between the first and second public spheres toward the end of the period through the eruption of civil movements and the countercultural occupation of symbolic and physical space, in which artists also played a significant role, was also to pave the way for the implosion of the system from the East European revolutions of 1989 to the final collapse of the Soviet Union two years later.

Accounts of the artistic production of the socialist period have frequently been structured around a sharp divide between, in the Stalinist era, Socialist Realism and modernism, and for the period from the 1960s onwards, official

art and the neo-avant-garde. Recognition of the importance of hybrid phenomena, such as Socialist Modernism, referring to the many cases in which
abstract art and modernist architecture served the ideological needs of the
socialist state, has complicated the understanding of art under socialism and
brought a revision of polarized views deriving from Cold War art history.
Reassessments of Socialist Realism have also stressed its roots in the modernist avant-garde's desire to transform the world and reframed it as an aspect
of modernity rather than a fatal exception, and as a movement with artistic
qualities and value, rather than relegating it to the category of artistically
irrelevant propaganda that does not merit proper analysis or preservation.
The reevaluation of the official art of late socialism also involves challenging
the assumption, cultivated by the art market since the fall of communism,
according to which the only art of any interest was produced by oppositional
artists, and in particular the heroic figures of the neo-avant-garde generation
of the late 1960s and early 1970s. On closer inspection, it turns out that the
divide between the "supported," "tolerated" and "forbidden" artists was in
practice quite fluid while, as de facto co-participants in the creation of the
visual culture of real existing socialism, there was significant common territory between official and unofficial artists.

The indistinct culture of the period in question, which is defined negatively
by virtue of having come after Stalinism and before the end of communism,
and which has been characterized in terms of a laconic ambivalence between
stagnation and immutability, fragility and vigor, bleakness and promise,[1] has
contributed to the fact that there is no succinct and fully adequate term to
describe it. The expression "actually existing socialism," which was first
prominently used by dissident Marxist theorist Rudolf Bahro in 1977, offered
at the time a critique of the functioning of socialism in practice measured
against the theory of socialism, particularly in the sense of the more humanist
version that could be extrapolated from Karl Marx's early writings.[2] It also
resonates with the idea that the socialist system in later years represented
a retreat from the maximalist aim of total transformation that characterized
the ideology of Stalinism, which was visualized in terms of concrete steps
toward the building of a literal socialist utopia that always remained just over
the horizon. "Actually existing socialism" described the status quo of everyday life under socialism, but drained of the potential for radical

1 Alexei Yurchak, *Everything Was Forever, Until It Was No More: The Last Soviet Generation*
(Princeton: Princeton University Press, 2005), 4.
2 Rudolf Bahro, *The Alternative in Eastern Europe* (London: New Left Books, 1979 [first
published in German, 1977]).

transformation, while the notion of the end state of communism migrated to ever more distant metaphorical and abstract realms. The disadvantage of the most readily available term, "late socialism," is that it already contains within it a teleological assumption about the inevitability of the collapse of the system, which cannot easily be read into either the lived experience of socialism as a stable, enduring environment, or its self-sufficient visual culture. The post-Socialist Realist era does though, from a stylistic point of view, share some of the characteristics of other "late" periods in art that saw a relaxation of naturalistic and idealized representation and a move to explore more complex subjects and emotions.

This chapter focuses on several illuminating aspects of the visual culture of late socialism from the end of Stalinism to the fall of communism, taking into account the geographical diversity of the socialist experience. The contours of the visual culture of the post-Stalinist urban landscape emerge strikingly through the changing features of the public monument, examined here through an in-depth discussion of emblematic public sculptures by three Hungarian artists who in different ways sought both to respond to the changing political requirements of art commissions and to reflect on the emergence of new social and cultural trends. The visuality of the socialist city was also significantly defined by changing approaches to urbanism, where the abandonment of the decorative excesses of Socialist Realist architecture did not simply result in a return to the conventions of international modernism, but rather opened up a path to experiments that sought to apply the potential of new building technologies to the particular needs of the socialist citizen. Yugoslavia and Poland provide striking examples of the rethinking of socialist urbanism, from the distinctive socialist-futurist design ethos of Dalmatian hotels of the 1960s to the still-relevant utopianism of Oskar Hansen's Linear Continuous System (LCS). Both sculptors and city planners reacted to the changing needs and expectations of the inhabitants of actually existing socialism, not least of which was a rise in living standards and the phenomenon of consumerism. The ideologically charged public space of Stalinism was replaced by the décor of socialist consumerism that, as the singularities of the East European version of Pop Art reveal, was based on scarcity rather than abundance. Finally, this chapter considers the crisis of late socialist visual culture in the late 1970s and 1980s, when the collapse of the boundaries between the first and second public spheres and the influx of nonsocialist ideas, products and behaviors, as well as the breakdown of censorship and loss of semantic and actual control of public space, were unmistakable signs of the rapid dissolution of actually existing socialism.

Plate 17. Deng Xiaoping (L) and Hu Yaobang (R), Beijing, September 1981. Stringer / Getty Images.

Plate 18. Funeral of Enrico Berlinguer, 13 June 1984. Crowds of mourners perform the clenched fist salute as the coffin is carried through Piazza Venezia in Rome. Mondadori Portfolio via Getty Images.

Plate 19. Leaders of the Warsaw Pact at a meeting of the Political Consultative Committee in Prague, 1983. From left: János Kádár, Todor Zhivkov, Yurii Andropov, Gustáv Husák, Erich Honecker, Nicolae Ceauşescu and Wojciech Jaruzelski. ITAR-TASS / Vladimir Musaelyan; Eduard Pesov. Photo by TASS via Getty Images.

Plate 20. East German television filming the celebration ceremony of the fortieth anniversary of the capitulation of Nazi Germany to the Soviet Union in World War II, 8 May 1985. Mehner / ullstein bild via Getty Images.

Monuments acted as barometers of the official art of the socialist system, although only in interaction with the more or less autonomous sphere of post-Stalinist artistic intentions and the changing social and cultural environment which, above and beyond ideology, was a factor in the formation and reception of public sculpture in Eastern Europe. The changes in monumental sculpture were some of the most visible indicators of the shift away from the tropes of Socialist Realism and were visible throughout the Eastern bloc and in all genres of official public art. The Lenin statues that replaced – on occasion physically and not just metaphorically – effigies of Stalin in public squares across Eastern Europe, and which in general did not aspire to a cultic function at the center of mass rituals, were joined by portraits of other communist leaders and partisan heroes, in what was a modernist-inflected return to the traditions of the boom in monuments to historical figures at the end of the nineteenth century.

In Eastern Europe, while in the 1950s Soviet soldiers had been the ubiquitous focus of complex war memorials, from the 1960s onward more abstract renderings of general concepts such as peace and liberation were much more common. The post-Stalin years also saw an exponential increase in decorative public sculpture that often contained an affirmative, civic message, but did not seek to convey a direct ideological meaning. Perhaps most telling of changes in monumental culture, however, was the genre of sculptures representing the working class, in which can be detected signs of the post-utopian outlook of late socialism, anxiety on the part of the party toward the latent power of workers expressed through strikes and uprisings, as well as the influence of changes to the world of work itself as a result of technological and social developments.

In the case of the most provocative monuments that tested the boundaries of political acceptability and aesthetic tolerance there was often a delay between the realization of the work and its erection in public space that reflected tensions within closed party committees rather than public discussion of their stylistic and ideological merits. Indeed, the public character of monuments made decisions around their planning and design especially sensitive issues, a situation compounded during times of political uncertainty. Such was the case with the *Martinász* or "Smelter" by József Somogyi (1916–93), which was cast in bronze in 1953, the year of Stalin's death, and only erected seven years later in the industrial new town that was at the time still called Sztálinváros, or Stalin Town. While in 1953 critics were able to recognize the work's expressive qualities, and the subject of the sculpture did not raise any objections, the artistic treatment of the genre of the industrial worker was considered to stray too far from the Socialist Realist norm to be acceptable for a permanent public position.

The subtle yet significant changes in the sculptural representation of the industrial worker heralded by Somogyi's *Martinász*, marking a loosening of the strict conventions of Socialist Realism, appear in sharp relief if the sculpture is compared to another work on a similar theme executed three years earlier. Depicting another key figure in the building of socialism, István Tar's *Welder* demonstrated the artist's successful attempt to fully comply with the strictures of the Stalinist model and shrug off accusations of "formalism" that had been directed at him by socialist art critics the previous year. The context was also important, as it was created for the First Hungarian Art Exhibition that was a "first" not only because it was followed the next year by a "second" national art survey, but also because it reflected the rapid implementation of the recommendations of a Soviet cultural advisor to intensify the pressure on artists to follow the model of Soviet Socialist Realism and turn away from modernism, to take measures to popularize Soviet art, to reform the art academy on Soviet lines, to exercise closer supervision of competitions and commissions, to control art criticism through a unitary art journal and to reform the artists' union. That Tar's *Welder* pushed all the right buttons for Socialist Realist art critics can be deduced from the following comments in the official art journal:

> The young welder good-humoredly raises his protective goggles to his forehead in order to change the blowtorch. He uses this short break in the work to quickly admire with satisfaction the results of his work so far; he has a broad smile on his face. This sympathetic, strong, pleasant figure personifies the members of the shock work brigades and the whole of communist youth.[3]

The rapid retreat from the reassuring image of a strong, enthusiastic, youthful, cooperative and universal metal worker to Somogyi's more sullen, laconic and introverted figure, although comprehensible to art critics, was too much for the director of the Dunaújváros Steel Works. According to later accounts, it was he who refused to allow the monument to be erected as originally planned at the entrance of the vast industrial plant, on the grounds that this "skinny, tired, ragged" smelter would not set a good example to the workers. As a result, Somogyi's *Martinász* sat out the dramatic events of the 1956 revolution hidden in a provincial factory basement, only to see the light

---

3 Gábor . Pogány, "Az I. Magyar Képzőmvészeti Kiállítás szobrászati anyaga," *Szabad Mvészet* 10 (Oct. 1950), 373.

of day again in 1958 when the statue of the forlorn furnace operator was unexpectedly dispatched to Brussels to stand in front of the Hungarian Pavilion at the first major world's fair since World War II. The dislocations caused by the suppression of the Hungarian Revolution in which many cultural and artistic figures were caught up and confusion over the status of Socialist Realism in Hungary in the wake of Nikita Khrushchev's policy of de-Stalinization, as well as the urgent need to shore up the legitimacy of the post-1956 Kádár regime,[4] came together to make József Somogyi an appropriate choice in this high-stakes bid to showcase Hungarian culture. As an internally circulated document outlining the concept for the pavilion reveals, the organizers, setting themselves the task of counteracting the image of life in socialist countries as "dreary and humourless," decided to stress Hungarian rather than socialist identity, while in place of "didactic diagrams" and portraits of the wise leader, items in a selection of "low-key" and "tasteful" exhibits were to be allowed to "speak for themselves."[5]

Somogyi also created one of a pair of *Dancers* that formed the centerpiece of the interior of the pavilion, and which thanks to their innovative installation on a massive concave wall, perfectly symbolizing the fascination in the period with the synthesis of the arts, earned a prestigious Grand Prix from the organizers.[6] In an irony of history, *Dancers*, a deliberately apolitical work created to legitimize the Soviet-imposed regime of János Kádár by two sculptors who were also responsible for several important Socialist Realist monuments, was acquired by a Belgian town where it stands in a public square to this day.[7] The inclusion of Somogyi's *Smelter* was in fact something of an afterthought and only happened because the authorities in Budapest got cold feet about the "concessions to Western formalist tendencies" that could be deduced from the advance plans for the pavilion.[8] The speed with which official tastes and artistic debate in Eastern Europe were evolving in the period can be seen from the fact that a statue that in 1953 was not sufficiently Socialist Realist to be erected in front of a factory in a provincial town was by 1958 enlisted to bolster the socialist credentials of the country abroad.

The statue of the *Smelter*, after its endorsement on the international stage, was finally erected in the city that was soon to be rechristened Dunaújváros,

---

4 For the importance of the "legitimacy deficit" in the decision of the Hungarian authorities to participate in the Brussels World Fair, see György Péteri, "Transsystemic Fantasies: Counterrevolutionary Hungary at Brussels Expo '58," *Journal of Contemporary History* 46, 1 (Jan. 2012), 137–60.

5 Extracts from "1958 Brussels World's Expo Newsletter nr. 5," are quoted ibid., 142–43.

6 The other artist responsible for this joint sculptural installation was Jenő Kerenyi.

7 Namely Namur, the capital of Wallonia. 8 Péteri, "Transsystemic Fantasies," 150, 153.

or Danube New Town, although not on the originally planned site in front of the steel works, or at a representative location in the center of town, but midway between the two in a residential district, suggesting a continued ambivalence about its appropriateness. The name of the work, *Martinász*, was also in fact more specific than suggested by the usual English translation as "Smelter," and referred to the specialized occupation of operator of an open-hearth furnace in the Siemens-Martin process that revolutionized steel production in the second half of the nineteenth century. To depict a "Martiner" rather than a generic iron worker was a step toward a more individualized treatment of the worker theme, and opened up the possibility of sculpting not a "muscle-bound, physically strong worker," but rather a "worker-intellectual."[9] In the less heroic atmosphere of the 1970s, art critics discovered still further qualities in the work, praising the "skinny Martiner" with "hand on hip" and a "tired-triumphant gesture" – a distinctly late socialist oxymoron – for revealing the "true, bitter pathos of real work."[10]

The Siemens-Martin process itself, which was the technology at the heart of the socialist heavy industry developed in cities across Eastern Europe on the model of Magnitogorsk, was already during its East European heyday in the 1950s considered an obsolete technology in Western Europe, where it had been replaced by the oxygen converter process. The open hearth furnaces of Eastern Europe, and the "tired-triumphant" workers who manned them, became in later decades symbols not of the heroic building of socialism, but rather of the technological malaise that undermined the system's claim to modernity. During the postcommunist era, the painful transition to a postindustrial economic model experienced by cities such as Dunaújváros has contributed to popular nostalgia for the era of the *Martinász*, with annual visits by school children and plans mooted in the early 2000s to relocate the sculpture to a more central location next to the city's Institute of Contemporary Art.

The changing conventions of the representation of the worker are also strikingly exemplified in Sándor Mikus's *Dalosok* ("Male Choir"), which was erected in front of the Csepel Car Factory in the outskirts of Budapest in 1961. Mikus had been one of the most successful sculptors of the Stalinist era in Hungary and the quickest to adapt to the strictures of Socialist Realism. Although he had no personal history of involvement in left-wing politics, and had in the 1930s been a marginal sculptor of small portrait busts, he emerged

9 Nóra Aradi, *Munkásábrázolás a magyar képzőmvészetben* (Budapest: Kossuth Könyvkiadó, 1976).
10 Rózsa Gyula, "Martinász – Szántó Kovács – Zrínyi," *Népszabadság* (15 Mar. 1970).

in the postwar era as a leading advocate of Socialist Realism. Most significantly, he was responsible for Budapest's Stalin statue, which was erected in 1951 and was briefly the central focus for mass celebrations on Stalin's birthday and other important socialist anniversaries. The destruction of the monument by anti-Soviet revolutionaries in 1956 was a deep blow to the artist, and in later years he worked to repair the decorative frieze that had been removed from the city center. Given his background and commitment to Socialist Realism, his approach to creating a monument for the Csepel Car Factory is particularly revealing of the changing demands and tastes of official commissions, and also of what was possible in the post-1956, post-Stalin years in terms of the representation of workers.

A guide to the interpretation of Mikus's *Male Choir* in terms of the artistic thinking of the period is provided by a leading authority of the time, art historian Nóra Aradi (1924–2001). Aradi was ideally placed to articulate the official line on art following the abandonment of Socialist Realism, and through her publications and role in public life played an important part in its formation. Having studied art history in Budapest from 1945 to 1950, she witnessed the imposition of Socialist Realism on the Hungarian art world and was well versed in its rules and methodology. She began her career at the Ministry of Culture as deputy head of the fine arts department in the year of Stalin's death, going on to head the department during the difficult period from 1957 to 1961. Over long years as a professor at the art history department of Eötvös Loránd University and as director of the Institute of Art History from 1969 all the way to 1990, she held a gatekeeper position over art historical interpretation and the careers of her subordinates, and published more than 700 books, articles, reviews and catalogue texts. Her writings from the period are exemplary of the nuanced official line toward public sculpture during the late socialist period.

Interpreting Mikus's statue group in her book on *The Depiction of Workers in Hungarian Fine Arts* from 1976, Aradi makes a number of observations that are worthy of analysis. First, she points out that the placing of the three statues on different levels and one behind the other is a means of conveying the idea of a "solid, unified crowd."[11] In the wake of the Hungarian Revolution of 1956, in which the Hungarian socialist state was overcome by the power of the crowd, which turned from a disciplined mass waving flags at socialist anniversaries in front of the Stalin statue to a revolutionary crowd whose first collective act was to pull down the edifice of the leader, the

---

11 Aradi, *Munkásábrázolás a magyar képzőmvészetben*, 200.

representation of the masses was problematic, just as gatherings of more than a handful of people were viewed with suspicion. A choir was in that sense among the least threatening of devices to represent a gathering of workers, as its members carry no weapons or tools, and notably are singing from a score rather than speaking for themselves.

The second observation made by this most prominent articulator of official art policy of the late socialist period is that the sculpture shows workers not in connection with the "working process" but in the "cultural phase."[12] This marked a distinct change from conventional Socialist Realist depictions of workers, who were almost always shown together with the tools of their trade and ideally engaged in productive labor. The exception to the rule was when artists set out to capture the gaze of the Stakhanovite during a momentary pause in heroic physical labor, when the shock worker glimpsed the utopian future of abundance and leisure that would be the ultimate reward for the Herculean effort of building socialism. The ideological rationale behind Socialist Realist depictions of the reading worker was to demonstrate the idea of progress and, similarly to paintings on themes such as workers and peasants at the opera, demonstrate that under socialism high culture was no longer the monopoly of the bourgeoisie. In the 1960s and 1970s, however, the decision to show workers engaged in cultural activities reflected the new priorities of post-Stalinist economic policy across the Eastern bloc, with a dramatic shift away from heavy industry toward the production of consumer goods. The evocation of a generic worker who could not be identified with a particular trade or branch of industry also reflected changes in the workplace and the spread of mechanized factory labor, and the decreasing importance both socially and ideologically of the stereotypical worker role models of macho heavy industry, such as the hammer-bearing iron worker, the smelter with his ladle of molten iron, or the drilling miner.

The ideal characteristics of the post-Socialist Realist worker are also conveyed by Aradi's final approving comments on the sculpture's evocation of the "new kind of human type and individual need" and avoidance of "all elements of external heroicization."[13] Through this opaque phraseology, typical of the ultra-cautious official art history of the time, can be perceived a shift from the New Man and Woman who were the ideal-types of the Socialist Realist utopia and whose needs were fully realized through selfless participation in the collective, to the more individualistic protagonists of

12 Ibid.   13 Ibid.

actually existing socialism, who as long as they did not challenge party rule were free to follow their own pursuits within a more variegated social reality. The "new kind of human type" did not correspond to the rebellious spirit of the revolutionary worker, heroism of the wartime partisan or self-empowering gestures of the builder of socialism, but was characterized instead by more modest ambitions and a benign social conformism, a tone that was perfectly conveyed by the singers in Mikus's featureless and banal *Male Choir*.

By the end of the 1960s, sculptors were again pushing the limits of what constituted an acceptable solution for the public representation of the work-ing class. István Kiss, whose *Republic of Councils Memorial* from 1969 was one of the most prominent public monuments erected in Budapest in the post-Stalin era, also created in the same year a model for a public sculpture entitled *Work* that did not garner such instant popularity. Depicting four male figures in overalls with their arms folded, communicating silently or telepathically without gestures or even exchanging glances, and with a large piece of industrial machinery under foot, the work evades straightforward ideological interpretation. These workers do not seem to be working, but rather just idly waiting around; the huge cog on the ground is not in the process of being constructed or moving, but seems only to provide a place to rest their feet. The group closes in on itself rather than looking out to the world, while the body language of folded arms could be interpreted as indicative of an attitude of mistrust, lack of self-confidence and defensiveness.

In a manner similar to Somogyi's *Martinász*, Kiss's *Work* was erected as a public monument only after a long delay, and again not in its planned location. While originally conceived at the end of the 1960s for the entrance of the Láng Machine Tool Factory on Vaci Way, in the end the sculpture was placed in 1982 at the nearby junction of two major roads in front of a newly constructed Party Building, with the slightly modified title of *Workers*. The choice of aluminum as the material for the sculpture matched the modernist style of the representative headquarters pictured in the back-ground in archive photographs. The building itself was the work of prize-winning architect Margit Pázmándy and included a 700-seat auditorium and a 120-seat committee room, as well as, on the second floor, 12 teaching rooms, each designed for 24 students for holding courses in Marxism-Leninism.[14] The lack of socialist ideological content, and Kiss's very ambivalent treatment

---

14 See "It Used to Be a Party Building . . .," Budapest city blog, fovarosi.blog.hu/2009/01/ 20/parthaz_volt_most_2_resz.

of the worker theme, has meant that, with the rebranding of the building in postcommunist times as first the Constitutional Court and currently the Hungarian State Treasury, the monument remains in place even today.

Public monuments were deployed at sites of political or historical symbolism, frequently to provide the focus for public rituals on red dates in the revolutionary calendar, but also as part of an urban ensemble to create a distinctively socialist built environment. To this end, sculpture, painting and design were enlisted to help buildings communicate a socialist message or ethos, although taking different forms during Socialist Realism and in the later period. While under Stalinism the idea of synthesis of the arts was interpreted narrowly through the widespread use of decorative sculptures and friezes on buildings, from the late 1950s onward traditional decoration was eschewed in favor of abstract motifs. These combined either folk traditions or futuristic styles with toned-down references to socialist culture, and were a feature both of the external decoration of buildings and of distinctive socialist interior design.

This shift could be understood in a Soviet context in terms of a timid return of what dissident cultural theorist Vladimir Paperny described in a samizdat publication as "Culture One," referring to the fascination with the architectural projects of the Leninist 1920s for horizontality, technology, biology, function and the immersion of the individual in the collective. In his account, "Culture One" was displaced in the early 1930s by "Culture Two," organized around a "hierarchical allocation of individualism" and rejection of the modernist ideals of the 1920s.[15] Although focusing primarily on the earlier period, Paperny noted both the rebirth of Culture One in the 1960s and the reemergence of Culture Two in the 1970s.[16] In wider terms, these returns could be understood as reflecting the alternation between the continuing relevance of avant-garde approaches and the conservative thread in late socialist culture, facing inward toward the cultivation of national traditions and exuding an image of stasis and inevitability. For the later period and in a wider geographical scope, a distinction can also be made between the radical, socially transformative ideals that represented one stream of the renewed Culture One, and the more formalist, depoliticized style of High Modernism, which drew on the aesthetic legacy of the architectural and artistic experiments of the 1920s.

15 Vladimir Paperny, *Architecture in the Age of Stalin: Culture Two* (Cambridge: Cambridge University Press, 2002), 110.
16 Ibid., 112.

The impulse to use architecture to structure all aspects of people's lives, inculcate socialist values and create the material basis for collectivity, which corresponded to the self-image of totalitarian society as an all-encompassing artwork or *Gesamtkunstwerk*, took on a post-*Gesamtkunstwerk* form in the later 1960s and 1970s, when East European architects renewed the search for far-reaching urban design solutions to the needs of actually existing socialism. While Stalinist attempts to control public space and impose a particular vision of socialism were articulated through neoclassical, "closed" architectural forms, in later years more organic and experimental architectural utopias came to the fore. These were typically presented and politically justified at the time as a return to the more humanistic roots of the young Marx and were influenced by philosophical movements such as existentialism and phenomenology, while also reflecting the rise of ecological thinking in response to environmental degradation. While the "socialist humanists" of Czechoslovakia and Yugoslavia were most loudly celebrated in the circles of the Western New Left, attempts to revise and soften communist ideology could be felt throughout the bloc in the post-Stalin years.

Adam Schaff, one of the most prominent Marxist theorists in Poland in the 1960s, voiced criticism of the economic materialism of "vulgar Marxism," which he accused of having "lost sight of the individual" by reducing man from being "a history-maker" and "master of his own choices" to being a *"mere* product, a statistical average, an executor of historical laws which are independent of his will."[17] The seizure of power by communist parties had, in Schaff's view, shifted the main goal from the "struggle against the old system" to the "task of creating new ways of life" and a return to the "central problem – how to make people happy."[18] A similar line was taken by Czech philosopher Milan Prúcha, who also argued for a return to the "humanist core of Marx's concept of communism," and focused on the problem of alienation, contrasting the standard situation in which "the active being of the individual is suffering" with the concept of "total man" based both on the abolition of exploitation and the division of labor and, more speculatively, on "making art a living form by the creation of a new type of social relationship."[19] For Croatian Praxis philosopher Gajo Petrović, the achievement of freedom within socialist societies implied more than the

---

17 Adam Schaff, "Marxism and the Philosophy of Man," in Erich Fromm (ed.), *Socialist Humanism: An International Symposium* (London: Allen Lane, 1967), 131.
18 Ibid., 135.
19 Milan Prúcha, "Marxism and the Existential Problems of Man," in Fromm (ed.), *Socialist Humanism*, 146–47.

"expropriation of the expropriators" and raising of living standards. His suggestion that we investigate instead the effect on human freedom of the ways in which we "communicate with nature and other men (technology) and the social forms in which that communication takes place (social organizations and institutions)" resonated strongly with the goals of radical experimentation in art, architecture and urbanism in the period.[20]

The new critical spirit that could be felt in the East European wing of neo-Marxist thought in the 1960s found its echo in attempts to remake the built environment, often using art and design as synthetic elements, in order to cater to the inner, individual needs of socialist citizens, as well as to overcome social alienation. While alienation was recognized as a common problem facing industrial, urban societies, idealistic urban thinkers in the East saw in socialism a greater potential to overcome its effects than under capitalism. As will be shown, some of the most illuminating architectural projects of late socialism were conceived not as a reaction to the urban design model of the 1950s, but rather in a critical relation to high modernism, with its technological, growth-oriented ethos, that by the early 1960s had replaced Socialist Realism as the de facto official style of Eastern Europe.

In that sense, the work of Polish architect and artist Oskar Hansen has been seen as an attempt to go beyond Cold War binary divisions, transcending both "the corrupting, authoritarian and bureaucratic mindset of existing communism" and "the corrosive materialism of Western capitalism."[21] Presented for the first time in 1967 at an exhibition in the Dom Artysty Plastyka in Warsaw, Hansen's Linear Continuous System proposed a new relationship between urban space, human individual and social community. Structuring the built environment around "organic patterns," his radical vision of the future city followed a series of "parallel belts," one for "residential-service," another made up of "agriculture and natural woods," "historical urban centres" and "the mining industry," while the third would be dedicated to "strenuous industry."[22] The belts would run alongside major rivers to secure a water supply, be connected by "collision-less transversal public transport" and be based on full employment. Over the long term, Hansen

20 Gajo Petrović, "Man and Freedom," in Fromm (ed.), *Socialist Humanism*, 253.
21 Joan Ockman, "Oskar Hansen's Radical Humanism: Open Form Against a Cold War Background," in Aleksandra Kedziorek and Łukasz Ronduda (eds.), *Oskar Hansen Opening Modernism: An Open Form Architecture, Art and Didactics* (Warsaw: Museum of Modern Art in Warsaw, 2014), 36.
22 See Oskar Hansen, "LSC: Linearny System Cigły," *Architektura* 4–5 (1970), quoted in translation in Andrzej Szczerski, "LCS or What Is a City?," in Kedziorek and Ronduda (eds.), *Oskar Hansen Opening Modernism*, 92.

anticipated that everyone would eventually abandon towns and cities, which would be preserved as tourist attractions, and relocate to the network-decentered, posturban belts.

Although Hansen at the time did not make any explicit reference to philosophical influences on his work, later reassessments of his legacy have pointed to correspondences with existentialist thought, which could be linked with the formative period the architect spent in Paris in the late 1940s, as well as the reversal of the Stalinist-era prohibition of the writings of Jean-Paul Sartre in Eastern Europe at the end of the 1950s, signaled by the publishing in Polish of his essay on "Marxism and Existentialism" in 1957.[23] Echoes of East European theorization of Socialist Humanism can also be detected, with Adam Schaff's reappraisal of the human individual as a relevant contemporary reference point for Hansen's description of LCS society as "classless, egalitarian and non-hierarchical," in which "everyone is dependent on the collective and the collective is dependent on the individual."[24] Of equal importance from today's perspective are the resonances of Hansen's work with newly appearing environmental concerns at the end of the 1960s.

The rejection of the traditional city represented a critical position toward both the capitalist and socialist versions of existing industrial society. Notably, the poster of his 1967 exhibition introducing LCS appropriately showed a graphic representation of a river with crowds of happy human faces on the banks, and key terms – security, culture, water, air, civilization, leisure and nature – floating in the current.[25] The authorities initially warmed to Hansen's proposals, recognizing in the LCS parallels with the "advanced socialist society" that was the political goal of the Polish United Workers' Party under Edward Gierek from 1970, an improved version of actually existing socialism that was to be achieved through the development of new technologies and consumer goods. However, Hansen's ecologically attuned vision of a postindustrial society based on individual creativity and a new nonhierarchical and postfamily form of social organization was ultimately at odds with the growth-oriented party policy of "second industrialization," which was based on the improvement of existing social and urban structures rather than their radical overhaul, and linked to the economic model of socialist consumerism.

23 "Marksizm i egzystencjalizm," *Twórczość* 4 (Apr. 1957), 33–79.
24 See Hansen, "LSC," 135, quoted in translation in Łukasz Stanek (ed.), *Team 10 East: Architecture in Real Existing Socialism* (Warsaw: Museum of Modern Art in Warsaw, 2014), 30.
25 Poster reproduced in Szczerski, "LCS or What Is a City?," 92.

The socialist consumer is a contradictory figure in the visual culture of late socialism. On the one hand, the improvement in living standards and levels of consumption of socialist citizens was a goal of post-Stalinist economic and social policy, with the commitment to provide for individual needs renewed periodically after periods of crisis. On the other, the proliferation of images of consumer goods in the socialist media during the 1960s and 1970s coincided with widespread shortages of the items themselves, and the growth of new social inequalities based on restricted access to both imported and Eastern bloc products. The question haunting the rise of red consumerism was whether it represented a complete capitulation to Western values, or whether there was still a specifically socialist dimension to an everyday culture based increasingly around desiring, and occasionally acquiring, consumer goods.

The existence of a socialist residue in the consumer culture of the 1960s and 1970s can be traced in the cult of the summer holiday, and the specific solutions found for seaside architecture on the Croatian and Bulgarian coasts. While new holiday developments were carried out with the aim of securing foreign currency from Western tourists, the urban design plans and architectural solutions went beyond the import of readymade models of the modern luxury hotel. While new hotel buildings synthesized elements of Western tourist culture, it has been pointed out that they did so in the context of "basic socialist premises, such as public ownership of land and property, and extensive rights and benefits for employees."[26] In Yugoslavia, for example, in the postwar period it was the state that provided workers and young people with cheap holidays in holiday homes constructed by the army, as well as major social and labor organizations. This spirit of social inclusiveness lived on in later hotel developments, according to which tourist complexes "were open to all and included public spaces designed to mediate between the collective and individual spheres."[27]

As a particular type of representative building under socialism, hotels meant for international guests offered more scope, as well as more generous design budgets, than commissions for party offices and public institutions. The interior of hotels offered an open field to continue and explore the

26 See Elke Beyer, Anke Hagemann and Michael Zinganel, "Introduction," in Elke Beyer, Anke Hagemann and Michael Zinganel (eds.), *Holidays After the Fall: Seaside Architecture and Urbanism in Bulgaria and Croatia* (Berlin: Jovis, 2013), 29.
27 Maroje Mrduljaš, "Building the Affordable Arcadia: Tourism Development on the Croatian Adriatic Coast Under State Socialism," in Beyer, Hagemann and Zinganel (eds.), *Holidays After the Fall*, 176.

modernist tradition of synthesis of the arts, which had been strongly advocated by the interdisciplinary group EXAT 51 in the early 1950s. The hotels built in Dalmatia and Istria in the 1960s have been described as virtual "museums of modern art," through their incorporation of the whole range of artistic media, from paintings, murals, reliefs and mosaics to "custom-designed furniture and textiles," with many of the commissions going to leading artists and designers.[28] The design of luxury hotels offered an opportunity to present an image of socialist modernity to the world, making use of new materials such as plastic furniture, and creating a futuristic environment that, through the emphasis on collective spaces, offered a particular East European version of the "technological sublime."[29]

The spread of consumer values in Eastern Europe, both as a result of government economic policy and due to the increasing permeability of culture across political borders, gave rise to anxiety on the part of the communist authorities, as well as prompting a response from cultural producers. Changes in the look and feel of life in socialist cities, with the advent at the end of the 1960s of "soft-sell advertising" and "brightly packaged and branded" products, as well as "lifestyle magazines promising socialist consumerism,"[30] were reflected on by artists, who developed a specifically East European version of Pop Art. Through paintings and collages, they noted the formal similarities between Western and Eastern consumerism, while going beyond an apolitical fascination with the surface banality of popular culture typical of the high Pop Art of the West, to turn their observations into a sharp political critique of either the contradictions of the socialist system or of its apparent sellout to capitalist values.

Serbian artist Dušan Otašević's *Towards Communism on Lenin's Course* from 1967 for example, showed Lenin pointing to a red star to his left, while on his right can be seen a "no right turn" sign, which could be read as an ironic warning against right-wing deviationism as well as an indication of shifting sands of late socialist ideology. Other works by the same artist focus on everyday acts such as shaving, eating ice cream and smoking, as well as the crude signs made by private shopkeepers in Yugoslavia at the time, that reflected the "the more naive and austere circumstances of an emerging

28 Ibid., 199–201.
29 For the "Western" version, see David E. Nye, *American Technological Sublime* (Cambridge, MA: MIT Press, 1990).
30 David Crowley, "Pop Effects in Eastern Europe Under Communist Rule," in *The World Goes Pop* (London: Tate, 2015), 33.

consumerism in a socialist socio-economic state."[31] By, for example, illustrating the entwinement of an uneasy consumerism with the official anti-capitalist ideology, artists both commented on and contributed to the emptying out of ideological meaning from the socialist public sphere. Such actions took their most dramatic form, however, when they left the gallery context to intervene in the contested space of the socialist city.

The apparatus of the controlled and fearful public spaces of Stalinism was both dismantled from above, through official policies of de-Stalinization under Khrushchev, and chipped away at by artistic actions to undermine the system's monopoly of meanings. In the 1960s, this frequently took the form of playful and poetic interventions with subtle and only indirect political allusions. Stano Filko and Alex Mlynárčik's *Happsoc*, for example, used a printed invitation card to declare the city of Bratislava to be an artwork from 2 to 8 May 1965, mimicking the official penchant for statistics by enumerating units of everything from women, men, dogs and balconies to washing machines, street lamps and tulips that constituted the city. In Prague, Milan Knížák staged surreal scenes on the streets near his studio, making use of everyday items and human figures to disturb the accepted reality of the city. One of the most elaborate of such actions, *A Walk Around the New World – A Demonstration for All the Senses*, on 13 December 1964, confronted passersby with a sculpture of old dresses hanging on a lamppost and a man lying on the cobblestones while playing a double bass.[32]

The invasion by Soviet and East European troops of Czechoslovakia in August 1968 to put down the brief flowering of "socialism with a human face," brought in its wake both terminal disillusionment with the socialist utopia on the part of left-leaning artists and intellectuals, and a new tone to artistic interventions in public space. By the mid 1970s, in the place of witty and absurdist tactics of urban disruption that flourished in the 1960s, the street became a site to express youthful alienation from both mainstream culture and the faith of an earlier generation of neo-avant-garde artists that the system could be reformed. This new attitude of profound disillusionment was exemplified by Željko Jerman's proclamation, written on a white sheet as part of an outdoor action by the Group of Six Authors in Zagreb, that: "This Is Not My World!" Rejecting the "optimism" and belief in the social function

31 Branislav Dimitrijević, "Pop Art and the Socialist 'Thing': Dušan Otašević in the 1960s," *Tate Papers* 24 (Autumn 2015), www.tate.org.uk/research/publications/tate-papers/24.
32 See Pavlína Morganová, *Czech Action Art: Happenings, Actions, Events, Land Art, Body Art and Performance Art Behind the Iron Curtain* (Prague: Charles University Press, 2014), 50–79.

of art of the late 1960s, the young artists left aside "socially engaged practice in favor of a more cynical and ironic approach."[33] On the whole it was not until the late 1980s that a new wave of protests and civic actions, in large part galvanized by environmental concerns, opened the way to a cautious reengagement by artists with the politics of the public sphere.

The ideological decay of the twilight years of the socialist system ultimately allowed a more diverse urban culture to emerge, in which artists, and the wider cultural underground, took symbolic and eventually literal possession of public space, remaking it in the image of the democratic upsurge of the revolutions of 1989. The dramatic end of actually existing socialism, and the rapid transition to a new economic and political system, rendered both the ebbs and flows of official art from the 1950s to the 1980s and the fluctuating appeal of socialism in its humanist guise to cultural producers momentarily irrelevant and invisible. With the cooling of ideological tempers and unraveling of established narratives, it is now possible to reassess the trajectories of official and nonconformist artists through the changing political, technological and ecological realities of a system that despite its apparent timelessness was nevertheless subject to historical transformation. We are also now able to better appreciate the incremental changes to the socialist public sphere since the Thaw, and the role of artists, architects and designers in reclaiming public space and the popular imagination through small-scale actions that prefigured the oppositional culture that emerged in the 1980s. Transversal connections also emerge between the concerns of progressive, experimental artists and those that worked in the more restricted setting of official commissions, with discernible echoes in the unspectacular public sculpture of late socialism of the era's fascination with the cosmos, technology, environmental concern and the inalienability of individual human freedom.

Bibliographical Essay

Research into the art history and wider visual culture of Eastern Europe and the Soviet Union since the 1960s has flourished in recent decades, with a raft of publications dealing with the careers of particular artists and movements, comparative accounts of the region as a whole, as well as research focusing on particular themes that cut across geographical

---

33 Maja Fowkes, *The Green Bloc: Neo-Avant-Garde Art and Ecology Under Socialism* (Budapest and New York: Central European University Press, 2015), 148–49.

boundaries. The most influential survey of the region remains Piotr Piotrowski's *In the Shadow of Yalta: Art and the Avant-Garde in Eastern Europe, 1945–1989* (London: Reaktion Books, 2009), while the artist-led project *East Art Map: Contemporary Art and Eastern Europe* (London: Afterall, 2006), initiated by Slovenian group IRWIN, was another wide-ranging attempt to insert the "missing" history of East European art into Western-oriented accounts. Among the many exhibitions that have contributed to the self-definition of East European art of the period, particular mention could be made of those that by focusing on particular issues challenged the predisposition to overpoliticize accounts of the art of the socialist era. These include the pioneering "Body and the East: From 1960s to the Present," curated by Zdenka Badovinac at Moderna Galeria, Ljubljana, in 1999, and ten years later, the self-reflective "Gender Check: Femininity and Masculinity in the Art of Eastern Europe," curated by Bojana Peijić at MUMOK in Vienna. Recent monographs that likewise deal with neglected aspects of the art history of the period include Klara Kemp Welch's *Antipolitics in Central European Art: Reticence as Dissidence Under Post-Totalitarian Rule 1956–1989* (London: I. B. Tauris, 2014), Pavlína Morganová's *Czech Action Art: Happenings, Actions, Events, Land Art, Body Art and Performance Art Behind the Iron Curtain* (Prague: Charles University Press, 2014) and Maja Fowkes's *The Green Bloc: Neo-Avant-Garde Art and Ecology Under Socialism* (New York and Budapest: Central European University Press, 2015). Another notable tendency has been to question the starkness of the divide between "official" and "unofficial" art, both by treating Socialist Realism as an artistic movement in its own right rather than as mere propaganda, such as in Matthew Cullerne Bown's *Socialist Realist Painting* (New Haven: Yale University Press, 1998), and by examining the complex relationship of artists, curators and art historians to the socialist art system, which is the focus of a special issue of *Third Text* edited by Reuben Fowkes on "Contested Spheres: Actually Existing Artworlds Under Socialism" (forthcoming 2017). The particularities of the mass culture of the Soviet 1980s have been analyzed by Alexei Yurchak in *Everything Was Forever, Until It Was No More: The Last Soviet Generation* (Princeton: Princeton University Press, 2005), an account that brings to light both points of convergence and disjuncture with the lived experience of socialism in the rest of the Eastern bloc. Research on the history of Soviet and East European design, architecture, urbanism, fashion and cinema also informs interdisciplinary approaches to the visual culture of socialism, such as David Crowley and Jane Pavitt (eds.), *Cold War Modern: Design*

1945–1970 (London: V&A Publishing, 2008), as well as, with its focus on the modern architecture of non-Russian soviet republics, Katharina Ritter et al. (eds.), *Soviet Modernism 1955–1991* (Vienna: Architekturzentrum Wien, 2012), while Łukasz Ronduda and Florian Zeyfang (eds.), *1,2,3 ... Avant-Gardes: Film/Art Between Experiment and Archive* (Berlin: Sternberg Press, 2007), have investigated the overlaps between experimental film and the visual arts.

14

Communist Propaganda and Media in the Era of the Cold War

STEPHEN LOVELL

As Nicholas J. Cull has noted in a chapter for another *Cambridge History*, the Soviets were "the old professionals in the culture game."[1] As the representatives of a revolutionary state they had had to fight for legitimacy and credibility in ways that more staid liberal nation-states had never had to contemplate. In the process they had also had to overcome severe social and technological disabilities. For all the Promethean rhetoric, the Soviet Union in the interwar period was a poor, traumatized and weakly educated country riven by social and ethnic divisions. Yet, even if there were sections of the population left untouched or unpersuaded by "Stalinist civilization," by the end of the 1930s the successes of the Soviet cultural project were already striking. Illiteracy had been slashed, a model of politically engaged mass journalism had been created, the Soviet entertainment industry (primarily cinema) had achieved takeoff and radio had spread to a critical mass of urban households.

World War II dealt a heavy blow to the cultural infrastructure the Soviet Union had built up with such difficulty over the previous decade. Radio personnel and film studios had to be evacuated east to Kuibyshev (Samara) and Alma-Ata (Almaty). Newspaper circulations were drastically reduced. Yet, despite all the upheaval, in this field as in others, the Soviet model proved remarkably resilient at its moment of greatest crisis. The radio network held up despite dislocation and bomb damage. Writers, artists and performers poured their energies into the cause, many of them reaching their audience face-to-face at the front. The war also helped to resolve a thorny matter of content: how to balance forward-looking revolutionary themes with the fact

I thank Jennifer Altehenger for helpful reading suggestions and comments on a draft.
1 Nicholas J. Cull, "Reading, Viewing, and Tuning In to the Cold War," in Melvyn P. Leffler and Odd Arne Westad (eds.), *The Cambridge History of the Cold War*, vol. II (Cambridge: Cambridge University Press, 2011), 439.

that any culture needs points of reference in the past and tradition. Almost immediately after the German invasion, the conflict could be referred to as a "great patriotic war," a gesture to the fatherland rather than the party as the source of loyalty and an overt reference to the original "patriotic war" in 1812, deep in the tsarist past.

Once it was over, the war became even more of a boon to Soviet propaganda. Now the Soviet triumph over Hitler could top all other points of propaganda reference – not just 1812 but even, before too long, 1917 itself. The party and patriotism were at last at one. Better still, the unfinished business of World War II led to a global polarization between communism and capitalism that made vivid and communicable the abstractions of Marxism-Leninism. Now the USSR was joined by the people's democracies in Eastern Europe and (from 1949) another communist behemoth in the form of the People's Republic of China (PRC). Together they could launch a concerted propaganda effort – which, in the immediate absence of "hot" war, seemed the best way to achieve advantage in the conflict with the liberal capitalist West.

Over the next two decades, from the mid 1940s to the mid 1960s, the USSR saw further striking advances in its media and propaganda capacity. As a contemporary observer noted, "The growth of radio and television during the years since Stalin died can best be described as a communications explosion."[2] Newspaper circulations went up, and dozens of new journals and magazines were established. The journalistic profession increased rapidly both in size and in sense of self-worth. The Union of Journalists had its first congress in 1959, when it numbered 23,000 members; by the time of its second congress in 1966 membership had almost doubled. For the first time the country started producing wireless radio sets in significant numbers; Soviet society was deemed fully "radiofied" by 1960. Cinema was experiencing a golden age, as the more diverse and vibrant output of the post-Stalin era was matched by a vast audience. By the 1960s, the USSR had more than forty studios spread over all fifteen union republics. Film output more than quadrupled from 38 full-length features in 1954 to 175 in 1967, while the number of projectors tripled from 52,300 in 1953 to 153,000 in 1967. The industry attained a new peak of 4 billion tickets sold in 1968, and box office figures held up well through the following decade. Most striking of all, television was fast becoming the most desirable consumer item for the Soviet

2 Gayle Durham Hollander, *Soviet Political Indoctrination: Developments in Mass Media and Propaganda Since Stalin* (New York: Praeger, 1972), 124.

person: Here was a medium that seemed to realize the propagandist's fondest dreams, bringing the message of the party into people's domestic universe in the form of spoken words and moving pictures. Transmission capacity grew from 3 stations in 1952 to almost 300 in 1971, including the powerful Ostankino Tower (opened 1967), which made Channel One truly a national broadcaster. Television was the main propaganda weapon in the new conditions of the Cold War in the more consumer-oriented 1960s: It both was itself a consumer item, thus demonstrating the capacity of socialist light industry to satisfy a more demanding and prosperous citizenry, and communicated better than any other medium the "private" issues (family, housing, welfare) that were central to the post-Stalin version of state socialism as to its liberal capitalist counterparts. The statistics tell the story better than anything else: The USSR had 44.1 inhabitants per set in 1960, but only 4.6 in 1975. Nor was the Soviet case extreme in the socialist bloc: Bulgaria had 1,577 inhabitants per set in 1960, but only 5.8 in 1975. Comfortably ahead of the rest was the German Democratic Republic (GDR): 16.8 people per set in 1960, down to a mere 3.2 in 1975.[3]

Yet, by the start of the period that mainly concerns us in this chapter – the second half of the Cold War – the golden age was already losing its sheen. Radiofication was not altogether a success story: Mass production of short-wave sets had in fact delivered the Soviet listener into the hands of the Western propagandists of Voice of America and Radio Liberty. Television was giving rise to some of the same anxieties about social atomization and trivialization as were voiced in the West, and they were even more troubling for a political system with such a strong edificatory mission. Finally, the presence of multiple other communist states around the globe did not necessarily help matters. Keeping these states "on message" in propaganda terms sometimes proved considerably more difficult than controlling their defense policy. In any case, propaganda and culture could not straightfor-wardly be transplanted from one society to another – not even to Poland, let alone to China. What exactly was "communist" about media and propaganda once all the local variation was taken into account?

---

3 Statistics in this paragraph are from Hollander, *Soviet Political Indoctrination*, 34–35, 102, 132; Kristin Roth-Ey, *Moscow Prime Time: How the Soviet Union Built the Media Empire That Lost the Cultural Cold War* (Ithaca: Cornell University Press, 2011), 26; and Sabina Mihelj, "The Politics of Privatization: Television Entertainment and the Yugoslav Sixties," in Anne E. Gorsuch and Diane P. Koenker (eds.), *The Socialist Sixties: Crossing Borders in the Second World* (Bloomington: Indiana University Press, 2013), 251, 253.

Essential common features can certainly be identified: The monopolization of the means of communication, the creation of a hierarchical propaganda apparatus, and the imposition of strict controls and sanctions (both before and after publication) were all core requirements of a communist media system in the late Stalin era and beyond. In places where communism was established after 1945, the new regimes wasted little time in imposing discipline on the media professionals at their disposal. It helped matters that in most cases they were rebuilding these professions from the ground up. In Poland, where the prewar intelligentsia was worst hit of all, the number of registered journalists more than doubled from 1949 to 1954.[4]

But suppressing ideologically incorrect messages was never sufficient. The Soviet model of propaganda was proactive and mobilizatory: Soviet people were to be actively engaged by the propaganda industry. As always, that left open the question of how best to mobilize. The answer depended on the character of the audience, which shifted over time. In earlier eras of Soviet history, the distinction between "agitation" and "propaganda" had been highly meaningful: Agitation tended to be face to face and oral, for the less politically literate audience, while propaganda usually meant print. As the Soviet population became more sophisticated in the postwar era, propaganda was conducted through a greater variety of printed material. Certainly, agitation remained a significant part of the Soviet communications repertoire in the 1960s and beyond, though it was generally pitched at a more educated audience than in the Stalin era: Grassroots face-to-face communication was still the best way of getting certain messages to stick, even if people on average spent less time in political meetings than earlier in the Soviet period.[5] But the advent of the audiovisual media had muddied the waters. Film and TV were certainly oral, but they did not allow the speaker to adapt to the particular requirements of the audience. Tub-thumping agitation, such as had been applied to peasants-turned-workers in the Stalinist 1930s, was no longer so effective. The rhetoric of propaganda had to become softer and more consensual for the more urbane audience of the Brezhnev era. From the mid 1960s onwards, Soviet broadcasters were more likely to address their audience as "friends" than as "comrades."

---

4 Jane Leftwich Curry, *Poland's Journalists: Professionalism and Politics* (Cambridge: Cambridge University Press, 1990), 40.
5 Hollander, *Soviet Political Indoctrination*, ch. 6.

In many ways, this audience was indeed less comradely. The readers, listeners and (especially) viewers of the Leonid Brezhnev era were on average younger than their predecessors, had more disposable income, and enjoyed more free time (notably after the introduction of a two-day weekend in the late 1960s). Many Soviet cinema-goers were "fans" in a sense entirely recognizable to an American contemporary, adopting a very personal and proprietorial relationship to their favorite stars.[6] The logic of individualization also touched that quintessential oracle of Soviet power, the radio. The postwar era saw a shift from wired broadcasting (according to which an audience, often collective, listened to the one available channel at a receiver point) to wireless. The Soviet Union invested in mass production of shortwave sets, which brought into being a more autonomous and individualized listening audience. Most worrying for the Soviet authorities was the fact that many of these liberated radio lovers were, despite concerted jamming campaigns, tuning in to Western stations. It was especially galling that the devotees of foreign radio were younger and better educated than average – precisely the section of the population that in another age would have been considered the ideological vanguard. To be sure, many of them were tuning in for music and entertainment rather than overt indoctrination, but this could often be a gateway to "hard" news and opinion.[7]

Television had the advantage that it was not so vulnerable to virtual border-crossing of this kind: One of the reasons it received so much investment from the Soviet government in the 1950s and 1960s was that it seemed so firmly national a medium. But it was also more intimate and domestic than radio had ever been; the Soviet propaganda authorities were forever preoccupied with the problem of the distracted, frivolous or generally "uncultured" viewer. Much closer to the communist ideal was the active, engaged, participatory viewer, but the problem here was how to keep the participation within prescribed limits. An outlier in communist Europe, in this as in other respects, was Yugoslavia, which in the 1960s made the mass media more dependent on advertising and introduced a higher degree of audience participation than would have been countenanced in the USSR. But even here audience activism was seen to get out of

6 Roth-Ey, *Moscow Prime Time*, 72–73.
7 Elena I. Bashkirova, "The Foreign Radio Audience in the USSR During the Cold War: An Internal Perspective," in A. Ross Johnson and R. Eugene Parta (eds.), *Cold War Broadcasting: Impact on the Soviet Union and Eastern Europe* (Budapest: Central European University Press, 2010), 109, 117–18.

hand, as demands for national autonomy threatened to pull the federation apart in the early 1970s.[8]

There was also the problem that the gap between design and implementation was perhaps greater in the field of culture than in any other domain of Soviet policy. The regime might have certain ideological desiderata, but how to turn these aims into palatable form was a task that had to be turned over to the established specialists in such matters – the "creative intelligentsia" of writers, artists, filmmakers and the like. Although Stalin had in the main been successful in creating a patriotic new Soviet intelligentsia, many members of the Soviet educated elite had become more independent-minded as a result of de-Stalinization. Although most of them remained patriotic, they were getting ideas above their station, and a few were threatening to cross the line into dissent. Coercion alone would not bring the requisite propaganda material, even if it could very effectively suppress the work of Vasilii Grossman, Aleksandr Solzhenitsyn or anyone else determined to take their own course in interpreting the Soviet past and present. Ingenuity was especially required in the wake of Prague 1968, which posed more of a challenge to the propaganda agencies than Budapest 1956 (where patriotic Soviets could say that Hungarian nationalists, a mere decade after their pact with Hitler, had strung up good communists). Especially in the sensitive border regions, the Soviet authorities were dealing with a population routinely tuning in to Western broadcasts. In 1966, the Estonian authorities estimated that at peak times more than two-thirds of the population were listening to foreign (mainly Finnish) radio.[9]

Nowhere in the Eastern bloc were the teething troubles of the new medium more acute than in the GDR. This country was in uncomfortably close proximity to a powerhouse of Western liberal capitalism, as well as to the main instruments of its mass media; worse still, it shared a language and a culture with this menacing neighbor. The competition from over the border led the GDR to launch its television service in the 1950s before it had any clear sense of what to do with it: The airwaves were just another kind of "territory" in the Cold War. In 1956, television was still a second-class medium relative to radio and the press, especially in the eyes of the party propaganda apparatus. It was only after the upheavals of that year in Hungary and Poland that television was taken seriously. Tapping its

---

8 Sabina Mihelj, "Audience History as a History of Ideas: Towards a Transnational History," *European Journal of Communication* 30, 1 (2015), 22–35.
9 Amir Weiner, "Foreign Media, the Soviet Western Frontier: Accounts of the Hungarian and Czechoslovak Crises," in Johnson and Parta (eds.), *Cold War Broadcasting*, 310.

rhetorical potential became an even more urgent task with the continuing crisis over Berlin after 1958 and the consequent risk of significant loss of morale and legitimacy. One of the main innovations of those years was a crime drama series called *Blaulicht* (a flashing police light), where the open border was a regular theme: Crime was here shown to be imported rather than home-grown, smuggled in by unsavory types from the Federal Republic of Germany (FRG). Shows like this prepared the population for the abrupt closing of the border in August 1961: The Wall had already been "normalized." In the later 1960s, East German television could enter a phase of consolidation and switch to the themes of *Heimat*, hard work, family – and patriotic devotion to the state.[10]

However traumatic the effects of the Berlin Wall for the families it separated, its discursive foundations were already in place. The events of August 1968 were a bigger test of communist propaganda: This was an armed intervention that brought with it a large-scale purge of personnel and dealt a crushing blow to intelligentsia morale in Czechoslovakia and elsewhere in the bloc. For this reason, the case of post-1968 Czechoslovak "normalization" is particularly valuable for understanding the mix of hard and soft power that East European communism used to persuade both the producers and the consumers of culture of its legitimacy and viability. The first phase of normalization was, of course, a swift and decisive purge of those who had been most caught up in the reformist fervor of 1968. But the second phase was the selective readmission of the reformist intelligentsia to the party or to their profession. The regime understood that it could not hope to gain support for, or at least acquiescence in, its new course unless it could call on the services of qualified and experienced writers, editors, camera operators and so on. But for the rehabilitated liberals this was a Faustian bargain: The price for resuming their careers was participation in recantation rituals of varying degrees of severity. Even filling in a screening questionnaire placed a person in a relationship of complicity with the regime. Phase three was the most subtle: The "normalized" TV profession set about producing crime dramas and soap operas that recast 1968 as a moment of collective hysteria and showed the forces of order displaying calm, reason and decency.[11]

---

10 Heather L. Gumbert, *Envisioning Socialism: Television and the Cold War in the German Democratic Republic* (Ann Arbor: University of Michigan Press, 2014), 14, 59, 92–93, 157.

11 Paulina Bren, *The Greengrocer and His TV: The Culture of Communism After the 1968 Prague Spring* (Ithaca: Cornell University Press, 2010).

But the repercussions of 1968 were felt across the bloc. The problem was not only the reputational damage caused by the Warsaw Pact intervention but also the growing sophistication and privatization of the mass media audience. How were the authorities to avoid losing control over information management without alienating readers and viewers through tedious or palpably false newspaper articles and television programs? How were the media to be directed and policed in the post-terror era? One possible solution was to look once again for "enemies" and take the route of xenophobic "patriotism"; this was tried in Poland at the very end of the Władysław Gomułka period, which saw an ugly lurch toward anti-Semitism, and to some extent in the USSR under head of broadcasting Sergei Lapin, himself a noted anti-Semite. But a more fruitful approach, and close to a common pattern after 1970, was to project an aura of modern professionalism and thereby to cultivate the loyalty of media professionals and audiences alike. The arrival in power of Edward Gierek in Poland and Erich Honecker in the GDR brought hopes that cultural restrictions would lessen. In theory, this meant that party hegemony could be exercised in a more subtle and ostensibly consensual way: As one historian of the GDR media puts it, this would be "censorship without the censor." Yet the softer technocratic rhetoric of media management in the 1970s was belied by the reality of constant meddling by the authorities. In the GDR, for example, newspaper editors received a stream of telephone instructions and were summoned every Thursday to the Central Committee for "argumentation" briefings; they were constantly "advised" which events and topics to cover, and in what light. After 1977, with the gap between economic reality and propaganda myth widening, controls became more explicit and oppressive, and Honecker interfered more and more, especially in the main party newspaper, *Neues Deutschland*. Nonetheless, as the most impressive study of the subject concludes, it is more helpful to think of the GDR media industry in the Honecker era as an authoritarian public-relations operation than as an old-fashioned exercise in agitprop.[12]

The Soviet Union, as the region's hegemon, did not find it quite so difficult to "normalize" the post-1968 order; although the intelligentsia might (and

---

12 Tomasz Goban-Klas, *The Orchestration of the Media: The Politics of Mass Communications in Communist Poland and the Aftermath* (Boulder: Westview Press, 1994), 126–27, 133–40, 147–49; Gunter Holzweissig, *Die schärfste Waffe der Partei. Eine Mediengeschichte der DDR* (Cologne: Böhlau, 2002), 1–2, 135–36; Anke Fiedler, *Medienlenkung in der DDR* (Cologne: Böhlau, 2014), 25, 281, 289, 421.

did) grumble, the wider population had few problems coming to terms with the country's imperial domination of Eastern Europe. Nonetheless, the TV age (which largely coincided with the post-1968 era) presented palpable challenges for the Soviet propaganda industry. In its overtly experimental phase, the late 1950s and early 1960s, TV professionals had a vanguard zeal, taking on the mantle of film in the 1920s: Their imagined ancestor was Dziga Vertov, not the aging grandees of the mature Soviet culture industry. TV had a "vibrant and egalitarian atmosphere" for those working there. It had the liveness and distance-transcending immediacy that had once been the distinguishing characteristic of radio, but also an intimacy, even domesticity, that radio had always struggled to achieve. At the same time, TV retained the traditional Soviet *mission civilisatrice*, which in practice was indistinguishable from the hegemony of the intelligentsia. The signature talk-and-music show of the 1960s, *Little Blue Flame*, was set in a café and gave creative types free rein.[13]

Television certainly seems to have been an exciting place to work in the Soviet 1960s, but it still had not found a way of meeting the main demands on the mass media in the Cold War era: to avoid political indiscretion and satisfy the censors; to match the competition from punchy Western media that were becoming ever more accessible to the Soviet audience through radio broadcasts; and to find a way of enthusing, or at least not boring, the audience of mature socialism. "Live" TV had a habit of going wrong, as in the disastrous case of an early game show in 1957 that ended with the audience storming the stage and a live chicken on the loose; the vulnerability of the medium to such shenanigans made the censor's hair stand on end and left TV professionals fearful of the consequences of even minor gaffes.[14] Yet, in international comparison, Soviet media remained ponderous: the slow response time was a serious liability in the era of Radio Liberty. Finally, intelligentsia hegemony was gratifying for writers and filmmakers, but did not necessarily provide engaging viewing material for the rest of Soviet society. The new field of media sociology, and in particular the modestly staffed audience survey unit within Gosteleradio, was delivering a clear bottom line: The unified Soviet public was more than ever a myth. The Soviet Union had audiences, not an audience, and many readers, viewers and listeners did not have higher education.

13 Roth-Ey, *Moscow Prime Time*, 124–25, 226, 245.
14 For an account of the 1957 mishap, see ibid., 249.

The years 1968–70 brought a profound transformation of Soviet media culture, and TV especially.[15] On the small screen, the 1970s looked and felt very different from the 1960s. Part of the change was due to a crucial technical innovation: the shift to largely prerecorded programming, which reduced the gaffe potential of the medium to a minimum. The student comedy competition *KVN*, a signature show of the 1960s and a byword for playful improvisation, became more rehearsed and made the switch to video in 1968.[16] From 1971, the informal café conversation of *Little Blue Flame* was superseded in the festive schedule by the more hierarchical, ritualized and populist *Song of the Year*. The authoritarian Lapin reined in intelligentsia excesses, outlawed domestic bad news and insisted on more stories featuring model workers.[17]

A long line of disaffected memoirists has commented on the ossification of public culture in the Brezhnev era and on the baleful effects of Lapin's rule in particular. To a significant extent, the contemporary perception of stagnation was inscribed in the cultural products of the time. Partly it was again a matter of technology: Greyness looked so much more striking in grainy colour than in the dynamic black and white of the Khrushchev era. In the second half of the 1970s, the TV appearances of the desperately infirm general secretary, though artfully stage-managed, only provided joke fodder. But the wistful, the mundane and the unheroic were prominent in the subject matter freely chosen by 1970s filmmakers and script writers. Soviet films were now more likely to show unresolved moral quandaries, petty workplace squabbles and extramarital indiscretions. Protagonists aged palpably, and the midlife crisis was a regular visitor on the big screen. The idiocies and limitations of Soviet life were subject to (mostly) fond parody. One of the most popular films of the era featured a blind-drunk protagonist who enters an apartment block in a typically anonymous Soviet *mikroraion* (housing estate on the edge of town), taking it for his own – but not realizing he is in a completely different city.[18]

Yet, to quote the leading historian of the subject, if the post-Stalin mass media were a failure, they were "a very successful failure."[19] "Stagnation" captures something important about the 1970s, but it is a loaded word;

---

15 This is one of the main arguments of Christine Evans, *Between Truth and Time: A History of Soviet Central Television* (New Haven: Yale University Press, 2016), on which much of my account of Soviet TV in the post-1968 era relies.
16 Roth-Ey, *Moscow Prime Time*, 260.   17 Evans, *Between Truth and Time*, chs. 3–4.
18 The film is *The Irony of Fate* (dir. El'dar Riazanov, 1975).
19 Roth-Ey, *Moscow Prime Time*, 1.

"stability" and "familiarity" might be alternatives. Like TV audiences elsewhere, many Soviet people were more interested in the quotidian than the public, and were happy to swap the utopian strivings of previous eras for low-key but affecting treatments of the world they already knew. The unheroic could by now serve to bolster a sense of Sovietness.

There was a lot more to 1970s TV than Brezhnev struggling to stay upright at the podium. Media professionals recall the iron hand of Lapin as well as his personal prejudices (directed not only at Jews but also at women unsuitably attired and men with excessive facial hair). But his arrival at Gosteleradio marked an institutional elevation for broadcasting, which now had de facto ministerial status and a powerful boss: Lapin was an insider in the Brezhnev regime.[20] Nor did the Lapin era put a stop to creative innovation in the broadcast media. The evening news broadcast, *Time*, had been launched in 1968 as a way to liven up (and, above all, speed up) Soviet coverage of events. In the 1970s it continued to present much shorter news items than had been the norm before 1968. Although the treatment of domestic news remained turgid, international news had far fewer constraints (and attracted much of the journalistic talent). Game shows continued under Lapin: *KVN*, with its too-clever-by-half student contestants, was discontinued (under circumstances that gave rise to dark suspicions about anti-Semitism) and replaced by shows more obviously directed at the working class. Yet in 1977 Soviet TV launched a new show, *What? Where? When?*, in which a team of markedly intellectual "experts" sat round a casino table and attempted to answer riddles sent in by the viewers, all this accompanied by jazzy live music. It would be hard to imagine a TV spectacle less congruent with the Soviet propaganda mission as conventionally construed.[21] At the same time, filmmakers were entirely giving up on their earlier ambition to combine moral and intellectual uplift with the mass audience: The cinema industry of the 1970s wholeheartedly embraced genre films and was bankrolled by smash hits with titles like *Pirates of the Twentieth Century*.[22]

But the greatest popular successes of the Soviet mass media in the 1970s came in the field of TV drama. The 1970s saw the flowering of the Soviet mini-series. The most successful example of the genre was *Seventeen Moments of Spring* (first broadcast in August 1973), which showed the capacity of the mature Soviet media to offer something for everyone. The series was an impeccable Cold War product: Set in Berlin in the last

20 On the semi-mythical figure of Lapin, see ibid., 217–22.
21 Evans, *Between* Truth *and* Time, chs. 6–7.
22 On the move to genre films, see Roth-Ey, *Moscow Prime Time*, 62–63.

days of World War II, it concerned the efforts of a Soviet spy to foil a plan by the Germans to agree a separate peace with the United States, thus preventing the Soviet takeover of East-Central Europe. Yet, with its melancholy protagonist, its longueurs and its loving depiction of "Western" life, the series could hardly be said to have pursued the theme of American treachery with the dedication it deserved. *Seventeen Moments* immediately became cult viewing for intelligentsia sophisticates, but it drew in most other groups in Soviet society as well.[23]

Thus, the notion of decline and ossification in Soviet media of the 1970s will not do. It has been fostered above all by the memoirs of the creative intelligentsia, who did indeed lose much of the cultural clout they had enjoyed in the early days of TV. In fact, television got more, not less, sophisticated in the Lapin era. That is not to say that it became unsocialist, or that it ever fully resolved the conflicting demands of ideology and entertainment. Soviet news was still boring, and newspeak was rife. But the medium had by now become more interesting than the message. The entertainment function was acknowledged as crucial by media professionals and government officials alike. Programming adopted the "layer cake" principle: A heavy slab of ideology had to be accompanied by the whipped cream of populism if it were to be digested by the audience. More importantly, the TV schedule fostered the "routinization of life" in mature industrial society. In the USSR and the GDR as in Britain or the United States, television set many of the parameters of life, both acknowledging and reinforcing an orientation to the less overtly political concerns of family, consumerism and the workplace; contrary to myth, most East Germans did not spend their time watching West German television (at least not until 1989, when the inability of communist media to make satisfactory sense of fast-moving events finally proved a clinching liability).[24] Even Yugoslavia, untethered to Soviet orthodoxy, whose media were unusually rambunctious in the 1960s, reined in the open-ended formats and audience participation in the 1970s, opting instead for fond depiction of small-town life, national myths and "safe" humor. The "retreat into privacy" seems to have been a pan-European, not just a Soviet or bloc-wide phenomenon.[25]

23 In addition to Evans, *Between* Truth *and* Time, ch. 5, see Stephen Lovell, "In Search of an Ending: *Seventeen Moments* and the Seventies," in Gorsuch and Koenker (eds.), *The Socialist Sixties*, 303–21.

24 Gumbert, *Envisioning Socialism*, 159, 161.

25 Mihelj, "The Politics of Privatization," 261, 263.

Television was certainly a special case, as the newest and most dynamic of the mass media. But similar debates on how to acknowledge audience tastes while upholding and promoting Soviet values took place in the more staid print media. Politizdat, ostensibly the most ideological publishing house in the USSR, which had been entrusted with publication of the canonical works of Stalinism and was rewarded with enormous print runs, launched in the late 1960s a new series of biographies of "fiery revolutionaries" with the aim of revitalizing its profile. Message was no longer to come at the expense of literary panache: "Stylistic sophistication" was deemed a prerequisite for books in the series. Editors and internal reviewers debated at length the balance to be struck between inventiveness and documentary accuracy, and between the private and public dimensions of the subjects' lives. In due course, the authors in the series would include such quintessentially post-Socialist Realist names as Okudzhava, Aksenov and Trifonov.[26]

Spurred by the Kosygin reforms, which introduced market elements into the press, Soviet journalists of the mid 1960s recognized that they could do better in attracting a readership. To improve their performance they enlisted the help of sociologists, who advised them on the real, rather than assumed nature of their audience. Many journalists were unwilling to retreat too far from the educative role that was central to their self-definition. Nonetheless, in the second half of the 1960s, there were signs of a new "sociological aesthetic" in Soviet newspapers, as the traditional Socialist Realist hero (by definition exceptional) was displaced by portraits of the statistically average representative of particular professions. Thereafter, with the weakening of market principles, Soviet journalists largely reverted to didactic type, but it had already become clear that this was a "post-heroic age."[27]

So far we have traced a common trajectory for the media of communist states in East-Central Europe: a shift from the public, the political and the forward-looking to the domestic, the traditional and the routine, and from propaganda to public relations, all of this conditioned by the rise of television. Certainly, there were significant differences between the various East

26 Polly Jones, "The Fire Burns On? The 'Fiery Revolutionaries' Biographical Series and the Rethinking of Propaganda in the Brezhnev Era," *Slavic Review* 74, 1 (Spring 2015), 32–56.
27 Simon Huxtable, "In Search of the Soviet Reader: The Kosygin Reforms, Sociology, and Changing Concepts of Soviet Society, 1964–1970," *Cahiers du monde russe* 54, 3 (2013), 623–42.

European societies and their media industries – from the technologically advanced GDR to backward Bulgaria. But for the most part these were countries with at least half a century of intensive urbanization behind them and a significant educated public. How, though, does our story change when it is forced to accommodate communism on a global scale, in particular the rise of a second communist hegemon in China in the 1960s?

The Chinese Communist Party (CCP) wasted little time in closing independent newspapers and publishers and imposing an information monopoly: a striking transformation given how commercially oriented the print media had been hitherto. It also established a propaganda bureaucracy. To this extent it clearly followed the Soviet model. As in the USSR, "propaganda" was anything but a dirty word, and many leading cadres had been closely involved in propaganda work before seizing power. The CCP had its equivalent of the Soviet Thaw in the Hundred Flowers campaign of 1956, but it abruptly reasserted control within months. Throughout these perturbations propaganda retained its pedigree: The leaders of Chinese communism had behind them two decades of intensive reflection on political tactics that were shaped by Gustave Le Bon and a global interwar debate on mass communications as well as by Soviet precedent. They also took account of the particularities of Chinese culture: its long tradition of hierarchical communication from the enlightened few to the subjected many and, more fundamentally, the more distant relationship between speech and writing than obtained in European cultures. If Bolshevik propagandists in the 1920s could tell themselves that their jargon would be understood by a mass newspaper-reading audience, no such delusions could be entertained by Chinese communists as they contemplated their overwhelmingly rural population and the formidable barriers to anything more than functional literacy in Mandarin. From the beginning, the Chinese propaganda system was unusual for the amount of information that it spread outward from the center by word of mouth. The Chinese communists did not make the same distinction as the Soviets between "propaganda" and "agitation."[28]

The CCP also had a different relationship to its intellectuals from its European counterparts. Certainly, the Bolsheviks were selective or ambivalent in their approach to the legacy of the Russian intelligentsia: They wanted its commitment to serve, not its oppositional sentiment. But from the mid

---

28 Nicolai Volland, "The Control of the Media in the People's Republic of China," Ph.D. dissertation (University of Heidelberg, 2003).

1930s a Soviet intelligentsia was deemed to be in existence, and for the most part it enjoyed high social prestige and a well-developed self-esteem.[29] By the mid 1960s, East European intelligentsias were swelling both in size and in their sense of their own dignity. Soviet journalists had a strong notion of themselves as agents of critical thinking and social, even moral improvement.[30] A similar professional ethos formed among Polish journalists in the 1950s and 1960s; its strength would be demonstrated in the early 1980s, when more than a third of the profession actively resisted the imposition of martial law.[31] In China, by contrast, intellectuals as a class were viewed with grave suspicion by Mao Zedong. Even if they were fully committed to serving the party, they did so in a cerebral and bureaucratic manner that was at odds with the Leader's charismatic authority.[32] From the very beginning, Mao had been acutely conscious of the unsophisticated character of the mass audience, emphasizing simple, inspiring slogans and visual material in preference to Marxist theory.[33] The formative Rectification Movement of the early 1940s, the ideological launchpad for the communist bid for power, had drummed into intellectuals that they must keep in mind the "mass" character of the audience when writing for the press. Ideas were to be generated by Mao and reinforced in study sessions, not developed or embroidered by a caste of intellectuals.[34]

Largely because it was willynilly staffed by intellectuals with arcane knowledge, the Propaganda Department was a significant casualty of the Cultural Revolution. But the alternative was hardly compatible with the long-term authority of the party: The red guard press, much as it tried to be more Maoist than Mao, was chaotic and practically unpoliceable.[35] The propaganda professionals made a creeping comeback over the following decade, presiding over an ideological order of striking rigidity. The "master texts" of the

29 The two main studies of the subject differ on many things but not on this point: See Vladimir Shlapentokh, *Soviet Intellectuals and Political Power: The Post-Stalin Era* (Princeton: Princeton University Press, 1990), and Vladislav Zubok, *Zhivago's Children: The Last Soviet Intelligentsia* (Cambridge, MA: Belknap Press of Harvard University Press, 2009).
30 Thomas C. Wolfe, *Governing Soviet Journalism: The Press and the Socialist Person After Stalin* (Bloomington: Indiana University Press, 2005).
31 Curry, *Poland's Journalists*.
32 For the case study of one prominent intellectual servant of Chinese communism who eventually fell victim to its anti-intellectualism, see Timothy Cheek, *Propaganda and Culture in Mao's China: Deng Tuo and the Intelligentsia* (Oxford: Oxford University Press, 1997).
33 Chan-tai Hung, *Mao's New World: Political Culture in the Early People's Republic* (Ithaca: Cornell University Press, 2011).
34 Volland, "The Control of the Media," ch. 2.   35 Ibid., ch. 7.

CCP had to be followed slavishly. Even during the Cultural Revolution, at least after its chaotic initial phase, local agencies were issued with lists of exactly which individuals were subject to criticism, and exactly what degree of vitriol should be directed at them. At more stable moments, the party elite devoted enormous attention to the semantic minutiae of their pronouncements, and expected these to be repeated to the word. Paraphrase was prohibited, while slips of the tongue were severely punished.[36]

The paradox was that this slavish literalism was achieved with a much smaller censorship bureaucracy than in the USSR. Even when it recovered from the depredations of the 1960s, the Propaganda Department never had a staff of more than 500. Formal prepublication censorship was applied only to a handful of central newspapers and books on a limited number of sensitive topics. For everything else, communist China operated a "responsibility system," passing the burden to editors and to the authors themselves. Not only was this arrangement far cheaper than the overcontrolling Soviet system, it also seems to have been more effective in suppressing undesirable content.[37] Conversely, the PRC seems to have gone even further than Soviet-style communist states in controlling access to information: The population was segregated according to what it was permitted to know, with the result that any Chinese public sphere was at best "highly fragmented."[38]

But for all the virtuosity they displayed in managing the internal production, distribution and use of information, the acid test of communist media and propaganda agencies was how well they fared in the international rivalry that defined the era. Despite the best efforts of communist censorship, information was crossing borders to an unprecedented extent – mainly through radio listening. Could Soviet media give their audience enough to withstand the siren call of Radio Liberty? Could China keep its master texts intact when globalized and audiovisual media were writing their own script?

In fact, communist thinking on media and propaganda had always been shaped by an awareness of Western developments – whether the growth of broadcasting infrastructure in the 1920s–30s or the emergence of public opinion research in the same era. Harold Lasswell taught briefly in China in 1937, and budding Chinese propagandists followed the Dewey–Lippmann

---

36 Michael Schoenhals, *Doing Things with Words in Chinese Politics: Five Studies* (Berkeley: University of California Press, 1992).
37 Volland, "The Control of the Media," ch. 4.   38 Ibid., 217.

debate.[39] By the mid Cold War era, Soviet media professionals were not shy in borrowing broadcasting knowhow from the West, whether the prime-time schedule or the round-the-clock music and news channel (known in the USSR as Maiak, and launched in 1964). The impression from the internal documentation of Gosteleradio and the Central Committee Department of Agitation and Propaganda is that the Soviet authorities were in reactive mode much more of the time than they would have cared to admit publicly. They anxiously monitored the extent of foreign radio listening. They made sure to put out their own most attractive programming at the times Soviet people might be most tempted to tune in to Voice of America. And of course they jammed.

How much this undermined communist rule in Eastern Europe is hard to say. Soviet citizens did not, on the whole, become dissidents by listening to Western radio. They could value foreign stations for their rock music and breaking news while still trusting their own government on its core ideological territory of state patriotism and social justice. East German viewers and listeners seem to have regarded the West German media as no less ideological than their own.[40] What does seem clear, however, is that communist propaganda in the other direction was of limited efficacy. The message put out by the GDR's Deutschlandsender, for example, was too much at variance with the experience of people in the FRG to have much effect beyond Western communists.[41] Ironically, the most successful external propaganda operation of the GDR was its domestic media system, which was defined by the imperative to keep up appearances for the West. Yet, while the optimistic account it gave of the East German economy may have helped to sustain a large foreign currency debt, the domestic population was not so easily fooled. By the mid 1980s, East Germans were rapidly losing trust in their media, finding no satisfactory treatment of the social and economic problems they saw around them.[42]

China had always been prepared to draw on the West as well as the Soviet model. Especially after 1968, there was no question that Beijing

39 Mareike Svea Ohlberg, "Creating a Favorable International Public Environment: External Propaganda (*Duiwai Xuanchuan*) as a Global Concept with Chinese Characteristics," Ph.D. dissertation (University of Heidelberg, 2013), 52, 54. In the 1920s, Walter Lippmann and John Dewey conducted a debate on the capacity of the democratic public for rational deliberation, with Lippmann taking the more skeptical view.
40 Gumbert, *Envisioning Socialism*, 159.
41 Klaus Arnold, *Kalter Krieg im Äther: Der Deutschlandsender und die Westpropaganda der DDR* (Münster, Germany: LIT Verlag, 2002).
42 Fiedler, *Medienlenkung in der DDR*, 324–25.

thought it had more to learn in propaganda terms from Washington and London than from Moscow. In the late 1970s, the prestige of external propaganda began to rise, as the Chinese authorities recognized the importance of projecting a positive image, both to secure foreign investment and to compete effectively with the sophisticated weapons employed by the other side; the US Information Agency saw its budget rise sharply early in the Ronald Reagan era. There was some cautious opening to Western radio and TV channels; more proactively, the English-language *China Daily* was launched in 1981 (with the articles written directly in English, not translated from Chinese); the pregnant phrase "national image" entered the discourse of the *People's Daily* in 1982. In this period, external propaganda was acting as the vehicle for a more responsive propaganda concept that took greater heed of the concerns of the audience. When Sino-American relations soured from 1982 onwards, the main propaganda target once again became the Third World rather than the West; student demonstrations of December 1986, for which hostile Western propaganda was blamed, clinched a turn away from external propaganda to the traditional focus of domestic propaganda. But the underlying principle – that it was a core mission of the CCP to project the image of a powerful and economically thriving state – lived on when China recovered from the turbulence of the late 1980s. External propaganda was identified as China's "weak link" in the early 1990s, and the mass media set about creating an aura of China as great power. Aiming to break the "Western public opinion monopoly," the Chinese authorities took up some cutting-edge political technologies. *China Daily* launched an online edition in 1995 (before the general public even had access to the internet), and in 1998 the Propaganda Department was renamed the Central Publicity Department. By the end of the decade China had achieved gratifying foreign-policy successes and seemed well on the way to the international recognition it craved. How much this was due to the more favorable "public opinion environment" created by external propaganda, rather than to Western *Realpolitik* and economic self-interest, is unclear. But the Publicity Department unquestionably rose in status as a result.[43]

The case of China reminds us that, for the sprawling, displaced, multi-ethnic and agrarian societies that Russia was in 1917 and China in 1949,

---

43 Ohlberg, "Creating a Favorable International Public Environment," in particular 232–33, 297–98, 320, 331, 337.

communism was above all a nation-building project. But by the last third of the twentieth century, however isolationist the instincts of the political class, that project could not be pursued in a narrowly "national" setting. Thanks above all to the increasingly globalized mass media, patriotism had to be at least a touch cosmopolitan. Propaganda was essential both for gaining the patriotic allegiance of the population at home and (when directed externally) for gaining international recognition as a major power. Even domestic propaganda had to take account of the rising education and sophistication of the audience, as well as its craving for entertainment, rapid response and information about the wider world. New technologies, above all the internet, made unviable preliminary censorship and even narrowly prescriptive agenda-setting of the traditional communist kind. In China, the scale and speed of media growth were indeed breathtaking. TV ownership rose from a negligible level at the start of the reform era in the late 1970s to more than 80 percent of households in 1996; the number of licensed broadcasting stations rose over the same period from 32 to 880, most of them regulated in the regions, not the center. Television advertising, an innovation of the early reform era, had become a worrying free-for-all in the 1990s, with many journalists crossing the line into corruption by accepting payment for favorable coverage of particular enterprises or provincial administrations. No wonder, in light of facts like these, that one scholar at the end of the millennium could write of the "crumbling" of the propaganda state, and of a "'public-sphere praetorianism,' a condition in which neither the state nor any other organized political force can impose order and purpose upon the initiation and circulation of society's communications messages."[44]

Yet, with the benefit of hindsight, we can say that the post-1989 period brought a renaissance, not a withering, of the propaganda state. Western apprehensions of Chinese "soft power" may be somewhat exaggerated: Old habits die hard, and Chinese propaganda for foreign consumption still suffers from a credibility deficit. But domestically the PRC has embraced to striking effect the techniques of public relations and what the Russians call *polittekhnologiia*.[45] From the 1990s onwards, soap operas have promoted a Chinese version of post-1989 "normalization." Commercialized populism in the press, far from undermining party hegemony, seems to dovetail

---

44 Daniel C. Lynch, *After the Propaganda State: Media, Politics, and "Thought Work" in Reformed China* (Stanford: Stanford University Press, 1999), 2, 9, 141.
45 The main argument of Anne-Marie Brady, *Marketing Dictatorship: Propaganda and Thought Work in Contemporary China* (Lanham, MD: Rowman & Littlefield, 2008).

nicely with self-assertive nationalism under the communist aegis.[46] Nor has the internet presented much of a threat to CCP dominance. The authorities have efficiently shut off the flow of information on topics that concern them (Taiwan, Tibet, democracy, dissidents) both by setting up firewalls and by forbidding the main domestic news portal (Sina.com) from generating its own reports on foreign news or even providing links to foreign news sites. But that still leaves many regions of the internet – human-interest stories, economic news, even pornography – that the authorities are largely content to leave in peace. The party is now confident enough not to micromanage the media, retaining for itself the right to intervene decisively whenever it sees fit but recognizing that to exercise that prerogative more often than necessary would be a sign more of weakness than of strength. In 2003, a historian surveying the entire trajectory of the Chinese system of propaganda was struck above all by the "substantial gain in self-confidence of the CCP" in the 1990s.[47]

In 1917, no one could have said for sure that communism, an ideology and political formation made by men soaked in newspaper ink, would be capable of adapting to the more diversified and individualized media of an audiovisual age. Radio and television drew the Soviet Union and the later communist states into a degree of competition and interaction with liberal Western media that was quite unthinkable in the age of print. The experience shaped communism profoundly. In several obvious ways, the comparison with Western media was not advantageous to the communist states: Their American, British and West German counterparts were better funded, more engaging, more entertaining and much faster in responding to events. The Soviet and East European media industries were forced into the most sincere form of flattery: They borrowed genres, styles and formats, most obviously in the introduction of a 24-hour music channel on Soviet radio in 1964. When the Soviet system became vulnerable (mainly because of political choices made by the top leadership in 1987–89), radio and television quickly became agents of disintegration. The parliamentary goings-on in the Congress of People's Deputies in 1989 made clear to the Soviet viewer that the party was no longer sovereign, while the last-ditch coup of August 1991 was much harder to sustain when the camera drew attention to Gennadii Yanaev's trembling hands. But

---

46 This I take to be the main implication of Yuezhi Zhao, *Media, Market, and Democracy in China: Between the Party Line and the Bottom Line* (Urbana: University of Illinois Press, 1998).

47 Volland, "The Control of the Media," ch. 10 (quotation from p. 580).

media were more a symptom than a cause of the decline of Soviet power. In China, a state where the communist regime clung firmly to the reins, radio, television and even the internet continued to function quite effectively as tools of hegemony. And, although communism "collapsed" in the Soviet Union, here too it is as easy to see continuity as rupture. Much is said about the KGB past of Putin, but another Soviet legacy seems just as pertinent: The foundations of Russia's "managed democracy" of the early twenty-first century were laid in the years of "developed socialism," which were also the years of maturity of the Soviet media industry.[48] Well before 1991, the class-based ideology of communism was mutating into the nation-based ideology of patriotism, and the mass-mobilizatory ethos of earlier Soviet propaganda was giving way to a more subtle mode of persuasion: one that acknowledged the viewer as an individual and adopted an informal, at times even playful tone, while carefully circumscribing the field of conceivable political action.

Bibliographical Essay

The best all-round study of the Soviet media industry is Kristin Roth-Ey, *Moscow Prime Time: How the Soviet Union Built the Media Empire That Lost the Cultural Cold War* (Ithaca: Cornell University Press, 2011). The important story of Soviet TV in its heyday is told in Christine Evans, *Between* Truth *and* Time: *A History of Soviet Central Television* (New Haven: Yale University Press, 2016). On the earlier medium of broadcasting, see Stephen Lovell, *Russia in the Microphone Age: A History of Soviet Radio, 1919–1970* (Oxford: Oxford University Press, 2015). Another branch of the post-Stalin culture industry forms the subject of Thomas C. Wolfe, *Governing Soviet Journalism: The Press and the Socialist Person After Stalin* (Bloomington: Indiana University Press, 2005).

Useful studies of other media systems in communist Eastern Europe include Tomasz Goban-Klas, *The Orchestration of the Media: The Politics of Mass Communications in Communist Poland and the Aftermath* (Boulder: Westview Press, 1994), Jane Leftwich Curry, *Poland's Journalists: Professionalism and Politics* (Cambridge: Cambridge University Press, 1990), Gertrude Joch Robinson, *Tito's Maverick Media: The Politics of Mass Communications in Yugoslavia* (Urbana: University of Illinois Press, 1977),

48 For more extensive reflections on the continuities, see Evans, *Between* Truth *and* Time, "Epilogue."

Heather L. Gumbert, *Envisioning Socialism: Television and the Cold War in the German Democratic Republic* (Ann Arbor: University of Michigan Press, 2014), Anke Fiedler, *Medienlenkung in der DDR* (Cologne: Böhlau, 2014), and Paulina Bren, *The Greengrocer and His TV: The Culture of Communism After the 1968 Prague Spring* (Ithaca: Cornell University Press, 2010).

The international perspective on communist media and culture is explored in a number of chapters in Anne E. Gorsuch and Diane P. Koenker (eds.), *The Socialist Sixties: Crossing Borders in the Second World* (Bloomington: Indiana University Press, 2013). On the challenge from abroad to communist broadcasting, see Michael Nelson, *War of the Black Heavens: The Battles of Western Broadcasting in the Cold War* (Syracuse: Syracuse University Press, 1997). For a more detailed collection, see A. Ross Johnson and R. Eugene Parta (eds.), *Cold War Broadcasting: Impact on the Soviet Union and Eastern Europe* (Budapest: Central European University Press, 2010).

On China, Nicolai Volland offers an excellent historical study of the CCP's "media concept'" in his Ph.D. dissertation, "The Control of the Media in the People's Republic of China" (University of Heidelberg, 2003). Michael Schoenhals, *Doing Things with Words in Chinese Politics: Five Studies* (Berkeley: University of California Press, 1992), is an illuminating study of the discursive rules of the game in communist China. The best place to start on more recent developments is Anne-Marie Brady, *Marketing Dictatorship: Propaganda and Thought Work in Contemporary China* (Lanham, MD: Rowman & Littlefield, 2008).

15

The Zones of Late Socialist Literature

POLLY JONES

The late socialist period across almost all of the Eastern bloc (except Romania and Albania) was unique for the coexistence and competition of three publishing industries: officially published literature, or gosizdat; samizdat, or literature printed or hand-typed, and distributed domestically outside official publishing because its style or content contradicted Socialist Realism; and tamizdat, texts by residents of socialist countries but first published outside the Eastern bloc, again usually because they flouted state doctrine.[1] All three types of publishing existed before the 1960s: Russian samizdat could trace its roots far back before the revolution, tamizdat scandals had occasionally erupted earlier in Soviet history, and socialist literature had already been firmly institutionalized, into its third decade on the Western fringes of the bloc and approaching its half-century in the Soviet Union. Throughout the late socialist period, the volume of samizdat and tamizdat never threatened to exceed the vast print runs and powerful publicity machine of gosizdat. Yet never before had socialist literature faced such competition for readers and critical prestige, and never had writers been faced with a genuine, if risky, choice of multiple "zones" through which to reach readers. The effects of this new publishing diversity were profound in terms of socialist literary institutions, identities and policies.

In the 1960s and 1970s, samizdat and tamizdat literature grew exponentially, producing what many Western and dissident observers saw as a gravitational shift from official literature to unofficial literature and a profound schism between these two worlds: The most politically daring, philosophically profound and aesthetically sophisticated works of East European fiction seemed now to appear in unofficial publications.[2] Yet others noted that the socialist

1 For a succinct outline, see D. Pospielovsky, "From 'Gosizdat' to 'Samizdat' and 'Tamizdat,'" *Canadian Slavonic Papers* 20, 1 (Mar. 1978), 44–62.
2 E.g. ibid.; Yurii Mal'tsev, *Vol'naia russkaia literatura, 1955–1975* (Frankfurt am Main: Posev, 1976); Abram Terts, "Literaturnyi protsess v Rossii," *Kontinent* 1 (1974), 143–90.

literary world had itself become more difficult to map, with works at its fringes and margins sharing some features with illicit publications: aesthetic experimentation, social, moral and political critique, and psychologically and ethically complex heroes. Such "grey zones" and "in-between literature" blurred the frontiers between official and unofficial publishing and thrived in many parts of the bloc, especially Hungary, Czechoslovakia and the Soviet Union, the main focus of this chapter.[3]

Late socialist culture is often mapped in complex spatial terms: the pluralization of the underground(s); living "outside" Soviet norms; "de-territorializing" ideology in public spaces; the existence of "oases" and "niches" of relative autonomy within intellectual life.[4] Yet literature, perhaps because it is so closely linked to personal freedom and (perhaps especially in Eastern Europe) imbued with a sense of moral mission, has often seemed to entail starker territorial divisions: crossing the "frontier" into samizdat and tamizdat; working either above or under ground; the impossibility of bridging two literary "worlds," one free, the other compromised aesthetically and morally.[5] Similarly, post-Stalinist writers' behavior has often been categorized into fixed "roles," from craven conformity to outright dissidence.[6]

In fact, though, such definitive choices of publishing outlets and literary identities were far from typical in late socialism. Indeed, the most strident claims about the stark divisions between official and unofficial literatures (and their associated behaviors) often issued from writers and critics who had already definitively moved into the underground, and were urging more of their colleagues and readers to do the same. However, such certainty eluded

3 E.g. Geoffrey Hosking, *Beyond Socialist Realism: Soviet Fiction Since Ivan Denisovich* (London: Granada Publishing, 1980); Deming Brown, *The Last Years of Soviet Russian Literature: Prose Fiction, 1975–1991* (Cambridge: Cambridge University Press, 1993); Nicholas Shneidman, *Soviet Literature in the 1970s: Artistic Diversity and Ideological Conformity* (Toronto: University of Toronto Press, 1979); Dennis C. Beck, "Gray Zone Theatre Dissidence: Rethinking Revolution Through the Enactment of Civil Society," *Journal of Dramatic Theory and Criticism* 23, 2 (Spring 2009), 89–109; Jiří Holý, *Writers Under Siege: Czech Literature Since 1945* (Brighton: Sussex Academic Press, 2008).
4 Alexei Yurchak, *Everything Was Forever, Until It Was No More: The Last Soviet Generation* (Princeton: Princeton University Press, 2006); Vladislav Zubok, *Zhivago's Children: The Last Russian Intelligentsia* (Cambridge, MA: Belknap Press of Harvard University Press, 2009); Edwin Bacon and Mark Sandle, *Brezhnev Reconsidered* (Basingstoke: Palgrave Macmillan, 2002).
5 E.g. Miklós Haraszti, *The Velvet Prison: Artists Under State Socialism* (New York: Basic Books, 1988); Yurii Mal'tsev, "Promezhutochnaia literatura i kriterii podlinnosti," *Kontinent* 25 (1980), 285–321, who claims that "authenticity" is absent from all officially published texts.
6 E.g. George Roseme, "The Politics of Soviet Literature," in John Strong (ed.), *The Soviet Union Under Brezhnev and Kosygin* (New York: Van Nostrand Reinhold, 1971), 176–92; Natalia Ivanova, "Nostal'iashchee," *Znamia* 9 (1997).

many of their contemporaries. For much of the 1960s and 1970s, as this chapter will argue, writers continued to move between these worlds, stretching their limits through protest against socialist institutions and literary controls, as well as through their literary texts. Indeed, the exact definition and aims of socialist literature had become somewhat unclear to officials, shaken by the ructions of the Thaw and influenced by the greater ideological pragmatism of developed socialism. Many writers' journeys into unofficial publishing were therefore prolonged, by their own uncertainties and by the inconsistent cultural policies of the authorities as they juggled concerns about rigor, readability, rival media and regime reputation. Some authors eventually journeyed further, out of the Eastern bloc and into yet another world: that of émigré publishing, with its links to Western anti-communism.

The Emergence of New Zones in the 1950s and 1960s

Socialist Realism, the official state aesthetic doctrine, was inextricably intertwined with Stalinism. It was ratified between 1932 and 1934 and was thereafter enforced through a characteristically Stalinist blend of repression with selective cooptation of older traditions and unorthodox authors and texts. Its core principle of depicting "reality in its revolutionary development" dictated optimism, celebration and emplotment of historical progress, not just in literature but in Soviet life. Literature projected the communist future while expressing the deepest urges of the Stalinist present: the desire to speed up progress toward communism; the realization of utopia; and the aestheticization of everyday life.[7] This doctrine was enforced especially stringently in the postwar Soviet Union, which was also when it was exported to the newly Sovietized Eastern bloc.

After Stalin's death, socialist cultures across Eastern Europe enjoyed "Thaws" of different temperatures and duration; late socialist literary institutions were crucially shaped by leaders' and writers' reactions to these Thaws and to their curtailment, completed by 1970 (and in some places much earlier). While the end of Stalinism had almost immediate effects in the German Democratic Republic (GDR) and Poland, for example, the region was more profoundly affected by Nikita Khrushchev's "Secret Speech" of 1956, which opened up myriad questions of central importance to the arts,

7 Yevgenii Dobrenko, *Political Economy of Socialist Realism* (New Haven: Yale University Press, 2007); Katerina Clark, *The Soviet Novel: History as Ritual* (Chicago: University of Chicago Press, 1981).

including professional autonomy, freedom to criticize and doctrinal diversity. In Poland and Hungary, in particular, it was writers who were at the forefront of these discussions and quickly pushed them beyond permissible limits. Fears of a Soviet Petofi Circle in turn drove the Soviet authorities to clamp down on the intelligentsia within months of the speech.[8] The threat posed by such literary and intellectual ferment curtailed fledgling attempts to revitalize and diversify socialist literature before they could bear much fruit. The later 1950s saw scant reform of socialist literary institutions and even at times seemed to herald a return to Stalinist persecution of writers, such as Boris Pasternak, forced to renounce the Nobel Prize and hounded by the Soviet authorities for tamizdat publication of *Doctor Zhivago* until his death in 1960.

However, the early 1960s saw renewed attempts to reform socialism and discard Stalinism, heralding new hope among the socialist intelligentsia. The Soviet Thaw was one of the shortest of the decade. Initiated by Khrushchev's return to de-Stalinization at the end of 1961, and spearheaded by the liberal literary journal *Novyi mir*, it peaked with publication of Solzhenitsyn's *One Day in the Life of Ivan Denisovich* (1962) and was already being constrained by the Soviet authorities before Khrushchev's ouster (1964). Even this "warmest" Soviet Thaw periodically froze over; when Vasilii Grossman submitted his epic historical novel *Life and Fate* to the journal *Znamia* in the early 1960s, both the editor and the party's ideological chief proclaimed it dangerously anti-Soviet and moved swiftly to destroy it, probably hastening the author's death. The first years of Leonid Brezhnev's leadership were characterized by uncertainty about state–intelligentsia relations in the new regime, gradually giving way to greater foreboding.

In Czechoslovakia, by contrast, the most important Thaw got underway in 1963 and peaked in 1967–68, with the lifting of censorship, the flourishing of extensive literary experimentation and critique (such as prison narratives and experimental youth prose) and the prominent involvement of writers and intellectuals in the Prague Spring. The latter were brought back under control only in early 1970. In Poland and Hungary, meanwhile, greater regime stability and greater awareness since the 1950s of the potentially catastrophic effects of liberalization meant that the transition from "Thaw" to late socialist "normalization" was smoother.

---

8 Polly Jones, *Myth, Memory, Trauma: Rethinking the Stalinist Past in the Soviet Union, 1953–1970* (New Haven: Yale University Press, 2013). The Petofi Circle was a Hungarian literary group that played a central role in the revolution of 1956.

The end of these Thaws of the 1960s – and with it, the dashing of hopes for a transformation of socialist literature and the socialist writer – was marked not just by the tightening of literary controls, but also by the growth of new literary institutions. In the Soviet Union, samizdat manuscripts had started to proliferate in reaction to the curtailment of the first Thaw, when harsh repressions against intellectuals in 1956–57 and the quashing of unofficial poetry readings had spurred writers to circulate documentation of these repressions, and then to found the first samizdat journals, such as *Sintaksis*, at the start of the 1960s. The first signals of Brezhnev's otherwise deliberately vague cultural policy were sent through repression of unofficial publishing, before most writers had seriously engaged in it. The landmark events signaling the end of the Thaw were the 1966 trial of Andrei Siniavskii and Yulii Daniel, for tamizdat publication of "anti-Soviet" works of literature and criticism, and the trial of Yurii Galanskov and Aleksandr Ginzburg in 1968, in part for samizdat offenses (these trials provoked political samizdat, such as the *Chronicle of Current Events*, to develop into a key forum for trial reportage). Solzhenitsyn's expulsion from Soviet literature in 1968–69 was punishment for the entwined sins of tamizdat, samizdat and political dissent, erasing memories of his brief but spectacular period of Soviet publication and acclaim earlier in the decade. The attacks on *Novyi mir* in 1969–70 only confirmed the new limits to Soviet literature and left many convinced that all outlets for Soviet publication had been closed.

In Czechoslovakia, the curtailment of the Prague Spring orchestrated around the same time as this final act of the Soviet "freeze" was more demonstrative, since the political involvement and radicalism of writers had been so much greater. Unlike the isolated Soviet signals of intolerance for literary disobedience, the Czechoslovak leadership orchestrated a massive purge of writers and literary institutions in 1969–70, expelling hundreds of writers, banning them from publication, and shutting down all literary journals. The latitude for official publications thus seemed tiny at the start of 1970, and there quickly sprang up samizdat journals and, later, samizdat publishing houses, such as Petlice and later Kvart. These would produce editions more professional and durable than anything circulated in Soviet samizdat (though the Czechoslovak network was on a much smaller scale than later Polish samizdat). By contrast, in Hungary, the initial transition to late socialism was marked by fewer demonstrative acts of repression, and by the affirmation of a certain tolerance for criticism (or "para-opposition") in official publications.[9] Samizdat here was much more limited as

9 George Schopflin, "Opposition and Para-Opposition: Critical Currents in Hungary, 1968–1978," in R. L. Tokes (ed.), *Opposition in Eastern Europe* (London: Palgrave Macmillan, 1979), 142–86.

a result, with limited circulation more typical for works that sailed close to official limits, such as the Gulag narrative of Jozsef Lengyel (*Confrontation*) and the bleak social portraiture of his fellow Hungarian, György Konrád (*The Case Worker*).

The "socialist Sixties" across the bloc were therefore varied in their intensity and duration, and in the repression used to end them and signal the dawn of a new era.[10] However, what followed the end of these Thaws was less diverse, the leaders of the bloc more unified (as they were militarily by the Brezhnev doctrine) in their desire to forestall another Prague Spring and catastrophic reverberations across the region. Normalization under János Kádár and Gustáv Husák, and "stability of cadres" and "developed socialism" under Brezhnev, all bespoke a desire to abandon hectic reforms while stemming any overt dissent before it could spread, as it had in 1968; writers and artists were viewed as a particular threat in this regard.

These policies could seem impossibly restrictive, making unofficial publishing the only viable option; the Soviet satirist Vladimir Voinovich observed that such restrictions were far more onerous for talented writers than for mediocre ones.[11] Conversely, though, they could be embraced or at least exploited, especially where the authorities sought to entice intellectuals to stay within, or reenter, official culture. The range of publishing outlets from which writers could choose – and they were diverse, as explored below – was now wider than ever before. Unofficial publishing had gained momentum and purpose from the curtailment of the limited liberalization of the 1960s, and would continue to grow and diversify throughout late socialism, but this growth saw persistent contestation over its borders, and further intersections with socialist literature.

Entering and Leaving Samizdat and Tamizdat

Despite the rapid rise of samizdat and tamizdat in the late 1960s, the dawn of late socialism was notable for writers' (and indeed theater directors' and musicians') attempts to expand, or at least not to shrink, the limits of socialist culture. Memories of the recent prestige and prominence of literature in the Thaw (its frustrations rapidly forgotten) fueled a desire to keep literature socially relevant and aesthetically innovative, and to keep open the channels

---

10 Anne E. Gorsuch and Diane P. Koenker, *The Socialist Sixties: Crossing Borders in the Second World* (Bloomington: Indiana University Press, 2013).
11 Olga Matich and Michael Henry Heim, *The Third Wave: Russian Literature in Emigration* (Ann Arbor, MI: Ardis, 1984), 48.

to as wide a public as possible. Many writers therefore had little desire to retreat fully into unofficial zones and instead petitioned the authorities in the late 1960s not to narrow the sphere of official publishing any further. These petitions were more collective and confident than letters that writers, such as Mikhail Bulgakov and Yevgenii Zamiatin, had dared to send to Stalin in the 1930s; they reflected the renaissance of the intelligentsia's sense of its identity and ideals in the Thaw, and the diminished fears of persecution during this "vegetarian," post-terror phase of cultural policy.

Collective writer protests greeted the Siniavskii–Daniel trial and the persecution of Solzhenitsyn, for instance, while the tightening of censorship occasioned a flurry of criticisms around the Third Writers' Union Congress in 1967, led by Solzhenitsyn but embraced by an eclectic range of writers including Georgii Vladimov and Vladimir Voinovich. More broadly political concerns also animated the liberal wing of the Soviet literary profession: In the late 1960s, writers including Solzhenitsyn, Lidiia Chukovskaia and Roy Medvedev wrote to the authorities to condemn censorship, stealthy bans on publication and a growing ideological conservatism for stifling public expression, fostering the spread of "lies" in official media, and fueling the growth of alternative publication outlets.[12] These protests, straddling aesthetic, social, political and moral concerns, were the closest equivalent to the writer Ludvík Vaculík's "Two Thousand Words" manifesto of 1968, which warned of the dawning of a more repressive era under a new Czechoslovak leadership.[13] Such open (if not exactly public) protest expressed writers' desire to continue the civic mission of the Thaw. Though these hopes were dashed, they nevertheless constituted the first signs of the emergence of a "parallel" or second public sphere in Eastern Europe, one more rooted in unofficial publishing and private socializing than ever before.

Despite the increasingly bleak outlook, the majority of writers of the period still sought publication in official venues rather than in the fledgling networks of samizdat and tamizdat. Indeed, late 1960s Soviet petitions against censorship and ideological dogmatism were often inspired by evidence of unexplained decisions to publish texts that would have seemed socialist (realist) only a few years earlier. This period represented the peak of unwilling migration of works into samizdat and/or tamizdat after prolonged attempts at official publication, as editors operated heightened "vigilance"

---

12 Leopold Labedz (ed.), *Solzhenitsyn: A Documentary Record* (Harmondsworth, UK: Penguin Books, 1972).

13 "Two Thousand Words," in Jaromír Navrátil (ed.), *The Prague Spring 1968: A National Security Archive Documents Reader* (Budapest: Central European University Press, 1998).

for lingering signs of the Thaw agenda and for contamination from the nearby Prague Spring. Among these thwarted authors in the Soviet Union were writers as diverse as Solzhenitsyn (*Cancer Ward*), Aleksandr Bek (*The New Appointment*), Aleksandr Tvardovskii (*By Right of Memory*), Konstantin Simonov (*100 Days of War*) and Vladimir Voinovich (*Chonkin*). The delays surrounding such texts meant that their manuscripts often started to circulate widely as samizdat, or appeared in tamizdat, even before the final decision on publication was reached, as happened with several of Solzhenitsyn's novels, for example.

However, this flux between the three types of publishing was not a purely transitional phenomenon. In the 1970s, too, writers often published in both official and unofficial outlets, because of failed publication attempts, but also due to their increasingly confident sense of what was suitable for each outlet, and of the ways in which the different "zones" of literature could be played off against one another to keep writers' identities unstable and to prolong their official (and more lucrative) publication careers. For example, Vasilii Aksenov continued to publish his works sporadically in Soviet outlets almost to the end of the 1970s, but his main project of the decade was the experimental novel about the intelligentsia and the Gulag, *The Burn*, which circulated in samizdat and tamizdat. Aksenov's contemporaries Anatolii Gladilin, Georgii Vladimov and Vladimir Voinovich likewise shifted back and forth between official and unofficial publishing for much of the 1970s. Writing for mainstream Soviet publications was a way to squeak their more marginal literary works into print and also helped to shield them from the harshest punishment for unofficial publishing (as well as from penury), at least until the authorities realized the extent of their underground activities.

Others stayed at the margins. Perhaps the most widely disseminated "greyzone" literature across the Eastern bloc was guitar poetry; the later rise of rock music in the 1970s and 1980s, which competed with guitar poetry but never eclipsed it, was a more clearly underground phenomenon. Drawing on the traditions of prison songs and lyric romance, influenced by Western folk music and rejecting the bombastic tone of Soviet mass song, the guitar songs of Bulat Okudzhava, Vladimir Vysotskii and Aleksandr Galich – and of countless less famous socialist "bards" – became the ubiquitous soundtrack to apartment parties and "wild tourism" in the 1960s and 1970s. The technology for copying songs on to cassettes (magnitizdat) was more widespread and harder to police than the typewriters of samizdat. The often minor-key music, amateur recording techniques and intimate lyrics of guitar poetry were all key to its success, creating a sense of authentic performance and communication.[14]

Of the three most famous Soviet bards, Okudzhava's publishing career was the most hybrid, his historical novels (see below) published in large print runs in the 1970s, but his guitar poetry at best tolerated and at worst banned for its preoccupation with marginal identities and un-Soviet emotions. Vladimir Vysotskii never received official recognition, despite being the biggest bard celebrity of all, his rough, passionate style of delivery as important to the cult around him as his confessional, sometimes allegorical lyrics. He was never fully defined as mainstream or dissident, yet survived on the margins of official culture (including work at the liberal edge of Soviet theater, the Taganka) for a remarkably long period until his death in 1980. Aleksandr Galich, meanwhile, illustrates that guitar poetry in its more politicized form could not endure on the margins. Instead, his caustic songs about Stalinism and Soviet hypocrisy led inexorably to performance bans by the end of the 1960s, exclusive use of samizdat and magnitizdat for song distribution and, by 1974, emigration (he died the same year).

Some writers, of course, wrote exclusively for samizdat, having given up entirely on official outlets by or even before the dawn of late socialism. Ludvík Vaculík found that publication of his works was possible only when socialism (and socialist literature) had been pushed to the limit: During the Prague Spring, his novel *The Axe* (1967) caused a sensation with its frank depiction of a journalist persecuted for attempting to report a suicide. That same year, he was expelled from the party, and the end of the Prague Spring then stoked his political activism while pushing his literary works definitively underground. His novel *The Guinea Pigs* (1970) started his career in samizdat (and initiated the Petlice publishing initiative) with a deeply sinister and suggestive meditation on cruelty and corruption. By the end of the 1970s, he had become so steeped in the culture of the Czechoslovak underground that he published a samizdat novel, *The Dream Book*, dramatizing samizdat and dissent. A similar trajectory from short-lived socialist publication to a total embrace of unofficial culture can be traced in the career of Vaculík's contemporary and frequent collaborator, Václav Havel. Their rapid move into samizdat went hand in hand, in the 1970s, with the evolution of the authors' position on "dissent" and the "parallel polis,"

---

14 Martin Daughtry, "'Sonic Samizdat': Situating Unofficial Recording in the Post-Stalinist Soviet Union," *Poetics Today* 30, 1 (2009), 27–65; Rachel S. Platonov, *Singing the Self: Guitar Poetry, Community, and Identity in the Post-Stalin Period* (Evanston, IL: Northwestern University Press, 2012).

culminating in the drafting of the Charter 77 petition and other seminal texts on dissent.[15]

In the Soviet Union, thanks to the longer and more tortuous development of cultural politics, there were fewer artists with such a clear-cut identification with unofficial culture. The author Venedikt Yerofeev was unusual, not only in exclusively publishing in samizdat, but also in viewing it as a way of "dropping out" from both socialism and politicization; his *Moscow to the End of the Line* (1969–70) was hailed for its carnivalesque irreverence, its sprawling, inebriated anecdotes and its ingenious and erudite intertextuality, representing a summation of intelligentsia underground culture. Its appearance in samizdat, its pages fragile and typesetting unprofessional, enhanced the sense of an authentic voice emerging entirely outside official publishing.[16]

However, others used samizdat and tamizdat to pursue more politicized agendas, exhibiting crossover with nonliterary samizdat such as the *Chronicle of Current Events*. Illustrative is Siniavskii (also known as Abram Tertz), whose trial and Gulag imprisonment were major preoccupations of political samizdat, and whose texts (ranging from polyphonic Gulag narratives to irreverent studies of Pushkin) appeared in literary samizdat and tamizdat throughout the 1970s and 1980s. Other politicized literary samizdat and tamizdat, by Solzhenitsyn, Mark Popovskii and Vladimir Maksimov, often displayed a peculiar fascination with Stalinism, one of the most taboo subjects of the 1970s and early 1980s and also one of the earliest themes to migrate into samizdat. Even writers who stayed in the Soviet fold for much longer than Solzhenitsyn had to use samizdat for their works on the topic. Georgii Vladimov's narrative of the Khrushchev-era Gulag closures, *Faithful Ruslan*, was told through the perspective of a loyal dog unable to adapt to life without "The Service," and represented not just one of the earliest samizdat works of Gulag fiction, circulating from 1964 onward, but also one of the most narratively inventive.

It is no surprise that far more politicized authors than Vladimov, such as Solzhenitsyn and Popovskii, intersected frequently with the dissident movement and political samizdat, nor that they were forced into emigration rather quickly (unlike their Czechoslovak counterparts). This political strand of samizdat has been criticized for generating not an alternative, but a mirror image, to socialist literature, retaining its politicized perspective and didacticism; what was

15 Jonathan Bolton, *Worlds of Dissent: Charter 77, the Plastic People of the Universe, and Czech Culture Under Communism* (Cambridge, MA: Harvard University Press, 2012).

16 Ann Komaromi, "The Material Existence of Soviet Samizdat," *Slavic Review* 63, 3 (Autumn 2004), 597–618.

needed, some argued, was a literature "outside" Soviet concerns (*vnesovetskaia*), rather than still fundamentally preoccupied with them.[17] Such politicization also meant that aesthetic experimentation was more limited, especially in prose works, though samizdat became the major forum for poetic innovation in the 1960s and 1970s. However, by the end of the 1970s, Soviet samizdat had matured (albeit under constant official pressure) to the point of generating a startlingly eclectic and confident body of prose and poetry, the *Metropol'* almanac. Compiled by a small team of writers including Vasilii Aksenov and Viktor Yerofeev in 1978, it brought together a deliberately broad range of writers and texts to give an "explicit, though far from exhaustive sense of the bottomless stratum of literature" now being rejected by Soviet publications, which had come to "form a kind of entire forbidden layer of national literature."[18] Through this "festive" celebration of the variety and breadth of this reluctantly unofficial literature, ranging from the songs of Vysotskii to the lyric poetry of Yevgenii Rein and the obscene stories of Yuz Aleshkovskii, the almanac evoked its impoverished opposite: the world of official literature, whose taboos by now stretched from Stalinism to sex, and where stylistic "formalism" of any kind was frowned upon.

In a similar spirit to the purportedly open petitions of the late 1960s, the almanac sought public dissemination, but was quickly suppressed by the KGB. However, even this open provocation evoked a somewhat uncertain response rather than blatant repression, targeting primarily junior participants through internal Writers' Union processes, which backfired with the refusal of famous authors, such as Aksenov, to stay within the union if the punishment went ahead. For Aksenov, the episode was the final twist in his long journey toward emigration, and he left months later, as did Aleshkovskii. While some participants, such as Fazil' Iskander, eventually salvaged a Soviet career, many other participants, such as Viktor Yerofeev, never again attempted to cross from samizdat to Soviet publication.

Policing the Zones of Literature

As the *Metropol'* episode demonstrates, mature socialism was a time when cultural controls had matured, especially in the Soviet Union, but they had also mushroomed, duplicating or contradicting each other. Writers and editors were sometimes able to exploit this bureaucratic complexity to play

17 Matich and Heim, *Third Wave*, 32.
18 Vasilii Aksenov and Viktor Yerofeev, *Metropol'. Literaturnyi al'manakh* (Moscow: Podkova, 1999).

institutions off against each other using the "telephone politics" of the period, but official literature was an oppressive and agonizingly unpredictable world.[19] Among the many instruments of control accumulated by this point were policing and surveillance, well-established bureaucratic bodies (such as the Writers' Union and the party's Department of Culture) and longstanding censorship (Glavlit, in the Soviet Union).[20] The *ex cathedra* judgements of leaders on writers and texts, characteristic of the Stalin and Khrushchev eras, were now largely supplanted by more anonymized, bureaucratized decision-making.

The least powerful of these bodies was now the censorship, increasingly viewed as fact-checkers rather than highly qualified analysts, whose decisions could be overruled. Nonetheless, the censors shored up their position some-what through cooperation with the military (which banned several "pessi-mistic" works about war) and Soviet ministries (such as the metal industry bosses who helped to ban Bek's *The New Appointment*). In some parts of the Eastern bloc, such as Czechoslovakia, there was no institutional censorship, meaning that editors were entrusted with policing the suitability of texts. In fact, even where censorship was legally enshrined, as in the Soviet Union, the role of editors in preemptive censorship grew enormously (and was privately satirized by writers as "hypercaution," or *perestrakhovka*).

By contrast to this dispersal of censorial authority, the powers of the police grew significantly in the period. In the two years after the crushing of the Prague Spring, the Czechoslovak secret police doubled in size and thereafter regularly harassed dissident and marginal writers, including Havel and Pavel Kohout. In the 1970s, especially after Yurii Andropov's appointment as police chief, Soviet writers on the margins, and especially those in contact with dissidents, were frequently searched, interrogated and intimidated by the KGB. Although officially intended as a form of "prophylaxis" to cure any incipient dissent, it often reduced writers to despair or anger, and eventually hounded many not just out of Soviet literature but out of the country, as happened with Vladimir Voinovich, Sergei Dovlatov, Georgii Vladimov and many others. After the trial of Siniavskii and Daniel, Soviet writers were rarely put on trial, however. Although the case against renegade authors was often constructed by the secret police, it would usually be heard by the Writers' Union; these internal politics aimed to keep writers inside official

19 Dirk Kretzschmar, *Politika i kul'tura pri Brezhneve, Andropove i Chernenko, 1970–1985* (Moscow: AIRO-XX, 1997).
20 John Gordon Garrard and Carol Garrard, *Inside the Soviet Writers' Union* (London: I. B. Tauris, 1990).

structures as well as to conceal disciplinary treatment from the outside world, a particular concern during détente.

By contrast, the more lenient policy that usually held sway in Hungary was punctuated by moments of demonstrative repression, such as the harassment of the Budapest School in 1973 and the 1974 trial of the writer Miklós Haraszti. The latter's offense consisted in writing a critical, allegedly anti-socialist account of factory life, *A Worker in a Workers' State* and in circulating it around friends for review while awaiting the verdict of official Hungarian publications. The author's trial, like that of Siniavskii and Daniel, witnessed a display of solidarity from writers (including György Konrád and Iván Szelényi) and a spirited defense of the socialist author's rights to criticize social inadequacies as well as to circulate a manuscript for comments without being accused of full-scale "alternative" publishing. The defense failed, and Haraszti thereafter produced exclusively samizdat and tamizdat.

The usual avoidance of blatant repression was not just out of concern for appearances; socialist authorities had a considerable stake in trying to keep writers, especially famous and talented figures, within the fold. Their public presence and publications advertised that socialist culture could generate works of high quality and cultivate prestigious writers despite the strident claims of Cold War Western media. They also, at least in theory, kept writers available to fulfill their traditional duties of propagandizing socialism and to attract readers to socialist culture and away from the increasingly alluring alternative media (in practice, though, many consumed both). In the 1960s and 1970s, the Soviet authorities increasingly recognized the importance of sophisticated, evocative and imaginative forms of propaganda in preventing the population from migrating to unofficial and often anti-Soviet media.[21] Andropov's policy as KGB chief, and later briefly as Soviet leader, aimed to encourage some intelligentsia creativity but also to keep a tight lid on anything approaching dissent, an unworkable combination. In other parts of the socialist bloc, too, new forms of propaganda were trialed, such as the involvement of prestigious writers (after recantation for the Prague Spring) in TV shows about normalization in Czechoslovakia.[22]

Given these complex dynamics of repression and cooptation, very few offenses committed by writers were enough in and of themselves to exclude

---

21 Polly Jones, "The Fire Burns On? The 'Fiery Revolutionaries' Biographical Series and the Rethinking of Propaganda in the Brezhnev Era," *Slavic Review* 74, 1 (Spring 2015), 32–56.

22 Paulina Bren, *The Greengrocer and His TV: The Culture of Communism After the 1968 Prague Spring* (Ithaca: Cornell University Press, 2010).

them from the official literary world. Many writers accumulated fat files of reports of misbehavior – ranging from petition-signing to samizdat and tamizdat publications – before being finally expelled. What the writer and dissident Lidiia Chukovskaia called "the process of exclusion" was often long, though at a certain point it became inexorable.[23] The rapid escalation of repression against figures such as Siniavskii and Daniel and Solzhenitsyn was thus atypical. Writers with less spectacular records of disobedience would often be invited to recant controversial views, to renounce foreign publication or to engage in other demeaning rituals of reinclusion in socialist literature, such as writing propagandistic works (in the Soviet Union, this notion of *sotszakaz* was widely satirized in intelligentsia circles).

In Czechoslovakia, one of the most notorious examples of such compromise was Bohumil Hrabal, who recanted on his previous reformist views and publicly affirmed his commitment to socialism in 1975, and was then allowed to publish certain works (though many continued to come out in samizdat, or in samizdat editions to compensate for censored official versions, such as his novel about the destruction of literature, *Too Loud a Solitude*). Several Soviet writers likewise spent much of the late 1960s and 1970s alternating between publication bans, as punishment for samizdat, tamizdat or association with dissidents or petition-signing, and temporary permission to publish.[24] Throughout the Brezhnev era and until his emigration to Paris in 1976, Anatolii Gladilin fell in and out of favor with editors and consequently disappeared and reappeared in Soviet publications; the same was true of Vasilii Aksenov throughout the 1970s.

To some, such rituals were no more noble than the conformity of mainstream writers. Vladimir Voinovich, having secured some time and sustenance with an official biography of Vera Figner in the early 1970s, defiantly continued to write works without a chance of Soviet publication (such as his multivolume political satire, *Chonkin*) and to sign political petitions. In 1974, he was finally expelled from the Writers' Union, though he remained in the Soviet Union until his emigration in the early 1980s. However inevitable such outcomes may seem in retrospect, the preceding negotiations at the margins of official literature played an important role in destabilizing the boundaries between official and unofficial writing and writers and in fueling "grey-zone" literature.

23 Lidiia Chukovskaia, *Protsess iskliucheniia. Ocherk literaturnykh nravov* (Paris: YMCA-Press, 1979).
24 Matich and Heim, *Third Wave*, 143.

The Challenge to Socialist Realism

Just as the core institutions of socialist literature – the Writers' Union, the censorship, party oversight – remained in place in late socialism, despite the seismic changes to the broader literary field, so too did Socialist Realism persist as the hegemonic doctrine. Yet it was widely debated in the period, as party authorities and literary critics grappled with the declining relevance of the Stalinist model and the difficulty of generating a workable literary doctrine for mature socialism. As a result, several key aspects waned in theoretical importance, and even more so in practical decision-making, shared and diluted across multiple bodies with different visions of what the doctrine now meant.

Narodnost', or popular accessibility, remained a powerful argument against formal(ist) experimentation, though this did not in fact prevent many complex narratives from appearing in official outlets, as below. However, socialist authorities now projected a more sophisticated vision of popular tastes and reading capabilities: After several decades of socialist power, the goal of cultural politics had moved beyond literacy toward literary connoisseurship. Moreover, personal improvement and pleasurable consumption were much more central to the post-Stalinist social contract, with reading one of the key embodiments of these promises.[25]

The need to show "reality in its revolutionary development," which had often meant the primacy of Romanticism over realism, was not renounced either. However, the doctrine of developed socialism, with its infinitely deferred communist future, meant that writers could legitimately focus on the present without showing that future, or even any kind of happy ending. This gradualism embedded in "developed socialism" and normalization also reduced the necessity for literature to be aggressively mobilizational or Promethean, as it had been in much of the Stalin era and in some Thaw-era works too (such as the scientist stories of Daniil Granin and Vladimir Dudintsev). The teleological thrust and hortatory tone of earlier literature now seemed to lag behind popular literary tastes, which the regime itself had helped to develop.

What was left, and most consistently enforced, was *partiinost'* (party-mindedness), always the most arbitrary element of the doctrine. In earlier periods, writers had periodically been rebuked for not showing the party leadership sufficiently (for example in Aleksandr Fadeev's *Young Guard*, and

25 Stephen Lovell, *The Russian Reading Revolution: Print Culture in the Soviet and Post-Soviet Eras* (Basingstoke: Macmillan, 2000).

Khrushchev-era "trench prose"). However, plenty of Stalin-era and post-Stalinist works were not just published, but praised, despite lacking a significant party presence. In fact, it was sometimes safer not to touch on the topic at all than to do so in a way that might attract the kind of controversy caused by Dudintsev's portrayal of corrupted party cadres in *Not by Bread Alone* (1956). By late socialism, therefore, there was ample precedent for a more capacious definition of "party-mindedness," connoting broad, if implicit, alignment with the party's goals, and the absence of criticism of the leadership. This policy automatically placed many overtly politicized works of samizdat well beyond the pale, but it generated some space to maneuver in official publications.

Social and moral criticism did not die out in late socialist literature and enjoyed a certain resurgence once the Thaws had been tamed and a doctrinal basis for developed socialism had been established, focusing on more modest and gradual, though still teleological and anti-capitalist transformation. Such criticism, sometimes not so different from that of the Thaw, could be justified, given the ever looser definition of Socialist Realism and its growing overlap with critical realism. In Czechoslovakia, published fiction began to revive traditions of social criticism within a few years of the end of the Prague Spring.[26] One of very few notable Czech writers able to pursue a socialist publication career relatively uninterrupted by the events of 1968–69, Vladimír Páral consistently explored urban alienation and moral corruption. His debut novel *Catapult*, published at the height of the Thaw in 1967, followed its young male hero on a chaotic journey through multiple marital affairs and attempts to acquire material goods and higher salaries, and ended with his death, propelled into a metal aeroplane door by his frantic motion. The novel satirized the hero's hedonism and egotism, yet also seemed sympathetic to his fundamental desire to "catapult" himself out of the banal routine of late socialist urban life. Páral's subsequent works included a five-volume examination of the alienation of modern life, told through the experience of *Homo statisticus*.

György Konrád's quasi-documentary novella, also on the theme of city life, *The Case Worker* (1969), was granted only a limited circulation and small print run in Hungary, and its author shifted into samizdat thereafter (and was banned from employment four years later). The novella was strikingly bold even for limited publication, determinedly focused on the "losers" of socialist

26 Robert Pynsent, "Social Criticism in Czech Literature of 1970s and 1980s Czechoslovakia," *Bohemia* 27, 1 (1986), 1–36.

society. The eponymous welfare-state bureaucrat absconds from the daily grind to live with a child orphaned by suicide, and returns to "normal" life and work only with great reluctance, even despair, at the end. Meanwhile, the late 1960s and 1970s Moscow stories of Yurii Trifonov, with their under-hand transactions of scarce goods and materialistic attitudes, could just about be justified as satirical contributions to the regime's delicate balancing act between increasingly consumption-based policies and the still reviled "petty-bourgeois" (*meshchanskii*) mentality, as was also true of many late Soviet films about consumerism.[27]

By contrast to these controversial representations of everyday urban life, works about rural life produced by the Soviet "village prose" movement enjoyed a relatively smooth transition from the Thaw to the early 1980s. This was partly down to the power of the Russian nationalist lobby, but also to the fact that these texts superficially aligned with socialist goals of tackling the backwardness of rural life. In fact, though, many published portrayals of the "village" portrayed it not so much as a space tragically neglected by socialist modernization, but as a fragile repository of values destroyed by such "pro-gress" elsewhere. The most striking example was Valentin Rasputin's *Farewell to Matyora* (1979), in which the building of a hydroelectric station leads to flooding and to the destruction of a sacred way of life and the moral foundations of Russia. Village prose has been likened to Stalinist Socialist Realism, in its evocation of a timeless pastoral idyll.[28] However, the apoca-lyptic time and tragic tenor of Rasputin's narrative suggested a desire to reverse, not merely slow, movement toward the "glorious future."

Many other works of published literature of the period also subverted official temporality, in different ways. Although "developed socialism" and "normalization" were modifications to the "charismatic" temporality of ear-lier socialist regimes, they maintained a fundamental forward thrust.[29] However, in many texts, the treatment of time was more complex, evoking regret and doubt rather than the triumphant unfolding of the dialectic. Yurii Trifonov's late socialist works embodied his philosophy of the "interconnect-edness" (*slitnost'*) of time periods and a poetics of retrospection and stream of consciousness. This was not fundamentally at odds with regime self-legitimation through the revolutionary past, but tended toward exploration

27 Natalya Chernyshova, *Soviet Consumer Culture in the Brezhnev Era* (London: Routledge, 2013).
28 Clark, *Soviet Novel*.
29 Stephen Hanson, *Time and Revolution: Marxism and the Design of Soviet Institutions* (Chapel Hill: University of North Carolina Press, 1997).

of guilt and regret, especially for the aging and declining male heroes in *House on the Embankment*, a Soviet literary sensation of the mid 1970s, or *The Old Man*, of the late 1970s, which both traced the present's moral decline to Stalinist and revolutionary terror. Trifonov's works appeared committed to improving Soviet morality while at the same time implying that the ethical problem lay at the heart of the regime; their multilayered, polyphonic texture concealed and complicated such interpretations, however, contributing to his impressive (though not total) success in publishing his works.

If such works staged retrospection, one of the most popular genres across the Eastern bloc, the historical novel, plunged readers directly into the past. There was nothing inherently subversive about writing about the distant past or different political systems, since late socialist regimes increasingly sought legitimacy in a broad range of predecessors. Interest in the pre-Soviet past represented one of the few points of common interest between the intelligentsia and socialist authorities, but their aims were often divergent. For many writers and readers of historical fiction, the past represented an alternative, an escape or a salutary lesson, rather than the source of an unalloyed ideal.

Some writers, such as the historian Natan Eidel'man were primarily interested in popularizing factual historical research, especially about the Decembrists. Yet, for the many literary writers who became hooked on historical research in the Brezhnev era, such investigation highlighted the psychological and ethical complexity of the past and pushed it beyond the schematic and tendentious "use" that socialist regimes made of it. Trifonov along with Yurii Davydov, another acclaimed Soviet historical novelist of the period, used novels set in the nineteenth century to explore moral and philosophical questions around political action (including terror) and ideology.

Other writers of historical fiction allegorized the socialist present and recent past. For instance, Bulat Okudzhava's interest in the Decembrists across several historical novels of the 1970s was partly rooted in parallels with the dissident movement, while Anatolii Gladilin's novel, *The Gospel According to Robespierre* (1970), drew daring parallels between French revolutionary and Stalinist terror. In other parts of the bloc, too, settings such as the Counterreformation, the Napoleonic era, the German occupation of the Czech lands and nineteenth-century Estonia were used by Jiří Šotola, Vladimír Körner, Ladislav Fuks and Jaan Kross respectively for veiled critiques of contemporary restrictions on freedoms and human rights.

Historical prose thus emerged, over the 1970s, as one of the leading genres of "Aesopian fiction." Such complex treatments of time and space are testament to the greater thematic flexibility of Socialist Realism, but they also indicate the degree to which published writing had to resort to circumlocution so as not to overstep the limits of the permissible. Some critics viewed such complex poetics as one of the key "benefits" of socialist literary controls, while others dismissed them as sad proof of the contortions and self-censorship necessary to stay within official boundaries.[30] In fact, while such complexity helped to evade charges of subversion, it also gave rise to richly polyphonic texts.

The works of Ladislav Fuks, who along with Vladimír Páral unusually managed to stay within "official" Czechoslovak literature throughout late socialism, are a case in point. Having survived the transition from the Prague Spring with his official reputation unscathed, Fuks continued to publish novels throughout the 1970s. His novel *Of Mice and Mooshaber* (1970) presented a hallucinatory picture of the eponymous heroine, mistreated by her family and fellow citizens. Mrs. Mooshaber spends her time tending graveyards, yet improbably emerges as the new ruler of her country after the popular overthrow of the ruling dictatorship, a fantasy with particular resonance after 1968. Fuks's works shared disorientating shifts of style and an uncertain grasp on reality, helping them to evade charges of subversion, but also expressing a deeper philosophy of openness.[31]

Chingiz Aitmatov, one of the most powerful and acclaimed late Soviet novelists, also exploited ambiguity and allegory to multiply interpretations of his texts. His 1980 novel, *The Day Lasts Longer Than a Hundred Years* was among the most temporally and spatially ambitious, and ambiguous, works of the period. At once the story of a Kyrgyz railway worker's attempts to preserve his culture's ancient traditions, a suggestive fable of interplanetary (non)communication, and a confrontation of memories of Stalinist repression, the novel spanned the ancient past, the Soviet era and the possible future of the world, while moving through Soviet space, across Cold War frontiers and beyond terrestrial space itself. Though analyzed as a creative recombination of Socialist Realist tropes from across the doctrine's long

---

30 E.g. the émigré press dispute: Mal'tsev, "Promezhutochnaia literatura," and Olga Shneerson, "Razreshennaia pravda," *Kontinent*, 28 (1981). On "benefits," see Lev Losev, *On the Beneficence of Censorship: Aesopian Language in Modern Russian Literature* (Munich: O. Sagner in Kommission, 1984).

31 Rajendra A. Chitnis, "Remaining on the Threshold: The Cunning of Ladislav Fuks," *Central Europe* 2, 1 (2004), 47–59.

history, it can also be seen as an amalgam of contemporary official and unofficial literature, including village prose, science fiction (as more famously practiced by the Strugatskii brothers) and memory fiction about Stalinism.[32] Aitmatov's interwoven but not fully resolved storylines epitomize the use of ambiguity and open-endedness to secure publication, and even critical acclaim, in the period.

To some observers, this social criticism, historical enquiry and stylistic experimentation seemed bold and even improbable: Had the editors and censors let it slip through unnoticed?[33] However, others suggested that they were not "in between" official and unofficial literature, but fundamentally complicit with the authorities, rooted in the same worldview.[34] Whatever the ultimate significance of this "grey-zone" literature, its undoubted peak across the Eastern bloc was the 1970s. In fact, though, this decade – especially its final years – also saw attrition of marginal texts and authors, whether through migration into the underground or emigration. Many Czech writers, including Kohout, Milan Kundera and Josef Škvorecký, had departed by the end of the 1970s, but Soviet emigration became especially widespread due to changed regulations on Jewish emigration and the ever more oppressive cultural restrictions in the late 1970s and early 1980s.

It is thus the early 1980s that might best be described as a time of stagnation of socialist culture, its creative forces depleted by these defections into other "zones" and its limits ever more strictly policed. Conversely, the last years before the changes of the late 1980s were a time when underground culture flourished as never before, including in Poland and Czechoslovakia. However, in the Soviet Union, émigré publishing was the main beneficiary, so large was the number of writers who had left for France, Germany, the United States and Israel.

All of these publishing worlds can be linked to the collapse of state socialism. Tamizdat publications fueled, and were fueled by, Cold War anti-communism, as the agendas of disillusioned writers chimed with the sentiments of Western publishers and readers and piled external pressure on the region. Domestically, the networks of samizdat were as important to the public sphere as the content of texts, allowing participants to imagine spaces

32 Katerina Clark, "The Mutability of the Canon: Socialist Realism and Chingiz Aitmatov's I dol'she veka dlitsia den'." *Slavic Review* 43, 4 (Winter 1984), 573–87.
33 Martin Dewhirst and Robert Farrell (eds.), *The Soviet Censorship* (Metuchen, NJ: Scarecrow Press, 1973), 17–22.
34 Mal'tsev, "Promezhutochnaia literatura."

of aesthetic and civic autonomy.[35] "Grey-zone" literature, despite its eventual decline, expressed a more flexible vision of socialist culture, while its minimal *partiinost'* suggested the increasing hollowness of official ideology. When even such limited boundary-pushing declined in the 1980s, the resulting stagnation served as a warning to revitalize socialist culture before its audience was lost entirely to alternative zones; however, in the Soviet Union, the succession of short-lived conservative leaders after Brezhnev and before Gorbachev hampered any such change.

The expansion of the limits of socialist culture and its attempted reintegration of social criticism and aesthetic creativity were fundamental to Mikhail Gorbachev's project of *glasnost'*. The rapid expansion of socialist culture across the Eastern bloc during the second half of the 1980s enticed many dissidents (such as Havel) and émigrés (such as Voinovich) back into public activities and also revitalized the careers of writers who had survived within precarious niches of late socialism (such as Sergei Zalygin and Grigorii Baklanov, who edited major Soviet journals and magazines during *glasnost'*). In literature, every taboo, from sex and drugs to criticism of Stalinism and socialism, was broken within a half-decade of reform, while the Soviet-era canon transformed equally rapidly thanks to publication of formerly prohibited works by Anna Akhmatova, Andrei Platonov, Osip Mandel'shtam, Vasilii Grossman, Aleksandr Solzhenitsyn and many others. However, socialist culture could tolerate for only so long this attempt to integrate previously separate zones, and its own foundations rapidly dissolved in the ever more radical changes of the time. The contours of the cultural map that emerged after the collapse of state socialism have proved far harder to trace than even the complex late socialist zones examined here.

Bibliographical Essay

On the institutionalization of Socialist Realism, see Katerina Clark, *The Soviet Novel: History as Ritual* (Chicago: University of Chicago Press, 1981), and Evgenii Dobrenko, *Political Economy of Socialist Realism* (New Haven: Yale University Press, 2007). Archive-based studies of the Soviet "Thaw" include: Polly Jones, *Myth, Memory, Trauma: Rethinking the Stalinist Past in the Soviet Union, 1953–1970* (New Haven: Yale University Press, 2013); Denis Kozlov, *The Readers of Novyi Mir: Coming to Terms with the Stalinist Past* (Cambridge,

---

35 Bolton, *Worlds of Dissent*; Ann Komaromi, "Samizdat and Soviet Dissident Publics," *Slavic Review* 71, 1 (Spring 2012), 70–90.

MA: Harvard University Press, 2013); Denis Kozlov and Eleonory Gilburd (eds.), *The Thaw: Soviet Society and Culture During the 1950s and 1960s* (Toronto: University of Toronto Press, 2013). On comparisons of Eastern bloc "Thaws," see Harold B. Segel, *The Columbia Guide to the Literatures of Eastern Europe Since 1945* (New York: Columbia University Press, 2003); Marcel Cornis-Pope and John Neubauer (eds.), *History of the Literary Cultures of East-Central Europe: Junctures and Disjunctures in the Nineteenth and Twentieth Centuries* (Amsterdam and Philadelphia: John Benjamins, 2004).

On the post-Stalinist intelligentsia, see Vladislav Zubok, *Zhivago's Children: The Last Russian Intelligentsia* (Cambridge, MA: Belknap Press of Harvard University Press, 2009); Boris Kagarlitsky, *The Thinking Reed: Intellectuals and the Soviet State 1917 to the Present* (London: Verso, 1989). Late Soviet cultural politics is currently analyzed mostly in memoirs and Russian-language scholarship, of which the most systematic is Dirk Kretzschmar, *Politika i kul'tura pri Brezhneve, Andropove i Chernenko, 1970–1985* [Politics and Culture Under Brezhnev, Andropov and Chernenko, 1970–1985] (Moscow: AIRO-XX, 1997). Older studies of Soviet literary institutions (John Gordon Garrard and Carol Garrard, *Inside the Soviet Writers' Union* [London: I. B. Tauris, 1990]; Martin Dewhirst and Robert Farrell [eds.], *The Soviet Censorship* [Metuchen, NJ: Scarecrow Press, 1973]) still contain valuable insights for the period. Useful overviews of Czechoslovak literary politics include Jiří Holý, *Writers Under Siege: Czech Literature Since 1945* (Brighton: Sussex Academic Press, 2008), and Milan Šimečka, *The Restoration of Order: The Normalization of Czechoslovakia 1969–1976* (London: Verso, 1984), while the normalization-era intelligentsia is analyzed in Jonathan Bolton, *Worlds of Dissent: Charter 77, the Plastic People of the Universe, and Czech Culture Under Communism* (Cambridge, MA: Harvard University Press, 2012), and Paulina Bren, *The Greengrocer and His TV: The Culture of Communism After the 1968 Prague Spring* (Ithaca: Cornell University Press, 2010). Writers' polemics against official culture include Alexander Solzhenitsyn, *The Oak and the Calf* (London: Collins and Harvill, 1980), and Miklós Haraszti, *The Velvet Prison* (New York: Basic Books, 1988).

Much valuable analysis of "official" literature appeared during and just after the period. On Soviet literature, see Deming Brown's *Soviet Russian Literature Since Stalin* (Cambridge: Cambridge University Press, 1978) and *The Last Years of Soviet Russian Literature: Prose Fiction, 1975–1991* (Cambridge: Cambridge University Press, 1993), as well as Nicholas Shneidman, *Soviet Literature in the 1970s: Artistic Diversity and Ideological Conformity* (Toronto: University of Toronto Press, 1979), and Geoffrey Hosking, *Beyond Socialist Realism: Soviet Fiction Since Ivan Denisovich* (London: Granada, 1980). The only book-length study of "Aesopian" language remains Lev Losev, *On the Beneficence of Censorship: Aesopian Language in Modern Russian Literature* (Munich: O. Sagner in Kommission, 1984). In addition to Segel, Holý and Cornis-Pope, wide-ranging accounts of Czechoslovak literature include Rajendra Chitnis, *Literature in Post-Communist Russia and Eastern Europe: The Russian, Czech and Slovak Fiction of the Changes, 1988–1998* (London: Routledge Curzon, 2005), and Robert Pynsent, "Social Criticism in Czech Literature of 1970s and 1980s Czechoslovakia," *Bohemia* 27, 1 (1986), 1–36.

Samizdat is an area of burgeoning interest, thanks to access to documents and interest in alternative public spheres: Jan C. Behrends and Thomas Lindenberger (eds.), *Underground Publishing and the Public Sphere: Transnational Perspectives* (Vienna: Lit, 2014), Ann Komaromi, *Uncensored: Samizdat Novels and the Quest for Autonomy in Soviet Dissidence* (Evanston: Northwestern University Press, 2015), and two special issues of Poetics Today, edited by Vladislav Todorov, "Publish & Perish: Samizdat and Underground Cultural Practices in the Soviet Bloc," 29, 4 (2008) and 30, 1 (2009). Tamizdat has received less attention, with the exception of the ground-breaking volumes Friederike Kind-Kovács, *Written Here, Published There: How Underground Literature Crossed the Iron Curtain* (Budapest: Central European University Press, 2014); and Friederike Kind-Kovács and Jessie Labov (eds.), *Samizdat, Tamizdat, and Beyond: Transnational Media During and After Socialism* (New York: Berghahn Books, 2013).

16

Feminism, Communism and Global Socialism: Encounters and Entanglements

CELIA DONERT

The promise of women's emancipation and equal rights under socialism exerted a powerful influence over global feminist movements during the twentieth century. Equality between men and women was central to the ideology of socialist regimes in the Soviet bloc and China, even though this aim was not always achieved in practice. By the early 1970s, when "second-wave" feminism emerged in the United States and Western Europe, women in most socialist countries enjoyed equal educational and employment opportunities, childcare facilities, access to abortion and extended maternity leave. Thus many of the demands of Western feminist movements after 1968 were already taken for granted by women living in socialist states. With the significant exception of China, where the economic reforms introduced by the post-Mao government were accompanied by the coercive and often violent one-child policy after 1979–80, the last two decades of state socialism witnessed a further expansion of measures to safeguard the social protection of motherhood and thus to boost flagging birth rates while enabling women also to work in paid employment. Despite the constraints and inadequacies of the paternalistic welfare policies implemented by socialist regimes, many women experienced the collapse of state socialism in 1989–91 as a loss of social rights as well as an era of tantalizing new freedoms, among them the possibility of establishing organizations that explicitly identified as "feminist."

This chapter explores the shifting relationship between feminism, communism and global socialism between 1968 and 1995. During this period, ideas about women's emancipation, women's rights and feminism circulated between East and West, as well as among the countries of the Soviet bloc, China and postcolonial states. The Vietnam War and the global protest movements around 1968 acted as a trigger for these transnational encounters, even though contacts between women across geographical and ideological borders could be strained and characterized by misunderstandings. Women's status in public and private life also became part of the ideological contest between governments during the Cold War.[1] International forums such as the United Nations' Decade for Women (1975–85) provided opportunities for feminist mobilization in international politics, as well as for communist regimes and postcolonial countries seeking to put forward their vision of women's emancipation in the larger context of struggles to define "equality" (of sex, as well as race and class). Ten years later, at the United Nations' Fourth World Conference on Women, held in Beijing in 1995, US First Lady Hillary Rodham Clinton gave a widely reported keynote speech in which she condemned the use of rape as a weapon of war and called for an end to gender discrimination and violence against women.[2] The speech was an implicit rebuke to the Chinese government and its denial of women's autonomy and reproductive freedom, and signaled a new era of transnational feminisms that sought to recognize "women's rights as human rights."

Recent scholarship has reignited debates about feminism, communism and global socialism with the aim of reevaluating the history of women's rights in socialist regimes vis-à-vis the achievements of Western feminism.[3] This new work has emerged in the context of the postsocialist retreat from structural solutions to the "problem of women" in favor of a liberal feminism premised on the protection of bodily autonomy. In many ways, these debates pick up on the vibrant discussions about women's emancipation under socialism that were already taking place during the Cold War. In the 1960s and 1970s, Western feminists looked for inspiration to the Soviet Union, Eastern Europe and China, seeing state socialism as both a positive and a negative example of state-sponsored women's liberation. The same was true for women's movements in the global South, whose visions of gender equality were often influenced by Maoism as well as Soviet communism. This chapter reflects upon these debates, as well as drawing on archival research and oral histories of women's experiences of state socialism that have challenged the notion that communist regimes simply imposed "emancipation" upon women, exploring instead how the social policies of post-Stalinist regimes

1 Celia Donert, "Women's Rights in Cold War Europe: Disentangling Feminist Histories," *Past & Present* 218, supplement 8 (2013), 180–202.
2 Valerie M. Hudson and Patricia Leidl, *The Hillary Doctrine: Sex and American Foreign Policy* (New York: Columbia University Press, 2015).
3 The best of this scholarship is collected in Francisca de Haan (ed.), "Ten Years After: Communism and Feminism Revisited," *Aspasia* 10 (2016), 102–68.

helped shape new gendered identities and subjectivities among socialist citizens.

Feminism and Global Socialism After 1968: Crisis and Critique

During the Prague Spring, the epicenter of the crisis within the Eastern bloc in 1968, impassioned debates about the official policy of female emancipation emerged in *Vlasta*, the Czechoslovak magazine for women. "Women's emancipation in today's meaning of the word is a complete degradation of womanhood," declared one article.[4] In the same year, the Czechoslovak Association of Women was reconstituted with a pro-reform communist at its head. The abolition of censorship created a brief opportunity for open discussion of questions about the gap between the revolutionary promises of socialism and the realities of everyday life for Czechoslovak citizens that had been simmering during the 1960s.[5] Animating these debates was a sense of frustration that the Czechoslovak state was not doing enough to implement its egalitarian ideals: Women's wages still did not match those of men, the gap between women's qualifications and their job prospects had not been closed, and investment in social services was insufficient. As a result, women were struggling to shoulder the double burden of paid work and caring responsibilities. At the same time, public discussions of women's role in socialist society registered the increasing influence of pro-motherhood and pro-family arguments advanced by experts in social policy, demography, psychology and education in post-Stalinist Eastern Europe.[6] To understand the stakes of the debate about women's emancipation in state-socialist Eastern Europe after 1968, it is necessary to situate these critiques in a longer history.

Equality between the sexes was a central element of socialist ideology. Patriarchal oppression was defined in Marxist-Leninist texts as a consequence

---

4 *Vlasta* 22 (1968), 15, cited in Denisa Nečasová, "Women's Organizations in the Czech Lands, 1948–1989: An Historical Perspective," in Hana Havelková and Libora Oates-Indruchová (eds.), *The Politics of Gender Culture Under State Socialism: An Expropriated Voice* (London: Routledge, 2014), 57–81.

5 For a brilliant analysis, see Paulina Bren, "Women on the Verge of Desire: Women, Work, and Consumption in Socialist Czechoslovakia," in David Crowley and Susan E. Reid (eds.), *Pleasures in Socialism: Leisure and Luxury in the Socialist Bloc* (Evanston, IL: Northwestern University Press, 2010).

6 Havelková and Oates-Indruchová (eds.), *The Politics of Gender Culture*; Celia Donert, *The Rights of the Roma: State Socialism and the "Gypsy Question"* (Cambridge: Cambridge University Press, forthcoming).

of capitalist class society or the lingering remnants of feudalism. Thus the abolition of private property and the socialization of reproductive as well as productive labor would destroy the hierarchies between the sexes. The Soviet Union, and after 1945 the people's democracies in Eastern Europe and Asia, introduced policies of full employment and access to education for women, as well as dismantling legal barriers to equality within marriage, decriminalizing abortion, liberalizing divorce and socializing child care.[7] Women, and especially married mothers, broke through traditional resistance to female participation in paid labor.[8] Attempts to open up traditionally male occupations to women – such as mining – often failed, due to societal resistance and the durability of male working-class identities and interests.[9] Women were encouraged to take lower-level managerial jobs but excluded from the top of the social hierarchy in political and professional life.[10] Much as in the West, the feminization of economic sectors such as textile production or service provision remained entrenched, and workers in these sectors received lower wages and less societal recognition for their labor than did those in heavy industry.

Yet despite these seemingly intractable inequalities, women were very far from being the victims of a "top-down" project of emancipation. Although it is easy to point to the gap between the rhetoric and reality of women's liberation under socialism, scholarship on the history of women's everyday lives in the Eastern bloc has demonstrated that the paternalistic social policies implemented by socialist regimes contributed to the formation of new modes of citizenship and subjectivity.[11] By the 1960s, the "problem" of women in state socialism was no longer viewed as a task for ruling communist parties to solve through mass mobilization and labor. Instead, experts in social policy introduced a range of measures that aimed to boost flagging birth rates and

7 Donna Harsch, "Communism and Women," in Stephen A. Smith (ed.), *The Oxford Handbook of the History of Communism* (Oxford: Oxford University Press, 2014), 488–504; Malgorzata Fidelis, *Women, Communism and Industrialization in Postwar Poland* (Cambridge: Cambridge University Press, 2010).
8 Donna Harsch, *The Revenge of the Domestic: Women, the Family and Communism in the German Democratic Republic* (Princeton: Princeton University Press, 2007).
9 Fidelis, *Women, Communism and Industrialization*; Mark Pittaway, *The Workers' State: Industrial Labor and the Making of Socialist Hungary, 1944–1958* (Pittsburgh: University of Pittsburgh Press, 2012); Jill Massino, "Workers Under Construction: Gender, Identity, and Women's Experiences of Work in State Socialist Romania," in Shana Penn and Jill Massino (eds.), *Gender Politics and Everyday Life in State Socialist Eastern and Central Europe* (New York: Palgrave Macmillan, 2009), 13–32.
10 Éva Fodor, *Working Difference: Women's Working Lives in Austria and Hungary, 1945–1995* (Durham, NC: Duke University Press, 2003), 156.
11 Penn and Massino (eds.), *Gender Politics and Everyday Life*.

offset fears about the psychological effects of maternal deprivation on children, while enabling women to continue working in paid employment, such as higher child benefits and paid maternity leave. Socialist regimes not only sought to mobilize women as workers and citizens, but also simultaneously constructed them as a group with special needs – above all, as mothers – which conferred particular responsibilities as well as privileges.[12]

The mass organizations for women that were established in the people's democracies of the Eastern bloc, and after 1949 in China, were entrusted with the task of mobilizing women for building socialism. Although the term "feminism" was typically rejected by ruling communist parties as a bourgeois Western concept, the Czech sociologist Hana Havelková has observed that socialist regimes "expropriated" presocialist feminist traditions on the grounds that the socialist state possessed the resources to implement their egalitarian agenda more effectively than nongovernmental women's organizations.[13] The extent to which women's organizations in the Soviet Union, Eastern Europe, Cuba, Southeast Asia and China can be characterized as "feminist" is a question that provoked intense debate among contemporary observers during the Cold War and continues to do so today.[14] The same is true for their status as "nongovernmental" organizations. Thus together with the trade unions and youth organizations, mass organizations for women shared the responsibility for organizing women in support of the overarching aim of building socialism. This tension between gender-based separatism and class solidarity reverberated through the long history of European socialist movements.[15]

Over the past decade, scholars such as Francisca de Haan, Kristen Ghodsee and Wang Zheng have argued that female activists in states as diverse as Bulgaria, Poland, Yugoslavia and Maoist China pursued socialist feminist goals that conflicted with the patriarchal views of male communist party leaders.[16] Premised on the observation that historians should not measure

---

12 Fodor, *Working Difference*, 156.
13 Hana Havelková and Libora Oates-Indruchová, "Expropriated Voice: Transformations of Gender Culture Under State Socialism," in Havelková and Oates-Indruchová (eds.), *The Politics of Gender Culture*, 3–27.
14 De Haan (ed.), "Ten Years After."
15 Marilyn Boxer, "Rethinking the Socialist Construction and International Career of the Concept 'Bourgeois Feminism,'" *American Historical Review* 112, 1 (Feb. 2007), 131–58, but also Susan Zimmermann, "A Struggle over Gender, Class, and the Vote: Unequal International Interaction and the Birth of the 'Female International' of Socialist Women (1905–1907)," in Oliver Janz and Daniel Schönpflug (eds.), *Gender History in a Transnational Perspective: Networks, Biographies, Gender Orders* (New York: Berghahn, 2014), 101–26.
16 Nanette Funk, "A Very Tangled Knot: Official State Socialist Women's Organisations, Women's Agency and Feminism in Eastern European State Socialism," *European*

communist women's organizations against a political and cultural ideal of female "autonomy" – itself a concept developed by Western second-wave feminism after 1968 – these studies seek instead to explore the goals of organizations such as the Anti-Fascist Women's Front of Yugoslavia in their historical context.[17] This important new scholarship has suggested that state-socialist women's organizations pursued these goals within the structures of the state and can thus be characterized as examples of "state feminism." In the People's Republic of China, Wang Zheng argues, activists in the All-China Women's Federation shifted from mobilizing women at the grassroots as a revolutionary group to acting as lobbyists within policymaking processes at the center of power: "'State feminism' in the Chinese socialist state, after all, is no less an expression of feminist contention within the state than it is in capitalist states."[18]

Whether or not socialist women's organizations are characterized as "feminist," it is clear that their function within the socialist state changed over time. By the late 1960s, the official women's leagues in Eastern Europe and the Soviet Union had become sites of sociability and social work, rather than revolution.[19] The Soviet system of state-run *zhensovety*, the women's councils initially set up in the 1920s, were revived by Khrushchev in the late 1950s to engage women's support for communist party policies and provide social services, such as distributing holiday vouchers and summer camp spaces for children. This reflected the broader shift in the Soviet bloc toward satisfying citizens' demands for a quiet life, consumer goods and privacy, all of which operated in deeply gendered ways. Fearful of rapidly declining birth rates, communist governments introduced pro-natalist policies such as higher child benefits and longer periods of paid maternity leave. Gendered divisions of work within the home were rarely addressed in public policy (exemplified by the East German policy of giving women – but not men – one day off work

Journal of Women's Studies 21 (2014), 344–60; Kristen Ghodsee, "Untangling the Knot: A Response to Funk," *European Journal of Women's Studies* 22 (2015), 248–52; Wang Zheng, *Finding Women in the State: A Socialist Feminist Revolution in the People's Republic of China, 1949–1964* (Berkeley: University of California Press, 2016); Basia Nowak, "Constant Conversations: Agitators in the League of Women in Poland During the Stalinist Period," *Feminist Studies* 31 (2005), 488–518.

17 Chiara Bonfiglioli, "Cold War Internationalisms, Nationalisms and the Yugoslav–Soviet Split: The Union of Italian Women and the Antifascist Women's Front of Yugoslavia," in Francisca de Haan et al. (eds.), *Women's Activism: Global Perspectives from the 1890s to the Present* (London: Routledge, 2013), 59–76.
18 Wang, *Finding Women in the State*, 48.
19 Basia A. Nowak, "'Where Do You Think I Learned to Style My Own Hair?' Gender and Everyday Lives of Women Activists in Poland's League of Women," in Penn and Massino (eds.), *Gender Politics and Everyday Life*, 45–58.

per month to do "their" housework).[20] Subjects such as domestic violence, which conflicted with the official determination to prove that socialism emancipated women, remained practically taboo.[21]

The apparent failure of socialist regimes to extend their revolutionary rhetoric to the private sphere constituted one of the major critiques of Western socialist feminists who looked to the Soviet bloc and China for sources of inspiration from the 1950s to the 1970s. Influenced by exile or emigration to Western Europe or the United States, or study visits to socialist regimes, scholars of the Soviet Union, China and Eastern Europe produced a wave of publications investigating the status and experiences of women in "really existing socialism."[22] To cite just two studies of women's status in socialist Czechoslovakia during the 1970s: Alena Heitlinger, an émigrée from Czechoslovakia, framed her study of *Women and State Socialism* in the larger context of the absence of democracy, while the American scholar Hilda Scott, a long-term resident in Czechoslovakia, focused on the implementation of equality policies in her 1975 study, *Does Socialism Liberate Women?*[23]

In her 1972 book, *Women, Resistance, and Revolution*, the British feminist Sheila Rowbotham articulated the importance of this critical reflection on women and really existing socialism for the self-understanding of women's liberation in the West.[24] However, in the light of increasing disillusionment with Soviet-style communism, Western socialist scholars increasingly looked to Maoism for an alternative model of women's liberation in the 1960s and 1970s. Women active in the civil rights and New Left movements saw in the Chinese Revolution a possibility for feminist "consciousness-raising" in the United States. After China opened up to Western researchers in the late 1970s, however, high expectations gave way to criticism.[25] Moreover, the embrace of Maoism by some French intellectuals after the failure of the 1968 revolutions in Paris and Prague resulted in texts such as Julia Kristeva's deeply controversial *About Chinese Women* (1977), which reproduced Orientalist

20 Myra Marx Ferree, *Varieties of Feminism: German Gender Politics in Global Perspective* (Stanford: Stanford University Press, 2012).

21 Monika Schröttle, *Politik und Gewalt im Geschlechterverhältnis* (Bielefeld: Kleine, 1999).

22 For example, Sonia Kruks, Rayna Rapp and Marilyn B. Young, *Promissory Notes: Women and the Transition to Socialism* (New York: Monthly Review Press, 1989).

23 Alena Heitlinger, *Women and State Socialism: Sex Inequality in the Soviet Union and Czechoslovakia* (Basingstoke: Macmillan, 1979); Hilda Scott, *Does Socialism Liberate Women? Experiences from Eastern Europe* (Boston: Beacon Press, 1974).

24 Sheila Rowbotham, *Women, Resistance, and Revolution: A History of Women and Revolution in the Modern World* (London: Allen Lane, 1972).

25 Ping-Chun Hsiung and Yuk-Lin Renita Wong, "Jie Gui – Connecting the Tracks: Chinese Women's Activism Surrounding the 1995 World Conference on Women in Beijing," *Gender and History* 10, 3 (Nov. 1998), 470–97.

stereotypes about "Eastern" women and was criticized by post-structuralist theorists such as Gayatri Spivak for displaying the classic "colonial benevolence" symptomatic of Western, first-world feminism.[26]

After 1968, feminism in the United States and Western Europe – particularly the radical and socialist feminism driven by women's dissatisfaction with the sexism of the New Left – evolved through intellectual and practical engagement with the promise of women's emancipation under really existing socialism, as part of a wider feminist critique of Marxist theory and politics.[27] The crisis of Marxism had similar repercussions in Eastern Europe, particularly in the relatively open public sphere of nonaligned Yugoslavia. Feminism in Yugoslavia, writes Zsófia Loránd, combined "elements of the Western second wave with current issues in Yugoslav society" and intellectual movements such as the Frankfurt School, the Budapest School of Lukács, local Marxist humanism and revisionism associated with the journal *Praxis*, and Lacanian psychoanalysis.[28] Located in the major cities of Belgrade, Zagreb and later Ljubljana, Yugoslav feminists organized an international conference in Belgrade in 1978 and summer schools in Dubrovnik. These events influenced the practice as well as the theories of activism. The Network of East–West Women in New York, for example, was cofounded after 1989 by activists such as the writer Slavenka Drakulič and American feminists such as Nanette Funk, who had participated in summer schools in Yugoslavia during the 1970s.[29]

Narratives that depict feminism as a Western import to Eastern Europe after 1989 – often also critiquing the perceived "weakness" of feminism in the region – thus obscure the extent to which feminist movements emerged out of an entangled history of translation and interpretation between East and

26 Julia Kristeva, *About Chinese Women*, trans. Anita Barrows (London: Marion Boyars, 1977); Gayatri Chakravorty Spivak, "French Feminism in an International Frame," *Yale French Studies* 62 (1981), 154–84; Richard Wolin, *The Wind from the East: French Intellectuals, the Cultural Revolution, and the Legacy of the 1960s* (Princeton: Princeton University Press, 2012).

27 On 1968, see Geoff Eley, *Forging Democracy: The History of the Left in Europe, 1850–2000* (Oxford: Oxford University Press, 2002); Robert Gildea, James Mark and Anette Warring (eds), *Europe's 1968: Voices of Revolt* (Oxford: Oxford University Press, 2013); Martin Klimke, Jacco Pekelder and Joachim Scharloth (eds.), *Between Prague Spring and French May: Opposition and Revolt in Europe, 1960–1980* (New York and Oxford: Berghahn, 2013).

28 Zsófia Loránd, "'A Politically Non-Dangerous Revolution Is Not a Revolution': Critical Readings of the Concept of Sexual Revolution by Yugoslav Feminists in the 1970s," *European Review of History – Revue européenne d'histoire* 22, 1 (2015), 120–37.

29 Zsófia Loránd, "Learning a Feminist Language: The Intellectual History of Feminism in Yugoslavia in the 1970s and 1980s," Ph.D. dissertation (Central European University, Budapest, 2014).

West (as well as North and South), as well as a dialogue between older traditions of feminist thought and the so-called second wave. This was true not only for women's liberation in Britain and the United States but also for feminist movements in West European states with strong communist parties, especially France and Italy.[30] Second-wave feminism sought to redefine the contours of the political, including the politicization of the private sphere of family and affective relationships, the creation of women as political subjects, and new forms of political mobilization.[31] And, similarly to feminists of the "first wave," they linked the private sphere to international politics. Thus, during the 1960s, organizations such as the Women's International League for Peace and Freedom and the US movement Women Strike for Peace reemerged from the networks of communist and progressive women that had been marginalized by the strident anti-communism of the early Cold War.

State Feminism, Third World Internationalism and the Second Wave: The UN Decade for Women

During the Vietnam War, women's organizations in the First, Second and Third Worlds mobilized in solidarity campaigns for peace, nuclear disarmament and sexual equality. Anti-Vietnam protests in North America revivified an older generation of pacifists within organizations such as the Women's International League for Peace and Freedom and Women Strike for Peace – many of whom had suffered anti-communist attacks during the 1950s – as well as young women politicized by civil rights and the New Left.[32] Members of Women Strike for Peace met representatives of the North Vietnamese Women's Union and the South Vietnamese communist-affiliated Women's Union of Liberation in Moscow and Jakarta in 1965. Vietnamese women were not, however, passive recipients of Western solidarity. North Vietnam and the Vietnamese Women's Unions actively deployed the image of Vietnamese women as a means of popular diplomacy to garner support abroad.[33]

---

30 Maud Anne Bracke, *Women and the Reinvention of the Political: Feminism in Italy, 1968–1983* (New York: Routledge, 2014); Kristina Schulz, *Der lange Atem der Provokation. Die Frauenbewegung in der Bundesrepublik und in Frankreich 1968–1976* (Frankfurt am Main: Campus, 2002).
31 Bracke, *Women and the Reinvention of the Political*, 6.
32 Judy Wu, *Radicals on the Road: Internationalism, Orientalism, and Feminism in the Vietnam Era* (Ithaca: Cornell University Press, 2013).
33 Lien-Hang Nguyen, "Revolutionary Circuits: Toward Internationalizing America in the World," *Diplomatic History* 39 (2015), 411–22.

Images of women and children under socialism were central to the public diplomacy of communist states throughout the Cold War, often in the wider context of campaigns in defense of world peace and anti-imperialism.[34] The Women's International Democratic Federation (WIDF) was the official representative of the international socialist women's movement globally. Founded in France in 1945, the WIDF secretariat moved to East Berlin in 1951. As the Cold War intensified, the WIDF contributed to popular mobilization and propaganda for the "Struggle for Peace," through which the Soviet Union made a powerful bid to assert its identity as moral leader of the global community.[35] Initially granted consultative status as an NGO at the United Nations Economic and Social Council (ECOSOC), the WIDF was stripped of its membership in the early 1950s after it participated in campaigns accusing American forces of committing crimes against humanity during the Korean War.[36] The organization continued to host World Congresses of Women in European capital cities throughout the 1950s and 1960s, despite friction between the national sections – in particular, the Italian communist women's organization (Unione Donne Italiane, UDI) – over WIDF support for Soviet foreign policy.[37] Only in 1967 did the WIDF regain consultative status at the United Nations.

From the outset, the WIDF explicitly framed itself as global and anti-imperialist, holding a Conference of Asian Women in Beijing just weeks after the creation of the People's Republic of China in 1949. During the 1950s and 1960s, the WIDF provided a network for women from the communist bloc and postcolonial nations, as well as Western Europe and the United States, to forge international contacts around issues such as women's rights, peace, racial equality and anti-imperialism. Solidarity campaigns, technical assistance and aid between the Second and the Third Worlds shaped the rise of global humanitarianism during the Cold War.[38] Such campaigns received significant popular support in states such as East Germany, although the

---

34 Catriona Kelly, "Defending Children's Rights, 'In Defense of Peace': Children and Soviet Cultural Diplomacy," *Kritika* 9, 4 (2003), 711–46; Paul Betts, "Socialism, Social Rights, and Human Rights: The Case of East Germany," *Humanity* 3, 3 (2012), 407–26.

35 Timothy Johnston, *Being Soviet: Identity, Rumour, and Everyday Life Under Stalin, 1939–1953* (Oxford: Oxford University Press, 2011).

36 Celia Donert, "From Communist Internationalism to Human Rights: The Women's International Democratic Federation Mission to North Korea, 1951," *Contemporary European History* 25, 2 (2016), 313–33.

37 Wendy Pojmann, *Italian Women and International Cold War Politics, 1944–1968* (New York: Fordham University Press, 2013).

38 Young-Sun Hong, *Cold War Germany, the Third World, and the Global Humanitarian Regime* (New York: Cambridge University Press, 2015).

humanitarian assistance offered by socialist regimes was characterized in practice by racism, paternalism and sexism that differed very little from the West.[39]

Within the United Nations and its specialized agencies, such as the International Labour Organization, communist regimes acted together with postcolonial countries to put the question of women's rights – as well as race – on the agenda.[40] The new countries that joined the UN in the 1960s, acting through the Non-Aligned Movement, swiftly pushed for a Convention on the Elimination of All Forms of Racial Discrimination (CERD). Delegates from the USSR, Hungary and Poland soon afterward proposed that the UN Commission on the Status of Women draft a declaration on the status of women modeled on CERD. Soviet bloc countries highlighted the emancipation of women in socialist regimes, and pushed for a draft that would require states to take affirmative action to raise women's status, in which they received support from secular leaders of Muslim countries such as Afghanistan. During the 1970s, the rise of détente between the Soviet Union and the West, and the emergence of the Southern states as a majority-voting bloc, changed the balance of power at the United Nations regarding the question of women's rights.[41]

In 1972, the WIDF proposed that the United Nations organize an International Women's Year.[42] The proposal, put forward by the Romanian delegate at the Commission on the Status of Women (CSW), coincided with the first in a series of global UN conferences on development-related themes, such as the environment and population.[43] A small number of second-wave feminists, such as Germaine Greer and Betty Friedan, challenged delegates at the 1974 World Population Conference in Bucharest to recognize the gendered dimensions of population control.[44] The UN World Conference on Women, held in Mexico City in 1975, brought second-wave feminists into

---

39 Ibid.
40 Lisa Baldez, *Defying Convention: US Resistance to the UN Treaty on Women's Rights* (New York: Cambridge University Press, 2014); Eileen Boris and Susan Zimmermann (eds.), *Women's ILO: Transnational Networks, Global Labour Standards and Gender Equity, 1919 to the Present* (Basingstoke: Palgrave Macmillan, forthcoming).
41 Baldez, *Defying Convention*, 55–61.
42 Raluca Popa, "Translating Equality Between Women and Men Across Cold War Divides: Women Activists from Hungary and Romania and the Creation of International Women's Year," in Penn and Massino (eds.), *Gender Politics and Everyday Life*, 59–73.
43 Devaki Jain, *Women, Development, and the UN: A Sixty-Year Quest for Equality and Justice* (Bloomington: Indiana University Press, 2005).
44 Matthew Connelly, *Fatal Misconception: The Struggle to Control World Population* (Cambridge, MA: Harvard University Press, 2008).

contact with representatives of the New International Economic Order and statist models of development in the Third World and the Soviet bloc.[45] At the NGO Tribune, meanwhile, activists clashed over questions such as social justice and reproductive rights, which Third World women perceived as part of the liberal equal rights ideology that Western feminists were presumed – often erroneously – to espouse.[46] The Mexico City conference resulted in the Group of 77 and the communist states adopting a controversial declaration that presented women's rights in the language of the NIEO, world peace and anti-Zionism.

In October 1975, the Soviet bloc organized its own World Congress of Women as the socialist contribution to International Women's Year. Held in East Berlin, the World Congress conceptualized women's equality as the embodiment of the socialist conception of human rights, understood as fundamental elements of social justice and entitlements. The story of the congress, therefore, chimes with recent scholarship that analyzes socialist "rights regimes" as a reflection of the changing relationship between socialist states and citizens, rather than measuring them against Western ideals of civil rights.[47] This complicates narratives that reduce local human rights politics in Eastern Europe during the 1970s to a narrowly conceived "Helsinki effect."[48]

Histories of the Helsinki network – Soviet and East European dissidents using the Conference on Security and Cooperation in Europe (CSCE) to criticize their governments for violations of civil rights – lend weight to the argument that human rights emerged as a global politics of morality in the 1970s as a result of disillusionment with the failed utopias of postwar politics, not least revolutionary socialism.[49] The archives of the East German government, as well as the Stasi, demonstrate the high degree of state involvement in the planning of this international event, as well as the surveillance of the delegates.[50] Despite restrictions on civil and political rights in the Soviet bloc, however, the vision of gender equality promised by state socialism still

45 Roland Burke, "Competing for the Last Utopia? The NIEO, Human Rights, and the World Conference for the International Women's Year, Mexico City, June 1975," *Humanity* 6, 1 (2015), 47–61.
46 Jocelyn Olcott, "Cold War Conflicts and Cheap Cabaret: Sexual Politics at the 1975 United Nations International Women's Year Conference," *Gender and History* 22, 3 (Nov. 2010), 733–54.
47 See Mark Philip Bradley, "Human Rights and Communism," in this volume.
48 Daniel C. Thomas, *The Helsinki Effect: International Norms, Human Rights, and the Demise of Communism* (Princeton: Princeton University Press, 2001).
49 Samuel Moyn, *The Last Utopia: Human Rights in History* (Cambridge, MA: Harvard University Press, 2010).
50 Celia Donert, "Whose Utopia? Gender, Ideology and Human Rights at the 1975 World Congress of Women in East Berlin," in Jan Eckel and Samuel Moyn (eds.),

retained a certain allure for women's organizations around the world during the era of détente.

Western women's organizations such as the Young Women's Christian Association (YWCA) moved swiftly to write the World Congress of Women out of histories of International Women's Year. For example, the Women's Tribune Centre set up in 1976 to organize follow-up activities after International Women's Year made no mention of the East Berlin Congress in its reports.[51] Yet the influence of socialist governments and mass women's organizations continued to shape the movement for recognizing women's rights as human rights. The landmark Convention on the Elimination of All Forms of Discrimination against Women (CEDAW), adopted by the UN General Assembly in December 1979, bore the influences of Soviet perspectives on gender equality and human rights. The documents adopted by the Copenhagen World Conference on Women in 1980 were even more strongly influenced by postcolonial and Soviet claims, referring explicitly to the advances made by women in centrally planned and postcolonial economies.

The World Congress in East Berlin provided a venue where women from socialist countries could make international contacts with delegates from elsewhere in the socialist bloc, as well as Africa, Asia and Latin America.[52] The loosening of restrictions on transnational exchanges between activists and social movements allowed new ideas about gender and sexual rights in Eastern and Western Europe to circulate across the Iron Curtain. During the cultural détente of the early 1970s, for instance, the massive Tenth World Festival Games of Students and Youth in East Berlin provided a forum for creating transnational alliances built around international gay solidarity.[53] By mid decade, the World Congress of Women was a far more official affair, but hosting an international conference under UN auspices nonetheless forced the German Democratic Republic (GDR) to open its doors to human rights organizations such as Amnesty International, whose representatives had hitherto been refused permission to enter the country. The UN

The Breakthrough: Human Rights in the 1970s (Philadelphia: University of Pennsylvania Press, 2014), 68–87.

51 Karen Garner, *Shaping a Global Women's Agenda: Women's NGOs and Global Governance* (Manchester: Manchester University Press, 2010).
52 Kristen Ghodsee, "Rethinking State Socialist Mass Women's Organisations: The Committee of the Bulgarian Women's Movement and the United Nations Decade for Women, 1975–1985," *Journal of Women's History* 24, 4 (2012), 49–73.
53 Josie McLellan, "Glad to Be Gay Behind the Wall: Gay and Lesbian Activism in 1970s East Germany," *History Workshop Journal* 74, 1 (2012), 105–30; Josie McLellan, *Love in the Time of Communism: Intimacy and Sexuality in the GDR* (Cambridge: Cambridge University Press, 2011).

411

Decade for Women and the Soviet ratification of CEDAW in the early 1980s inspired the transformation of the Soviet Women's Committee by obliging the USSR to seek out and support experts on women's status who could represent the Soviet Union's new face abroad.[54]

In post-Mao China, too, the 1980s were also a decade of slow changes in the role of the Women's Federation. Along with many mass organizations, the federation was inactive during the Cultural Revolution and was reconstituted only after the death of Mao. During the 1980s, a new discourse about femininity and gender differentiation emerged in China.[55] The status of women was only one of a wide variety of social and political issues that became subjects of public discussion after having been taboo during the Cultural Revolution. Questions relating to sexuality, marriage, family life, divorce and violence fueled the public discussion of gender discrimination, as did the increasing availability of information from Western countries that accompanied political liberalization. The development of an active women's movement in the West and its effect on China made the discussion of women's issues in the 1980s profoundly different from previous discussions, such as those that had taken place in the mid 1950s.[56] In this context, the Women's Federation began to play a more active role as an advocate for women, particularly in cases of infanticide, abuse, employers' attempts to impose prolonged "maternity leave" on female workers and economists' proposals for the withdrawal of women from the workforce to solve the problem of urban unemployment.[57] At a moment when female scholars were again debating feminism, the federation also sponsored women's studies programs in some cities.[58] Even though women's studies emerged as a discipline during the 1980s, the Women's Federation retained an institutional monopoly on women's organizing.

The economic reforms and "opening" of China to the global capitalist system under the post-Mao government resulted, notoriously, in the introduction of a "one-child" policy in 1980. Although birth rates had fallen dramatically in the 1970s (from around six children per woman to three) scientists and policymakers feared that continued population growth would

54 Valerie Sperling, *Organizing Women in Contemporary Russia: Engendering Transition* (Cambridge: Cambridge University Press, 1999).
55 Emily Honig and Gail Hershatter, *Personal Voices: Chinese Women in the 1980's* (Stanford: Stanford University Press, 1988).
56 Ibid. 57 Ibid., 319.
58 Wang Zheng, "Gender, Employment and Women's Resistance," in Elizabeth J. Perry and Mark Selden (eds.), *Chinese Society: Change, Conflict and Resistance* (London: Routledge, 2003), 162–86.

threaten modernization and China's status as a global power. The population problem was reframed in Malthusian terms as "too many people of too backward a type."[59] After a nationwide sterilization campaign provoked violent resistance, in 1984 the policy was quietly "perfected" to allow two children for rural couples whose first was a girl.[60] In the United States, the birth and population program was folded into Cold War narratives that represented the People's Republic of China as a brutal totalitarian state.[61] The "coercion narrative," Susan Greenhalgh has written, gained new impetus in the mid 1980s when it was taken up by a newly emerging coalition on the right in American politics: "[C]onservative Republicans and right-to-life advocates, many with strong anti-communist sentiments, made China's population policy their *cause célèbre* in a public crusade against abortion."[62] Some linked the issue of coercion to American support for the UN Population Fund which had established a program in Beijing in 1979, claiming that the United States should not fund a UN agency that supported coercion in China.

The history of independent or unofficial women's organizing during late socialism challenges some of the familiar narratives explaining the role of dissident movements in contributing to the erosion or collapse of communism. During the last years of state-socialist rule, a small number of independent women's organizations was established in Eastern Europe and the Soviet Union. The writings of a Soviet women's group established for a brief period in Leningrad in the late 1970s were published in the West with enthusiastic endorsements by feminists such as Robin Morgan, but were practically unknown in the Soviet Union itself. Dissident life was deeply gendered, since so much dissident work was conducted within the private spaces of the home.[63] Well-known movements such as Charter 77 in Czechoslovakia and Solidarity in Poland depended on gendered divisions of labor between activists and their families through long periods of political work, strikes, arrests and prison sentences.[64] Women frequently took on the role of supporting families and cultivating social networks while male

---

59 Susan Greenhalgh, *Just One Child: Science and Policy in Deng's China* (Berkeley: University of California Press, 2008).
60 Susan Greenhalgh, *Cultivating Global Citizens: Population in the Rise of China* (Cambridge, MA: Harvard University Press, 2010).
61 Ibid.   62 Ibid., 5.
63 Padraic Kenney, "The Gender of Resistance in Communist Poland," *American Historical Review* 104 (1999), 399–425.
64 Shana Penn, *Solidarity's Secret: The Women Who Defeated Communism in Poland* (Ann Arbor: University of Michigan Press, 2005).

"dissidents" conducted their political work.[65] In the GDR, meanwhile, approximately 100 women's organizations organizing around ecology, sexuality and peace were founded during the 1980s, especially in cities such as Berlin, Halle and Leipzig. During *perestroika* (1985–91) a small number of independent women's organizations was established in the Soviet Union. Some activists split from the Soviet Women's Committee (SWC) and the state-run *zhensovety* to set up their own organizations. When the Soviet state collapsed in 1991, the SWC collapsed with it, leaving its successor organization, the Union of Russia's Women (URW), to inherit its legal rights and property.

Toward Beijing: Postsocialism, Violence and Women's Human Rights

After the fall of the Berlin Wall, around 1,000 East German women formed an Independent Women's Union (Unabhängiger Frauenverband, UFV) calling for the integration of women's issues into a reformed socialism in the GDR under the slogan: "You Can't Build a State Without Women" (*Ohne Frauen ist kein Staat zu machen*).[66] The founding principles of the UFV, drafted by the young historian and ethnographer Ina Merkel, criticized the state for its patronizing treatment of mothers, appealed for the freedom to work part-time and the possibility of creating a nonpatriarchal family, more opportunities for women in the workplace and a democratic grassroots voice in politics.[67] In the Soviet Union, Moscow-based feminists organized the First Independent Women's Forum in spring 1991 in Dubna, a city outside Moscow. Attended by around 200 people, the forum brought together dozens of new women's groups from across the Soviet Union to discuss questions such as violence against women (raised for the first time on a national scale) and the exclusion of women from the reform process.[68] The forum attracted international attention to the Soviet women's movement. International aid followed, beginning in the early 1990s as a modest

65 Marketa Spiritová, *Hexenjagd in der Tschechoslowakei. Intellektuelle zwischen Prager Frühling und dem Ende des Kommunismus* (Cologne: Böhlau, 2010); Jonathan Bolton, *Worlds of Dissent: Charter 77, the Plastic People of the Universe, and Czech Culture Under Communism* (Cambridge, MA: Harvard University Press, 2012).
66 Cordula Kahlau (ed.), *Aufbruch! Frauenbewegung in der DDR. Dokumentation* (Munich: Frauenoffensive, 1990).
67 Myra Marx Ferree, *Varieties of Feminism: German Gender Politics in Global Perspective* (Stanford: Stanford University Press, 2012).
68 Sperling, *Organizing Women*, 103.

trickle and becoming a torrent mid decade as "gender mainstreaming" entered the development lexicon as a central element of programs supporting democratization.[69]

Feminist activism in postsocialism, Magdalena Grabowska has written of Poland, emerged not simply as a result of the democratic revolution of 1989, but at the intersection of three revolutions: the failed socialist revolution promising the total emancipation of women, the self-limiting revolution of Solidarity and the conservative revolution of the church, nationalism and neoliberal economic reform during the 1990s.[70] The so-called transition from socialism to capitalism offered new opportunities to some women – such as those with particular skills or working in sectors such as tourism – but overall resulted in disproportionate rates of female unemployment and loss of pension rights, as well as the withdrawal of subsidized services such as child care, at a moment when prices were rising.[71] Women's employment, child care, pensions and divorce regulations were all affected by radical revisions to public policy by postsocialist governments during the 1990s, in ways that were often detrimental to women.[72] Thus even as women had criticized the failures of socialism to guarantee the equal rights of women, many experienced the collapse of socialism as a much greater loss of rights.

The autonomous women's organizations that emerged during and imme-diately after 1989 evolved from small groups of close friends relying on voluntary participation and exchange of skills and knowhow into localized and professionalized social service organizations or nongovernmental orga-nizations that were dependent for funding on the state, international private foundations or donors such as USAID or, from the late 1990s, the European Union.[73] NGO feminism in Central and Eastern Europe today has become professionalized and bureaucratized, with contradictory consequences: On the one hand, such organizations are able to reach out to a wider range of audiences, but at the same time, their activities tend to follow the

---

69 Julie Hemment, *Empowering Women in Russia: Activism, Aid, and NGOs* (Bloomington: Indiana University Press, 2007).

70 Magdalena Grabowska, "Bringing the Second World In: Conservative Revolution(s), Socialist Legacies, and Transnational Silences in the Trajectories of Polish Feminism," *Signs* 37, 2 (2012), 385–411.

71 Katja Guenther, *Making Their Place: Feminism After Socialism in Eastern Germany* (Stanford: Stanford University Press, 2010), 12; Kristen Ghodsee, *The Red Riviera: Gender, Tourism and Postsocialism on the Black Sea* (Durham, NC: Duke University Press, 2005); Susan Gal and Gail Kligman, *The Politics of Gender After Socialism: A Comparative-Historical Essay* (Princeton: Princeton University Press, 2000).

72 Guenther, *Making Their Place*.

73 Katja Guenther, "The Possibilities and Pitfalls of NGO Feminism: Insights from Postsocialist Eastern Europe," *Signs* 36, 4 (2011), 863–87.

project- and reform-oriented agendas of their donors. Nonetheless, women frequently experienced the fact of working in a feminist organization as itself a political act, at a time when women's work in general was being devalued.[74]

Abortion became a flashpoint for the redefinition of women's rights after 1989, and indicative of a broader shift around the politics of reproduction and sexuality in a period of economic and political liberalization. Abortion was among the first issues raised by virtually all of the postsocialist governments in East Central Europe.[75] During German reunification, the liberal East German abortion policy was pitted against the more restrictive Article 218 of the West German Basic Law. In Poland, abortion was constantly on the parliamentary agenda (reflecting debates about reproductive politics that reached back to de-Stalinization in the 1950s). A private adoption market in babies, not all of whom were unwanted by their mothers, emerged in Romania.[76] The dynamics of reproductive politics and of sexual rights had repercussions internationally as well as domestically, as postsocialist state responses to International Monetary Fund or World Bank advice on such matters were viewed as a barometer of democratization.[77] In China, meanwhile, global philanthropic foundations such as the Ford Foundation began to promote sexual rights in sexual health programs that invoked the vocabulary of rights, accountability, fairness, respect, dignity and sexual happiness.[78] By the mid 1990s, Greenhalgh has argued, China began to phase out overtly coercive campaigns in its family policy in favor of a new concern with broader questions of population governance.[79]

Violence against women in postsocialist states became newly visible as a target for the interventions of Western feminist organizations, as well as domestic women's groups. Domestic violence is one of the "most contested and suppressed topics in the contemporary postcommunist region," but activism to reduce it has "been in many ways one of the most successful encounters between local activists and international organizations or

74 Guenther, *Making Their Place*.
75 Gail Kligman and Susan Gal, "Gendering Postsocialism: Reproduction as Politics in East Central Europe," in Sorin Antohi and Vladimir Tismaneanu (eds.), *Between Past and Future: The Revolutions of 1989 and Their Aftermath* (Budapest: Central European University Press), 198–215.
76 Ibid.   77 Gal and Kligman, *The Politics of Gender*.
78 Leon Rocha, "The Question of Sex and Modernity in China," in Vivienne Ko and Michael Stanley-Baker (eds.), *Handbook of Chinese Medicine* (London: Routledge, forthcoming); Joan Kaufmann et al., "Gender and Reproductive Health in China: Partnership with Foundations and the United Nations," in Jennifer Ryan et al. (eds.), *Philanthropy for Health in China* (Bloomington: Indiana University Press, 2014), 155–74.
79 Greenhalgh, *Cultivating Global Citizens*.

movements."[80] Rape and violence against women during the civil war in Yugoslavia led to solidarity campaigns, humanitarian actions and a successful effort to recognize sexualized violence as a crime of war.[81] Yet at the same time, conflicting interpretations of wartime rape of women in Bosnia (and, to a lesser extent, Croatia) became a highly contentious issue among women activists in the former Yugoslavia and internationally. On the one hand, rape figured in ethnonational narratives of the war and of collective identities, as Bosnian religious and nationalist leaders called for compassion toward the victims but did not challenge the patriarchal interpretation of the meaning of the rapes and their connection to nationhood.[82] On the other, women activists saw Western NGOs as promoting a moral hierarchy of victims and aggressors that created the Bosnian Muslim female victim of wartime rape as passive and blameless, while eliding the ethnic dimension of the conflict by ignoring the rape of Serb women.[83]

A similar unease about the liberal feminist embrace of "violence against women" as a central claim for recognizing women's rights as human rights has been voiced in critiques of international responses to the "Natasha trade," or the apparent explosion of sex trafficking from the Soviet Union and Eastern Europe.[84] The collapse of communism in Eastern Europe in 1989 provided new resources – geographical and human – for the sex trade and traffic, as a result of political and economic liberalization as well as internal and international militarism.[85] The commodification and exploitation of sex as one form of labor has increased as European borders become more porous and labor more flexible, write Gail Kligman and Stephanie Limoncelli, with the former socialist countries catapulted into the global economy and women disproportionately affected by unemployment and the loss of social benefits.[86] These developments have led socialist feminists to criticize what

---

80 Katalin Fábián (ed.), *Domestic Violence in Postcommunist States: Local Activism, National Policies, and Global Forces* (Bloomington: Indiana University Press, 2010), 3.

81 Catharine MacKinnon, "Post-Modern Genocide: Rape and Pornography," in Alexandra Stiglmayer (ed.), *Mass Rape: The War Against Women in Bosnia-Herzegovina* (Lincoln: University of Nebraska Press, 1994).

82 Elissa Helms, *Innocence and Victimhood: Gender, Nation, and Women's Activism in Postwar Bosnia-Herzegovina* (Madison: University of Wisconsin Press, 2013).

83 Dubravka Zarkov, "Feminism and the Disintegration of Yugoslavia: On the Politics of Gender and Ethnicity," *Social Development Issues* 24 (2003), 59–68.

84 Jennifer Suchland, *Economies of Violence: Transnational Feminism, Postsocialism and the Politics of Sex Trafficking* (Durham, NC: Duke University Press, 2015).

85 Gail Kligman and Stephanie Limoncelli, "Trafficking Women After Socialism: To, Through, and from Eastern Europe," *Social Politics* 12, 1 (2005), 118–40.

86 Ibid.; for a cultural analysis, see also Anca Parvulescu, *The Traffic in Women's Work: East European Migration and the Making of Europe* (Chicago: University of Chicago Press, 2014).

they perceive as a misguided embrace of sexual rights and questions of bodily autonomy over social justice in the global campaign to recognize women's rights as human rights, launched at the UN Conference on Human Rights in Vienna.[87]

Violence against women was a central slogan at the 1995 Fourth World Conference of Women in Beijing, the largest of the UN conferences on women to date and famous as the occasion of Hillary Clinton's speech on "women's rights as human rights." The conference was significant for post-socialist women's organizations, not least in China itself. Since the 1980s, feminist activists had been seeking a new language and institutional relationship in which to articulate "women's questions" in relation to the state, including the All-China Women's Federation.[88] Wang Zheng and Ying Zhang found that, for the burgeoning women's NGOs in post-Maoist China, the existing Women's Federation – with its 90,000 paid officials and staff nationwide, "has become a substantial institutional resource that they can utilize as long as the necessary connections are available."[89] Supported by funding from Western donors such as the Ford Foundation, post-Mao feminists strategically drew on the term "gender equality" rather than "feminism," which was historically rejected by the Chinese Communist Party, or "equality between men and women," which in their analysis "connotes the control of women by an authoritarian socialist patriarchy."[90]

In conclusion, the history of the encounters and entanglements between feminism and communism from 1968 until 1995 also places the history of Second and Third World women in a broader global perspective. Over the past decade, scholars have revived debates about the achievements of the women's movement under state socialism, seeking to insert the history of Second World women into narratives that have focused unduly on the experiences of second-wave feminism in the West. While this is a debate that is only just beginning, it seems clear that the urgency with which scholars of gender are now engaging with the historical relationship between communism and feminism in the twentieth century is a response to the precipitous retreat from structural solutions to the "problem of women" across the postsocialist world. To understand the ways in which questions of social

87 Suchland, *Economies of Violence*.
88 Ping-Chun Hsiung, Maria Jaschok and Cecilia Milwertz with Red Chan (eds.), *Chinese Women Organizing: Cadres, Feminists, Muslims, Queers* (Oxford: Berg, 2001).
89 Wang Zheng and Ying Zhang, "Global Concepts, Local Practices: Chinese Feminism Since the Fourth UN Conference on Women," *Feminist Studies* 36 (2010), 40–70.
90 Ibid.

justice and sexual democracy jostle with each other in current debates about women's human rights, this chapter has argued, it is essential to grasp the active role played by official and unofficial women's organizations in national and international politics during the last decades of socialist rule.

Bibliographical Essay

An excellent introduction is provided in Donna Harsch, "Communism and Women," in Stephen A. Smith (ed.), *The Oxford Handbook of the History of Communism* (Oxford: Oxford University Press, 2014), 488–504; Shana Penn and Jill Massino (eds.), *Gender Politics and Everyday Life in State Socialist Eastern and Central Europe* (New York: Palgrave Macmillan, 2009); Éva Fodor, *Working Difference: Women's Working Lives in Austria and Hungary, 1945–1995* (Durham, NC: Duke University Press, 2003); Hana Havelková and Libora Oates-Indruchová (eds.), *The Politics of Gender Culture Under State Socialism: An Expropriated Voice* (London: Routledge, 2014); Michel Christian and Alix Heiniger (eds.), "Dossier: femmes, genre, et communisme," *Vingtième Siècle. Revue d'Histoire* 2 (2015) (special issue); Sandrine Kott and Françoise Thébaud (eds.), "Le 'socialisme reel' à l'épreuve du genre," *Clio: Femmes, Genre, Histoire* 41 (2015) (special issue). On the postwar period, see Malgorzata Fidelis, *Women, Communism and Industrialization in Postwar Poland* (Cambridge: Cambridge University Press, 2010), and Donna Harsch, *The Revenge of the Domestic: Women, the Family and Communism in the German Democratic Republic* (Princeton: Princeton University Press, 2007), while the sexual revolution in East Germany is explored in Josie McLellan, *Love in the Time of Communism: Intimacy and Sexuality in the GDR* (Cambridge: Cambridge University Press, 2011). On the gendered nature of dissent and resistance, see Padraic Kenney, "The Gender of Resistance in Communist Poland," *American Historical Review* 104 (1999), 399–425.

State feminism in Eastern Europe and China is debated in Francisca de Haan (ed.), "Ten Years After: *Communism and Feminism Revisited*," *Aspasia* 10 (2016), 102–68; Chiara Bonfiglioli, "Cold War Internationalisms, Nationalisms and the Yugoslav–Soviet Split: The Union of Italian Women and the Antifascist Women's Front of Yugoslavia," in Francisca de Haan et al. (eds.), *Women's Activism: Global Perspectives from the 1890s to the Present* (London: Routledge, 2013), 59–76; Basia Nowak, "Constant Conversations: Agitators in the League of Women in Poland During the Stalinist Period," *Feminist Studies* 31 (2005), 488–518; Wang Zheng, *Finding Women in the State: A Socialist Feminist Revolution in the People's Republic of China, 1949–1964*

(Berkeley: University of California Press, 2016); Francisca de Haan, "Continuing Cold War Paradigms in the Western Historiography of Transnational Women's Organisations: The Case of the Women's International Democratic Federation (WIDF)," *Women's History Review* 19, 4 (Sep. 2010), 547–73; Celia Donert, "Women's Rights in Cold War Europe: Disentangling Feminist Histories," *Past & Present* 218, supplement 8 (2013), 180–202.

Contemporary studies by émigré scholars, or observers of communist regimes during the Cold War, include Alena Heitlinger, *Women and State Socialism: Sex Inequality in the Soviet Union and Czechoslovakia* (Basingstoke: Macmillan, 1979); Hilda Scott, *Does Socialism Liberate Women? Experiences from Eastern Europe* (Boston: Beacon Press, 1974); Maxine Molyneux, *Women's Emancipation Under Socialism: A Model for the Third World?* (Brighton: IDS Publications, 1981); Sonia Kruks, Rayna Rapp and Marilyn B. Young, *Promissory Notes: Women and the Transition to Socialism* (New York: Monthly Review Press, 1989).

East–West transnational connections between female activists after 1968 are explored in Judy Wu, *Radicals on the Road: Internationalism, Orientalism, and Feminism During the Vietnam Era* (Ithaca: Cornell University Press, 2013); Zsófia Lóránd, "'A Politically Non-Dangerous Revolution Is Not a Revolution': Critical Readings of the Concept of Sexual Revolution by Yugoslav Feminists in the 1970s," *European Review of History – Revue européenne d'histoire* 22, 1 (2015), 120–37.

On the gendered dimensions of socialist internationalism, see Young-Sun Hong, *Cold War Germany, the Third World, and the Global Humanitarian Regime* (New York: Cambridge University Press, 2015); see also Quinn Slobodian (ed.), *Comrades of Color: East Germany in the Cold War World* (New York: Berghahn, 2015); Alena Alamgir, "Recalcitrant Women: Internationalism and the Redefinition of Welfare Limits in the Czechoslovak–Vietnamese Labor Exchange Program," *Slavic Review* 73, 1 (2014), 133–55; Celia Donert, "From Communist Internationalism to Human Rights: The Women's International Democratic Federation Mission to North Korea, 1951," *Contemporary European History* 25, 2 (2016), 313–33.

Cold War conflicts over women's rights at the UN are explored in Lisa Baldez, *Defying Convention: US Resistance to the UN Treaty on Women's Rights* (Cambridge: Cambridge University Press, 2014), especially chs. 2 and 3. More broadly, see Eileen Boris and Susan Zimmermann (eds.), *Women's ILO: Transnational Networks, Global Labour Standards and Gender Equity, 1919 to the present* (Basingstoke: Palgrave Macmillan, forthcoming), and Devaki Jain,

Women, Development, and the UN: A Sixty-Year Quest for Equality and Justice (Bloomington: Indiana University Press, 2005). For a state-socialist perspective, see Kristen Ghodsee, "Rethinking State Socialist Mass Women's Organisations: The Committee of the Bulgarian Women's Movement and the United Nations Decade for Women, 1975–1985," *Journal of Women's History* 24, 4 (2012), 49–73; Celia Donert, "Whose Utopia? Gender, Ideology and Human Rights at the 1975 World Congress of Women in East Berlin," in Jan Eckel and Samuel Moyn (eds.), *The Breakthrough: Human Rights in the 1970s* (Philadelphia: University of Pennsylvania Press, 2014), 68–87; Raluca Popa, "Translating Equality Between Women and Men Across Cold War Divides: Women Activists from Hungary and Romania and the Creation of International Women's Year," in Penn and Massino (eds.), *Gender Politics and Everyday Life*, 59–73.

On feminism and postsocialism, see Valerie Sperling, *Organizing Women in Contemporary Russia: Engendering Transition* (Cambridge: Cambridge University Press, 1999); Katalin Fábián (ed.), *Domestic Violence in Postcommunist States: Local Activism, National Policies, and Global Forces* (Bloomington: Indiana University Press, 2010); Julie Hemment, *Empowering Women in Russia: Activism, Aid, and NGOs* (Bloomington: Indiana University Press, 2007); Elissa Helms, *Innocence and Victimhood: Gender, Nation, and Women's Activism in Postwar Bosnia-Herzegovina* (Madison: University of Wisconsin Press, 2013); Jennifer Suchland, *Economies of Violence: Transnational Feminism, Postsocialism and the Politics of Sex Trafficking* (Durham, NC: Duke University Press, 2015); Wang Zheng and Ying Zhang, "Global Concepts, Local Practices: Chinese Feminism Since the Fourth UN Conference on Women," *Feminist Studies* 36 (2010), 40–70; Katja Guenther, *Making Their Place: Feminism After Socialism in Eastern Germany* (Stanford: Stanford University Press, 2010); Myra Marx Ferree, *Varieties of Feminism: German Gender Politics in Global Perspective* (Stanford: Stanford University Press, 2012).

17

The Communist and Postsocialist Gender Order in Russia and China

MARKO DUMANČIĆ

Wherever they emerged, communist parties proclaimed gender equality as a central tenet of their agenda. Communists prophesized vanquishing class injustice and gender disparity in the same breath; these missions were, at least rhetorically, one and the same. Vladimir Lenin unambiguously equated patriarchal oppression with oppression by the bourgeoisie: "There cannot be, nor is there, nor will there ever be real 'freedom' as long as there is no freedom for women from the privileges which the law grants to men, as long as there is no freedom for the workers from the yoke of capital, and no freedom for the toiling peasants from the yoke of the capitalists, landlords and merchants."[1] Communist parties consistently assured their audiences that they intended to liberate women from domestic drudgery, opening up paths to full and unrestricted participation in public life. The most famous slogans of the Cultural Revolution confidently proclaimed women's emancipation: "Men and women are the same. Whatever men can do, women can do, too," and "Women hold up half the sky."[2] However tempting it might be to make a definitive statement on the extent to which communists turned this egalitarian rhetoric into practice, this chapter will avoid passing judgement and instead discuss the direction and content of the changes communist party policies effected vis-à-vis gender relations.[3] The effect of communist

---

1 Vladimir I. Lenin, *Collected Works*, vol. XXX, 4th English edn. (Moscow: Progress Publishers, 1965), 120.
2 Quoted in Sharon K. Hom (ed.), *Chinese Women Traversing Diaspora: Memoirs, Essays, and Poetry* (New York: Taylor & Francis, 1999), 84.
3 Donna Harsch makes a compelling case that communist regimes failed to bring about true equality between men and women: Donna Harsch, "Communism and Women," in Stephen A. Smith (ed.), *The Oxford Handbook of the History of Communism* (Oxford: Oxford University Press, 2014), 488–504. Martin King Whyte explains the difficulty of making definitive pronouncements about the liberation, or lack thereof, of Chinese women under communism: Martin King Whyte, "The Perils of Assessing Trends in Gender Inequality in China," in Barbara Entwisle and Gail E. Henderson (eds.),

parties on women's sociopolitical and economic status should continue to be debated but it provides only one side of the gender equation;[4] the policies communists initiated altered the individual and collective existence of the sexes, effectively transfiguring both halves of the gender order – well into the postsocialist era. This chapter thus discusses communist femininities *and* masculinities in tandem in order to provide a full overview of how communist authorities – sometimes unintentionally – altered dynamics *between* and *within* sexes. As one of the founders of masculinity studies, R. W. Connell, points out, "Masculinities do not first exist and then come into contact with femininities; masculinities and femininities are produced together in the process that constitutes a gender order."[5] The critical analysis of women *and* men under communism makes more transparent both the dynamism of communist gender policies and how the legacy of state-sponsored feminism continues to affect gender trends in contemporary China and Russia.

Three periods can most clearly showcase how and why ideas about men and women changed either in direct response to governmental policies or as a result of the unintended social, political and cultural phenomena these policies caused. During the revolutionary era in the USSR (1917–53) and the People's Republic of China (1949–76), Soviet and Chinese societies underwent a militarization of civilian life, which had a profound impact on both sexes.

Re-Drawing Boundaries: Work, Households, and Gender in China (Berkeley: University of California Press, 2000), 157–70.

4 A substantial literature exists discussing the position of women in Soviet and Chinese societies under communism. For China, see Marilyn B. Young (ed.), *Women in China: Studies in Social Change and Feminism* (Ann Arbor: University of Michigan, 1973); Margery Wolf, Roxane Witke and Emily Martin (eds.), *Women in Chinese Society* (Stanford: Stanford University Press, 1975); Elisabeth J. Croll, *Feminism and Socialism in China* (New York: Routledge, 1978); Phyllis Andors, *The Unfinished Liberation of Chinese Women, 1949–1980* (Bloomington: Indiana University Press, 1983); Judith Stacey, *Patriarchy and Socialist Revolution in China* (Berkeley: University of California Press, 1983); Margery Wolf, *Revolution Postponed: Women in Contemporary China* (Stanford: Stanford University Press, 1985). For the Soviet Union, see Gail Warshofsky Lapidus, *Women in Soviet Society: Equality, Development, and Social Change* (Berkeley: University of California Press, 1978); Richard Stites, *The Women's Liberation Movement in Russia: Feminism, Nihilism, and Bolshevism, 1860–1930* (Princeton: Princeton University Press, 1978); Susan Bridger, *Women in the Soviet Countryside: Women's Roles in Rural Development in the Soviet Union* (Cambridge: Cambridge University Press, 1987); Mary Buckley, *Women and Ideology in the Soviet Union* (Ann Arbor: University of Michigan Press, 1989); Wendy Goldman, *Women, the State and Revolution: Soviet Family Policy and Social Life, 1917–1936* (Cambridge: Cambridge University Press, 1993); Barbara Evans Clements, *Bolshevik Women* (Cambridge: Cambridge University Press, 1997).

5 Robert W. Connell, "Globalization, Imperialism, and Masculinities," in Michael S. Kimmel, Jeff Hearn and Robert W. Connell (eds.), *Handbook of Studies on Men and Masculinities* (London: Sage, 2005), 72.

While men were expected to submit fully to party dictates in collective life, disavowing any personal attachments or individual interests, women were either absorbed into the national economy or, in the Soviet and East European context, expected to play the starring role in the state-sponsored motherhood cult by raising loyal and capable workers. The revolutionary phase proved to be radical in its aim to advance women's liberation, but continued to privilege traditional masculinity, emphasizing the martial masculine experience as superior and universal. Male citizens, however, did not always benefit from this arrangement, since their social identities were wholly governed and defined by a bureaucratic rank order. In public life individual men played a supporting role to party demands, and in the domestic realm they were also a largely peripheral element, obligated and expected to provide little besides financial support.[6]

The Stalinist and Maoist eras thus ushered in a novel gender-relations paradigm in which masculinity and femininity were not defined exclusively in relation to each other, but were also delineated in their relationship to the state. The new communist authorities relied on a triangular gender order in which the state performed the role of the "third gender," as both men and women outlined their sociopolitical roles in relation to each other as well as to the party's norms and expectations.[7] The state became a kind of universal patriarch to which both men and women were subjugated. Although communist parties were not unlike centralized bureaucracies in modern capitalist societies in terms of their determination to regulate their citizens' gender identity and sexual practices, they differentiated themselves in that they were publicly – at least during the revolutionary periods – committed to toppling the existing gender order. Most communist parties staked their legitimacy on achieving gender parity, and therefore their level of involvement in the regulation of daily life was distinctive in its level of invasiveness. In the Soviet case, this dynamic was most evident in Central Asia, where the Bolsheviks waged a controversial and often coercive "deveiling campaign," organizing mass meetings at which thousands of women ceremonially burned their veils in the late 1920s.[8] China's Iron Girls (*tie guniang*) and female Red Guards

---

6 Sergei Kukhterin, "Fathers and Patriarchs in Communist and Post-Communist Russia," in Sarah Ashwin (ed.), *Gender, State, and Society in Soviet and Post-Soviet Russia* (London: Routledge, 2000), 73–91.
7 Zhanna Chernova, "The Model of 'Soviet' Fatherhood: Discursive Prescriptions," *Russian Studies in History* 51, 2 (2012), 37.
8 Marianne Kamp, *The New Woman in Uzbekistan: Islam, Modernity and Unveiling Under Communism* (Seattle: University of Washington Press, 2006); Douglas Northrop, *Veiled Empire: Gender and Power in Stalinist Central Asia* (Ithaca: Cornell University Press, 2003).

exemplified the party's commitment to gender parity by placing women at the front lines of economic revolution as well as political and social conflict.

In the second (late socialist) reform era (1953–91 for the USSR and 1976–90 for China), a "crisis of masculinity" evolved into a prominent topic of discussion in artistic and intellectual circles in the two countries. In both national contexts, the "gender panic" discourse constituted a rebuke of the parties' female emancipation politics that had emerged during the revolutionary period, charging that men had become overly feminized because state policies encouraged women to become overly masculine. From the late 1950s in the USSR and the late 1970s in the People's Republic of China (PRC), the Maoist and Stalinist privileging of a collective proletarian gender identity would be challenged by a search for specifically national(ist) manhood and womanhood. The cultural politics of "remasculinization" and the reestablishment of a "natural balance" between the sexes began under Nikita Khrushchev and continued under Leonid Brezhnev, receiving full expression in the literary subgenre called "village prose" (*derevenskaia proza*). In China, a similar kind of self-conscious inward turn came through most clearly during the 1980s through the "seeking roots" literature and films (*xungen*) as well as "northwestern wind" (*xibei feng*) music.[9] Both *xibei feng* rock musicians and village-prose proponents advocated a return to a bifurcated gender order in which Russianess/Chineseness was represented by rural folk culture that allegedly remained pristine and unaffected by imperial decadence, communist ideology and/or Western excesses.

While the transition to globalized capitalism has certainly led to major changes in both Russia and China, it would be misleading to say that the reorientation to a market system has erased the communist legacy or muted the "gender panic" of the late socialist period. Much as communist reforms could not fully eradicate the patriarchal views of gender, capitalism has not wholly undermined sociopolitical ideas about gender that evolved under communism – especially those relating to women's equality in the labor market. In fact, as Chinese and Russian popular cultures move away from official socialist conceptions of gender, there is simultaneously an expansion and contraction of possibilities to actualize one's gender identity. On the one hand, millennial capitalism and the culture of neoliberalism have multiplied the number of sites where gender can be explored, debated and negotiated. Expressions of individual desires have proliferated in the

9 Jin Zhaojun, "Feng cong nali lai? Ping getan "xibeifeng"' [Where Is the Wind Coming From? Commenting on the Pop Scene's Northwest Wind], *Renmin ribao* (23 Aug. 1988).

mass media, internet chat rooms, parliamentary debates and televised reality shows; this public process legitimizes the notion of personal desire and competes with remnants of the socialist notion of class consciousness.[10] Janet Elise Johnson and Jean C. Robinson accurately note that, "instead of one highly problematic gender ideology, there are a variety of gender ideologies much more free from state control."[11] On the other hand, much as gender equity under communism was projected to parallel the disappearance of class differences, under capitalism gender differentiation has resumed its function as a marker of class distinctions. This reorientation has impacted both sexes, but has had a particularly dramatic impact on the scope of women's agency.

The Revolutionization of Gender Roles Under Stalin and Mao

Reacting to their countries' past (military) humiliations and feeling encircled by foreign capitalist powers, Bolsheviks and Maoists created an under-siege mentality that permeated social and political reality. Moreover, for most Soviet and Chinese communist leaders, revolutions and civil wars constituted a formative experience; they therefore tended to organize society in a way that blurred lines between civilian and army life. In this emotionally charged and paranoid context, women found themselves in a paradoxical position; rhetorically, the communists used the female sex concurrently as a symbol of both backwardness and historical progress. As Gail Hershatter and Wang Zheng accurately point out: "The 'woman question' provided language, symbols, policy imperatives, individual aspirations, and visions of national modernity as well as dystopic imaginings of calamitous alternatives."[12] From the late nineteenth century onward, Chinese intellectuals used the image of the foot-bound, cloistered and uneducated woman as shorthand for China's national weakness and an explanation for the country's semi-colonial status. Similarly, the iconic image of the Russian *baba* – ignorant and uneducated woman – became "a foil to, and assistant of, the (universal, gender-neutral) comrade in the

10 Lisa Rofel, *Desiring China: Experiments in Neoliberalism, Sexuality, and Public Culture* (Durham, NC: Duke University Press, 2007).
11 Janet Elise Johnson and Jean S. Robinson, "Introduction," in Janet Elise Johnson and Jean S. Robinson (eds.), *Living Gender After Communism* (Bloomington: Indiana University Press, 2007), 11.
12 Gail Hershatter and Wang Zheng, "Chinese History: A Useful Category of Gender Analysis," *American Historical Review* 113, 5 (2008), 1409.

creation of a new Soviet order."[13] The Bolsheviks and Maoists used the longstanding discourse that pegged women as backward and anti-revolutionary in order to engender policies that aimed to liberate women to become productive citizens. The "uplift" of women was a key to strengthening the nation and staving off colonization. Mao in particular pushed women to occupy stereotypically masculine professions, extolling female model workers (*nüjie diyi*) during the 1950s as well as the Iron Girls during the 1960s.[14] Within the official lexicon of Maoist China, the female tractor driver represented the arrival of a socialist modernity that shattered the fetters of Confucian, feudal and capitalist worldviews and their attendant patriarchal forms. Some female Red Guards were also noted by contemporaries for being especially brutal in confronting supposed traitors of the revolution.[15] Marxist doctrine on gender relations and economic exigency prompted communist parties to create unprecedented opportunities for financial independence for women of all walks of life. Between 1929 and 1935, of the 4 million Soviet women who began to work for wages, nearly half entered industrial occupations. By 1935, 42 percent of all industrial workers in the USSR were women. The demand for labor during the First and Second Five-Year Plans was so intensive that, in 1932 and 1933, women constituted the *only* new source of labor.[16]

Although some critics dismiss these phenomena as forced masculinization and desexualizing of women, the practice demonstrated a genuine potential to disrupt the gender binary and to lead to a practice of "female masculinity," which, as Judith Halberstam explains, does not constitute a poor imitation of virility, but represents a meaningful and intentional staging of hybrid and minority genders.[17] More to the point, female Soviet Red Army soldiers during World War II and female Red Guards during the Cultural Revolution demonstrate that force, combat and violence did not constitute an exclusively male domain. At a minimum, the 120,000 Soviet women

13 Elizabeth A. Wood, *The Baba and the Comrade: Gender and Politics in Revolutionary Russia* (Bloomington: Indiana University Press, 1997), 9.
14 Tina Mai Chen, "Female Icons, Feminist Iconography? Socialist Rhetoric and Women's Agency in 1950s China," *Gender and History* 15, 2 (2003), 268–95.
15 Emily Honig, "Maoist Mappings of Gender: Reassessing the Red Guards," in Susan Brownell and Jeffrey N. Wasserstrom (eds.), *Chinese Femininities, Chinese Masculinities: A Reader* (Berkeley: University of California Press, 2002), 255–68; Emily Honig, "Socialist Sex: The Cultural Revolution Revisited," *Modern China* 29, 2 (2003), 143–75.
16 Wendy Goldman, *Women at the Gates: Gender and Industry in Stalin's Russia* (Cambridge: Cambridge University Press, 2002), 1.
17 Judith Halberstam, *Female Masculinity* (Durham, NC: Duke University Press, 1998).

combatants and millions of female Red Guards testify to the fact that Stalinist and Maoist authorities never had a uniform or consistent discourse regarding women's social roles and personal identity.[18] Moreover, in practical terms, the Iron Girl movement went far beyond the original intentions of the organizers and became a dynamic political field in which lower-class women were able to initiate challenges to local gender practices as well as make claims to social recognition for their contributions.[19] The working-class image of the Iron Girl also became an inspirational role model for a whole generation of young (rural) women who aspired to live an independent life on an equal footing with men.

Complicating the narrative of women's emancipation is the fact that Soviet and Chinese women bore a double burden, expected as they were to shoulder domestic and professional obligations. The cult of motherhood and domesticity was particularly potent under Stalin.[20] While female fertility was openly celebrated and child-bearing elevated to a state responsibility, domestic labor performed almost exclusively by women was "rendered invisible and the time performing it made women less able to rise to supervisory positions."[21] The androcentrism and tokenism that defined the party's attempts to create a gender balance in the workplace as well as the home also characterized the realm of politics. Although a quota system aimed to ensure that women filled approximately 30 percent of parliamentary seats, by the 1960s and 1970s Soviet women never exceeded 5 percent of the membership of the highest party organs and constituted less than 4 percent of urban and district party first secretaries.[22] Men remained overrepresented in the party and governmental apparatus and also occupied key positions in the economic, cultural and academic spheres at the expense of their female counterparts. Although millions of women gained access to social and educational mobility, men statistically and in real terms dominated society and government. The communist experiment in achieving gender equity thus led to a paradoxical legacy. While women were granted full legal equality and were

---

18 Anna Krylova, *Soviet Women in Combat: A History of Violence on the Eastern Front* (Durham, NC: Duke University Press, 2011); Honig, "Maoist Mappings of Gender."
19 Emily Honig, "Iron Girls Revisited: Gender and the Politics of Work in the Cultural Revolution," in Entwisle and Henderson (eds.), *Re-Drawing Boundaries*, 97–110.
20 David L. Hoffmann, "Mothers in the Motherland: Stalinist Pronatalism in its Pan-European Context," *Journal of Social History* 34, 1 (2000), 35–54.
21 Elisabeth J. Croll, *Changing Identities of Chinese Women: Rhetoric, Experience, and Self-Perception in Twentieth-Century China* (Hong Kong: Hong Kong University Press, 1995), 44.
22 Joel C. Moses, "Women in Political Roles," in Dorothy Atkinson, Alexander Dallin and Gail W. Lapidus (eds.), *Women in Russia* (Hassocks, UK: Harvester, 1978), 334.

also given the opportunity to realize themselves in previously male-centered occupations, men's monopoly in these arenas remained unchallenged as did notions that women should assume exclusive responsibility for the domestic and familial spheres.

Even as women entered the public, i.e. masculine, realm as signifiers of modernity, progress and scientific advancement, Soviet intellectuals in the 1920 and 1930s and their Chinese counterparts of the 1950s and 1960s tended to privilege exclusively masculine communities over female ones, classifying traditionally feminine traits and preoccupations as anti-revolutionary. While domesticity, femininity, nature and the family were objects of scorn for Bolsheviks and Maoists, the public arena, science, productive labor and masculinity were established as ideals. The foundation for the new society early communists envisioned was based on "the hallmarks of a traditionally masculine ethos: production rather than reproduction, participation in the historic process rather than domestic ahistoricity, heavy industry, construction, and, of course, 'the struggle.'"[23] Mao and the intellectuals under Mao similarly rejected China's Confucian tradition as it related to masculine identities. Kam Louie has shown that Chinese constructs of masculinity are best examined through the *wen–wu* binary, which distinguishes a scholarly, sophisticated and intellectual masculinity (*wen*) from the militant, unworldly and practical one (*wu*).[24] Because *wen* was more highly prized during the imperial period, encouraging as it was of order, civility and pacifism, it was marked for particular scorn by Maoist activists. Mao openly derided *wen*, identifying it as the main culprit of China's humiliation at the hands of Western imperial powers during the late nineteenth and early twentieth centuries. Consequently, Maoist culture prized *wu* masculinity, which hewed closely to the figure of the soldier and warrior, rejecting *wen* masculinity as inadequate for the task of achieving communism.

Stalin, like Mao, extolled square-jawed, muscular and virile masculinities, privileging men as default historical and sociopolitical agents. At the same time, the images of hypermasculine supermen, especially under Stalin, coexisted with male bodies that were amputated, paralyzed or near death. As Lilya Kaganovsky explains, depictions of ostentatious but dramatically mutilated masculinities did not constitute a contradiction; rather, "the two forms of masculinity exist together . . . together they create the ideal Stalinist

23 Eliot Borenstein, *Men Without Women: Masculinity and Revolution in Russian Fiction, 1917–1929* (Durham, NC: Duke University Press, 2001), 3, 17.
24 Kam Louie, *Theorising Chinese Masculinity: Society and Gender in China* (Cambridge: Cambridge University Press, 2002).

man: hyperbolically strong, yet without arms or legs; committed to the cause, yet permanently chained to his bed; visionary, yet blind."[25] If women were asked to make their sexuality invisible in professional settings and submit to a masculinized culture, men were asked to "conquer time and space along both horizontal and vertical axes" on behalf of Stalin and Mao.[26] Although men were the privileged sex in public spaces, this was no brotherhood of equals, especially since no man could match the mythical omnipotence of the two Great Leaders.

Paralleling the limitations men experienced in the public and professional domains were the controls the party imposed on men's activities in the family realm. Communist authorities did not advance the patriarchy of individual men; in fact, they wished to delegitimize the power of individual heads of households in order to weaken society's opposition to the party's power monopoly. Thus, even though the communist state remained patriarchal in terms of its superstructure, it effectively debilitated the power of individual patriarchs. By ensuring job prospects and child support for female citizens, communist authorities divorced men from their familial obligations, relegating them almost entirely to the public sphere, in which their autonomy was also constricted. Since the state appropriated the role of primary head of household, men came to play second fiddle in the marital and familial contexts; their role was reduced to bringing home (one of) the paycheck(s) or paying alimony and child support. Rather than the household patriarch, husbands and fathers legally, economically and culturally became interchangeable appendages of the communist nuclear family.[27]

The "Gender Panic" of the Late Socialist Era

As Soviet and Chinese societies entered the phase of late socialist reform after Stalin's and Mao's dictatorships, the bonds between the state and gender identity began to change direction. As a reaction to the seemingly limitless power of centralized bureaucracies and state-sponsored feminism, intellectuals and cultural elites began to discuss the state's overreach, couching it in

25 Lilya Kaganovsky, *How the Soviet Man Was Unmade: Cultural Fantasy and Male Subjectivity Under Stalin* (Pittsburgh: University of Pittsburgh Press, 2008), 4.
26 Helena Goscilo and Andrea Lanoux, "Introduction," in Helena Goscilo and Andrea Lanoux (eds.), *Gender and National Identity in Twentieth-Century Russian Culture* (DeKalb: Northern Illinois University Press, 2006), 7.
27 Elena Zdravomyslova and Anna Temkina, "Gosudarstvennoe konstruirovanie gendera v sovetskom obshchestve," *Zhurnal issledovanii sotsial'noi politiki* 1, 3–4 (2003), 306–07.

the language of a masculinity and femininity "crisis." Although centered on men's deficiencies, discussions of a masculinity crisis were also implicitly misogynistic in the sense that they advocated constraining women's agency in the public arena; they depicted women as either idealized expressions of the national spirit (in Russia's case) or as playing supporting roles in men's attempts to change their inferior position vis-à-vis the state (in China's case). The fear that an overly strong state had had a debilitating effect on the nation's men and women was combined with fears that the local economy was not competitive in a global economic system. As the Soviet economy gradually opened itself up during the 1960s, and the Chinese during the 1980s, each country and its men were being explicitly compared, within and without, to Western economies and masculinities.

Soviet "village prose" was a paradoxical post-Stalinist phenomenon. On the one hand, it rejected the idealization of Soviet (rural) life propagated under Stalin only to create an equally mythical bucolic idyll that supposedly encapsulated Russia's pure national essence. On the other hand, village-prose writers informed "the Soviet reading public of grave miscarriages of justice, state terrorism, and vast ecological damage" at a time of cultural conformity and massive repression.[28] This literary genre rejected the idea that modernization, industrialization and urbanization changed society for the better, resolving the tension between old and new in favor of the former and unfavorably comparing the social alienation of urban life with the social harmony of the village. Village-prose authors expressed their opposition to the Soviet state in explicitly gendered terms, blaming men for the squandering of an environment that was encoded as female. Barbara Heldt encapsulates the gendered dynamic of village prose best when she avers that, "although the Soviet system stands accused, it has a gender – a largely male bureaucracy is set against female Nature. Russia, as the Good Mother, is threatened with imminent destruction by the Soviet Union, who, as the Wicked Stepmother, has taken Russia's place and is destroying her children."[29]

The ecological and social justice message of village prose is partly offset by its exclusive nationalistic/xenophobic politics and its conservative view of women. Village-prose writers place older (Russian) village women at the forefront of opposition to male-inspired state policies and therefore elevate

28 David Gillespie, "Is Village Prose Misogynistic?," in Rosalind Marsh (ed.), *Women and Russian Culture: Projections and Self-Perceptions* (New York: Berghahn Books, 1998), 241.
29 Barbara Heldt, "Gynoglasnost: Writing the Feminine," in Mary Buckley (ed.), *Perestroika and Soviet Women* (Cambridge: Cambridge University Press, 1992), 167.

them to positions of moral leadership and guidance that men in the Soviet age had been unable to occupy. Nonetheless, village-prose writers domesticate, idealize and desexualize their heroines, rejecting any other form of feminine identity as inauthentically Russian. While (saintly older) women figure prominently in village prose, men are depicted as either corrupt or defeated; they play the role of either mindless, unethical, phony bureaucrats or depressed, bamboozled, defeated Russian "blokes." Village-prose writers thus understand Soviet power as having destroyed the best of Russian national culture through its revolutionary modernization drive, turning its men into alcoholics and its women into consumerist sellouts. Even in the world of the popular joke (*anekdot*), the frustrated Russo-Soviet male identity was salvaged only through the subjugation of women and ethnic minorities by the dual processes of stereotyping and scapegoating.[30]

The anxiety about communist sexual politics having perverted "natural" sex roles was present as much among social scientists as it was among writers. Soviet scholars began discussing a crisis of masculinity after the publication of a 1970 article by the Soviet demographer Boris Urlanis. Building on his insights, the discussion of the "masculine crisis" evolved during the final two decades of the Soviet regime. Commentators pointed to a number of benchmarks to buttress their call to "protect men": Men lived shorter lives than women, suffered higher instances of alcoholism and experienced much higher mortality rates.[31] Hidden from sight was the intellectuals' implicit condemnation of official policies that created this deplorable state of affairs. The between-the-lines criticism accused the Soviet state of having both an oversized effect on men's private lives and a negligible influence on their wellbeing. Within the public sphere men thus emerged as casualties, rather than social agents who proactively shaped their own fates. Because the communist apparatus was (ostensibly) so dedicated to resolving the woman question, problems specific to the male portion of the population were not frequently addressed on a policy level, let alone in practice. Underlying the discourse on the male crisis was the idea that the system had fundamentally undercut men's autonomy. Because their rights – to property, political action and freedom of conscience – had been restricted,

---

30 Michelle Smirnova, "Multiple Masculinities: Gender Performativity in Soviet Political Humor," *Men and Masculinities*, www.academia.edu/29270372/Multiple_Masculinities_Gender_Performativity_in_Soviet_Political_Humor.

31 David Leon et al., "Huge Variation in Russian Mortality Rates in 1984–1994: Artefact, Alcohol or What?," *Lancet* 350, 9075 (1997), 383–88; D. Wasserman and A. Värnik, "Reliability of Statistics on Violent Death and Suicide in the Former USSR, 1970–1990," *Acta Psychiatrica Scandinavica* 98 (1998), 34–41.

it was difficult to imagine how men could have developed the ability to become independent and responsible agents.[32] The flip side of the masculinity crisis was a panic about "masculinized women" who were accused of causing a spike in male hooliganism and alcoholism.[33]

The "gender panic" that was on full display during the 1970s and 1980s in the USSR was also present in spades in China at the start of the reform era, which heralded Deng Xiaoping's drive to delegitimatize the Cultural Revolution. As economic reforms accelerated during the 1980s, Chinese intellectuals, writers and media shifted "from glorifying the Iron Girls as a model of working-class women's capability and strength to disparaging them as a disreputable symbol of women's masculinization."[34] Part and parcel of Deng's campaign to negate the Cultural Revolution was the discrediting of Maoist notions of socialist femininity. At a 1986 meeting of scholars discussing the status of women in China, there was open opposition to Iron Girls being a feminine ideal; male academics in particular asserted that a masculine woman was a "mutant" and that capable women should be different from men in that "they have their own special charm, for example exquisiteness and depth of emotions and well-developed imagistic thinking."[35] This rejection of the Maoist female ideal was not simply misogynistic but also represented a denunciation of a rural working-class female identity celebrated during the 1960s and 1970s; it diminished the value of female labor and wished to erase it from public view.

The other side of the "gender panic" coin could be seen in the intellectuals' discussion of a "masculinity crisis." Zhang Xianliang's 1985 novel *Half of Man Is Woman (Nanren de yi ban shi nüren)* revolves around an intellectual who had suffered twenty years of forced labor under Mao for writing poetry; he becomes a symbol of anxiety paralyzing post-Maoist China since his inability to properly discharge his marital duties stands in for the feebleness of the country's intellectual stratum in general. In one of the novel's famous dream sequences, a castrated horse gives voice to the disappointment with China's intellectual class more generally: "I even wonder if your entire intellectual

32 Elena Zdravomyslova and Anna Temkina, "The Crisis of Masculinity in Late Soviet Discourse," *Russian Social Science Review* 54, 1 (2013), 40–61.

33 Beth Holmgren, "Toward an Understanding of Gendered Agency in Contemporary Russia," *Signs* 38, 3 (2013), 537.

34 Wang Zheng, "From Xianglin's Wife to the Iron Girls: The Politics of Gender Representation," in David S. G. Goodman (ed.), *Handbook of the Politics of China* (Northampton, MA: Edward Elgar, 2015), 298.

35 Marilyn Young, "Chicken Little in China: Some Reflections on Women," in Arif Dirlik and Maurice Meisner (eds.), *Marxism and the Chinese Experience: Issues in Contemporary Chinese Socialism* (Armonk, NY: M. E. Sharpe, 1989), 262.

community isn't emasculated. If even ten percent among you were virile men, our country would never have come to this sorry state."[36] The response to the critique expressed in *Half of Man Is Woman* could be most clearly seen in the proliferation and popularity of rock music. The performers' public personae, together with the aural dynamics of the genre, cumulatively expressed deep-seated anxieties and vocal demands that Chinese men restore their dignity. It would not be an exaggeration to say that rock music served as a kind of soundtrack to the events leading to the Tiananmen Square protests. Open rebellion was the predominant sentiment featured in 1980s rock songs.[37] By celebrating uncompromising individuality, bold action, and brutal straightforwardness, rockers and their audiences challenged both the communist authorities and the Confucian insistence on self-control, submission and discipline. While insisting on male autonomy, rock musicians were unapologetically misogynistic and often equated state oppression with the kind of pressure they imagined women exert on their male partners. Both the state and women became "the other" that actively sought to limit men's autonomy and field of action.

The popularity of rock music also served as a vent for the frustration Chinese men felt as China came into increasing contact with Western culture, especially via Taiwan and Hong Kong. The sense of emasculation grew during the late 1980s as China's economic and technological backwardness relative to the West came into sharp relief. The West's dominance certainly evoked the trauma of China's humiliation during the 1920s and 1930s. By accentuating China's mainland culture, rock music combated the sense that the West was again violating the nation's autonomy. Chinese rockers self-consciously adopted "the vocal style and melodic characteristics associated with the rural area of northern Shaanxi province, one of the most backward but historically significant geographic areas in China and the Party's headquarters in the course of the anti-Japanese resistance in the years 1937–45. The style thereby articulated its Chineseness, in other words its independence from the West."[38] This development resulted in a hybrid subgenre that came to be called *xibeifeng*, or Northwest Wind. *Xibeifeng* announced the rejection of Western culture while mirroring Western rock conventions. Rock performers thus defined post-Maoist masculinity in ways that rejected Maoist notions of gender equity, compromise with political

36 Zhang Xianliang, *Half of Man Is Woman* (New York: Viking, 1988), 129.
37 Quoted in Nimrod Baranovitch, *China's New Voices: Popular Music, Ethnicity, Gender, and Politics, 1978–1997* (Berkeley: University of California Press, 2003), 117.
38 Ibid., 128–29.

authorities, and Western-style modernity. This kind of masculinity resonated with the late 1980s for two reasons. First, it provided solace and a cultural compass to a populace that was feeling increasing concern about the pace of reform and the dramatically shifting socioeconomic landscape. Second, it assuaged anxieties about the feebleness of Chinese men in the post-Mao period. It demonstrated that the Maoist state had not entirely castrated male autonomy and that Chinese masculinities were capable of competing with Western, Japanese and Hong Kong masculinities.

Postsocialist Gender Norms

From the late 1980s in Russia and the mid 1970s in China, the emphasis on class and class struggle began to lessen and was replaced with consumerist values compatible with the emerging market economy. In both Russia and China, the state "shed many of its previous provisions and responsibilities, forcing the individual to be increasingly self-reliant, competitive, and disembedded" from the former paternalistic redistributive socialist system.[39] What succeeded it was a "powerful and widespread cultural model that promised upward mobility for all youth, regardless of their gender or socioeconomic backgrounds."[40] The Chinese and Russian cultural repertoires adjusted to the cataclysmic break in national politics and economics: "In place of industrial workers, peasants, and ... soldiers who triumph over class enemies and adverse material conditions in pursuit of the collective cause of communism, we now see on center stage entrepreneurs who inhabit the brave new world of luxury hotels, board rooms, jet travel, golf courses, and good-looking young females. Such ... representations ... contribute to the making of a new cultural imaginary in keeping with the latest official ideological configuration."[41] Even more important is the fact that gender has become central to the delineation of class difference and material status. If, under communism, the state was committed to erasing class differences by making gender invisible in the public sphere (or, to put it differently, erasing female sexuality for women engaged in politics and manual labor), in the postsocialist era new gendered relationships have again become central in making class

---

39 Yunxiang Yan, "The Chinese Path to Individualization," *British Journal of Sociology* 61, 3 (2010), 509.
40 Vanessa Fong, *Only Hope: Coming of Age Under China's One-Child Policy* (Stanford: Stanford University Press, 2004), 101.
41 Xiaoying Wang, "'A Time to Remember': The Reinvention of the Communist Hero in Post-Communist China," *New Literary History* 34 (2003), 133.

difference visible. Paradoxically, the rhetoric of gender equity continues not only to be promoted by the state, but also to be consistently articulated by the Russian and Chinese populations at large.

This shift simultaneously signifies a move away from socialist sexual politics and an entrenchment of gender norms that transpired under Stalin and Mao. On the one hand, the liberalization of the economic systems and the partial democratization of public and political spaces led to a legitimization of personal desire. Although the state still exerts a powerful influence on the media, the multiplication of gender subjectivities in public forums has advanced, if at a fitful pace. On the other hand, the belief in innate, biologically determined gender differences, which gained sway under the guise of a "masculinity/gender crisis" during late socialism, has continued to dominate popular opinion. The notion of fixed gender difference based on biology has been actively supported by state actors and buttressed by the reemergence of Confucian and Russian Orthodox cultural principles, which propagate ideas about the naturalness of gender hierarchies. While the postsocialist era has ushered in a shift toward the retraditionalization of gender norms, the democratization and globalization of the public forum have expanded possibilities for creating alternative and/or hybrid gender identities.

The ambiguous results of the transition to capitalism come through with particular clarity in the scholarship on women's and men's positions in the labor force. In both national contexts, women occupy a liminal space, being widely acknowledged as tough competitors and worthy assets, but in reality often discriminated against and marginalized. As early as the *perestroika* period, as the Soviet economy contracted, Mikhail Gorbachev asked women to stay at home to fulfill their familial and marital obligations.[42] Ever since the late 1980s, Russian women have occupied a precarious position in the national labor economy as the shift to market capitalism slashed employment in state-sponsored industries; hiring was scant and layoffs were massive for female laborers. Russian women endured regular harassment, discrimination and double standards and for women to even articulate "notions of autonomy and a concept of women's interests unrelated to their role as mothers require[d] immense courage."[43] Another testament to women's vulnerability was the exploitation of women's bodies: through

---

42 Holmgren, "Toward an Understanding of Gendered Agency," 537.
43 Michelle Rivkin-Fish, "Pronatalism, Gender Politics, and the Renewal of Family Support in Russia: Towards a Feminist Anthropology of 'Maternity Capital,'" *Slavic Review* 69, 3 (2010), 710–11.

global sex trafficking, the mail-order bride business and pornography.[44] Although not all women involved in these ventures fall into the docile victim vs. gold-digger binary, the sexual politics of the postsocialist era clearly left women with fewer options. In terms of both socioeconomic mobility and personal autonomy, women fared worse than their male counterparts and lost some of the ground they had gained during the socialist period, when their cause was supported by the (now collapsing) centralized state.[45]

Yet, despite such sociocultural barriers, Russian women are finding ways of competing with their male counterparts. A 2011 survey indicated that growing numbers of Russian women with higher education were starting their own businesses and that the gender gap in first-time business ownership was showing signs of narrowing.[46] Moreover, according to a 2014 international business report, Russia has the highest proportion of women in senior management globally, totaling 45 percent, a figure that has held fairly stable since 2004. Taking into account that the global average is 24 percent, this outcome is notable.[47] Russia and former communist states in Eastern Europe boast a thriving culture of female entrepreneurship at least in part due to "a legacy of the Communist ideal of equality of opportunity"; "consequently we find women well represented in ... emerging industries such as financial services and technology."[48] Although being a businesswoman in postsocialist Russia means having difficulty finding a spouse, securing professional connections or even counting on support among friends, female entrepreneurs have proven successful because they changed their self-perceptions rather than changing the economic and cultural barriers facing them; they have become well versed in utilizing the affirmative vocabulary they acquired in an array of globally circulating motivational seminars and media that have appeared in Russia during the past two decades.[49]

44 Eliot Borenstein, *Overkill: Sex and Violence in Contemporary Russian Popular Culture* (Ithaca: Cornell University Press, 2008).

45 Ericka Johnson, *Dreaming of a Mail-Order Husband: Russian–American Internet Romance* (Durham, NC: Duke University Press, 2007).

46 O. Verkhovskaya and M. Dorokhina, *Global Entrepreneurship Monitor: Russia 2010* (St. Petersburg: St. Petersburg University, 2010), 29, www.gemconsortium.org/country-profile/104.

47 Ama Marston, *Women in Business: From Classroom to Boardroom* (London: Grant Thornton International Ltd., 2014), https://www.grantthornton.jp/pdf/press/IBR2014_WiB_report_en.pdf.

48 Dominic King, *Women in Business: The Path to Leadership* (London: Grant Thornton International Ltd., 2014), www.grantthornton.global/globalassets/1.-member-firms/global/insights/ibr-charts/ibr2015_wib_report_final.pdf.

49 Andrea Mazzarino, "Entrepreneurial Women and the Business of Self-Development in Global Russia," *Signs* 38, 3 (2013), 623–45.

Chinese women face obstacles and opportunities similar to those of Russian women. Numerous quantitative and qualitative studies point to increasing inequalities for women in the workplace since the beginning of the reform period.[50] For example, state figures show that 63 percent of employees laid off by state enterprises in 1995 were women, and that they had only a one in three chance of finding a new job.[51] Perhaps the situation is most dire for the new class of female workers that has emerged in China in the past two decades known as "working girls" (dagongmei). During the 1980s and 1990s in particular, these young women, usually in their late teens and early twenties, moved from rural areas to urban centers to work in factories, engaging in low-paid, physically exhausting manual labor for three to five years before returning home.[52] Although rural women as well as men are migrating to urban areas to work, they are heavily regulated once they reach their destinations; the household registration system and accompanying discriminatory restrictions control migrants' movement, employment, ferti-lity, education and housing.[53]

Scholars such as Pun Ngai and Tamara Jacka explain that these women are not simply passive victims of a patriarchal and capitalist system. Rather, they enter these arrangements fully aware of the dire conditions awaiting them and endure the sweatshop labor in order to resist the fate of their rural family life. Migrant women experience a sense of autonomy from rural patriarchal authority when they migrate to the city – even as they end up exploited by the capitalist market economy and discriminated against by urban residents. Increasing numbers of dagongmei remain for years and even decades in the city, convinced that migration enables a change in fate. Ultimately, although many "working girls" have benefited from the professional prospects that have opened up in the post-Mao market economy, their achievements remain largely unacknowledged or deemphasized.[54]

50 Björn Gustafsson and Shi Li, "Economic Transformation and the Gender Earnings Gap in Urban China," *Journal of Population Economics* 13 (2000), 305–29; Jieyu Liu, *Gender and Work in Urban China: Women Workers of the Unlucky Generation* (London: Routledge, 2007).

51 Alicia S. M. Leung, "Feminism in Transition: Chinese Culture, Ideology and the Development of the Women's Movement," *Asia Pacific Journal of Management* 20, 3 (2003), 367.

52 Pun Ngai, *Made in China: Women Factory Workers in a Global Workplace* (Durham, NC: Duke University Press, 2005).

53 Tamara Jacka, *Rural Women in Urban China: Gender, Migration, and Social Change* (Armonk, NY: M. E. Sharpe, 2006).

54 Minglu Chen, *Tiger Girls: Women and Enterprise in the People's Republic of China* (Abingdon, UK: Routledge, 2011).

Like postsocialist femininity of the *dagongmei*, Chinese masculinity is built on a similar degradation of rural, working-class identities. Since the early 1990s the appeal of an urbanized, cosmopolitan and consumerist masculinity has predominated because it is closely related to Confucian conceptions of *wen* maleness and because the government's emphasis on neoliberal values has made this model more attractive. Newly empowered entrepreneurs have come to represent a new male ideal of the market era and are highly favored in the marriage market.[55] In popular discourse, individual men's economic failure is interpreted as a lack of virility.[56] Geng Song and Derek Hird precisely pinpoint this dynamic in observing that Chinese men "are taking on the appearance, mannerisms, and voca-bularies of the slick, smart, market-oriented, 'global' white-collar man. They appear to be – at least to the outside world – the bright, young, tolerant, squeaky-clean products of an educated vanguard, bringing China 'into line' with glossy models of respectable and respected corporate masculinities."[57] It is also significant that this refined and polished version of Chinese masculinity is as much a factor of state intervention as it is of market forces and, more specifically, of female consumers. As Mao's revo-lution catapulted women into the public sphere and as Deng's reforms ensured women would play a major consumerist role in the country's capitalist economy, female consumers have become a major determining factor in how men look and conduct themselves. But rather than simply imitating Western-style modernity, the Chinese pursue capitalism with a "distinctive national character." By distinguishing itself from its ideologi-cal foes, the Chinese Communist Party accentuates the country's long civilization and advances the image of China as a proud "spiritual civiliza-tion" (*jingshen wenming*). Unlike the West, which is cast as crassly materialist and lacking refinement, China and its men are symbolized by *wen*-like civility, harmony and humanism. In short, the ideals of Chinese masculinity in the postcommunist period have been closely aligned not only with the interests of the state but with an obvious nod to Confucian values that Mao had fought so hard to discredit.

---

55 Suowei Xiao, "The 'Second-Wife' Phenomenon and the Relational Construction of Class-Coded Masculinities in Contemporary China," *Men and Masculinities* 14, 5 (2011), 611.

56 James Farrer, *Opening Up: Youth Sex Culture and Market Reform in Shanghai* (Chicago: University of Chicago Press, 2002); John Osburg, *Anxious Wealth: Money and Morality Among China's New Rich* (Stanford: Stanford University Press, 2013).

57 Geng Song and Derek Hird, *Men and Masculinities in Contemporary China* (Leiden: Brill, 2014), 144.

The transition to neoliberal capitalism has similarly reshaped hegemonic Russian masculinity so that the national masculine ideal hews closely to established standards of international/transnational business masculinity. As much as the communist revolutions sought to create a new kind of individual, so becoming a successful entrepreneur requires following a model that is not limited to learning business practices, but also "means learning a whole set of norms that demarcate everyday practices, dispositions, and one's relationship to the self and to the world."[58] No less than their Chinese counterparts, Russian businessmen have to learn to submit themselves to the disciplinary effects of the new neoliberal regime of truth and power that rules not only the Russian, but also the global corporate universe. It would seem that the competitive and individualized world that extolls risk-taking and ingenuity would be foreign to the last Soviet generation, i.e. "the young builders of communism" who were born between the late 1950s and the early 1970s. However, the logic of economic neoliberalism, although different in content from socialism's stress on collectivism, is similar in practice. The last Soviet generation internalized the dominant discourse of late capitalism because it offered a totalizing logic that had particular appeal in the ruins of Soviet socialism. Even as autonomy was being praised as a central virtue of a postcommunist era, in reality Soviet-style hierarchies were being replaced with those governing the corporate world.[59]

The Russian business culture mirrors the hierarchical organizational structure of party organization as well as the ideology of male chauvinism on display in the late socialist genre of village prose. Moreover, the machismo of the Russian entrepreneur is firmly rooted in practices inherited from the 1980s Soviet black market and the calamitous days of Boris Yeltsin's shock therapy.[60] During the Yeltsin era, a very thin layer of society reaped financial benefits from the proto-capitalist changes, and earned the moniker "New Russians." Because lawlessness and brute force characterized the transition from planned to capitalist economy, it is not surprising that the majority of the (male) participants in the commercial sphere came from the criminal underground, which was itself a product of the Soviet-era black market. Muscular, worked-out bodies, short haircuts, leather jackets or two-piece

58 Alexei Yurchak, "Russian Neoliberal: The Entrepreneurial Ethic and the Spirit of 'True Careerism,'" *Russian Review* 62, 1 (2003), 73.
59 Elena Meshcherkina, "New Russian Men: Masculinity Regained?," in Ashwin (ed.), *Gender, State and Society*, 105–17.
60 Vadim Volkov, *Violent Entrepreneurs: The Use of Force in the Making of Russian Capitalism* (Ithaca: Cornell University Press, 2002).

tracksuits, exaggerated masculine behavior and prison jargon very soon became the most visible hallmarks of postcommunist masculinity. Although presented by their critics as simple thugs, these men came to play a crucial role in the origins of Russian capitalism. The adaptability of these organizations was demonstrated by the fact that, by the late 1990s, they had, by and large, shifted into semi-legitimate spheres, often morphing into private security services and protection agencies. By the early 2000s, the law-abiding and restrained entrepreneur commanding a boardroom became the dominant cultural standard for Russian modernity. Despite the polished veneer, however, homophobia, sexism and machismo remain staples of Russia's male-dominated business class.

The male-centered universe of the Russian entrepreneurial class parallels and embodies the hypermasculinity of the Vladimir Putin era. This can be most clearly seen in the promotion of Putin's masculinity cult, which began to develop with the onset of the second Chechen war in 1999. Displaying "Russianness" through force and unabashed virility has become the most dominant trait associated with postsocialist Russia. Years of being economically dependent on the West and facing international and domestic challenges to its authority under Yeltsin's two terms have produced the need to project an image of strength and demand the same of the nation's men. This agenda takes different forms – whether in Putin's many photographed adventures, the ceaseless promotion of the bear as the ultimate symbol of the country's forcefulness, or intervention in international conflicts, such as the Syrian civil war.[61] An intimate link exists between the state's mandate to turn Russian men into fearless, but loyal subjects and the state's desire to reclaim its global standing. This discourse has seeped into the logic of foreign policy, where emasculation of opponents has become standard fare. Whether discussing Ukraine, Poland or Georgia, Russian media degrades its adversaries by feminizing them.[62] The same approach is applied to internal dissenters, who, according to the Kremlin, want to return Russia to the subservience and weakness that characterized the 1990s. These attitudes are, of course, not new but a carryover from the gender discourse of the late socialist period, when men were pronounced endangered by village-prose writers and social scientists alike.

61 Valerie Sperling, *Sex, Politics, and Putin: Political Legitimacy in Russia* (Oxford: Oxford University Press, 2014).
62 Oleg Riabov and Tatiana Riabova, "The Remasculinization of Russia? Gender, Nationalism, and the Legitimation of Power Under Vladimir Putin," *Problems of Post-Communism* 61, 2 (2014), 23–35.

Rather than being limited to confirming Putin's political legitimacy, the advancement of the *muzhik*, the ordinary Russian "bloke," as the archetypal masculine model serves an important symbolic role in containing the influence of Western culture. With the national humiliations of the 1990s still fresh in the populace's minds, distinguishing between Western and Russian models of masculinity symbolically and practically distances Russia from the West. Simply put, by privileging the trope of the *muzhik*, the Putin regime is remasculinizing the Russian body national while feminizing outsiders, whether domestic or foreign. The clearest manifestation of this trend is the Russian neologism "Gayropa," which identifies homosexuality as the quintessential characteristic the democratic, secular and liberal order that EU member states symbolize.[63] The Russian propaganda machine has depicted the EU's championing of LGBT rights as the death knell of not only the nuclear family but also of "Western civilization" itself. In contrast, by upholding a strict gender binary and restricting the rights of sexual minorities, the Putin regime has proclaimed itself to be the stronghold of moral principles, the protectors of which are the morally upright (and heterosexual) Russian *muzhiks*.

Conclusion

When they came to power, the Bolsheviks and the Chinese communists set out to liberate women and put the sexes on equal footing. They shared the goal of realizing Mao's pronouncement that "Female comrades can do whatever male comrades can do." In a sense, what the Soviet and Chinese Communist Parties tried to do was not only to erase the patriarchal cultures steeped in Confucian and Russian Orthodox tradition, but also to eradicate the view that human characteristics could be dichotomized into masculine and feminine. Needless to say, this was a tall order, one of even utopian magnitude. Nonetheless, communist regimes and their successors have profoundly transformed men and women's lived realities and the national symbolic orders over the course of the twentieth century and into the new millennium. As increasing numbers of women entered the labor force, female citizens and workers not only became prominent as symbols of communist-style modernity but also changed women's perception of their sociopolitical roles – even as true gender equality failed to materialize. To the extent that women found work to be personally fulfilling, socially relevant

---

63 Ibid., 29.

and financially liberating, men could no longer play the role of unchallenged familial patriarch. Moreover, within the context of a bureaucratic party-state, male citizens had to submit to the vertical hierarchy of the party apparatus. Thus, even as a large proportion of women remained subordinated to men's monopoly in private and public realms, the communist party and state apparatus was powerful enough to assert its prerogatives and shape the dynamics between the sexes. As such, during the revolutionary period the communist party could be said to have played the role of the "third gender."

The transition to neoliberal capitalism heralded a reform of socialist gender relations but not their eradication, especially since the Chinese and Russian state apparatus maintain control of the media and much of economic activity. Nonetheless, there was a definite shift away from the socialist state playing the role of the third gender to a more individualized gender order shaped by the impact of the market. Simultaneously, however, echoes of independent women engaged in the public sphere and (both mental and manual) labor remain firmly entrenched in popular consciousness; this legacy both rekindles reactionary anxieties about the imbalance of the "natural" gender order and engenders opportunities for women to challenge men's monopoly on power. Despite the fact that the market has increased the possibilities for hybrid and alternative gender identities, the perceived threat of the West's economic dominance has strengthened support for a neotraditional gender order. Although Chinese and Russian authorities propagate transnational business masculinity as essential to their postcommunist identity, equally as important to postsocialist states is a widely shared sense of nationalist exceptionalism. While China and Russia understand themselves to be participating in the global market, a hegemonic masculine identity clearly divorced from Western-style modernity has emerged as the postsocialist states define themselves against the West. As they articulate their nations' distinct form of capitalist development, the postsocialist regimes create idealized hybrid masculinities in which entrepreneurial intelligence is mixed with strains of virulent machismo or a sense of cultural superiority.

Suggested Readings

Ashwin, Sarah (ed.), *Gender, State and Society in Soviet and Post-Soviet Russia* (London: Routledge, 2000).

Ashwin, Sarah and Tatyana Lytkina, "Men in Crisis in Russia: The Role of Domestic Marginalization," *Gender and Society* 18, 2 (2004), 189–206.

Baranovitch, Nimrod, *China's New Voices: Popular Music, Ethnicity, Gender, and Politics, 1978–1997* (Berkeley: University of California Press, 2003).

Goldman, Wendy, *Women at the Gates: Gender and Industry in Stalin's Russia* (Cambridge: Cambridge University Press, 2002).

Harsch, Donna, "Communism and Women," in S. A. Smith (ed.), *The Oxford Handbook of the History of Communism* (Oxford: Oxford University Press, 2014), 488–504.

Hinsch, Bret, *Masculinities in Chinese History* (New York: Rowman & Littlefield, 2013).

Honig, Emily and Gail Hershatter, *Personal Voices: Chinese Women in the 1980s* (Stanford: Stanford University Press, 1988).

Jacka, Tamara, *Rural Women in Urban China: Gender, Migration, and Social Change* (Armonk, NY: M. E. Sharpe, 2006).

Louie, Kam, *Theorising Chinese Masculinity: Society and Gender in China* (Cambridge: Cambridge University Press, 2002).

Ngai, Pun, *Made in China: Women Factory Workers in a Global Workplace* (Durham, NC: Duke University Press, 2005).

Riabov, Oleg and Tatiana Riabova, "The Remasculinization of Russia? Gender, Nationalism, and the Legitimation of Power Under Vladimir Putin," *Problems of Post-Communism* 61, 2, (2014), 23–35.

Rivkin-Fish, Michelle, "Pronatalism, Gender Politics, and the Renewal of Family Support in Russia: Towards a Feminist Anthropology of 'Maternity Capital,'" *Slavic Review* 69, 3 (2010), 701–24.

Geng Song and Derek Hird, *Men and Masculinities in Contemporary China* (Leiden: Brill, 2014).

Sperling, Valerie, *Sex, Politics, and Putin: Political Legitimacy in Russia* (Oxford: Oxford University Press, 2014).

Yurchak, Alexei, "Russian Neoliberal: The Entrepreneurial Ethic and the Spirit of 'True Careerism,'" *Russian Review* 62, 1 (2003), 72–90.

Zdravomyslova, Elena and Anna Temkina, "The Crisis of Masculinity in Late Soviet Discourse," *Russian Social Science Review* 54, 1 (2013), 40–61.

Bibliographical Essay

The fields of women's studies and critical studies on men and masculinities have had an uneven trajectory. While scholarship on the position of women in the USSR and the PRC traces its roots to the late 1960s and early 1970s, critical studies on Chinese and Russo-Soviet masculinities did not emerge until the late 1990s. While women's studies constitute a fundamental part of both communist and postcommunist studies, the scholarship on the masculinity side of the gender equation remains in a relatively nascent phase.

For the evolution of Russian and Soviet women's history, see Barbara Engel Alpern, "New Directions in Russian and Soviet Women's History," in Pamela S. Nadell and Kate Haulman (eds.), *Making Women's Histories: Beyond National Perspectives* (New York: New York University Press, 2013), 38–60. For the development of scholarly studies on Chinese women in both China and the West, see Gail Hershatter and Wang Zheng, "Chinese History: A Useful Category of Gender Analysis," *American Historical Review* 113, 5 (2008), 1404–21. The position of women under communism is analyzed in Donna Harsch, "Communism and Women," in Stephen A. Smith (ed.), *The Oxford Handbook of the History of Communism* (Oxford: Oxford University Press, 2014), 488–504.

A useful overview of scholarship on Russian and Soviet masculinities emerges in Barbara Evans Clements, Rebecca Friedman and Dan Healey (eds.), *Russian Masculinities in History and Culture* (Basingstoke: Palgrave, 2002). A theoretical and *longue durée* approach to Chinese masculinity receives coverage in Kam Louie, *Theorising Chinese Masculinity: Society and Gender in China* (Cambridge: Cambridge University Press, 2002).

Two works that delineate the Soviet and Chinese Communist Parties' paradoxical attitude toward women, as simultaneously sociopolitically regressive elements and embodiments of historical progress and social change, see Elizabeth A. Wood, *The Baba and the Comrade: Gender and Politics in Revolutionary Russia* (Bloomington: Indiana University Press, 1997); and Tina Mai Chen, "Female Icons, Feminist Iconography? Socialist Rhetoric and Women's Agency in 1950s China," *Gender and History* 15, 2 (2003), 268–95.

Evaluations of Soviet women's contribution to Stalin's industrial revolution and of their World War II combat roles are presented, respectively, in Wendy Goldman, *Women at the Gates: Gender and Industry in Stalin's Russia* (Cambridge: Cambridge University Press, 2002), and Anna Krylova, *Soviet Women in Combat: A History of Violence on the Eastern Front* (Durham, NC: Duke University Press, 2011). The transformation of women's sociopolitical roles under Mao receives scrutiny in Emily Honig, "Socialist Sex: The Cultural Revolution Revisited," *Modern China* 29, 2 (2003), 143–75, and Emily Honig, "Iron Girls Revisited: Gender and the Politics of Work in the Cultural Revolution," in Barbara Entwisle and Gail E. Henderson (eds.), *Re-Drawing Boundaries: Work, Households, and Gender in China* (Berkeley: University of California Press, 2000), 97–110.

For the fundamental transformation the masculinity ideal underwent during the first three decades of Soviet rule, see both Eliot Borenstein, *Men Without Women: Masculinity and Revolution in Russian Fiction, 1917–1929*

(Durham, NC: Duke University Press, 2001), and Lilya Kaganovsky, *How the Soviet Man Was Unmade: Cultural Fantasy and Male Subjectivity Under Stalin* (Pittsburgh: University of Pittsburgh Press, 2008). For the Chinese revolutionary project's impact on the social construct of masculinity, see Bret Hinsch, *Masculinities in Chinese History* (Lanham, MD: Rowman & Littlefield, 2013), 151–70.

The various elements of the late socialist Soviet masculinity crisis are featured in Elena Zdravomyslova and Anna Temkina, "The Crisis of Masculinity in Late Soviet Discourse," *Russian Social Science Review* 54, 1 (2013), 40–61. Two studies that identify the rapidly changing gender politics after Mao's death include Nimrod Baranovitch, *China's New Voices: Popular Music, Ethnicity, Gender, and Politics, 1978–1997* (Berkeley: University of California Press, 2003), as well as Wang Zheng, "From Xianglin's Wife to the Iron Girls: The Politics of Gender Representation," in David S. G. Goodman (ed.), *Handbook of the Politics of China* (Northampton, MA: Edward Edgar, 2015).

For an overview of how men's domestic roles changed after the fall of the Soviet Union, see Sarah Ashwin and Tatyana Lytkina, "Men in Crisis in Russia: The Role of Domestic Marginalization," *Gender and Society* 18, 2 (2004), 189–206. The emergence of the neoliberal entrepreneurial ethos and its impact on gender relations are covered in Andrea Mazzarino, "Entrepreneurial Women and the Business of Self-Development in Global Russia," *Signs* 38, 3 (2013), 623–45, and Alexei Yurchak, "Russian Neoliberal: The Entrepreneurial Ethic and the Spirit of 'True Careerism,'" *Russian Review* 62, 1 (2003), 72–90. The hypermasculine and ethnoexclusivist politics of the Putin era is examined in Oleg Riabov and Tatiana Riabova, "The Remasculinization of Russia? Gender, Nationalism, and the Legitimation of Power Under Vladimir Putin," *Problems of Post-Communism* 61, 2, (2014), 23–35.

The realities of female entrepreneurs in China receive treatment in Minglu Chen, *Tiger Girls: Women and Enterprise in the People's Republic of China* (Abingdon: Routledge, 2011). Monographs on women factory workers include Pun Ngai, *Made in China: Women Factory Workers in a Global Workplace* (Durham, NC: Duke University Press, 2005), and Tamara Jacka, *Rural Women in Urban China: Gender, Migration, and Social Change* (Armonk, NY: M. E. Sharpe, 2006). For a comprehensive treatment of contemporary Chinese masculinities, see Geng Song and Derek Hird, *Men and Masculinities in Contemporary China* (Leiden: Brill, 2014).

PART III

*

TRANSFORMATIONS
AND LEGACIES

18

Make Some Get Rich First: State Consumerism and Private Enterprise in the Creation of Postsocialist China

KARL GERTH

Who created postsocialist China? Starting in 1978, conventional histories explain, bold national leaders led by Deng Xiaoping, who took power that year, initiated a major transformation of Chinese society and foreign relations, known as the "market reforms and opening" or simply "the reforms" and "the reform era."[1] Leaders once again permitted small private plots for farming and small-scale private enterprises. Millions of farmers became better off. And millions of "self-employed, household-run businesses" (hereafter, I use the Chinese term, *getihu*) responded to the policy change from the top by establishing everything from dumpling stalls to interprovincial agricultural produce transport. Thanks to the policy changes initiated by Deng Xiaoping, conventional histories continue, these private farmers and businesspeople helped transform China from a land of socialist economic stagnation and consumer deprivation to one of dynamic markets and consumer plenty.

In recent years, scholars have challenged the Deng-led narrative of the postsocialist era by highlighting changes from below, experiments and risks taken first by local farmers, even in secret, and then by mom-and-pop private businesses in the countryside and cities.[2] Even the Chinese Communist Party (CCP) now sanctions such grassroots interpretations of change. The 48-part TV biopic, *Deng Xiaoping at the Crossroads of History* (2014), heavily emphasizes

---

1 "Reform" (*gaige*) or "reform and opening" (*gaige kaifang*) are the terms used by the Chinese government for the major policy changes that began in the late 1970s. I periodically place the term "reform" in quotations to flag the word as reflecting the party-state's promotion of the "policy changes," a more neutral term.
2 See Kate Xiao Zhou, *How the Farmers Changed China: Power of the People* (Boulder: Westview Press, 1996).

the commune where unauthorized decollectivization and private farming on household plots began. Hundreds of millions of people living in the country-side on rapidly disbanding communes led the way, as the chapters in this book by Carl Riskin as well as Mark Selden and Ho-fung Hung detail. At the same time, this biopic also narrates stories of local entrepreneurs such as the student who sold Chinese crepes, or *jianbing*, from a cart in Beijing in the late 1970s and early 1980s.[3] In these newer bottom-up interpretations, local change – rural and urban – paved the way for national change. Stated differently, change often came despite rather than as a result of national policies.

Yet bottom-up interpretations of the post-1978 era have two shortcomings of their own. First, they mention but do not explain the critical role of the Chinese state in promoting, condoning or, at the very least, looking the other way during the reintroduction of grassroots privatization of the state-controlled economy, that is, the rebirth of the market economy populated by small-scale businesses that gave way to the state capitalism and profit-oriented, massive corporations in the 1990s.[4] Local and national policy implementation was critical. Important initiatives came from below, but they flourished with the approval and direction of China's communist leadership. Second, such inter-pretations still focus on Chinese people in their capacities as workers and producers and, therefore, on production as the driver of history. But mom-and-pop shop proprietors and soon other merchants also changed China in their capacity as highly touted leading consumers in the mass media and popular imagination – the figurative Joneses that other Chinese wanted to catch up with, let alone keep up with. Although the vast majority of *getihu* remained poor, their desires, and the unintended consequences of their strug-gles to fulfill those desires, transformed China in the 1980s. And the state was central to the creation of institutions that promoted and protected consumer-ism and consumers, particularly *getihu*.

3 Thanks to Matthew Wills for suggesting I look at *Deng Xiaoping at the Crossroads of History* and for other suggestions on sources. See Chris Buckley, "Xi Jinping the Hidden Star of a TV Series About Deng Xiaoping," sinosphere.blogs.nytimes.com/2014/08/27/xi-jinping-the-hidden-star-of-a-tv-series-about-deng-xiaoping/?_.
4 I follow sociologist Ho-fung Hung's use of the term "capitalism" and his preference for seeing capitalism in China as a modified version of capitalism rather than a unique one that will challenge the existing global order. Hung distinguishes between markets and capitalism: "Whereas a market economy is grounded on exchange and competition among small producers, concerned more about livelihood than profit, capitalism is driven by profit maximization and wealth accumulation" (Ho-fung Hung, *The China Boom: Why China Will Not Rule the World* [New York: Columbia University Press, 2015], 8).

My focus here is on the evolving processes through which the state reauthorized and promoted market economy and consumerism, and the far-reaching consequences of the reemergence of small-scale private enterprise, long suppressed by the state, in postsocialist China. In the 1980s – that is, a decade before the widespread return of multinational corporations (MNCs) and the concurrent Chinese state attempts to create consolidated domestic competitors in the 1990s – the heart of revived markets and consumerism was the state-managed creation of a new class of local entrepreneurs, the *getihu*, and the revalorization of "bourgeois lifestyles," as they had been labeled and attacked during the previous decades, associated with modestly successful *getihu*.[5] In my account, this state-sponsored consumerism, or simply "state consumerism," becomes a primary force transforming postsocialist China. The postsocialist state directly and indirectly promoted this consumerism; but Chinese society also embraced consumerism, as it had done even during the height of the socialist era and despite the anti-consumerist rhetoric of that time. This does not mean that the Chinese state now embraces any and all consumerism as the new driver of the economy. Indeed, as an endless stream of Chinese and foreign economic reports point out, the Chinese state has been slow to shift from an economy centered on exports and state investment to a domestic-consumption-led economy.[6] In fact, state policies have taken it in the opposite direction by dismantling the social welfare state of the socialist era for those largely in cities lucky enough to have jobs at state-owned industries, making it more difficult to transfer wealth – and therefore purchasing power – into the hands of hundreds of millions of Chinese consumers.

A critical feature of the 1980s was the tension between how to benefit from and simultaneously restrain capitalist cultural influences and imports – that is, limit what had previously been labeled and attacked as "bourgeois consumerism." This tension helps explain the transitional policies underlying the early postsocialist era such as the creation of SEZs (Special Economic Zones), the promotion of Chinese cultural alternatives to popular imports, and the periodic mass campaigns such as the "Anti-Bourgeois Liberalization"

5 For an overview of Chinese efforts to build competitive MNCs, see Peter Nolan, *Is China Buying the World?* (Boston: Polity Press, 2013).
6 One such report to gain Chinese and international attention is World Bank and Development Research Center of the State Council of the People's Republic of China (eds.), *China 2030: Building a Modern, Harmonious, and Creative High-Income Society* (Washington, DC: World Bank, 2012). The complete report is available at www.worldbank.org/content/dam/Worldbank/document/China-2030-complete.pdf.

of the late 1980s and the "Anti-Spiritual Pollution" of 1983 – which included attacks not only on pornography, but also on new hairstyles, clothing and facial hair. But quickly changing national and local realities made yet another radical policy shift away from markets and consumer-led economic and social development less possible or likely. Take the ties of trade. The "reform" mantra had a second half: "market reform *and* opening to the outside world," that is, encouraging trade and investment from capitalist countries. Between 1971 and 1975, international trade tripled, with the vast majority of that trade conducted with noncommunist countries (85 percent). The trade deficit rose so quickly that imports were sharply curtailed in 1975, briefly slowing China's new strategy of importing capital and technology to speed economic development. China was so committed to foreign trade and foreign direct investment (FDI) by the end of the 1970s that some labeled the policies the country's "great leap outward."[7] Consequently, a better sign for China's new direction at the end of 1978 than the oft-cited Third Plenum and reemergence of Deng was the announcement on 15 December 1978 that the United States and China would establish formal diplomatic ties at the start of the new year.

Throughout the 1980s imported capital, products and culture continued to spread quickly. There was significant growth of FDI, particularly into the successful SEZs located in Guangdong and Fujian provinces, but also the influx of foreign products and brands, rapidly expanding the consumerism that had survived throughout the entire socialist era. By 1984, for instance, Volkswagen, IBM, Gillette, Coca Cola, Beatrice Foods and many other MNCs had operations in China. Trademark registrations provide a useful measure of the shift from a few to a plethora of branded products in China. In 1980, the Chinese government received 20,000 trademark applications, a number that by 1993 had reached 132,000.[8] In every area of Chinese life, new brands appeared, greatly expanding the vocabulary of a revived consumerism.

In addition, the state encouraged the advertising industry, the manufacturer of modern desire and disseminator of this vocabulary of consumerism. Above all, in China's postsocialist society, advertising created alternative narratives of the good life, narratives centered on personal happiness through acquisition and consumption rather than politics and work. Branded products

7 Carl Riskin, *China's Political Economy: The Quest for Development Since 1949* (Oxford: Oxford University Press, 1987), 259–60.
8 China State Council Information Office, White Paper, "New Progress on China's IPR Protection," Xinhua, 21 Apr. 2005.

spread hand in glove with advertising during this period. When David Ogilvy, dubbed the "Father of Advertising," visited China in the early 1980s, he was struck by the near-absence of advertising. Print advertisements looked like specification sheets, containing little more than detailed, technical information about a product and no evocative images. The few commercials on Chinese television mostly featured industrial products such as electric motors rather than consumer goods. The rare big billboard proclaimed the latest in communist propaganda. Ogilvy noted that the most important advertising medium in China was radio, "the communal speaker system reaching 75 percent of the population" that would broadcast advertisements, one right after another, twice a day. There were fewer than seventy ad agencies in all of China, with a quarter of those producing advertisements for Chinese goods overseas.[9] The change was staggering, even to contemporary observers. By the late 1990s, advertisements, along with brands, were everywhere.

Advertising and brands created new meanings in the marketplace but also contributed to tremendous consumer anxiety, a historical driver beyond the direct control of central planners. But policymakers helped create this new force: The implementation of the "household responsibility system" devolved the risks and rewards of household agricultural work and local enterprises, usually in market-oriented versions of the former collective enterprises, from the state to family leaders and enterprise managers. This policy change sanctioned the first wave of economic winners, most conspicuously decollectivized farmers with access to urban markets for their crops. The policies also created anxious losers, people disadvantaged by policy changes that, for example, undercut the security of state-sector workers.[10]

Thus the 1980s saw the postsocialist rebirth of the consumer marketplace closely associated with China in subsequent decades, namely, countless consumer-product scandals in China and abroad. Over the course of the 1980s, policymakers replaced fixed prices and distribution via state "work units" (*danwei*) with market prices and individual purchases. This environment created new consumer issues, including resentment and fear of unfair pricing, sales of imitations through deceptive

9 David Ogilvy, *Ogilvy on Advertising* (London: Prion Books, 2007), 187–88.
10 According to Frederick Teiwes and Warren Sun, Deng lagged behind even Hua Guofeng in supporting the household responsibility system: *Paradoxes of Post-Mao Rural Reform: Initial Steps Toward a New Chinese Countryside, 1976–1981* (New York: Routledge, 2015), 4.

packaging, food adulteration, false advertising claims, product liability, and warranty issues. Reemerging markets became sources of media scandals and popular panics and rumors. For instance, in the summer of 1985, a scandal erupted over the sale of supposedly dirty imported used clothing that was sold as new. A Beijing textile and clothing association investigation concluded that the clothing was not only filthy but also came from sick people. That winter twenty cities and counties participated in operations to search and destroy the offending clothing, called "foreign trash."[11]

Amid the growing number of market-related consumer scandals, it was unsurprising to see the state initiate a top-down "consumer movement" to further push policies designed to protect the interests of Chinese people as consumers with individual or family interests rather than as citizens participating in setting a national agenda. Indeed, in the 1980s, the Chinese term for "consumer" became much more popular. State-promoted consumerism helped develop the idea of Chinese people as "consumers" in the academic, bureaucratic and social spheres. In 1979, the government invited the American consumer advocate Ralph Nader for a two-week visit to China.[12] China's most important consumer association, the Chinese Consumers' Association (CCA), was established in 1983 as a quasi-state-sponsored consumer protection organization. By the end of the 1990s, the CCA had 3,000-plus local branches across China, had accepted over 6 million consumer complaints and had established a nationwide complaint hotline. Local consumer-protection efforts also began in the 1980s. In 1987, the northeast city of Shenyang passed the first local consumer-protection laws, and dozens of provinces and cities quickly enacted similar ones. The Shanghai Supreme Court agreed to accept consumer lawsuits in 1986, and an individual consumer won a case in the Nanjing Intermediate Court in 1987 against a department store over a defective television. In Sichuan, four people were given death sentences for selling a poisonous beverage that killed twenty-five people.

As the state embraced consumerism during the 1980s, the CCP recast itself as defender not of workers, farmers and others previously exploited by capitalism and imperialism but rather of new middle-class consumers.

---

11 For an account of a peddler who sold such clothing in Beijing, see Sang Ye, *China Candid: The People on the People's Republic* (Berkeley: University of California Press, 2006), ch. 1.

12 Randall E. Stross, *Bulls in the China Shop and Other Sino-American Business Encounters* (New York: Pantheon, 1990), 257.

The party-state established regulatory agencies such as the National Administration of Industry and Commerce (similar to the US Federal Trade Commission), which regulates trademarks and advertisements; the Commodity Inspection Bureau, which creates standards and requires companies to add product warnings and maintenance information; and the China Standards Bureau (similar to the US Consumer Product Safety Commission). Beginning in 1986, China officially established a yearly Consumer Rights Day in China (15 March). In short, new forms of state administration reflected the importance of consumers and consumerism.

The State of the Market, the Market of the State

The Chinese state did more than simply create institutions to manage and promote the market economy and consumerism. Its involvement in constructing markets determined who got rich first, that is, who got to consume what. In the 1980s, the state's role in making some rich first was more subtle, leading scholars such as the Massachusetts Institute of Technology business school professor Yasheng Huang to interpret the 1980s as a hopeful decade of mom-and-pop-led entrepreneurial capitalism. In contrast, during the 1990s, state-owned enterprises (SOEs) became profit-oriented corporations much more directly linked to the state; the resurgence of state control over the economy crushed entrepreneurial capitalism and created the "state capitalism" of China that dominates the Chinese economy down to the present. But this critical state role was there throughout the 1980s, even as markets displaced state provisioning. To paraphrase Honoré de Balzac, behind every new Chinese fortune, even the comparatively modest mom-and-pop fortunes of the 1980s, there was a state policy making some rich (and others poor).

State policies deregulating prices, for instance, created instant winners and losers. It was a dramatic change. By the end of the 1980s, the idea of price stability, a hallmark of the socialist era, had become a legacy. Inflation returned. Initially, the postsocialist era saw a shift from fixed prices, strictly controlled and unchanging, to three types of price policies: prices set by the government, prices set by businesses but fixed within a range, and prices set entirely by the market. Such policies created consumer problems, giving rise to the perception that prices were unfair and manipulated by the politically connected and ruthless rather than determined simply by naturally occurring "free markets." By the middle of the 1980s, with most prices no longer fixed by the state, an intensive market culture of negotiation, instability and uncertainty emerged. Market culture seemed to pop up everywhere, with self-employed peddlers (i.e. *getihu*) on every corner of city streets and commerce in formerly commerce-free places.

Despite the romanticization of the early postsocialist era as a "Golden Age for free markets," the state played a critical role in constructing those markets. From the start of the postsocialist era, the state facilitated the success of non-state-owned enterprises (non-SOEs): local township and village enterprises (TVEs), a marketized extension of the former collective whose numbers grew from 1.5 million in 1978 to 12 million by 1985.[13] TVEs were successful not because the state left the these businesses to live or die in free markets but rather because the state implemented a dual-price structure in the early postsocialist era that effectively forced SOEs to continue to sell at low prices but allowed TVEs to sell at higher market prices. Moreover, very few TVEs had to pay taxes, unlike SOEs.[14] They also did not have the extensive health and welfare costs of workers at SOEs. As a consequence of state policies favoring TVEs, rural production and incomes grew rapidly in the first years of the new era, peaking in 1985.[15] In other words, the first to get rich – namely, farmers with access to markets and those profiting from TVEs – were the direct beneficiaries of state policy, not of state withdrawal from the economy, as Yasheng Huang famously argued.[16]

The state also indirectly structured market opportunities. The Chinese market was still fragmented in the 1980s as a direct consequence of socialist-era policies, when the central-planning philosophy emphasized local and regional self-sufficiency for nearly all products. This system created an inefficient transportation infrastructure and local governments that protected state- and collectively owned businesses. With the existence of only a handful of national brands and products, many of them holdovers from the presocialist era, this fragmentation created opportunities for

13 TVEs were not necessarily owned by local governments and former communes, but tended to be located in townships and villages, the successors to teams and brigades. Ownership varied. See Yasheng Huang, *Capitalism with Chinese Characteristics* (New York: Cambridge University Press, 2008).
14 Wang Hui, "The New Criticism," in Wang Chaohua (ed.), *One China, Many Paths* (New York: Verso, 2003), 67.
15 Martin Hart-Landsberg and Paul Burkett, *China and Socialism: Market Reforms and Class Struggle* (New York: Monthly Review Press, 2005), 45–50. Agricultural incomes grew by 15 percent a year from 1978 to 1984, but slowed to 2 percent by the end of decade.
16 Huang, *Capitalism with Chinese Characteristics*. My critique draws on Joel Andreas, "A Shanghai Model?," *New Left Review* 65 (Oct.–Nov. 2010), 63–85.

small-scale enterprises to make and move local products between subnational internal markets.[17]

Many of the provisioning policies of the socialist era lingered on into the 1980s and early 1990s, maintaining a state role in structuring consumerism. Even in cities, the state still subsidized consumption, though often indirectly. Some Chinese consumers could afford higher levels of consumption because the government supplied, or at least heavily subsidized, essentials, including food, and ensured availability via a rationing system. The government also heavily subsidized necessities, such as housing, clothing and transportation. True, as China moved to a market economy, such subsidies for urbanites with jobs at SOEs, known as the "labor aristocracy," were reduced and eventually eliminated. In 1988, for instance, work units started selling housing to their occupants. But even here, the state policy ensured these were sold in ways that limited price and ensured affordability, allowing these early postsocialist consumers to buy other things.

The state also subsidized consumerism directly via the generous expense accounts of employees of ministries, the armed forces, schools, state-owned enterprises and other public organizations. This consumption was estimated at US$ 16.6 billion in 1994, of which about one-quarter remained unreported, and included products such as automobiles, furniture, electrical appliances and office supplies as well as health care and entertainment. In 1993, for example, the Chinese imported some 100,000 cars; expense accounts paid for 99 percent of them.[18] But these benefits also extended more modestly to urban workers. During the early postsocialist era, consumption was often done not through the individual or the family but rather via work units. SOEs used resources to buy consumer goods such as video recorders, TVs, radios and many other products for factory leaders and even workers as in-kind bonuses in lieu of cash.[19]

17 Many stories of early *getihu* were involved in moving products between different parts of China. For examples on how such *getihu* supplied Shenyang in the 1980s, see Liu Zhiqing, "Ziyou gouda: guanyu getihu jingji quan de baogao he sikao" [A Land of Freedom: A Report and Reflections on the *getihu* Economic Circles], initially published in *Yalujiang zazhi* 9 (1988), reprinted in Wang Lingxu (ed.), *Ziyou guodu: gongshang getihu shenghuo jishi* [A Land of Freedom: A Record of the Business *getihu* Economy] (Shanghai: Shanghai Academy of Social Sciences Press, 1993).
18 Rick Yan, "To Reach China's Consumers, Adapt to Guo Qing," *Harvard Business Review* 72, 5 (Sep.–Oct. 1994), 66–74.
19 Sociologist Andrew Walder has demonstrated in his now classic work that perks sustained the clientelist system at the heart of Chinese society: *Communist Neo-Traditionalism: Work and Authority in Chinese Industry* (Berkeley: University of California Press, 1986).

State policies indirectly shaped consumerism by creating ideal conditions for smuggling. Reminiscent of presocialist-era treaty ports, SEZs modeled on East Asian export zones were set up to lure foreign businesses and export-oriented Chinese enterprises with lower tax rates, fewer labor and environmental regulations, and duty-free imports. The regulations allowed duty-free imports to foreign companies and Chinese work units, which were expected to import supplies and raw materials and then export finished products to earn hard currency. At a time of high tariffs, this was an extremely valuable market advantage. In reality, SEZs created ideal conditions for speculators and smugglers who, for instance, imported cars for as little as US$ 8,000 duty-free and then sold them for US$ 20,000–30,000 in Beijing and Shanghai.

Hainan Island, a newly created province and SEZ, became a natural haven for smugglers and corrupt officials in 1980. As in the socialist era, Chinese work units continued to send delegations on "business trips" to make opportunistic purchases and buy whatever they could find, which would later facilitate luxurious lifestyles for cadres but also ease transactions between work units by using smuggled goods as bribes.[20] The same forms of smuggling and black-market activities occurred in other SEZs. For instance, although set up to promote exports, the vast majority of Shenzhen's products (approximately 70 percent) were sold on the domestic market rather than exported, often on the black market and for hard currency.[21] The most notorious outcome was the high-profile smuggling case of 1985, when smugglers used navy ships to transport foreign cars, TVs, video recorders and motorcycles into the duty-free port of Hainan.

The People's Liberation Army (PLA), another part of the Chinese state, also shaped consumerism. For instance, the PLA owned 20,000 enterprises by the end of the 1980s and was finally forced to divest from commercial activity in 1998, though not before earning the nickname "PLA, Inc."[22] These activities should be seen partially as a socialist era holdover. Even during the Cultural Revolution decade (1966–76), the supposed height of anti-capitalist modernity, General Lin Biao had instructed the PLA to become

20 Jim Mann, *Beijing Jeep: The Short, Unhappy Romance of American Business in China* (New York: Simon & Schuster, 1989), 145–46.
21 Hart-Landsberg and Burkett, *China and Socialism*, 49.
22 See Cao Haili, "1998 nian Jiang Zemin xuanbu 'Jundui bu zai jing shang' zhenjing shijie" [News of Jiang Zemin Declaring "the Army Is No Longer in Business" Shocks the World], in *Yinbiao song 1998 kaishi* [Exploding Start from 1998] (Beijing: Shijie zhishi chubanshe, 1999).

a "big school," training workers and farmers in agriculture and sideline production. In the first years of the Cultural Revolution, most army units in the PLA became self-sufficient in meat and vegetable production. By 1971, as many as 600,000 soldiers were involved in industrial production. Markets created opportunities to sell their product and the "military-business complex" grew especially quickly in the 1984–89 period, when the PLA moved into light consumer goods, manufacturing everything from baby carriages to pianos and washing machines. Likewise, the PLA became an export powerhouse, with its factories exporting hundreds of products, including more than 30 million pairs of shoes by the mid 1980s.[23]

Thus the earliest, highest-profile consumers in the postsocialist era included the PLA and others connected with the government and party. Their consumption had political implications. The PLA military-industrial complex was at the heart of the dual-track price system and "official racketeering" scandals of the 1980s, a central complaint during the 1989 Tiananmen demonstrations. PLA units and soldiers used their special access to government-subsidized scarce goods, which they then resold on the open market for quick profits. This was especially problematic in the late 1980s, as China transitioned from price controls to market prices, sparking instant inflation, itself a big incentive for consumers to spend before the money lost its value. PLA corruption was also used to fund unauthorized building projects such as officers' quarters, personal automobiles, feasts and countless other forms of consumption.[24] Corrupt consumption became ubiquitous. It also became politically useful. With participation so common, nearly all cadres were vulnerable to accusations of corruption, as forms of consumption became telltale signs of bourgeois lifestyles and/or corruption. Prime Minister Zhao Ziyang's love of golf, for instance, was used as indisputable evidence of his bourgeois tendencies during the conservative counterattack surrounding the post-Tiananmen crackdown in 1989.[25] Indeed, high-end consumption by officials (and their children) remains as politically dangerous today under President Xi Jinping and his anti-corruption campaigns as it was in earlier periods.

These state policies impacted on everyday consumerism. Fear of inflation in the mid 1980s, for instance, spurred a specific form of consumption.

23 James C. Mulvenon, *Soldiers of Fortune: The Rise and Fall of the Chinese Military-Business Complex, 1978–1998* (New York: Routledge, 2001), 47–48, 57.
24 Ibid., 61.
25 Seth Faison, *South of the Clouds: Exploring the Hidden Realms of China* (New York: St. Martin's Press, 2004), 97–100.

Consumers feared that the lifting of price controls would also lift prices, making their savings worth less. "Panic purchasing" (*qianggou feng*) ensued, especially for alcohol and cigarettes in August 1988, when price controls were lifted.[26] Consumers also sought to convert their cash into consumer goods as quickly as possible as a hedge against inflation, creating consumer binges for TVs, washing machines, refrigerators and cassette recorders. One American reporter in China at the time, James Mann, described the result as a consumer "frenzy."[27] Once again, though, such frenzies had also existed in a different form in the socialist era of shortages. Consumers then feared that they would miss out on the limited opportunities to buy something rather than because they worried about inflation, which had been nearly nonexistent in the socialist era. Or they coveted the product on offer, especially hard-to-obtain famous brands of bicycles and watches, which helps explain the devotion to those same brands in the postsocialist era when they have become readily available. When the Japanese wristwatch manufacturer Seiko, a brand that had continued to have underground appeal throughout the socialist era, opened a store in Beijing, it attracted 5,000 visitors a day.[28]

The consumer situation changed dramatically in the 1980s in Chinese cities, from one in which products of any quality were in short supply to one in which there was a glut of low-quality domestically made products, a glut exacerbated by the easy availability of higher-quality, competitively priced smuggled goods, especially in the free-for-all early days of the post-socialist era. Despite massive efforts, in the early 1980s, local governments fought a losing battle against smuggled foreign goods, especially with the simultaneous emergence of private peddlers. But by the mid 1980s officials claimed the tide had turned against smugglers, reflecting broader changes in the market.[29] A massive increase in products led to the market shift in the mid 1980s from a sellers' market to a choosy consumers' market. The 41 million wristwatches produced in 1985 represented a nearly 10 percent increase over the previous year. Other previously hard-to-buy products such as bicycles saw bigger increases, growing by 13 percent between 1984 and 1985 to 32 million. The production increases were even greater for washing machines, refrigerators, cameras, cassette recorders and other previously

26 For a description of the panic purchasing by a Xinhua reporter, see Chen Yun, "Xinhuashe bei pi" [Xinhua Criticized], *NewsQQ* (28 Oct. 2009), news.qq.com/a/2009 1028/000576.htm.
27 Mann, *Beijing Jeep*, 144.   28 Stross, *Bulls in the China Shop*, 249.
29 "Customs Brings Smuggling Under Control," *Xinhua News Agency* (3 Aug. 1986).

unavailable consumer goods.[30] In major cities such as Tianjin, by 1985 most homes had a black-and-white TV (and 16 percent had a color TV, up from none at the start of the decade). While under 10 percent had refrigerators, the percentage of households with refrigerators was growing quickly, up from zero at the start of the decade.[31]

Unsurprisingly, as pent-up desire for previously hard-to-acquire goods was finally met, consumers began to want new things, creating an inflation of desires, another driver of postsocialist social and economic change well beyond the control of national leaders. By the mid 1980s, the "Three Big-Ticket Items" of the socialist era (bicycles, wristwatches and sewing machines) had been replaced with the "Four Big-Ticket Items": color TVs, double cassette recorders, double-door refrigerators and washing machines. As an official for the Ministry of Commerce said, "People are buying products they didn't dare dream of a decade ago. They think they are essential to a better way of life."[32] Such desires extended to other products associated with a bourgeois lifestyle: carpets, pajamas and even wallpaper.

Geti Who? State-Supported Grassroots Change in Postsocialist China

The most important contribution of the Chinese state to revived consumerism was its role in reinvigorating the class of those who wanted – and could afford – the must-have items such as refrigerators and TVs as well as the new consumer luxuries such as blue jeans and disco dancing. Beginning in the 1970s, millions of new *getihu* became a primary force spreading not only private enterprise but also the corollary, the revived consumerism made possible by economic success.[33] In 1978, there were only 150,000 private

---

30 "1985 Economic, Social Statistics Revealed," *Xinhua News Agency* (28 Feb. 1986).

31 "Tianjin Residents Possess More Consumer Goods," *Xinhua News Agency* (26 Feb. 1986).

32 "Consumers More Affluent, More Demanding," *Xinhua News Agency* (8 Oct. 1986).

33 At first, *getihu* were the only category of people allowed to engage in private-sector activity. To avoid ideological debates over capitalism existing in an avowedly socialist economy, they were limited to fewer than eight employees, not including the owner and family members, a seemingly artificial limit but actually drawn from Marx (Susan Young, *Private Business and Economic Reform in China* [Armonk, NY: M. E. Sharpe, 1995], 5). But in 1987 Beijing allowed for a second classification of private entrepreneur – the *siying qiye*, or "private enterprise," with more than seven employees. Once again, this measure simply legalized what had already been happening at the grassroots level; private enterprises had already exceeded the seven-employee limit. See Susan McEwen, "New Kids on the Block," *China Business Review* 21, 3 (May–Jun. 1994), 35–39.

businesses; a decade later, there were more than 14 million *getihu*.[34] These numbers grew so fast in part because legalization of *getihu* effectively recognized – and attempted to regulate – private economic activity that was already occurring.[35] In contrast to the socialist-era revolutionary ideology of equality, in which displays of wealth were at times deemed crimes against the state or, at the very least, an indication of "thought problems," this accelerating privatization of the economy symbolized by the spread of *getihu* immediately produced new classes of relatively prosperous Chinese who demanded Coke, Pierre Cardin shirts and countless other new consumer goods. Of 1,490 *getihu* households in a single district of Tianjin by 1984, for example, 946 had acquired televisions, 433 cassette recorders, 90 refrigerators and 48 motorcycles.[36]

The simple existence of modestly well-off people who profited from market transactions and manifested their new economic power in consumerism reflected a profound transformation in China. At the end of the socialist era and into the 1980s, China had been egalitarian relative to capitalist countries. But it was also desperately poor, and the income gap was large between the richer cities and the countryside, which was squeezed to support cities via low state-set prices for agricultural products and state subsidies for urban housing, welfare and medical care. At the same time, the "household registration system" (also known in English by its Chinese name, *hukou*) posed obstacles to rural residents seeking better-paying jobs in cities even as the rural migrant population surged. But, as a result of new social and economic policies making possible gains for the newly well off, starting in the 1980s and becoming more pronounced in the 1990s, China became a much more visibly unequal country.[37]

Different classes of China's newly prosperous and wealthy consumers emerged at various stages of the postsocialist policies.[38] After farmers and those connected with successful TVEs, the first group to appear was the

34 Young, *Private Business*, 6.
35 Ole Bruun, *Business and Bureaucracy in a Chinese City: An Ethnography of Private Business Households in Contemporary China* (Berkeley: Institute of East Asian Studies, 1992), 48.
36 Marcia Yudkin, *Making Good: Private Business in Socialist China* (Beijing: Foreign Languages Press, 1986), 30.
37 See Carl Riskin, "China's Human Development After Socialism," in this volume; and Andrew Walder, *China Under Mao: A Revolution Derailed* (Cambridge, MA: Harvard University Press, 2015), 331. China was the most inegalitarian socialist country in the 1970s, with a Gini coefficient of 0.33, a number that peaked at 0.491 in 2008 and then trended downward. Of course, 0.33 is not a high level.
38 Xiaowei Zeng, "Market Transition, Wealth and Status Claims," in David S. G. Goodman (ed.), *The New Rich in China: Future Rulers, Present Lives* (London: Routledge, 2008), 53–70.

small-scale household entrepreneurs (the *getihu*), who led China's initial service and petty retailing revolution. As many of the 17 million young people "sent down to the countryside" before and during the Cultural Revolution decade returned to Chinese cities seeking work, the Chinese government officially recognized that massive urban unemployment had to be addressed, but it was not prepared to allocate massive state resources to solve the problem. In February 1979, the Central Committee of the CCP approved a report by the State Administration for Industry and Commerce that advised the central government to allow unemployed people with urban "household registrations" to start their own private businesses, but restricted such businesses to repair, services and handcrafts. Initially, as leaders felt ambivalent about abruptly reembracing private enterprise, *getihu* were forbidden to hire workers, a restriction that was quickly ignored and gradually changed as the range and size of private businesses expanded.[39] Virtually every business surveyed by Ole Bruun in Chengdu in the late 1980s had employees that were not, as they were required to be, registered. Such "employees" seldom included workers hired off the streets but rather were neighbors, distant relatives and former coworkers.[40] By 1985, *getihu* numbered nearly 10 million. Roadside bicycle-repair shops, food stalls and fruit vendors appeared everywhere. In the countryside, home to three-fourths of these new enterprises, individuals set up fishing ponds, restaurants, repair shops and other small businesses.

Getihu pushed economic changes into unauthorized areas by playing a role in the black markets mentioned above. For instance, enterprising people contracted formerly collectively owned boats to conduct smuggling operations. In the mid 1980s, two such boats alone were discovered by customs officials to have 10,000 wristwatches, while two other boats stopped by Guangzhou officials had more than 2,000 Japanese cameras.[41] Moreover, as limits on the number of allowable employees expanded, so did the numbers employed in the private sector, reaching more than 18 million by 1988.[42]

39 Chen Guanren, "'Wenge' you Zhongguo shoujia siying fandian: Yuebin fandian" [Yuebin Restaurant, the First Privately Owned Restaurant in China After the Cultural Revolution], initially published in *Zhongwai shu zhai* 3 (2010), 32–35, www .zwszzz.com/DCFB/bkview.asp?bkid=191395&cid=630477.
40 Bruun, *Business and Bureaucracy*, 62.
41 "Guangdong Smuggling Cases Fewer but Bigger," *Xinhua News Agency* (21 Mar. 1986).
42 The trends and statistics for the establishment of *getihu* are summarized in Wu Nan, "Gaige kaifang hou de xiahai jingshang yanjiu" [A Study of the Trends of Going into Business After the Start of the Reform and Opening Era] (M.A. thesis, Liaoning University, 2011).

The early years for *getihu* were a time of anxious consumerism, as a local saying in Chengdu conveyed: "What your stomach contains, no one can take away from you."[43] They feared yet another policy reversal on private enterprise, cognizant that any reversal might close their businesses and confiscate their earnings. One peddler even worked his anxieties into the name of his business. In September 1980, in the Yangpu District of Shanghai, an unemployed youth set up a stall named the "Long and Short Pavilion" (Changduan ting) selling dumplings and snacks. The proprietor explained that "the business will last a long time if the policy stays in place; it will be short-lived if the policy changes."[44] This anxiety constrained consumption. According to the sociologist Thomas Gold, who conducted interviews with *getihu* in the 1980s, most "had little confidence in the life expectancy of the policy that spawned them. They therefore set out to earn as much money as they could, consuming it aggressively in the expectation that their halcyon days were numbered."[45] After decades of state-sanctioned attacks on private enterprise as "tails" of capitalism, unsurprisingly, this newly affluent group was accorded low social status. While some *getihu* became better off than state workers, few became part of the newer, wealthier aristocracy that began to emerge by the late 1980s.[46]

The richer among the new wealthy were generally much more directly connected to the state than those who began as *getihu*. A second and more successful group among the wealthy consumers emerged with the reforms of 1985, when the government allowed state enterprises to sell their surplus products and keep the profits. As noted, this promptly created a dual-track price structure for commodities: a lower price for quotas earmarked for the state and a higher market price, often 200 or 300 percent higher. Tens of millions of Chinese exploited these price differentials, the most successful being the politically connected, especially the children of high-ranking officials, the "princelings" (or the "princeling party"), holding provincial and national offices, who used their connections to gain control over public resources and to ensure state buyers even for bad products. Such speculation

43 Quoted in Bruun, *Business and Bureaucracy*, 44.
44 Chen Guanren, "'Wenge' you Zhongguo shoujia siying fandian: Yuebin fandian." See also Zhang Xutang, "Cong Weimeiguan dao Changduan ting yi 20 nian guanyu get canguan de baodao fengbo" [From Delicious to the Long and Short Pavilion: 20 Years of Reporting on *getihu* Restaurants], *Xinwen jizhe zazhi* 6 (2000), 52–53.
45 Thomas Gold, "Urban Private Business and China's Reforms," in Richard Baum (ed.), *Reform and Reaction in Post-Mao China: The Road to Tiananmen* (New York: Routledge, 1991), 94.
46 Zhahui Hong, "Mapping the Evolution and Transformation of the New Private Entrepreneurs in China," *Journal of Chinese Political Science* 9, 1 (Spring 2004), 26–27.

within this dual-track price structure became known as "official racketeer-ing," and its practitioners were labeled profiteers or wheeler-dealers. During the 1980s, this racketeering generated as much as 600 billion *yuan* in profits, while those who got rich by it were labeled parasites, responsible for the rapid inflation that followed the price reforms of the late 1980s. As noted, such official racketeering, rather than only or primarily a lack of political freedom and vague ideas of "democracy," was a leading complaint fueling the Tiananmen Square demonstrations of 1989.

But those early state-connected wheeler-dealers were poor compared to the land speculators who gained their riches starting in the late 1980s. The latter became China's first billionaires. As with official racketeering, land speculators relied on political connections to gain the right to purchase choice parcels of land and secure loans from state-owned banks. Chinese land developers are seen by most Chinese as completely dependent on state connections. They use connections so that they need pay only a small fraction of the value of land expropriated from urban residents and farmers in areas surrounding cities and obtain unsecured low-interest loans from state banks to finance construction. According to one report, 90 percent of China's billionaires (measured in *yuan*) are princelings, including nearly all of the richest developers in China – nine of the top ten real estate magnates and thirteen of the richest fifteen owners of construction companies in Shanghai.[47] Many Chinese blame this group for the inflation of the late 1980s and the inflated Chinese housing market thereafter, which has made home ownership prohibitively expensive and slowed the spread of a broader, middle-class consumerism.[48]

Although not as directly dependent on state connections as subsequent wealthy groups, even modestly successful *getihu* also had forms of state support, including crucial but subtle local official and state media support. Such was the case with the woman credited with opening Beijing's first private restaurant in the aftermath of the Cultural Revolution on 30 September 1980. Liu Guixian lived near the famous shopping street of Wangfujing in Beijing with her husband Guo Peiji, a cook at a state-owned engine factory. The couple had five children, none of whom had jobs or even

---

47 "90 Percent of China's Billionaires Are Children of Senior Officials," *China Digital Times* (2 Nov. 2006).
48 Outside the timeframe of this chapter is a fourth category of the new rich: former managers of state-owned enterprises (SOEs) who became wealthy during the rapid and notably corrupt conversion of public enterprises into private and stockholder-owned companies beginning in the late 1990s. See Minxin Pei, "How China Is Ruled," *American Interest* 3, 4 (Mar.–Apr. 2008), 44–52.

job prospects. Liu heard a news story about a couple in northeast China selling dumplings (*baozi*) on the street that they had made themselves. As with other early *getihu*, Liu's business had state backing. Cadres at Beijing's Dongcheng District Industrial and Commercial Bureau wanted to comply with national directives and help launch new businesses as well as endorse such *getihu* as examples for others to follow. When Liu Guixian went to submit an application, although there was as yet no official license, the cadres allowed her to start the restaurant despite not having an official license to issue.[49]

Official permission was not the only obstacle. Liu Guixian also lacked the ration coupons necessary to stock her restaurant. After a local reporter covered her story, she was given grain and oil rations by a stranger. But she still needed a longer-term solution to secure supplies. Once again, the state helped. Beijing's Dongcheng District Industrial and Commercial Bureau dispatched a senior cadre of the bureau, a man identified only as a Mr. Suo, under pressure to implement the policy, to help find a solution. Mr. Suo went to the Dongcheng Food Bureau to reassure them that the restaurant was a pilot project and had official permission. Eventually the food bureau gave Liu special permission to buy grain, flour and oil. Mr. Suo also helped her secure a 500-yuan bank loan by cosigning, and this at a time when private bank loans were extremely rare. He even helped her select an appropriate name, steering her away from her initial choice, "Green Flower" (Cuihua), which sounded like a traditional brothel name, in favor of "Pleasing Guests" (Yuebin). By National Day on 1 October 1980, the restaurant was ready to open. Despite rain, the line for a seat at the four tables stretched out the door. By the time she closed, the restaurant had made more than 40 yuan in profit, a sum roughly equal to her husband's monthly salary.

Repeating the pattern of "reforms" following on-the-ground realities, although the business was technically against the rules limiting the scope of private enterprises to service and repair, Liu Guixian's restaurant received tacit state endorsement in the state media when Wang Daren, a reporter of *Beijing Evening News*, publicized the new venture. National and international media attention followed. News of a privately established restaurant attracted American Embassy officials, who made a regular reservation. The US Embassy even made a promotional map and distributed it to other

---

49 For the basis of the story, I rely on Chen Guanren, "'Wenge' you Zhongguo shoujia siying fandian: Yuebin fandian."

embassies. With those group reservations, Liu and her husband made thousands in profits each month. As they recalled the magnitude of their new wealth, they earned enough every day to buy the once-coveted but hard to obtain Flying Pigeon brand bicycle.

As with *getihu* around China, Liu and her family encountered other problems, especially the envy and animosity of neighbors. Most people on her street disapproved of her opening a restaurant. One person believed that, as a private businessperson, Liu was by definition a "capitalist" opposed to the CCP. Another neighbor suggested Liu was a spy for foreign countries. Reflecting the widespread uncertainty about national policies, neighbors warned her that she would regret it someday and that the government would eventually close private businesses such as hers. The stigma extended to her family. Classmates of her youngest son stopped visiting after the restaurant opened. The boy also was given the cold shoulder by neighborhood children; another child called him "a pioneer in the restoration of capitalism" (*zibenzhuyi fubi ji xianfeng*).

Reversing decades of anti-capitalist news coverage, the state media attempted to teach Liu's neighbors and everyone else of the legitimacy of private enterprise in a "socialist" country.[50] The publication of such articles in state newspapers signaled official support for the changes underway even before policy officially sanctioned them.[51] Private restaurants in other Chinese cities had raised similar issues for policymakers and confronted the same problems well before the Pleasing Guests restaurant opened in Beijing. On 12 July 1980, months before Pleasing Guests debuted, for example, Chen Guigen, an unemployed youth in Shanghai, overcame his fears of being labeled a "capitalist tail" and opened a private restaurant named Delicious. To encourage others to follow Chen's example, the next day Zhang Xutang, the director of news at a leading newspaper, *Wenhui bao*, published a front-page story, and a month later the *People's Daily* picked up the story. His restaurant created a public debate on issues such as: Should private restaurants be legal? If private restaurateurs get rich first, would it affect Chinese socialism? Could Chen Yungen, the younger brother of Chen Guigen as well as a chef at a state-owned restaurant, work for his older brother's private restaurant in his own time? The Shanghai City Hall Office of Finance and Trade convened meetings with related departments including labor, industry and commerce, tax,

50 Yudkin, *Making Good*, 27, 42.
51 Zhang Xutang, "Cong Weimeiguan dao Changduan ting yi 20 nian guanyu get canguan de baodao fengbo." See *Wenhui bao* (13 Jul. 1980) and *RMRB* (10 Oct. 1980).

house management and food bureaus to discuss conflicts and issues raised by Delicious. Official policy on private restaurants eventually caught up with local realities. On 4 November 1980, the Beijing government decided to allow individuals to enter food and petty retailing businesses. Moreover, on the eve of the Chinese New Year Festival the following year, Liu Guixian was told that national and municipal leaders would pay her a traditional ceremonial visit to wish her well in the new year, another endorsement of the policy changes her restaurant represented.

The unraveling of direct state control over the economy accelerated through small acts of defiance or desperation, often with the complicity, tacit agreement or active support of local officials. A *getihu* proprietor in Wenzhou, for instance, wanted to buy clothing in Shanghai and Guangzhou, where the selection was better and more fashionable. But at that time, police officers checked the documents of travelers in bus stations and harbors. *Getihu* needed letters from bureau-level or higher authorities to buy ship tickets. *Getihu* such as Ye Yongguo got his local industrial and commercial bureau (the Wenzhou Industrial and Commercial Bureau) to provide a letter of introduction authorizing him to buy clothing on their behalf, which allowed Ye to buy ship tickets. Other *getihu* then followed his example, and indeed Wenzhou became a national leader in promoting the activities of *getihu*.[52]

Although much wealthier businesspeople such as factory owners and property developers quickly displaced *getihu* as symbols of the Chinese wealthy, *getihu* were critical to the rapid expansion of consumerism. The modestly successful ones were local and exposed ordinary Chinese people throughout the country, in cities and villages, to the new lifestyles available to those with the money to buy them. As Peng Mingyin, a *getihu* proprietor running a cured meat business in Jinan told an investigator in the early 1980s: "Look, a colour TV, 1,700 yuan! Tape recorder, 600 yuan. Look, high-quality tea . . . Outside, I have a Suzuki motorcycle. I can afford to buy a car but – no place to park it. If they asked me to be head of the province, I wouldn't do it. He makes only 200 yuan a month."[53]

And *getihu* lifestyles became the objects of envy and emulation. As exemplified by their higher disposable incomes and more luxurious

52 You Chengyong, Xiao Xinhua and Wang Danrong, "Wenzhou getihu: shichang xianxingzhe. Huanyuan Zhongguo diyi dai getihu de nei duan lishi" [Wenzhou *getihu*: Market Pioneers. The History of China's First Generation of *getihu*], *Wenzhou Daily* (7 Jan. 2008), 1.
53 Yudkin, *Making Good*, 1.

lifestyles, *getihu* created local envy. Deng Xiaoping had famously stated in 1985 and other years that China must "first allow one group of people to get rich."[54] That happened. But it also created difficult-to-address problems. Envy inspired many popular expressions, including "It's better to sell eggs than to work developing nuclear bombs."[55] Thus a hallmark of Chinese consumerism in the early postsocialist era was the continuity of negative associations with those who had nice things, which had been especially prominent during the first few years of the Cultural Revolution decade. In the socialist era, having and even desiring nice things could signify corruption, illegal activity or simply ideological incorrectness. In the early postsocialist era, in addition, having nice possessions could also suggest an engagement in commerce by one who probably came from a lower-class, or had a politically problematic class, background and was thus willing to take the risk of becoming a low-status but higher-income *getihu*. As I have argued elsewhere, there was a popular love–hate relationship with *getihu* and other newly rich: They were envied for their access to new consumer lifestyles but often reviled for how they had become wealthy.[56]

Conclusion

Sanctioning *getihu* became a new way for the Chinese state to continue to shape and endorse consumerism. As more than 10 million "educated youth" (*zhiqing*) returned to Chinese cities from their rustication, joining the already swollen ranks of those waiting years for government-assigned jobs, allowing very small-scale private enterprise in the form of *getihu* was an inexpensive fix. In addition, *getihu* filled innumerable holes in the Chinese economy, particularly in basic services ranging from bicycle repairs to restaurants and

---

54 Deng Xiaoping used this phrase with a visiting American delegation in 1985 and again with the prime minister of New Zealand in 1986: "Deng Xiaoping: Rang yibufenren xian fuqilai" [Deng Xiaoping: First Allow One Group of People to Get Rich], *Zhongguo Gongchandang xinwen wang*, cpc.people.com.cn/GB/34136/2569304 .html. The oft-repeated phrase "to get rich is glorious" may be apocryphal and instead comes from the title of a best-selling English-language book about China at that time (Orville Schell's *To Get Rich Is Glorious* [New York: Pantheon, 1984]), but conforms with other quotations justifying inequality as necessary to economic development. See Evelyn Iritani, "Great Idea but Don't Quote Him," *Los Angeles Times* (9 Sep. 2004).

55 Interview, Mrs. Wang Yushi (b. 1955 in Ji'nan) conducted by her daughter, Feng Ying, on 8 Aug. 2014; follow-up questions on 18 Aug. 2014.

56 Karl Gerth, "Lifestyles of the Rich and Infamous: The Creation and Implication of China's New Aristocracy," *Comparative Sociology* 10, 4 (2011), 488–507.

food stalls. Moreover, a *getihu* from Shenyang claimed that his produce transport business preempted social problems associated with food-price spikes. For instance, in 1987, the price for green peppers doubled in local markets. One enterprising *getihu* quickly sourced several tens of thousands of the vegetables from Guangdong and Guangxi provinces, on the other side of the country, which reduced the price below its prespike level.[57] In effect, *getihu* such as these became effective ways for the state to "outsource" or "subcontract" its own former responsibilities.

As this chapter argues, *getihu* symbolized the shift to a postsocialist country that occurred across the 1980s. *Getihu* became local symbols of the advantages of market "reforms" and the justification for further market policies such as the expansion of the private economy at the expense of the state-controlled economy, whether in the privatization of state-owned enterprises in the cities or in the disbanding of communes in the countryside. Of course, the vast majority of *getihu* did not get rich quickly (or at all). But in the state-controlled mass media and the popular imagination, *getihu* became symbols of a surefire pathway to prosperity: individual initiative. This shift had political implications critical for understanding the transition to postsocialism. Blame for individual economic problems such as unemployment or a low standard of living – and responsibility for ameliorating it – shifted onto the individual and his or her relationship to markets, rather than to the state and its handling of the economy. Can't find a job? Exercise your own initiative and find your own source of income such as selling homemade dumplings on a street corner, as the proprietors of the Long and Short Pavilion did. And that solution – self-reliance – had its complement in consumerism. Can't afford betrothal gifts? Or, unlike your neighbors, can't afford a color TV, a refrigerator, washing machine or even a cassette recorder – the new must-have Four Big-Ticket Items? Start a business and, with your earnings, buy status.

It would be easy to describe the foregoing as the natural consequence of the shift from socialism to capitalism in the 1980s. Once upon a time, the state was responsible for everything; then the market took command. But such a conclusion overlooks the critical role the state played in creating *getihu* and promoting the positive values associated with them and with the market during the transitions of the 1980s. This state role extended from the national top, particularly in the "reform and opening" policies, to their local implementation in the "smashing of the iron rice bowl" of employment

---

57 Liu Zhiqing, *Ziyou gouda—guanyu getihu jingji quan de baogao he sikao.*

in state-owned enterprises. Neither at the national nor at the local level did the state "get out of the way" and allow markets to reappear spontaneously. Despite his famous mandate that China "let some get wealthy first," Deng Xiaoping and the Chinese state did not simply step aside and "let" anyone become wealthy. State policies and their implementation smoothed the path for some to get wealthy first and, in fact, directly or indirectly pushed them to try.

Bibliographical Essay

On the political economy of the early transition to postsocialism, see Joseph Fewsmith, *Dilemmas of Reform in China: Political Conflict and Economic Debate* (Armonk, NY: M. E. Sharpe, 1994); Barry Naughton, *Growing out of the Plan: Chinese Economic Reform, 1978–1993* (Cambridge: Cambridge University Press, 1995); and his influential textbook, *The Chinese Economy: Transitions and Growth* (Cambridge: MIT Press, 2006 [updated edition forthcoming]). See also Carl Riskin, *China's Political Economy: The Quest for Development Since 1949* (Oxford: Oxford University Press, 1987). A leading government economic advisor throughout the era, Wu Jinglian, has also written a helpful survey: *Understanding and Interpreting Chinese Economic Reform* (Mason, OH: Thomson Higher Education, 2005).

The abandonment of the state-dominated economy and reestablishment of markets has had many critics on the left. See Martin Hart-Landsberg and Paul Burkett, *China and Socialism: Market Reforms and Class Struggle* (New York: Monthly Review Press, 2005). These criticisms were often leveled concurrently with the new policies. See, for instance, Michel Chossudovsky, *Towards Capitalist Restoration? Chinese Socialism After Mao* (London: Macmillan, 1986), and the writings of William Hinton, especially *The Great Reversal: The Privatization of China, 1978–1989* (New York: Monthly Review Press, 1990).

For a thorough critique of the myth of a Deng-initiated "reform era," which nonetheless emphasizes the top-down origins of the changes, see the work jointly written by the leading authorities on elite politics in Mao and transitional eras, Frederick Teiwes and Warren Sun, especially *Paradoxes of Post-Mao Rural Reform: Initial Steps Toward a New Chinese Countryside, 1976–1981* (New York: Routledge, 2015) and *The End of the Maoist Era: Chinese Politics During the Twilight of the Cultural Revolution, 1972–1976* (Armonk, NY: M. E. Sharpe, 2007).

For a bottom-up interpretation of the transition to the market economy that emphasizes unauthorized decollectivization rather than experiments by regional and local leaders, see Kate Xiao Zhou, *How the Farmers Changed China: Power of the People* (Boulder: Westview Press, 1996). This view has been popularized by Frank Dikötter in *The Cultural Revolution: A People's History, 1962–1976* (New York: Bloomsbury, 2016). Studies of the rural transformation that acknowledge the impact of local officials include Jonathan Unger, *The Transformation of Rural China* (Armonk, NY: M.E. Sharpe, 2002). Long-term case studies similarly demonstrate the critical role of local officials. See, for instance, Edward Friedman, Paul G. Pickowicz and Mark Selden, *Revolution, Resistance, and Reform in Village China* (New Haven: Yale University Press, 2005), and Marc Blecher and Vivienne Shue, *Tethered Deer: Government and Economy in a Chinese County* (Stanford: Stanford University Press, 1996), 63–85.

The best-known proponent of the Golden Age of small-scale private enterprise in the 1980s is Yasheng Huang, *Capitalism with Chinese Characteristics* (New York: Cambridge University Press, 2008). For a thorough critique, see Joel Andreas, "A Shanghai Model?," *New Left Review* 65 (Oct.–Nov. 2010). Another study that downplays the role of the state in the economic transformation is Victor Nee and Sonja Opper, *Capitalism from Below: Markets and Institutional Change in China* (Cambridge, MA: Harvard University Press, 2012). For a balanced assessment of the relationship between TVEs and the state, see Jean C. Oi, *Rural China Takes Off: Institutional Foundations of Economic Reform* (Berkeley: University of California Press, 1999).

The best academic studies of *getihu* were published by social scientists who observed the implementation of the policies during the 1980s. The most influential is the work by Dorothy J. Solinger, especially *Chinese Business Under Socialism: The Politics of Domestic Commerce, 1949–1980* (Berkeley: University of California Press, 1984). For a helpful overview of the specific policy changes – and the range of attitudes toward them – in the early development of *getihu*, see Dorothy J. Solinger, "Commerce: The Petty Private Sector and the Three Lines on the Early 1980s," in Dorothy J. Solinger (ed.), *Three Visions of Chinese Socialism* (Boulder: Westview Press, 1984), 73–111. Particularly valuable for its use of interviews conducted in the early 1980s is Marcia Yudkin, *Making Good: Private Business in Socialist China* (Beijing: Foreign Languages Press, 1986). For the implementation in a smaller town, see Ole Bruun, *Business and Bureaucracy in a Chinese City: An Ethnography of Private Business Households in Contemporary China* (Berkeley: Institute of East Asian Studies, 1992).

Sociologist Thomas Gold has written several articles on *getihu* based on personal observation. See, for instance, "Urban Private Business and China's Reforms," in Richard Baum (ed.), *Reform and Reaction in Post-Mao China: The Road to Tiananmen* (New York: Routledge, 1991), 84–103. Likewise, scholar-journalist Orville Schell's *To Get Rich Is Glorious* (New York: Pantheon, 1984) captures the Zeitgeist of the early transition and is based on extensive interviews.

Finally, China's first generation of postsocialist entrepreneurs has spawned many Chinese popular works and biographies of success stories. See the collection reprinted in Wang Lingxu (ed.), *Ziyou guodu: gongshang getihu shenghuo jishi* [A Land of Freedom: A Record of the Business *getihu* Economy] (Shanghai: Shanghai Academy of Social Sciences Press, 1993).

19

China's Human Development After Socialism

CARL RISKIN

In 1979 China was a deeply wounded country recovering from successive rounds of social conflict and turmoil almost unprecedented in a country not at war. It was still a very poor country, far behind its East Asian neighbors in economic development. Thirty-five years later it had become a globalized economic superpower with the second-largest GDP in the world – largest if measured by purchasing power parity (PPP). It had entered the ranks of middle-income countries, and much of its population lived in the information age. Everything seemed to have changed – except the continuing rule of the communist party, albeit a party quite different than that of Cultural Revolution days. This chapter begins with the redefinition of "socialism" and consequent reorganization of the economy that occurred during the transition from the collective "Mao" period to the reform era and then discusses the ensuing record of human development.[1]

Soviet socialism, the only proven model available to the young People's Republic of China in 1949, was soon criticized by Mao Zedong for being overcentralized, elitist and bureaucratic.[2] Mao came to reject the central command planning which China had learned from the Soviet Union, on these same grounds. Command planning treated the entire national

I thank Mark Selden and Isabella Weber for very helpful comments on an earlier draft of this chapter.

1 "Human development" refers to economic and social changes that foster the flourishing of people's talents and capabilities. Principal ingredients of human development include increases in nutrition, health, life expectancy and level of education, as well as in freedom from constraints imposed by poverty, illness or tyranny, or by gender, race or other kinds of discrimination, and in relative economic and social equality. The concept itself was derived to counteract the widespread practice of measuring economic development by the sole standard of GNP or GDP per capita. See hdr.undp .org/en/content/what-human-development.

2 Mao Zedong, *A Critique of Soviet Economics* (New York and London: Monthly Review Press, 1977).

economy as if it were a single large enterprise. Such planning could work effectively only in a simple economy beginning to industrialize. In those circumstances, it even had the advantageous ability to change the inherited economic structure by contravening market signals. But as the economy grew and became more complex, the vast amounts of information it required became an insuperable obstacle. Nor did it foster efficiency or stimulate innovation, and its implicit incentives produced hoarding and other behavioral pathologies. János Kornai called the result of all this the "shortage economy," in which demand was essentially infinite and scarcity endemic.[3] It is not surprising that estimates of total factor productivity growth in China over the years of the central planning regime found it to be zero or very low.

The problems of central planning are the subject of a vast literature, some of which debates the merits of a more decentralized form of market socialism.[4] Going back to Vilfredo Pareto in the early twentieth century, the debate has engaged a distinguished list of scholars across the ideological spectrum: Ludwig von Mises, Eugen Boehm von Bawerk, Friedrich Hayek, Oscar Lange, Abba Lerner, Maurice Dobb, Abram Bergson, Alec Nove, János Kornai, Joseph Stiglitz[5] and many others. It was enriched by the contributions of economists living in the "actually existing socialist" world, in Europe including Lange, Kornai, Ota Šik and Włodzimierz Brus,[6] and in China Sun Yefang, Xue Muqiao, Wu Jinglian[7] and Wang Xiaoqiang, who all brought to the discussion a familiarity with the irrationalities, disproportions, disincentives and behavioral pathologies of their various national systems.

Mao Zedong had also rejected the idea of market socialism. To him, markets inevitably strengthened selfish individualism at the expense of collective solidarity. He did his best to eliminate them altogether during the Great Leap Forward (1958–60), acquiescing in their limited restoration only in the wake of the crisis and famine his policies had produced.

---

3 J. Kornai, *Economics of Shortage* (Amsterdam: North-Holland, 1980).
4 D. M. Levy and S. J. Peart, "Socialist Calculation Debate," in S. N. Durlauf and L. E. Blume (eds.), *The New Palgrave Dictionary of Economics*, 2nd edn. (Basingstroke: Palgrave Macmillan, 2008).
5 J. Stiglitz, *Whither Socialism? The Wicksell Lectures* (Cambridge, MA, and London: MIT Press, 1994).
6 W. Brus and K. Laski, *From Marx to the Market: Socialism in Search of an Economic System* (Oxford: Clarendon Press, 1989); J. Kornai, *The Socialist System: The Political Economy of Communism* (Oxford: Oxford University Press, 1992).
7 B. Naughton (ed.), *Wu Jinglian: Voice of Reform in China* (Cambridge, MA: MIT Press, 2013).

Rejecting both markets and Soviet-style central planning, and at times even the idea of economic incentives in any form, Mao was left with no practical means of organizing and coordinating a national economy. During the Great Leap and the Cultural Revolution decade (1966–76) coordination among producers, suppliers, buyers and sellers fell by the wayside. Enterprises and localities, in the absence of coherent planning, were forced to become self-sufficient, and the "comprehensive" firm providing for its own needs became a model of "self-reliance." This "Maoist model" of economic organization produced the disasters of the Great Leap, the famine of 1959–61 and the Cultural Revolution – results that did not recommend its continuation after Mao's death. Yet by the late 1970s the orthodox Soviet central planning approach had also proved deeply flawed in theory and practice and no longer seemed a feasible alternative.

The end of the Cultural Revolution brought a renewed interest in Marxist classics other than the few propagated by Mao.[8] Chinese intellectuals in this new ferment rediscovered Marxism's economic determinist side, the view that socialism could emerge only in an economically advanced country, with the corollary that premature social change would be both impossible and pernicious. China, a very poor and backward country, was only in the "primary stage of socialism,"[9] and its main task must be to develop the forces of production. Deng Xiaoping reflected this view when he stated that, "Socialism means eliminating poverty. Pauperism is not socialism, still less communism," and "the fundamental task for the socialist stage is to develop the productive forces."[10] Debates about utopian communism were put off to a distant future when China would have achieved "an overwhelming abundance of material wealth"[11] by becoming a developmental state.[12] The argument for communist power was a pragmatic one: that it was the only means to maintain stability and build a strong and prosperous nation.

8 M. Meisner, "The Chinese Rediscovery of Karl Marx: Some Reflections on Post-Maoist Chinese Marxism," *Bulletin of Concerned Asian Scholars* 17, 3 (1985), 2–16.
9 Su Shaozhi and Feng Lanrui, "Wuchan jieji qude zhengquan hou de shehui fazhan jieduan wenti" [On the Stages of Social Development After the Proletariat Takes Power], *Jingji Yanjiu* 5 (1979), 14–19.
10 Deng Xiaoping, "Build Socialism with Chinese Characteristics" 30 Jun. 1984, in Spencer C. Tucker (ed.), *Cold War: A Student Encyclopedia*, vol. V (Santa Barbara, CA: ABC-CLIO, 2008), 2744.
11 Ibid.
12 A. K. Bagchi, "The Past and the Future of the Developmental State," *Journal of World-Systems Research* 6, 2 (2000) (special issue), Part 1, 398–442.

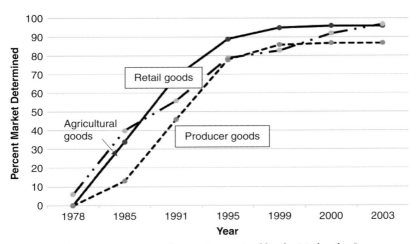

Figure 19.1. Changing Proportion of Prices Determined by the Market, by Sector
Source: Plotted from data given in N. R. Lardy, *Markets over Mao: The Rise of Private Business in China* (Washington, DC: Peterson Institute for International Studies, 2014), Tab. 1.1.

A state-guided market capitalism would be the vehicle for this development. Over the ensuing years, private enterprise and the role of the market in fact grew increasingly prominent while the state progressively stepped back from direct control of the economy and encouraged market forces to play a paramount role.[13] By the early 2000s, prices that in 1978 had been virtually all state-set had become overwhelmingly market-determined (see Fig. 19.1).

In agriculture, the large collective farms of the 1970s ("people's communes") were dismantled and the fields returned to individual family farms. Under China's constitution, farmland is owned by the village, which is considered a collective organization. Farmers have property rights to the use of their land under a system of thirty-year leases. Marketing of agricultural output now takes the form of sales to small private traders. The mandatory sales quotas of the past are gone, leaving agriculture largely a private market-based activity.

However, farmers' property rights are only partial. Cash-strapped local governments can gain revenue by confiscating land with minimal compensation to the displaced farmers and reselling it at a high price to developers.

13 N. R. Lardy, *Markets over Mao: The Rise of Private Business in China* (Washington, DC: Peterson Institute for International Studies, 2014).

Such "land grabs" have been the source of tens of thousands of local protests by peasants.

In industry, private ownership of firms, entirely absent after the mid 1950s, began reappearing in the 1980s. By 2012 there were almost 6 million registered private firms, comprising 70 percent of all enterprises and becoming "the major driver of China's economic growth, employment, and exports."[14] In industry, while the state retained control of some key industries, the output share of state enterprises fell from about three-quarters in 1978 to one-quarter in 2011.[15]

The rigid five-year plans of the past are gone, but unlike other postcommunist countries China has retained planning of a sort, including five-year plans. These are now complementary to markets and meant to convey governmental policy objectives. Various kinds of levers are used to achieve these, including consultation, taxes and subsidies, and incorporation of plan objectives in the criteria for promoting cadres.[16]

The state's fiscal capacity had been weakened by the decentralizing reforms of the late 1970s and 1980s, and the ratio of government revenue to GDP fell below 11 percent in 1995. Tax reform in 1994 finally began to rebuild fiscal capacity, aided by the rapid growth of the economy, and by 2013 government revenue had recovered to almost 23 percent of GDP, of which almost half went to the center. The progressive, redistributive policies of the new century owe their existence to the center's restored fiscal capacity.

Human Development in the Mao Years

During the turbulent years 1950–76, the lives of those who survived the famine and political violence of the period did improve. Human development took the form of increases in social consumption, such as public health and education. Millions of children received vaccinations, infant and child mortality fell rapidly and infectious diseases began to succumb to modern medicine. Life expectancy at birth grew by more than 50 percent, from forty-one or forty-two years in 1950 to the mid to

---

14 Ibid., 66. 15 Ibid., 76.
16 S. Heilmann and O. Melton. "The Reinvention of Development Planning in China, 1993–2012," *Modern China* 39, 6 (2013), 580–628; Hu Angang, "The Distinctive Transition of China's Five-Year Plans," *Modern China* 39, 6 (2013), 629–39; B. Naughton, "The Return of Planning in China: Comment on Heilmann–Melton and Hu Angang," *Modern China* 39, 6 (2013), 640–52.

upper sixties by 1978. Basic literacy also spread more widely through the population.[17] Private consumption, however, did not advance. Food consumption per capita was still very low in 1979, no better than in 1955, with more than 90 percent of calories coming from basic staple grains. Housing conditions in the cities deteriorated: With city populations more than doubling and limited construction of new housing, the average per capita living space in urban China declined from 4.5 to 3.6 square meters[18] – in Shanghai it fell to under 3 square meters. The Maoist goal for Chinese socialism was to serve the people, yet it neglected to improve their food and housing levels.

Economic inequality probably declined (there are no reliable statistics) because of the disappearance of property income and the leveling effect of collectivization. Equality for women advanced due to legal gains, such as the Marriage Law (1950), which gave women formal equality with men in marriage and divorce, and because more women received an education and employment. China was still an extremely poor country in 1979, on the verge of the reform period, yet observable poverty seemed less desperate and destitute than, say, that of India.

Human Development in the Reform Era

Since the late 1970s, however, China has experienced the fastest economic growth in recorded history over some three and a half decades, going from producing 2 percent to 16 percent of the global economy, with deceleration coming only after average per capita GDP (in PPP dollars) had grown by some forty times. With this growth came a myriad of changes that made the China of 2015 unrecognizable from the vantage point of 1978. First and foremost, the great majority of the population experienced a huge improvement in living standards, along with advances in longevity and nutrition, and greatly expanded personal freedom – all principal components of "human development."

Food consumption standards and housing conditions are vastly superior today compared with 1978. Consumer goods and services of all kinds that could not be found anywhere in the 1970s are available to the population.

---

17 Adult literacy, reported to be only 20 percent in 1950, had grown to 65.5 percent in 1982. See World Bank, World Development Indicators (www.econstats.com/wdi/wdiv_817 .htm), and T. Plafker, "China's Long – but Uneven – March to Literacy," *New York Times* (12 Feb. 2001).

18 Wang Feng, "Housing Improvement and Distribution in Urban China: Initial Evidence from China's 2000 Census," *China Review* 3, 2 (2003), 121–43.

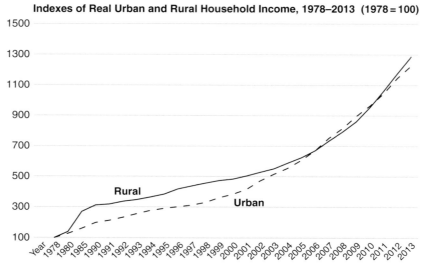

Figure 19.2. Growth of Real Urban and Rural Household Income, 1978–2013
Source: *Statistical Yearbook of China 2014*, Table 6.4, at Chinadataonline.org.

The population is also connected to the world via the internet, although the government has become sophisticated in suppressing information that it does not want people to have. Life expectancy has increased substantially. Women have gained along with men, although old prejudices have resurfaced.[19] Income inequality has soared, but tens of millions of people have escaped from poverty. Perhaps the biggest negative factor in postreform human development has been the devastation of the natural environment (see below).

Figure 19.2 shows the growth of household income in urban and rural China, both increasing by about twelvefold over thirty-five years, an average annual growth rate of about 7.5 percent. The urban–rural income gap is higher in China than in most developing countries. Because the population registration (*hukou*) system adopted in the late 1950s prevented rural-to-urban migration,[20] and because the state provided substantial subsidies to urban state workers, the gap was high even in the Mao years. The early 1980s

19 United Nations Development Programme, *China: National Human Development Report 1997* (Beijing: UNDP, 1998).
20 K. W. Chan and W. Buckingham, "Is China Abolishing the *Hukou* System?," *China Quarterly* 195 (2008), 582–606; K. W. Chan and Z. Li, "The *Hukou* System and Rural–Urban Migration in China: Processes and Changes," *China Quarterly* 160 (1999), 818–55.

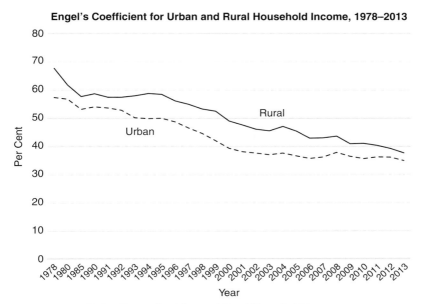

Engel's Coefficient for Urban and Rural Household Income, 1978–2013

Figure 19.3. Engel's Coefficient for Urban and Rural Household Income, 1978–2013
Source: *Statistical Yearbook of China 2014*, Table 6.4, at Chinadataonline.org.

reforms were concentrated in the rural population, however, and the gap narrowed. Much of the rural gain came from reallocation of resources made possible by the breakup of the people's communes and the resumption of individual household farming. Suppressed markets reopened, and farmers could produce whatever was most profitable. The resulting resurgence of higher-value crops, fruits and vegetables, poultry, pork, etc., greatly raised farmer income. Although that surge in income ended after such "low-hanging fruit" had been picked, rural income continued to improve (Fig. 19.2).

The average Chinese diet, extraordinarily spartan in 1978, made great gains in quality, quantity and diversity. As Figure 19.3 shows, Engel's coefficient – the proportion of income spent on food – fell markedly for both urban and rural populations, an indicator of improved wellbeing.

Education

Education expanded rapidly in the 1950s, its goals fluctuating between enlarging enrollments to achieve broad basic literacy, and emphasizing the skills needed for industrial and technical development. In the mid 1960s the Cultural Revolution closed universities. No undergraduates were admitted for six years, and a generation of students lost the opportunity for higher education. Many middle and primary schools also closed for sustained periods, to reopen with a curriculum dedicated to "eliminating class differences, whether urban–rural, worker–peasant, or intellectual–manual," rather than to academic achievement.[21] Urban middle-school students were sent to the countryside to learn from the peasants. Vocational, technical and teacher-training schools were all shut down.

Conversely, primary-school enrollments grew to 90 percent, and junior and senior middle-school enrollments also rose,[22] as new policies promoted access to education without cost for the rural population. The Cultural Revolution goal was "to promote a radical socialist agenda of eradicating social differences."[23]

All this changed beginning in the late 1970s. The goal of education was redefined to promote economic development, modernization and science and technology. Emphasis was put on improving teacher training and educational quality, aligning education with the needs of the emerging market economy, restoring vocational and technical education and decentralizing its finance and management. "Key" schools at various levels were established to accommodate the most talented, best-prepared or best-connected students. Tertiary education and the number of students attending university were vastly expanded. Economic returns to education, which had been virtually zero at the end of the collective era, rose in the 1990s and became substantial.

These developments tended to reverse the socially equalizing changes of the Cultural Revolution decade. For instance, tuition and fees rose as the government share of total educational expenditures fell. Regional disparities in educational spending widened as poor areas were unable to raise nongovernmental resources. Private schools emerged and became an important part of the mix. Yet, from the mid 1980s on, a series of policies has addressed the problem of widening inequality of educational opportunity by first

21 E. C. Hannum, J. Behrman, M. Wang and J. Liu, "Education in the Reform Era," in L. Brandt and T. G. Rawski (eds.), *China's Great Economic Transformation* (Cambridge and New York: Cambridge University Press, 2008), 216.
22 J. Knight, T. Sicular and Ximing Yue, "Educational Inequality in China: The Intergenerational Dimension," in S. Li, H. Sato and T. Sicular (eds.), *Rising Inequality in China: Challenges to a Harmonious Society* (Cambridge and New York: Cambridge University Press, 2013), 142–96.
23 Hannum et al., "Education in the Reform Era," 218.

propounding and then substantially achieving universal compulsory nine-year education with no tuition or fees for rural students. This has enhanced educational opportunities for poor rural communities, although there is still substantial inequality in regional middle-school enrollment rates and in financing for public education.

The long-term story of Chinese education since 1949 is one of "phenomenal educational expansion" producing an increasingly well-educated population in ways that have facilitated both the country's rapid economic/technical modernization and its expanding global role.[24]

Urbanization

China has undergone massive urbanization in the reform period. In 1978 the urban population numbered 178 million people. By 2014 this number had reached 749 million, over 54 percent of the total population. Thus, more than 500 million rural residents have become urban dwellers, with all of the economic, social, environmental and political consequences brought by that shift.[25] Urbanization has been the cause and occasion for an unprecedented buildup of infrastructure throughout the country: housing, factories, roads, bridges, tunnels, electrical and communications lines, railways (both high speed and conventional), ports and airports, subway systems, cellular towers and so on.

In relative terms, however, China's urbanization fell short of other late developers, such as Japan and South Korea, which at China's current GDP per capita had attained much higher urbanization rates.[26] The *hukou* system (see above) left China extraordinarily underurbanized in 1980 when fewer than 20 percent of the population lived in cities and towns. Urbanization has been catching up ever since and is projected to reach 60 percent by 2020 and 70 percent – or 1 billion people – by 2030.[27]

However, some 260 million migrants live in towns and cities – more than a third of the total urban population – as second-class citizens lacking urban

---

24 Ibid., 243.
25 According to the World Bank, natural increase accounted for about 15 percent of urban population growth from 2000 to 2010, while net migration accounted for 43 percent and the reclassification of rural localities to urban accounted for 42 percent. See World Bank, *Urban China: Toward Efficient, Inclusive and Sustainable Urbanization* (Washington DC: World Bank, 2014), 75.
26 Ibid.
27 See www.bloomberg.com/news/articles/2014–03-24/china-s-urbanization-loses-momentum-as-growth-slows.

registration and most without access to services from schooling to health insurance.[28] As the injustice of a two-class system becomes ever more apparent, support for *hukou* reform has been growing. The system has been softened and tweaked in various ways, but it still creates an underclass of urban residents who retain their rural registration even after years or decades of living and working in the cities.

Housing

Housing construction has been especially notable because it had been so neglected during the collective period. Between 1949 and 1978, annual investment in housing construction came to only 1.5 percent of GDP. China's reform leaders gave priority to housing construction. In the 1980s investment in housing climbed to 7 percent of GDP and by 2012 urban per capita living space was 32.9 square meters, more than nine times its 1980 level. In the countryside, soaring incomes in the 1980s led to a great surge of house-building as peasants invested their newly acquired wealth in this safest possible asset in a still-volatile political landscape. Thus, in contrast to the collective period, both food consumption and housing space – two fundamental components of wellbeing – have made rapid progress.

Poverty Reduction

According to the World Bank up to half a billion people have been lifted out of extreme poverty during the reform era. This accomplishment derived first and foremost from China's extraordinary economic growth, and then from the pro-rural and pro-poor nature of its growth model from 1978 to 1985. Other government policies helped, such as higher purchase prices for agricultural goods, abolition of rural taxes and fees, funding of basic education and new social insurance policies for the rural population.[29] The national headcount rate of poverty in 2010 was 11.2 percent at the

28 World Bank, *Urban China*.
29 A. R. Khan and C. Riskin, *Inequality and Poverty in China in the Age of Globalization* (Oxford: Oxford University Press, 2001); C. Riskin, "The Fall in Chinese Poverty: Issues of Measurement, Incidence and Cause," in J. K. Boyce, S. Cullenberg, P. K. Pattanaik and R. Pollin (eds.), *Human Development in the Era of Globalization: Essays in Honor of Keith B. Griffin* (Northampton, MA: Edward Elgar, 2006), 31–43; World Bank, *From Poor Areas to Poor People: China's Evolving Poverty Reduction Agenda – An Assessment of Poverty and Inequality in China* (Washington, DC: World Bank, 2009); Li, Sato and Sicular (eds.), *Rising Inequality in China*.

World Bank's US\$ 1.90/day poverty line,[30] and in 2013 it was 8.5 percent at China's national poverty line.[31]

Urban China had been largely poverty-free in the Mao era because the cities were closed to poor rural migrants while every urban resident was guaranteed a job from the end of middle school to mandatory retirement age (generally sixty years old for men, fifty-five for women) and a secure pension thereafter. Toward the end of that era, however, many middle-school graduates suffered long waits for work assignments due to administrative dysfunction and the slowing pace of economic growth. Although these young people were classified as "waiting for work," they were in fact unemployed. Only in the late 1970s was unemployment openly acknowledged to be large although numbers remained elusive.

In the 1980s and early 1990s a contradiction developed between the shift from planning to markets, on the one hand, and the presence of an immobile urban labor force beyond the reach of market forces, on the other. Workers' entire lives were governed by their work unit (*danwei*), from which they received wages, housing, schooling and pensions, as well as various subsidies and even scarce consumer goods. Workers could be fired only under the most extraordinary circumstances, for a dismissed worker would be cast into a societal vacuum, losing identity and means of subsistence. This institutional setup provided great security to full-status urban workers along with wages and benefits that far exceeded peasant income.[32]

In official doctrine, workers were "the masters of their enterprises." The cost of this system, to both workers and the economy, was that it made the labor force immobile. Workers could not move or change jobs. In the Mao years even the idea of seeking a better job would have been condemned as individualism at odds with "serving the people." Redundancy in the urban workforce became an income-maintenance mechanism in the 1970s. Rather than fire workers and give them unemployment compensation, the state kept them employed and paid them. With no markets governing production, neither the compensation of workers nor the capital investment

---

30 At 2011 PPP prices.
31 International Food and Development (IFAD), www.ruralpovertyportal.org/country/statistics/tags/china.
32 C. Riskin, *China's Political Economy: The Quest for Development Since 1949* (Oxford: Oxford University Press, 1987). A corps of contingent workers lacking security and benefits, and paid less as well, grew up at the end of the collective period. They were pioneers of the large army of rural–urban migrants who now constitute a lower class of urban workers, earning more than in their home villages but less than full-status urban workers, and lacking both benefits and ordinary public services.

plans of enterprises depended on profitability, and so it made little difference that workers might have little to do for their pay.

Such an institutional setup could not survive in a market environment with state-owned enterprises (SOEs) facing competition from imports and a growing private sector. The reform and restructuring of SOEs and collective enterprises that began in the mid 1990s and continued into the early years of the new century privatized most small public enterprises and reorganized or consolidated large ones,[33] turning them into joint stock companies. One of the most striking results of the reform was the layoff of some 43 million erstwhile "masters of their enterprise."[34] The previous "social contract" between state and workers was abandoned. Although unemployment was now openly acknowledged, the tens of millions of workers laid off by their *danwei* were not included in its ranks. Estimates of actual unemployment – including laid-off workers – rose from about 7 million in 1993 to 16 million in 1995–96. Layoffs continued at a high rate before finally tapering off after 2000, when one estimate of the true unemployment rate put it at 12.3 percent.[35] Another study found the overall rate surpassing 12 percent – and 15 percent for women – in 2001.[36]

The *danwei* itself had provided the urban social safety net before the breaking of the "iron rice bowl" of lifetime job security in the 1990s. Now, with unemployment soaring, the rudiments of a broad social insurance system were erected to replace it. Most laid-off workers at first received small subsistence stipends from their former enterprises, but eventually local governments established Reemployment Service Centers (RECs) that broke the formal (and psychological) links between laid-off workers and their former work units. The RECs became the workers' new *danwei*, provided them with a basic living allowance and helped them seek new jobs. After three years, those who were still unemployed were transferred into a new unemployment insurance program for two more years, after which they could apply for relief from a newly established urban anti-poverty program called the Minimum Livelihood Guarantee program (*dibao*). This provided meager relief under often-humiliating circumstances. All of these new

---

33 This policy was called *"zhua da fang xiao"* or "grasp the large and let go of the small": World Bank, *China Economic Update June 2015* (Washington, DC: World Bank, 2015).
34 J. Giles, A. Park and C. Fang, "How Has Economic Restructuring Affected China's Urban Workers?," *China Quarterly* 185 (2006), 61–95.
35 A. Hussain, "Urban Poverty in China: Measurement, Patterns and Policies" (Geneva: International Labour Office, 2003), 23.
36 Giles, Park and Fang, "How Has Economic Restructuring."

programs were locally funded, and thus dependent upon the state of local finances. In wealthy Shanghai benefits were far more generous than, say, in Heilongjiang province in the depressed northeast, where the subsistence stipend paid by the local REC in the late 1990s came to only 6 percent of the worker's former wage.

SOE reform risked but did not ignite the widespread turbulence and resistance that the government feared. After several years of continuing layoffs and mass unemployment, the situation stabilized. Older workers were offered early retirement, young ones were retrained and found new jobs or "jumped into the sea" – i.e. left the public sector to try working on their own – a decision made more feasible by the maintenance of a very high growth rate. And those who were in neither of these categories were moved into the new social insurance-cum-relief programs.

SOE reform eliminated job security, universal pensions and virtually free health care, and ushered modern poverty and insecurity into China's urban environment. Employment became dependent on labor market conditions. The fast economic growth of the years up to and immediately following the Great Recession of 2008–09 kept demand for labor strong, and wages rose rapidly. In such a high-growth environment – especially in the nonstate sector and in the export-producing enclaves of the coastal regions – jobs were added quickly enough to absorb some of the laid-off workers in addition to the flood of rural migrants seeking employment.[37] Yet urban poverty was now institutionally possible, not only among the migrant workers whose only feasible reaction to losing a job was often to return to their home village. Now job loss, injury, illness or bad luck could deprive even full-status urban workers of their livelihood and threaten them with poverty.

What is the incidence of such urban poverty? Quite low, according to the evidence. Since the Chinese government does not publish regular data on this, we must look to independent research. One study for the year 1998 by the Asian Development Bank[38] found an urban poverty rate of 4.7 percent for that year, excluding migrants from the urban population, and 5.8 percent if migrants are included. Albert Park and Dewen Wang found that in 2004 and 2005 large cities had an average poverty rate of 3.8 percent and small cities

37 M. W. Frazer, "State-Sector Shrinkage and Workforce Reduction in China," *European Journal of Political Economy* 22 (2006), 435–51.
38 A. Hussain, *Urban Poverty in China: Measurement, Patterns and Policies* (Geneva: International Labour Office, 2005).

6.6 percent.[39] Such urban poverty rates are far below those of most other developing countries and, indeed, below those of the United States, which of course uses a much higher poverty line.[40] The average urban poverty rate for the World Bank's US$ 1.08/day (1993 PPP) poverty line among eighty-seven low- and middle-income countries in 2002 was 24.6 percent, many times higher than the highest estimate for China. Even taking into account cross-national differences in poverty definitions and measurement practices, China's urban poverty rate is very low in comparative context.

Inequality

Under the 1980s mantra of "letting some get rich first," income inequality has grown, ultimately reaching a level alarming enough to trigger serious state efforts to combat it. Since 2008, due in part to such efforts, it has appeared to moderate.

At the end of the collective era in the late 1970s China's income distribution was in some respects highly egalitarian. The estimated rural Gini coefficient in 1979 was a low 0.26 and the urban an even lower 0.16 in 1981. However, the latter figure was partly the result of the government's success in barring rural-to-urban migration. China kept poverty confined to the countryside, which produced an unusually wide urban–rural income gap. Peasants in general were disadvantaged relative to city residents. Not only did urban incomes greatly exceed theirs, but the array of government-supplied urban benefits provided a high degree of security that peasants lacked. The estimated national Gini coefficient in 1979, reflecting the wide urban–rural income gap, was 0.33, which exceeded both the urban and rural measures taken separately. Indeed, the pronounced urban–rural gap raised overall national inequality to a level not notably different from that of other Asian countries.[41]

39 A. Park and D. Wang, "Migration and Urban Poverty and Inequality in China," *IZA Discussion Paper* 4877 (2010). See their Table 3. The study uses the World Bank's US$ 2 per day poverty line. For a summary of studies of urban poverty in China, see ibid., n. 1.

40 The poverty rate in the United States was 14.8 percent in 2014. See C. DeNavas-Walt and B. D. Proctor, *Income and Poverty in the United States: 2014*, Current Population Reports, US Census Bureau (Washington, DC: US Government Printing Office, 2015), 13.

41 Riskin, *China's Political Economy*; World Bank, *China: Socialist Economic Development* (Washington, DC: World Bank, 1983); World Bank, *China: Long-Term Issues and Options* (Washington, DC: World Bank, 1985), vol. 1, Annexes A–E; N. Dillon, *Radical Inequalities: China's Revolutionary Welfare State in Comparative Perspective* (Cambridge, MA: Harvard University Press, 2015).

Income distribution was quite equal *within* communities and work units, where politics and ideology imposed very narrow class and status differences. *Among* localities, however, the weakness of central planning and redistribution permitted differentials based on local conditions to flourish. Inequality took other forms as well. The late William Hinton, who spent decades observing China closely, once remarked that, "Anything created by a peasant who lives in the administrative sphere of a higher official, if it will enhance the latter's career, can be moved, removed, manipulated, or expropriated by that official just as if he were the lord of a feudal fief."[42] Very few people were privileged to ride in a curtained limousine, travel abroad or live behind high walls in Zhongnanhai, the complex in Beijing where China's senior leaders reside.

The first half-decade of the reform era brought a decline in income inequality as reform began in the countryside, decollectivizing rural life in general while also raising farm prices. Farmers were encouraged to produce profitable crops, and markets in which to sell them were freed up. Large amounts of cheap fertilizers and other farm inputs were supplied. Farm incomes soared for several years, reducing the urban–rural gap and thus overall national inequality. Farm output grew by an average annual rate of 9 percent between 1978 and 1984. Much of this growth was temporary, as resources were shifted from low-value staple crops to higher-value fruits, vegetables, poultry, etc. "Raising chickens has become one of the avenues leading to wealth,"[43] although that avenue would soon be closed by market saturation.

By 1985 the growth spurt in farm incomes had ended, and the urban–rural gap widened again. The government turned its attention from agricultural reform and launched a "coastal development strategy" to attract foreign direct investment (FDI) and build an export engine for China's growth. The economy rapidly integrated into the global market. Trade was substantially liberalized and the export share of GDP, which had grown little between 1979 and 1985, then doubled by 1995. FDI had hardly figured in China's economy before 1985, while ten years later China was receiving almost 40 percent of all FDI going to low- and middle-income countries.[44] Accession to the World Trade Organization in late 2001 brought more FDI and an even greater emphasis on exports. The strategy produced growth of unprecedented speed and longevity, but it was disequalizing growth. From

42 W. Hinton, "Village in Transition," in M. Selden and V. Lippit (eds.), *The Transition to Socialism in China* (Armonk, NY, and London: M. E. Sharpe, 1982), 98–115.
43 See Riskin, *China's Political Economy*, 292.
44 Khan and Riskin, *Inequality and Poverty in China*, 5.

1988 to 1995, the estimated national Gini coefficient of income distribution rose from 0.38 to 0.45, an increase of 18 percent in seven years.

Globalization increased the income gap between eastern coastal provinces and the interior, as FDI came mainly to the developed east, where most exports were also produced. Income per capita in the eastern coastal provinces was 75 percent higher than in the poorer west in 2007.[45] However, regional income inequality in general – among all provinces – did not trend upward and may actually have fallen.[46] The "western development strategy" introduced in 2000 was the first major attempt to address the east–west gap, bringing large infrastructure investments to western and central China.

Rural population peaked in size in 1995 and fell substantially thereafter. Among the remaining rural dwellers, off-farm wage employment began to spread more widely, raising rural incomes. Further relaxation of *hukou* restrictions allowed increasing streams of rural migrants to flow into coastal cities to work. The new *dibao* program began providing living allowances to poor urban residents. Taxes and subsidies became less regressive. For these and other reasons, the Gini coefficient remained constant from 1995 to 2002, as inequality in both rural and urban incomes fell slightly, while a still-rising urban–rural gap offset those changes in the national measure.[47]

Inequality became a widely discussed public issue in the late 1990s and early 2000s, when the "restructuring" and privatization of state enterprises were in full swing and the weakness of China's social safety net became a pressing issue. For instance, the old enterprise-based urban pension system could not survive the state enterprise reform. Struggling SOEs in the early 1990s could not meet their pension obligations, and many retired workers were paid late or not at all. In the mid 1990s a new pension system was introduced, financed by a combination of government and enterprise contributions plus mandatory individual accounts.

---

45 Li, Sato and Sicular (eds.), *Rising Inequality in China*, 68. Incomes are adjusted for regional cost of living differences. Without this adjustment, regional differences would be greater.

46 C. Li and J. Gibson, "Rising Regional Inequality in China: Fact or Artefact?," Working Papers in Economics 12, 9 (Department of Economics, University of Waikato, New Zealand, 2012).

47 A. R. Khan and C. Riskin, "China's Household Income and Its Distribution, 1995 and 2002," *China Quarterly* 182 (Jun. 2005), 356–84. The Gini coefficients cited here for 1995 and 2002 omit migrants from the samples used and do not take regional price differences into account. The 2002 China Household Income Project (CHIP) round was the first that administered a special survey of migrants and included them in distribution estimates, so no comparison on that basis with 1995 is possible.

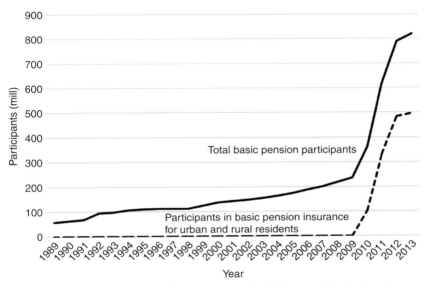

Figure 19.4. Increase in Coverage of Basic Pensions for Workers and Residents, 1989–2013
Source: *Statistical Yearbook of China 2014*, Table 24.30, at Chinadataonline.org.

Several policies begun in the early 2000s were aimed at fostering a more equitable, rural-focused and environmentally sustainable strategy of development. A new cooperative medical insurance program was finally put in place for the rural population; its coverage expanded to 99 percent of the eligible population by 2013.[48] For the first time in China's history, a serious effort began to provide social security for the rural population as well as the urban. As Figure 19.4 shows, total social security-type coverage – including both urban employee pensions and the new social security program for both urban and rural residents – rose to about 820 million people by 2013. Yet only about 242 million workers had pension coverage, less than one-third of the total labor force of 770 million, and it has proved rather unreliable. The China Labour Bureau asserts that the government has failed to enforce labor laws, including those prescribing employer contributions to the pension fund, and has instead been shifting the burden of social insurance contributions onto individuals.[49]

48 National Bureau of Statistics of China, *China Statistical Datasheet 2014* (Beijing: National Bureau of Statistics of China, 2014), sec. 22, p. 20. However, amounts paid to beneficiaries were still very small.
49 China Labour Bureau, "China's Social Security System," *China Labour Bulletin* (2015), www.clb.org.hk/content/china%E2%80%99s-social-security-system.

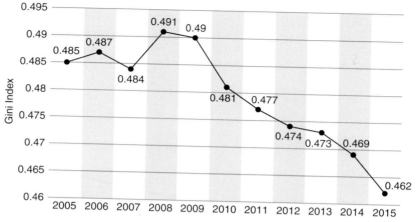

Additional Information:
China; National Bureau of Statistics of China; 2005 to 2015

Figure 19.5. Is Inequality Falling?
Source: National Bureau of Statistics for China, as reported by Statista, www.statista.com
/statistics/250400/inequality-of-income-distribution-in-china-based-on-the-gini-index.

In addition to the urban–rural gap (still large even if somewhat reduced), a notable contributor to income inequality has been the growing differentiation of socioeconomic classes. Indeed, the increase in income differences between social classes accounts for the entire increase in the Gini coefficient from 1988 to 2002.[50] This should not be surprising, yet is rarely discussed. Chinese society has acquired a class character such that one's identification as worker, peasant or member of the urban or rural elite is a strong predictor of one's relative income, while the gaps between the incomes of different classes have widened rapidly.

Despite this, the national Gini coefficient for income distribution, after peaking at 0.491 in 2008, fell for six straight years to 0.462 in 2015 (Fig. 19.5). This is only a 6 percent (3 percentage point) decline, but its persistence suggests that China's growth model may be evolving toward one generating less inequality.

Consistent with the falling Gini, the incomes of poorer deciles of the population grew faster than those of richer deciles between 2007 and 2013. This is explained in part by the narrowing of the urban–rural income gap over

50 V. Vakulabharanam, "Chinese Inequality Turns Full Circle: Trends of Inequality in Post-Revolution China," unpublished paper, University of Massachusetts at Amherst, 2015.

that period.[51] Evidently, the rapid spread of rural off-farm wage employment and the growth of rural business income, inter alia, helped lift rural income at more than three times the urban rate.[52] The proliferation of equalizing policies and programs described above, including new social insurance laws and policies, which have continued to advance in size, coverage and resources, may also have contributed to the decline in national income inequality.

Population

From 1950 to 1970, China's death rate (per 1,000) fell from 18 to 7.6, a decline of nearly 60 percent. At the same time, fertility remained high (5.8 children per woman) while effective public health measures increased life expectancy from the low forties in 1950 to the sixties in 1970. The result of these trends was a population "explosion" of 278 million people between 1950 and 1970 – a 50 percent increase. In the 1970s, however, even before the draconian one-child policy was imposed, birth rates fell sharply from 35 (per 1,000) in 1969 to 21 in 1978 – a 40 percent reduction in just nine years. The one-child policy, adopted in 1979, restricted births in most cases to one per family and imposed an enforcement regime that included intrusive interference in women's reproductive decisions and heavy penalties for violations. In the years since, fertility and population growth rates have fallen further. The total fertility rate in 2014 was 1.55, well below the replacement rate, and the annual rate of natural increase fell to 5.43 per 1,000 (or 0.54 percent). Population is still growing very slowly due to the large cohort still in the reproductive age range as well as to rising longevity.[53] But the "intrinsic rate of growth," a measure based only on the underlying fertility and mortality drivers of population growth, has been increasingly negative since the late 1980s.[54] Except for the age structure, that is, the population would already be decreasing in size, and it will start to do so around 2030.

51 Li Shi, "The Latest Changes in Income Inequality in China," UNU-WIDER 30th Anniversary Conference, www1.wider.unu.edu/30thanniversary/sites/default/files/IGA/Shi.pdf.
52 Communication from Terry Sicular. Complete analysis of the rural income spurt is still under way by the CHIP team.
53 Life expectancy in 2014 was 75.4 years, with women enjoying a four-year advantage over men. See www.cia.gov/library/publications/resources/the-world-factbook/fields/2102.html#ch.
54 F. Wang, B. Gu and Y. Cai, "The End of China's One-Child Policy," *Studies in Family Planning* 47, 1 (2016), 83–86.

Although the "one-child policy" is often credited with the reduction in fertility, Amartya Sen argues that socioeconomic change, not the state's coercive policies, was chiefly responsible.[55] In Taiwan, for instance, with similar cultural parameters to the mainland, the total fertility rate dropped to 1.12, well below the mainland's 1.55, although Taiwan had no coercive policies to limit births. Instead, economic development, urbanization and increasing educational and employment opportunities, especially for women, sharply reduced fertility. That is very likely the story on the mainland, as well. What the one-child policy did do, however, was distort the sex ratio of the population, as rural people, for whom a son has been crucial for old-age survival,[56] engaged in sex-selective abortion or inferior care for infant girls. In 2014, the ratio of births by sex was about 116 boys to 100 girls, well above the normal ratio of 105 to 100. This has produced a cohort of Chinese men unable to marry. In October 2015, the party announced the end of the one-child policy and its replacement by one permitting two children "as an active response to an ageing population."[57]

China's population is thus heading for some shrinkage, which will have significant consequences for economic growth and for the ability to sustain and expand welfare for the growing proportion of aged people. Already, the number of young workers entering the labor force and the absolute size of the labor force itself are declining as the number of retirees exceeds that of new entrants. This has contributed to rising wages despite a decline in economic growth rates in 2014 and 2015. China must raise labor productivity so that a smaller working share of the population will be able to support the growing elderly cohort without a deterioration in living standards.

The Environment

In one way, China's hypergrowth of three decades plus has been devastating to the wellbeing of its people and to the rest of the world, as well. Growth was pursued to the neglect of protection of the natural environment, which has been heavily damaged. Air quality in Chinese cities is reminiscent of the deadly London fog (smog) that was tolerated until the 1950s. China is the

---

55 A. Sen, "Women's Progress Outdid China's One-Child Policy," *New York Times* (2 Nov. 2015).
56 Traditionally, girls marry out of their family and village and become responsible for their husband's family.
57 Xinhua as reported by Reuters, *World News*, 30 Oct. 2015.

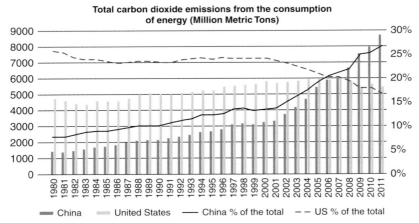

Figure 19.6. Carbon Dioxide Emissions, 1980–2011
Source: Image by The Climate Group, with elaboration from the Energy Information
Administration of the United States data, www.theclimategroup.org/what-we-do/news-
and-blogs/china-will-launch-worlds-biggest-carbon-market-in-2016/.

world's largest emitter of sulfur dioxide (SO_2), a gas that exacts a heavy toll on
public health, damages crops, forests and soils, and acidifies lakes and
streams. A recent conservative estimate by the World Bank put the cost of
air pollution in premature death and morbidity at 3.8 percent of China's GDP.
In August 2016, the Health Effects Institute released an international cooperative study of the impact on health of emissions of fine particulate matter
(PM 2.5) from coal burning and other sources. The study concludes that
916,000 premature deaths in China in 2013 were caused by such emissions
alone.[58] China is also the highest emitter of greenhouse gases that trap warm
air at the earth's surface and cause climate change with devastating potential
results for the globe as a whole. Much of China's air pollution and greenhouse gas emissions can be traced to its reliance on coal, the nation's only
cheap and abundant fossil energy source. China is responsible for about half
the world's total combustion of coal for energy, and coal is the biggest
contributor to carbon dioxide (CO_2) emissions (see Fig. 19.6). China's size,
emphasis on heavy industry and reliance on dirty coal have made its greenhouse gas emissions a major threat to itself and the world as a whole.

58 Health Effects Institute (HEI), "Burden of Disease Attributable to Coal-Burning and
Other Major Sources of Air Pollution in China," GBD MAPS Working Group, Special
Report 20 (2016), www.healtheffects.org/publication/burden-disease-attributable-
coal-burning-and-other-air-pollution-sources-china.

China's local air pollution challenges, viewed in historical context, are manageable. The worst SO_2 levels in major Chinese cities in the early 2000s were below those of Tokyo in 1968, Seoul in 1990 and New York in 1972. Total suspended particulates (TSP) are lower and have begun falling at an earlier stage of development than in those cities. The urban air pollution problem is thus not unprecedented in scale and has begun to trend downward as the state puts remedial measures in place.[59] Yet even while total emissions may decline, the susceptibility of an aging population to health impacts such as cancers, heart attacks and strokes from pollution is likely to increase over the coming years.[60]

Water also poses a big problem. More than half the water in the seven main rivers of China is unfit for human consumption. Groundwater depletion and the use of polluted water by industry are taking a toll on both the economy and human health. Water pollution can be traced to the heavy use of chemicals in agriculture as well as the more general practice of dumping chemical and other wastes into rivers and streams. The serious water shortage in northern China stems from the draining of aquifers by northern cities as well as from the use of highly water-intensive Green Revolution farm technologies. Coal mining also contributes to water scarcity by requiring prodigious amounts of water.

In responding to the northern water shortage China has relied on an environmentally questionable fix – the South–North Water Transfer Project taking water from the Yangzi River to northern cities – and has put less emphasis on water conservation and the use of economic incentives to reduce water use. The price of water has been rising and administrative controls are increasing, but more of both will no doubt be required. Moreover, because agriculture accounts for well over half of total water demand in the north, some curtailment of farming activity there is likely to be necessary to meet the challenge posed by chronic overuse and long-term drought.[61]

Another big environmental challenge is posed by desertification, as land erosion (mostly from agriculture) has allowed the Gobi desert to march eastward. "Desertified land areas ... [total] at 1.839 million km², taking up 19.16% of the total territory of China, or 69.77% of the total land territories of 13 provinces, autonomous regions and municipal cities in Northwest,

59 D. H. Perkins, *The Economic Transformation of China* (Singapore, Hackensack, NJ, and London: World Scientific, 2015), 416–18.
60 Health Effects Institute (HEI), "Burden of Disease Attributable."
61 Perkins, *The Economic Transformation of China.*

Northern and Northeast China."[62] China combats desertification with tree-planting campaigns and other ecological improvement strategies which, according to the UN Convention to Combat Desertification, have had some success in controlling the problem.

China has responded to the many dimensions of its severe environmental challenge by enacting laws and establishing a governmental network to protect the environment, but enforcement has been an ongoing problem. Large investments in clean energy sources, such as wind and solar power, as well as in nuclear power have begun reducing the dependence on coal, relative to total energy consumption. In 2015, the slowdown in economic growth produced an unprecedented decline in total CO_2 emissions of 2.5 percent.[63]

In keeping with the "new normal" of lower-than-double-digit growth, China has been trying to shift the structure of its economy away from dirty heavy industry and toward cleaner services. This and other structural choices, such as that between more mass transit and a bigger auto industry, could have a large bearing on the country's environmental future. At this writing, China is preparing to introduce the world's largest national carbon market by 2017, capping carbon emissions and allowing them to be traded among major emitters, their price providing an incentive for reduction.

Nevertheless, despite growing excess capacity in the coal industry, China has continued to approve the construction of new coalmines. While Xi Jinping stresses the need for "supply-side structural reforms" including the shutdown of heavy industrial enterprises with much excess capacity, the country continues to rely on massive expansion of bank credit such as gave rise to that capacity in the first place. Demand for clean air at home, global pressure to lower greenhouse gas emissions, and increasing awareness of China's own vulnerability to climate change – including rising sea levels and failing fresh water supplies – have led to ambitious plans and actions to reduce emissions. Yet the entrenchment of the old dirty model and fear of a slowing economy make local implementation of such a shift difficult.

62 Y. Yang, L. S. Jin, V. Squires, K. Kim and H. Park (eds.), *Combating Desertification and Land Degradation* (Changwen, Republic of Korea: United National Convention to Combat Desertification, 2011).
63 See R. Garnaut, "Global Development in the Twenty-First Century," *Policy Quarterly* 11, 2 (2015), 3–14; E. Wong, "Statistics from China Say Coal Consumption Continues to Drop," *New York Times* (3 Mar. 2016), A5; J. Matthews, "China's Continuing Renewable Energy Revolution – Latest Trends in Electric Power Generation," *Asia-Pacific Journal* 14, 17, 6 (1 Sep. 2016).

As one relatively optimistic scholar of China's substantial efforts to "green" its energy sector concludes, it is still "an open question" whether these will be sufficient for China and the world to avoid the most devastating impacts of climate change.[64]

Conclusion

Communism could not deliver a utopian society in Mao's lifetime, but the Chinese Communist Party has presided over rapid growth and much human development since as well as over many of the same aberrations as capitalism, including rising inequality, environmental destruction and political oppression. The competence that produced growth and rising living standards has bought it political legitimacy, according to opinion surveys. However, that legitimacy has been threatened by environmental deterioration, rampant corruption, unjust use of power (land grabs) and high and growing inequality, which increasingly exhibits a class character. Here, too, unabated growth kept these threats under the threshold of social and political instability, giving the party and state time to deal with them. As one of the few ruling communist parties to survive the end of the Cold War, the party recognizes that its legitimacy is fragile and contingent. It has not dared to commence a discussion about the values and institutions that should undergird good governance. Xi Jinping's anti-corruption campaign, overtly a response to the erosion of party legitimacy, has been accompanied by the suppression of criticism and dissent, restrictions on access to information on the internet, and a general retreat from the idea of a more open political system. These are all impediments to human development. The balance sheet is thus a complicated one. As China advances from the "primary stage of socialism" toward becoming a wealthy society, it will be interesting to see whether Marxism informs its social development from within or merely the analysis thereof, from without.

Bibliographical Essay

Human development, its meaning and its measurement are discussed in every annual Human Development Report (HDR) issued by the United

64 Matthews, "China's Continuing Renewable Energy Revolution." Of course China is not alone in being responsible for slowing climate change. The US responsibility, in particular, is also great while the United States to date has done less than China to develop alternative sources of energy.

Nations Development Programme since the first one appeared in 1990. In addition, each report focuses on a particular aspect of human development. These can be found at the HDR web site, hdr.undp.org/en. Since 1997, a national HDR for China has been issued every few years by UNDP China, and these are available at www.cn.undp.org/content/china/en/home/library/human_development.html?rightpar_publicationlisting_7_start=3. The first one, for 1997, contains a broad survey of human development in China to that date.

There is a vast literature on the critique of central planning and the feasibility of market socialism. One convenient summary of this long debate can be found in D. M. Levy and S. J. Peart, "Socialist Calculation Debate," in S. N. Durlauf and L. E. Blume (eds.), *The New Palgrave Dictionary of Economics*, 2nd edn. (Basingstroke, UK: Palgrave Macmillan, 2008). An introduction to the way central planning was done in China from the 1950s to the early 1980s can be found in D. H. Perkins, "The Centrally Planned Command Economy (1949–1984)," in G. Chow and D. H. Perkins (eds.), *Routledge Handbook of the Chinese Economy* (London and New York, Routledge, 2014), 41–54, and online at www.routledgehandbooks.com/doi/10.4324/9781315767475.ch3#sec3_2. The deterioration of central planning under Mao Zedong is discussed in C. Riskin, "Neither Plan nor Market: Mao's Political Economy," in W. A. Joseph, C. Wong and D. Zweig (eds.), *New Perspectives on the Cultural Revolution* (Cambridge, MA: Harvard University Press, 1991), 133–52.

The most comprehensive introduction to China's evolving economy of the reform period is B. Naughton's *The Chinese Economy: Transitions and Growth* (Cambridge, MA: MIT Press, 2006). Look for the appearance of a thoroughly revised second edition, which is in press at this writing. G. C. Chow's *China's Economic Transformation*, 3rd edn. (Oxford and Malden, MA: John Wiley & Sons, 2015), touches usefully and briefly on many different aspects of China's economy, as well as on technical issues (e.g., ch. 6.2 "Dynamic Properties of the Multiplier-Accelerator Model").

Poverty alleviation and the reduction of economic inequality are two core components of human development. The work of the China Household Income Project has thrown light on both topics. See S. Li, H. Sato and T. Sicular (eds.), *Rising Inequality in China: Challenges to a Harmonious Society* (Cambridge: Cambridge University Press, 2013); B. Gustafsson, S. Li and T. Sicular (eds.), *Inequality and Public Policy in China* (Cambridge: Cambridge University Press, 2010); A. R. Khan and C. Riskin,

Inequality and Poverty in China in The Age of Globalization (Oxford: Oxford University Press, 2001); C. Riskin, R. Zhao and S. Li (eds), *China's Retreat from Equality: Income Distribution and Economic Transition* (Armonk, NY: M. E. Sharpe, 2001). A new book from this project, discussing the results of the 2013 survey of household income and related topics in China, is currently (August 2016) being prepared.

The World Bank has also contributed to the understanding of poverty and inequality in China, especially work by M. Ravallion and S. Chen. See, for example, M. Ravallion, "An Emerging New Form of Social Protection in 21st Century China," in S. Fan, R. Kanbur, S.-J Wei and X. Zhang, *Oxford Companion to the Economics of China* (Oxford and New York: Oxford University Press, 2014), 441–45.

Demographic aspects of China's human development are insightfully discussed in F. Wang, B. Gu and Y. Cai, "The End of China's One-Child Policy," *Studies in Family Planning* 47, 1 (2016), 83–86. The enormous internal migration of workers from poorer rural areas to coastal cities and the problem of the population registration system are discussed by D. Davin, *Internal Migration in Contemporary China* (London: Palgrave Macmillan, 1999), and K. W. Chan, "Internal Labor Migration in China: Trends, Geography and Policies," in United Nations Population Division, *Population Distribution, Urbanization, Internal Migration and Development: An International Perspective* (New York: United Nations Publications, 2012), 81–102. See K. W. Chan and W. Buckingham, "Is China Abolishing the *Hukou* System?," *China Quarterly* 195 (2008), 582–606, while Charlotte Goodburn considers more recent reforms in "The End of the *Hukou* System? Not Yet," University of Nottingham, China Policy Institute Policy Paper 2 (2014), at www.nottingham.ac.uk/cpi/documents/policy-papers/cpi-policy-paper-2014-no-2-goodburn.pdf.

An excellent summary of the evolution in healthcare policy and status in China can be found in W. C. Hsiao, "Correcting Past Health Policy Mistakes," *Daedalus* 143, 2 (special issue on "Growing Pains in a Rising China") (Spring 2014), 53–68. The same issue of *Daedalus* includes an informative discussion by M. W. Frazier of recent social policy in general: "State Schemes or Safety Nets? China's Push for Universal Coverage," 69–80. Changing policy on education and the intergenerational transmission of education are closely discussed in J. Knight, T. Sicular and Y. Ximing, "Educational Inequality in China: The Intergenerational Dimension," in Li, Sato and Sicular (eds.), *Rising Inequality in China*, 142–96.

The problem of environmental degradation in China has been much written about. A good place to start might be R. L. Edmonds, "The Environment in the People's Republic of China 50 Years on," *China Quarterly* 159 (special issue on "The People's Republic of China After 50 Years") (Sep. 1999), 640–49. A Council on Foreign Relations Backgrounder, "China's Environmental Crisis," can be found at CFR.org. It includes suggestions for further reading. E. C. Economy, *The River Runs Black: The Environmental Challenge to China's Future*, 2nd edn. (Ithaca: Cornell University Press, 2010), is a useful comprehensive discussion. The *China Human Development Report* (*CHDR*) for 2009–10 has as its theme, "Sustainable Future: Towards a Low-Carbon Economy and Sustainable Society," while the 2013 *CHDR* deals with the topic of "Sustainable Cities." They can both be found at the UNDP-China website. A relatively upbeat account of China's efforts to "green" its energy production and curtail greenhouse gases can be found in J. Matthews, "China's Continuing Renewable Energy Revolution – Latest Trends in Electric Power Generation," *Asia-Pacific Journal* 14, 17, 6 (1 Sep. 2016).

20

China's Postsocialist Transformation and Global Resurgence: Political Economy and Geopolitics

HO-FUNG HUNG AND MARK SELDEN

China's Transformations

China's socioeconomic transformation and global resurgence are best dated from the United States–China opening of the early 1970s, which facilitated the country's entry into the capitalist world economy, initiated the rapid expansion of trade and led to the first groping steps toward market predominance. From 1978, the pace of transformation accelerated with the dismantling of collective farms and restoration of a household-centered rural economy in the early 1980s, together with the growth of township and village enterprises and the freeing of rural workers, previously bound to their villages, to migrate in search of predominantly urban jobs in manufacturing, construction and trade. In the late 1980s urban price reform opened major commodities to market forces. In the 1990s, privatization of significant numbers of state-owned enterprises (SOEs) resulted in layoffs of state workers and the end of job security for the remaining employees who, for the first time, were hired on term contracts (three years in most cases), and faced competition from massive numbers of rural migrant workers. Throughout these successive stages, decentralization, markets and exports remained priorities while some 300 million rural migrants swelled China's urban population. With the decline in central planning and regulation, local governments expanded their reach by allowing local circuits of capital accumulation to plug into global circuits through foreign trade and foreign direct investment (FDI) inflow, and by replacing a centralized state revenue system with a decentralized one under which local governments retained larger portions of tax revenue and public enterprise income, while central government subsidies declined.[1]

In this decentralized regime, local governments became a driving force of economic growth and planning while competing for private investment and bank loans. This spurred diverse local strategies of wealth accumulation. Some local governments directly encouraged and sponsored collective township and village enterprises or turned state-owned enterprises within their jurisdiction into profit-oriented units, resulting in "local corporatism" or "local state entrepreneurialism."[2] Prospering localities facilitated private and collective industrial enterprises, including foreign enterprises, and relied on the tax generated in the private sector for revenue. Others, however, engaged in predatory practices by extorting taxes, fees or favors from local residents and economic actors, or siphoning off the resources of the party-state through appropriation and reselling of state assets or obtaining credits from state-owned banks.[3] Most local governments adopted a mix of these approaches.

Throughout the 1980s, with the important exceptions of major coastal cities such as Shanghai, Tianjin and Shenzhen, the local entrepreneurial state frequently lacked sufficient startup capital, technical knowhow and marketing expertise to stimulate private-sector development. It could, however, channel cheap rural labor to domestic and foreign investors in its own territories. This took such forms as opening local SOEs to foreign capital and management in the form of joint ventures and development of industrial parks in major coastal cities. Equally important, however, was relaxing the restraints on movement, market and entrepreneurship, allowing and eventually encouraging villagers to take advantage of myriad new opportunities for labor and enterprise.[4] Notably since the 1990s, China's growth has been strongly driven by FDI centered in the export sector.[5] By 2004, almost 60 percent of Chinese exports were manufactured in foreign-funded

---

1 Susan L. Shirk, *The Political Logic of Economic Reform in China* (Berkeley: University of California Press, 1993).
2 Jean C. Oi, *Rural China Takes Off: Institutional Foundations of Economic Reform* (Berkeley: University of California Press, 1999).
3 Thomas Bernstein and Lü Xiaobo, *Taxation Without Representation in Contemporary Rural China* (Cambridge: Cambridge University Press, 2003).
4 See Karl Gerth, "Make Some Get Rich First: State Consumerism and Private Enterprise in the Creation of Postsocialist China," in this volume.
5 George Lin, *Red Capitalism in South China: Growth and Development of the Pearl River Delta* (Vancouver: University of British Columbia Press, 1997); You-tien Hsing, *Making Capitalism in China: The Taiwan Connection* (New York: Oxford University Press, 1998).

enterprises, and this percentage was even higher for products with higher value-added such as electronics. It is a startlingly high figure compared with other Asian countries in similar stages of takeoff – 20 percent for Taiwan in the mid 1970s, 25 percent for South Korea in the mid 1970s and 6 percent for Thailand in the mid 1980s. Measured in terms of the ratio between FDI and gross capital formation, China's FDI dependence has been among the highest in Asia since the 1990s.[6]

Major legacies of the development trajectory of the early decades of the People's Republic of China (PRC) – namely transfer of the rural surplus to drive state capital accumulation centered in industry and the cities while suppressing mass consumption, the existence of a huge reservoir of rural surplus labor resulting from the spatial segregation of a household registration system (*hukou*) that kept villagers bound to the land and the collective, and a low-wage and disciplined industrial labor force – subsequently made China a magnet for international investment. Cooperative medical care and mass education offered by the People's Communes ensured the abundant rural surplus labor would be more literate and healthier than their counterparts in other developing countries at comparable levels of development. Attractions for foreign capital included not only China's apparently unlimited supplies of cheap labor but also the capacity of local governments to provide favorable terms and to expedite the establishment of international operations in China.[7] At the same time, the collective and state guaranteed basic security at low income levels in city and countryside while raising life expectancy and becoming by the 1970s "one of the world's most egalitarian societies."[8]

Relaxation (but not abolition) of the *hukou* system of population control facilitated labor mobility. From the 1980s rural migrants were encouraged to work in the cities but were denied access to many benefits guaranteed to state-sector urban workers including free health care, subsidized housing, generous pensions, lifetime employment and free access to public education in city schools. The social reproduction of rural migrant laborers remained the responsibility of their home villages, allowing employers to

---

6 Ho-fung Hung, *The China Boom: Why China Will Not Rule the World* (New York: Columbia University Press, 2016), 56.
7 Barry Naughton, *Growing Out of the Plan: Chinese Economic Reform, 1978–1993* (Cambridge: Cambridge University Press, 1995).
8 Mark Selden, *The Political Economy of Chinese Development* (Armonk, NY: M. E. Sharpe, 1993); Carl Riskin, Renwei Zhao and Shih Li (eds.), *China's Retreat from Equality: Income Distribution and Economic Transition* (Armonk, NY: M. E. Sharpe, 2001). See also Carl Riskin, "China's Human Development After Socialism," in this volume.

minimize the wage level necessary for their survival. Voices calling for total abolition of the *hukou* system to ensure migrant workers access to full urban entitlement have been strong at the level of central government, but in the absence of subsidies to pay for these services, local governments, which benefit from the availability of cheap labor without bearing the cost of their reproduction, have vigorously resisted such calls.[9]

In the midst of profound economic transformation, the center retained control of the most valuable state industries and banks and macroeconomic regulatory functions including setting interest and exchange rates and preferential policy toward certain regions, all important legacies of the socialist era that continue to the present. However, its direct control over the economy receded, as local states became the leading agents or direct regulators of capital accumulation centered on both domestic and international capital, and as the scale and scope of state enterprise were cut back.

With market transition from the early 1980s, following the end of collective agriculture and the commune system together with the rise of township and village enterprises, rural households gained access to jobs in local enterprises and labor in coastal factories. State-sector workers, little touched by the institutional changes of the early reform, benefited from rising incomes and the availability of new consumer goods in the market. In short, in the first stage of reform up to the mid 1980s, most segments of the population, but particularly villagers, benefited from new economic opportunities. Despite permanent minimum wage work, exclusion from major benefits enjoyed by urban workers, and facing oppressive working conditions and long working hours, China's rural migrant workers were drawn to higher incomes in the cities.

From the mid 1990s, far-reaching changes undercut the position of state workers as SOEs were turned into autonomous profit-making units depriving workers of the security and benefits that the socialist system had assured. Rather than abolishing the state sector as it had done with the communes in 1983, managerial authority of many nonessential SOEs was initially transferred from the central government to local managers, while

9 Feiling Wang, *Organizing Through Division and Exclusion: China's Hukou System* (Stanford: Stanford University Press, 2005), ch. 7; Dorothy Solinger, *States' Gains, Labor's Losses: China, France, and Mexico Choose Global Liaisons, 1980–2000* (Ithaca: Cornell University Press, 2009); Tiejun Cheng and Mark Selden, "City, Countryside and the Dialectics of Control: The Origins of China's Hukou System, 1949–1960," *China Quarterly* 139 (Fall 1994), 644–68.

prices of most industrial products and raw materials were allowed to float on the market.[10]

At the same time, rampant inflation reaching just short of 20 percent in 1988 led to falling living standards among workers and peasants. Popular discontent precipitated by deepening class divisions created an explosive situation that was ignited by students calling for political liberalization in 1989 and extended to militant workers.[11]

Though the liberalization and democratization demands made by students during the 1989 hunger strike at Tiananmen Square captured media attention around the world, the movement was far from limited to Beijing and to those political demands. Student protests which sprang up in major cities across the country were frequently joined by citizens from all walks of life, including state workers and some segments of the state elite whose interests were sacrificed in the reform process.[12] Many demands were more social than political, ranging from checking corruption and commodity speculation by cadres and state managers to protecting workers' rights in reconstituted state-owned enterprises. Where protesting students employed Western-style language and symbols of liberal democracy to demand fundamental changes in the socialist system, some workers took to the streets carrying portraits of Mao Zedong to express opposition to the undermining of workers' rights enshrined in state enterprises. Viewed in this light, the uprising in 1989 not only involved a quest for Western-style liberal democracy, but was also a call for the protection of society against the expansion of a self-regulating market that jeopardized workers' rights and welfare; in other words, for some it included a vision of socialist democracy at the very moment when socialism and the Soviet bloc were collapsing in Eastern Europe.[13]

In the following decade, in the wake of the state crackdown on the demonstrators of 1989, the first massive layoffs of workers in SOEs took place, followed by privatization of many state enterprises, resulting in the

10 Tiejun Wen, *Women daodi yao shenme* [What Do We Want?] (Beijing: Huaxia chubanshe, 2004), 37.
11 Hui Wang, *China's New Order: Society, Politics, and Economy in Transition* (Cambridge, MA: Harvard University Press, 2003); Selden, *The Political Economy of Chinese Development*, 206–30.
12 Jonathan Unger (ed.), *The Pro-Democracy Protests in China: Reports from the Provinces* (Armonk, NY: M. E. Sharpe, 1991).
13 Wang, *China's New Order*.

permanent loss of job security for all workers. For the first time, state workers who had enjoyed lifetime employment faced competition for jobs from rural migrant workers.

Despite growing social dislocation, the 1990s were characterized by a paradoxical social peace, the product of state repression in the wake of Tiananmen and other protests together with promotion of new forms of nationalist ideology. Discarding earlier official nationalist ideology with its overtones of national liberation and solidarity with developing nations and national liberation movements, a more chauvinistic nationalism emerged that sought to restore China's past imperial glory and "center-of-the-world" status.[14] The political and ideological framework designed to ensure the smooth unfolding of economic liberalization was succinctly articulated in two official slogans in the 1990s: "stability above everything" (*wending yadao yiqie*) and "realize the great resurgence of the Chinese nation" (*shixian zhonghua minzu de weida fuxing*). But for Chinese workers, both those in SOEs and rural migrant workers, there was little stability.

Imbalance, Crisis, Rebalance

China's rapid economic growth and social transformation from the 1980s were facilitated by export-oriented investment. By the new millennium, China had become the most dynamic center of capital accumulation and a leading manufacturing and trading nation with the world's highest sustained growth rates. This coincided, however, with growing economic imbalances as a result of excess investment in unproductive state enterprises, low levels of domestic consumption and growing social polarization, all of which threatened sustainability and social harmony.[15] This imbalance increased at the peak of China's boom years in the 2000s and paved the way for the economic slowdown that followed the 2008 Lehman Brothers crisis in the United States, resulting in financial turmoil in China's real estate and stock markets, and excess capacity that threatened continued industrial growth in 2015.

With state-owned banks continuing to deliver easy credit to insolvent or profligate SOEs, roughly 40 percent of which incurred losses in 2006

14 Peter Hays Gries, *China's New Nationalism: Pride, Politics, and Diplomacy* (Berkeley and Los Angeles: University of California Press, 2004); Suisheng Zhao, *A Nation-State by Construction: Dynamics of Modern Chinese Nationalism* (Stanford: Stanford University Press, 2004), 248–90.
15 Hung, *The China Boom*, Table 6.4.

according to government figures, sectoral overinvestment resulted in a proliferation of nonperforming loans.[16] The gains in social and political stability as a result of job creation and layoff prevention must be set off against the long-term economic effects of overinvestment in industry and construction as witnessed by the proliferation of ghost high rises in major cities, that is, vast rows of unoccupied high-rise apartment blocks. In contrast to the state sector, many private enterprises, even successful ones, found it difficult to obtain loans from state banks.[17]

With high-speed growth over three decades, China advanced from producing 2 percent to 16 percent of the global economy while increasing per capita GDP (in purchasing power party [PPP] dollars) fortyfold.[18] The East Asian Tigers – Taiwan, South Korea, Hong Kong and Singapore – during their initial industrial takeoff in the 1950s, like China, were governed by authoritarian regimes. Nevertheless, redistributive policies such as land reform and provision of free education helped make it possible for the fruits of economic expansion to reach the lower classes, including the rural population.[19] Substantially rising income and consumption levels and reduction in urban–rural income disparity in the 1980s made possible the creation of sizeable domestic markets in the newly industrializing economies, which buffered them against the vagaries of the world market, while providing infant industries with sufficient internal demand before they could compete internationally. The result was rising income levels that brought per capita incomes in their economies to levels comparable to many of the world's high-income countries while maintaining relatively low levels of income disparity, a performance in both rising incomes and equality that China could not match despite its dynamic growth.

In the 1990s China took important steps to strengthen its position in world markets. In 1993 it unified foreign exchange rates, devalued the currency and further opened foreign investment, all preparatory to meeting stringent US-imposed standards that would permit China's entry into the World Trade Organization (WTO). By 2001, China had gained important trade advantages while confronting new challenges.[20]

16 Ibid., ch. 6.
17 Kellee S. Tsai, *Back-Alley Banking: Private Entrepreneurs in China* (Ithaca: Cornell University Press, 2002), 29–35.
18 See Riskin, "China's Human Development After Socialism," in this volume.
19 Stephen Haggard, *Pathways from the Periphery: The Politics of Growth in the Newly Industrializing Countries* (Ithaca: Cornell University Press, 1990), 223–53.
20 Barry Naughton, *The Chinese Economy: Transitions and Growth* (Cambridge, MA: MIT Press, 2007).

If the economy was registering important gains, China's pursuit of market-driven growth from the 1990s onward exacerbated social polarization. Class, urban–rural and regional disparities (particularly coastal and inland) all expanded in the 1990s, hand in hand with rapid economic growth, one of whose consequences was extraordinary wealth concentrations in the hands of the 0.001 percent of a growing group of multimillionaires. With mass migration of village youth to the coastal areas and the cities, poverty intensified in the rural hinterlands, offset in part by transfer payments to the village. At the same time, the old bastions of state industry such as the northeast China rustbelt confronted massive layoffs, plant closures and unemployment.[21] As jobs created by export-oriented global capital could not increase as rapidly as those disappearing from battered state-owned factories, in the absence of robust Chinese consumption, China would experience a net loss of manufacturing jobs from the mid 1990s. The share of manufacturing in total employment never reached the levels found at the peak of manufacturing employment in the smaller newly industrializing economies, and already in the 1990s China's service sector narrowly surpassed manufacturing in its contribution to GDP, while agriculture steadily declined.[22]

Villagers-turned-workers in coastal boom towns and cities faced new problems. In the 1990s and afterward, given the vast pool of surplus labor migrating to the cities, China did not experience wage gains comparable to those of other East Asian newly industrializing economies during their rise. Rural migrants comprised the fastest-growing sector of industrial labor, nearly all of them working at state minimum wages in the private sector and retaining few of the benefits enjoyed by an earlier generation of state workers even as state workers faced privatization of SOEs and layoffs from the late 1990s. China's manufacturing wage as a percentage of US manufacturing wage stagnated at approximately 5 percent and remained far below the level of earlier East Asian industrializers during their periods of highest growth (see Fig. 20.1.) Nevertheless, in the new millennium, annual increases in the state minimum wage (with the exception of 2008 when world recession led to large-scale layoffs of workers) steadily boosted worker income.

---

21 Ching Kwan Lee, *Against the Law: Labor Protests in China's Rustbelt and Sunbelt* (Berkeley: University of California Press, 2007).
22 Peter Evans and Sarah Staveteig, "The Changing Structure of Employment in Contemporary China," in Deborah Davis and Feng Wang (eds.), *Creating Wealth and Poverty in Postsocialist China* (Stanford: Stanford University Press, 2008), 69–83.

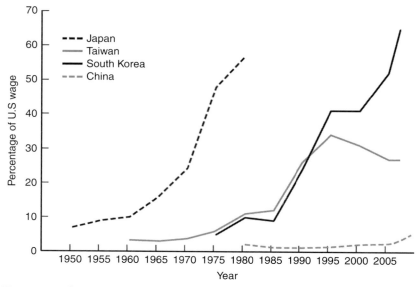

Figure 20.1. China, Japan, Taiwan and South Korea Hourly Manufacturing Wage as a Percentage of US Hourly Manufacturing Wage in Periods of High Growth, 1950–2010
Source: Ho-Fung Hung, *The China Boom: Why China Will Not Rule the World* (New York: Columbia University Press, 2016), Tab. 3.2.

Japan, Taiwan and South Korea all rapidly closed the income gap with the United States during their periods of most rapid postwar growth while reining in economic inequality. For example, Taiwan reduced income disparity indicated by the decline in Gini coefficient during its takeoff years from a range of 0.5–0.6 in the 1950s to 0.3–0.4 in the 1970s. By contrast, China's Gini coefficient grew from 0.33 in 1980 to more than 0.45 in 2007, placing it among the highest income disparities in the world, approaching that of the United States. The share of wage income in China's GDP fell from 53 percent in 1998 to 41.4 percent in 2005, driving the declining share of consumption in GDP. China's consumption lagged far behind the exuberant growth in investment and GDP. In recent years, fixed capital formation as a share of GDP approached 50 percent, while the share of household consumption has dropped to 30 percent. This means that China's economic growth remains disproportionately export-dependent.

Earlier East Asian developmental achievements were also initially based on high investment and low consumption rates. But China's fixed-asset investment rate, which has been above 40 percent of GDP and reached

45 percent in 2009, was far higher than Taiwan's and South Korea's rates at their peaks of industrial growth in the 1970s of 25–35 percent. China's private consumption share of GDP, below 40 percent and falling since 2004, was much lower than Taiwan's (50–60 percent) and South Korea's (60–70 percent) in the 1970s.[23] The low consumption rate above all of China's rural migrant workers and those villagers who remained in the countryside is a product not only of low wages but also of the fact that many rural migrants, lacking welfare, health and retirement benefits, require high savings to support themselves in old age.

In recent years, economic imbalance, precarity of labor, accumulation of bad loans, massive capital flight and concern about profitless growth have led many analysts not only to question the sustainability of the China boom but also to anticipate an imminent economic crisis. Rising state revenue from the export-led economic boom has thus far made it possible to bail out the state banks and state enterprises even at a time of slowing growth. Beneath the surface, however, reliance on state revenue to support the banks, together with lagging domestic consumption, constrains government capacity to lower taxes or invest in social programs that are especially urgent for villagers, rural migrants and laid-off workers.

The US economic crisis of 2008 struck a blow at China's exports with growth rates of exports declining from 22 percent in 2007 to –10 percent in 2009. When the global financial crisis struck, China's export engine stalled and its export-dependent manufacturing sector contracted sharply across the board. China then laid off workers in coastal industries. In Guangdong province alone, 62,000 factories closed in 2008, and by early 2009 some 23 million or 17 percent of the 140 million rural migrant workforce was unemployed, forcing many to return to their villages.[24] As Kam Wing Chan observes, rural migrant workers served the function of a Marxian industrial reserve army that could be easily recruited in periods of expansion and sent home in periods of contraction to live off their small plots of land until jobs could be found. However, with little work available in the countryside, most soon returned to the cities, aided by, among other things, government-financed construction projects. The experience of crisis underlined the important role both of the state in sustaining growth and of the countryside in providing reproduction costs for the rural migrant population

23 Hung, *The China Boom*, Figures 3.5–3.7.
24 Kam Wing Chan, "The Global Financial Crisis and Migrant Workers in China: 'There Is No Future as a Labourer; Returning to the Village Has No Meaning,'" *International Journal of Urban and Regional Research* 34, 3 (Sep. 2010), 665–67.

including child rearing and support for the elderly, thus reducing the financial burden on the state and corporations.

In response to the world economic crisis of 2008, the central government initiated stimulus by swiftly rolling out a US$ 570 billion fiscal stimulus package to revive growth. This stimulus was not primarily directed toward social spending, such as financing of medical insurance and social security to raise disposable income and hence purchasing power of workers and farmers, encourage consumption and reduce inequality. In fact, barely 20 percent was allocated for social spending. The largest share went to investment in capital construction such as high-speed rail, highways and housing projects. The assumption was twofold: This would provide jobs until exports revived, and rural migrant workers would support themselves in the interim back in the village on small agricultural plots. Little was done to support small and medium-sized labor-intensive enterprises that might have provided jobs and boosted domestic consumption, thus reducing export dependence.

China's leaders belatedly recognized that a key to decreasing export dependence lay in raising consumption of working people through redistribution of a larger share of income from capital to employees, including the extension of welfare provisions to rural migrant workers and to village-based farmers. From 2005 efforts were made to fuel a takeoff of domestic consumption by boosting the disposable income of villagers and urban workers. Early initiatives included the abolition of agricultural taxes, an increase in government procurement prices of agricultural products and investment in rural infrastructure. From 2009, the state focused on annual increases in the minimum wage and encouragement of investment in poorer regions, especially the west (with the Go West program). These measures provided a certain stimulus to consumption, especially among the rural poor and rural migrants yet, in the absence of an expansive welfare program fully incorporating villagers and migrant workers, the intertwined problems of rural poverty, inequality and precarity continue to hold back Chinese consumption and development.

Slightly improved economic conditions and employment opportunities in the agricultural sector since 2008 slowed the flow of rural–urban migration, as shown by rising rural local income (both farm and nonfarm) compared with migrant labor remittances in household income. Despite the fact that hundreds of millions of migrants have left the countryside, agricultural income, while declining steadily as a percentage of rural income, continues to provide the largest share of rural income even as remittances have risen steadily since the 1980s (see Fig. 20.2).

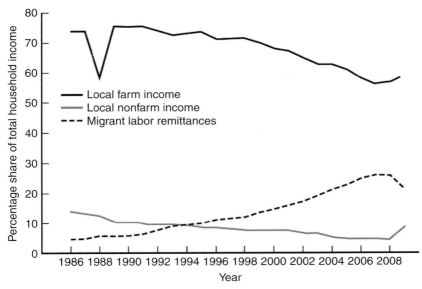

Figure 20.2. Sources of Rural Household Income
Source: Ho-Fung Hung, *The China Boom: Why China Will Not Rule the World* (New York: Columbia University Press, 2016), Fig. 6.6.

This was one factor behind a sudden labor shortage in coastal industry, leading many economists to conclude that the "Lewis turning point" – that is, the point at which rural surplus labor was exhausted as a result of a demographic transition rooted in part in China's flawed (and in 2015 terminated) one-child family planning policy – had finally arrived.[25] It remains debatable whether such a turning point has been reached or is just imminent. But a tightening of the labor market was reflected in the steady state-mandated increase in China's minimum wage which has driven the increase in manufacturing wages since 2005. The livelihood of workers was further protected by a New Labor Contract Law implemented in 2008. Despite sporadic enforcement by local governments intent on attracting investment, it became a weapon workers could sometimes wield to win concessions from employers.

Beginning in 2010, a wave of labor unrest, including strikes, riots and worker suicides, swept through China's industrial sunbelt in the south, impacting the largest international companies, notably Honda, Walmart,

25 Cai Fang and Du Yang (eds.), *The China Population and Labor Yearbook*, vol. I, *The Approaching Lewis Turning Point and Its Policy Implications* (Leiden: Brill, 2009).

Apple and electronics manufacturer Foxconn. With unrest widely reported in Chinese and foreign media, and with pressures from the Guangdong Federation of Labor, a number of global companies made significant wage concessions. In this and other instances, the Chinese state countenanced unrest at individual plants and sometimes pressured employers to ensure limited worker gains. At the same time, the state moved aggressively to prevent sustained movements or regional or national unrest by denying protesters the opportunity to extend demands across an entire city, region or industry. The All China Federation of Labor Unions, the agency of government–corporate power, retained a monopoly on representation, with rare exceptions wielding power in support of management. In spring 2011, the National People's Congress approved a new five-year plan that pledged to raise workers' wages as a share of GDP and enhance social and workplace protection of workers. The results include sustained annual hikes in the minimum wage at a time when labor availability has begun to decline. The bedrock of China's state capitalism, however, remains cooperation among foreign enterprises, the local Chinese state and the unions under circumstances in which workers are denied the rights to collective bargaining, to strike and to formation of independent unions. The state has simultaneously strengthened its legal codes while pressuring aggrieved workers and other protesters to take their individual cases off the streets and to the courts, even while denying workers the power inherent in class-action suits.

China's economic dynamism has made possible its resurgence to the position of number 2 in world GDP (it of course ranks far lower in per capita GDP) and a major economic power measured by trade, investment and infrastructure construction throughout the Asia-Pacific and beyond. It has also made possible the reduction of absolute poverty and an advance to lower-middle-income status while reversing the long-term trend toward rising income inequality each year since 2008.[26] Despite these gains, in contrast to Taiwan, Korea, Hong Kong and Singapore, all of which rose within a few decades to the ranks of high-income countries, China has barely achieved middle-income status in per capita terms, US$ 14,238 in 2015 PPP terms.[27] It has also experienced higher levels of income inequality than any of the Four Tigers.

26 See Riskin, "China's Human Development After Socialism," in this volume.
27 World Bank, GDP Per Capita PPP (2015), data.worldbank.org/indicator/NY.GDP.PCAP
.PP.CD?order=wbapi_data_value_2014±wbapi_data_value±wbapi_data_value-last
&sort=desc.

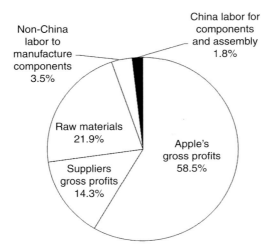

Figure 20.3. Breakdown of Profits on the Apple iPhone.
Source: Adapted from Kenneth L. Kraemer, Greg Linden and Jason Dedrick, "Capturing Value in Global Networks: Apple's iPad and iPhone," 2011, econ.sciences-po.fr/sites/def ault/files/file/Value_iPad_iPhone.pdf, p. 5.

China's performance as an industrial power and the world's leading exporter rests heavily on the advanced technologies of Japan, Korea, the United States and other nations. This is illustrated by its assembly of the iPhone, the world's most lucrative consumer product, and other electronic goods. While the electronic object in your pocket informs you that it was "made in China," Chinese workers capture only a few dollars per iPhone (1.8 percent) of the price. Most important is that, while final assembly and some manufacturing took place in China, the highest share of value-added and profit goes to Japanese and Korean firms which produced such critical and technologically sophisticated components as the touch screen and microprocessors in South Korea, Japan and Malaysia, and the manufacture and assembly of the iPhone and many other electronic products are organized in China by the Taiwanese firm, Foxconn, the world's largest industrial employer. This illustrates the fact that China's efforts to gain control of the commanding heights of technology are still in their early stages. Above all, Apple, which produces no part of the final product, captures the overwhelming share of profits as the designer and marketer, an extraordinary 58.5 percent of the price of an iPhone (see Fig. 20.3).[28]

28 Jenny Chan and Mark Selden, "China's Rural Migrant Workers and Labour Politics," in Yingjie Guo (ed.), *Handbook on Class and Social Stratification in China* (Cheltenham, UK: Edward Elgar, 2016), 362–82.

China has, however, emerged as a major regional economy and the biggest trading partner of most Asian and Pacific countries. It also provides many neighboring countries with investment, loans and other economic assistance, notably through infrastructure developments involving railroads, roads, dams, harbors and other projects that link recipients, expand trade and form part of a grandiose Chinese vision of a New Silk Road to strengthen land and water links from Asia to Europe and beyond.

For all China's expansive economic and financial position in the Asia-Pacific and beyond, far from significantly challenging the US-led world economic order, its resurgence since the 1970s has been framed within the parameters of the capitalist world system dominated by the United States. Not only does the dollar reign supreme but US, European and Japanese corporations and consumers are major beneficiaries of Chinese growth and trade. China is symbiotically bound to the United States not only by its 30 percent share of Chinese exports (including reexports from Hong Kong) but also by China's purchase of US$ 2 trillion of treasury bonds, which underwrites continued massive US trade deficits. China also adheres to rules largely dictated by the United States, ranging from the International Monetary Fund (IMF) and World Bank to the WTO and UNCLOS (United Nations Convention on the Law of the Sea).

China's resurgence can be dated from the 1949 reunification of the country (with the important exception of Taiwan) and the end of foreign invasion under the PRC. It continued with socialist construction in the 1950s and accelerated from the 1970s with China's formal entry into the ranks of the great powers (a UN Security Council seat and the United States–China opening) and has been driven by sustained economic growth in the course of transformation from a collective-socialist model to one that may best be understood as state-capitalist. That transformation is notable for the appearance of powerful new social and economic forces as China emerges as a regional power and makes strides toward becoming a global economic and trading power. But it is equally striking for the emergence of new social, economic and environmental contradictions.

If China's large economy has achieved global reach, its continued development is challenged by formidable obstacles including the world's highest emissions of greenhouse gases and pollution of air, water and soil so severe as to threaten its economic and consumption goals, calling into question the premises of the rush for industrialization and development.

Indeed, the impact of breakneck industrialization on air, water and soil constitutes a direct challenge to the very growth model that it has pioneered.

In response, the state has launched the most ambitious program for curbing coal production and consumption of oil, natural gas and other sources of greenhouse gases. Whether the center can enforce the closure of polluting coal and other mines and implement its ambitious solar- and wind-power agenda will be critical factors in determining the viability of China's growth model.[29]

We have noted China's passage from among the most egalitarian nations to one characterized by extremely unequal patterns of wealth and income distribution including regions of stark poverty centered in rural areas in general and western regions in particular. Per capita income of urban residents in China today is more than three times that of rural residents, and the per capita income of the wealthiest part of China, the Shanghai region, is more than five times that of the poorest province, Guizhou.[30] Illustrative of persistent inequality is the fact that average life expectancy in Shanghai, the wealthiest part of China, was eighty years old, while the figures in Yunnan, Qinghai and Tibet in the poor western interior are all below seventy, according to United Nations human development indicators.[31] China, in short, is a nation whose character is shaped by both social class and spatial contradictions, notably those between capital and labor and between city and countryside. At the same time, the class structure is masked by scholarly and official analysis which recognizes only an emerging middle class while denying the distinctive place of both the very rich and the working-class poor.[32] Its ambitions domestically, regionally and globally may outstrip its capacities.

For more than three decades, a capitalist boom fueling rising incomes as well as life expectancy has enabled the state to defuse tensions arising from social cleavages by expanding opportunities and particularly the expectation of opportunity for the downtrodden while creating a "stability-maintenance" regime in which local governments buy off and repress contentious collective actions.[33] Facing a new context of economic slowdown and rising social protest, the Chinese state has thus far maintained a tight grip on power through a combination of securing the allegiance not only of the prospering classes but also that of workers and farmers who hope to rise in an expanding

---

29 John A. Mathews, *Greening of Capitalism: How Asia Is Driving the Next Great Transformation* (Stanford: Stanford University Press, 2016).

30 Hung, *The China Boom*, 92, 94.   31 Ibid., Table 4.1.

32 David S. G. Goodman, *Class in Contemporary China* (Cambridge: Polity Press, 2014), ch. 4.

33 Ching Kwan Lee and Yonghong Zhang. "The Power of Instability: Unraveling the Microfoundations of Bargained Authoritarianism in China," *American Journal of Sociology* 118, 6 (2013), 1475–1508.

economy and whose isolated protests have focused on immediate gains rather than being a fundamental challenge to either capital or the power of the state.[34] The issues confronting the 70-million-strong Chinese Communist Party (CCP) are not, however, confined to the domestic economic and social spheres but are deeply imbricated with nationalism and China's growing global power.

China in Regional and Global Geopolitics

In the three decades following World War II, Asia, and China in particular, was the storm center of East–West conflict as reflected in United States–China contention in the Chinese Civil War, the US–Korean War and the United States–Indochina War. From the early 1960s, the Chinese–Soviet conflict and US stalemate in Indochina paved the way for a United States–China opening that in turn facilitated China's entry on the world political stage and its economic resurgence. Following its defeat in Indochina in 1975, the United States became embroiled in successive wars in the Middle East and Central Asia while, for the first time since the 1840s, East Asia and the western Pacific entered a period of relative peace.

Is China's geopolitical resurgence best understood as a new stage in the historic Chinese empire or Sinocentric regional order which exercised hegemony throughout much of Asia and the western Pacific for protracted periods prior to the nineteenth century, or in terms of the socialist–capitalist conflict shaping the geopolitics of the post-World War II postcolonial era? The historical regional order with China at its center can be contrasted with a Westphalian conception rooted in the conflicts among modern nation-states. We assess China's geopolitical transformation in light of the passage from the Chinese–Soviet alliance in the 1950s to Chinese–Soviet conflict since the 1960s, and from US–Chinese conflict to the United States–China opening in the 1970s to the new millennium in which deepening US–Chinese economic and financial ties go hand in hand with deepening geopolitical competition centered on the western Pacific and the South China Sea. China's attempt in the new millennium to exercise control of the South China Sea and the Philippines' lawsuit in the Permanent Court of Arbitration in The Hague, which successfully

---

34 Bruce Dickson, *The Party's Dilemma: The Chinese Communist Party's Strategy for Survival* (Oxford: Oxford University Press, 2016).

contested Chinese claims, have taken place against a background of expanded US naval maneuvers to ensure its hegemonic position in the region at the center of the Barack Obama administration's attempted "pivot to Asia."

As historian Takeshi Hamashita has argued, dynastic China's worldview posited a universalism in which no absolute distinction was drawn between entities "inside" and "outside" the empire, in contrast to a Westphalian worldview of competing nations.[35] China's historical worldview is best represented by concentric circles with the emperor and the capital at the center, surrounded by directly governed provinces and, at the periphery, tribute vassals, with others beyond the pale who might eventually become tributary regions. This world order, at its peak in the sixteenth to eighteenth centuries, was predicated not on the logic of economic extractions by the center as in the manner of nineteenth- and twentieth-century imperialism, but on reciprocity with the center (China) frequently subsidizing the periphery in exchange for fealty demonstrated in tributary missions to the imperial capital, and preservation of a Sinocentric hegemonic order as the condition for regional peace. In this system, rulers of tributary states derived legitimacy from the endorsement of the Chinese emperor, and the loyalty of tributary states was instrumental to the security and economic welfare of the Chinese empire. In contrast to Western colonialisms, the Chinese tributary system was far less intrusive: predicated neither on settler colonialism nor on domination and transformation of local economies. Nevertheless, Manchu forces and their Mongol allies greatly expanded the territorial scope of the Qing empire by the eighteenth century with the conquest of Tibet, Xinjiang and Mongolia.

This tributary order was destroyed by Western and then Japanese imperialism initiating a century of warfare that destroyed the Qing empire as a result of foreign invasion and wars (from 1840), followed by internal rebellions (1860s) and dynastic collapse (1911). It would not be reversed until the founding of the People's Republic in 1949, and international recognition of the PRC as the government of China in the 1970s followed by China's expansive role in the world economy and the geopolitics of East Asia and the western Pacific.

During China's economic resurgence in the 1980s, Deng Xiaoping advanced a strategy of lying low (*tao guang yang hui*), that is, focusing

---

35 Takeshi Hamashita, *China, East Asia and the Global Economy: Regional and Historical Perspectives*, eds. Mark Selden and Linda Grove (London: Routledge, 2008).

on economic development and refraining from asserting political and military power in recognition of the nation's limited military strength. In that era, China's foreign policy pivoted on cooperation with the United States, at times even serving US geopolitical interests, notably in pressuring the Soviet Union. Right after Deng assumed the leadership mantle, China went to war with Vietnam, in response to Vietnam's 1978 invasion of China-backed Cambodia under the Khmer Rouge. After dealing a blow to Vietnam and withdrawing its forces, Beijing continued to support the Khmer Rouge guerrillas resisting the Vietnam-backed government in Phnom Penh.

Following its defeat in Vietnam in 1975, the United States looked to China to check the expansion of Vietnam's influence in Southeast Asia, which it viewed as a Soviet proxy. China's war with Vietnam and its support for Khmer Rouge guerrillas in Cambodia, while serving China's interest in competition with the Soviet Union, fit the American post-Indochina War Asia strategy well.[36] In return, the United States supported China's developmental goals, in sync with US business interests, and China's geopolitical goal of securing the return of Hong Kong from British rule. This dynamic of United States–China collaboration in the 1980s is reflected in historian Mark Elvin's recollection of his advocacy for the autonomy of Hong Kong in the context of the 1997 sovereignty handover. Contacting President Ronald Reagan through a colleague who had known him during his time as governor of California, Elvin enquired "through him whether there was any chance of the US being willing to apply pressure to help in this effort. The contact worked, and the answer was unequivocal: there was no chance at all, as doing so would risk damaging American business interests in China."[37]

This collusive relationship between China and the United States (and the West in general) weakened in the aftermath of the 1989 Tiananmen crackdown, when US policymakers debated sanctioning China. But after the collapse of the Soviet Union, China's leadership solidified relations with American and global business interests by accelerating market reform and opening to international investment.[38] Major American business interests formed a formidable lobby that helped the administration of Bill Clinton to delink the annual renewal of China's most-favored-nation status from

36 Henry Kissinger, *On China* (New York: Penguin Book, 2012), chs. 13–14.
37 Mark Elvin, "The Historian as Haruspex," *New Left Review* 52 (Jul.–Aug. 2008), 83–109.
38 Hung, *The China Boom*, ch. 3.

human rights consideration,[39] opening the road to China's permanent most-favored-nation status for the United States and its accession to the WTO in 2001.

In the late 1990s, China's growing strength gave it confidence to challenge US geopolitical supremacy, above all in the western Pacific. This was manifested first in China's missile testing over the Taiwan Strait coinciding with Taiwan's first democratic presidential election in 1996, and subsequently in China's increasing assertiveness of sovereignty over the South China Sea. The United States responded to the first challenge by sending a carrier group through the Taiwan Strait. The second challenge culminated in the spy plane incident when a Chinese fighter jet collided with a US reconnaissance plane over the South China Sea, leading to the crash of the China fighter jet and the forced landing of the US spy plane on China's Hainan Island. But just as United States–China tensions were building, the US "War on Terror," triggered by the terrorist attack of 11 September 2001 and the subsequent Afghanistan and Iraq Wars, shifted US geopolitical priorities to the Middle East and Afghanistan. As a result, the George W. Bush era was notable for improved relations in an effort to secure China's assistance in addressing many thorny issues in Asia, notably the North Korea nuclear crisis, rising China–Japan tensions over the Diaoyu/Senkaku Islands, and South China Sea territorial conflicts involving China and the Philippines, among others.

With the United States tied down in the Middle East, and with China's growing global reach in trade, investment and search for resources, Beijing became more assertive in projecting its political and military power to protect its growing overseas interests and challenge the United States' hegemonic reach, notably in the western Pacific and the South China Sea, but also extending to regions far from its historical periphery including Africa, Latin America and Central Asia.

The connection between the global expansion of Chinese capital and China's desire to expand its military power regionally and globally is best articulated in the 2013 National Defense White Paper that stated explicitly for the first time that protecting China's overseas interests had become a core mission of the People's Liberation Army, as

> [w]ith the gradual integration of China's economy into the world economic system, overseas interests have become an integral component of China's

39 David M. Lampton, "America's China Policy in the Age of the Finance Minister: Clinton Ends Linkage," *China Quarterly* 139 (Sep. 1994), 611–29.

national interests. Security issues are increasingly prominent, involving overseas energy and resources, strategic sea lines of communication, and Chinese nationals and legal persons overseas.[40]

China earlier played an important role in the United States–Korea and United States–Indochina Wars, in both cases helping to thwart US designs on China's borders and demonstrating that China was a military force to be reckoned with. This reality was reinforced by China's development of nuclear weapons in 1964 and air and naval power in recent years. Yet, in contrast to the United States, during the past half-century China has neither forged strong alliances nor established extensive overseas military bases.

With the rapid growth of China's navy and air force and the extension of its power in the South China Sea, the robust United States–China economic relationship is now challenged by deepening geopolitical conflict in the western Pacific. At the same time, the US and Chinese economies remain deeply integrated, presenting for both Beijing and Washington a dilemma between conflict and cooperation and posing uncertainty for United States–China relations that is widely recognized as the most important bilateral relationship in the international system.

China's increasing role in challenging and reshaping the economic and geopolitical order in East Asia and the western Pacific is not a reincarnation of the historical tributary-trade framework, though it does restore a measure of centrality to China's regional position. It is very much a function of an expansive global trade and investment profile, the legacies of twentieth-century wars and conflicts, and a changing regional geopolitical order shaped by the 1982 United Nations Convention on the Law of the Sea, which transformed what were once open seas into realms controlled by nations. Particularly striking are the vast territorial gains of the United States (which has been the major beneficiary of UNCLOS, although it has refused to ratify the treaty) and Japan, while China was the major loser among the powers.[41]

China's growing regional air and naval presence and territorial claims are centered in the area of its historical reach. However, where China was long the sole dominant power in the historic Sinocentric tributary-trade order through the eighteenth century, it presently encounters

40 Chinese Information Office of the State Council, 2013.
41 Gavan McCormack, "Much Ado over Small Islands: The Sino-Japanese Confrontation over Senkaku/Diaoyu," *Asia-Pacific Journal* 11, 21 (3) (27 May 2013), japanfocus.org/-Gavan-McCormack/3947/article.html.

US power in the Pacific predicated on naval and air superiority rooted in a network of military bases and alliances that encircles China. It also encounters other nations, notably Japan and South Korea, which possess economic, technological and geopolitical strengths as well as far higher income levels and alliance relationships with the United States. Above all, the logic of China's expansive reach, still centered in the regions of its historical periphery, is constrained by the Westphalian system of sovereign nation-state economic interests in global capitalism, as well as post-Cold War networks of alliances. China has emerged as the dominant trade, investment and construction power throughout the region, and its military strength grows apace. This is not, however, a revival of a Sinocentric tribute-trade system; rather it takes place within the parameters of a Westphalian competition for power with China and the United States at its center and played by the rules of an international order that is dominated by the United States through the world trade system, UNCLOS and the United Nations among other institutions.

A number of Asian states with deep economic ties to China have responded to China's expansive moves in the South China and East China Seas by strengthening security ties with other regional powers, notably the United States, but also Japan, Australia, Philippines, Vietnam and India. For its part, as US–Russian relations grow tense over Ukraine, China and Russia have sought to strengthen their relationship and in July 2016 engaged in joint naval exercises.

At the same time, together with European and other nations, with the exception of the United States and Japan, all the above-mentioned US allies have responded positively to China's 2015 initiative to establish the US$ 100 billion China-centered Asian Infrastructure Investment Bank (AIIB), China's boldest international financial initiative to date. China touts the bank as financing many projects under the "One Belt, One Road" concept that Xi Jinping floated in 2013 to build a series of ports, roads and railways to link China and Europe over maritime and land routes and strengthen China's already formidable trade, investment and construction ties with neighboring states. The AIIB is the first major institutional challenge to the US-dominated international economic order, one that could both strengthen China's trade, infrastructure and investment ties with multiple nations and also enhance intra-regional ties. With the United States and Japan as the only powers to oppose the bank, efforts to prevent others from joining failed. Indeed, China has emerged as the world's biggest lender to developing countries. China's Development Bank and the Export–Import Bank provided US$ 684 billion in loans between 2007 and 2014, more than the next six international lenders.[42] Both the AIIB and China's defeat at the International Court of Justice over its territorial claims in the South China Sea illustrate dimensions of how conflicts are playing out in geopolitical, financial and trade arenas.

To be sure, multiple challenges await the AIIB and the many infrastructure projects that China proposes to finance. First, although it is the largest investor, China is unlikely to dominate the institution as the United States dominated the Bretton Woods institutions after World War II. For all its economic and financial power, China lacks the overwhelming economic and military-political edge to control the AIIB in contrast to US political-economic supremacy over its Cold War allies in the early postwar years, when all major rivals and allies were in ruins and the United States financed the war recovery of its allies. Second is the viability of the ambitious projects of the One Belt, One Road initiatives, many of which involve politically unstable regions such as Pakistan and Central Asian states, and areas in which other regional powers like India have been actively courting, such as Sri Lanka. With high political risks and competition from China's geopolitical rivals, many of these projects, together with the AIIB that is expected to finance them, could fail.

If China's most expansive economic and geopolitical initiatives of recent decades have centered in the Asia-Pacific, in its search for markets, resources and investment opportunities, it has also extended its reach to Europe, the Americas and Africa in ways that invite comparison with those of other nations from the age of imperialism to the present. China is the world leader in investing not only in African natural resources, but also in land, and Chinese laborers and farmers as well as managers, by some estimates 1 million people, have moved to Africa. The region could become another front in US–Chinese conflict as the United States establishes a military position throughout the region, with a particular eye on North Africa and the Middle East.[43]

Critics have charged China with launching a new imperialism in Africa. For example, in March 2013, the then governor of the Central Bank of Nigeria,

42 Robert Soutar, "China Becomes World's Biggest Development Lender," *China Dialogue* (25 May 2016), www.chinadialogue.net/article/show/single/en/8947-China-becomes-world-s-biggest-development-lender.
43 Nick Turse, *Tomorrow's Battlefield: US Proxy Wars and Secret Ops in Africa* (New York: Dispatch Books, 2015).

which has been one of the African countries heavily reliant on Chinese loans for its development, warned in the *Financial Times* that, by embracing China, Africa is "opening itself up to a new form of imperialism." He also stated that, "China takes from us primary goods and sells us manufactured ones. This was also the essence of colonialism."[44] At the same time, China's growing African presence has not only stimulated African economies but also provided alternatives to domination by the old imperial powers, at times by propping up African dictatorships. In December 2015 Xi Jinping completed a triumphal Africa tour. Beijing has not limited its African turn to trade and diplomacy. It also joined forces with international mercenaries to defend its African interests. In 2014, Erik Prince, the founder and former CEO of US security firm XE Services (formerly Blackwater), which was heavily involved in the second US invasion of Iraq, became the chairman of a Hong Kong-based logistics and risk management firm. The firm, Frontier Services Group, has close ties and interlocking directors with China's biggest state-owned conglomerate, CITIC. Its main business is to provide security services to Chinese companies throughout Africa.[45] China's African initiatives as well as its far-reaching New Silk Road projects well illustrate the distance from the regional tributary-trade order of the eighteenth century.

In recent decades we note a double movement in which the United States–China relationship, with its synergies and contradictions, has become the world's most important not only in economic and financial but also in geopolitical terms. This has been a period of China's resurgence and relative US decline, the latter illustrated by successive and simultaneous costly, destructive and abortive or inconclusive wars in the Middle East and Central Asia. The United States nevertheless retains by far the most powerful military machine, the dollar securely holds its position as the global currency and, together with its strong alliance and base network and its hegemonic reach, the country continues to shape the dominant global narrative in the WTO, UNCLOS and the United Nations, the IMF and the World Bank. Stated differently, for all its growing power and reach, there is scant evidence that China is on the

---

44 Lamido Sanusi, "Africa Must Get Real About Chinese Ties," *Financial Times* (11 Mar. 2013).

45 Sébastien Le Belzic, "Erik Prince: 'Je suis en mission pour l'économie chinoise en Afrique,'" *Le Monde* (3 Sep. 2015), www.lemonde.fr/afrique/article/2015/03/09/erik-prince-je-suis-en-mission-pour-l-economie-chinoise-en-afrique_4589827_3212.html#flD GY016kUxJSPco.99.

verge of replacing or even significantly challenging the United States as the dominant global power even as it is squarely positioned to shape outcomes in the Asia-Pacific.

The Chinese economic boom and the rebound of the Chinese economy after the global crisis of 2008 that battered the US economy heightened Beijing's self-confidence in putting aside Deng Xiaoping's "lying low" strategy. The CCP has recently become more aggressive in building on its economic strengths in Asia and in other developing countries to challenge both its neighbors and US geopolitical interests head on, as exemplified by its assertive action regarding the sovereignty disputes over the South China Sea and over the Diaoyu/Senkaku Islands. With the Chinese economic boom slowing, and with the international backlash against China's military assertiveness in Asia and the Pacific, the United States has signaled its intentions to strengthen its political, military and economic ties with countries to balance China's influence through its "pivot to Asia" and Trans-Pacific Partnership, even as it faces continuing military challenges in numerous, seemingly endless Middle Eastern wars. For its part, a state-capitalist China whose communist party retains a firm grip on power confronts multiple domestic and international challenges, but at this writing none that threatens its demise or points the way toward fundamental political change.

Bibliographical Essay

China's recent rise as a regional and global geopolitical power can be traced back to its regional centrality in the early modern world. For a discussion of this centrality and its loss in 1800–1950 as the background to China's contemporary resurgence, see Takeshi Hamashita, *China, East Asia and the Global Economy: Regional and Historical Perspectives*, eds. Mark Selden and Linda Grove (London: Routledge, 2008), and Giovanni Arrighi, Takeshi Hamashita and Mark Selden (eds.), *The Resurgence of East Asia: 500, 150 and 50 Year Perspectives* (London: Routledge, 2008).

For the dynamics of the rise of the East Asian Tigers during the Cold War as a prelude to China's economic boom, see Stephen Haggard, *Pathways from the Periphery: The Politics of Growth in the Newly Industrializing Countries* (Ithaca: Cornell University Press, 1990).

For the nature of contemporary China's state-capitalist economic boom, see Barry Naughton, *Growing out of the Plan: Chinese Economic*

Reform, 1978–1993 (Cambridge: Cambridge University Press, 1995); Barry Naughton, *The Chinese Economy: Transitions and Growth* (Cambridge, MA: MIT Press, 2007); Nicholas R. Lardy, *Markets over Mao: The Rise of Private Business in China* (Washington, DC: Peterson Institute for International Economics, 2014); Bruce J. Dickson, *Wealth into Power: The Chinese Communist Party's Embrace of China's Private Sector* (New York: Cambridge University Press, 2008); You-tien Hsing, *Making Capitalism in China: The Taiwan Connection* (New York: Oxford University Press, 1998); Susan L. Shirk, *The Political Logic of Economic Reform in China* (Berkeley: University of California Press, 1993); Mark Selden, *The Political Economy of Chinese Development* (Armonk, NY: M. E. Sharpe, 1993).

For the nature of state-capitalist transformation and the communist party-state's handling of challenges from below and the nature of state-capitalist transition, see Bruce Dickson, *The Party's Dilemma: The Chinese Communist Party's Strategy for Survival* (London: Oxford University Press, 2016); Ching Kwan Lee, *Against the Law: Labor Protests in China's Rustbelt and Sunbelt* (Berkeley: University of California Press, 2007); David S. G. Goodman, *Class in Contemporary China* (Cambridge: Polity Press, 2014); Elizabeth Perry and Mark Selden (eds.), *Chinese Society: Change, Conflict and Resistance*, 3rd edn. rev. and enlarged (London: Routledge, 2010); Sebastian Heilmann and Elizabeth J. Perry (eds.), *Mao's Invisible Hand: The Political Foundations of Adaptive Governance in China* (Cambridge, MA: Harvard University Press, 2011); Dorothy Solinger, *States' Gains, Labor's Losses: China, France, and Mexico Choose Global Liaisons, 1980–2000* (Ithaca: Cornell University Press, 2009); Joseph Fewsmith, *The Logic and Limits of Political Reform in China* (New York: Cambridge University Press, 2013); Teresa Wright, *Accepting Authoritarianism: State–Society Relations in China's Reform Era* (Stanford: Stanford University Press, 2013); Ya-sheng Huang, *Capitalism with Chinese Characteristics: Entrepreneurship and the State* (Cambridge: Cambridge University Press, 2008).

For China's increasing influence in the global economy and global politics (but also the limits of Chinese growth), see Ho-fung Hung, *The China Boom: Why China Will Not Rule the World* (New York: Columbia University Press, 2016); Deborah Brautigam, *The Dragon's Gift: The Real Story of China in Africa* (New York: Oxford University Press, 2011); Kevin Gallagher, *The Dragon in the Room: China and the Future of Latin American Industrialization* (Stanford: Stanford University Press, 2010); Cai Fang and Du Yang (eds.), *The China Population and Labor Yearbook,* vol. I, *The Approaching Lewis Turning Point and*

Its Policy Implications (Leiden: Brill, 2009).For nationalist upsurge amidst China's geopolitical rise, see Suisheng Zhao, *A Nation-State by Construction: Dynamics of Modern Chinese Nationalism* (Stanford: Stanford University Press, 2004); Peter Hays Gries, *China's New Nationalism: Pride, Politics, and Diplomacy* (Berkeley: University of California Press, 2004).

21

Communism and Environment

DOUGLAS R. WEINER

The first venue where state power was seized by followers of Marx and Engels was in Russia in November 1917. During the "environmental decade" of the 1960s and 1970s scholars first wondered whether communist states might have developed in an environmentally more sensitive way than capitalist ones. Most concluded that not only did communist regimes fail to realize the theoretical advantages of a *dirigiste* system, their careless practices brought about, in the words of Murray Feshbach and Fred Friendly, Jr., an "ecocide."[1] Even some Soviet authors agreed.[2]

"Environmentally sensitive development," however, is not easily defined. There is no "natural" standard for environmental purity or pollution apart from different individuals' or societies' ideas of acceptable risk.[3] Efforts to curtail resource wastage, to promote the sustained use of renewable resources and recycling, to protect habitats and life forms and to control pollution have together come under the broad rubric of "environmental protection." Yet, humans, like all living things, cannot escape transforming

1 Murray Feshbach and Alfred Friendly, Jr., *Ecocide in the USSR: Health and Nature Under Siege* (New York: Basic Books, 1992); D. J. Peterson, *Troubled Lands: The Legacy of Soviet Environmental Destruction* (Boulder: Westview Press and RAND, 1993). The earlier works include Marshall Goldman, *The Spoils of Progress: Environmental Pollution in the Soviet Union* (Cambridge, MA: MIT Press, 1972); Philip R. Pryde, *Conservation in the Soviet Union* (Cambridge: Cambridge University Press, 1972), and his *Environmental Management in the Soviet Union* (Cambridge: Cambridge University Press, 1991); and Charles Ziegler, *Environmental Policy in the USSR* (Amherst: University of Massachusetts Press, 1987).
2 Mikhail Lemeshev, *Vlast' vedomstv – ekologicheskii infarkt* (Moscow: Progress, 1989), translated as *Bureaucrats in Power – Ecological Collapse* (Moscow: Progress, 1990); Aleksei Iablokov and Rolf Edberg, *Tomorrow Will Be Too Late: East Meets West on Global Ecology* (Tucson: University of Arizona Press, 1991); Ze'ev Volf'son (Boris Komarov), *The Destruction of Nature in the Soviet Union*, trans. Michael Hale and Joe Hollander (London: Pluto Press, [1980]), orig. publ. as *Unichtozhenie prirody: obostrenie ekologicheskogo krizisa v SSSR* (Frankfurt-am-Main: Posev, 1978).
3 See Mary Douglas and Aaron Wildavsky, *Risk and Culture: An Essay on the Selection of Technical and Environmental Dangers* (Berkeley: University of California Press, 1982).

our environment.[4] The idea that we should think about the likely environmental effects of our activity has roots only as far back as seventeenth-century Europe.[5] Moreover, the various policies subsumed under "environmental protection" reflect widely divergent concerns: human health, resource availability into the future, and ethical and esthetic concerns about nonhuman life forms and landscapes. Some societies could be concerned with one, or two, but not all of these issues.

Finally, concern does not necessarily translate into desired outcomes. A society might set concentration thresholds for individual chemicals, but still be unable to control the dangerous effects of their combined action.[6] In the absence of complete scientific knowledge and technical capacity to achieve our environmental goals, there will always be a gap between ideals or concerns and outcomes. Consequently, it is difficult to assign "environmental" rankings to regimes.

Early Soviet Policies

Soviet environmental management has varied by time period, with the earlier period characterized by uniquely forward-looking policies for their day. The Bolsheviks seized power with a desire to impose a "planned," scientifically grounded order – including resource management – in place of a rapacious and anarchic capitalist one. Initially, the new regime heeded the voices of tsarist-era trained scientists, mostly botanists, zoologists and geographers, who forcefully championed habitat protection.[7] Responsibility for nature protection was delegated to the People's Commissariat (ministry) for Education. Additionally, the Soviet regime in 1918 enacted a "Law on Forests" that created a category of

4 Willliam R. Dickinson, "The Holocene Legacy," *Environmental History* 5, 4 (Oct. 2000), 483–502.
5 See Richard Grove, "Conserving Eden: The (European) East India Companies and Their Environmental Policies on St. Helena, Mauritius, and in Western India, 1660 to 1854," *Comparative Studies in Society and History* 35 (Apr. 1993), 318–35.
6 See Shepard Krech III, *The Ecological Indian* (New York: Norton, 1999), "Introduction" and "Epilogue."
7 For an extended treatment of the late tsarist period, see Feliks Robertovich Shtil'mark, *Istoriografiia rossiiskikh zapovednikov (1895–1995)* (Moscow: Logata, 1996); Douglas R. Weiner, *Models of Nature: Ecology, Conservation and Cultural Revolution in Soviet Russia* (Bloomington: Indiana University Press, 1988); and Vladimir E. Boreiko, *Istoriia okhrany prirody Ukrainy: X vek–1980. Izdanie vtoroe* (Kiev: Kievskii ekologo-kul'turnyi tsentr, 1997) and his *Ocherki o pionerakh okhrany prirody*, 2 vols. (Kiev: Kievskii ekologo-kul'turnyi tsentr and Tsentr okhrany dikoi prirody SoES, 1996).

protected forests and limited cutting in provinces with low percentages of forested land, although research has established that the law was unevenly observed.[8]

The world's first national environmental regulatory body, the Interagency State Committee for Nature Protection (1925–31), had a nominal right to protest and delay implementation of economic projects and targets that were found to harm ecological values unacceptably. The Education Commissariat additionally sponsored the world's first network of protected territories (*zapovedniki*) exclusively dedicated to the ecological and scientific study of "wild" nature. These were imagined as baselines (*etalony*) of healthy natural communities against which changes in surrounding, once-similar but human-affected areas could be compared. Scientists could then recommend for each ecological region of the country forms of land use that caused the least measurable (or visible) biotic changes. By 1933 there were seventy republic- and local-level reserves across the Soviet Union with a total area of 6 million hectares (about 15 million acres). Ironically, this binary of "healthy" pristine nature and "corrupting" human society flew in the face of the Marxian dialectical view and was based on premises that scientists now hold as faulty.[9]

Limited conservation activism was also permitted in the 1920s. The All-Russian Society for the Protection of Nature (Vserossiiskii obshchestvo okhrany prirody, VOOP) was founded in 1924; its journal *Okhrana prirody* (Protection of Nature) began publishing four years later. Extensive foreign contacts were forged.[10]

Building on prerevolutionary public health activism, the communist regime created a Commissariat of Public Health which in 1923 published "Regulations on Levels of Purity of Wastewater" and conducted chemical and hydrobiological assays on hundreds of rivers, ponds and wells.[11] Here, too, foreign efforts were closely studied.[12]

---

8 On the forest law, see Brian Bonhomme, *Forests, Peasants, and Revolutionaries: Forest Conservation and Organization in Soviet Russia, 1917–1929* (Boulder: East European Monographs, 2005); Stephen C. Brain, *Song of the Forest: Russian Forestry and Stalin's Environmentalism* (Pittsburgh: University of Pittsburgh Press, 2011); Weiner, *Models of Nature*, 24–25.

9 On the rejection of static, equilibrium-based models of ecological communities, see Daniel Botkin, *Discordant Harmonies: A New Ecology for the Twenty-First Century* (New York: Oxford University Press, 1990).

10 See Weiner, *Models of Nature*, 31–84.

11 Mikhail Vladimirovich Poddubnyi, *Sanitarnaia okhrana okruzhaiushchei sredy v Rossii i SSSR v pervoi polovine XX veka. Seriia: istoriia okhrany prirody, vypusk 16* (Kiev: Kievskii ekologo-kul'turnyi tsentr and Tsentr okhrany dikoi prirody SoES, 1997).

12 Ibid., 17. Dr. Alice Hamilton, then an assistant professor of medicine at Harvard University and later a pioneer in environmental toxicology in the United States, visited

The Stalin Era

Prospects both for nature protection and for control of industrial pollution were stunted by Joseph Stalin's revolution from above. Because it opposed target quotas for procurement of timber and marine mammals, the Interagency State Committee for Nature Protection was abolished in 1931. Eight years later, vice-premier of the USSR Andrei Yanuar'evich Vyshinskii famously propounded that pollution standards were not needed either: "We have the Stalin Constitution. That is sufficient to ensure that our public hygiene and public health are the best in the world!"[13]

The Legacy of Marx and Engels

To understand the environmental attitudes and policies of communist regimes from the 1960s, we must first grasp the principles upon which all Soviet-type regimes were constructed. These signally include these regimes' selective borrowing – or rejection – of the ideas of Marx and Engels. As presumptuous as were those philosophers' claims to have founded the one correct "science" of society,[14] their understanding of the "man–nature" relationship was precocious. Today, the idea of the Anthropocene is accepted without fuss, but when Marx and Engels in 1845–46 advanced the idea that humans and "nature" had cocreated each other, it was truly a novel conception.[15] Marx referred to "nature" as "man's body" and to humans as "the mind of nature," overturning the stark division between humans and "nature" generally held.

Moscow in 1925, where she was hosted by the Institute for Occupational Diseases. Her observations, contained in Alice Hamilton, "Industrial Hygiene in Moscow," *Journal of Industrial Hygiene* 7, 2 (Feb. 1925), 47–61, were highly laudatory: "It would seem that we are justified in looking forward to great things in this field to come out of Russia" (61). See also K. F. Meyer, "Some Observations on Infective Diseases in Russia," *American Journal of Public Health* 47 (Sep. 1957), 1083–92.

13 Poddubnyi, *Sanitarnaia okhrana okruzhaiushchei*, 27.
14 For lucid critiques of the assumptions and claims of Marxism, see Leszek Kołakowski, *Main Currents of Marxism*, vol. I, *The Founders* (Oxford: Oxford University Press, 1978); Andrzej Walicki, *Marxism and the Leap to the Kingdom of Freedom: The Rise and Fall of the Communist Utopia* (Stanford: Stanford University Press, 1995); and Alexander Yakovlev (Aleksandr Nikolaevich), *The Fate of Marxism in Russia* (New Haven: Yale University Press, 1993).
15 Karl Marx and Friedrich Engels, *The German Ideology. Part One, with selections from Parts Two and Three and supplementary texts*, ed. with an introduction by C. J. Arthur (New York: International Publishers, 1970), esp. 61–63. For a clear explanation of their view, see Kołakowski, *Main Currents*, 134–37, which also includes a discussion of relevant sections of Marx's Paris manuscripts of 1844.

Engels argued that humans could gain some knowledge of the world by using experience rather than a priori metaphysics.[16] "Practice ... is the criterion of truth," he noted; we can only learn about the world through our interaction with it. Yet, Engels rejected the idea that humans could *fully* comprehend the totality of the universe.[17] For one thing, nature is always in flux, and humans can never be sure of the sphere of validity of the natural laws we discover.[18] And, although Engels believed that all products of the universe could be explained through some interaction of matter and energy, he also held the door open to the notion that humans were not always able to provide adequate explanations of causality at any given time.

Humans – social beings – have used collectively organized labor from our earliest days to wrest food and other products from our surroundings, and have transformed those surroundings in the process, argued Engels. But, for that to be successful, "our mastery of nature [ought] not resemble that of a conqueror," for "nature, in order to be mastered, must be obeyed." To proceed heedlessly was to risk unwanted consequences:

> Let us not, however, flatter ourselves overmuch on account of our human victories over nature. For each such victory nature takes its revenge on us. Each victory, it is true, ... first ... brings about the results we expected, but in the second and third places it has quite different, unforeseen effects which only too often cancel the first ... Those who spread the potato in Europe were not aware that ... they were at the same time spreading scrofula. Thus at every step we are reminded that we by no means rule over nature like a conqueror over a foreign people, like someone standing outside nature – but that we, with flesh, blood and brain, belong to nature, and exist in its midst, and that all our mastery of it consists in the fact that we have the advantage over all other creatures of being able to learn its laws and apply them correctly.[19]

Engels remained optimistic, however, that human understanding would eventually undermine the false dichotomy of man and nature:

> [A]fter the mighty advances made by the natural sciences in the present century, we are more than ever in a position to realise, and hence to control, also the more remote natural consequences of ... our ... production activities. But the more this progresses the more will men not only feel but

16 Friedrich Engels, *The Dialectics of Nature* and *Ludwig Feuerbach and the End of Classical German Philosophy* (London: Electric Book Co., 2001).
17 See the fine discussion again in Kołakowski, *Main Currents*, 376–98.   18 Ibid., 395.
19 See www.marxists.org/archive/marx/works/1876/part-played-labour/. This is from F. Engels, *The Part of Labor in the Transformation from Ape to Man*, trans. Clemens Dutt (Moscow: Progress Publishers, 1934).

also know their oneness with nature, and the more impossible will become the senseless and unnatural idea of a contrast between mind and matter, man and nature, soul and body, such as arose after the decline of classical antiquity in Europe and obtained its highest elaboration in Christianity.[20]

Marx and Engels had no place for the veneration of "pristine" nature.[21] Nevertheless, they were sensitive to the dialectical or mutually transforming feedback processes of human society and the rest of the material world. However, that and their caution regarding the limits to human knowledge, plus their cognizance that all choices are tradeoffs, were all disregarded by their followers, who understood the founders more simplistically. Despite the attraction of some early Soviet scientists and philosophers to the more sophisticated aspects of Marx's and Engels's thinking, communist political leaders and regimes – like market societies – saw "man" and "nature" as things apart, with the latter to be vanquished by the former.[22]

Although nature protection activists tried to enlist Engels's dictum that nature, to be commanded, must be obeyed, the era of the five-year plans ushered in a new dichotomization of humans and nature sponsored by the regime. Reflecting this, writer Maksim Gorkii declared "a war to the death" against nature, railing that "the blind drive of nature to produce on earth every kind of useless or even harmful trash – must be stopped and eradicated."[23] Conservation was accused by an influential party critic of constituting "a land mine under socialist agriculture,"[24] and the leading scientific ecologist and conservation activist, Vladimir Vladimirovich Stanchinskii, was arrested in 1933.[25]

The Soviet Political Economy and Resource Use

To understand the environmental policies of mature Soviet-type states, we must examine not only philosophies of nature but the actual system of

20 Ibid.
21 Karl Marx, *Capital*, vol. III, trans. Ernest Untermann (Chicago: Charles H. Kerr and Co., 1909), 954, quoted in Erich Fromm, "Foreword," in Karl Marx, *Early Writings*, trans. and ed. T. B. Bottomore (New York: McGraw-Hill, 1964), ii.
22 See Loren R. Graham, *Science, Philosophy and Human Behavior in the Soviet Union* (New York: Columbia University Press, 1987).
23 Maksim Gor'kii, "O bor'be s prirodoi," *Izvestiia* (12 Dec. 1931).
24 Arnosht Kol'man, "Sabotazh v nauke," *Bol'shevik* 2 (1931), 75.
25 Douglas R. Weiner, *A Little Corner of Freedom: Russian Nature Protection from Stalin to Gorbachev* (Berkeley: University of California Press, 1999), 44–46; Vladimir Yevgen'evich Boreiko, *Don Kikhoty. Istoriia, liudi, zapovedniki* (Moscow: Logata, 1998), 223–39.

political economy of those states. The Stalinist and post-Stalinist economic system was based on a labor- and resource-intensive organization of inputs designed to produce a large but limited array of products. Targets were set by central planners in Gosplan USSR, the state planning agency, under the supervision of the Soviet Communist Party's Central Committee, to take the Soviet example. If Marx had described "communism" as the transcendence of the "kingdom of necessity," then to attain that goal regime leaders drilled that there first had to be a massive expansion of the "means of production," understood as heavy industry. Replacing capitalism's "fetishism of commodities" was Soviet-type regimes' fetishism of heavy industrial growth.[26]

These priorities were not simply ideological; they were symbolic. Huge hydroelectric dams (Dneprstroi, Volga dams at Stalingrad [Volgograd] and Kuibyshev [Samara]) were constructed to rival the Boulder (Hoover) and Grand Coulee dams; together with massive canal projects (Moscow–Volga, Volga–Don, Fergana), they served to create visible symbols of communist progress.[27] Engineers who argued that smaller thermal-generating plants would be more cost-effective were ignored or repressed as were biologists who warned about the effects of these projects on fisheries and other biota. Ironically, the fulminating smokestacks of more industrialized Western nations served as the Soviet model.[28]

---

26 See especially Thomas Remington, *Building Socialism in Bolshevik Russia: Ideology and Industrial Organization, 1917–1921* (Pittsburgh: University of Pittsburgh Press, 1984); also, Paul R. Gregory (ed.), *Behind the Façade of Stalin's Command Economy: Evidence from the Soviet State and Party Archives* (Stanford: Hoover Institution Press, 2001). Lenin famously redefined communism as "Soviet power plus electrification of the whole country." See his "Nashe vneshnee i vnutrenee polozhenie i zadachi partii," in Lenin, *Polnoe sobranie sochinenii*, vol. XLII (Moscow: Gos. Izdatel'stvo politicheskoi literatury, 1965), 30.

27 See Weiner, *Models of Nature*; Loren R. Graham, *The Ghost of the Executed Engineer: Technology and the Fall of the Soviet Union* (Cambridge, MA: Harvard University Press, 1993); Anne D. Rassweiler, *The Generation of Power: A History of Dneprostroi* (Oxford: Oxford University Press, 1988); Paul R. Josephson, *Industrialized Nature: Brute Force Technology and the Transformation of the Natural World* (Washington, DC: Island Press, 2002).

28 See readings in previous note. Thomas F. Remington, in his *Building Socialism*, 19, writes: "[The Bolsheviks] cultivated an ideology of technological modernism which linked the accumulation of national power to the liberation of society's resources from underdevelopment. Lenin, in particular, translated the older socialist ideals of justice and equality into formulas of collective power through industrial progress. Industrialism provided the mechanistic images of Lenin's vision of society: a society grown into the state, a state in which, to be sure, power was itself shared with the masses and social choice was disaggregated into millions of discrete but automatic responses . . . [N]o chaos would be tolerated."

Labor and natural resources were treated as free goods. Because "attractive pictures of stateless communism" increasingly seemed a vision of the far distant future,[29] the task of the moment was growth at the fastest speed possible.[30] A central goal linked to this was building the military-industrial complex, a response to the pervasive belief among communists that the Soviet Union was encircled by irreconcilable enemies.[31]

Marshall Goldman notes in his pioneering study that Soviet economic doctrine did not admit in principle that its system could generate externalities, i.e. social costs of production.[32] Additionally, the price structure set by Gosplan often encouraged vast waste of resources. Thus, owing to low land rents, it was cheaper for an extractive enterprise to move to a new site rather than fully exploit an existing mine or well.[33] There were no mechanisms for collaboration between oil- and gas-extraction firms, and therefore much of the natural gas tapped at oil wells was simply flared off.[34]

Moreover, the enterprises of the five-year plans were heavily polluting.[35] Added to these were the environmentally questionable agricultural practices associated with collectivization, which was carried out in order to supply tribute to pay for industrialization. Nikita Khrushchev's Virgin Lands Program (1954), for example, led to significant topsoil erosion owing to the absence of soil-conservation measures.[36]

One partial exception under Stalin was forest policy, which protected forests in major watersheds of European USSR in order not to jeopardize the effectiveness of hydroelectric dams, which could be harmed by erosion

---

29 Ibid., 143. 30 Ibid.
31 Mark Harrison, "Providing for Defense," in Gregory (ed.), *Behind the Façade*, 81–110. For the more recent, postwar period, see Valerii I. Bulatov, *Rossiia. Ekologiia i armiia* (Novosibirsk: TsERIS, 1999).
32 Goldman, *Spoils of Progress*, 46–63.
33 Ibid., 48. See also Marshall Goldman, *Petrostate: Putin, Power and the New Russia* (New York: Oxford University Press, 2008), 41–42.
34 Goldman, *Petrostate*, 42–43.
35 Paul Josephson, Nicolai Dronin, Ruben Mnatsakanian, Aleh Cherp, Dmitry Efremenko and Vladislav Larin, *An Environmental History of Russia* (Cambridge: Cambridge University Press, 2013), 76. See also Marc Elie, "Desiccated Steppes: Droughts, Erosion, Climate Change, and the Crisis of Soviet Agriculture, 1960s–1980s," in Nicholas Breyfogle (ed.), *Eurasian Environments: Nature and Ecology in Imperial Russia and the Soviet Union* (Pittsburgh: University of Pittsburgh Press, forthcoming).
36 Pryde, *Environmental Management*, esp. 198–202; Goldman, *Spoils of Progress*, 167–73. See esp. Ihor Stebelsky, "Agricultural Development and Soil Degradation in the Soviet Union: Policies, Patterns, and Trends," in Fred Singleton (ed.), *Environmental Problems in the Soviet Union and Eastern Europe* (Boulder: Lynne Rienner, 1987), 71–96.

and silting.[37] Other exceptions included isolated, unsuccessful experiments in closed-cycle, waste-free ore extraction.[38]

One environmentally "friendly" feature of Soviet life that persisted throughout the entire Soviet period was the scarcity of private automobiles and a reliance on a dense and serviceable network of urban mass transit and passenger rail. Nevertheless, Soviet vehicles were much more heavily polluting than Western ones owing to their greater average age and less efficient combustion.[39]

Soviet Environmental Issues 1960–1991

More often than not, Soviet development tradeoffs yielded short-term advantage with heavy disregard for serious long-term costs. A classic example was the decision to turn Central Asia into a supplier of the Soviet Union's cotton needs.

Although cotton as an export crop in Central Asia predated the tsarist conquest of the region,[40] Lenin promoted the notion that Central Asian cotton would ensure self-sufficiency for the Soviet regime.[41] Stalin revived earlier plans to harness the Amu-Dar'ia and Syr-Dar'ia Rivers for irrigation. Beginning with the Great Fergana Canal, irrigation was extended westward to Turkmenistan, building the unlined Karakum Canal, whose seepage rate is 50 percent. It diverts up to 30 percent of the Amu-Dar'ia's annual flow. Much of the formerly best agricultural lands were poisoned due to soil salinization owing to overwatering and poor drainage.[42]

37 Brain, *Song of the Forest*, esp. 115–26. Afforestation and the planting of shelter belts was not restricted to the Soviet Union or to communist nations but has been undertaken by many countries.
38 Andy Bruno has described this in *The Nature of Soviet Power: An Arctic Environmental History* (Cambridge: Cambridge University Press, 2016), esp. 97, 111.
39 See the informative discussions in Goldman, *Spoils of Progress*, 130–34; Pryde, *Environmental Management*, 22–24.
40 Jeff Sahadeo, "Cultures of Cotton and Colonialism: Politics, Society and the Environment in Central Asia, 1865–1923," unpublished paper, AAASS 2003 Annual Convention, Toronto, Canada; Muriel Joffe, "Autocracy, Capitalism and Empire: The Politics of Irrigation," *Russian Review* 54, 3 (Jul. 1995), 366–89.
41 Sahadeo, "Cultures of Cotton and Colonialism."
42 On the Aral Sea crisis and the problem of cotton-based agriculture in Central Asia, see Tom Bissell, "Eternal Winter: Lessons of the Aral Sea Disaster," *Harper's Magazine* (Apr. 2002), 41–56; Robert G. Darst, Jr., "Environmentalism in the USSR: The Opposition to the River Diversion Projects," *Soviet Economy* 4, 3 (1988), 226–27; Nikolai Ivanovich Chesnokov, *Dikie zhivotnye meniaiut adresa* (Moscow: Mysl', 1989); John C. K. Daly, "Global Implications of Aral Sea Dessication," *Central Asia – Caucasus Analyst* (8 Nov. 2000); Eric Sievers (ed.), *EcoStan News*, www.ecostan.org/library/;

More dramatically, the relentless withdrawal of water from the two rivers has resulted in a regional environmental catastrophe: the disappearance of the Aral Sea. Barely fifty years ago Aral was the fourth-largest lake in the world and covered an area of 66,000 square kilometers with a volume of 1,061.6 cubic kilometers and a salinity level of 10 parts per 1,000. Since the early 1990s Aral has consisted of two shrinking ponds whose area together was 28,687 square kilometers in 1998 with a volume of 181 cubic kilometers. Owing to evaporation, salinity in the lake has increased more than fourfold. This destroyed the fishery, which once yielded an annual catch of 40,000 metric tons. Large, rusting trawlers lie stranded on the dry seabed.

The entire regional landscape has undergone disastrous transformation. A toxic lake, Sarykamysh, with an area of 3,000 square kilometers and 26 cubic kilometers of waste, was formed by the discharge of drainage water from the cotton fields, and the tugai floodplain, a species-rich habitat of tall reeds, tamarisks, poplars, willows and oleasters, desiccated.

The desiccation of the Aral Sea has been a human health catastrophe. From the exposed seabed tens of millions of tons of sand laden with salts, pesticides, fertilizers and other chemicals (DDT, hexachloro-cyclohexanes/ b-isomer Lindane, Toxaphene, phosalone pesticide, PCBs, dioxins), as well as precipitates from irrigation wastewater, are carried annually to fields and towns. Worst hit has been the Autonomous Republic of Karakalpakstan (in Uzbekistan), in the direct path of the prevailing northerly winds. A recent statistic noted that 111 children per 1,000 die before their first birthday. As clean water has disappeared, viral hepatitis and typhoid fever and other diarrheal diseases have become widespread, as have anemia, psychoneural retardation, acute respiratory diseases, cancers and especially tuberculosis.[43]

Feshbach and Friendly, *Ecocide in the USSR*; Michael H. Glantz (ed.), *Creeping Environmental Problems and Sustainable Development in the Aral Sea Basin* (Cambridge: Cambridge University Press, 1999); Ulrike Grote (ed.), *Central Asian Environments in Transition* (Manila: Asian Development Bank, 1997); "Receding Waters May Expose Soviet Anthrax Dump," *Austin American-Statesman* (2 Jun. 1999); Philip P. Micklin (ed.), "The Aral Crisis," *Post-Soviet Geography* 33, 5, special issue (May 1992); Pryde, *Environmental Management*; and Erika Weinthal, *State Making and Environmental Cooperation: Linking Domestic and International Politics in Central Asia* (Cambridge, MA: MIT Press, 2002).
43 Philip Whish-Wilson, "The Aral Sea Environmental Health Crisis," *Journal of Rural and Remote Environmental Health* 1, 2 (2002), 29–34.

Another environmental problem raised by the Aral is the safe disposal of stored chemical and biological weapons on Vozrozhdenie Island, once located in the middle of the lake and now connected to the shore. An accidental release could trigger a worldwide pandemic.

The party bosses of Central Asia sought to counteract the damage by proposing a transfer of water from northward-flowing Siberian rivers such as the Irtysh and Ob' to their region as irrigation for cotton continued unabated. First proposed under Stalin and approved by the Politburo in 1966, the "Sibaral" canal, dubbed "the project of the century," would have stretched for 2,200 km across the Turgai watershed, delivering water to the Aral. Because the entire country was its "patrimony" and therefore its testing ground, the Soviet Communist Party leadership endorsed the project along with a similar project to divert northward-flowing European rivers and waters southward, to irrigate Ukraine, Kalmykia and the North Caucasus, and to stem a further drop in the level of the Caspian Sea. Soviet planners never considered foreseeable tradeoffs and never consulted with stakeholders or considered their opinions.

Public opposition to these plans gathered force from the 1970s among liberal intelligentsia and students, Russian nationalists and the general public.[44] Most militant were the student brigades for nature protection – the *druzhiny* – who called out the semi-official All-Russian Society for Nature Protection as a fraud. In the face of an insistent public outcry on the heels of the Chernobyl accident, the new Soviet leader – Mikhail Sergeevich Gorbachev – canceled the project on 20 August 1986, the first such regime policy retreat owing to popular resistance.

Other massive Brezhnev-era water- and earth-moving schemes and industrial projects served as nuclei for growing public protest. One such "great project" was the walling off of the Kara-Bogaz-Gol, a shallow arm of the Caspian Sea, in order to evaporate the water and mine the salts on the sea floor. This had to be reversed once it was clear that the airborne salts posed a major threat to agricultural land and to people.[45] Another was the "Damba," one of the biggest earth-moving projects of all time, an earth and stone dam across the Gulf of Finland to protect the city of Leningrad from hundred-year inundations from the Baltic Sea. This, too, resulted in unwanted consequences: Algal blooms appeared along the Leningrad littoral

44 Darst, "Environmentalism in the USSR."
45 See Theodore Shabad, "Soviet Plugs Caspian Leak, Then Restores It," *New York Times* (28 Nov. 1984), A-15.

owing to the absence of flushing from the gulf.[46] Public hearings in the Leningrad City Soviet in 1990 forced major alterations in the design.

The litany of grand projects of the Brezhnev era up to Gorbachev (October 1964 to March 1985) also included the Katun Hydroelectric Power Station, the Volga–Chograi Canal, the Baikal–Amur Railroad and the industrial development around Lake Baikal.[47] All threatened vulnerable habitats, but none acquired such domestic and international notoriety as the situation of Lake Baikal, the world's deepest lake, which contains about 800 endemic species found nowhere else.

To develop eastern Siberia, the Khrushchev regime initiated the construction of a massive hydroelectic station at Bratsk on the Angara River. A plan to widen the mouth of Lake Baikal where its waters feed the Angara to increase water flow through the turbines was aborted after scientists objected, but industrial development was begun around the periphery of the lake. In 1966 and 1967 the Baikalsk and Selenginsk cellulose factories at the southern end of the lake began operations over domestic and international protest. A decade later, in conjunction with the Baikal–Amur Mainline Railroad (BAM), a variety of military-related industries were sited around the northern rim. Despite a multitude of regime blue-ribbon commissions and injunctions against damaging the lake, thermal and heavy-metal pollution continued unabated. No one knows precisely the tolerances of the lake's myriad life forms for the growing array of toxic effluents, thermal changes and changes in dissolved oxygen and other gases.

Another feature of communist rule was the extreme lack of information available to the public concerning resource exploitation and environmental risks. A decree of the Central Committee of 1957 prohibited the reporting "of forest fires, industrial accidents, military accidents, infant mortality, or radioactive pollution."[48] Routine Soviet practices ensured environmental

46 There are no scholarly studies on the Damba to my knowledge. See en.wikipedia.org/wiki/Saint_Petersburg_Dam.
47 On the Baikal–Amur Railroad, see Christopher J. Ward, *Brezhnev's Folly: The Building of BAM and Late Soviet Socialism* (Pittsburgh: University of Pittsburgh Press, 2009). There is a large literature on Baikal. Good places to start are Feshbach and Friendly, *Ecocide in the USSR*; Josephson et al., *An Environmental History of Russia*; Pryde, *Environmental Management*; Goldman, *The Spoils of Progress*; Weiner, *A Little Corner of Freedom*, 355–73; Volf'son (Komarov), *The Destruction of Nature*, 3–19.
48 Josephson et al., *An Environmental History of Russia*, 142. This is drawn from Vladimir Yevgen'evich Boreiko, *Belye piatna istorii prirodookhrany*, 2nd edn. (Kiev: Kievskii ekologo-kul'turnyi tsentr, 2003), 289.

censorship.[49] What information was provided was not always reliable. It took a disaster of the cataclysmic proportions of Chernobyl to eliminate much of the censorship surrounding environmental issues.

Chernobyl itself was connected to the USSR's larger energy dilemmas. Energy commitments to Eastern Europe and Cuba, combined with the need to export large quantities of oil to pay for food imports, plus the general energy inefficiency of the Soviet economy and wasteful extraction and transport of fossil fuels, led the USSR to turn to nuclear power to meet its own energy needs.[50] As a consequence the reactors at Chernobyl, for example, were allowed to go on line without a backup emergency cooling system; the bungled attempt to retrofit that two years later was the cause of the reactor's meltdown.[51] No doubt the autocratic style of decision-making is an extremely important part of the story of the Soviet environmental legacy. Yet no discussion can avoid another key factor: the pervasive militarization of the Soviet state from its beginnings.[52] Dominating the Soviet economy was its military-industrial complex.[53] The Soviet regime continued the production of chemical and biological weapons.[54] Public costs included the accidental release of anthrax near the city of Sverdlovsk (Yekaterinburg, pop. 1 million) in April 1979, causing 64 officially reported (and, according to one scholarly estimate, 36,000) deaths.[55]

Products of the 440 active and 85 demobilized atomic power stations (55 more are under construction), spent fuel and toxic wastes now amount to 8,700 tons in about 100 storage sites.[56] Extensive regions were affected by the atmospheric and subterranean testing of nuclear weapons, most notably eastern Kazakhstan, where 450 nuclear tests (119 above ground) were

49 Vladislav Larin, Ruben Mnatsakanian, Igor' Chestin and Yevgenii Shvarts, *Okhrana prirody Rossii. Ot Gorbacheva do Putina* (Moscow: Scientific Press Ltd./KMK, 2003), 32–34. Most environmental information was classed as "DSP," or for internal use only.
50 Thane Gustafson, *Crisis amid Plenty: The Politics of Soviet Energy Under Brezhnev and Gorbachev* (Princeton: Princeton University Press and Rand Corporation, 1989).
51 Zhores A. Medvedev, *The Legacy of Chernobyl* (New York: W. W. Norton, 1990).
52 Sheila Fitzpatrick, "The Civil War as a Formative Experience," in Abbott Gleason, Peter Kenez and Richard Stites (eds.), *Bolshevik Culture: Experiment and Order in the Russian Revolution* (Bloomington: Indiana University Press, 1985), 57–76.
53 Bulatov, *Rossiia. Ekologiia i armiia*, 20.
54 Vladimir Birstein, *The Perversion of Knowledge: The True Story of Soviet Science* (Boulder: Westview Press, 2001), 121–22.
55 Bulatov, *Rossiia. Ekologiia i armiia*, 62. S. N. Volkov, in his study "Spetssluzhby i biologicheskoe oruzhie v dvukh izmereniiakh," *Mir, demokratiia, bezopasnost'* 12 (1998), 38–55, and his *Yekaterinburg. Chelovek i gorod. Opyt sotsial'noi ekologii i prakticheskoi geourbanistiki* (Yekaterinburg, Russia: Yekaterinburgskii gumanitarno-ekologicheskii litsei, 1997), estimates the number of fatalities at 36,000.
56 Bulatov, *Rossiia. Ekologiia i armiia*, 51.

conducted between 29 August 1949 and 19 October 1989. Exposure to radiation affected hundreds of thousands of people. Another eighty nuclear tests have taken place on the fragile Arctic archipelago of Novaia Zemlia, whose mainland and shallow shelf also constituted a "dumping ground for enormous amounts of radioactive and mixed waste": up to 17,000 containers (150,000 cubic meters of liquid radioactive waste) plus old or damaged nuclear reactors, some with fuel.[57]

Additionally, controlled nuclear explosions were used to control oil-well fires, to increase oil and gas flow rates and to control methane seepage into coalmines.[58] More than 9 million hectares in Russia alone, not counting Kazakhstan, have been badly polluted by the space program.[59] At least sixteen large regions of the former Soviet Union were badly polluted.[60] In many cities birth defects reached disturbing levels.[61]

On the other hand, the USSR's network of protected territories, including inviolable *zapovedniki* created from Lenin's time, but ravaged under Stalin and Khrushchev, *zakazniki* – or temporary areas designed to protect particular biotic resources, *pamiatniki prirody* – or protected natural features, and *natsional'nye parki* or tourist-oriented national parks, all expanded from the 1960s.[62] However, these were troubled by pervasive episodes of poaching.[63]

Inspired by the work of Ulrich Beck,[64] sociologist Oleg Yanitskii characterizes Russia as the ultimate "risk society" which had sustained "genetic damage" during the long period of totalitarianism.[65] "Over the course of eighty years," Yanitskii writes, "[the USSR] was used as a testing ground for the most divergent model schemes of modernization." By the fall of the communist regime an area occupying 2.5 million square kilometers of the

---

57 Anna Scherbakova and Scott Monroe, "The Urals and Siberia," in Philip R. Pryde (ed.), *Environmental Resources and Constraints in the Former Soviet Republics* (Boulder: Westview Press, 1995), 74.
58 Alexander Yemelyanenkov, *The Sredmash Archipelago* (Moscow: IPPNW-Russia and IPPNW-Sweden, 2000), 26–34.
59 Ibid., 26.
60 Philip R. Pryde, "Environmental Implications of Republic Sovereignty," in Pryde (ed.), *Environmental Resources*, 12, 14.
61 Boris I. Kochurov, "European Russia," in Pryde (ed.), *Environmental Resources*, 50.
62 Feliks Robertovich Shtilmark, *History of Russian Zapovedniks, 1895–1995*, trans. G. H. Harper (Edinburgh: Russian Nature Press, 2003), esp. 151–97.
63 Ibid. See also Weiner, *A Little Corner of Freedom*.
64 Ulrich Beck, *Risk Society: Toward a New Modernity* (London: SAGE, 1992).
65 Oleg Nikolevich Yanitskii, *Rossiia. Ekologicheskii vyzov (obshchestvennoe dvizhenie, nauka, politika)* (Novosibirsk: Sibirskii khronograf, 2002), 41; and also Yanitsky, *Russian Greens in a Risk Society* (Helsinki: Kikimora, 2000), and Yanitskii, *Sotsiologiia riska* (Moscow: Izdatel'stvo LVS and Institut sotsiologii RAN, 2003).

territory of the Russian Federation, or 15 percent, was considered to represent "an acute ecological situation."[66] This encompassed 20 percent of the nation's population (about 60 million people), while 68 cities were deemed "dangerous" by Goskompriroda, Gorbachev's new State Committee for Environmental Protection. In sixteen cities, the concentration of air pollutants was more than fifty times the norm.[67] Safe drinking water was a particularly low priority, with only 30 percent of wastes satisfactorily treated and with such major cities as Baku, Riga and Dnepropetrovsk without sewage systems.[68] In Russia alone, 1 million tons of lethal chemicals were stored in dubious conditions of security at more than 3,500 sites. Nuclear sites, aside from the region affected by Chernobyl, include Kyshtym in the Urals, site of a 1957 disaster,[69] Krasnoyarsk, Tomsk oblast and the eastern coast of Novaia Zemlia, to name only the most seriously polluted areas.[70] By official admission, the Soviet environmental legacy was a grim one.

Eastern Europe

Latitude for independent environmental policies in Eastern Europe was severely constrained by the needs of the Soviet economy, which broadly determined East European economic priorities, and by the Soviet economic model itself that was imposed on the region. Most scholarly studies conclude that the sensitivity of East European regimes to environmental values was low.[71] Many of the works speak of a "crisis"; perceptions of heightened risk

---

66 N. N. Kliuev (ed.), *Rossiia i ee regiony. Vneshnye i vnutrennye ugrozy* (Moscow: Nauka, 2001), 42 ("ostraia ekologicheskaia situatsiia").

67 Ann-Mari Sätre Åhlander, *Environmental Problems in the Shortage Economy: The Legacy of Soviet Environmental Policy* (Aldershot, UK: Edward Elgar, 1994), 6–8.

68 Ibid., 15.

69 Zhores A. Medvedev, *Nuclear Disaster in the Urals* (New York: Vintage, 1979).

70 Feshbach and Friendly, in their *Ecocide in the USSR*, 138, point out that only 1–2 percent of the energy budget was devoted to maintaining natural gas pipelines. A leak in one line, ignited by a spark, resulted in an explosion equal to 10,000 tons of TNT – half the force of Hiroshima – on 3 June 1989, destroying two passenger trains in the Urals and killing 300 people.

71 Joan DeBardeleben, *To Breathe Free: Eastern Europe's Environmental Crisis* (Washington, DC: Woodrow Wilson Center Press, 1991); Fred Singleton (ed.), *Environmental Problems in the Soviet Union and Eastern Europe* (Boulder: Lynne Rienner, 1987); Joseph Alcamo (ed.), *Coping with Crisis in Eastern Europe's Environment* (Carnforth, UK: Parthenon, 1992); Andrew Tickle and Ian Welsh (eds.), *Environment and Society in Eastern Europe* (Harlow: Longman, 1998); Barbara Jancar, *Environmental Management in the Soviet Union and Yugoslavia: Structure and Regulation in Federal Communist States* (Durham, NC: Duke University Press, 1987); Raymond Dominick, "Capitalism,

propelled activism in Poland, East Germany, Hungary, Yugoslavia and other countries.[72]

Joan DeBardeleben argues that the Stalinist model generated even greater environmental stress in Eastern Europe than it did in the Soviet Union. To blame were poorer endowments of mineral resources, open space and water, a higher population density, rapid and poorly planned urbanization, and overreliance on highly polluting, sulfur-rich lignite (brown coal), particularly under the pressures of reducing foreign debt (higher grades of coal were exported).[73]

China

Like Eastern Europe, the People's Republic of China took its development template initially from the Soviet Union. The Chinese were assisted by Soviet engineers and economic advisors until Mao Zedong's partial rejection of the Soviet emphasis on urban industrialization – as opposed to agriculture – during the Great Leap Forward. Despite Mao's break with Khrushchev and his successors, great family resemblances remained between Chinese and Soviet ways of managing the environment. In the mold of Stalin, Mao engaged in mass campaigns to reshape human attitudes through the transformation of the face of the landscape. Similarly, Mao disregarded long-term implications of policies for short-term advantage. The success of his encouragement of population growth as a weapon in the struggle against Soviet "revisionism" and American capitalism led his successors to impose coercive limits on the number of children per couple. Mao likewise repressed scientists who counseled against his population policy and his drive to "defeat" and remold nature through sheer human will.[74] Ill-advised hydropower stations on the Yellow River, such as Sanmenxia, and in other areas of northern China turned into expensive debacles.

Communism, and Environmental Protection: Lessons from the German Experience," *Environmental History* 3, 3 (Jul. 1998), 311–32.
72 Barbara Hicks, *Environmental Politics in Poland: A Social Movement Between Regime and Opposition* (New York: Columbia University Press, 1996); Barbara Jancar-Webster (ed.), *Environmental Action in Eastern Europe: Responses to Crisis* (New York: M. E. Sharpe, 1993).
73 DeBardeleben, "Introduction," in *To Breathe Free*, 3.
74 The best extended analyses of this are found in Judith Shapiro, *Mao's War Against Nature: Politics and the Environment in Revolutionary China* (Cambridge: Cambridge University Press, 2001); and David Pietz, *The Yellow River: The Problem of Water in Modern China* (Cambridge, MA: Harvard University Press, 2015).

Deforestation, overdraft of water resources and soil exhaustion and erosion were unwanted legacies of his rule. Even a campaign to eliminate sparrows, viewed as competing with humans for the harvest, was pursued. The human costs of Mao's policies, like Stalin's, were enormous; upward of 15 million people were estimated to have perished from famine and disease as an unplanned consequence of the Great Leap Forward in 1959–61.[75] Similar to Soviet campaigns, wetlands were drained, grasslands plowed and irrigation expanded to create more arable land with similar deleterious consequences for the productivity of fisheries, especially in lakes and streams.[76] Enormous amounts of chemical pesticides and fertilizers created leaching of nitrates into soils and water basins, eutrophication and high levels of toxic residues in food, soil and water.[77]

In another parallel with Soviet experience, Mao built the massive military-industrial complex at Panzhihua in the mountainous Sichuan region at huge human cost (more than 5.4 percent of the workforce perished from 1965 to 1975); filters were never installed at the steel plant, and the valley was prone to temperature inversion.[78] Panzhihua polluted the headwaters of the Yangzi River. In another military-related campaign, 200,000 "educated youth" were exiled to the most ecologically rich and sensitive area of China, southern Yunnan, to clear-cut the tropical forest to plant rubber plantations. A catastrophic decline for the many rare mammals, birds, insects and plants for which the area is among their last habitats resulted.[79] Ironically Yunnan rubber is also uneconomical. Atmospheric tests of atomic bombs polluted areas in western Qinghai province.

To be fair, there were both real and intended improvements in public health and environmental quality. The period before the Great Leap Forward was marked by a halving of the death rate by 1957 owing

---

75 Shapiro estimates 35 to 50 million deaths in this period: *Mao's War*, 89. Maurice Meisner in his *Mao's China and After: A History of the People's Republic* (3rd edn.; New York: Free Press, 1999), 237, notes that official mortality statistics released in the early 1980s indicate a death toll of 15 million, but notes a credible estimate by Judith Bannister of 35 million. See her *China's Changing Population* (Stanford: Stanford University Press, 1987). On the anti-sparrow "Four Pests" campaign that began in 1958, see Shapiro, *Mao's War*, 86. Per capita grain output declined from 306 kg in 1957 to 240 kg in 1962, greater than 20 percent. See Richard Sanders, "The Political Economy of Environmental Protection: Lessons of the Mao and Deng Years," *Third World Quarterly* 20, 6 (Dec. 1999), 1202.

76 Shapiro, *Mao's War*, esp. 95–139.   77 Sanders, "The Political Economy," 1203.

78 Shapiro, *Mao's War*, 139–93. Particular emissions were 218 times greater than the national recommendations (154).

79 Ibid., 169–85.

to greater food security and improvements in hygiene, including the composting of night soil.[80] The first five-year plan of 1953 called for the recycling of industrial wastewater, while laws were passed in 1956 prohibiting the siting of industries upstream from major cities and urging the development of technologies that reduced emissions.[81] Similar to other communist countries, these laws were hortatory and did not result in improvement in air or water quality. Concern over unwanted consequences of development resurfaced only after the ebbing of the Cultural Revolution. Under the patronage of Premier Zhou Enlai, China participated in the 1972 Stockholm Conference on the Human Environment, sponsored by the United Nations, and in the following year convoked a National Environmental Conference in Beijing.[82] This resulted in the creation of a first-ever governmental body, the Environmental Protection Leading Group of the State Council. Nevertheless, as Judith Shapiro and Vaclav Smil have concluded, the Mao years were ones in which there was very little concern about the collateral effects of agricultural and industrial policies for human health or habitat and species survival.[83]

Interestingly, the market reforms that were ushered in by Deng Xiaoping spurred major spikes in deforestation and in all pollution indicators, relative to the Mao period. Richard Sanders marks an even richer irony: "[W]hat advances *were* made in terms of environmental research, monitoring and protection were achieved as a result of tradi-tional 'command-and-control' policies, and ... their successes were limited or negated by the drives towards liberalising markets and priva-tisation which occurred at the same time."[84] Indeed, the breakup of the communes in the 1980s undercut integrated pest management and biogas development.[85]

80 Judith Banister, "Population, Public Health and the Environment in China," *China Quarterly* 156 (Dec. 1998), 987.
81 Sanders, "The Political Economy," 1204.   82 Ibid.
83 Vaclav Smil, *The Bad Earth: Environmental Degradation in China* (New York: M. E. Sharpe, 1984).
84 Sanders, "The Political Economy," 1209.
85 Ibid., 1210. See also Richard Louis Edmonds, "The Environment in the People's Republic of China 50 Years on," *China Quarterly* 159 (Sep. 1999), 640–49, for an overview of the Deng period and the emergence of an awareness of environmental downsides to growth. On pest management, see Sigrid Schmalzer, *Red Revolution, Green Revolution: Scientific Farming in Socialist China* (Chicago: University of Chicago Press, 2016), esp. 53–64.

Cuba

Cuba provides a good window on the specifically "communist" contributions to environmental spoliation for a number of reasons, argue the authors of the most extensive study on the subject.[86] Essentially, none of the conventional contributing causes to environmental deterioration in capitalist-oriented developing countries – population growth, income inequality, extreme poverty and unequal access to resources – is present in Cuba.[87] Instead, we can see the Soviet communist model of capital-intensive agriculture in isolation: disregard by central planners of local environmental conditions, lack of citizen involvement in decision-making, an absence of a feeling of stewardship, the structure of bonuses for managers, and the occasional uninformed, meddlesome technical decisions by Fidel Castro and other leaders. Adding to this are the defects of implementing laws and decrees; they are often simply declarative.[88] Of course, the authors admit, the ultimate model for capital-intensive agriculture is the American one, which generates similar environmental tradeoffs on a larger scale throughout most of the globe.[89]

After Fidel Castro's entry into Havana in January 1959 his new regime soon aligned with the USSR. Although Soviet-style emphasis on heavy industry was abandoned by 1964, light industry, particularly sugar refining and cement works, was expanded and nickel mining also increased. Employing Soviet and East European technology, these industries have generated much pollution, affecting rivers and coastal areas.[90]

The most serious environmental issues in post-1959 Cuba stem from the continuing predominance of agriculture. Soviet-style irrigation projects in Cuba resulted in soil waterlogging because of the absence of proper drainage, soil salinization and the salinization of underground waters owing to overpumping and the invasion of seawater.[91] Soviet-style state farms utilized copious amounts of agricultural chemicals; integrated pest management was only seriously applied after 1991, after the onset of the "special period" when cheap fertilizers, fuel and farm machinery became unavailable.[92]

---

86 Sergio Diaz-Briquets and Jorge Pérez-López, *Conquering Nature: The Environmental Legacy of Socialism in Cuba* (Pittsburgh: University of Pittsburgh Press, 2000).
87 Ibid., 4–5.   88 Ibid., 5.   89 Ibid., 6.   90 Ibid., 164–202, esp. 201–02.   91 Ibid., 111–37.
92 Ibid., 109.

However, by contrast with his predecessors and with regimes in Latin America,[93] Castro's 1959 Reforestation Plan increased forest cover on the island to 18 percent of the country's area.[94] About 64 percent of that is under some form of protection. Nine national parks were added to the preexisting five, and 200 protected areas of various types on 12 percent of the country's area were created; about 2 percent of national territory is strictly protected.[95] One multiple-use area, the Gran Parque Nacional Sierra Maestra, has sought to incentivize the 200,000 people who live there to join cooperatives with lower-impact activities such as aquaculture.[96] Cuba is a signatory of CITES, and through its National Commission for Environmental Protection and the Rational Use of Natural Resources (COMARNA) – from 1994, CITMA, the Ministry of Science, Technology and the Environment – Cuba has established the requirement of environmental impact statements for major projects. Finally, in the 1990s Cuba amended its constitution to mandate the goal of sustainable development.

Because communist countries have found themselves in situations of relative commercial isolation and partial autarky, they have promoted recycling of scarce resources. Cuba, owing to both the United States' commercial embargo and the withdrawal of Soviet support (1991), has been particularly energetic, using cafeteria and agricultural wastes to produce animal feed and sugar cane husks for particle board, to name just two programs.[97] Although there are no nongovernmental conservation organizations in Cuba, individual activists such as Antonio Núñez Jimenez, a friend of Fidel Castro, convinced the leader to halt construction of a hydroelectric dam that could have disrupted a sensitive habitat.[98] Additionally, in recent years organizations such as the MacArthur Foundation and the Environmental Defense Fund have collaborated with the Cuban regime on environmental issues.[99]

Public health has been a priority, and Cuba has both the lowest infant mortality rate and lowest rate of mortality for poverty-related diseases in Latin America, with a high life expectancy at birth of seventy-four years.[100]

93 Eduardo C. Santana, "Nature Conservation and Sustainable Development in Cuba," *Conservation Biology* 5, 1 (Mar. 1991), 13–16, quote 13; 50 percent of flowering plants and 32 percent of vertebrates are endemic to its 1,600 islands.
94 Ibid. Cuba's forest cover was 56 percent in the late 1800s but only 14 percent by 1959.
95 Ibid.   96 Ibid., 14.   97 Ibid.
98 Saleem Ali, "Greening Diplomacy with Cuba," *National Geographic* (16 Jun. 2012), voices.nationalgeographic.com/2012/06/16/greening-diplomacy-with-cuba/.
99 Ibid.   100 Santana, "Nature Conservation," 14.

Population growth is near zero. As may be seen, the environmental record has been mixed, depending on the issue examined.

Ultimately, because communist societies' goals have been largely borrowed from those of the capitalist world, they share many of the same features of resource management, beginning with a reliance on fossil fuels and nuclear energy. Until the 1970s, when Western societies were still governed by the ideals of keeping private profit balanced with the protection of common property resources, labor rights and public health through regulation, there was a difference in environmental decision-making and risk management between Western societies and the communist states, favoring the West. Communist countries' environmental laws were declarative, their singular focus on large-scale industrial and agricultural development was wasteful and heavily polluting, and the political leadership often meddled in scientific issues to overrule informed counsel.

More recently, the regulatory state in the West has been tottering. Communism's worse environmental reputation may turn out to be an artifact of an anomalously progressive period in Western societies combined with the fact that communist countries could not export risk and so had to pollute their own people.[101]

Commenting on Eastern Europe, both Joan DeBardeleben and Andrew Tickle and Ian Welsh notably reject the idea that a market-based society alone is sufficient to guarantee significant reduction of the pollution of air, soil and water. "Market mechanisms in Western countries," observes DeBardeleben, "have not provided effective safeguards against environmental deterioration either."[102] "While market signals and pressures may have encouraged individual firms to reduce the waste of resources," she continues, "they have not discouraged the same firms from sloughing off the costs of pollution onto society." And she adds that the very "imperative to growth" of market societies encourages continuously expanding consumption and the "production of throwaway commodities, forces that are not at all inherent in a centrally planned system."[103] Newly released consumerist aspirations in Eastern Europe lead DeBardeleben to a skeptical

---

101 Regrettably, there is little written in Western languages about environmental management either in the Korean People's Democratic Republic (North Korea) or communist Southeast Asia.
102 DeBardeleben, *The Environment and Marxism-Leninism: The Soviet and East German Experience* (Boulder: Westview Press, 1985), 12.
103 Ibid.

view that environmental protection will soon become a top priority in the region, despite the fact that it served as a salient argument in the struggle to topple communism.[104]

Paul Josephson's argument, that "pluralist states have developed institutions that are far more responsive to environmental problems than [communist or postcolonial regimes], largely because of broader access by citizens to information . . . and because of the creation of legal, scientific, and other institutions to mitigate environmental problems," is theoretically persuasive.[105]

Nevertheless, although communist regimes have not upheld pollution control and habitat protection as high priorities, accusations of "ecocide" must be put in comparative perspective. Western market states "followed the same paths of breakneck development and profligate use of natural resources," observe Josephson and his coauthors.[106] Broadening the lens helps to put this in perspective. Because the communist regimes did not have the benefit of overseas colonies or, later, a network of commercially exploitable and dependent developing countries, they had to site the production of dangerous chemicals on their own territories, unlike Union Carbide, for example, which set up operations in Bhopal. Large amounts of toxic waste, until the 1990s, were routinely shipped from the First World to Africa.

Josephson's argument must also be amended to account for changes within the democratic market polities themselves. With the ascendancy of corporate-friendly governments and corporate-owned media in industrialized countries, information to citizens has been reduced and environmental regulation itself has been weakened. One need go no further than Flint, Michigan, where the city's water supply was compromised to save money following the imposition of direct rule by the state's governor.[107] Regarding nuclear issues, the silences and censorship within Western democracies have been more the rule than the exception. Both the Oak Ridge National Laboratory in Tennessee and the CIA, for example, recognized that a major nuclear accident had occurred in Kyshtym in the southern Urals in 1957, but suppressed their reports so as not to undermine support in the

104 Ibid., 13.
105 Paul Josephson, *Resources Under Regimes: Technology, Environment, and the State* (Cambridge, MA: Harvard University Press, 2005), 20.
106 Josephson et al., *An Environmental History of Russia*, 12.
107 Julia Lurie, "A Toxic Timeline of Flint's Water Fiasco," *Mother Jones* (16 Jan. 2016), www.motherjones.com/environment/2016/01/flint-lead-water-crisis-timeline.

United States for nuclear power.[108] Perhaps the most direct parallel to Soviet practice was the censorship regime at the Hanford plutonium-processing plant in Washington state, in which doctors colluded in falsifying radiation sickness and where the press was obstructed from learning the degree of the radioactive pollution of the Columbia River. Indeed, Kate Brown structures her book, *Plutopia*, on the chilling similarities between the Soviet and American nuclear weapons programs and their environmental effects.[109] And the Fukushima (TEPCO) nuclear reactor meltdown has now given market societies their own Chernobyl.

Much has been made of the penchant for communist regimes to attempt very large scale reengineering of their landscapes. Certainly, the Volga and Dnepr have been turned into chains of hydroelectric stations, reservoirs and irrigation canals in adjacent arid lands. Irrigation has caused the almost complete desiccation of the Aral Sea, and the Soviet regime seriously considered damming the Ob'–Irtysh river system and constructing a gigantic pumping station and canal to transfer water to replenish the depleted water of the inland sea. Arguably the Chinese government's construction of the Sanxia (Three Gorges) Dam, together with plans under study since the 1950s for enormous water transfers from the south to north China represent risky legacies of a Stalinist mode of thinking.

Yet, the great Hoover (Boulder) Dam was begun in the 1920s, the Tennessee Valley Authority reshaped the upper South as radically as anywhere, and the Columbia River has, in the words of Richard White, been turned into an "organic machine," while the US Bureau of Reclamation has dammed and canalized just about every available watercourse in the American West. And this is only to speak of the United States.

Without a doubt the communist command economy was inherently more wasteful of labor and resources and more polluting per unit of usable product than market societies. This waste was a consequence not only of defective products but also of profligate energy use in production and what Ferenc Fehér, Agnes Heller and György Markús called the "goal-function" of communist economies.[110] Within these "dictatorships over needs,"

108 Paul Josephson, *Red Atom: Russia's Nuclear Power Program from Stalin to Today* (New York: W. H. Freeman, 2000), 279.
109 Kate Brown, *Plutopia: Nuclear Families, Atomic Cities, and the Great Soviet and American Plutonium Disasters* (Oxford: Oxford University Press, 2013).
110 Ferenc Fehér, Agnes Heller and György Markús, *Dictatorship over Needs: An Analysis of Soviet Societies* (Oxford: Basil Blackwell, 1983).

investment was largely geared not to the most efficient production but to investments that could be best controlled by the commanders of the economy and that would promote the reproduction of the regime politically. State-owned enterprises were favored over cooperatives, despite the 40 percent higher efficiency of the latter, especially in agriculture.[111] This is why large-scale, inefficient "projects of the century" were favored by those regimes.

Yet the argument that communist states were an order of magnitude more "environmentally delinquent" than market societies is not easily supported. As in market societies, concerns in communist regimes about human health, habitat preservation, species extinction and planetary environmental systems all took a back seat to shorter-term development goals. From the perspective of a planet facing human-forced climate change and other big problems, those differences will seem increasingly minute.

Bibliographical Essay

As of this writing, there is no book-length study that examines environmental history and resource management across all major communist regimes in a comparative framework. The bulk of scholarship focuses on the Soviet Union, and here a serviceable broad-stroke overview may be found in Paul Josephson, Nicolai Dronin, Ruben Mnatsakanian, Aleh Cherp, Dmitry Efremenko and Vladislav Larin, *An Environmental History of Russia* (Cambridge: Cambridge University Press, 2013). For an in-depth analysis of Soviet environmental policies from 1917 to the First Five-Year Plan era, see Douglas Weiner's *Models of Nature: Ecology, Conservation and Cultural Revolution in Soviet Russia* (Bloomington: Indiana University Press, 1988). That work and its sequel, *A Little Corner of Freedom: Russian Nature Protection from Stalin to Gorbachev* (Berkeley: University of California Press, 1999), also explain the diverse roots and significance of nature protection activism in the Soviet context, focusing foremost on the struggle around protected territories (*zapovedniki*). This struggle is also treated in the work of an activist, Feliks Robertovich Shtil'mark, *The History of Russian Zapovedniks, 1895–1995*, trans. G. E. Harper (Edinburgh: Russian Nature Press, 2003).

111 Ibid., 66–67.

Another fine historical work is Stephen C. Brain's *Song of the Forest: Russian Forestry and Stalin's Environmentalism* (Pittsburgh: University of Pittsburgh Press, 2011), which puts Stalin's forest-protection measures into context in addition to documenting a unique, peasant-oriented Russian approach to forest management.

Environmental histories of Soviet geographical regions for the post-Khrushchev period have thus far focused on the Arctic, researched by Paul Josephson, *The Conquest of the Russian Arctic* (Cambridge, MA: Harvard University Press, 2014), and Central Asia, whose various late Soviet agricultural problems are analyzed in chapters by Marc Elie and Julia Obertreis in Nicholas Breyfogle (ed.), *Eurasian Environments: Nature and Ecology in Imperial Russian and Soviet History* (Pittsburgh: University of Pittsburgh Press, forthcoming).

In addition to Weiner's *A Little Corner of Freedom*, environmental activism in Russia, especially among university students, is the subject of the opus of Oleg Nikolaevich Yanitsky, notably his *Russian Environmentalism: Leading Figures, Facts, Opinions* (Moscow: Mezhdunarodnyje Otnoshenija Publishing House, 1993). Environmental activism as a vehicle for nationalist struggles is addressed by Jane I. Dawson's *Eco-Nationalism: Anti-Nuclear Activism and National Identity in Russia, Lithuania and Ukraine* (Durham, NC: Duke University Press, 1996).

More policy-oriented works have chronicled and analyzed Soviet resource and environmental policies and problems of the post-Khrushchev final decades. These include Ze'ev Volf'son (Boris Komarov), *The Destruction of Nature in the Soviet Union*, trans. Michael Hale and Joe Hollander (London: Pluto Press, [1980]), originally published as *Unichtozhenie prirody, Obostrenie ekologicheskogo krizisa v SSSR* (Frankfurt-am-Main: Posev, 1978); Marshall Goldman's *The Spoils of Progress: Environmental Pollution in the Soviet Union* (Cambridge, MA: MIT Press, 1972); Philip R. Pryde's *Environmental Management in the Soviet Union* (Cambridge: Cambridge University Press, 1991); Murray Feshbach and Alfred Friendly, Jr., *Ecocide in the USSR: Health and Nature Under Siege* (New York: Basic Books, 1992); Murray Feshbach's *Ecological Disaster: Cleaning Up the Hidden Legacy of the Soviet Regime* (New York: Twentieth Century Fund Press, 1995); Mikhail Lemeshev, *Vlast' vedomstv – ekologicheskii infarkt* (Moscow: Progress, 1989), translated into English as *Bureaucrats in Power – Ecological Collapse* (Moscow: Progress, 1990); D. J. Petersen, *Troubled Lands: The Legacy of Soviet Environmental Destruction* (Boulder: Westview Press and RAND, 1993); and Barbara Jancar's *Environmental Management in the Soviet Union and Yugoslavia* (Durham, NC: Duke University Press, 1987).

A number of works focus on one resource. Thus, Brenton M. Barr and Kathleen E. Braden in their *The Disappearing Russian Forest: A Dilemma in Soviet Resource Management* (Totowa, NJ: Rowman & Littlefield, 1988) focus on post-1960 overharvesting. For a broad look at Soviet nuclear problems, the reader is directed to Alexander Yemelyanenkov, *The Sredmash Archipelago* (Moscow: IPPNW/SLMK, 2000), and Sonja D. Schmid, *Producing Power: The Pre-Chernobyl History of the Soviet Nuclear Industry* (Cambridge, MA: MIT Press, 2015), while an excellent social, political and technological dissection of the Chernobyl accident may be found in Zhores A. Medvedev, *The Legacy of Chernobyl* (New York: W. W. Norton, 1990). Kate Brown's *Plutopia: Nuclear Families, Atomic Cities, and the Great Soviet and American Plutonium Disasters* (Oxford: Oxford University Press, 2013) compares the social and epidemiological ramifications of the Soviet and American plutonium production programs.

Although the question of ideology is raised in many of the works cited here, Joan DeBardeleben's *The Environment and Marxism-Leninism: The Soviet and East German Experience* (Boulder: Westview Press, 1985) compares regime and intelligentsia environmental discourse in those states to ask whether official ideology could accommodate a more environmentally sensitive approach to development, although, as Ferenc Fehér, Agnes Heller and György Markús, *Dictatorship over Needs: An Analysis of Soviet Societies* (Oxford: Basil Blackwell, 1983), argue, official dogma may not be the actual operating software of Soviet regimes.

On Eastern Europe, see Joan DeBardeleben, *To Breathe Free: Eastern Europe's Environmental Crisis* (Washington, DC: Woodrow Wilson Center Press, 1991), and on activism specifically see Barbara Hicks, *Environmental Politics in Poland: A Social Movement Between Regime and Opposition* (New York: Columbia University Press, 1996), and Barbara Jancar-Webster (ed.), *Environmental Action in Eastern Europe: Responses to Crisis* (New York: M. E. Sharpe, 1993).

Concerning the People's Republic of China, the Mao period is examined in Judith Shapiro's lively *Mao's War Against Nature: Politics and the Environment in Revolutionary China* (Cambridge: Cambridge University Press, 2001), and in David Pietz, *The Yellow River: The Problem of Water in Modern China* (Cambridge, MA: Harvard University Press, 2015), while for a comparison with the Deng Xiaoping years see Richard Sanders, "The Political Economy of Environmental Protection: Lessons of the Mao and Deng Years," *Third World Quarterly* 20, 6 (Dec. 1999), 1201–14. Finally, there is one monograph devoted to the environmental history of Communist Cuba, that of Sergio Diaz-Briquets and Jorge Pérez-López, *Conquering Nature: The Environmental Legacy of Socialism in Cuba* (Pittsburgh: University of Pittsburgh Press, 2000).

22

Legacies of Communism: Comparative Remarks

JAN C. BEHRENDS

There are many legacies of communism. The communist movement, communist power in the Soviet Union, in Eastern Europe and throughout the world, changed over time and had numerous regional variants. Many observers would also agree that there is something distinctly postcommunist or post-Soviet about the societies that emerged after the collapse of the party-states in Europe in 1989–91. Communist power has left a specific footprint on Eurasian politics and societies that can be examined.

Still, this is not the whole picture. While communist regimes have collapsed throughout Eurasia, they continue to exist in other parts of the world. More than a quarter of a century after the disintegration of the Soviet empire, communist rule survives in China, Vietnam and Cuba as well as in North Korea. In China alone 70 million people are members of the Chinese Communist Party. There communist power is as much a Maoist legacy as it is a current reality. At the same time, however, the international communist movement – for much of the twentieth century and well into the 1980s a potent political actor – has been confined to history.[1] In most Western countries as well as in the developing world, communist parties have become marginal, while successor organizations of most of the former party-states can no longer be considered communist. Even in Russia itself the successor to the once-mighty party is just another pawn in the Kremlin's political game. In Eastern Europe former communist parties have adopted various nationalist or populist political positions. Thus, a century after the October

---

1 See e.g. Michel Dreyfus (ed.), *Le siècle des communismes* (Paris: Seuil, 2004); Robert Service, *Comrades! A History of World Communism* (Cambridge, MA: Harvard University Press, 2007); David Priestland, *The Red Flag: Communism and the Making of the Modern World* (London: Penguin Books, 2009); Archie Brown, *The Rise and Fall of Communism* (London: Random House, 2010); Silvio Pons, *The Global Revolution: A History of International Communism 1917–1991*, trans. Allan Cameron (Oxford: Oxford University Press, 2014).

Revolution the legacies of the communist movement and of communist power vary greatly and are often contradictory. What can we focus upon?

In the years following the collapse of communist power in Europe a dominant narrative was established: The "peaceful revolution" in Eastern and Central Europe and the mostly nonviolent Soviet collapse were celebrated as the civil end to a violent century. Francis Fukuyama famously declared the "end of history" which was achieved through a "worldwide liberal revolution."[2] According to this narrative, the West had regained the optimism lost in 1914 and was bound to triumph on a world-historical scale after 1989. Others just claimed that Europe had learned the lessons of the twentieth century and had become a community of civil states.[3] Peaceful change remained the key focal point.[4] On close inspection, however, these interpretations were questionable from the beginning. Neither the rise of communist China after 1989 or Putin's Russia, nor the wars in the former Yugoslavia, fit the interpretation. Yet it took the Russian war against Ukraine in 2014 to discredit this interpretation and to acknowledge that the temptations of authoritarianism, geopolitics and the perils of war are still present in Europe – especially but not exclusively in the post-Soviet space.[5] The looming question is how recent developments are tied to the communist past.

While communist power after 1917 changed over time and varied depending on locality its aftermath is equally hard to assess. The nature of the historical legacy itself remains contentious. There is not one comprehensive methodology that can be followed to explore the historical consequences of communist rule. We rather need to ask "why . . . certain institutional forms, ways of thinking, and modes of behavior appear to have persisted . . . while others have fallen by the wayside."[6] This chapter examines the political consequences of communism for both postcommunist societies and those in which communist parties still rule. It explores differences between the former USSR, Eastern Europe and China and takes into account factors such

---

2 Francis Fukuyama, *The End of History and the Last Man* (London: Penguin Books, 1992).
3 See James J. Sheehan, *Where Have All the Soldiers Gone? The Transformation of Modern Europe* (Boston, MA: Houghton Mifflin, 2008), 147–221.
4 Stephen Kotkin, *Armageddon Averted: The Soviet Collapse, 1970–2000* (Oxford: Oxford University Press, 2001); Padraic Kenney, *A Carnival of Revolution: Central Europe 1989* (Princeton: Princeton University Press, 2003).
5 Andrew Wilson, *Ukraine Crisis: What It Means for the West* (New Haven: Yale University Press, 2014); Jan C. Behrends (ed.), *The Return to War and Violence: Case Studies on the USSR, Russia, and Yugoslavia, 1979–2014* (London: Routledge, 2017).
6 Stephen Kotkin and Mark R. Beissinger, "The Historical Legacies of Communism: An Empirical Agenda," in Mark R. Beissinger and Stephen Kotkin (eds.), *Historical Legacies of Communism* (Cambridge: Cambridge University Press, 2014), 3.

as the length of communist rule and the aftermath of cataclysmic events such as collectivization, state terror, forced labor and national uprisings. I will further argue for a distinction between the long-term effects of Stalinism and the consequences of late socialism. Finally, I would like to point out that the years immediately following the collapse of communist power appear to have been crucial for shaping its legacy. Thus, legacies of communism themselves are fluid and constantly (re)made. They date back to the time after the revolution that brought down communist party rule in many countries, they include the era of late socialism and they were shaped decisively in the 1990s.

Societies Transformed and the Party-State: The Legacy of Revolution and Stalinism

The most lasting legacy of communist rule is the Leninist party-state. Instead of withering away – as Karl Marx had predicted – the modern state was transformed by Vladimir Lenin and the Bolsheviks. The "dictatorship of the proletariat" turned out to be the rule of a hierarchically structured party that dominated the state and declared war not merely on the remnants of the old regime but on independent society as such.[7] The communist party controlled both the army and the secret police – the main enforcers of state power. From the beginning of communist power in late 1917 the unrestrained use of violence, the desire to control economic activity, to subjugate civil society and to control public and private spaces became trademarks of this type of statehood. The party-state formed the basis for the social transformations that communist parties aspired to.

While the councils ("soviets") had been momentous as representatives of soldiers and workers during the Russian Revolution, they were quickly limited to a decorative role. The party was at the core of this modern type of dictatorship. The Bolsheviks had shown that a small yet determined group from the margins of the political spectrum could take over a state and defend its hold on power for an indefinite time. A new type of regime was formed; its state machine as well as the federal structure of the USSR adopted in 1922 were an influential paradigm and impressed friends and enemies in Europe and beyond.[8] In 2016, this Leninist party-state model is still ruling in China,

---

7 Steven G. Marks, *How Russia Shaped the Modern World. From Art to Anti-Semitism, Ballet to Bolshevism* (Princeton: Princeton University Press, 2003), 299–332.
8 Brown, *The Rise and Fall of Communism*, 103–14; Gerd Koenen, *Utopie der Säuberung. Was war der Kommunismus?* (Berlin: Fest, 1998), 95–110.

Cuba, North Korea and Vietnam. As a blueprint it certainly impacted also on noncommunist dictatorships around the globe.

The Leninist state placed a small group of leaders at the center of political power. Party and state had a militarized structure and were organized around chains of command, with the party leader taking the role of commander-in-chief. Lenin and Stalin created this system during the Russian Civil War.[9] In reality, however, the functioning of the party apparatus was more complicated than its hierarchical structure. While on paper the party had a formalized structure, internal party politics were highly informal. They could be broken down into personal and regional networks of strongmen that controlled segments of the party-state as well as economic resources. Within these webs of patron–client relationships personal trust and loyalty outweighed institutional frameworks and ideological differences.[10] To outsiders the internal dealings of the party-state remained opaque. This lack of transparency contributed to the widespread perception that power and society were strictly separated spheres – "us" and "them" – a characteristic divide for dictatorships in general and communist rule in particular. Those who held power were sometimes respected but more often feared. This fear of the party-state and its security services led to widespread distrust of the state and its intentions, especially during the founding phase of communist state, but to a lesser degree also after revolutionary radicalism waned.

During Stalinism and the great terror, fear also structured relationships *within* the party-state. Even in the higher echelons of power nobody could feel immune from arrest and persecution. Although mass reprisals would finally stop after the deaths of Stalin and Mao, the aftermath of these cataclysmic events continues to be felt. The party-state's terror did not just destroy careers, families and lives; for decades to come it shaped society and served as a reminder of the arbitrary power of the state. Those living under communist rule in the USSR and China had experienced how totalitarian ambition translated into mass violence. The losses and the insecurity experienced continue to shape politics and societies.[11] Few families remained untouched by decades of upheaval, and most had to keep silent about their

9 See Stephen Kotkin, *Stalin: Paradoxes of Power, 1878–1928* (New York: Penguin Press, 2014), 227–660.

10 For a *longue durée* perspective, see J. Arch Getty, *Practicing Stalinism: Bolsheviks, Boyars, and the Persistence of Tradition* (New Haven: Yale University Press, 2013).

11 Polly Jones, *Myth, Memory, Trauma: Rethinking the Stalinist Past in the Soviet Union, 1953–1970* (New Haven: Yale University Press, 2013); Andrew G. Walder, *China Under Mao: A Revolution Derailed* (Cambridge, MA: Harvard University Press, 2015), 315–44.

losses for decades. Millions fell victim to the repeated attempts to cleanse society, and even in Eastern Europe, where repression was experienced on a lesser scale, it had a lasting impact on society. Those who had perished could not publicly remember, and those who survived remained scarred for life.

The destruction of the traditional ruling classes under Stalinist rule – the nobility as well as the clergy and parts of the intelligentsia – could not be reversed. New social and ethnic groups advanced under communist power. To a somewhat lesser degree this was also true for East European countries. Thousands of the old elites fled, only a few surviving in niches, while even fewer returned from exile after 1989–91. None of the postcommunist states reintroduced the monarchy as a national symbol, and few gave returnees from exile a prolonged chance in politics. Precommunist structures and traditions were often hard or impossible to resurrect. Here, again, the duration of communist rule and the proximity to the West seem to make a difference. While East Europeans of the 1990s could still imagine a political life before communism, this was much harder in the former USSR. There were, for example, no remnants of Russian liberalism to return to. Seventy years of party rule and isolation had wiped out any experience with pluralistic systems. This proved to be an important distinction between Eastern Europe and Russia – with Ukraine being a borderland between these two areas.

The change of elites during the decades after the revolution was accompanied by rapid social transformation triggered through policies such as collective agriculture or industrialization. Peasants became city-dwellers, but they brought rural culture to the towns. Migration became a mass experience in a "quicksand-society" (Moshe Lewin) where neither policies nor personnel seemed to last. Cities grew, were rebuilt and transformed according to Stalinist aesthetics.[12] What the populations witnessed was not the emergence of a rational and planned new order. Rather, from the beginning communist policies were often improvised and determined by situational contingencies.[13] This nature of communist power contributed to a sense of uncertainty that tainted social life. The population learned how to live through extraordinary times; they adapted to new, mostly unwritten rules, learned when to speak up and when to remain silent, what

12 See, e.g., David L. Hoffmann, *Peasant Metropolis: Social Change and Identities in Moscow, 1929–1941* (Ithaca: Cornell University Press, 1994).
13 For a panorama of the Soviet case, see Sheila Fitzpatrick, *Everyday Stalinism: Ordinary Life in Extraordinary Times, Soviet Russia in the 1930s* (Oxford: Oxford University Press, 1999).

to remember and what to forget instead – and passed this knowledge on to their children. Thus, the mores and values of societies under communist rule were shaped. A characteristic political and social fabric emerged. And it persisted even after the death of the revolutionary leaders. Thus, the revolution and its radical phase did not merely leave a mark on history; its impact on societies, their structures and their values continues to be felt beyond the lifetimes of Lenin, Stalin and Mao.

The New Normal: Late Socialism's Continued Legacy

Communist rule changed profoundly after the death of Stalin. The process of de-Stalinization had several consequences. First and foremost it meant the end of mass violence and terror by communist states in Europe and in the USSR. China and other Asian countries, however, resisted the new path taken by Moscow. The result was that after 1956 the communist world witnessed unprecedented pluralism. Stalinism – especially in a Maoist guise – continued to be an option, but myriad other national roads to socialism opened up as well. The end of terror and mass mobilization in the Soviet Union and Eastern Europe meant that another type of communism could be created, one that was no longer the product of notions of civil war.

Those who survived the camps and internal exile were gradually released during the 1950s and readmitted into society. The momentous consequences of this process for (post-)Soviet societies are still poorly understood. We now know that the history of forced labor did not end with the liberation of millions of prisoners. The liberated prisoners brought legacies of their violent experiences back into the mainstream of society.[14] Many of those who returned had trouble adjusting to everyday life in the USSR and continued to live according to the rules and the criminal culture of the camps. While mass violence by the party-state ended, low-scale criminal violence permeated society. A new culture of criminal gangs emerged whose roots can be traced back to bonds forged and values adopted in the Gulag.[15] The aftermath of the Gulag is not only memories of what man

---

14 Miriam Dobson, *Khrushchev's Cold Summer: Gulag Returnees, Crime and the Fate of Reform After Stalin* (Ithaca: Cornell University Press, 2009).
15 Svetlana Stephenson, *Gangs of Russia: From the Streets to the Corridors of Power* (Ithaca: Cornell University Press, 2015).

endured in the camps;[16] rather, the camps left a concrete mark on society by criminalizing it.

The initial revolutions did not live up to their promises and hardly eased social problems in the USSR and China. They merely created islands of authoritarian modernity in still predominantly agrarian societies. Only under Stalin's and Mao's successors did living standards rise and everyday life become more predictable. Late socialism began to deliver results in crucial areas such as housing policy as well as in consumption. More tranquility and security were to be coupled with more prosperity even for some of those not in the *nomenklatura*. Yet in the countryside and in neglected areas poverty continued to be the norm. These economic and social realities of the 1960s and 1970s are still relevant today because they reshaped the population's relationship with and expectations of the state. The late socialist order came to be seen as a provider of work, education, housing and limited consumption. The population began to judge leaders by what they could deliver. The party-state's legitimacy became tied to consumption and social welfare. More than before, economic hardship and social crises became threats to the regimes. Soviet and East European societies – while still plagued by shortages – became accustomed to the provisions of a welfare state with free social services.[17] This experience first put a strain on communist power and then limited the possibilities of postcommunist governments. After the end of communist power in the Soviet Union and Eastern Europe a rollback of the welfare state was not acceptable. Rather, the free public services and a safety net for the poor and the elderly were certainly seen as accomplishments of socialism worth defending.

From the times of Stalin and Mao the building of heavy industry had been at the core of the communist modernization project. Gigantic steel works stood famously for economic achievement. The lack of competitiveness vis-à-vis the West, aging machinery and a largely superfluous array of enormous enterprises formed a legacy of Stalinism that shaped late socialism.[18] After the regime's collapse, these state-owned plants were often doomed, yet in countries such as Russia, Ukraine and Poland steel works, shipyards and the defense industry also represented much of the national wealth. In many cases

---

16 For biographical accounts, see Paul Hollander (ed.), *From the Gulag to the Killing Fields: Personal Accounts of Political Violence and Repression in Communist States* (Wilmington, DE: ISI Books, 2006).

17 János Kornai, *Economics of Shortage* (Amsterdam: North-Holland Publishers, 1980).

18 See, e.g., Stephen Kotkin, *Steeltown USSR: Soviet Society in the Gorbachev Era* (Berkeley: University of California Press, 1991).

the state was ready to shed its responsibility for heavy industry. Yet, the privatization of socialist industries tended to be controversial and problematic, not least as it put on the line the jobs of workers who could not easily be integrated into other workplaces. The social consequences for a once-favored, now-neglected working class posed a threat to social stability. Already in the 1980s industrial towns had become depressing reminders of the Stalinist past. The pride of Magnitogorsk or Nowa Huta was gone. In these places one could observe despair and the atomization of society in exemplary fashion. Nevertheless, where these plants and the mono-towns built around them were not successfully privatized, they often continued to rely on state subsidies – and continue to be a factor in postcommunist economic life.

Despite the end of mass repression, societies under communist rule did not simply liberalize after Stalin. They retained many distinct features that stemmed from the Stalinist period but played out differently in the decades after 1956. The workplace – whether a factory, institute or collective farm – continued to be a central place that administered most provisions and social services such as housing, child care and access to holiday resorts. Social relations revolved around work: This held true in the USSR as well as in Eastern Europe. In 1987 Finn Sivert Nielsen published a panorama of Soviet life under late socialism.[19] Nielsen observed that people lived their lives on separate "islands." He described how they could congregate and exchange rare goods and commodities in a country where public spaces were regulated and autonomous civic organizations could not be founded. The limited opportunities of socialist subjects often led to frustration because of constant shortages, inefficiencies and incongruities of the system. For much of the population everyday life was about getting the best out of one's connections, building a private life at the dacha or escaping the distinct "greyness" of reality through consumption of vodka – both at the workplace and after hours.[20] Today, late socialist habits continue to shape both private life and public behavior.

The end of isolation and autarchy imposed by Stalinism and the early Cold War meant a greater exposure to the West, its people, values, products and

19 Finn Sivert Nielsen, *The Eye of the Whirlwind: Russian Identity and Soviet Nation-Building. Quests for Meaning in a Soviet Metropolis* (Oslo: Department of Social Anthropology, 1987).
20 Mark Lawrence Schrad, *Vodka Politics: Alcohol, Autocracy, and the Secret History of the Russian State* (Oxford: Oxford University Press, 2014), 216–73; Alena V. Ledeneva, *Russia's Economy of Favors: Blat, Networking and Informal Exchange* (Cambridge: Cambridge University Press, 1998).

lifestyles. Certainly more porous borders shattered many myths of Stalin's propaganda. Western influence as well as black-market trading in all sorts of Western things – ideas and commodities – emerged as a parallel world to socialist economics.[21] Yet in the official sphere scarcity remained a primary factor. We may argue that these realities prepared at least part of the population of Eastern Europe and the USSR for life after communism. Personal initiative was rewarded in this parallel universe, and commercial ties could be established.[22] However, with the exception of Poland and Hungary, much of this enterprise was officially illegal or happening in a grey zone. Officials periodically suppressed these activities. Certainly trade and small-scale enterprise continued to be seen as problematic by many who hewed to the official value of equality. Acquiring additional assets and living a prosperous life could thus be devalued or partially criminalized. The party-state's campaigns against illegal income and "speculation" contributed to these views that continued to be held long after the end of party rule.

Paradoxically, this increased openness toward the West coincided with a growing nationalism, especially in Central and Eastern Europe but also in many republics of the USSR. Countries which had been multiethnic societies with strong minorities before World War II became less diverse as a result of the Holocaust and ethnic cleansing during the last months of and immediately after the war. Despite Sovietization of the political system the party-state's propaganda after 1945 used strong national themes and even at times copied slogans of the radical right from the interwar era.[23] This could be seen in the pan-Slavic propaganda of the 1940s as well as in the embrace of national history and its heroes in countries such as Poland and Hungary.[24] Nationalist rhetoric was one way to reach out to a population deeply suspicious of the USSR and of communism. It shaped the identity of generations growing up under communist rule. Within the Soviet bloc, national stereotypes, far from

21 Friederike Kind-Kovács and Jessie Labov (eds.), *Samizdat, Tamizdat and Beyond: Transnational Media During and After Socialism* (New York: Berghahn Books, 2013).
22 For examples from Moscow, see Lois Fisher-Ruge, *Nadezhda Means Hope: Views from Inside the Soviet Union* (London: Weidenfeld & Nicolson, 1989).
23 Marcin Zaremba, *Komunizm, legitymizacja, nacjonalizm. Nacjonalistyczna legitymizacja władzy komunistycznej w Polsce* (Warsaw: Trio, 2001); Martin Mevius, *Agents of Moscow: The Hungarian Communist Party and the Origins of Socialist Patriotism 1941–1953* (Oxford: Oxford University Press, 2005); Yitzhak M. Brudny, *Reinventing Russia: Russian Nationalism and the Soviet State, 1953–1991* (Cambridge, MA: Harvard University Press, 2000).
24 Jan C. Behrends, "Nation and Empire: Dilemmas of Legitimacy During Stalinism in Poland (1941–1956)," *Nationalities Papers* 37, 4 (Jul. 2009), 443–66.

being diminished, continued to thrive. The official internationalism of the bloc was often decorative and devoid of meaning. National sports teams and national history became beacons of collective pride. Ethnic homogeneity and social equality as well as a lack of migration contributed to a sense of a closed community where "others" did not belong. Although officially nonexistent, racism and xenophobia were widespread behind the Iron Curtain. The growing exchange with the "Third World" exposed these tendencies in socialist societies.[25] There were often disputes with foreign visitors which centered on the fight over rare resources as well as sexual relations. Exchange students and foreign workers were often discriminated against. Decades of nation-building under communist rule fostered the idea of ethnic communion; the imagined socialist nation was closed to migrants. Ethnic nationalism and xenophobia are part of the communist heritage in Europe and in the post-Soviet space.

In some respects, the legacy of late socialism in Eastern Europe and the former USSR decisively differ. One important factor is the experience of war and militarized violence. After decades of peace the Soviet Union invaded Afghanistan in December 1979 – a war that would shape Soviet as well as post-Soviet societies in different ways. European Soviet allies did not participate in military action in the Hindu Kush. They continued to foster large armed forces until 1989, when they quickly disarmed. Demilitarization was part of the escape from communism. Central European countries prepared to join NATO and depoliticized their armed forces while the former Soviet army was merely downsized: It remained largely unreformed and closely tied to those in power. Already during *perestroika* and on an even larger scale under Russia's first post-Soviet leader, Boris Yeltsin, the military fought on the southern periphery. After 1991 the army viewed itself as a force of order that was needed in troubled times. It took Yeltsin's side during his confrontation with the Supreme Soviet – Russia's elected parliament – in October 1993, and thereafter the armed forces became a pillar of his rule.

The 1979 invasion of Afghanistan marked the beginning of a series of often extremely violent and unconventionally fought "wild wars,"[26] mostly in Central Asia and the Caucasus. Crucially, from 1994 onward the Russian

---

25 Constantin Katsakioris, "The Soviet–South Encounter: Tensions in the Friendship with Afro-Asian Partners, 1945–1965," in Patryk Babiracki and Kenyon Zimmer (eds.), *Cold War Crossings: International Travel and Exchange Within the Soviet Bloc, 1940s–1960s* (College Station: Texas A&M University Press, 2014), 134–65.

26 The term is developed in Wolfgang Sofsky, *Violence: Terrorism, Genocide, War* (London: Granta Books, 2003).

armed forces were used internally to forcibly preserve the unity of the state.[27] The conflict in Chechnya (1994–96, 1999–2008) was marked by illegitimate violence on the side of the insurgents and the Russian army.[28] The nature of this war certainly put a burden on a Russia in transition and indeed on the whole post-Soviet realm. Yet that it came to such massive abuse of civil rights, war crimes[29] and mass violence was not inevitable: It was the Russian leadership in Moscow that chose the use of force over negotiation. In 1993 blood was shed in political battles.[30] In itself, the battle for the parliament was a defining moment. Further, both Boris Yeltsin in 1994 and Vladimir Putin in 1999 hoped that short victorious military campaigns would boost their popularity and crush the forces of opposition and independence. The wars in Afghanistan and Chechnya helped reverse the trend toward a more civil order in Russia.

Yet, the experience of military violence not only meant loss, suffering and death. It also triggered civic movements such as the Soldiers' Mothers in Russia.[31] Moreover, when looking at the Russian protest movement of 2011 we may argue that the insistence on civility that characterized the demonstrations also stemmed from the experience of violence – both communist and postcommunist. Paradoxically, the continuity of violence has also bred a wide civil consensus of nonviolence among parts of the population.[32] Going to war is not popular, and there were good reasons for hiding Russia's involvement and its losses first in Afghanistan, then in Chechnya and Ukraine, from the public.

In the post-Soviet space, the experience of violence was not limited to the military. On the everyday level, postcommunist states saw a rise in crime and criminal violence after 1989–91. Often, this was linked to the weakness of the state after the end of socialism. Still, this phenomenon is also tied to decades of communist rule. The role of former Gulag inmates has already been mentioned. Veterans of Afghanistan and other wars also joined organized

---

27 Mark Galeotti, *Russia's Wars in Chechnya, 1994–2009* (Oxford: Osprey, 2014).
28 Valery Tishkov, *Chechnya: Life in a War-Torn Society* (Berkeley: University of California Press, 2004).
29 Emma Gilligan, *Terror in Chechnya: Russia and the Tragedy of Civilians in War* (Princeton: Princeton University Press, 2010).
30 Vladimir Gel'man, *Authoritarian Russia: Analyzing Post-Soviet Regime Changes* (Pittsburgh: University of Pittsburgh Press, 2015), 50–56.
31 Overall, the weakness of civil society should be considered a legacy of communist power: Marc Morjé Howard, *The Weakness of Civil Society in Post-Communist Europe* (Cambridge: Cambridge University Press, 2003).
32 Mischa Gabowitsch, *Protest in Putin's Russia* (London: Polity, 2016).

crime.[33] But late socialism itself is also part of the picture. Corrupt practices and powerful organized crime existed already in the 1970s. Many criminal organizations that thrived during the transition have roots dating back to late socialism.[34] The demoralization through decades of repression, the disorientation of the 1990s and postcommunist fatigue certainly added to the often-unbearable presence of organized crime in everyday life.[35] After the fall of communism, many from the security apparatus joined forces with criminal gangs. There was widespread collusion between both sides that had already begun during the old regime.[36] Thus, postcommunist societies were often influenced by criminal structures dating back to late socialism, which seized the opportunities offered by unregulated capitalism and state failure.

The 1980s and 1990s: How Endgames and Transitions Shaped Legacies of Communism

The growing difference between various forms of communist rule became dramatically visible on 4 June 1989: While the tanks of the People's Liberation Army cleared Beijing's Tiananmen Square of protesters, the Polish population cast their vote in the first partially free election in Poland since World War II.[37] While the military in Beijing's center destroyed the student-led protest movement, Polish citizens overwhelmingly elected representatives of the anti-communist opposition to the Sejm. The same Polish Communist Party that not even a decade ago had silenced Solidarność with tanks, mass arrests and the imposition of martial law would not prevent the formation of a democratic government in Warsaw.[38] In contrast to the rulers of late socialist Poland, who had lost faith in their project as well as their backing from Moscow, Chinese party chieftain Deng Xiaoping and many of his lieutenants were members of China's revolutionary generation: Deng pushed for a violent response against some more moderate communists who had greater sympathy for the demonstrators and were reluctant to kill their fellow citizens.

33 Vadim Volkov, *Violent Entrepreneurs: The Use of Force in the Making of Russian Capitalism* (Ithaca: Cornell University Press, 2002), 11–13.
34 Stephenson, *Gangs of Russia*, 16–23.
35 For a vivid account, see David Satter, *Darkness at Dawn: The Rise of the Russian Criminal State* (New Haven: Yale University Press, 2003).
36 Volkov, *Violent Entrepreneurs*, 126–54.
37 Ezra F. Vogel, *Deng Xiaoping and the Transformation of China* (Cambridge, MA: Harvard University Press, 2011), 595–640.
38 Stephen Kotkin, *Uncivil Society: 1989 and the Implosion of the Communist Establishment* (New York: Modern Library, 2009), 100–31.

The summer of 1989 illustrates the different political options that communist regimes had at the time.[39] The Chinese party chose to crack down in order to continue authoritarian modernization. Simultaneously the Soviet leadership, in disarray, desperately tried to reform its economy as well as the political system, while Polish communists agreed to step down and become one player in a contested political field. Although the party controlled the army and police until the end in the Soviet and Polish cases, it abstained from the use of force. During the autumn of 1989, communist Europe generally followed the Polish path. After the fall of the Berlin Wall on 9 November, the disintegration gained momentum and the remaining regimes fell in quick succession.[40]

Clearly, the decision taken by the Polish communists in the spring of 1989 was made possible by Mikhail Gorbachev's attempts to modernize and civilize the Soviet system from above. Gorbachev had ruled out the use of the Soviet army to preserve communism in Eastern Europe.[41] The Soviet leader's growing frustration with the stubbornly unreformed Soviet Communist Party rank and file led him to introduce a partially competitive election in the USSR in 1988. Gorbachev's accelerated reforms – at once undermining the CPSU's authority and the federal structures of the USSR – paved the way for the collapse of the European Soviet empire in 1989 and the Soviet Union in 1991.[42] Still, these processes took different shapes in the USSR and in Eastern Europe, leading to diverging forms of political order throughout the former Soviet bloc. While the collapse in Central Europe was mostly peaceful, there was always the option to use force, as during the putsch against Nicolae Ceauşescu in Romania or, much more dramatically, during the Yugoslav Wars that took place throughout the 1990s.[43] And there was the possibility for communist elites to walk out of the communist party and grab power for themselves.

39 For comparative perspectives, see Peter Nolan, *China's Rise, Russia's Fall: Politics, Economics and Planning in the Transition from Stalinism* (Basingstoke: Palgrave, 1995); Minxin Pei, *From Reform to Revolution: The Demise of Communism in China and the Soviet Union* (Cambridge, MA: Harvard University Press, 1994).
40 For an overview of the political process, see Mark Kramer, "The Demise of the Soviet Bloc," *Journal of Modern History* 83, 4 (Dec. 2011), 788–854.
41 Jan C. Behrends, "Oktroyierte Zivilisierung. Genese und Grenzen des sowjetischen Gewaltverzichts 1989," in Martin Sabrow (ed.), *1989 und die Rolle der Gewalt* (Göttingen: Wallstein, 2012), 401–23.
42 On Eastern Europe, see e.g. Kotkin, *Uncivil Society*; on the Soviet collapse, see Kotkin, *Armageddon Averted*; Serhii Plokhy, *The Last Empire: The Final Days of the Soviet Union* (New York: Basic Books, 2014).
43 For a comparative view, see Sabrow (ed.), *1989 und die Rolle der Gewalt*.

In retrospect, the disparities between 1989 in Eastern Europe and 1991 in the Soviet Union are striking. While the revolutions in Eastern Europe were characterized by growing dissent, social movements, dialogue and the advent of political pluralism, the backroom deals of 1991 in the USSR had a much different character.[44] In the Soviet Union communist power was ended by the August putsch and Yeltsin's countercoup in the second half of that year.[45] There was no all-union round table in 1991, but secret negotiations in the Belarusan backwater Belavezha between representatives from Belarus, Ukraine and Russia. While former functionaries such as Yeltsin, Leonid Kravchuk and Nursultan Nazarbaev seized power and wealth in their republics, dissidents-turned-politicians such as Václav Havel or Lech Wałęsa aspired to a moral revolution in Czechoslovakia and Poland. Thus, the drive for liberalization of the political order and for confronting the communist past was much larger in Eastern Europe.

In this way, the endgames of communism determined its legacy. While the nation-states of Eastern Europe set out to dismantle the pillars of the Leninist state, former Soviet republics – with the notable exception of the Baltic states – were more reluctant to embrace political change. In the 1990s Eastern Europe set out to join NATO and the EU and had to fulfill strict criteria in order to gain membership. In contrast, the post-Soviet states often failed to reform key institutions of communist rule such as the army or the secret services. Economic reform and liberal experiments by themselves, however, could not pave the way to a more civil order.[46] In both Eastern Europe and the former Soviet republics, where Leninist power structures were not dissolved after the fall of party rule, they turned out to be powerful and long-lasting legacies of communism.

After 1989–91 the political culture of the party-state proved to be more influential than its ideological foundations.[47] Personal power continued to outweigh institutional mandates throughout Eastern Europe, in the post-Soviet space and in China. More often than not, politics was less about concrete policies and agendas. Rather, it was dominated by national and

---

44 On 1989, see Philipp Ther, "1989: eine verhandelte Revolution, Version: 1.0," *Docupedia-Zeitgeschichte* (11 Feb. 2010), docupedia.de/zg/1989?oldid=106114.

45 See Ignac Lozo, *Avgustovskii putch 1991 goda. Kak eto bylo* (Moscow: ROSSPEN, 2014).

46 For an inside account of the early 1990s in Russia, see Petr Aven and Alfred Kokh, *Gaidar's Revolution: The Inside Account of the Economic Transformation of Russia* (London: I. B. Tauris, 2015). For the economic and political transformation of Eastern Europe including Ukraine, see Philipp Ther, *Die neue Ordnung auf dem alten Kontinent. Eine Geschichte des neoliberalen Europa* (Berlin: Suhrkamp, 2014).

47 On political practices and their social consequences, see e.g. Catherine Verdery, *What Was Socialism, and What Comes Next?* (Princeton: Princeton University Press, 1996).

regional actors able to distribute resources among their supporters.[48] Different political cultures certainly mattered here – the moral standards of the former opposition in Central Europe, critical media and an emerging public sphere could serve as a counterweight to these traditions. Still, the old practices proved hard to surmount. A specific style of doing politics continued to dominate in postcommunist countries: institutions – political parties, parliaments, independent courts – proved hard to build. They remained weak while those (male) networks once formed under communism turned out to be durable as well as flexible. Personal networks and informal practices inherited from socialism but also reinvented might actually have been even more influential in post-Soviet economic practice than before and also prospered in other realms of social life such as culture and sports.[49]

The precarious status of institutions resulted in a weak rule of law.[50] The anticipated expansion of the realm of "liberty and property" did not materialize because there were no courts able to guarantee either. Where communist power had subdued the judiciary and turned it into a political instrument, rebuilding it remained a challenge many states failed to meet. This was also due to the strong standing of the procuracy and the (secret) police under communist rule. The KGB and the East German Stasi – to name the most infamous examples – carried much weight, and it took great efforts to dismantle their structures and to investigate the many ways in which they had penetrated society. Naturally, this proved to be easier in Germany where the communist East voted to join the larger Federal Republic than in Russia or other post-Soviet states where the structures of the KGB remained largely unscathed and where Yeltsin was able to use the old structure to consolidate his power.[51]

In the long run, the question of lustration and the buildup of alternative security structures were crucial for the political system.[52] Where the secret police remained largely untouched they could shake off the traditional

---

48 The example of 1990s St. Petersburg is examined in Karen Dawisha, *Putin's Kleptocracy: Who Owns Russia?* (New York: Simon & Schuster, 2015), 36–162.

49 Alena V. Ledeneva, *How Russia Really Works: The Informal Practices That Shaped Post-Soviet Politics and Business* (Ithaca: Cornell University Press, 2006).

50 See e.g. Brian D. Taylor, "From Police State to Police State? Legacies and Law Enforcement in Russia," in Beissinger and Kotkin (eds.), *Historical Legacies of Communism*, 128–51.

51 On the KGB's failed transition, see Amy Knight, *Spies Without Cloaks: The KGB's Successors* (Princeton: Princeton University Press, 1996).

52 See e.g. Agnès Bensussan, Dorota Dakowska and Nicolas Beaupré (eds.), *Die Überlieferung der Diktaturen. Beiträge zum Umgang mit den Archiven der Geheimpolizeien in Polen und Deutschland nach 1989* (Essen: Klartext, 2004).

oversight by the party and even expand their power. Lustration itself was often a painful process marred by political intrigue, denunciation and power play. The debate about the content of secret police files poisoned public discourse in many postcommunist states. Yet, ultimately lustration was the way to liquidate hidden Stalinist structures and come to terms with the past. Overall the communist secret police could be dismantled and its legacy overcome, but it clearly took political will and struggle. The legacy of the communist police state therefore varied by country: On the one hand, there was the German model of the Gauck-Behörde with its law-based access to secret files and state-sponsored research on the Stasi; on the other hand, there was Russia, where the secret police proved to be more influential in the postcommunist state than the communist party and where KGB methods of fabricating *kompromat*, or compromising material, became part of the political game.[53]

The size of the anti-communist opposition was also decisive. In most countries it consisted only of a few hundred to a few thousand activists. The main exception is Poland where a complete countersociety had emerged since the 1970s, partially under the umbrella of the Catholic Church, partially supported by an oppositional milieu that was able to build its own "underground" institutions. From the 1970s onward Polish opposition activists could develop alternatives to the party-state and its values and were ready to take political responsibility. In Czechoslovakia the former opposition activist Václav Havel was elected president, although he would remain somewhat on the margins of a political field dominated by postcommunist practices.[54] Still, a figure like Havel at the helm of the state provided guidance, legitimacy and authority during the difficult 1990s. Havel and Wałęsa in Poland and Vytautas Landsbergis in Lithuania certainly defined themselves and their political agenda differently than Yeltsin or Leonid Kuchma in Ukraine. They were state-builders, not just power brokers. Overall, it made a decisive difference whether a strong opposition including prominent public actors had emerged during late socialism and whether these groups were willing to enter the political arena or whether they stood on the sidelines as most of the Russian intelligentsia did.

The first sociological studies of (post)communist societies claimed that *Homo sovieticus* did exist – demoralization and lack of ambition among citizens were seen as a result of decades of communism.[55] Although Yuri

---

53 Ledeneva, *How Russia Really Works*, 58–90.
54 See Michael Žantovský, *Havel: A Life* (London: Atlantic Books, 2014).
55 Yuri Levada, *Sovetskii prostoi chelovek. Opyt social'nogo portreta na rubezhe 90-kh* (Moscow: Mirovoi okean, 1991); Boris Dubin (ed.), *Rossiia nulevykh: politicheskaia*

Levada's epic study of ordinary Soviet men certainly had its shortcomings, his team's research provided valuable insights into late socialist Soviet society. Levada's analysis allowed a glimpse into the frustration, anger and isolation of the Soviet subject, the limited potential for initiative and change, the deep imprint of paternalism and violence on people's values that separated the USSR even from many places in Eastern Europe. Initially, the social collapse of the 1990s only strengthened these characteristics. Yet, the end of communism also opened ample opportunity for those able and willing to decide their own fate. The negative picture of the 1990s – in Russia, by now a state-sponsored view – tends to exclude any emancipatory tendencies from the picture of this decade.

Different Shades of Authoritarian Rule: Varieties of Postcommunist Regimes

The optimistic assumption of the early 1990s was that postcommunist societies would – despite economic hardship and political quarrels – strive to build democratic institutions, honor the principles of liberty and property, and combine them with a reformed version of the European welfare state. Yet any overview will show that a variety of dissimilar regimes emerged. The aspirations of the elite, political traditions, the length of communist rule and influences from the outside – e.g. from NATO and the EU – were certainly among the decisive factors differentiating the outcomes.[56]

Integration into Western institutions such as the European Union was an important incentive to break with the authoritarian traditions of communism and build a law-based state. For Central and Eastern Europe as well as the Baltic countries, such policies could be promoted as a "return to Europe." Still, post-1989 political leaders in Eastern Europe were walking a tightrope: They had to be reformers and conservatives at the same time. While they were expected to fundamentally change the economic system and produce long-awaited prosperity, they were also expected to guarantee stability and preserve those social benefits of late socialism that the population valued. Needless to say, this was at best difficult. In those countries that opted for

---

kul'tura, istoricheskaia pamiat', povsednevnaia zhizn' (Moscow: ROSSPEN, 2011). For an oral history perspective with similar results, see Svetlana Alexievich, *Secondhand Time: The Last of the Soviets* (London: Random House, 2015).

56 For a systematic comparison, see Timothy Frye, *Building States and Markets After Communism: The Perils of Polarized Democracy* (Cambridge: Cambridge University Press, 2010).

democratic elections and a parliamentary system, the difficulties associated with postcommunism often led to repeated changes in government.[57] In Central Europe in the 1990s it was nearly impossible for any political party to get reelected. Even in Poland frustrated voters voted the ousted (post)communists back into power – something unthinkable in the immediate aftermath of 1989 when the representatives of the old regime were discredited and resented.

What at the time was often perceived as instability in some countries effectively paved the way to procedures that were more democratic. As governments changed and power was peacefully transferred, institutions could develop. This was the case in central Europe from Slovenia to Poland and in the Baltic states. But even here the road to democracy was hardly smooth. As early as the 1990s, states like Slovakia under Vladimír Mečiar flirted with authoritarian rule. On the whole, though, the region's transformation under neoliberal auspices brought initial pain but also midterm economic success.[58] The economy but also society and culture evolved more rapidly in Poland with its spirit of reform than, for example, in post-Soviet Ukraine where the influence of Soviet legacies initially remained strong. However, twenty-five years later the states of Eastern and Central Europe have still not fully caught up to their Western aspirations. Some – such as Hungary under Viktor Orbán and the Poland of Jarosław Kaczyński – are once again drifting toward an authoritarian order.[59]

Most post-Soviet states – with the notable exception of the Baltic countries – took a quite different road. After 1991, Central Asia and the Caucasus suffered from weak statehood, lack of legitimacy and continued repression. Here Gorbachev's *perestroika* took a very different form than in the Slavic republics. It resulted primarily in the rise to power of local party elites who saw little reason to liberalize the political order. Their main purpose was to stay in power, seek rent and eliminate the opposition. There was no (real or imagined) pre-Soviet order to return to. In these regions the attempt to build new institutions was at best half-hearted. In most instances local party chieftains continued as autocratic rulers of sovereign states. In the best case they strove for some version of authoritarian modernization, as in Kazakhstan under Nazarbaev, while in the worst case communist rule was transformed

---

57 See Padraic Kenney, *The Burdens of Freedom: Eastern Europe Since 1989* (London: Zed Books, 2006).

58 Ther, *Die neue Ordnung*, 86–121.

59 For a critical analysis of Viktor Orban's Hungary, see Bálint Magyar, *Post-Communist Mafia-State: The Case of Hungary* (Budapest: Central European University Press, 2016).

into outright despotism as in the Turkmenistan of *Türkmenbaşi*, Saparmurat Niyazov. Generally, the hybridity of these regimes may be noted. They combine elements of the Soviet past with authoritarian features, autocratic power and attributes of Western statehood. Some of the states, such as Kyrgyzstan and Georgia, did attempt to reform themselves and flirted with accountable government and democracy. Others remained stagnant and repressive through a long post-Soviet winter.

The Slavic heartland of the Soviet Union is yet another case. Under the leadership of Boris Yeltsin and with the decisive support of Ukraine, the federal structures of the USSR were dismantled. This did not mean, however, that the regime leaderships had concrete plans for the future. Rather, they improvised, and the power struggles between the existing networks and interests intensified. In Russia President Yeltsin exemplified that staying in power was much dearer to him and his entourage than liberal reform or nation-building.[60] As noted above, it was an unprecedented move in 1993 to use the army's tanks in the power struggle with the Supreme Soviet. In retrospect, it was a decisive caesura: The storming of Moscow's White House and the invasion of renegade Chechnya in 1994 signaled the end of liberal reform and the "civilizing from above" begun by Gorbachev.[61] From 1993 onward, President Yeltsin allied himself to the army and the former KGB as well as those oligarchs who had financed his reelection campaign.[62] While some reformers remained part of his team, his priorities had shifted. The new constitution, written for Yeltsin and introduced in 1994, marked a return to the country's autocratic tradition. The parliament – the new Duma – was awarded only limited influence, while the president's office came to represent state power. The attempts to build a system of checks and balances were scrapped. In retrospect it becomes clear how the politics of the 1990s served to discredit notions of democracy and liberalism in the eyes of much of the Russian population. For many, these concepts came to equal corruption, lawlessness and a weak state.

Yeltsin's political system meant more than the return to autocracy. After his rigged reelection of 1996, a new type of political order emerged. Through control of the mass media and political parties, "virtual politics" – the rule of spin doctors and "political technology" – was established in Russia and later

60 On Yeltsin's tenure, see Lilia Shevtsova, *Yeltsin's Russia: Myth and Reality* (Washington, DC: Carnegie Endowment for International Peace, 1999).
61 Behrends, *Oktroyierte Zivilisierung*.
62 Anders Åslund, *Russia's Capitalist Revolution: Why Market Reform Succeeded and Democracy Failed* (Washington, DC: Peterson, 2007).

to a certain degree also in Ukraine.[63] "Active measures" by those holding power prevent genuine political contests because of constant interventions. While democratic institutions remain formally in place, they are divested of their meaning. A pluralistic and democratic facade with several parties, a supreme court and a parliament was erected to hide the fact that major decisions were taken exclusively in the Kremlin and increasingly by Yeltsin and his associates, dubbed at the time his "family." The spin doctors who controlled the mass media went to great lengths to spread political narratives. From 1996 onward, free and fair elections disappeared from the political landscape of Russia. Rather, various political parties were launched by the Kremlin to sabotage the political contest. In 1999, the "family" decided on Vladimir Putin as the successor to the ailing Yeltsin.[64] His election as president in the beginning of 2000 affirmed a decision taken in the Kremlin. A new authoritarian culture emerged that relied heavily on mass media.[65] Their influence on the public, however, is often more sophisticated than in the times of Soviet agitprop. In the background rent-seeking elites divided up resources and enriched themselves.[66] Open contests in politics are as despised as in Soviet times. This political system of the late Yeltsin and early Putin years was clearly influenced by Soviet traditions and political practices. The strict control of mass media and the political process, informal networks at the top and in the regions, and the strong position of the army and secret police as well as contempt for competitive politics were all trademarks of the Soviet system. Although the framework changed, the paternalism toward society and the urge to control remained in place. "Virtual politics" with all its machinations may well be considered the agitprop of the twenty-first century.

With Vladimir Putin's return to the presidency in 2012 the re-Sovietization of political culture gained new momentum. Political repression against real or imagined oppositionists, restrictions on civil society and censorship of the media increased. Moreover, for the first time since the end of communism in Russia, political mobilization of society was revived in the broad anti-Western and anti-Ukrainian campaigns that accompanied Moscow's aggression. Political traits of the Soviet era were

---

63 On the concept of virtual politics, see Andrew Wilson, *Virtual Politics: Faking Democracy in the Post-Soviet World* (New Haven: Yale University Press, 2005).

64 Ben Judah, *Fragile Empire: How Russia Fell in and out of Love with Vladimir Putin* (New Haven: Yale University Press, 2014), 7–168.

65 Ulrich Schmid, *Technologien der Seele. Vom Verfestigen der Wahrheit in der russischen Gegenwartskultur* (Berlin: Suhrkamp, 2015).

66 For details, see Dawisha, *Putin's Kleptocracy*.

reinstated: e.g. mass festivals and parades, the leader cult, the cult of the "Great Fatherland War" and show trials as well as mass organizations that were founded with the purpose of supporting state policies.[67] What Russians dub *sistema*, the political order, bears many marks of the Soviet past. The informal circle at the top is undoubtedly yet not exclusively influenced by Soviet ideals.[68] Clearly, the presidential administration is the contemporary equivalent to the Central Committee of the CPSU – in both form and function. Overall, Russia's recent history exemplifies that many traits of the Soviet system could be revived and that the elites once again view them as tools to consolidate the authoritarian state. The imperial tradition – in both Soviet and tsarist symbols – became the main tool with which to legitimate postcommunist power.

The developments in Belarus and Ukraine indicate that there were alternatives to Moscow's post-Soviet path. Since 1994 Belarus under Aleksandr Lukashenko has adopted an authoritarian model of statehood that legitimizes itself by embracing Soviet-style paternalism. The elites have promised to shield the population from the perils of change and impertinence brought about by globalization. Minsk provides its population with basic goods and services and has created a distinctly Brezhnevite atmosphere in the country.[69] Those not content with this course are marginalized or driven out of the country. Ukraine is the only major Soviet republic that has seen the emergence of competitive politics – although the influence of regional strongmen ("oligarchs") has remained strong, and rent-seeking continues to be a problem despite the uprisings of 2004 ("Orange Revolution") and 2014 ("Euromaidan"). Still, the question remains why Ukraine has developed into a more pluralistic polity than other Soviet republics and how strong local identities and an active civil society could emerge. It remains to be seen if Ukrainian society will manage to overcome its Soviet heritage in politics and government. As long as the country keeps the presidential model, it will be prone to repeating the authoritarian experience. Overall, the legacy of Soviet rule, clearly, did allow for different paths after 1991. It is still an open question how historians can explain these disparities.

---

67 On Putin, see Steven Lee Myers, *The New Tsar: The Reign and Rise of Vladimir Putin* (New York: Simon & Schuster, 2015).

68 See for insights Mikhail Zygar, *All the Kremlin's Men: Inside the Court of Vladimir Putin* (New York: Public Affairs, 2016).

69 Andrew Wilson, *Belarus: The Last Dictatorship in Europe* (New Haven: Yale University Press, 2011).

Some Conclusions

From a 21st-century perspective the Chinese Revolution might be viewed as more monumental than the Russian October.[70] In many ways it continues to shape the present time. In contrast to postcommunist Russia, post-Mao China has taken center stage in the global arena. By radically embracing economic globalization, Chinese leaders have delivered the authoritarian modernization communism failed to achieve in other parts of the world.[71] Large parts of the population have left their traditional agrarian way of life, moved to cities and have made their country the workshop of the world. In metropolitan areas, consumption and lifestyles have often reached Western levels. Economic exchange has opened the country to Asia and the wider world. The rise of the Chinese model, however, carries a price: The party-state remains repressive and does not offer its citizens political rights. The communist party stands above the constitution. Nevertheless, it has overseen three decades of economic growth as well as the consolidation of China as a major international power rivaled only by the United States. Thus, the whole idea of the collapse of communism may be viewed as a European narrative. From Asia the story is more about the transformation of the Chinese regime into a world power. In China the communist revolution of 1949 brought back the centralized state that had not existed for almost a century. Therefore Chinese communism has to be assessed separately from that in Europe and other parts of the world. Since the 1980s it has emerged as an order *sui generis* that has emancipated itself from the Soviet model. It remains to be seen whether China will indeed emerge as an authoritarian challenge to the West.[72]

A quarter of a century after the fall of communism in Europe and the former USSR, the picture remains mixed. Clearly decades of communist power have left their footprint on these societies. In Europe we may distinguish between the results of Stalinist rule and the legacies of post-1956 late socialism. While Stalinism reshaped societies violently, late socialist practices and mentalities are influential. They include an authoritarian impulse, the

---

70 For a stimulating comparative historical perspective on Russia and China, see Perry Anderson, "Two Revolutions: Rough Notes," *New Left Review* 61 (Jan.–Feb. 2010), 59–96; Gerd Koenen, "Der Kommunismus in seinem Zeitalter. Versuch einer historischen Verortung," *Osteuropa* 63 (2013), 9–38.
71 Walder, *China Under Mao.*
72 See Larry Diamond, Marc F. Plattner and Christopher Walker (eds.), *Authoritarianism Goes Global: The Challenge to Democracy* (Baltimore: Johns Hopkins University Press, 2016).

weakness of institutions and civil society, xenophobia, widespread demoralization and distrust, and rent-seeking elites as well as violent conflicts in the
post-Soviet space. On the more positive side, a craving for social justice and
economic equality, support for a welfare state and the ability of the populace
to deal with sometimes repressive, sometimes merely dysfunctional states
remain. These findings, however, should be taken as merely a starting point
from which to thoroughly scrutinize the often-enigmatic postcommunist
condition – a condition both similar and distinct in the various places that
share the experience of communist power.

Bibliographical Essay

Over the past decades the aftermath of communism in Europe has been
discussed widely. Initially, the historical optimism of such public intellectuals
as Timothy Garton Ash or Francis Fukuyama had a strong impact on the
perception of 1989–91. Right after the revolution a master narrative about
peaceful change and embrace of a liberal order was established that has long
prevailed among the Western public. This normative perspective was also
echoed in political science ("transition to democracy") where yet another
wave of global democratization was studied. The term "third wave of
democratization" was coined by the otherwise more skeptical Samuel
P. Huntington and proved influential: see Samuel P. Huntington, *The Third
Wave: Democratization in the Late Twentieth Century* (Norman: University of
Oklahoma Press, 1991). Transformation studies argued that urbanization,
education and the rise of a middle class favored the development of
a liberal order, that the United States as well as the European Union served
as models and that local "snowball effects" could be observed. For an overview, see e.g. Raj Kollmorgen, Wolfgang Merkel and Hans-Jürgen Wagener
(eds.), *Handbuch Transformationsforschung* (Wiesbaden: Springer, 2015).
Implicitly, this approach suggested that new political and social systems
emerged after 1989–91 and that they could be approached without a deeper
understanding of the old regime. While individual studies may still be
valuable, the approach taken in the 1990s should today be historicized and
analyzed as a product of that particular time.

Few studies have explicitly tackled the difficult question of how revolutionary upheaval and Stalinism still shape (post)communist societies today.
A possible exception is foreign policy, where a *longue durée* perspective has
a lengthy tradition. See e.g. Robert Legvold (ed.), *Russian Foreign Policy in the
Twenty-First Century and the Shadow of the Past* (New York: Columbia

University Press, 2007). A model for such a perspective is Miriam Dobson's study of Gulag returnees that explains how the release of millions from the camps impacted on Russian society: *Khrushchev's Cold Summer: Gulag Returnees, Crime and the Fate of Reform After Stalin* (Ithaca: Cornell University Press, 2009). Only in hindsight do we come to understand the significance of the spreading of violent and criminal culture from the camps into society. Other such studies, however, are still lacking. Therefore we do not yet understand the full political as well as cultural impact of decades of mass violence on postcommunist societies. Psychological terms such as "trauma" are merely descriptive and add little to our understanding of the historical phenomenon.

The past decades have produced a number of books that have marked the historicization of the transformation and that may be read as contributions to the debate about legacies of communist power. Catherine Verdery was among the first to connect the old order and the new regimes: See her *What Was Socialism, and What Comes Next?* (Princeton: Princeton University Press, 1996). Stephen Kotkin's monographs about the post-Soviet space and Eastern Europe serve as an introduction to the debate: *Armageddon Averted: The Soviet Collapse, 1970–2000* (Oxford: Oxford University Press, 2001) and *Uncivil Society: 1989 and the Implosion of the Communist Establishment* (New York: Modern Library, 2009). In cooperation with Mark Beissinger, Kotkin has also edited a volume that was the first attempt to systematically explore the legacies of communism in several countries: Mark R. Beissinger and Stephen Kotkin (eds.), *Historical Legacies of Communism* (Cambridge: Cambridge University Press, 2014). Vladimir Gel'man has written a comprehensive history of postcommunist politics in Russia, *Authoritarian Russia: Analyzing Post-Soviet Regime Changes* (Pittsburgh: University of Pittsburgh Press, 2015), while both Padraic Kenney, *The Burdens of Freedom: Eastern Europe Since 1989* (London: Zed Books, 2006), and Philipp Ther, *Die neue Ordnung auf dem alten Kontinent. Eine Geschichte des neoliberalen Europa* (Berlin: Suhrkamp, 2014), offer comparative introductions on the recent history of Eastern and Central Europe. Exploring the legacy of Deng, Ezra F. Vogel provides a similar overview for the Chinese case: Ezra F. Vogel, *Deng Xiaoping and the Transformation of China* (Cambridge, MA: Harvard University Press, 2011). To understand the social structure as well as the values that prevail in postcommunist societies the sociology of Finn Sivert Nielsen, Yuri Levada and Boris Dubin as well as the work of Svetlana Alexievich present milestones of research on the post-Soviet space. See Finn Sivert Nielsen, *The Eye of the Whirlwind: Russian Identity and Soviet Nation-Building: Quests for Meaning in a Soviet Metropolis* (Oslo:

Department of Social Anthropology, 1987); Yuri Levada, *Sovetskii prostoi chelovek. Opyt sotsial'nogo portreta na rubezhe 90-kh* [Regular Soviet Man: Social Experiences at the Beginning of the 1990s] (Moscow: Mirovoi okean, 1991); Boris Dubin (ed.), *Rossiia nulevykh. Politicheskaia kul'tura, istoricheskaia pamiat', povsednevnaia zhizn'* [Russia in the 2000s: Political Culture, Historical Memory, Everyday Life] (Moscow: ROSSPEN, 2011); and Svetlana Alexievich, *Secondhand Time: The Last of the Soviets* (London: Random House, 2015). In more recent years, interest in the study of post-communism has been stimulated by the rise of China and by Russia's aggression against Ukraine as well as by the comparative study of authoritarian regimes that characterize most postcommunist states: Larry Diamond, Marc F. Plattner and Christopher Walker (eds.), *Authoritarianism Goes Global: The Challenge to Democracy* (Baltimore: Johns Hopkins University Press, 2016).

23

State Communism at 100: Remembering and Forgetting the Russian Revolution

JAN PLAMPER

The October Revolution, no matter how much we differ in its interpretation, was a milestone on the path toward the first communist state in human history. Like any revolutionary state, the founding of the Soviet Union was accompanied by iconoclasm – by the toppling of tsarist statues, the tearing down of portraits and the prohibition of old religious and monarchic holidays. Like any revolutionary state, the Soviet Union then filled the built environment with its own statues, created its own portraits and established new holidays. And, like any revolutionary state, the Soviet Union in its self-descriptions professed to have created the new from scratch, in a kind of big bang of signifiers, whereas in reality the new was the result of a recombination of preexisting elements.

To gain an understanding of Soviet communism and its legacy, it is, then, worth taking a close look at some of these (partially) new statues, portraits and holidays. Let us start with the annual cycle of Soviet holidays and its evolution over time. In the Soviet Union the anniversary of the October Revolution marked the absolute high point of the calendar of celebrations. It was celebrated from 1918 onward and later ranged in importance even ahead of 9 May, the day of victory over Hitler's Germany in World War II. People had both days of the October Revolution, 7 and 8 November, off work, and these involved commemorative events across the entire country, 7 November with a military parade on Red Square in Moscow. In late 1991 the Soviet Union imploded, and instead of Moscow there was now a multiplicity of capitals. Accordingly, the culture of celebrations was also decentralized. From then on, the former Soviet republics dealt with the memory of

For conversations on this topic, I am grateful to Dietrich Beyrau, Alexander Etkind, Alexei Evstratov, Juliane Fürst, Mischa Gabowitsch, Boris Kolonitskii, Nikolai Mikhailov, Nikolay Mitrokhin, Igor Narskii, Stephen A. Smith and Andrei Zorin.

the October Revolution as they pleased – in Belarus, Kyrgyzstan and Transnistria, for example, people to this day celebrate the "Day of the Great Socialist October Revolution."

Out of an anti-Soviet impulse, Boris Yeltsin, the president of the largest successor state, the Russian Federation, curtailed the double-dip holiday by 24 hours: From 1992 onward only 7 November was celebrated. The military parade on Red Square was suspended, so that no military parades at all took place on Red Square between 1991 and 1994. It was only on 9 May 1995, during the fiftieth anniversary of the victory, that another parade was carried out in the country's symbolic center, though without military technology. This is the way it stayed until 2008. In other parts of the Russian Federation, post-Soviet, syncretic celebratory practices formed which invariably contained some Soviet elements. Among the latter was a laying of wreaths at the Lenin monument on Lenin Square, so long as this monument had not been destroyed and the place not renamed. After Yeltsin defeated his communist competitor Gennadii Ziuganov in the presidential elections of 1996, he deemed the anti-communist political forces strengthened to such an extent that he dared to recode the revolutionary holiday. On 7 November 1996 he signed a decree that renamed it the "Day of Accord and Reconciliation."

However, and contrary to the Yeltsin command's intentions, the "Day of Accord and Reconciliation" (now the "Day of Unity") never shed its revolutionary meanings – after all, it was created as a response to a date in the Soviet calendar, and 7 November in collective memory continued to remain connected with "Red October." To this day many people and political groups celebrate 7 November in their particularist commemorative practices as a distinctly Soviet day, from pensioner communist sectarians with their Stalin portraits on Red Square, to the Communist Party of the Russian Federation (Kommunisticheskaia partiia Rossiiskoi federatsii, KPRF), a serious political force with real support among voters of various ages. On 7 November the KPRF leadership appears at rallies in red tracksuit jackets that have the party's logo on their left side, the Nike swoosh on the right and red KPRF scarves, probably produced by a machine from capitalist South German Baden-Württemberg in an embroidery factory normally making items for football fans.[1] During the 1990s, when the media were still relatively free and uncensored, pictures of particularist commemorations "from

---

1 See cdn15.img22.ria.ru/images/106206/48/1062064816.jpg (2015).

below" began circulating, such as those of the elderly protesters with Stalin portraits on and around Red Square, thus keeping the revolutionary memory of 7 November alive.

There was one institution that could not but take issue with the continued Soviet framing of 7 November: the reempowered Russian Orthodox Church. No matter how many compromises the church had made with the Soviet state, no matter how mired it had become in the Soviet secret services, from its perspective 7 November marked the beginning of an awful, godless time. Most likely, though it is hard to tell, the church initiated the rescheduling of the holiday. In 2004 the interreligious committee of the Russian parliament, the Duma, got things started by proposing 4 November as an alternative. It reasoned that 4 November 1612 was the day on which the Muscovites ousted the Polish Rzeczpospolita from Moscow, ended the "Time of Troubles" and established the Romanov dynasty.

The date and the accuracy of the historical events were disputed from the very beginning. Several historians pointed out that Kuzma Minin and Dmitrii Pozharskii had not reconquered Kitai-Gorod and the Kremlin on this day. The major points of reference in 2004, however, were not the opinion of professional historians, but two historical events that could serve as precedents. For one thing, it was the very first Romanov tsar, Fedor Mikhailovich, who declared 4 November as the day on which Moscow was reconquered. What is more, the second Romanov tsar, Aleksei Mikhailovich, designated 4 November the religious holiday of the Our Lady of Kazan Icon, one of Orthodoxy's most revered icons. In so doing Aleksei Mikhailovich wanted to commemorate the birth of his first son, who was born on 4 November 1648 (and died a year later while still a child) – originally the Our Lady of Kazan Icon day was celebrated in the summer.

More Duma committees and parties joined the legislative initiative of the interreligious committee, youth organizations supported the project by demonstrating in the provinces and on 29 September 2004 the patriarch personally intervened: "This day reminds us how in 1612 Russians [*rossiiane*, a term denoting all Russians regardless of ethnic background, which was reinstated in the post-Soviet era; *russkie* describes ethnic Russians only] of different faiths and different ethnic backgrounds overcame their differences, defeated the dangerous enemy, and led the country to a stable civil peace."[2] (To be sure, the patriarch made this statement at a time when ethnic tensions

2 See www.afonru.ru/news/2015_09_10/4/.

were on the rise and attacks by ethnically Russian extreme rightists on ethnically Caucasian or Central Asian Russians became rampant – despite the fact that all shared Russian citizenship and were *rossiiane*.) At the same time – and this line became dominant – 4 November was meant to symbolize the victory over the "Polish–Lithuanian interventionists" in 1612. To quote an official explanatory briefing (dated 12 October 2004) associated with the draft legislation, "On 4 November 1612 the warriors of the people's volunteer corps stormed Kitai-Gorod and thus liberated Moscow from the Polish interventionists, demonstrating an example of heroism and the unity of the entire people, irrespective of background, belief and status in society."[3] As this quotation shows, the reinterpretation of the holiday came along with an orientation toward an exterior enemy who needed to be expelled from Russia. Thus 4 November was firmly placed in today's central unifying historical myth, the victory over Hitler, and the holiday of 9 May. Victory Day is the only Soviet myth that has weathered all zigzags and changes of the decades since 1945 and from which the majority of former Soviet citizens, no matter whether they reside in Moscow, Minsk or Mogilev, Brighton Beach, Berlin-Marzahn or Be'er Sheva, define their identity, if only for the horrendous loss of lives – 27 million Soviet dead is the number that is considered accurate today. The creation of the 4 November holiday thus meant, as it were, the foundation of a second Victory Day, a second 9 May. The quotation's emphasis on ethnic and religious harmony and on classlessness also shows that the shrill, revolutionary tone of 7 November was meant to be over-written and a kind of social symphony created in its stead.

The legal change was definitively decided in late 2004 and "Unity Day" (literally, "Day of the Unity of the People") celebrated for the first time in 2005. Since then a new celebratory culture has come into existence, and yet it is still unclear whether this day will ever be accepted. During its first year 2005 polls revealed that 92 percent of Russian citizens did not know what was being celebrated. As late as 2011 18 percent still told the independent, credible pollsters from the Levada Center that they planned on celebrating the old revolutionary holiday on 7 November. Only 16 percent said they would celebrate the new Unity Day. Similarly, in 2011 half of those interviewed spoke negatively about the abolishment of the revolutionary holiday.

---

3 "Poiasnitel'naia zapiska, K proektu Federal'nogo zakona 'O vnesenii izmeneniia v stat'iu' 1 Federal'nogo zakona 'O dniakh voinskoi slavy (pobednykh dniakh) Rossii,'" www .lawmix.ru/lawprojects/49350/.

The only authentic Unity Day that they spoke of was 9 May.[4] When in 2015 the tenth anniversary of 4 November was celebrated, there were – despite authentic patriotism in the wake of the annexation of Crimea, despite state investments in balloons and flags in the white, blue and red of the Russian tricolor, which were waved in the entire country, despite state-controlled media – still voices that said Unity Day "had not taken root. The majority of people simply sees it as an additional day off from work during the gloomy November season."[5]

So much for the revolutionary holiday of 7 November. Let us now try and map the wider memory landscape of communism and the revolution: What will be the locus of 1917? Where is it likely to be situated in the commemorative topography of 2017 during the 100th anniversary? What does this tell us about the fate of communism in the first state that made it a lived and political reality?

Gosudarstvo, or The State – The Power, and the Glory, for Ever and Ever

If there is a leitmotif that runs through the polyphony, or cacophony, of the Putinite politics of memory, it is that of étatism – *gosudarstvennost'*. In many ways this term is a carryover from communist times, tailored, to be sure, to the needs of global capitalism. The term signifies the belief in the intrinsic power of a strong state. It further signifies a privileging of the executive over the legislative and judiciary powers, a trust in the capability of the state to be in the best position to solve social tasks, and a deep mistrust of federalism. It finally signifies the necessity of economic intervention and making sure that a part of the gains from selling natural resources ends up in state coffers in order to fulfill the state's many tasks. So much for the level of state representations.

It is a different question altogether that in reality the tasks of the state are executed by a mafia-like coterie of people that came into being not through meritocratic principles, but through loyalty, family relations and common socialization, especially in the KGB; that his clique uses the state as a vehicle for its personal enrichment and not for the fulfillment of social, welfare-state tasks; and that it has destroyed the division of powers and censors the fourth

---

4 See vz.ru/columns/2011/11/7/536568.html (Mikhail Solomatin, 7 Nov. 2011).
5 See www.gazeta.ru/comments/2015/06/11_e_6837529.shtml (11 Jun. 2015). On the unified celebrations with balloons and flags see e.g. www.dni.ru/society/2015/11/4/319567 .html (4 Nov. 2005).

power, the media, specifically in order to hide its personal enrichment from the population.[6]

The strong state as an intrinsic value is of course difficult to reconcile with the destruction of the state in the two revolutions of 1917. Consequently everything discontinuous – anything resembling a break or caesura – needs to be downplayed and the formation of a new strong state, the Soviet state, emphasized. That is why all *gosudarstvenniki*, the étatists, strive to shorten the distance between 1917, the end of the tsarist empire, and 1922, the beginning of the Soviet Union, as much as they can and emphasize the natural continuity between the two empires. In so doing, the communism of the world's first communist state also moves into the background.

It is in endowing the strong, continuous state with religious legitimacy that the Russian Orthodox Church enters the picture. And here the Archimandrite Tikhon plays a special role. Tikhon heads the Sretenskii Monastery in Moscow and is rumored to be Putin's confessor. What is known for certain is that he has accompanied Putin on many of his foreign travels and is considered a likely successor of Patriarch Kirill. The 1958-born Tikhon, or Georgii Shevkunov by secular name, had just graduated from the Gerasimov film school in Moscow when, in 1982, he claims to have experienced some kind of epiphany. After this he got himself baptized and became a priest and later a monk. The film school part in his career is significant because Tikhon has developed into one of the leading propagandists of the Kremlin and the church. In 2011 he published a bestseller *Unholy Holies*, which in 2012 sold more than 1 million copies and even beat the Russian translation of *Fifty Shades of Grey*.[7] His popularity, however, is first and foremost founded on his film *Death of an Empire: The Byzantine Lesson* of 2008, which deserves a closer look.

This movie is a technically elaborate pastiche of documentary, computer animations and reenacted, docudrama-type scenes. What the viewer sees is first of all Tikhon himself in the role of raconteur-cum-flaneur, who is at one point placed in his black frock in front of Istanbul's Hagia Sophia; at another he can be seen walking through a crowd of people on Venice's San Marco Square and a few cuts later he is montaged in a Venetian gondola. In between there are 3D computer animations of Constantinople during its prime; original black-and-white scenes of the victory against the Teutonic Knights

6 See Karen Dawisha, *Putin's Kleptocracy: Who Owns Russia?* (New York: Simon & Schuster, 2014); Mikhail Zygar, *All the Kremlin's Men: The Four Metamorphoses of Vladimir Putin* (New York: PublicAffairs, 2016).

7 Charles Clover, "Putin and the Monk," *Financial Times Magazine* (25 Jan. 2013).

on the ice of Lake Peipus from Sergei Eisenstein's 1938 *Alexander Nevsky*; collages of icons and artwork; scenes in which little plaster figurines reenact drunken binges of late Byzantine decadence (at one point we see a torture scene reenacted in the original location, the Turkish catacombs; at another point a young boy of African descent in a Byzantine, but actually Roman, toga, deeply immersed in a manuscript) – all in order to underscore the peaceful multiethnicity and intellectual prowess of the empire.

The film's message can easily be summarized. Byzantium was the greatest empire that ever existed, Russia is its legitimate, natural successor – this is of course the old theory of Moscow, the Third Rome. Byzantium was destroyed by external enemies who copied its scientific and other achievements and then used them against Byzantium itself. Rather than continuing the religious, Eastern Orthodox tradition, they only utilized Byzantine technology to accumulate superfluous material things; instead of souls they possessed only coldness, and instead of multiethnic harmony they were capable only of monoethnic hatred. Byzantium fell apart because it failed to solve the problem of the successor, i.e. the problem of *preemstvennost'*; this issue had become acute under Vladimir Putin and Dmitrii Medvedev the year before the film appeared because of the restriction to two elected terms of office for the president. All of Russia was worried about Putin's *preemnik*, or successor.

The film's often-pseudohistorical Russian language, reminiscent of Church Slavonic, is enriched by elements from the present. Thus we hear that Venice is in the clutches of a "financial oligarchy" (an allusion to the post-Soviet oligarchs); that the "eternal problem of all empires" is the "separatism in the peripheries" (an allusion to Chechnya and Georgia); that the good Byzantine tsar Basil II "unrelentingly built a vertical of power" (an allusion to Putin) and bequeathed to his successor "a kind of stabilization fund" (an allusion to the stabilization fund created on the model of Norway's sovereign wealth fund by Putin's minister of finance Aleksei Kudrin). In sum, stability, a strong state, a single religion, which others convert to, the great social symphony and a lot of soul – these form "the Byzantine lesson."

Martyrology

Tikhon is also the mastermind behind another project. There are plans to build a new cathedral on the territory of his Sretenskii Monastery, and not just any cathedral, but Moscow's tallest. It will be even taller than the cathedral in the vicinity of the Kremlin, the Cathedral of Christ the Savior, which Stalin had demolished in 1931 and which was rebuilt faithfully to the original in 1995 and inaugurated in 2000. This new, tallest Moscow cathedral on the premises of Sretenskii Monastery will be dedicated to the "Martyrs of the Revolution."[8]

Martyrology is another dominant framework in the church, both regarding the memory of 1917 in particular and the entire Soviet period in general. In it the revolution figures as an ill that came from outside and broke into a healthy, Russian Orthodox-majority society. Closely connected with martyrology are conspiracy theories – of the revolution as a Jewish conspiracy, a Masonic conspiracy, a Judeo-Masonic conspiracy, a conspiracy of Wilhelmine Germany, a "Western" conspiracy of the allied British, Americans and Japanese (see more below) and so on. In the martyrological framework, the church was forced to go either underground or into exile, and individual church representatives were murdered, tortured and killed in the Gulag.

Importantly, this is not a victim narrative: The key feature of martyrdom is that it is positively charged. This is encapsulated by the motto of the priests and monks imprisoned on the Solovetsky Islands in the White Sea, the Ur-Gulag, as early as under Lenin: "What do we need the charms of liberty, our happiness lies also on the Solovki" (*Chto nam prelesti svobody, shchast'e nam i v Solovkakh*).[9] Paradoxically, this ended up legitimating the revolution and the anti-religious policy of the Bolsheviks. Both were interpreted as a higher, transcendental fate and had to be suffered rather than resisted. Ultimately this created a religiously charged moral-historical entanglement between Russian Orthodoxy and the apparatchik representatives of the Soviet state, also, in a way, legitimating the former KGB agent Putin.

Some clergymen treat the connection between Putin and his confessor Tikhon with humor: "In our confessions there is not very much specific information. You just say 'I stole' or 'I fornicated.' Maybe you add a few specific details like how much and how often. But you don't need to be very specific. If Father Tikhon is captured by some foreign intelligence service and tortured, there would not be much he could tell them."[10] On a more serious note, beyond martyrology there is of course another – second – connection

8 See izvestia.ru/news/546146; www.pravoslavie.ru/60331.html; www.the-village.ru/village/city/situation-comment/134659-kommentariy-dnya; red-sovet.su/post/15876/roc-celebrate-century-of-revolution-1917.
9 See back cover of Irina Reznikova, *Pravoslavie na Solovkakh. Materialy po istorii Solovetskogo lageria* (St. Petersburg: Memorial, 1994).
10 Evgenii Nikiforov in Clover, "Putin and the Monk."

that points to a much closer, direct personal relationship between the church and the Soviet state. As is well known, many Russian priests who served in Soviet times were KGB informants. It is proven that the post-Soviet Russian Orthodox patriarchs – both Alexis II, who was elected in 1990 and his successor, Kirill I, inaugurated in 2009 – were KGB agents. This is why more liberal church circles do not hesitate to speak of the guilt that the church burdened itself with. These circles claim real victim status for the clergy members who were repressed in state violence as opposed to the martyr narrative; they do not charge the suffering with metaphysical meaning.

Conspirology

With the rise of the internet, conspiracy theories have become more popular than ever, and yet Russia's *konspirologiia* likely occupies a leading place in the world. It is the basis of state-historical narratives: America or "Gayropa" – all evil comes from outside. This is just as true for Napoleon's Russian campaign of 1812 as it is for the collapse of the Soviet Union: In the former case it was "the West" that invaded the Russian territory; in the latter it was "the West" that incited the republics to secede from the Soviet Union in order to then incorporate them into its own sphere of influence of NATO and the EU.

At first glance, however, the October Revolution is not particularly well suited for conspiracy theories since the responsible Bolsheviks created the glorious Soviet empire and the KGB. And yet a lot of conspiracy interpretations feed into the official historical narratives, not to mention the unofficial ones. For one thing, the old thesis of the revolution (and hence the introduction of a communist system) as a conspiracy of politicians from the liberal parties and the Freemasons, with a lot of overlap between the two groups, is being reactivated. These groups allegedly weakened the tsarist empire from inside and ultimately also from the outside, since they were allegedly connected with international Freemasonry. For instance, the cultural institute Russkiy mir, a soft-power tool of cultural diplomacy, which was founded in 2007 as an equivalent of the Goethe and Cervantes Institutes, is instrumental in spreading this conspiracy theory.[11] Sometimes the liberals and Freemasons get mixed together with the Bolsheviks and the

11 Vera Tolz, "Modern Russian Memory of the Great War, 1914–1920," in Eric Lohr et al. (eds.), *The Empire and Nationalism at War* (Bloomington, IN: Slavica Publishers, 2014), 278–80.

German Wilhelmine Empire, and later Britain and the USA, especially when the Brest-Litovsk Peace Treaty and the Russian Civil War are concerned: They allegedly cut vitally necessary body parts off the Great Russian Empire, particularly by pushing it out of Eastern Europe. In this variant of the conspiracy theory, the Russian liberals look more like handmaidens of Anglo-American governments, ones who strove for a unipolar world and ultimately global dominance.[12] It is important to remember that none of these historical narratives strictly adheres to logic, stringency or purity. Putin, for instance, in summer of 2012 in front of military officials mentioned the "the national betrayal by the Bolshevik leadership" as a cause of Russia's defeat in World War I – despite the great esteem in which he holds the Soviet empire and its secret services.[13]

The conspiracy theories that get circulated on the Russian internet or in popular books is another thing altogether, even if the boundary between official and unofficial representations of history often gets blurred. In popular literature, cyclical historical theories are rampant.[14] For adherents of these cyclical theories the parallels are all too obvious: In 1914 in the west of the empire a short war began that first gave a boost to the tsar's popularity; in 2014 in the south of the empire a short war began in Crimea that first gave a great boost to the president's popularity. Three years later the structural problems of the tsarist and Putinist regimes had become so obvious that these were swept away, and deservedly so. There is only one kind of interpretation that official representations stay clear of in post-Soviet times: anti-Semitic ones. Anti-Semitic interpretations of the revolution flourish on the web and elsewhere, often by reactivating older texts, often from the revolutionary epoch itself, such as the *Protocols of the Elders of Zion*.[15]

Color Revolutions

Today's memory of the Russian Revolution is haunted by the possibility of a revolution in contemporary Russia, a revolution by the Putin system and its

12 See Nataliia Narochnitskaia, *Velikie voiny XX veka stoletiia. Reviziia i pravda istorii* (Moscow: Veche, 2010).
13 Tolz, "Modern Russian Memory," 257.
14 See, e.g., voprosik.net/cikly-rossijskoj-istorii/. For a skeptical assessment of cyclical theories of history, see *Istoriia i antiistoriia. Kritika "novoi khronologii" Akademika A. T. Fomenko. Analiz otveta A. T. Fomenko*, 2nd edn. (Moscow: Yazyki russkoi kul'tury, 2001).
15 See Marlène Laruelle, "Conspiracy and Alternate History in Russia: A Nationalist Equation for Success?," *Russian Review* 71, 4 (Oct. 2012), 565–80.

ruling economic-political elite. This potential revolution in contemporary Russia surfaces in a variety of forms. For one thing, it is well known that the current elite is extremely dismissive of the so-called color revolutions of the 2000s – Georgia's Rose Revolution of 2003, Ukraine's Orange Revolution of 2004, Kyrgyzstan's Tulip Revolution of 2005 and most recently Ukraine's Euromaidan in 2014. There were also the protests in Moscow and other major Russian cities in 2011–12 following the Medvedev–Putin job swap – which transpired in late September 2011 and was perceived as anti-constitutional by large parts of the voting population – and the rigged Duma elections of 4 December 2011. The protests lasted until well into the spring, even beyond the 4 March 2012 presidential elections, and became known as the "Snow Revolution."

The current elite denies the legitimacy of all of these color revolutions by depicting them as the result of negative outside intervention – as orchestrated by Western secret services and Russian nongovernmental organizations, which in turn are also represented as puppet organizations of Western secret services. The anti-foreign agent law (signed by the reelected President Putin in July 2012) was, then, only the next logical step. The purported attempts at external influence are placed in long continuities – beginning with the Revolution of 1917 when "the West," the Entente, allegedly intervened, leading to the downfall of the tsarist empire. There was a spectacular case in which a line of continuity was constructed that can only be called phantasmatic: In April 2015 the University of Nottingham historian Sarah Badcock's doctoral student was expelled from Russia on the grounds that she had entered the country for doctoral research in the archives with a tourist rather than a scholar's scientific visa. In reality, the Russian news agency *LifeNews* reported, the doctoral student was a foreign spy and a stooge of her doctoral supervisor who "works on subjects the purpose of which is the West's attempt to create in Russia the conditions for a 'color revolution.'" Badcock and her supervisee both work on 1917. An American colleague of Badcock's commented wryly that the supposed causal nexus between research on the Russian Revolution and the sponsoring of a color revolution against Putin is as plausible as the claim that "Starship Enterprise might have successfully countered the Hunnic invasions."[16]

16 See www.theguardian.com/world/2015/apr/03/british-student-laura-sumner-ordered-leave-russia-media-speculate-spying.

Since 2014, however, the internal and external political situation of Russia has deteriorated further. Wars in eastern Ukraine and Syria, a serious conflict with Turkey after a Russian fighter jet was shot down in November 2015 and a massive economic crisis have created a situation in which, in early 2016, an early end of the Putin regime is discussed more and more often.[17] Sociopolitically, Russia has become even more polarized. Even if Putin's popularity reached an all-time high after the annexation of Crimea, minorities are radicalizing, on both the left and the right – in early 2016 a group formed under "the Donetsk People Republic's" separatist leader Igor Strelkov that calls itself "Committee of 25 January" based on its founding date. Many of these radicals are counting on a revolution in 2017, a vision of the future that is partly founded on the popular cyclical ideas about history. The key question is whether these radicals will manage to mobilize larger segments of society – this is not that far-fetched, especially if the general population's economic situation continues to worsen and at the same time new photographs of opulent palaces in Crimea or new luxury presidential airplanes with white leather seats and the double eagle logo, their own onboard fitness studios, and golden sinks and faucets continue to surface in the public sphere.[18]

What About Professional History-Writing?
Irrelevant

In Soviet times for professional historians studying "Red October" meant studying the holiest of holies. To be sure, Soviet historiography of 1917 was subject to ebbs and flows, to changes so momentous that they would merit their own scholarly investigation. Now, it bears noting that these traditionally influential historians of the revolution, who are still institutionally based at the historical institutes of the Academy of Sciences in Moscow and St. Petersburg, have not been consulted in the preparations for commemorating 1917. While professional Russian historians of the revolution are inundated with

17 See, e.g., from a pro-Western, economically liberal perspective, www.ryzkov.ru/in dex.php?option=com_content&view=article&id=28414&catid=11:2011-12-26-10-30-14 &Itemid=6; http://www.mk.ru/politics/2015/09/18/revolyuciya-2017-goda.html (18 Sep. 2015). For a different perspective, see the sociologist Lev Gudkov: www.m k.ru/politics/2015/08/06/pochemu-v-2017-godu-v-rossii-ne-budet-revolyucii.html (8 Aug. 2015).
18 See home.bt.com/news/world-news/tsar-putins-100m-planes-cause-outrage-among-russian-taxpayers-11363971207607.

invitations to Western centenary conferences during 2017, there is no interest in them in their own country.

Yet there is plenty of interest in history and a highly active Russian politics of memory. Suffice it to recall here a few milestones of the étatization of this memory. In 2007 a Kremlin-supported new history schoolbook appeared, which explained the victory in World War II largely as a result of Stalin's forced industrialization.[19] In February 2009 Russia's president at the time, Dmitrii Medvedev, called for "criminal liability" in the case of "denying the USSR's victory in the Great Patriotic War," and in May of that year a "Presidential Commission of the Russian Federation to Counter Attempts to Falsify History to the Detriment of Russia's Interests" was founded.[20] In February 2013 Putin called for a unified schoolbook that would end the pluralism of various textbooks used in Russian schools and that would be "free of inner contradictions and double entendres."[21] One of the "inner contradictions" that figured prominently in the guidelines of the historians' commission was the large "loss of human lives" in World War II. Suggestions that the staggering numbers of casualties in the war might at least partially be the result of Stalin's misguided policies, his insufficient preparations for the upcoming showdown with Nazi Germany (being caught by surprise on 22 June 1941) and his strategic mistakes as supreme commander will not appear on the pages of the unified schoolbook.[22] In 2014 an article by the German doctoral student Sebastian Stopper, who had defended his history thesis on partisans during World War II in the Briansk region, was placed, right after Mussolini's writings, on the Russian Ministry of Justice's "list of extremist materials." The real reason was that Stopper had proven that a German general was not killed by partisans in 1943 but instead had died a natural death in 1979.[23] And in March 2016 Sergei Mironenko, the Russian

19 On this, see the essays by David Brandenberger, Vladimir Solonari, Boris Mironov and Elena Zubkova in the special issue *"Ex Tempore:* Toward a New Orthodoxy? The Politics of History in Russia Today," *Kritika: Explorations in Russian and Eurasian History* 10, 4 (2009). The quotation about Stalin as "an effective manager" does not figure in Filippov's school textbook. On the genealogy and circulation of this canard, see svpressa.ru/blogs/article/110256/.

20 See www.bbc.com/russian/russia/2009/05/090519_medvedev_history.shtml; rg.ru/2009/05/20/komissia-dok.html.

21 See graniru.org/Politics/Russia/President/m.236312.html; rg.ru/2013/04/25/uchebnik-anons.html; latitude.blogs.nytimes.com/2013/02/25/the-single-logic-of-continuous-rus sian-history/.

22 See www.reuters.com/article/us-russia-history-idUSBRE9AH0JK20131118; http://poli t.ru/article/2013/09/18/history/.

23 See www.spiegel.de/politik/ausland/russland-stuft-deutschen-historiker-stopper-als-extremisten-ein-a-974971.html; www.zeit.de/2015/18/kriegsende-1945-gedenken-russland/komplettansicht.

archival administration's long-serving director, was fired because his institution had issued a publication that cast doubt on the myth of General Ivan Panfilov's (and the Panfilovites') defense of Moscow in 1941.[24] In a word, the boundaries of interpretation are narrow for World War II because it is *the* site of memory; in the case of the Russian Revolution they are quite flexible because the revolution is considered less important.

Hence "a screaming silence" will dominate the forms of official memory of Red October in 2017, according to revolutionary historian Nikolai Mikhailov (Academy of Sciences, St. Petersburg). Not silence, but "eclecticism" with some elements condemning the revolution, and others praising it, will dominate official memory, opines his colleague Boris Kolonitsky (European University, St. Petersburg). They are in agreement that, if any official commemoration does take place, it will be produced outside academic, professional history. For instance, no official commemorative commissions, which professional historians might have been invited to, have been formed. And while the Ministry of Culture has allegedly provided a lot of money for popular films on the revolution, professional historians have not been consulted, nor has it transpired among them what these films are about.

Time and again one issue has been a bone of contention between official commemoration and professional history in contemporary Russia: the new (old) sacralization of power, here embodied in the monarchy. "How can one speak critically about Nicholas II in public after he was canonized on 20 August 2000?," asks Kolonitsky. The canonization of historical actors is a problem few Western historians have to contend with, at least so far. Since Charlie Hebdo it has become less absurd for artists and scholars in the West that the practice of their secular professions might "violate religious feelings." Here Russia might become, much like after 1917, a laboratory for the future for Paris, London or Berlin.

Summary and Prospect

One year before the 100th anniversary of the Russian Revolution that engendered the world's first communist state, the picture on the ground is a heterogeneous one, made up of a variety of often-contradictory memories. Among these are the Putin government's fear of a color revolution-like regime change; the positive meaning of the October Revolution for a part of the current elite, whose roots go back to Soviet institutions and the KGB;

24 See www.the-american-interest.com/2016/06/06/in-putins-russia-history-is-subversive/.

and the negative meaning of both 1917 revolutions for the Russian Orthodox Church. The government does not have to take into consideration nostalgic revolutionary memory "from below," since such revolutionary memory lacks broad support in the population. Revolutionary nostalgia is restricted to the KPRF and real, large-scale, popular memory initiatives, as those that defend the memory of the Great Patriotic War are noticeably absent. There are no signs, for instance, that Sergei Kurginian's Soviet nostalgic organization "Essence of Time" (Sut' vremeni) has adopted the revolution as a cause, even though it envisions a Russian Orthodox-cum-Communist "USSR 2.0" with global messianic aspirations.

But it is clear that the centenary will not be forgotten, even if the state chooses to practice "screaming silence." Unresolved historical-symbolic problems, such as Lenin's dead body in the country's symbolic center on Red Square, ensure in very concrete, physical fashion that the anniversary is kept alive. Whether one likes it or not, 1917 is "marked," and this markedness is driven not least by a strong cyclical-historical subterranean current, instantiated in cultural products, such as Olga Slavnikova's novel *2017* from 2006, a love/environmental disaster story set in the capitalist Riphean (read: Ural) Mountains in which the city authorities, in honor of the centenary, stage a costumed fight between members of the Red Cavalry and the White Guards that gets horribly out of hand. Or the 2012 Russian-American dystopian science fiction film *Branded*, known as *Moscow 2017* in Russian – a title based on a scene in which the main protagonist, a marketing executive, calls our present age the "era of marketing" and credits Vladimir Lenin with starting it, pointing to Soviet advertising and propaganda.[25] This trend also moves another year into focus: 1937. The impending eightieth anniversary of the pinnacle of Stalinist violence is always present in all emancipatory memory initiatives of 1917. Liberation – and indeed Soviet-style communism – can end, two decades later, in a bloody tsunami of terror. That too belongs to the legacy of communism.[26]

25 Further, see (in the field of the arts) e.g. Rosalind Brodsky's time travel project at the London Institute for Militronics and Advanced Time Interventionality (IMATI), in which she travels from 2017 back to the Moscow of 1917: Suzanne Treister, "From Fictional Videogame Stills to Time Travelling with Rosalind Brodsky, 1991–2005," in Andy Clarke and Grethe Mitchell (eds.), *Videogames and Art* (Bristol: Intellect Books, 2007), 138–41.

26 One of the fears of the Putin–Medvedev government seems to be that "genuine" civil society will usurp the memory of 1937 and thus render this memory hard to channel and control. Hence the – liberal, at first glance – condemnation of the repressions, encapsulated in the cipher 1937, during summer 2015 are best understood as a controlled étatization of the memory of Stalinism. See www.themoscowtimes.com/article.php?id=528254 (19 Aug. 2015).

Bibliographical Essay

The Russian Revolution was at the heart of Soviet and Western historical research from the beginning of Soviet-style communism until its very end on 31 December 1991. Writing about the revolution always meant taking an ethical-political stance and situating oneself within the bipolar politics of the Cold War. In the post-Soviet period the revolution became depoliticized – and insignificant: The center of research gravity moved first to Stalinism during the 1930s, then to the war years, later to the postwar period, and more recently to the Khrushchev and Brezhnev periods. Only as the centenary of the revolution came closer was there a spate of new books and articles on the Russian Revolution with the crescendo likely reaching its height in 2017 itself. The memory of 1917 – collective and group memories, and the politics and symbols of memory, as well as speculative forecasts about what these variegated practices of commemorating the revolution might look like in 2017 – have yet to become the subject of monographic research, although the first journalistic treatments have appeared, most of them online.

With the approaching centenary, new surveys of the historiography of the Russian Revolution and its legacy for communism have been published. In a 2015 special issue of the journal *Kritika*, S. A. Smith provides a state-of-the-art overview, forcefully arguing for a recovery of the central category of class that typified all of the historical actors in 1917 and more so than in any other revolution – this category had moved out of sight during the new cultural history of the Russian Revolution: "The Historiography of the Russian Revolution 100 Years on," *Kritika: Explorations in Russian and Eurasian History* 16, 4 (2015), 733–49. In the same issue Boris Kolonitsky, arguably the most important Russophone author writing on the Russian Revolution today, criticizes the preponderance of memoiristic accounts of the revolution and thus the lapse into the main interpretations of the historical actors and the political currents they embodied. He also bemoans the emphasis on elites that comes with the rise of the memoir genre in Russian post-Soviet history-writing of the revolution – less powerful, less literate people thus move out of focus: "On Studying the 1917 Revolution: Autobiographical Confessions and Historiographical Predictions," *Kritika: Explorations in Russian and Eurasian History* 16, 4 (2015), 751–68. Other influential surveys of the historiography written from the perspective of cultural history (and after the end of the Soviet Union) include Stephen Kotkin, "1991 and the Russian Revolution: Sources,

Conceptual Categories, Analytical Frameworks," *Journal of Modern History* 70, 2 (Jun. 1998), 384–425, and, from the perspective of social history (and during the early 1980s before the end of the Soviet Union) by Ronald Suny, "Toward a Social History of the October Revolution," *American Historical Review* 88, 1 (Feb. 1983), 31–52. The historiographical sections in Sheila Fitzpatrick, *The Russian Revolution* (Oxford: Oxford University Press, 1982), Rex A. Wade, *The Russian Revolution, 1917* (Cambridge: Cambridge University Press, 2000), and S. A. Smith, *The Russian Revolution: A Very Short Introduction* (Oxford: Oxford University Press, 2002), still remain excellent places to start. Edward Acton, Vladimir Cherniaev and William Rosenberg (eds.), *Critical Companion to the Russian Revolution 1914–1921* (London: Arnold, 1997), contains superb surveys of Russian-language work as well.

The general historiography of the Russian Revolution over the past five or so decades was for the most part dominated by social-historical studies that downplayed the role of high politics and individuals: e.g. Leopold Haimson's key essays from 1964 and 1955 republished as *Russia's Revolutionary Experience, 1905–1917: Two Essays* (New York: Columbia University Press, 2005) and *The Russian Marxists and the Origins of Bolshevism* (Boston, MA: Beacon, 1968), and the many works by Alexander Rabinowitch, beginning with *Prelude to Revolution: The Petrograd Bolsheviks and the July 1917 Uprising* (Bloomington: Indiana University Press 1968). During the 1990s and 2000s several (partly Lotman- and Geertz-, partly Foucault-inspired) cultural-cum-political histories appeared: Richard Wortman, *Scenarios of Power: Myth and Ceremony in Russian Monarchy*, vol. II (Princeton: Princeton University Press, 1995); Mark D. Steinberg, *Moral Communities: The Culture of Class Relations in the Russian Printing Industry 1867–1907* (Berkeley: University of California Press, 1992); Mark D. Steinberg, *Proletarian Imagination: Self, Modernity, and the Sacred in Russia, 1910–1925* (Ithaca: Cornell University Press, 2002); Mark D. Steinberg, *Petersburg Fin de Siècle* (New Haven: Yale University Press, 2013); Peter Holquist, *Making War, Forging Revolution: Russia's Continuum of Crisis, 1914–1921* (Cambridge, MA: Harvard University Press, 2002); and now also Jonathan Smele, *The "Russian" Civil Wars, 1916–1926: Ten Years That Shook the World* (Oxford: Oxford University Press, 2016). Holquist's influential work, especially, has shifted the focus from October to the civil war and more generally from the revolution as an event to *longue durée* practices such as surveillance that enveloped all of the fighting parties in the civil war, including the Bolshevik Reds and monarchist Whites. Regional studies have expanded since the 1980s – these have been mitigating against the Petrograd-centrism of the historiography and highlighting the complexity and diversity on the ground beyond the major urban centers: Donald J. Raleigh, *Revolution on the Volga: 1917 in Saratov* (Ithaca: Cornell University Press, 1986); Orlando Figes, *Peasant Russia, Civil War: The Volga Countryside in Revolution (1917–1921)* (Oxford: Clarendon Press, 1991); Sarah Badcock, *Politics and the People in Revolutionary Russia: A Provincial History* (Cambridge: Cambridge University Press, 2007). Popular, widely read accounts include both the conservative, political history by Richard Pipes and a new social history in which a cast of characters stands in for social groups: Richard Pipes, *The Russian Revolution* (New York: Knopf, 1990); Orlando Figes, *A People's Tragedy: The Russian Revolution: 1891–1924* (New York: Penguin Books, 1998).

Comparative histories of the communist revolutions in Russia and China are far and few between, not least for lack of language competency – S. A. Smith is the sole exception: *Revolution and the People in Russia and China: A Comparative History* (Cambridge: Cambridge University Press, 2008); but also see the collection by William G. Rosenberg and Marilyn B. Young (eds.), *Transforming Russia and China: Revolutionary Struggle in the Twentieth Century* (New York: Oxford University Press, 1982). Most recently comparative and entangled histories of empires include Michael Reynolds, *Shattering Empires: The Clash and Collapse of the Ottoman and Russian Empires 1908–1918* (Cambridge: Cambridge University Press, 2011); Sean McMeekin, *The Russian Origins of the First World War* (Cambridge, MA: Belknap Press of Harvard University Press, 2011); and Joshua A. Sanborn, *Imperial Apocalypse: The Great War and the Destruction of the Russian Empire* (Oxford: Oxford University Press, 2014). The centenary itself will furnish synthetic works by master historians of the revolution: Dominic Lieven, *Towards the Flame: Empire, War and the End of Tsarist Russia* (London: Allen Lane, 2015); S. A. Smith, *Russia in Revolution: An Empire in Crisis, 1890 to 1928* (Oxford: Oxford University Press, 2017); Mark D. Steinberg, *The Russian Revolution, 1905–1921* (Oxford: Oxford University Press, 2017); Laura Engelstein, *Russia in Flames: War, Revolution, Civil War, 1914–1921* (New York: Oxford University Press, 2017).

As for the memory of the Russian Revolution, Frederick Corney's *Telling October: Memory and the Making of the Bolshevik Revolution* (Ithaca: Cornell University Press, 2004) was a milestone in retracing early Bolshevik commemorative practices, showing that October before the mid 1920s was not a central site of memory and had to be actively implanted in collective memory. More generally on the Putin-era politics of history, especially as relates to the 2007 Filippov textbook, see the articles by David Brandenberger, Vladimir Solonari, Boris Mironov and Elena Zubkova in the special issue, *"Ex Tempore*: Toward a New Orthodoxy? The Politics of History in Russia Today," *Kritika: Explorations in Russian and Eurasian History* 10, 4 (2009). On conspirology and cyclical theories of history, see Marlène Laruelle, "Conspiracy and Alternate History in Russia: A Nationalist Equation for Success?," *Russian Review* 71, 4 (Oct. 2012), 565–80.

24

Thirty Years After: The End of European Communism in Historical Perspective

CHARLES S. MAIER

"A spectre is haunting Europe . . . " The most famous phrase to emerge from the revolutions of 1848 has come true in a totally unintended way: 170 years later, communism in Europe is just a spectre, a ghostly memory. This movement – which seemed so frightening during 1848, the Paris Commune of 1870–71, the aftermath of World War I and the Spanish Republic of 1936–39, which took power in Russia in 1917 and was imposed on Eastern Europe after 1945 – has become merely history and no more than hardly remembered at that. To be sure, nominally communist regimes still govern China, North Korea, Vietnam and Cuba – but in diverse ways radically different from the original Marxist-Leninist model.

How do we explain this millennial collapse? This chapter attempts an interpretation that focuses on the global transformations of political economy that not only led up to 1989, but have continued their transformative impact until the present. State socialism was an economic system that saw itself in perpetual competition with "capitalism." It judged itself comparatively, as have its historians, but even without yielding to the comparative framework it must always look different with the passage of time.

To focus on political economy is not to dismiss ideas and politics, but to relate them to the institutions that structured material conditions. Citizens in Eastern Europe resented the regime of controlled information, secret police and informers, one-party rule, arbitrary denial of privileges, and the whole apparatus of repression, even if some had sympathized earlier with social goals. The transformations in the Soviet Union unfolding under Mikhail Gorbachev gave hope that Moscow would not again repress the protests against these instruments of rule as it had in Berlin in 1953, in Budapest in 1956 and in Prague twelve years later and that had led General Wojciech Jaruzelski to impose martial law in Poland in 1982. The possibility of successful protest, it slowly became evident, was finally clear.

Intellectuals certainly recalled their disillusion with the ideals that had led them to embrace state socialism: "[C]hildren of the twentieth century, who had come to thirst for belief . . . carried away by frightful and beautiful plans for transforming the world, aware of themselves as belonging to an elite and simultaneously fascinated by being part of a community, a member of a collectivity," gradually or suddenly awoke.[1] But individual dissent did not bring down the system. It led to applause from the West and jail sentences at home. Collective solidarities had to be formed anew and energized as they had been in Poland in 1981 and again at the end of the 1980s. In a system that depended on barbed-wire frontiers, borders had to be opened, as they were in Hungary in the summer of 1989 – a breach that catalyzed a frantic emigration. And citizens had also to mobilize on the streets at home, as they did by the autumn of 1989 in the German Democratic Republic (GDR), and thereafter in Czechoslovakia.

For a decade after the collapse, or what came to be called "the transition" (or *Wende* in German), political analysis suggested that the organizations of civil society – the collective organizations that had resisted regime control – had successfully reasserted their aspirations and their demands. Trade unions and the church in Poland, peace organizers and then peaceful street protesters in the GDR, nationalists in Hungary and courageous intellectuals in Czechoslovakia had by dint of peaceful protest brought down the self-coopting guardians of party orthodoxy.[2] Despite the somewhat unfortunate term "implosion," which deprecated the role of the activists, sometimes intentionally, this was true; the courageous organizers and protesters transformed the political landscape. The "round tables" endowed them for critical months with a quasi-constitutional institution. But their activity became efficacious only under certain conditions. Significantly, the organizations of civil society and the political groups that emerged so dramatically and encouragingly in the late 1980s did not really function well over the long run. Poland's Solidarność, the Czech Civic Forum, the GDR's New Forum and all the other organizations

---

1 Carola Stern, *In der Netzen der Erinnerung. Lebensgeschichten zweier Menschen* (Reinbek bei Hamburg: Rohwolt, 1989), 11–13.
2 On "civil society" and the opposition to the communist regimes of Eastern Europe, see John Ehrenberg, *Civil Society: The Critical History of an Idea* (New York: New York University Press, 1999), 173–98, and further reading in the Bibliographic Essay.

soon fractured and found it difficult to perpetuate their coalitions of protest. This chapter thus asks what ambient conditions allowed civil society to reclaim a voice that for a decisive moment could transform the regimes they lived under.

Undoubtedly a major order of causation was economic; the centrally planned economies performed badly in comparison with the Organisation for Economic Co-operation and Development (OECD) states. And comparison was integral to the metric that the state-socialist societies themselves insisted on. They continually pointed to achievements in themselves: industrialization in Eastern Europe, recovery from the devastation of World War II, the production of durable goods, some showpiece urban centers and buildings. But citizens who could travel or received news from the West understood that progress took place far slower, consumer goods, varieties of food, access to apartments and automobiles were scarcer and slower, and what was on offer was of inferior quality. Total factor productivity was significantly lower. Most telling, the gap seemed to widen, not close. Perhaps the most encompassing account of the reason for this inadequacy was provided by the Hungarian economist János Kornai in his theoretical summa, *The Socialist System*.[3] Kornai laid bare the reasons for the perennial scarcities and unprofitable enterprises that characterized central planning and the Soviet-dependent countries that constituted Comecon or the Council for Mutual Economic Assistance (CMEA).

But economic causation should not be taken as merely a matter of prices and wages, output and consumption, or even the uncloseable productivity gap vis-à-vis the OECD. Economics incorporates moral and political assumptions, notions of legitimacy and justice, or illegitimacy and injustice. Supporters of the state-socialist regimes could argue that inequality had been narrowed, especially in comparison with the West. They could point to educational access, collective child care and in some cases land reform. But the particular inequalities that ruling party officials enjoyed – even though they were usually far smaller in terms of income and privilege than Western corporate leaders preserved – remained galling enough and could give rise to a literature on the creation of a "new class." The collapse of communism, taking place as it did without violent resistance, involved a recognition that whatever legitimacy the ideology and the regimes might

3 János Kornai, *The Socialist System* (Oxford: Oxford University Press, 1992), but see also Kornai, *By Force of Thought: Irregular Memoirs of an Intellectual Journey* (Cambridge, MA: MIT Press, 2006).

once have enjoyed had long since evaporated. As Christoph Hein's Lancelot told King Arthur in his allegorical 1989 drama, *Knights of the Round Table*, "the people outside ... no longer believe in our justice and our dream ... For the people the knights of the round table are a pile of fools, idiots, and criminals."[4] This bitter acknowledgement (which of course was resisted by many of the displaced old guard, particularly in the GDR) meant abandoning the claim that a single party – especially one that had to rely on its own secret police and, at critical moments of opposition, ultimately on Soviet soldiers – really was fit to shape complex modern societies.

The socioeconomic world that communism ruled in Eastern Europe was far from the one their ideology had originally imagined. Historically, the communist parties were a creation of the era of coal and iron and steel and the heroic decades of industrialization, then of semi-legality in Eastern Europe and finally of wartime resistance. Fittingly their most ruthless leader took "steel" as the basis of his revolutionary name. Communist self-images stressed the fundamental class divisions between workers and bourgeoisie. The Marxist commitment to a labor theory of value made it cumbersome to work with concepts of demand or marginal utility. Bourgeois finance retained a certain sleight-of-hand: "All that is solid melts into air." Soviet economic planners worked with input–output tables that linked the diverse physical inputs and outputs of the economy, but the system paid less attention to the cost of capital as the measure of tradeoffs between present and future. Central planners decreed quantities and fixed prices they believed would cover costs, but enterprises hoarded inputs and, as Kornai explained, made scarcity integral to the system. Despite their professed internationalism, the regimes remained focused on the transformation of national economies.

All the premises that earlier had helped make Marxian economics plausible were changing from the mid 1960s through the 1980s. Globalization, the digital revolution and the displacement of iron and steel production and of basic consumer goods to economies with lower labor costs demanded reform of the so-called Fordist or mass-production economies, West and East. But the Western economies could turn to market incentives to restructure their industries and shift their resources; and they were wealthy enough to support workers and families through

---

4 Christoph Hein, *Die Ritter der Tafelrunde. Eine Komödie* (Frankfurt am Main: Luchterhand Literaturverlag, 1989).

an admittedly painful and often conflictual transition. It made more sense (at least according to the logic of Western capitalism) to leave large segments of the working and middle classes as a slack resource subsisting on welfare for a sustained period than to preserve noncompetitive industries. The state-socialist economies in the Soviet orbit, in contrast, found it difficult to simply shut down noncompetitive sectors or rely on market incentives and profits to generate new initiatives. Despite skilled labor and some advanced technological sectors, Soviet-style economies clung to a suicide pact with obsolescence.

Ideological erosion ineluctably accompanied the material ones. Communism, as a variant of socialism, always held out the promise of future abundance, not just in the sense of steady growth as did the Western OECD economies, but as a qualitative "leap forward," overtaking capitalism. It privileged the future over the present, and the credibility of its future ran out. The West's vision of the future, expressed in terms of continual incremental growth, remained more believable, although its own credibility may be ending as well.[5] Communism was an artifact of nineteenth- and twentieth-century industrial modernity – precisely therefore seized on by national movements that wanted to impose modernity – and it succumbed as the traits of industrial society (theorized by sociologists from Max Weber to Raymond Aron) yielded to what by the 1960s Daniel Bell and others were labeling postindustrial.[6]

The standard narrative suggests, moreover, that the fall of the communist parties, especially the Communist Party of the Soviet Union, and indeed the dissolution of the Soviet Union itself explain the disappearance or attrition of Western communist parties in Italy and elsewhere. But the evolution of the Italian party – its migration via the "Oaktree," then the "left," to the Democratic Party – and the numerical reduction of the French communists were not merely consequences of the disarray in the Kremlin. The Spanish and Italian parties had embarked on their independent course as Eurocommunists in the mid 1970s – responding in part to the opening of the post-Franco political system in Spain and the vision of a "historical compromise" in Italy, which despite the shared resistance to terrorism, could never really

---

5 See the recent history of the growth idea as institutionalized by Western economics: Matthias Schmelzer, *The Hegemony of Growth: The OECD and the Making of the Economic Growth Paradigm* (Cambridge: Cambridge University Press, 2016).

6 Raymond Aron, *Trois essais sur l'âge industriel* (Paris: Plon, 1965); Daniel Bell, *The Coming of Post-Industrial Society: A Venture in Social Forecasting* (New York: Basic Books, 1973).

be consummated. Western communism, observers generally decreed, lost its vocation with the end of the Soviet Union.

But it was not the collapse of the communist parties in Eastern Europe and the Soviet Union that undermined the communist parties in the West. Rather, the collapse of the ruling communist parties in the East and the reorientation of socialist parties in the West followed a more general loss of collectivist or leftist vision, East and West, during the 1970s and 1980s. "The times they are a-changin'," as Dylan had sung in the mid 1960s. But they were no longer changing in the way the Sixties generation had expected. The collapse of any credible social-democratic redistributionist policies in the 1970s and 1980s undermined the claims of all ideologies on the left and exerted its impact in the communist world. Lyndon Johnson's Great Society had run aground in Vietnam. The "stagflation" of the 1970s seemed to condemn Keynesian "demand management." When Margaret Thatcher declared, "There is no alternative," many among the Western left protested, but in effect acquiesced. Neither did the *tiersmondiste* vision of peasant revolution recruit mass enthusiasts once the Cultural Revolution gave way to Deng Xiaoping's reforms in China. Fidel survived, but Che perished. The grand sweep of a global left that had seemed on the offensive since the turn of the tide in World War II up through the end of the 1960s faltered in the 1970s, its great ideas (diverse as they were) exhausted.

Against that backdrop of ideological ebb and flow, the central thesis of this chapter is that the economic crisis that overtook communism was not a test for communism alone. Rather, it was part of a major systemic transition in the global political economy that has played out in different ways across the world and that everywhere has forced the abandonment or modification of all political settlements and economic doctrines. Looking ahead from the 1970s, three different regional paths were to open up. The countries of East Asia could take over the tasks of mass production, whether of steel or autos or the other goods that Western economies imported in quantity. In South Korea, Japan, Indonesia and elsewhere, interlocking family conglomerates provided organizational structure. China's post-Mao leadership under Deng Xiaoping embarked on their own state-capitalist variant. Deng understood that his rapidly developing country might preserve his party's political hold but still allow capitalist incentives to help transform its economy.[7] Early

---

7 See Ezra F. Vogel, *Deng Xiaoping and the Transformation of China* (Cambridge, MA: Harvard University Press, 2011).

enterprise zones in the Guangzhou region led the way to the unleashing of state-owned enterprises and private firms from central direction. In the long run China could also draw upon a vast countryside labor reserve no longer available in Western Europe and North America. So might other countries in the "global South," although they used market and tax incentives and not political control.

In a second fundamental evolution, West European and North American economies revealed the capacity to undergo the painful transitions required as they ceded basic industries to East Asia and emerging economies. A capital market that could respond to new incentives and the ability to shut down unprofitable industries and reallocate labor – or to support it when "redundant" – allowed economic survival and adaptation. As the years since the 1980s revealed, this was not an easy path: It often left blighted cities or "rustbelts," along with disaffected middle- and working-class groups, including youth, who have since faced high unemployment, stagnant wages and less-qualified jobs. At the same time, the Western economies relied increasingly on migrants from the less-developed economies outside their borders to fill low-wage service occupations, whether the demanding specialized skills of health care, or the less-qualified tasks in mass food preparation that replaced housewives now working outside the home, the custodial jobs required by urban development, the burgeoning security services and the cash registers of retail outlets. Over the long term such a labor market allowed the proliferation of consumer goods and even basic education, but also growing inequalities within societies.

The third path, which ended in a blind alley, was that taken by the Soviet and East European state-socialist economies that sought to preserve the industrial structures inherited from the postwar years within a planned economy. The socialist economies confronted labor as a force too potentially explosive to break up, but remained unable to provide the quality of life in the West (not to speak of the freedoms). They guaranteed employment and preserved heavy industry at tremendous ecological cost, but, without competitive products, they could not acquire the consumer goods their people yearned for and which the West and Japan produced far less expensively. Capitalism allowed liquidation that protected shareholders but laid off workers; the CMEA economies evaded bankruptcy with what Kornai termed soft budget constraints. These economies ended up in different destinations after the transition. GDR state assets were placed in a *Treuhandgesellschaft* (trusteeship corporation) and sold off as individual properties to Federal Republic of Germany (FRG) firms that would absorb their short-term losses. Czech, Slovak and Hungarian industry had already sought to integrate partially with the West and after the transition could serve as *maquiladora* subsidiaries of Western firms or make a go of it as relatively low-wage manufacturers in the more competitive European environment. In Bulgaria, Romania and above all Russia, the large public-sector firms ended up often in the hands of new oligarchs, who were allied with the postcommunist leadership.[8]

The events of 1989–91 – the transitions in Eastern Europe and the Soviet Union – were interpreted as a political triumph for liberal democracy, as indeed they were. But they also comprised one of the major episodes of adjustment that the world economy and its political frameworks have undergone in the long arc of global development from the 1960s to today. The same changes whose progress as of the 1970s and 1980s helped undermine the centrally planned economies continued to intensify and severely challenged the capitalist economies of the early twenty-first century. The advent of a post-Fordist economy (to use that short-hand term for a stage of development that was less dependent on assembly lines, more diverse in terms of manufactured output, and more reliant on advanced electronic components and services and on a labor force that was harder to organize collectively) helped to undermine state socialism. Its continued development challenged capitalist economies. So too did the continuing geographical transformation of the global economy, notably the reemergence of Asian countries, particularly China but also Southeast Asia, Japan and South Korea, as powerful centers of industrial production. Employment structures changed and vast numbers of workers migrated, not only from country to city, but also internationally and across continents. As part of this massive reshuffling of work opportunities, the inherited representation of labor was significantly weakened. These changes had to transform the assumptions and expectations on which perhaps seventy years of economic and political objectives had been constructed. What the Italian sociologist Aris Accornero has dubbed the century of labor, in which societies organized themselves toward production and work, became

8 On outcomes of the transition, see Gérard Roland (ed.), *Economies in Transition: The Long-Run View* (Basingstoke: Palgrave-Macmillan in association with the UN University-World Institute for Development Economics Research, 2012).

transformed.[9] The craft and industrial trade unions that had defended a more collective organization of the economy were diminished in numbers and often in the radicalism of their claims. The final dimension of these epochal transformations was the vast expansion of financial capital as a generator of speculative wealth and in effect the lubricant of all the other changes, an elusive trend whose role was often obscured. I will return to the revolution of financial capital, but must first comment on the original dislocations, West and East, that opened up at the end of the 1960s and intensified through the following decade.

The economic circumstances that undermined state socialism are covered in André Steiner's chapter and other publications and need not be repeated here. State socialism was a blunt instrument, more suitable for rapid industrialization, reconstruction and infrastructural projects than for progressing to a sophisticated consumer economy. It was imposed on Eastern Europe after devastating wartime destruction (Czechoslovakia excepted). The new regimes in Eastern Europe confronted a peasantry resentful at collectivization, which was successfully resisted in Poland. They had no source of foreign capital equivalent to the surpluses that the United States could provide. Whereas Western Europe moved quickly to build an interlocked regional economy under the benevolent hegemony of US foreign (and military) assistance, the East European economies set about the transformation from agriculture to industrialization that the Western economies had undertaken in the previous century. East European progress from 1949 to 1973 was significant, with growth rates running at almost 4 percent until the 1960s, but the gap between West and East seemed to increase.

Central planning led to dilemmas of production and distribution that the Western powers did not have to cope with. No price system equilibrated supply and demand or signaled when output of commodities was too high or insufficient. The need to meet plan quotas, dictated from the center, led to hoarding and perpetual scarcity. The consolidation of firms and the nationalization of enterprise stifled the artisanal trades that were required for quality to be maintained. By the 1960s communist economists were advocating a degree of autonomy for state firms with the right to retain profits. Some called for the freeing of prices to inaugurate a "market socialism" that would allow market-clearing prices, even as it preserved

9 Aris Accornero, *Era il secolo del lavoro* (Bologna: Il Mulino, 1997), 22, notes that the industrial struggles in the 1970s gave the appearance that working-class power was increasing, but in fact the tertiary sector was becoming more important.

public ownership. But partial attempts to institute these policies led to bottlenecks and shortages, not an easier modern economy. And when the political events associated with the Prague Spring threatened to undermine communist party influence throughout Europe the reforms were reversed.[10] Could a more radical reliance on a price system have rescued the socialist economies? Kornai remained skeptical: "The truth was that only a capitalist economy could operate a genuine – not a sham or simulated – market economy ... Were not the reformers fostering illusions? Were they not raising vain hopes in many naïve, benign people with semi-socialist convictions that professed 'anti-capitalist,' Marxist-Leninist principles could all be reconciled?"[11]

Communism failed the tests of political and economic reform in an increasingly competitive world that it itself encouraged. Instead, the Soviet Union relied on a transitory surplus of a key natural resource, petroleum, to reconsolidate its imperial hold. So long as the Soviets kept the price of oil below the high world-market prices (the latter politically determined by the OPEC price hikes of 1974 and 1979), the satellites drew some benefit as the USSR delivered petroleum to its satellites below world-market prices. East Germany exploited its own lignite deposits to generate electricity and sold the refined Soviet oil to Western Europe to earn needed Western currency. But as the real world-market price of oil tended to stabilize, the advantage Moscow's partners could draw became less important.

At the same time the Soviets attempted to run their own protected or neomercantilist zone for trade and exchange – the Council for Mutual Economic Assistance – to create greater interdependence among their satellites and minimize the goods and services purchased from the West in Western currencies. Intra-Comecon debts were to be settled in notional exchange rubles. In fact, however, each economy found that to satisfy consumer expectations, they needed Western goods and assistance, thus requiring convertible currencies.[12] The systemic strains were concealed by

---

10 For Evsei Liberman, see Emil Bej, "Some Aspects of Industrial Planning Under Brezhnev–Kossygin Rule," *Jahrbuch der Wirtschaft Osteuropas* 13, 1 (1989), 176–97; for Ota Šik, see his *Plan and Market Under Socialism* (White Plains, NY: International Arts and Sciences Press, 1967) and his post-Prague Spring thoughts, *The Third Way: Marxist-Leninist Theory and Modern Industrial Society*, trans. Martin Sling (London: Wildwood House, 1976).
11 Kornai, *By Force of Thought*, 279.
12 Randall Warren Stone, *Satellites and Commissars: Strategy and Conflict in the Politics of Soviet-Bloc Trade* (Princeton: Princeton University Press, 1996). See also Michael Marrese and

borrowing abroad: Edward Gierek's Polish government embarked on a credit spree from 1970 onward, following violent clashes with workers protesting austerity programs. The GDR quickly followed. "Increasing foreign trade means we increasingly confront the principles of the world market," as Alfred Neumann, one of the East German Politburo's old-timers warned the Council of Ministers when the fragile system began to crumble. "Increased indebtedness to the nonsocialist world is not possible. We've gone as far as we can politically. Otherwise we'll get into a situation that is politically dangerous, and in that case our comrades in the Volkspolizei and the Ministry for State Security won't be any help at all."[13] Egon Krenz, who replaced Erich Honecker in October 1989, reported that debt service on the US$ 26.5 billion owed in 1989 would require more than 60 percent of export earnings. The debt, another critical insider, Gerhard Schürer, charged, had begun to spiral in the early 1970s when Honecker had succeeded Walter Ulbricht and the Eighth Party Congress approved the "unity of social and economic policy," a generous commitment to social policy as well as investment. Hungary allowed state enterprises to produce for their own profit once they fulfilled a state quota. By the late 1980s they finally accepted that they had incurred a major debt burden.

The sense of panic probably exceeded the real impact of the debt; what the Central Committees suddenly comprehended was that they had no plausible strategy for diminishing the burden. Emerging markets have confronted periodic debt crises and have survived, albeit by enduring harsh recessions (Argentina, Brazil, Southeast Asia). But deprivation of living standards threatened renewed political upheavals that the East European regimes believed they could not incur. The workers' and peasants' states lived in fear of their own subjects. The Soviets also had to become the privileged purchaser for

Jan Vanous, *Soviet Subsidization of Trade with Eastern Europe: A Soviet Perspective* (Berkeley: University of California Press, 1983); and Vlad Sobell, *The CMEA in Crisis: Toward a New European Order* (New York: Praeger, 1990). For the economic difficulties as experienced by East Germany in particular, see Charles S. Maier, *Dissolution: The Crisis of Communism and the End of East Germany* (Princeton: Princeton University Press, 1997), ch. 2.

13 Sitzung des Ministerrats vom 19. Okt. 1919: Bundessarchiv, DC 20 1/3/2861, Bl. 89, cited in Maier, *Dissolution*, 59. There is a large literature on the growing indebtedness of the Eastern bloc. For citations as well as a summary, see André Steiner, *The Plans That Failed: An Economic History of the GDR*, trans. Ewald Oser (New York: Berghahn, 2010); and Stephen Kotkin, "The Kiss of Debt: The East Bloc Goes Borrowing," in Niall Ferguson, Charles S. Maier, Erez Manela and Daniel S. Sargent (eds.), *The Shock of the Global: The 1970s in Perspective* (Cambridge, MA: Harvard University Press, 2010), 80–93.

CMEA goods even as they undertook a missile-modernization program – they were overstretched by the 1980s, which placed before them a choice they could hardly evade: Either dismantle the planned economies or run them by tightening political compulsion – the attempted answer of the Yurii Andropov interlude. All these challenges were occurring as a host of developments were transforming the technological possibilities of society: The transistors of 1947 were followed by integrated circuits. Home computers that offered 264 kilobytes of RAM would be exponentially improved. Ronald Reagan's commitment to the Strategic Defense Initiative ("Star Wars") threatened to ratchet up the claims of military expenditure.

Still, the difficulty of Western economies attracted just as much attention in the 1970s. The working-class militance of the late 1960s in France and Italy, then the impact of the OPEC oil price hike, unleashed a decade of inflation and significant unemployment. The international architecture of capitalism also seemed at risk as the United States abandoned its commitment to currency convertibility in 1971 and forced a new system of parities as it transitioned to free exchange. The capitalist economies of the 1970s, in which governments felt that allowing greater inflation could reduce unemployment (a relationship summarized by the famous Phillips Curve), seemed only to generate sustained inflation. The OECD nations resorted to state-supervised wage-bargaining between unions and employer confederations – a pattern of political wage-setting dubbed neocorporatism that appeared to be a waystation to a planned economy. Labor delegations as well as industrial confederations chafed under the discipline. The Keynesian political economy seemed headed for a corporatist euthanasia.

Conservatives blamed excess wage hikes and an overdeveloped welfare state for changing capitalist incentives as well undermining entrepreneurial mentalities. Growth would be hard to restore as long as unions were powerful and pressed for generous social expenditures. States were overburdened, commentators for the Trilateral Commission argued, and the capacity for private investment reduced. Critics from earlier left positions argued that contemporary capitalism made consumption, not innovation and entrepreneurship, central to the economy. Capitalism had eroded its own moral and behavioral premises.[14]

---

14 Among other statements, see Daniel Bell, *The Cultural Contradictions of Capitalism* (New York: Basic Books, 1976).

By the end of the 1970s, more economists accepted the monetarist idea that central banks must stabilize the quantity of money by refusing to finance government deficits. They slowly abandoned Phillips Curve analyses. Exponents of the newer school of "expectations" argued that resolutely ending the belief in future monetary accommodation of their demands on the part of unions, employers and state bureaucrats would break the cycle of inflation. More importantly, at the end of the 1970s unhappy electorates rejected this twilight economy in Britain and the United States and installed Margaret Thatcher and Ronald Reagan. German Social Democrats were ousted by a hairline parliamentary vote in the Federal Republic in 1982; the socialist government of François Mitterrand, which had campaigned in 1981 on a program reminiscent of the prewar Popular Front, abandoned its strategy two years later in order to preserve the monetary alignment of the franc with the Deutschmark. The Italians moved beyond their congealed communist–Christian Democratic confrontations of convenience, abandoned efforts at a "historic compromise" and installed reformist "lay" governments drawn from and led by the smaller groups of the center-left in a coalition with the Christian Democrats. Even the Bank of Italy gained independent status, and the Bank of England gained greater autonomy from the Exchequer. The Western economies toughed out a recessionary period in the early 1980s as they endeavored to tighten monetary supplies. Governments achieved a significant stabilization of public expenditure.

Although welfare states were not dismantled, the political forces that had sustained them effectively lost the political power they had gained in the 1960s and 1970s. Whether the British coalminers or the US air traffic controllers, labor unions began their long slide from overt influence, retaining power primarily among public-sector workers. Central banks gained independence as wage indexation was modified, which meant that market outcomes had to be accepted. These reforms gave market economies the breathing space to survive, even as technology transformed them. The steel and coal sector was shut down in large measure and abandoned to the rising Asian economies.

The 1980s brought a sense of recovery to the nonsocialist economies: After initial recession, reforms seemed to lower inflation and reinvigorate production. Likewise, the European Union renewed its advance with the Single European Act, the Schengen border regime and, by 1992, the Maastricht accord and agreement on a common currency. The Western political economies seemed triumphantly affirmed by the recovery of the late 1980s, even as the centrally planned economies became increasingly discredited. The fear of communist geopolitical advance in Afghanistan, in Angola and briefly in Portugal dissipated. Gorbachev's policies of *glasnost'* and *perestroika* suggested that fundamental communist reforms were imminent; the Polish government opened talks with Solidarity representatives; the Hungarians maneuvered closer to the West. By 1990–91, Germany was unified, Václav Havel was president of Czechoslovakia, the Warsaw Pact disbanded and even the Soviet Union fragmented. Outside Eastern Europe, democracy also appeared momentarily triumphant in South Africa and South America: Under left-center governments democratic capitalism, now rebranded as "market democracy," was trump, communism a discredited memory. On the local level, Western cities arrested their apparent slide into shabbiness, crime and impoverishment and began a process of rejuvenation, gentrification and renewal.[15]

From the perspective of thirty-five years later, the East–West comparison, so decisively favorable to the West, seems more ambiguous. The recovery of the 1980s and 1990s was genuine, but also began the process that led to the great crisis and long difficulties that have marked Western economies since 2007. The unhealthy trends of the 1970s in the OECD economies that seemed most telling were the rate of inflation and the expansion of public credit. The 1980s and 1990s saw the taming of inflation and the stabilization of public debts. Labor representatives were cajoled into acceptance of anti-inflationary measures as they came to realize that nominal pay hikes did not translate into real gains; and in any case those unions that resisted were defeated in spectacular confrontations. But how could governments win the adherence of the financial and industrial interests that had also come to depend on easy credit?

Aggregate statistics suggest that national governments and central banks accomplished this task only by allowing the private banking sector and investors to create a compensatory mass of credits over the next years. The liquidity that public authorities and independent central bankers sopped

---

15 Not unrelatedly, another fundamental prediction of modernization theorists was also going awry, and with important political consequences. Confident predictions that modernity meant increasing secularism received a significant blow as political Islam secured a major success with the Iranian Revolution in 1979. But if in Iran it overturned a compliant pro-Western ruler, it gained further transnational influence with armed resistance to the Soviet occupation of Afghanistan.

up in the public sector they allowed to expand in the private sector. Private financial institutions were unleashed in every conceivable way, whether through lowered reserve requirements or new authorization to take on investment banking and lend abroad.

The readily available time series suggest a break in trend in the 1980s and a continuation of expansion thereafter: US nonfinancial corporate business debt (that is borrowing by firms not themselves in the banking business) rose modestly from US$ 174 billion (milliard) in 1970 to US$ 439 billion in 1980, hardly an increase in real terms when discounted for the cumulative inflation of the decade. By 1980 it was US$ 1,024 billion or US$ 1.24 trillion in US usage, then US$ 2.97 trillion in 2000 and US$ 5.53 trillion in 2015.[16] A related measure – the domestic credit provided by the financial sectors of every country to its own economy (including its housing sector) – also rose as a percentage of global GDP: from 80.3 percent in 1970 to 88.6 percent (1980), to 126 percent in 1990, 164 percent in 2000, 169 percent in 2010 and 180 percent in 2015. US borrowing somewhat outpaced global debt – up to 187 percent in 2010 and 195 percent in 2015.[17] Investment simultaneously poured into countries abroad: Global foreign direct investment (FDI) was US$ 10.2 billion in 1970, US$ 51.5 billion in 1980, US$ 196.3 billion in 1990, US$ 1.42 trillion in 2000 and US$ 3.0 trillion in 2007. It fell to US$ 1.4 trillion by 2009 and was back to US$ 2.0 trillion in 2015. In percentages of GDP this represented 0.5 percent in 1970 and virtually the same in 1980, but 0.9 percent in 1990, 4.3 percent in 2000 and 4.14 percent in 2006; after tumbling in the years of the 2008–14 recession, it was back to 2.7 percent in 2015. Most of these funds represented rich countries investing in other rich countries, although the emerging economies (BRICs) won an increasing share.[18]

Financial rules were decisively relaxed. As Piergiorgio Alessandri and Andrew O. Haldane point out, a centuries-old dependency was reversed. Whereas states had earlier depended on banks, banks came to depend on states.[19] At the same time banking assets grew enormously. UK banking-sector assets remained about 50 percent of GDP from 1850 to the mid 1960s,

16 FRED (Federal Reserve Bank of St. Louis), Non-Financial Corporate Business Debt, fred.stlouisfed.org/series/NCBDBIQ0275 (accessed 29 Aug. 2016).
17 International Monetary Fund, International Financial Statistics and Data Files, and World Bank and OECD GDP estimates, data.worldbank.org/indicator/FS.AST.PRVT .GD.ZS (accessed 18 Aug. 2016).
18 For the raw numbers in current US dollars, see data.worldbank.org/indicator/BX.KLT .DINV.CD.WD (accessed 28 Aug. 2016). For FDI as a percentage of GDP, see data .worldbank.org/indicator/BX.KLT.DINV.WD.GD.ZS. The term "BRICs" refers to Brazil, Russia, India and China.
19 "Banking on the State" (Bank of England, Nov. 2009).

climbed to 100 percent during the 1970s, reached about 250 percent by the end of the 1980s and about 550 percent by 2006. Returns on bank equity jumped from below 10 percent on average from 1920 to 1970 to about 20 percent in the 1970s and, after a temporary reversal in the late 1980s, surged up toward 30 percent at the end of the 1990s until 2006. Volatility on returns grew, and the central bank's support as measured by its balance sheet grew to World War II levels from the early 1990s on.

This compensatory monetary loosening, it must be emphasized, was a bipartisan policy promoted by "New Democrats" in the United States and "New Labour" in Britain. It found its major exponents in the policies of the Bill Clinton administration. The Mexican financial bailout of 1994, the subsequent effort to offset the Southeast Asia financial collapse, the repeal of the Glass–Steagall prohibition on fusing commercial and investment banks, and the periodic lowering of the Federal Reserve's interest rates to keep the equities markets advancing (or recovering) were the product of a regime that believed deeply in market democracy. All this meant that the potential for a vast expansion of credit and monetary equivalents went in search of opportunities to earn a profit – whether in emerging markets or the American housing sector, or in the stock market.

Indeed, looking back, one can discern a significant but unavowed change in the underlying parameters that financial authorities relied on to determine policy. The gold standard before World War I and the amended gold exchange standard between the wars gave priority to the fixed exchange values of currencies even at the cost of high employment. After the experience of the 1930s and World War II, macroeconomic management tended to switch from a gold standard to an implicit full-employment standard as the orienting variable. Once this "Keynesian" phase seemed to unleash unacceptable levels of inflation, central bankers restored price and exchange-rate stability as the regulative parameter in the 1980s, a priority written into the mandate of the European Central Bank. But policymakers of the 1990s followed a more contradictory course. Although the goal of price stability remained publicly inscribed, the implicit goal of policy (in the regulative sense) really became the performance of the equity markets – what might be called the Greenspan standard after the Republican banker who served as chairman of the Federal Reserve Board from 1987 until 2006, thus from Nixon through Clinton and into the George W. Bush administration. Reconciling a stable exchange rate with an implicit objective of stock-market advance meant that inflationary pressures found their outlet in asset markets rather than wages or consumer prices. This meant, as well, a continuing increase in housing prices, in a period when encouraging home ownership was likewise advanced by the federal agencies for guaranteeing home mortgages (so-called Freddie Mac and Fannie Mae) as well as private lenders. Forging a social consensus to carry policy forward meant undermining resistance on the one-time left (whether through New Democrats or New Labour) and granting the privileges of creating money to the private financial sector.

This does not mean that that the prosperity of the 1990s and early 2000s was spurious, but it was hostage to the conviction that growth must continue indefinitely. Certainly technological revolution connected with computers, electronics, miniaturization of components and telecommunications surged ahead, as did innovation in logistics. The medical sector claimed an ever greater share of GDP. Travel and hospitality services also grew, but transformation of output could outpace the retraining and redeployment of workers. Manufacturing and industry continued to migrate off shore. The United States' huge shopping centers, which provided employment for immigrants and African Americans as assembly lines shut down, sold what was woven and knitted and constructed elsewhere. China, which produced less than 20 percent of world steel output in 1970, would produce more than a third of a doubled steel output by 2006 and half the world's steel by 2015.

Most significant when considering the economic crisis that began in the United States in 2007, but then came to afflict Europe, too, was the mobilization and creation of financial capital as a source of wealth in its own right. Between the 1980s and 2006, Western capitalists restored the confident belief in ever increasing future payouts. Securitization of mortgages and debt seemed to create wealth far beyond the underlying value of hypothecated assets. Despite the financial time-bomb it concealed, subprime lending had a point: It was part of a program to broaden the groups who had a stake in asset holding. Freddie Mac and Fannie Mae were instruments of social change. Along with the growth of vast pension funds invested in equities and commercial paper, the financial and equity markets promised continuing enrichment. They made future returns far more important in the financial calculations of millions of families, especially when these families came to believe that future wealth was becoming relatively costless in the present.

Thus the Atlantic economies escaped their constraints by creating a vast amount of credit in the private sector, both for the American housing market and for commercial activity. This was a solution that was likely to increase tendencies toward inequality, as analyzed by Thomas Piketty in his recent bestseller.[20] Why did the financial economy – what David T. Bazelon had once called the paper economy – sustain apparent prosperity for so long? Viewed from a global perspective, the US and Western soft-money coalition was able to export many of the inflationary tendencies and difficulties to the emerging markets, contributing to financial crises by 1994 in Mexico (which Washington then helped to contain), by 1997 in Thailand and Indonesia, and Russia in the following year. Of course these difficulties were preprogrammed, as it were, by policy errors at home. Nonetheless, pressing credits on vulnerable economies helped produce their inflation, increased domestic debt, and led to default and/or devaluation and widespread misery. After 2008 those emerging economies fared better – in part because of the orthodox remedies that they accepted from the International Monetary Fund, in part too because of major rescue packages as in the case of the Mexican turmoil in 1994.[21] But precisely because the emerging markets behaved more prudently, the advanced capitalist economies had less ability to export the crisis. There was no Third World or ex-socialist economy large enough and precarious enough to take the fall for Western capital.

The adverse consequences were thus postponed until the period after 2008, when the contraction of debts required or led to a policy of austerity across the European countries. The West was not to escape a serious crisis, but could postpone it and work through it without any serious ideological challenge. In contrast to the global conditions prevailing when the socialist economies slowed down, there was no longer any systemic alternative to the market economies that might apparently promise an easier economic outcome. Throughout the postwar decades, the communist political economies could not isolate themselves from comparisons with the more efficient economies in the West. In particular the German–German juxtaposition, where the GDR depended upon credits from the FRG to avoid a social explosion, continually revealed the weakness of a centrally planned economy. But during the crisis of 2008 to 2015 (lasting as long as the world depression from 1931 until 1938), there was no rival economic system that beckoned on the left: State socialism was discredited and abandoned by the 1990s. While the outgoing Bush

20 Thomas Piketty, *Capital in the Twenty-First Century* (Cambridge, MA: Harvard University Press, 2014). Piketty's claim that the tendency for returns on capital to continually grow at the expense of wages and salaries is less well demonstrated than his history of how it has done so in recent decades.
21 See Ray Kiely, *The BRICs, US "Decline" and Global Transformations* (Basingstoke: Palgrave Macmillan, 2015), for analysis of the United States–BRICs relationship.

administration and the incoming Obama administration managed to pump enough liquidity into the banks to prevent a systemic collapse, the consequences were harsh. Partial fiscal stimulus (under the so-called TARP) was adopted as an emergency measure by the two US administrations but was largely precluded by the rules of the Eurozone and the EU. Since the united German economy, with its commitment to current account surpluses and balanced budgets (a social democratic government, after all, had trimmed the welfare system with the so-called Hartz IV reforms), seemed to function so robustly, there was no pressure to resort to Keynesian remedies. Discontent instead would manifest itself more in populist movements on the right than in radical doctrines on the left. Few people yearned for a return to state socialism. The centrally planned economies were afflicted by hopeless impediments – what Kornai had summarized as the economics of scarcity. From the viewpoint of information theory, they systemically distorted feedback from consumers and producers; they skewed incentives and immobilized enterprises. There should be no nostalgia.

Still, thirty years after the crisis of European communism, it is appropriate to reflect on the triumph of capitalism from the 1980s through 2006: Was the continued confidence in a leveraged future, based on the expansion of easy finance, justified or not? It presupposed the indefinite continuation of ever-increasing growth and productivity, which benefited from continuous technological innovation (the digital revolution of the era) and ironically on the vigor of China's state-capitalist advance. And as the West embraced financialization, it produced inequalities that were ineluctably to generate a populist backlash. What sort of calculus justified a bank president or the chairman of a pharmaceutical firm earning 350 times the mean per capita income, above all when so many families had to scrape by on far less? Aside from questions of equity, another consequential issue loomed: What might be the consequences of the "secular stagnation," i.e. the end to continuous growth, that some economists now predicted? Growth rates – the regulatory parameter that had eclipsed all others in the postwar decades – seemed either unable to be sustained, or increasingly inadequate as a measure of "the wealth of nations." With employment and remuneration far more precarious for so many, the meaning of growth was less clear. Were the innovations of the computer age as significant as they were transformative? Robert Gordon's persuasive study suggests that in fact after 1970 the digital innovations contributed less to general productivity and economic progress than had earlier inventions:

railroads, automobiles, air travel, containerization, air conditioning, antibiotics.[22] The percentage of GDP devoted to finance, that is to moving claims to paper wealth, grew enormously. It changed the structure of living patterns – "world cities" grew in number and size even as the global countryside was emptying. The world of work – that basic value orientation that had been so central since the proverbial expulsion from Eden – was less central. Consumption and leisure activities and social communication replaced the intense productivism of the earlier epoch. Communism suffered first from this civilizational transformation, for it had defined its role with respect to the world of labor and work. But a doctrine and set of practices that had seemed plausible during the era of industrialization, first in Europe, then among still largely peasant societies (and those often emerging from colonialism), made less sense by the late twentieth century. Whether the capitalist political economies, the great winners of 1989–91, can themselves remain unchanged is the great question that remains. In any case, historians of the future will see the outcomes for both communism and contemporary capitalism as aspects of the epochal economic transition that postindustrial society has embodied.

A decade and a half into the twenty-first century, we can look back upon the intense political conflicts of the twentieth century and ponder the fates of the great ideological movements. If communism considered as an economic system contended with capitalism, considered as a political system it confronted both fascism and multiparty democracy. In Europe fascism was defeated by communism and democracy in tandem after the greatest war in history. Forty-five years thereafter democracy apparently triumphed over communism without a final struggle. (The communist regime in China, of course, did not yield: 1989's demonstrations in Beijing were crushed. Still Chinese communism was on its way to developing a new hybrid authoritarian structure that allowed for capitalism without democracy.) As of this writing, nearly thirty years on, the anti-communist victories of 1989 seem more problematic. Authoritarianism without a mass party has recovered in Russia. And even in countries earlier designated as "the West" the question arises whether, even without a credible communist threat, fascist-like appeals might not revive as a political alternative that confronts democracies buffeted by recession and prone to inequality. The enduring power of market

---

22 Robert J. Gordon, *The Rise and Fall of American Growth: The US Standard of Living Since the Civil War* (Princeton: Princeton University Press, 2016).

capitalism to perpetuate liberal democracy, growth and affluence may yet be tested anew.

Bibliographical Essay

On the general economic record of the socialist governments after 1945, see László Bruszt, "Postwar Reconstruction and Socio-economic Transformation," in M. C. Kaser (ed.), *The Economic History of Eastern Europe 1919–1975*, vol. III, *Institutional Change with a Planned Economy* (Oxford: Clarendon, 1986). See also Barry Eichengreen, *The European Economy Since 1945* (Princeton: Princeton University Press, 1945). For theoretical reflections, see János Kornai, *By Force of Thought: Irregular Memoirs of an Intellectual Journey* (Cambridge, MA: MIT Press, 2006.); and János Kornai, *The Socialist System: The Political Economy of Communism* (Oxford: Oxford University Press, 1992). On the economic predicament of the GDR and its wider implications, see Charles S. Maier, *Dissolution: The Crisis of Communism and the End of East Germany* (Princeton: Princeton University Press, 1997).

On "civil society" and the opposition to the communist regimes of Eastern Europe, see John Ehrenberg, *Civil Society: The Critical History of an Idea* (New York: New York University Press, 1999), 173–98; Andrew Arato, "Civil Society Against the State: Poland 1980–1981," *Telos* 47 (Spring 1981), 23–47; Jean Cohen and Andrew Arato, *Civil Society and Political Theory* (Cambridge, MA: MIT Press, 1992); John Keane (ed.), *Civil Society and the State: New European Perspectives* (London: Verso, 1988); Vladimir Tismaneanu, *In Search of Civil Society: Independent Peace Movements in the Soviet Bloc* (New York: Routledge, 1990); and Vladimir Tismaneanu, *Reinventing Politics: Eastern Europe from Stalin to Havel* (New York: Free Press, 1992); as well as essays by Václav Havel, Adam Michnik and the US Helsinki Watch Committee, *Reinventing Civil Society: Poland's Quiet Revolution, 1981–1986* (New York: US Helsinki Watch Committee, 1986).

On Western ideas of growth, see Matthias Schmelzer, *The Hegemony of Growth: The OECD and the Making of the Economic Growth Paradigm* (Cambridge: Cambridge University Press, 2016). For discussions of the long inflation of the 1970s, see Leon Lindberg and Charles S. Maier (eds.), *The Politics of Global Inflation and Stagnation* (Washington, DC: Brookings Institution Press, 1987). On the economic impact of the 1970s and its consequences for Soviet-type economies, see Niall Ferguson, Charles S. Maier,

Erez Manela and Daniel S. Sargent (eds.), *The Shock of the Global: The 1970s in Perspective* (Cambridge, MA: Harvard University Press, 2010).

For an assessment of the postcommunist economic transition in some East European countries and in Russia, see Gérard Roland (ed.), *Economies in Transition: The Long-Run View* (Basingstoke: Palgrave Macmillan in association with the UN University-World Institute for Development Economics Research, 2012). On the Chinese transition, see Ezra F. Vogel, *Deng Xiaoping and the Transformation of China* (Cambridge, MA: Harvard University Press, 2011).

Index

Poland
  communist regime in
    collapse of 567–68
    and Catholic Church 321
    and women's movement 415
    and democratization 230–32
    dissidents/opposition against 23–24,
      25–26, 28, 37, 571
    shipyard workers 42
    Solidarity movement (Solidarność)
      45–46, 230–32, 236
    economic policies of 205, 207, 212, 216,
      218, 219–20, 223, 226, 227, 228
    journalists in 368
    labor unrest 42, 206
    propaganda of 361
    religious policies of 318
  Jaruzelski coup in (1981) 193
political economy, global transition of 605–20
  and collapse of communism in East Europe
    11, 600, 602–4
political reforms, by Gorbachev 255–59
politicization, of Soviet literature 385–86
politics
  and collapse of communism in East Europe
    600–2
  leftist 176, 605
    see also New Left movement
  postcommunist 277, 569–70, 575
Politizdat (publisher, Soviet Union) 366
polycentrism 183
Pons, Silvio xiv, 10–11
Pop Art, communist 349–50
Popovskii, Mark 385
popular religion, in China 322, 328
population policies, in China 412–13, 416,
  494
Pór, György 32
Portugal
  Communist Party in 189
  US military aid for 101
post-Soviet states
  communist legacies in 569, 573–74
    authoritarianism 572–76
  politics of 277
  see also Russian Federation/post-Soviet
    Russia
poverty, in China
  reduction of 484–88, 499–500
  rural areas 488
"The Power of the Powerless" (essay, Havel)
  170–71
Prague Spring (1968) 25, 36–37, 201, 401

legacy of 178–79, 184–86, 202, 350–51,
  360–62
  Soviet invasion 38, 44
price policies, in postsocialist China 455–56,
  464–65
Prince, Erik 525
privatization
  Chinese policies of 449–50, 465, 467–68,
    505–6
  of heavy industry 562–63
propaganda
  Chinese 367–71, 372–73, 374, 375
  communist 14, 356–57, 360–62, 371–72, 373,
    374–75
  Czechoslovak 360
  East German 359–60, 361, 370
  Polish 361
  Soviet 315–16, 354–56, 357, 374
    post-Stalinist 358–59, 361–66, 370, 388
protest movements
  of 1960s 24–30
  and communism 8–9
  and Cuban Revolution 30
  cultural 34–36
  legacy of 43–44
  see also peace movement; Vietnam War;
    women's movement
  in post-Soviet Russia 566
Protestantism
  in China 325, 328
  in East Germany 318–19, 321
Prúcha, Milan 345
psychiatry, Soviet repressive use of 303
public health
  in China 500, 545–46
  in Cuba 548–49
  in Soviet Union 531
public sphere in communist countries, visual
    culture in 334, 351–53
  architecture 13–14, 344–50
  late socialist 335–37, 350–51
  sculptures/monuments 337–44
  Socialist Realism 333–35, 337–38, 340–41,
    342–43
publishing industry
  late socialist 376–77
    unofficial 376–77, 380, 381–86, 395–96
  Soviet 366
Putin, Vladimir 17, 275
  presidency of Russia/Russian Federation
    by 275, 441–42, 575–76, 590–92
  and Tikhon 588–89
  on World War I 590